W9-AUV-425

PROSPECTS FOR SOVIET SOCIETY

DK 274.3
K 1968
K3

Prospects for Soviet Society

EDITED BY
ALLEN KASSOF

PUBLISHED FOR THE
Council on Foreign Relations
by

FREDERICK A. PRAEGER, *Publishers*
New York · Washington · London

DEC 4 1968

127160

FREDERICK A. PRAEGER, PUBLISHERS
111 Fourth Avenue, New York, N.Y. 10003, U.S.A.
77–79 Charlotte Street, London W. 1, England

Published in the United States of America in 1968
by Frederick A. Praeger, Inc., Publishers

Copyright © 1968, by Council on Foreign Relations, Inc.

*All rights reserved, including the right to reproduce this
book or any portion thereof in any form. For information,
address Frederick A. Praeger, Inc., Publishers,
111 Fourth Avenue, New York, N.Y. 10003*

Library of Congress Catalog Card Number: 67–20485

The Council on Foreign Relations is a nonprofit institution devoted
to the study of political, economic, and strategic problems as related
to American foreign policy. It takes no stand, expressed or implied,
on American policy. The authors of books published under the
auspices of the Council are responsible for their statements of fact
and expressions of opinion. The Council is responsible only for determining that they should be presented to the public.

For a list of Council publications see pages 583–586.

Translations from *The Current Digest of the Soviet Press*, published weekly
at Columbia University by the Joint Committee on Slavic Studies appointed
by the American Council of Learned Societies and the Social Science Research Council. Copyright 1959, 1961, 1963, 1964, 1965, 1966, and 1967, the
Joint Committee on Slavic Studies. Reprinted by permission.

Printed in the United States of America

Preface

The idea for this book on the future of Soviet society grew out of a series of discussions in 1963 and 1964, first sponsored by the Council on Foreign Relations on the initiative of Philip E. Mosely and later carried on by the American Council of Learned Societies. Scholars and journalists specializing in Soviet affairs, most of whom had recently returned from the Soviet Union, presented papers or informal remarks on a variety of topics and discussed current developments with a number of Council members and guests.

When it was proposed in 1964 that I edit a collection of some of the papers, I suggested instead a more ambitious volume that would provide scholars and laymen with a systematic analysis of recent trends in the Soviet Union. Discussions with John C. Campbell of the Council and with Professor Cyril Black (who had served as chairman of the earlier meetings) then led to a decision to devote our efforts to the larger issue of change and the future. The timing turned out to be more propitious than we knew. Just as preparations were underway for the first authors' meeting, the news of Khrushchev's ouster was announced, heralding another turning point in Soviet history and once again raising the question of its further course.

The authors, together with a number of others interested in the subject, met at the Council in January 1965, to plan the volume and to talk over the outlines of the proposed chapters. During the year, we prepared first drafts and met again in January 1966, to assess the results. Revisions were completed early in 1967, and the collective manuscript was edited, assembled, and brought up to date by the beginning of the summer. We have thus had an unusual opportunity to consult with one another at critical stages of the project. It was our hope from the very beginning to turn out something more than an assortment of papers. We aimed at a genuinely collaborative work that would reflect the fact that the authors have listened to one another very carefully.

The Council's interest in foreign affairs provided the point of departure, but it is our contention that a sound assessment of Soviet society itself is the first necessity in understanding its international behavior in the years ahead. Accordingly, we have emphasized the domestic scene, although in various chapters the authors discuss the foreign implications of their topics. John Campbell, who represented the Council throughout the project, has contributed a separate chapter devoted specifically to the Soviet Union in its international setting.

No one has yet devised dependable techniques for the prediction of human affairs, let alone the fate of entire societies. We do not claim to have accomplished any miracles of fortune-telling, nor has it been our purpose to be encyclopedic. But we have done our best to apply an array of specialized talents to the analysis of past and present conditions from which the future will flow, and to sketch its probable shape. Naturally, the degree of certitude varies from one area to the next. Topics such as population and manpower, which lend themselves to quantitative measures and are inherently limited with respect to rates and magnitude of change, allow extended forecasts, while political trends, for obvious reasons, are subject to rapid, frequent, and unforeseen shifts. Generally speaking, we have had in mind a span of approximately a decade or two as a working guideline, but there is variation from one paper to the next according to how well the topic lends itself to long-range treatment, and depending on the willingness of individual authors to combine a certain boldness with the traditional caution of professional scholars.

My contribution, in addition to over-all organization and editing, takes the form of an introductory essay, brief introductions to the topical sections, and a concluding chapter in which I bring together the findings of my colleagues. I have tried to avoid imposing a merely mechanical uniformity upon the contributions, preferring to give the widest scope to the individual authors in treating their subjects. The resulting differences in approach, in the detail of documentation, and in levels of abstraction, I have welcomed as stylistic and substantive strengths of our presentation. At the same time, I believe that we have achieved a genuinely organic unity in content and presentation, which the reader will find evident if he reads the essays in sequence.

On behalf of my colleagues, I would like to express our gratitude to the institutions and individuals who have contributed to the creation of this book, first of all to the Council on Foreign Relations for its generous sponsorship. The continuous interest and support of the American Council of Learned Societies and especially of its President, Frederick Burkhardt, are also deeply appreciated. The encouragement and constructive criticism of those who attended our two planning sessions were very important in shaping our work, and it is a pleasure to record the participation of Frederick C. Barghoorn, Harry Boardman, Walter Connor, Alexander Dallin, George Fischer, Col. Edward C. Foote, Welles Hangen, Col. Immanuel Klette, David W. MacEachron, Gregory Massel, Philip E. Mosely, Robert I. Owen, and Harry Schwartz.

Finally, I owe a personal debt to Robert Valkenier, the Council's editor, with whom I worked side by side in preparing the manuscript for publication.

ALLEN KASSOF

Princeton, N.J.
July 1967

Contents

PART ONE

Soviet Society After Fifty Years

1.

Persistence and Change

ALLEN KASSOF

The fiftieth anniversary of the Bolshevik Revolution provides a singularly appropriate occasion for the appearance of a book on the Soviet future. The contributions by the eighteen scholars represented here, however, have been motivated by more than a coincidence of timing. As the Communist regime marks its first half-century, the society it has created is once again undergoing a period of profound and far-reaching change.

Most of the earlier turning points in Soviet history were dramatic, sometimes violent, and of obviously epoch-making proportions. They entailed radical and sudden changes for millions of people, massive assaults upon established life patterns, the uprooting of whole populations, widespread privation, gigantic leaps from age-old backwardness to social and economic modernity. They were invoked in the name of a messianic ideology that sought to revolutionize not only an entire, sprawling society, but ultimately all societies. They called forth a passionate advocacy born of utopian aspirations, yet often took place in a murderous atmosphere of Byzantine intrigue.

If the current scene is remarkable for the almost total absence of such clear signs that history is in the making, then appearances are deceiving. The seeming quietude of the mid-1960s stems from the special nature of more subtle, but no less extensive, changes that we are now beginning to perceive in Soviet society.

The basic issue is that the crisis of modernization—which has formed the background of virtually every important development in Russia since (and, indeed, before) the October Revolution—is now fundamentally resolved. The secure place of the Soviet Union as a ranking world power is only an outward reflection of the

3

maturation of social institutions at home: the creation of a skilled, literate citizenry endowed with attitudes and motivations appropriate to life in the era of advanced technology; a highly productive educational system; a powerful and growing economic base; a network of urban complexes implying the human specialization and mobility that are essential characteristics of modern life. The social transformation that had eluded successive generations of Communist leadership has been achieved. The magnitude of the Soviet accomplishment, however uneven and flawed, is underscored by the fact that comparable levels are still beyond the reach, if not the dreams, of most people of most of the world.

One of the crowning ironies of our times (and perhaps of the history of human society in general) is that the solution to one set of problems almost invariably creates others more complex. Having successfully joined the ranks of industrial societies, the Soviet Union today is faced with unprecedented organizational dilemmas. Some of them resemble issues current in the older industrial societies, others arise from the uniqueness of the Soviet experience, none has an obvious solution. It is the quest for answers to new and difficult problems, then, that accounts for the appearance of relative calm in Soviet society. The simplistic political formulas and the barricade-storming mentality of earlier years have by no means evaporated, but they are becoming less and less relevant to the needs of a delicately balanced and highly interdependent social order. This new uncertainty has opened the door to experimentation and innovation that are partly intentional, partly beyond the control of the leadership, and that set the scene for change in the years to come.

The new climate in the Soviet Union did not come about overnight, but is only the latest consequence of the flow of events. Nevertheless, its stages have coincided with changes in leadership style and personnel that punctuate the transition. The landmark, of course, is the death of Stalin in 1953.

Virtually every institutional pattern in the Soviet Union today has its origin in the Stalinist period. The Soviet citizen who left his country in the late 1930s and returned tomorrow would surely discover drastic changes in the political atmosphere and in many details of daily life. But the outlines of the system, the established ways of getting things done, would be thoroughly familiar to him. The durability of this social structure, however, has not been matched by the durability of the Stalinist political culture itself. About the time of Stalin's death, many observers concluded that the society was near a breaking point—the creative initiative of the population sapped by a capricious, tyrannical irrationality, and the loyalties of the most ardent Communists threatened by waves of terror that promised to sweep away even Stalin's closest associates.

The successor regime, eventually under Khrushchev, very quickly recognized the need to dismantle at least the most extreme Stalinist inventions in order to minimize mass discontent during their own uncertain accession and to restore a degree of momentum to the society as a whole. The amnesties of 1953 and the subsequent dissolution of the forced labor camps were only first steps in a remarkable thaw that was to include an outright denunciation of Stalin himself and that opened the way to irreversible change.

Despite the well-founded anxieties that must have prompted the new leadership to take such risks, the Khrushchev period was generally marked by an optimism that has since disappeared. There was an air of expectancy that, with Stalin out of the way, a fundamentally sound system, until then dragged down by the ruinous machinations of an ingenious but misguided ruler, would soon realize its full promise. (The mood extended far beyond the Kremlin, finding expression, for example, among idealistic students who labeled themselves Leninists and who saw in the return to original principles a sure path from the distortions of Stalinism to the achievement of the good society.) Khrushchev's exhortations to the populace, the frequent shifts in administrative structure, the crash programs for solutions to a variety of economic and social problems, and other measures all seem to have been based on the assumption that success was always just around the corner, that the pieces would fall neatly into place once the key steps were devised and carried out. And, indeed, a series of successes in the mid-1950s might have appeared for a time to warrant the hope.

This initial optimism, however, was soon tempered by a growing realization that the complexities of running an entire society do not easily yield to adjustments in administration and that even the most enthusiastic leadership cannot alter reality by decree or persuasion. Claims that the Soviet Union would overtake and surpass the United States in the near future gave way to frenetic efforts merely to maintain the rate of earlier accomplishments. In the end, Khrushchev was ignominiously dismissed amid charges that his policies had amounted to hare-brained schemes. The epithet, motivated by the desire of the new leadership to discredit the old, was by no means accurate. Khrushchev had in fact not only managed the staggering task of leading the Soviet Union from its self-imposed international isolation, but had guided the potentially explosive transition from Stalinism with, all things considered, remarkable effectiveness.

In the process, nevertheless, it had become increasingly clear that the system itself might require more fundamental adaptations than had been anticipated. Obvious and acceptable alternatives were being exhausted, yet none of them proved to be altogether satisfactory. Khrushchev's downfall, of course, represented a personal defeat, but it was only incidental to a general reappraisal that began toward the end of his tenure and that is likely to continue for some time.

Present tensions stem from sources as wide and varied as the society, but fall into several main categories. The most obvious (although not necessarily the most important) issue concerns the production and allocation of economic resources. Briefly, the planning and management techniques that worked (effectively, if not very efficiently) during earlier stages of economic development have proved inadequate to more modern needs. Declining rates of economic growth in general and an extremely poor experience in agriculture in particular have been the result.

The quest for more suitable organizational practices is complicated not only by the inherent difficulty of devising new forms, but by the inertia of habit and tradition, in the Soviet case compounded by a prescriptive ideology that rules out whole ranges of possibilities on political grounds even though they may be feasible from a purely technical-rational point of view. The disputes that have surrounded the really quite modest introduction in recent years of what has come to be known as Libermanism—a system of economic accountability at the enterprise level—suggest how deep Soviet sensitivities are on this score and presage the difficulties that are likely to attend more extensive reforms.

Questions of allocation are no less vexing than those of production, for the pent-up expectations of Soviet citizens at all levels for visible improvements in the standard of living compete with the established emphasis on reinvestment and rapid growth. It would be a gross exaggeration to say that the Soviet government will simply have to accede to consumers' demands, yet some degree of accommodation has already taken place, and the appetite is only likely to grow in the eating. Such pressures to fulfill old promises significantly reduce the regime's flexibility in domestic economic undertakings, as well as in the kinds of civilian and military commitments that may be made in the foreign arena. Finally, the issue of how much of the national product is to be devoted to mass consumption raises the further question of how and to whom that share shall be distributed, with all of the political complications implied by the unequal access to wealth in a society that purports to be Communist.

A second major focus of tension concerns techniques of social, political, and cultural control. Stalinism, though by no means devoid of important elements of persuasion, relied on systematic terror and coercion to an unprecedented extent. The official revelations of the 1950s confirmed the worst suspicions as to the number of direct victims, and hardly anyone was unaffected by the atmosphere of fear and caution. It produced a situation that has been described as the institutionalization of anxiety, in which the individual is so uncertain of the consequences of even the most innocent act that his behavior becomes almost totally constrained. The costs of such mass psychic paralysis, carried to an extreme in the Stalin years, threatened to outweigh any conceivable advantages to the regime. Finding a viable substitute for coercion, however, has proved more difficult than abandoning it. In the first place, it is no longer a technique that can be turned on and off at the convenience of the leadership, whose pointed disassociation from Stalinism amounts, in effect, to a public renunciation of its most detested features. Then there is the serious question, even if such a return were contemplated, about the consequences of the popular uproar that would probably follow.

Meanwhile, the controlling effects of terror and coercion are eroded by the passage of time. While much of the older generation is still understandably cautious, if only out of vivid recollection, younger citizens have no such personal memories and are more and more disposed to regard a terror-free society as a normal state of affairs. The situation might be less urgent were it not for the fact that precedents for alternative forms of social order, based more on voluntaristic impulses, were historically weak in the prerevolutionary Russian autocracy, and the Communist system of single-party rule has been consistently hostile to the development of associational resources that might otherwise be expected to fill the vacuum. The absence of professional, occupational, regional, or ethnic groupings with a meaningful degree of organization is one example; the severely truncated legal system is another. It is also important to remember that the party continues to rule out autonomies beyond the immediate scope of its own authority as posing a direct danger, and that it vigorously represses them. In effect, its dilemma arises from the effort to preserve intact the institutional forms that have emerged since the 1930s without wishing or being able to resort to the full complement of political instrumentalities that accompanied their rise, and steadfastly refusing to acknowledge the legitimacy of any but its own voice in setting goals for the society and prescribing the means by which they are to be realized. To put it another way, the party faces the challenging task of maintaining a society which it can mobilize for its own purposes by persuasion and administration rather than by coercion. The feasibility of the change in methods remains to be seen.

This incongruence (which is aggravated by the existence within the leading group of varied and shifting opinions as to where the outer limits of liberalization can or should be drawn) is partly responsible for the ferment that has affected many segments of the population in recent years. The most highly publicized episodes have involved elements of the intellectual, scientific, and artistic communities, which have engaged in a seesaw struggle to establish and legitimize areas of autonomy. Equally important, though less visible, pressures are being felt in all corners of the society as individuals and groups begin to assert particular interests against the successful tradition of centralization. None of this is to say that the party is necessarily in immediate or even long-range jeopardy. (Considering the predictions that were once made to the effect that the Soviet system would collapse in the absence of Stalin, we should be at least skeptical about sweeping expectations.) Still, the strains generated by this ambiguity are gathering momentum and are certain to be a cause of further social and political change.

A third focus of tension concerns a variety of social problems that are by no means peculiar to the Soviet scene but are to some degree associated with the rise of urbanism generally: delinquency, crime, family disorganization, alcoholism, mental illness, individual alienation, and the like. They merit mention in the Soviet case because their very existence contradicts the ideological expectations of Communists and because the Soviet leadership has, therefore, been poorly prepared to cope with them. The insistence that social ills are the exclusive property of capitalist societies is at the basis of the miscalculation. During the Stalin years they were simply not acknowledged at all, or were attributed to "survivals of capitalism" that were supposed to disappear with the advent of full communism. In recent years there has been a grudging recognition that more than temporary repressive measures or the mere passage of time will be required, and the appearance of sociology as a legitimate applied discipline after decades of total banishment is one example of this reorientation. But many years will be required to alter fundamentally the habit of treating social ills as though they were not there. Meanwhile, the accumulation of problems entails high costs in the form of wasted human resources and implies defects in social planning that are a potent source of trouble.

The search for effective solutions in each of these three areas is also made difficult by the peculiar unevenness of social and economic development, which is such a pervasive feature of Soviet life as to constitute in some respects a separate problem. Among the examples are the mixture of highly advanced technologies in some sectors with virtually primitive techniques in others; the disproportionately large rural population relative to the Soviet Union's rank among world industrial powers; the striking differences in cultural level between the European peoples of the U.S.S.R. and many of its non-Slavic populations elsewhere (especially in Central Asia); the gap between the relative affluence of a substantial segment of the technical and bureaucratic intelligentsia and the hardships experienced by ordinary workers and peasants; the sharp discontinuities between the welfare and educational facilities of the cities and the backwardness of the village. The existence of such contrasts means that a mode of solution that may be appropriate at one level will only lead to trouble when applied to others. In this respect, Soviet policy-makers are required to cope not with a single, homogeneous society, but in effect with a series of sub-societies requiring sometimes distinct, and even mutually contradictory, treatment.

Turning from domestic to international aspects of the Soviet situation, we find a fourth major category of sources of potential change. Although the competitive dangers of relations among states have injected into Soviet foreign policy, almost from the very beginning, a powerful element of pragmatism that has sometimes been lacking in Soviet internal policies, the events of recent years undoubtedly have violated a number of ideologically inspired expectations held by the Soviet leadership and are therefore leading to serious re-evaluations. Among the most important factors have been the surprising vitality and duration of recovery in Western

Europe in the aftermath of World War II; the capacity and determination of the United States to confront Soviet power in the postwar years; the disappointments encountered in trying to extend Soviet power into the third world; and, most significant, the weakening of Soviet hegemony in the socialist bloc and the open—and probably irreparable—dispute with Communist China. These developments have already altered somewhat the practical, if not the doctrinal, posture of defensiveness and hostility vis-à-vis the West as the Soviet Union seeks to conventionalize and stabilize its international position.

The connection between foreign and domestic behavior is indirect at best, but there is no question about their interrelatedness. To cite the obvious, a sharp increase in international tensions is likely to result in intensified sociopolitical controls at home, while the prospects of favorable international developments tend to encourage, though by no means to guarantee, liberalization on a broad front. There are, of course, far more subtle effects; for example, the growth of cultural and commercial contacts with the West entails the exposure of Soviet officials, scientists and scholars, artists and writers, and even average citizens to fresh world views and styles of life that, in a formerly closed society, have an influence quite out of proportion to their still limited scope. Naturally, domestic developments also have a reciprocal influence on international behavior; it has even been argued that the Soviet leadership from time to time has intentionally magnified international tensions for the purpose of diverting popular restiveness and to create a garrison atmosphere that would enhance political controls at home. However that may be, the intertwined nature of domestic and foreign developments is axiomatic and has to be considered in assessing future probabilities.

Before turning to the kinds of changes that these and other sources are likely to generate, it would be well to see them in perspective. In the effort to look behind the monolithic façade that the Soviet Union presents to the outside world, we must be on guard against going to the other extreme of exaggerating the significance of strains and imbalances. Although the possibility of cataclysmic developments can never be entirely ruled out, the demonstrated durability of the Soviet system suggests that the burden of proof rests with those who predict revolutionary changes in the short run. It is also worthwhile to recall that at least some of the problems current in the Soviet Union can be encountered in most contemporary large-scale societies in one form or another.

The catalogue of comparable cases would be extensive. Stress is a permanent feature of all modern societies, but the recent historical record suggests that, short of suffering military defeat, they are generally able to preserve their basic structures over extended periods of time.

Provided that we keep this caution in mind, it is appropriate to emphasize that there are, after all, a number of special factors in the Soviet situation that make it more than usually vulnerable to pressures toward change. The concentration of policy-making and executive powers essentially in the hands of a single, all-pervading, and authoritarian political party, although in some respects an important advantage in initiating and enforcing broad socio-economic programs, also means that decisions better handled in other systems at middle and lower levels tend to become entangled in cumbersome bureaucratic machinery that impedes effective administration. Moreover, the insistence that the party is the only legitimate source of wisdom tends to stifle fresh ideas and approaches from independent sources that are essential if substitutes are to be found for old ways that have outlived their usefulness or have simply failed. Coupled with this structural monopoly of power is a highly inclusive ideology which, even when it is not faithfully observed, places severe limitations upon innovation. The party, which began its life as an instrument of rapid social change, has become perhaps the chief source of conservatism in Soviet society today.

Then, too, the extreme penetration of politics into areas which, in the West, have typically been regarded as lying beyond the legitimate scope of governmental authority or concern in effect transfers into the public realm whole spectrums of problems that might otherwise be handled voluntarily or, for better or worse, simply ignored. This pattern sometimes turns moderately troublesome issues and conflicts into manufactured or genuine crises, and the commotion that ensues can be highly self-destructive. One of the most notorious and costly affairs of this type was the virtual demolishment of Soviet biology during the Lysenko episode, when forcible official backing of a scientific charlatan on utterly irrational grounds set the field back for decades.

These and similar characteristics reduce the flexibility of the Soviet system in its response to the need for adaptation, and probably account for the impression that policy-makers and administrators are constantly moving from one crisis to the next. If we also consider that the organizational and material resources of the society have long been under the stress of overcommitment in the interests of forced growth, then we can appreciate why the Soviet Union suffers from a certain brittleness in the face of its changing internal and external environments.

*   *   *

Identifying the main sources of social change in the Soviet Union only leads to the far more difficult question of the direction it may take and the rate at which it is likely to occur. To suggest some of the answers is the main purpose of our volume, and I shall return in the conclusion to an evaluation of the evidence presented in my colleagues' chapters. A measure of the challenge—and the peril—that we face in trying to reach a sound and justified consensus on the probable shape of the future is given by the enormous range of possibilities that have been indicated from time to time by observers of various persuasions.

At one extreme is the expectation that the Soviet system, however the details of its structure may be modified, will remain essentially unaltered in the future. The persuasiveness of this position stems from the undeniable fact that societal patterns do, in fact, tend to persist and that the surest way to predict tomorrow is to describe today. Its limitation is that there are endless tomorrows.

Applied to the Soviet case, persistence prediction is usually associated with the view that modern totalitarianism, once it is thoroughly entrenched, is virtually permanent, that it is capable of adapting to new requirements without fatal disruptions, that its total nature by definition establishes an effective impermeability to alternative forms of social organization. Presented in this form, of course, the argument involves weightier considerations than mere persistence and has to be taken very seriously on its own merits.

At the opposite extreme is the view that the entire Bolshevik experience has been a temporary historical detour on the universal highway to modernization, that Stalinism was a passing aberration, and that the end is already in sight. In its popular form this view holds that the Soviet Union will become increasingly like the American and European societies as the success of hard-won industrialization is reflected in a rising standard of living and increasingly bourgeois tastes and outlook. It is in this connection that we hear assertions to the effect that the development of "capitalist" tendencies in Soviet economic management demonstrates that the Soviets have seen the light, that willingly or unwillingly they must adopt the time-tested methods of the West, and that happy political consequences will follow in due course. Alternatively, under the label of the "convergence" theory, there is the expectation that the Western societies on the one hand, and the Soviet Union (and Communist countries generally) on the other, are both moving toward an as yet undefined, hybrid societal type lying somewhere between their present positions. The underlying assumption is that form follows function and that, since all large-scale industrial societies face increasingly similar needs generated by the universal imperatives of science and technology, their structures must eventually reflect a corresponding similarity. This, too, is an argument that may very well account for at least certain types of anticipated change and, in its more thoughtful forms, cannot be lightly dismissed.

To say that the most likely course of events lies somewhere between these two poles is true enough, but that prediction covers so much ground that it is not particularly helpful. Narrowing the range of probabilities within useful and meaningful limits is the task that we have set for ourselves. The burden of this task is carried by my colleagues in the chapters that follow. Their assignment is to weigh the record of past and present in order to suggest where it may be leading. It would be folly to claim that the topics we were able to include within the confines of a single volume exhaust every important aspect of Soviet life, yet, taken as a whole, they touch upon the key issues that are likely to shape the future.

We begin, in Professor Black's contribution, with the essential matter of placing the Soviet Union in comparative perspective.

2.

Soviet Society: A Comparative View

CYRIL E. BLACK

I. COMPARABILITY AND UNIQUENESS

The central problem of modernizing societies is the adaptation of their institutions to the changes in function that result from the growth of knowledge. This is as explicitly the aim of Soviet as of other modernizing leaders; and one may gauge the pattern of adaptation peculiar to Soviet society in terms of the emphasis on selected aspects at the expense of others, as reflected in differential rates of change. The substance of these changes must be studied in terms of the domestic Soviet scene, drawing on the considerable wealth of information reported and interpreted by Soviet and foreign scholars, but their evaluation depends in large measure on comparisons with other societies that have grappled with similar problems.

It is one of the rules of the comparative method that entities should be of the same general order of magnitude and should possess certain main characteristics in common if one wishes comparisons to be meaningful. Yet it is not easy to follow this rule in comparing societies, for each is in some significant degree a special case, and the Soviet Union is more nearly unique than most. As the largest country in the world in area, the second largest in gross national product, and the third largest in population, it is in certain important respects comparable only to the relatively few major powers that encompass a similar range of resources and conditions. On a per capita basis, the Soviet Union may also properly be compared to a large number of societies that are reasonably close in levels of political, economic, and social development and in historical experience.

Within these limits, and in those areas where reasonably sound

14

statistical and general information is available, it is possible to estimate the levels of development of the various sectors of Soviet society, the means by which these levels have been achieved, and the rates of change in the past and in the near future. The experience of comparable societies provides the most reliable basis for judging the significance of estimates that evaluate the Soviet program of modernization in terms of achievements and costs. When comparisons are made with societies whose resources and problems are of a very different order from those of the Soviet Union, the results are of interest less as a yardstick than as an illustration of the range of levels and experience that exist among contemporary societies.

Many problems beset the comparison of societies. One is the difficulty of obtaining reliable statistical data. There is now a substantial literature on problems relating to the accuracy of statistics and the difficulty of comparing statistics of societies where different criteria of selection, organizational structure, and purchasing power of currencies must be taken into account. Indeed, no statistics come very close to the degree of accuracy that the untutored layman might expect. It is also difficult to identify satisfactory bases of comparison, for such concepts as "gross national product," "defense," "consumption," "books," "physicians," "engineers," and "students" are all matters of definition that vary from society to society and from specialist to specialist. Even after these discrepancies have been adjusted, it must be borne in mind that no two countries are at the same level of development; no two have identical systems of legislation, education, or values; no two are entirely comparable in their conception of professional, ethnic, or income groups; and no two currencies have the same purchasing power. The best recourse under the circumstances is to use the most accurate statistics that one can find, to describe the problems that may be particularly significant in individual cases, and to bear in mind throughout that the reliability of these comparisons is at best relative.[1]

The statistical comparisons made in this study are drawn from the available specialized sources and prepared by international organizations and by independent scholars in the United States and Western Europe. These, in turn, are based primarily on the official statistics of the various countries, and only occasionally on independent studies made within these countries. In the case of the U.S.S.R., virtually all the evidence is drawn ultimately from official Soviet statistics.

Comparisons with other societies have always played an important role in Soviet official statements and have been cited in numerous works of scholarship and propaganda, but only in very recent years has sophisticated statistical work been published on the problem of comparisons. The appointment in 1961 of a Scientific Council on Economic Competition Between the Two Systems and Problems Facing the Less Developed Countries, under the Academy of Sciences of the U.S.S.R., promises to result in important contributions to this field. Although these new studies are primarily theoretical in their approach, the conclusions reached thus far may be regarded as superseding earlier Soviet studies and are cited where appropriate. As with earlier Soviet studies, the statistical work of the new Scientific Council has concentrated primarily on comparisons of the U.S.S.R. with the United States, and thus has only a limited applicability to the subject of this paper.[2]

II. THE INTERNATIONAL ENVIRONMENT

The problems of comparability and uniqueness should be explored not only in terms of the statistics of domestic development. The formative experiences of the peoples of the Soviet Union—experiences that help to explain the role of the international environment in creating the values and institutions that have prevailed in the twentieth century—should also be taken into account on a comparative basis.

Prominent among these formative experiences have been the unification by the grand dukes of Moscow of the Eastern Slav principalities that came under Mongol rule in the thirteenth century; and the gradual extension of Muscovite rule to include the remaining East Slavs and many other peoples as well in a state that now embraces some fifteen major and almost a hundred minor nationalities. Of similar significance was the establishment and maintenance of a country of imperial dimensions in a setting of initially more powerful countries—Sweden, Poland, and Turkey in the seventeenth and eighteenth centuries; France in the eighteenth and nineteenth; and Germany in the nineteenth and twentieth—that were perceived by Russian leaders as threatening powers seeking to dismember and on occasion to occupy the lands of Russia. There was likewise the difficult problem of integrating a multinational state in which the Great Russians constituted only 44 per cent of the population in 1900 and 55 per cent in 1960, and where the major national minorities lived in borderlands adjacent to rival and often hostile countries. To these formative experiences one should also add a prevailing sense of backwardness in science, technology, and economic development, based on a level of living markedly lower than that of the principal members of the European system, by comparison with which Russia has measured itself.

None of these formative experiences is unique to Russia, when stated generally, but their particular pattern and quality is not reproduced in any other country. Problems of political unification have been faced by all countries, but among those at a similar level of development perhaps only Poland, Germany, Austria-Hungary, and Yugoslavia had comparable difficulties in nation-building. The creation of a state in a hostile environment is also a universal experience; but the fact that Russia is one of the few among the more than 130 sovereign states in existence today with a continuous territorial existence, free from foreign rule in modern times, reflects great stability as a state. England and its overseas heirs and France among the early modernizing societies, and China, Japan, Turkey, and Thailand, and perhaps a few others among those that modernized later, have likewise enjoyed territorial continuity in modern times. All other countries of the world, in one degree or another, have since the eighteenth century been newly established and have undergone extensive reorganizations of territory and foreign occupation for longer or shorter periods of time.

The creation of a modern society characterized by ethnic diversity is perhaps a more unusual experience, for nation-building has more often than not tended toward ethnic uniformity. Among modern multinational states, the Hapsburg and Ottoman empires failed conspicuously; and India and Nigeria, among many in Asia and Africa that are seeking to integrate diverse groups, are still being tested. Yugoslavia, Belgium, Lebanon, and Cyprus have survived several crises in handling their minority problems and may face others in the years ahead. The United Kingdom has achieved such stability that one does not think of it as a multinational state, although it was not so long ago that the Irish question stood high on the world agenda of nationality problems. The ethnic diversity of the countries of the New World is of a different order from those in which ethnic groups live in geographically distinct regions, and involves problems of assimilation rather than federalism.

Russia's position as a latecomer to modernization is of course shared by the great majority of the countries of the world, all of which are seeking to overtake if not surpass those that are more advanced. What is relatively unique about the Russian case, however, is its direct rivalry and participation with the advanced countries in the European political system since the eighteenth century, and the consequent need to exercise power at a European level on the basis of a per capita wealth that has been significantly lower than that of its peers. It is significant in this connection that throughout the twentieth century Russia has ranked highest among the major powers in the proportion of its national income that it has devoted to defense expenditures.[3]

A full delineation of Russia's political personality in world-wide comparison would require a wealth of detail that would go well beyond the limits of this essay, but suffice it to say that the Russian political experience has been sufficiently different from that of the societies of Western and Central Europe, or of the United States, or of the societies of Latin America, Asia, and Africa, and that comparisons should be based on the assumption of a predominantly different political culture. To categorize Russia as "non-Western" in contrast to "Western," "socialist" rather than "capitalist," "developing" rather than "developed," "totalitarian" rather than "democratic," or—to use Marxist-Leninist terminology—"democratic" in contrast to "imperialist" conceals more than it reveals. These simple dichotomies are not entirely devoid of meaning, but they are so crude and undiscriminating that they have no place in a comparative study.

An evaluation of the effect of these formative experiences is important since the view that Soviet leaders have of their own society is based essentially on a comparison with the advanced societies of Western Europe and the New World. The overarching motivation of Soviet domestic policy has been to "overtake and surpass" the more advanced countries, and in this respect probably only Japan among the major countries of the world has been as strongly motivated. Policy-makers in West European countries have either regarded their rate of development as adequate or, as in the case of Spain and Portugal, have not been seriously concerned with the problem. The countries of Eastern Europe have, by force of circumstance, sought to modernize in close relationship with a major power or group of powers—with the French system in the 1920s, with the German in the 1930s, and with the Soviet since 1945. The countries of Latin America, with a few exceptions (Argentina, Costa Rica, Mexico, and Uruguay, in particular), and the countries of Asia and Africa, Japan again excepted, are still at too early a stage of development to regard overtaking, let alone surpassing, as a practical problem.

The Soviet Union has thus been in the critical position of envisioning the possibility of achieving West European levels of per capita production and consumption, but only after an effort extending into the still distant future and calling for per capita sacrifices significantly greater than those required in the more advanced countries. This effort of economic development was as characteristic of the late empire as of the Soviet period, and there are many continuities in the general line of state policy in this regard since the 1880s.[4]

An important consequence of the adoption of the particular program of modernization that has come to be known as Marxism-Leninism was the ideological isolation of the Soviet Union from countries with which it had customarily maintained normal relations. This isolation was to have profound consequences on domestic policies. The Soviet leaders, like many others, have dealt with other countries on two levels. On one level, they have sought to maintain the security interests that have come to be considered normal by leaders of most nations: stable frontiers, assurance of favorable conditions for economic growth, annexation of territories when justified by national traditions, and participation in alliance systems and international institutions.

At another level, Soviet leaders have sought to maximize for their country what they have considered to be the inevitable consequences of revolutionary developments in world politics. While many countries operate in some degree on two such levels, seeing for themselves a role in world affairs that goes beyond mere maintenance of their security interests, the Soviet Union has carried policies on both levels to greater extremes than most. Probably no country except Germany in the twentieth century has made more drastic demands for territorial change in Eastern Europe, and none since France during its revolutionary phase has sought to make such dramatic use of ideological forces.

In the management of security interests, the Soviet leaders have normally exercised great caution in the use of military power. They have sought to avoid the use of armed forces beyond their frontiers, and have been prepared to compromise when the alternative might lead to war. The series of nonaggression pacts concluded with neighboring countries in the 1920s and which later served to stabilize the European and Asian frontiers of the Soviet

Union, and the nonaggression pact with Germany in 1939, had as their essential purpose to avoid involvement in the approaching war.

In their attitude toward the crisis in 1939 the statesmen of the U.S.S.R. showed no more foresight than those of the West European states, and for this they paid an enormous price. The outstanding exception to this rule of restraint was the Soviet attack on Finland in 1939, and it appears likely that the Soviet leaders regarded this as a pre-emptive measure with limited objectives. The occupation of Eastern Europe at the end of World War II occurred in pursuit of an enemy that had attacked the Soviet Union, and the postwar line of demarcation between the spheres of influence of the Soviet Union and the Western democracies has been substantially that which their armed forces reached at the time of Germany's defeat. Since World War II, the principal case of the employment of military power at a distance from Soviet borders has been the attempt to establish missile bases in Cuba. It is still a matter of controversy whether Soviet leaders regarded this as a deliberate act of provocation, or simply misread the rather indecisive American official statements and thought they were undertaking a venture that did not involve great risks. This was in any case an exceptional event in Soviet military policy and one that seasoned foreign observers would not have ventured to predict on the basis of past Soviet behavior.

At the ideological level, Soviet policy has been much bolder and has employed sophisticated methods for taking advantage of the crises of modernization abroad. It has sought to influence, and on occasion dominate, the policies of other countries through the international network of Communist parties. By the mid-1920s these parties had come in large measure under direct Soviet control, and were dominated by well-trained and generally loyal cadres. Associated with this core of organizers, as party members or as fellow-travelers in a variety of front organizations, was a larger group of followers varying in size and influence from country to country. Through these instrumentalities, the Soviet leaders sought to weaken governments that obstructed Soviet policies, turn governments against each other, separate colonies from empires, conduct espionage, and infiltrate the upper levels of bureaucracies. Not infrequently Communist parties sought actively to overthrow governments and to gain power for themselves, either alone or with other parties in coalitions known as "popular fronts."

The fact that the Soviet leaders were able to create such an

extensive and influential organization reflects an understanding of the strategic uses of political violence and an awareness of the vulnerabilities of societies in the process of rapid change, but in the perspective of fifty years the costs of this revolutionary policy appear to have outweighed its benefits. Of the other countries that eventually came under Communist rule, the Communist parties gained power without direct intervention by Soviet troops in five—Albania, China, Cuba, North Vietnam, and Yugoslavia. Three of these became active opponents of the Soviet Union within a few years' time, and the remaining two—Cuba and North Vietnam—have not been significantly valuable as Soviet allies. In the remaining eight countries where Communists have come to power, they owe their position primarily to the presence of Soviet armed forces. Even these governments, since the Stalin era, have been no more cooperative than are the members of other coalitions that operate on the basis of more relaxed principles.

Throughout the period of Soviet rule, the pursuit of ideological objectives has tended to place a great burden both on security interests and on domestic policies of development. The stated policy of supporting revolutionary movements, although not vigorously pursued for long periods, has served to increase the insecurity of other nations and in turn to make them more antagonistic to the Soviet Union. In regard to Germany, the proximity of a revolutionary Russia was one of the main factors in the success of National Socialism, and in due course Germany became Russia's principal enemy. Similarly, the degree of temporary security achieved after World War II with the creation of a bloc of Communist-governed states embracing a third of the world's population must be balanced against the great cost of matching the military power developed by the United States and the NATO coalition in response to what was perceived as a challenge to their security by the Communist bloc.

At the same time, there has been a gradual trend in the course of the half-century of Soviet rule away from a highly ideological view of the world toward one that sees other nations in more restrained and comparative terms. What appears incongruous to observers from the more advanced societies is not the theoretical outlook of Marxism-Leninism, which in its way seeks to describe and harness to Soviet needs the revolutionary implications of the world-wide process of modernization, but rather the view that Russia is in the forefront of this movement and represents a model that all others should follow. In the first years after the seizure of power there ap-

pears to have been a genuine belief that "world revolution" was at hand. This belief wore off rapidly in the 1920s, and Stalin was happy to settle for a world in which Russia could devote its attention to domestic development. The theory of world revolution now became more an instrument of foreign policy than an article of faith. As such, it played a vital role after World War II in creating a sense of community for the members of the Soviet bloc and in motivating Soviet attempts to manipulate revolutionary movements when they occurred in other parts of the world. Stalin's successors continued to nurture Marxism-Leninism, and indeed for the first time wove it into a more or less coherent doctrine, but more than ever they gave highest priority in their allocation of resources to Soviet domestic development. Ideology was not weakened, but was rather transformed to serve the needs of a great power seeking prosperity in a relatively stable world. International law and organization, rejected in the early 1920s as "bourgeois," and reluctantly adhered to in the 1930s, were by the 1960s accepted as the normal framework of international relations.

By comparison with its peers, the Soviet Union has been motivated by insecurity to a substantially greater degree—an insecurity stemming both from Russia's formative experiences in history and from the domestic position of a government that has relied heavily on police power. The Soviet leaders have differed from their contemporaries also in their adherence to an ideology significantly lacking in pragmatism. Although they have gained world leadership of a Communist movement, numbering 44 million members in 87 countries in 1966, of whom 41 million were in the fourteen Communist countries,[5] their policies have also greatly heightened the normal tensions of international relations and bore a substantial responsibility for the coming of World War II. The world Communist movement may well have been a burden rather than a benefit to Soviet policy.

By comparison with the Russian Empire in the generation before the Revolution, the Soviet Union isolated itself to a greater extent from the international community. As already suggested, this isolation—with roots in traditional policies, but greatly intensified as a result of the Soviet outlook—had profound consequences for domestic developments: it increased the per capita burden of maintaining national security, and it deprived the country of the economic benefits that would have followed from more normal political and commercial relations. In these respects the Soviet Union stands almost alone among the major countries of the world.

Only China, in the 1960s, has carried self-isolation to greater lengths and (excepting as unworthy of comparison the self-defeating nationalism of Germany and Japan in the 1930s) has been guided by an ideology even less sensitive to the complex realities of the world around it. In both cases the domestic costs have been very high.

III. POLITICAL CULTURE: FORMS AND FUNCTIONS

The political culture that informs Soviet policy-making—the heritage of ideas and institutions that Soviet leaders bring to the political process—is deeply rooted in the traditional belief that political authority should be vested in the central government and should be exercised boldly in support of a national policy, with the state predominating over other interests.

Both Soviet and foreign scholars, although they disagree on many points of emphasis, are inclined to stress the central theme in the Russian experience of the consolidation of political authority in response to divisive forces at home and threats from abroad. The continuity between the autocratic power of the emperors and the centralized party in the U.S.S.R. is one that stands out clearly in contrast to the experience of most other societies in modern times. This historically central role of the state was matched by a corresponding weakness of all other forms of organization: territorial subdivisions, religious bodies, political parties, social and occupational strata, labor unions, cooperatives, and business enterprises. Indeed, one may conjecture whether the Russian polity was not so predisposed to the centralization of authority by the time of World War I that only a group of leaders as single-mindedly devoted to the exercise of political power as the Bolsheviks could have hoped to bring order out of the chaos resulting from Russia's repeated defeats in 1914–17.

The Communist Party has greatly intensified and integrated the centralization of authority inherited from the empire, but it has not changed its fundamental character by comparison with other societies. Political scientists sometimes classify the Soviet Union, the other Communist states, National Socialist Germany, and Fascist Italy as "totalitarian." As a simple description of a highly centralized system of controls, a good case can be made for such a classification. But these societies differ greatly as to both traditional heritage and level of development. What is serviceable as a descriptive term is thus markedly lacking in explanatory value. Only in the case of China might one seek a meaningful parallel with Russia in relating a Communist government with totalitarian authority to the heritage of a centralized bureaucratic empire.

The more detailed characteristics that flow from this centralized institutional system may be summarized in terms of the results of a recent cross-polity survey using computer techniques. As reflected in this survey, the U.S.S.R. is one of 32 polities (of 110 studied) that share to a greater or lesser extent a mobilizational style, in the sense that its main purpose is to mobilize resources and skills to meet problems deemed to be of national urgency. It is among 16 polities (of 90) that are totalitarian, in contrast to 23 that are authoritarian, and 51 that are constitutional. It is one of the 22 (of 83) that have enjoyed governmental stability since World War I. It is one of 27 (of 108) where sectional feeling is particularly strong. It is one of 42 (of 80) that have a relatively stable political system. It is one of 6 countries (of 114) in which the federal structure is more formal than effective. It is one of 46 (of 106) in which the horizontal power distribution is negligible.[6]

The Soviet Union is also one of 43 polities (of 98) where the government is not effectively representative even though it is representative in form. Its electoral system is one of 43 (of 82) that are noncompetitive. It is one of 11 (of 99) in which no genuinely autonomous opposition groups are tolerated. It is one of 40 (of 100) in which interest articulation is expressed chiefly by institutional groups rather than by groups outside of the party-state system. It is one of 30 (of 97) where the political leadership may be characterized as elitist, in the sense that party membership is generally a prerequisite to responsible office. It is one of 28 (of 100) where the legislature is wholly ineffective since it is not independent of the party-state. It is one of 31 (of 108) where the military establishment supports the government. It is also one of 66 (of 101) where the police is politically significant.[7]

An interesting quantitative measure of the functioning of the system is provided by comparative statistics on votes in national elections as percentage of voting-age population. The U.S.S.R. ranks highest by this standard, with 99.6 per cent voting in 1958. The achievements of other one-party systems with compulsory voting are almost as high, but Italy also ranked high with 92.9 per cent in 1963 and the Netherlands with 92.1 per cent in 1959. By contrast, 78 per cent voted in the United Kingdom in 1959, 71.2 per cent in Japan, and 64.4 per cent in the United States in 1960,

and only 10.4 per cent in South Africa in 1961 and 1.9 per cent in Rhodesia in 1958.[8]

The bureaucracy underlying this political system has been characterized as a party-state bureaucracy, in contrast to representative, military-dominated, ruler-dominated, and ruling bureaucracies.[9] Characteristic is the close control exercised by the party over the bureaucracy through its monopoly of appointments and, at the upper level, through the overlapping of party and state appointments. This coincidence of party and state at the highest level was exemplified by the roles of Stalin and Khrushchev as both General Secretary of the Party and Chairman of the Council of Ministers in 1941–53 and 1958–64, respectively. As a party-state bureaucracy, the Soviet system is similar in general terms to the thirteen other states ruled by Communist parties and to perhaps half a dozen other movement-regimes where a single party exercises a monopoly of political power.

While the Soviet administrative system is thus relatively unique from a structural standpoint, in its functional characteristics it manifests significant similarities to other systems, as reflected in administrative behavior and representation of interest groups. A recent study finds that Soviet administrative behavior is similar to that prevailing in Western Europe in a number of respects. In the realm of industrial production and foreign trade, hierarchical command principles prevail in both cases—although in the administration of welfare, by contrast, Soviet lines of command tend to be blurred by a multiplication of controls. The importance of informal relations among bureaucrats, including persisting associations among former classmates in educational institutions, is considerable in both the Soviet and the West European bureaucracies. The two systems are also similar in that departures from hierarchical principles usually occur when a staff or functional agency acquires authority by reporting directly to the top of the command structure.

The two systems are significantly different, however, in the realm of communication. Vertical communications are seriously overloaded in the Soviet system because of the practice of requiring many reports to the central authorities and of encouraging lower officials to request permission from their superiors before exercising authority. There is a marked shortage of clerks and stenographers in the Soviet system, and a correspondingly greater reliance on oral communication. There is also a much greater dependence by bureaucrats on relationships with the ruling party, as well as a tendency toward solidarity of the various ethnic groups within the administration.[10]

The Soviet party-state bureaucracy also performs functions similar to those of its counterparts in societies at a similar or more advanced level of development, even though its institutional methods are quite different. Although the Communist Party is often thought of as an undifferentiated organ that decides and commands as a single man, it has in fact always been rent by controversies stemming in part from differences over ideology and policy, and in part from the need to reconcile many divergent interests. The Communist Party is like the human nervous system in that it has a central organ for receiving and sending messages—the Central Committee, with its Politburo and Secretariat, supported by a staff or "apparatus"—as well as a communications system—the nation-wide network of party officials, with 300,000 primary party organizations as the nerve ends that maintain contact with the functioning organisms of the society.

No less than the administrative systems in Western Europe and the United States, the Soviet system must in determining policy take into account the interests of heavy industry, light industry, agriculture, the armed forces, the police, science and technology, consumers, and health, education, and welfare. The competition for scarce resources is in fact more intense in the Soviet Union than in other societies at a comparable level of development, and controversy is correspondingly acute. The interests that in a representative bureaucratic system find expression through political parties, labor unions, professional bodies, and organized pressure groups, channeled through elected representatives in legislative and administrative bodies, are in the Soviet Union channeled through the party-state hierarchy until they reach the Central Committee and its Politburo. The staff of the Secretariat of the Central Committee is in fact organized in some twenty departments, most of which specialize in overseeing and communicating with one or more of the major interest groups within the society. Even within the Politburo, comprising in 1967 eleven members and nine alternate members, the roles of the top leaders tend to be functionally specialized with reference to the leading interest groups.

The Soviet party-state system thus performs the function of articulating and aggregating diverse interests, but the means used differ from those in other societies. It has established a hierarchy of interest groups in which heavy industry, science and technology, and the armed forces normally have a privileged status. The perplexities of allocating resources among interest groups are as burdensome in the Soviet Union as in representative systems, and it is probably fair to say that the differences among alternative proposals considered within the Politburo are as great or greater than those that divide the Democratic and Republican parties in the United States, the Conservative and Labor parties in the United Kingdom, or the moderate and non-Communist left-wing parties in Western Europe. The pressure to keep these differences behind closed doors is nevertheless very great, and the image presented to the outside world has been one of unanimity punctuated by occasional purges.

Since the Stalin era there has been an increasing tendency for high officials to air policy differences in the press. These public expressions of controversy are still rather veiled, however, and analysts must read the national and provincial press very systematically if they are to gain more than a casual understanding of the issues and participants in these continuing debates. In any event, for those interested in the theory of comparative modernization, the differences between the Soviet and other systems provides one of the best illustrations of the diversity of forms by means of which similar functions can be performed.

IV. MOBILIZATION FOR ECONOMIC DEVELOPMENT

Forms and functions are lifeless without a goal and a program to guide the choice among the options available to a society. In the Soviet Union this goal and program are provided by the ideology of Marxism-Leninism, which maintains that "the creation of the appropriate material and technical basis is the principal link in the chain of economic, cultural, and social tasks that have to be accomplished during the transition to communism."[11] The pursuit of this goal is the common thread that runs through the many twists and turns of Soviet policy over a period of half a century, and the Communist Party sees as its principal role the mobilization of Soviet society for economic development.

The comparative position of Soviet society in the economic realm is easier to define than in the political, and its relatively high rate of growth is well documented. The rate of growth of the Soviet Union in net national product for its best periods, 1928–40 and 1950–58, has been estimated at 5.2 per cent per year. This is comparatively quite high, although it has been exceeded over long periods by the United States and Australia in the nineteenth century and by Japan and South Africa in the twentieth. On a per capita basis the growth of the United States and Australia was lower than that of the Soviet Union, however, because of the large influx of population into these countries. That of Japan and South Africa, on the other hand, was higher on a per capita as well as on a net basis.[12]

The estimates of rates of growth for the postwar period alone are 7.2 per cent for gross national product and 6.8 per cent for net national product for the period 1950–58,[13] and 5.7 per cent for gross national product for the period 1950–60.[14] Rates of a similar order of magnitude in the postwar period are found in about a dozen other countries. Some are countries badly damaged by the war, such as Japan, West Germany, Austria, and Burma; others are those receiving extensive foreign aid, such as Greece, Turkey, Jamaica, and Israel. Others yet are countries, such as Venezuela, that could exploit a major national resource.[15] All of them had rates of growth twice or more as great as the more industrialized countries not damaged by the war. On the other hand, countries like Bolivia, Argentina, Paraguay, Morocco, and Syria have had declining rates of growth that went as low as minus 2.2 for Syria.[16]

The growth rate of the Soviet gross national product has been declining since 1958, however, due to a lagging agriculture and to accumulating inefficiencies in industry. The Soviet average annual growth rate in the years 1958–64 has been estimated at 5.3 per cent. This is somewhat above that of the United States (4.4) and the United Kingdom (3.9) in the same period, but below that of other major countries—among which Japan ranks highest at 12.0 per cent.[17]

The evaluation of the economic performance of an economy is a complex matter, since it must be compared with others not only in terms of its over-all purpose but also of the use that it makes of labor, capital, and technology in different branches of the economy. A study comparing the Soviet Union and the United States in this respect reaches the conclusion that in the use of new technology the Soviet Union lagged behind the United States about 25 years in 1963, the lag ranging from 5 to 40 years in individual indices. It also appears that the more rapid growth of the Soviet national product before 1962 was due primarily to the large Soviet input in fixed business capital. This, in turn, reflects the ability of the

Soviet government to keep the standard of living down in the interest of capital formation.[18]

Perhaps more significant as an indication of the Soviet economic effort is the percentage of the gross national product that it has been able to devote to gross domestic capital formation. Although the Soviet Union is only twentieth in rank among 77 countries for which such information was available in 1955, its percentage of 24.1 ranked relatively high among societies at its level of industrialization. It was surpassed by Yugoslavia (31.2 per cent), East Germany (31.1 per cent), Japan (29.2 per cent), Poland (24.8 per cent), and the Netherlands (24.3 per cent), among others, for varying periods in the 1950s. West Germany, New Zealand, and Switzerland had about the same rate of gross capital formation as the U.S.S.R. in the 1950s. The latter surpassed by a considerable margin, however, the United States (17.8 per cent), and the United Kingdom (15.2 per cent), not to mention the Philippines (8.7 per cent), and Indonesia (5.0 per cent).[19]

International comparisons of gross national product are particularly difficult because of differences in the purchasing power of currencies.[20] On the basis of dollar values at market prices, the U.S.S.R. ranked fifth in 1964 among major countries in per capita gross national product adjusted to market prices, behind the United States, France, Germany, and the United Kingdom. About a dozen other smaller countries in Europe, not included in the study cited, would also rank higher than the Soviet Union on a per capita basis. Italy and Japan, on the other hand, ranked slightly below Russia in this comparison.[21]

The question of the relative standing of the Soviet economy is the subject of a continuing debate, in which the chief protagonists are the Joint Economic Committee of the Congress of the United States and the Scientific Council on Economic Competition Between the Two Systems and Problems Facing the Less Developed Countries, attached to the Soviet Academy of Sciences. The American economists, who have advanced most of the concrete propositions thus far, maintain that in 1964 the Soviet gross national product (in dollar values at market prices) was approximately 47 per cent as large as that of the United States, and that this proportion has not changed significantly since 1958.[22] The Soviet specialists, for their part, maintain that the Soviet national income was 46 per cent of that of the United States in 1955 and over 60 per cent in 1961. Differences in computing national income and rates of growth lie at the heart of these contrasting estimates, and the Soviet economists deny that the rate of growth since 1958 of the Soviet gross national product has been declining.[23]

The burdens resulting from the high Soviet rates of investment and growth are reflected in the drastic decline in the share of household consumption and communal services in the gross national product from an estimated 85 per cent in 1928 to 55.8 per cent in 1950, with only a small rise thereafter. Long-term declines of this type normally accompany industrialization, but in other countries it has been a much more moderate decline of 10 to 20 percentage points over a period of three to eight decades. In the U.S.S.R., by contrast, the decline was 30 points in a little over two decades.[24]

The consequences of this pattern of development are also reflected in estimates that suggest that real wages, net of taxes and bonds, declined drastically between 1928 and 1948; and urban per capita purchases of goods and per capita housing space declined moderately in the same period. Per capita purchases of services and per capita industrial output of consumer goods increased only slightly between 1928 and 1948. Although these trends were certainly affected by the economic effort during World War II, they appear to reflect principally the underlying economic policy of the government. Not until the 1950s did the Soviet level of real wages, per capita purchases, and per capita output of consumer goods rise significantly above the 1928 level.[25] It should be noted in this connection that the 1928 level of the economy was little higher than in 1913. A comparative study that assigns the purchasing power of hourly wages in terms of food in the U.S.S.R. an index number of 100 for 1928 and 1950, estimates that the corresponding indices for Austria were 90 and 200, for France 112 and 221, for Sweden 176 and 450, for Great Britain 200 and 443, and for the United States 370 and 714.[26]

A comparison of patterns of consumption with selected West European countries between 1950 and 1962 finds that Soviet per capita consumption of food, clothing, housing, and durables was generally between 40 and 60 per cent of that in France, Germany, and the United Kingdom, depending on the category, and averaged a little over one-half. By comparison with Italy, Soviet consumption was higher per capita in housing and durables, almost as high in food, and about three-quarters as high in clothing. In the period from 1955 to 1962, Soviet over-all per capita consumption declined somewhat by comparison with France, Germany, and Italy, but rose by comparison with the United Kingdom.[27] A more detailed per capita comparison with the United States, by product and service group for 1955, shows a total consumption of 26.2 per cent of that of the United States, and a total consumption exclusive of health and education services of 23.2 per cent. In individual items, Soviet consumption was much higher in alcoholic beverages and cereal products and potatoes, while it equaled that of the United States in public transportation. Per capita consumption of fish, sugar, and confectionary products, and of health and education services stood at about one-half that of the United States.[28] Similar estimates for 1963 place Soviet per capita consumption at 29 per cent of the United States level.[29]

A critical factor in the Soviet pattern of growth has been the problem of agricultural production. No general comparative studies are available, but a comparison with the United States provides some indications of the dimensions of the Soviet problem. This comparison for 1963 indicates that the Soviet Union has 75 per cent more sown crop land than the United States, and 7.5 times the annual average employment in agriculture. It uses only 31 per cent as many tractors, however, 38 per cent as much commercial fertilizers—or 24 per cent per area sown—and 50 per cent as much electricity. The total Soviet production of major grains in 1963, a poor year for Soviet agriculture, was 47 per cent that of the United States. The average Soviet production of grains for 1955–59, which were good years, was 63 per cent of the American. In livestock commodities, Soviet production was higher than that of the United States in mutton, butter, and wool, but 10 to 56 per cent of the American level in other products. Such a comparison, although it does not take climate and soil fertility into account, highlights the central problem of Soviet agriculture: high input of manpower and land, and low input of technology.[30] The low performance in agriculture may be regarded as a significant part of the price paid for rapid industrialization.

As regards the related question of the distribution of income, on which information is only fragmentary, the general experience that distribution of income is more unequal in less developed than in more developed countries appears to be borne out in the Soviet case. Estimates of distribution of income indicate that in the Soviet Union it is at about the same level of inequality as in other countries where the share of the labor force in agriculture is between 40 and 50 per cent. At the same time it has a greater inequality of income distribution than countries with a similar per capita income.[31]

A major economic mechanism for accumulating savings in the interest of high investment and rapid growth is the tax system. There is no satisfactory comparative study of tax systems, but it is generally recognized that the Soviet tax rate is by a substantial margin the highest among comparable countries. The principal source of revenue is the turnover tax, a form of sales tax that bears particularly heavily on consumer goods. This tax amounted to 36.8 per cent of the retail trade turnover in 1963, and was as high as 77.8 per cent in 1947. Since this is a tax on consumer goods, it especially affects lower income groups and may take as much as fifty per cent of their outlays for certain products. Deductions from the profits of state enterprises is the other major source of revenue. The personal income tax is moderately progressive, but is at a relatively low rate and provides only 7 per cent of state revenues as compared with 38 per cent in the United States.[32]

V. Dimensions of Social Change

The most striking feature of Soviet social development has been the many-faceted adjustment to the planned industrialization starting in the late 1920s, which resumed, after a lapse of fifteen years, the process of rapid economic growth and social change that had characterized Russia from the 1880s to World War I.

One of the most profound social consequences of industrialization was the very rapid shift of the labor force from agriculture to industry. It has been estimated that a shift of labor comparable to that which took place in the U.S.S.R. in the twelve years between 1928 and 1940, took from thirty to fifty years in the countries of Western Europe and the English-speaking world that industrialized earlier. Seen in another way, the number of years it took for the share of the agricultural sector in the labor force to decline proportionately as much as in the thirty years between 1928 and 1958 in the U.S.S.R., was over sixty years in the United States, Norway, and Denmark, and fifty to sixty years in Sweden, Canada, and Japan.[33]

This transformation of the labor force is reflected in the rapid annual rate of increase of 0.71 per cent for the period 1926 to 1959 in the population in cities over 20,000. Similar figures for varying but comparable periods indicate that among fifty countries for which figures are available only four, Venezuela, Panama, Poland, and Ireland, had a higher rate of urban growth. A considerable number came close to the Soviet percentage rate, such as Nicaragua (0.70), West Germany (0.67), New Zealand (0.65), Japan (0.64), and Greece (0.61). Others were much further down the scale, such as France (0.24), Italy (0.23), India (0.18), and the United States (0.18). In others yet, such as Belgium, Malta and Gozo, Austria, and Morocco, for a variety of reasons, the percentage of the population in cities over 20,000 declined.[34]

Social mobility is a subject on which sociologists have as yet failed to do much basic research, or to define very adequately the terms and categories on the basis of which comparisons can be made. Indeed, no studies of social mobility have been made within the Soviet Union, and the only empirical evidence we have is based on a study of 765 Soviet emigrés. From this fragmentary data a few comparative judgments may nevertheless be ventured. The U.S.S.R. has a high rate of mobility from manual to nonmanual strata and from manual to elite strata. These two trends are understandable in the light of the rapid industrialization and the role of the Communist Party in destroying and bypassing the traditional elite. Both the United States and France have a comparable, but somewhat lower, rate of mobility from manual to nonmanual strata; and the United States also has a high rate of manual movement into the elite strata. The similarity in these respects of the United States and the U.S.S.R., although for different reasons, is interesting to note. All other societies that have been studied have a substantially lower rate of upward mobility.[35]

The occupational structure that has resulted from the social impact of industrialization is difficult to compare with that of other countries except in a most general way because of lack of adequate statistics. As regards the breakdown between nonmanual and manual occupations, in advanced societies such as the United States, New Zealand, and Sweden, the proportion of employment in nonmanual occupations in 1960–61 was 42.3, 36.7, and 33.2 per cent, respectively. In Japan, which is at about the same level of development as the U.S.S.R., the corresponding percentage is 28.2. In the U.S.S.R., the percentage in nonmanual occupations was 17.7 in 1939 and 20.1 in 1959. As regards the division of the manual category between industry and agriculture, in the advanced societies from about 5 to 15 per cent of the labor force is in agriculture. The corresponding figure is over 30 per cent for the Soviet Union and about the same for Japan.[36]

Instructive comparisons can also be made in the field of education, although these must necessarily be quantitative rather than qualitative. As regards higher education, the total number of students receiving full-time higher education at all levels in 1959–60 per 10,000 population has been estimated at 55 for the U.S.S.R. This is lower than the numbers for Canada (69), Sweden (71), and the United States (126); but it is higher than France (49), New Zealand (48), the Netherlands (47), West Germany (45), Australia (44), and Great Britain (31).[37]

An estimate on a somewhat different basis that compares the number of students enrolled in higher education in 1960, or the closest year for which statistics are available, finds that with 539 students per 100,000 population the U.S.S.R. ranked fifteenth among 105 countries. The fourteen countries with a higher enrollment include Uruguay (541), Japan (750), Argentina (827), Puerto Rico (1,192), the United States (1,983), and many of the countries of Western Europe. Countries with a proportionately smaller enrollment in higher education range from Belgium (536), West Germany (528), the United Kingdom (460), and Czechoslovakia and Switzerland (398), to India (220), China (69), Haiti (29), Ethiopia (5), and Rhodesia and Nyasaland (3). These figures exclude students enrolled in evening and correspondence courses, which comprise about one-half of the students engaged in higher education in the U.S.S.R.[38] It should be noted that comparisons such as these of total numbers of students tend to discriminate against the more efficient educational systems, such as those of Western Europe, where courses of study are tightly organized and students complete them in the normal period with relatively little wastage.[39]

A more accurate basis of comparison is provided by the number of students entering and completing higher education. The percentage of the relevant age group entering higher education in the U.S.S.R. in 1958–59 was 6 per cent for full-time courses and 12 per cent for all levels of higher education. The English-speaking and advanced West European countries all had equivalent or higher rates, ranging as high as 18 and 24 per cent for Canada and 30 and 35 per cent for the United States.[40] Figures for the completion of higher education in 1961–62 in all subjects and at all levels were 8 per cent of the age group in the U.S.S.R., as compared with 9 in Australia, 10 in Great Britain and New Zealand, 15 in Canada, and 17 in the United States. France, Sweden, West Germany, and the Netherlands had lower rates of completion, however, with 7, 7, 5, and 4 per cent of the age group, respectively. In science, engineering, and agriculture alone, however, the U.S.S.R. had the highest rate of completion at 5 per cent of the age group, with the other countries ranging from 2 to 4 per cent.[41]

Comparisons of expenditures for higher education are untrustworthy on account of problems of rates of exchange and national differences in purchasing power as related to the costs of higher education. Estimates of public expenditures on higher education as a percentage of gross national product about 1960 indicate a range between 0.8 per cent for the U.S.S.R., the United States, Great Britain, and Australia, and 0.3 per cent for France.[42] It should be noted in this connection, however, that private (in contrast to public) expenditures on higher education are 6 per cent in France, 10 in Great Britain, 31 in the United States, and 39 per cent in Canada of total expenditures on higher education.[43] Estimates of expenditures on higher education per student that take both public and private expenditures into account do not appear to exist, but from the limited information available it is apparent that Soviet expenditures per student are within the range of those in the English-speaking and advanced West European countries.[44]

An interesting attempt to rank countries according to quantitative indicators of human resource development is the Harbison-Myers scale. In constructing this scale, seventy-five countries were ranked in four groups on the basis of a composite scale based on the arithmetic total of (a) enrollment in secondary education as a percentage of the age group 15 to 19, adjusted for length of schooling, and (b) enrollment in higher education as a percentage of the age groups multiplied by a weight of five. The weighting of higher education reflects the emphasis of this scale on the development of skilled manpower. In this context the U.S.S.R. is in the group of sixteen most advanced countries, with a composite index of 92.6. The higher indices are those of Canada (101.6), France (107.8), Japan (111.4), the United Kingdom (121.6), Belgium (123.6), the Netherlands (133.7), Australia (137.7), New Zealand (147.3), and the United States (261.3). Ranking below the U.S.S.R. in this group of countries are Finland (88.7), West Germany (85.8), Israel (84.9), Argentina (82.0), Sweden (79.2), and Denmark (77.1).[45]

In the realm of research and development efforts, a comparative study has reached some tentative conclusions despite serious problems of comparability. In terms of manpower, the Soviet Union employs about a million people in research and development, as compared with a million and a quarter in the United States and half a million in Western Europe. A comparison of expenditures for research in 1962, taking into account differences in research costs, indicates that Soviet expenditures are about four-fifths of those of the United States and almost twice those of Western Europe. If the comparison were limited to civil research the lag of Western Europe would be much less, since much of the American and Soviet efforts are devoted to military and space research.[46]

As for the percentage of population aged 5 to 19 enrolled in primary and secondary education, the U.S.S.R. ranked thirty-ninth among 124 countries for which information was available in 1960. Its enrollment of 57 per cent of the age group compared with 73 per cent for Japan, 80 for the United Kingdom, 81 for the United States, and 89 for Iceland. Lower rankings included 41 per cent for China, 29 for India, and 2 for Niger.[47] In secondary education alone, however, Soviet enrollments were substantially higher than those of the major West European countries but lower than those in the United States.[48] With respect to literacy of the population aged 15 and over, there were more than twenty countries above the 95 per cent level estimated for the U.S.S.R. in 1959. Literacy in China was estimated at 47.5 per cent of those aged 15 or over in 1950, in India at 19.3 in 1951, and in Mozambique at 1.0 in 1950.[49]

In the realm of communications, the U.S.S.R. in 1960 ranked twenty-sixth in newspaper publication among 125 countries for which information is available, with a daily newspaper circulation of 172 per 1,000 population. The United Kingdom ranked first with 506, Japan sixth with 416, and the United States thirteenth with 326. China, on the other hand, ranked seventy-ninth with a daily circulation of 20 per 1,000, and Upper Volta last with 0.1.[50] In regard to radios, the U.S.S.R. in 1960 ranked twenty-fourth among 118 countries, with 205 sets per 1,000 population. The United States was first with 948, the United Kingdom ninth with 289, Japan fortieth with 106.7, and Upper Volta again last with 0.8.[51] Ranking with respect to television sets was much the same, with the U.S.S.R. twenty-fifth among 69 countries with 27.5 sets per 1,000 population in 1961. The United States was again first with 306.4 sets, Japan in this category was eighth with 98, and India sixty-ninth with 0.001. Cinema attendance in the U.S.S.R. was 17.7 per capita in 1960, giving it a rank of fifth among 104 countries for which such information is available. Countries ranking higher were Israel, Australia, Lebanon, and Hong Kong, the highest, with an attendance of 22.8 per capita. The United States, often thought of as the home of the cinema, ranked nineteenth with a per capita attendance of 11.8; Japan was twenty-sixth with 9.2, China seventy-third with 2.2, and Laos last with a per capita attendance of 0.4.[52]

The problem of comparing book publication is more complex because of problems of definition. According to Soviet practice, all publications with five pages or more are classified as "books-or-pamphlets." In the United States, on the other hand, publications of forty-nine pages or more are classified as books and those from five to forty-eight pages are classified separately as pamphlets. Another difference is that in the U.S.S.R. unchanged reprintings of old books are counted as new books, which is not the case in the United States and Western Europe. The U.S.S.R. also includes in its book statistics a wide variety of free publications, including administrative instructions, construction plans, and catalogues; this is not the case in other countries. Finally, Soviet statistics include as new titles translations of the same book into its many minority languages.

A discriminating comparison that takes these differences into account reaches the conclusion that in 1961 the U.S.S.R. *produced* 5.55 copies per capita of books and pamphlets of over four pages, and the United States *sold* 6.05 copies per capita of books of over forty-eight pages, not counting municipal, state, federal, and industrial publications. It appears that a number of West European countries do as well or better per capita. The question of the comparative cost of books is also a controversial matter, depending as it does not only on the purchasing power of currency but also on wage and salary levels. A comparison taking these factors into account reaches the conclusion that most categories of books were less expensive in the United States than in the U.S.S.R. in terms of the hours of work required in the two countries to earn the purchasing price.[53]

In matters of public health, the U.S.S.R. ranked thirteenth among 79 countries in 1958–59, with a life expectancy of 72 years for females at birth. Representative higher rankings were Czechoslovakia at 72.3 years, the United States at 73 years, and Sweden, the highest, at 75.2 years. Lower rankings included Japan at 69.9 years, Turkey at 50.4, India at 32.2, and Mali, the lowest, at 26.0.[54] The U.S.S.R. had 35 infant deaths per 1,000 live births in 1960, ranking twentieth after the Netherlands, which had the lowest rate of 16.5 infant deaths in 1960, and thirtieth above India, with 225 infant deaths in 1951. The United States, by comparison, had 26.4 infant deaths per 1,000 live births in 1959, Japan had 37.7 in the same year, and Yugoslavia had 100 in 1958.[55] Interesting figures are also available in regard to inhabitants per physician and per hospital bed. The U.S.S.R. had one physician for every 578 inhabitants in 1959, ranking in this respect second only to Israel with one for 400. By comparison, the United States had one physician for 780 inhabitants, Czechoslovakia ranked third with one for 620, Japan one for 930, India one for 5,200, China one for 8,700, and Ethiopia, the lowest, one for 117,000.[56] In such comparisons the quality of physicians, in terms of length of training and degree of specialization, is not taken into account. In regard to hospital beds, the Soviet ratio of one per 140 inhabitants in 1960 was surpassed by twenty-five countries, including all the English-speaking and advanced West European countries. Ireland ranked highest, with one hospital bed per 70 inhabitants. The ratio in most other countries was much lower, as reflected in one hospital bed per 1,800 inhabitants in China, one per 2,200 in India, and one per 8,100 in Afghanistan.[57]

Comparative estimates relating to the general problem of the changing role of women in society do not seem to be available. This is due in part to the lack of statistics and more particularly to some confusion as to what answers should be sought. Of the many issues involved in the emancipation of women in modern times, those concerning education and professional employment are most amenable to study. Since manual labor has included women in all societies and at all times, the controversial problems have tended to center on the accessibility to women of professional and managerial occupations with compensation equal to that received by men. A unique feature of Soviet society in this regard is the enrollment of women in higher education, which rose from 30 per cent of the students in 1930 to 40 per cent in 1940 and 80 per cent in the mid-1940s, and then declined to 50 per cent in 1950 and about 40 per cent in 1960. This trend was accompanied by an at-work rate of almost 90 per cent in the 1950s for women with a higher education. In the postwar years women have earned about one-quarter of the higher degrees in science and engineering, have occupied some 38 per cent of the faculty positions in Soviet higher institutions, and comprise 36 per cent of all scientific workers and 32 per cent of all engineers. At the same time, very few women have advanced to top positions in scholarship, science, and engineering. This role of Soviet professional women, which surpassed that of any West European country in the period 1930–55, was due principally to war losses and to political purges. Since 1955 the professional role of women in the U.S.S.R. has not been significantly different from that in the advanced countries.[58]

As regards the labor force in general, as distinct from employment in the professions, the underlying fact is that in 1946 it comprised 100.9 million females as compared with 75.1 million males in the U.S.S.R. The surplus of women over men both in the population as a whole and in the working-age population will continue beyond 1980.[59] The U.S.S.R. ranked highest among sixty-nine countries in the proportion of women among wage and salary earners, with 46.7 per cent in 1959. Other countries within ten percentage points were the Barbados, Jamaica, Ecuador, Haiti, and Finland. The United States ranked nineteenth with 30.5 per cent, and Japan twentieth with 30.3 per cent, and the range of the West European countries in general was between 23 and 34 per cent.[60]

Divorce rates, in contrast to many other social indices, tend to correlate more with cultural traditions than with the level of industrialization or urbanization. In 1962, for instance, the Soviet Union had 1.3 final divorce decrees per 1,000 population. This compares with rates of below 1 per 1,000 in England, France, Japan, and Greece, and of over 2 per 1,000 in the United States, Egypt, and Rumania.[61]

It would be interesting to compare, if one could, the prevalence of crime and other forms of social disorganization, but adequate statistical data do not appear to be available. One would expect the U.S.S.R., as a society still half-rural and half-urban, to have a relatively lower incidence of the social problems most characteristic of highly urbanized societies—irrational murder and assault, illegitimacy, homosexuality, suicide, and traffic accidents. At the same time, one might expect somewhat higher rates of murder and assault of relatives and acquaintances, burglary, and other crimes associated with rural and urban communities where people work under conditions of unusual stress and deprivation. In the present state of our knowledge it would doubtless be a mistake to assume a close correlation between social disorganization and urbanization, and a thorough examination of this question on a cross-cultural basis is one of the challenges that still confront students in anthropology, sociology, and social psychology.

If one could, it would also be interesting to compare the use of forced labor in the Soviet Union, where it was widespread from the 1930s to the 1950s, with its use in other countries. The available data do not, however, permit satisfactory comparisons.[62]

VI. A Retrospective Appraisal, 1917–67

The broad outline of the comparative position of Soviet society that emerges from the available data will not surprise persons knowledgeable about Soviet affairs, but only in recent years have world-wide comparative indices been prepared that permit one to explore in some detail the nuances of the relative standing of the U.S.S.R. in terms of its ranking in regard to other countries, the balance of achievements and costs, and the pattern of modernization represented by Soviet policies.

Rankings

One conclusion that can be drawn is that on a per capita basis the U.S.S.R. ranks in measurable economic and social indices about twentieth among the 130 or more countries for which reasonably adequate information is available. This is more than an impressionistic ranking, for a number of careful calculations have been made in an attempt to compare societies on the basis of composite indices. The Russett scale, for example, ranks 107 societies on the basis of levels of per capita gross national product and then divides them into five groups or stages in such a way as to maximize the consistency of eight variables. These variables are per cent urban population, per cent literacy, higher education per 100,000, inhabitants per physician, radios per 1,000, per cent voting, per cent in military service, and the expenditure of central government, social security, and public enterprise as a percentage of gross national product. According to this scale the most developed group of fourteen countries—in effect the English-speaking and advanced West European countries—are in the stage described as "high mass-consumption" societies. The next level comprises thirty-six identified as "industrial revolution" societies, which includes Czechoslovakia, the U.S.S.R., East Germany, Italy, Poland, and Japan, among others, in that order. The U.S.S.R. ranks sixth from the top in this second group, and twentieth from the top in the entire list of 107 countries.[63] The Central Statistical Administration of the U.S.S.R., on the basis of its own calculations of national income per capita, ranks the Soviet Union fourteenth—placing it ahead of Belgium and the Netherlands, among others.[64]

These indices that rank countries with per capita product or income as a key factor are the simplest to construct, but as a basis of comparison they suffer from all of the distortions that result from differences in purchasing power and rates of exchange when national incomes are converted into U.S. dollars. One attempt to avoid this difficulty is represented by the Niewiaroski scale, which seeks to establish the relative level of living of countries by selecting and weighting items significant to basic living conditions that can be measured in physical quantities. This scale uses nine economic and five social variables, and these are reduced by means of factor analysis to a common component which is expressed in relation to an index number of 100 for the United States. On this basis, the U.S.S.R. ranks twenty-first (of 88) in the economic scale, twenty-fourth in the social scale, and twenty-first in the combined scale, with indices of 46, 43, and 52, respectively. The twenty countries with higher levels of living than the U.S.S.R. include the English-speaking and advanced West European countries, and East Germany, Czechoslovakia, Finland, and Israel. Japan ranks twenty-second, just below the U.S.S.R., in the combined index, with its rank of eighth in the social index compensating for its rank of thirty-first in the economic index. On this scale, India ranks seventy-fifth, and Ethiopia, the lowest.[65]

Another composite index, based on an analysis of the ranking of 95 countries with reference to 43 indices of economic development, ranks the countries in terms of four basic patterns. Of these patterns the first two, technological and economic-demographic, are particularly relevant to our appraisal. In the technological pattern, based on indices of accessibility, transportation, trade, external relations, technology, industrialization, urbanization, national product, and the organization of population, the U.S.S.R. ranks in the second of five groups of 19 countries each. In the economic-demographic pattern, based primarily on birth and death rates, population growth rates, population densities, and population per unit of cultivated land, the U.S.S.R. again ranks in the second of five groups of 19 countries.[66]

This measurement of comparative levels of living may be compared with the Bennett scale, which ranked 31 countries in terms of consumption levels for the period 1934–38. The Bennett scale was constructed by ranking the countries in each of nineteen indicators of physical quantities of consumption, health, communications, and transportation, and then reducing the rankings to a single indicator by scoring countries according to their ranking in the nineteen indicators together and converting this to a percentage of the United States score. On this basis the U.S.S.R. ranked fourteenth (of 31), with a consumption level at 33.6 per cent of that of the United States. By comparison, Argentina, Czechoslovakia, Cuba, and Japan ranked seventh, eighth, ninth, and tenth, respectively.[67]

As regards earlier periods, estimates for eleven advanced countries indicate that in terms of changes of rates of growth per decade Russia was seventh highest in national product before World War I and fifth highest in the period 1913–54; and in rate of growth in per capita product it ranked ninth highest in the prewar period and third highest (after Sweden and Japan) in the period 1913–54. Its change in comparative standing since the beginning of the five year plans is reflected in estimates that it produced 8.1 per cent of world income in 1938 and 11.1 per cent in 1949, and that in the same period its relative income per capita rose from 102 to 133 per cent of the world level. The relative position of the United States, Canada, Australia, and New Zealand improved considerably more in this same period, but that of all other regions declined.[68]

This per capita ranking of about twentieth among the countries of the world in 1967 must, of course, be distinguished from a ranking in gross terms, in view of Russia's position as the largest country in area and the third most populous. In terms of gross industrial production Russia's world position has risen from fifth to second in rank since 1917. Due to the highly centralized character of the political system, this power is even more impressive in those areas that the government has selected for a special effort. The per capita level of development of a country is only indirectly related to its effectiveness in international relations, in which factors of size and organization are of vital importance. Thus China, with perhaps little more than one-tenth the per capita national income of the Soviet Union, and an even smaller proportion of that of Belgium or Denmark, is nevertheless a world power of great importance. To compare the per capita level of societies is not to deny the importance of gross national income and production in international relations, but rather to stress a related but distinct aspect of development.

In the perspective of fifty years, the comparative ranking of the U.S.S.R. in composite economic and social indices per capita has probably not changed significantly. So far as the rather limited available evidence permits a judgment, the U.S.S.R. has not overtaken or surpassed any country on a per capita basis since 1917 with the possible exception of Italy, and the nineteen or twenty countries that rank higher than Russia today in this regard also ranked higher in 1900 and 1917. The per capita gross national product of Italy, which is just below that of the U.S.S.R. today, was probably somewhat higher fifty years ago.[69]

In significant respects the Soviet Union has at the same time closed the gap separating it from the more advanced countries, although the statistical evidence is again limited. The Soviet gross national product has increased substantially since 1950 by comparison with that of the United States, for instance, although the extent of this increase is still a matter of debate between the economists of the two countries.[70] It is perhaps more pertinent that in certain important individual indices, such as heavy industry and technological education and research, the U.S.S.R. has not only closed the gap but surpassed some of the countries that were well ahead of it in 1917. These significant gains, at the same time, must be balanced against lags in other indices of development. Since all of the more advanced societies have been developing rapidly in the course of the past half-century despite many ups and downs, and a good deal more rapidly than the less-developed societies, it has taken great efforts and sacrifices on the part of the government and peoples of Russia to maintain the ranking of the Soviet Union in this arduous competition. Among the major, later-modernizing societies, probably only Japan has improved its relative standing more markedly than the Soviet Union over a period of half a century.[71]

Achievements and Costs

No less significant than the generalized ranking based on composite indices in the evaluation of Soviet society is an appraisal of the pattern of development reflected in the distinction between those areas where Soviet accomplishment is relatively high, surpassing countries at comparable levels of gross national product per capita, and those where it is relatively low. In making this distinction it is important to recognize that certain of the areas of high achievement are due to the nature of the Soviet political system—such as the high per cent of participation in national elections and the relative stability of the government. Other characteristics, such as the high expenditure on defense, may be attributed to the position of the U.S.S.R. as a great power. The large proportion of women in the labor force also appears to be due more to circumstances of war and revolution than to other factors.

Taking these qualifications into account, there are at the same time significant areas of high per capita ranking that can be attributed primarily to the policies of development adopted by the party-state. The most striking area of achievement is in the rate of economic growth, where the U.S.S.R. ranked ahead of all the major countries in the 1950s except West Germany and Japan. This comparatively high rate of growth is not being maintained, however, in the 1960s.

Closely related to this rapid growth rate is the Soviet pattern of development in the realm of social change. The shift within the labor force from agriculture to industry was twice as rapid as in the English-speaking and advanced West European countries, and the rate of urban growth was among the highest. This was accompanied by one of the highest rates of movement from manual to nonmanual and to elite strata.

The U.S.S.R. also surpasses a number of more advanced countries in enrollment in higher and secondary education, and especially in education devoted to science, technology, and agriculture. It ranks high also in expenditures on higher education per student and on research, and generally in human resource development. It may likewise be noted, although it is not very important, that in cinema attendance per capita the U.S.S.R. ranks among the highest. It no doubt also ranks high in the production and distribution of books, although adequate comparative figures are not available. Similarly, as has been noted, in such aspects of public health as life expectancy and the ratio of physicians to the population, the U.S.S.R. ranks relatively high.

In other respects the U.S.S.R. ranks relatively lower than its general ranking on the basis of gross national product per capita would lead one to expect. It ranks thirty-eighth among 93 countries in the per cent of its labor force in agriculture, and twenty-ninth among 120 in the per cent of its labor force in cities over 20,000. The share of household consumption and communal services dropped much more drastically than in other countries during the period of most rapid growth, and remains relatively low. Real wages also declined rapidly between 1928 and 1948, and only in the 1950s began to rise significantly above the 1928—and hence the 1913— level. The distribution of income within Soviet society has also been significantly more unequal than in countries at a comparable level of development, and lower income groups are taxed more heavily. The growth of purchasing power in hourly wages in terms of food between 1928 and 1950 was much lower than that in any of the English-speaking and advanced West European countries. In enrollment in primary schools the U.S.S.R. ranks relatively low.

These various respects in which the U.S.S.R. ranks relatively low may be considered as the cost of the relatively high rate of industrial growth and of investment in higher education, technology, and public health. In quantitative terms, this cost finds expression in lower wages, higher taxes, poorer housing, and a variety of acute shortages that are familiar to persons acquainted with Soviet life. These costs are borne primarily by the lower-income groups, in contrast to an elite that lives relatively comfortably and free from progressive taxation.

In political terms, the costs of Russian achievements have been reflected in the momentous purges of the 1930s and continued political terrorism into the 1950s. Political oppression of this character has been surpassed among major countries only by Germany in the 1930s and 1940s and China in the 1950s and 1960s. Other countries at a similar or more advanced level have achieved an equivalent or better record of development at a significantly lower cost in human lives and hardship.

The conclusions that one draws from such a balance-sheet of achievements and costs depend on one's goals and values. Those concerned with human welfare and rights will be appalled by the cost. Marxist-Leninists, and technocrats who place a high value on economic development, may admire the ability of the Soviet leaders to hold down the level of living of so many people for so long in the interest of a high rate of growth. Students of comparative modernization, for their part, will note that other societies have achieved similar results at a substantially lower cost, and will seek to discover whether there is something inherent in the Russian traditional heritage and resource base that made these sacrifices necessary.

The Soviet Pattern of Modernization

A comparative appraisal of Soviet society cannot fail to consider in what respects its pattern of development is characteristic of Communist societies in general. It is interesting to note in this connection that few of the characteristics of the Soviet political structure are unique to Communist countries. Thus, to repeat figures given above, although only 14 countries are under Communist rule, the number with totalitarian governments is 16, 28 have legislatures that depend wholly on the state, 30 have an elitist political leadership, 32 have a mobilizational style, 42 have a relatively stable party system, 46 have a negligible distribution of horizontal power, and in 66 the police is politically significant.

The absence of a clear distinction between Soviet and non-Soviet, or more generally Communist and non-Communist, patterns of development raises the question of what political characteristics are in fact unique to Communist societies. Three of these may be distinguished. One is a monopoly of political power by a Communist party. This monopoly undoubtedly lies at the heart of Marxism-Leninism, both in theory and in practice, and one could not regard as Communist a country in which the monopoly was not preserved intact.

The second characteristic is the effort to assert state control over all aspects of economic and social life. One may nevertheless question whether in the economic realm it is not a unique attribute more in form than in substance. Its original role in Marxism was as a means to an end—more equal distribution—rather than as an end in itself. Students of societies that are more industrialized but have maintained the principle of private property, have long since realized that the meaning of ownership in these societies has been greatly changed by the growth in the legal power of the government to restrict use of property. These matters are difficult to compare, but there are significant ways in which governments in free enterprise countries exercise greater control over property—through legal controls other than ownership—than is exercised in the U.S.S.R. and other Communist countries. It is in this sense that ownership of the means of production in the U.S.S.R. may be regarded as more formal than real. Moreover, the fourteen Communist countries vary considerably in the ways in which control of the means of production is exercised in practice. Within the U.S.S.R. itself, the means by which the state exercises its control through ownership has changed significantly in the 1960s, and it is likely that these means will become increasingly pragmatic and diversified in the next decade or two within the framework of an administered society.

The third characteristic of Communist societies is a policy of modernization that places an unusually heavy stress on rapid industrialization and on social factors regarded as essential to economic growth. This characteristic is less distinctively Communist than the monopoly of political power or the ownership of the means of production. A comparable level of mobilization of skills and resources has been achieved by less dramatic means in a number of major countries, including the United States, Sweden, Germany, Australia, and Japan, and by several smaller countries. There is also a considerable diversity among Communist countries in their ability to mobilize skills and resources. China, which has employed as ruthless mobilizational techniques as any Communist society, experienced a virtual stagnation in economic and social development between 1958 and 1962.

The question of the unique attributes of Communist societies is closely related to the question of the distinguishing features of "socialism." This is a term that means different things to different people. Those who are not adherents of Marxism-Leninism generally support one of two definitions: the vesting of ownership and control of the means of production in the community as a whole; or the distribution per capita of the goods produced on the basis of some test of equality, including government policies designed to promote social welfare. Marxist-Leninists, on the other hand, regard common ownership of the means of production as characteristic of both socialism and communism. They consider socialism to be a lower phase of the Communist social formation, in which goods are not produced in sufficient quantity to be distributed according to needs, and distinguish a higher phase—communism proper—in which production will be adequate for such distribution.

The problems involved in comparing ownership and control of means of production in different types of societies have already been noted, and it does not seem possible to compare societies in this regard on any precise basis. As regards distribution of goods, however, the available evidence indicates that there is a more equal distribution in a considerable range of countries, including the English-speaking and advanced West European societies, than in the U.S.S.R. Distribution appears to be a function more of the level of economic development than of the policies of the government, and the degree of equality of distribution is not significantly greater in "socialist" Denmark or Sweden, or in "labor" England, than in "capitalist" United States.[72] Indeed, due to the high rate of investment and the disproportionate emphasis on heavy industry over many years, distribution of goods is in all likelihood more unequal in the U.S.S.R. than in many countries at a comparable level of gross national product per capita, and also more unequal than in Japan, which has a somewhat lower per capita product.

If the U.S.S.R. cannot be considered uniquely "Communist" or "socialist," how can one evaluate the characteristics of its society in a world-wide comparative context? It may be seen as a society whose configuration in 1967 results from a unique heritage of national power and autocratic tradition; a per capita resource base in agriculture that is relatively low by European standards but quite high by Asian or African; and a base in industrial raw materials that was discovered to be quite high once natural resources were fully explored. On the basis of these traditions and resources the Tsarist government achieved a relatively high rate of economic growth and social change in the decades preceding World War I, and this rate was resumed on a more intensified basis after 1928. This second developmental drive was significantly influenced by the theories of Marxism-Leninism, but it was neither as different from the effort before the Revolution nor as closely related to what is usually considered to be "Marxism," "socialism," or "communism," as is commonly thought. In other words, the characteristics peculiar to Soviet society resulting from a unique pattern of resources and inherited traditions are more striking than those that it shares with other societies. As a model, it is useful only to the limited extent that other societies share its attributes.

In concluding this retrospective appraisal of Soviet society, two observations of a more theoretical character are called for. One is that the Soviet Union provides a good example of the role of historically evolved institutions in contemporary affairs. Not only political and social values, but also habits of work and occupational patterns that derive from the resource base of a society, play a profound role in the way in which it develops. The central theoretical issue confronting students of comparative modernization is thus not the one frequently asked of how a given society will move toward a fixed institutional pattern—Western, Soviet, or other, depending on the point of view—but rather how can its own institutions be adapted to the changing functions made possible by the growth of knowledge in modern times.[73]

The second and related observation is that, given the profound influence of historically evolved institutions, the institutional patterns of different societies should not be expected to converge in the foreseeable future. The functions that they perform will converge, but the institutional means by which these are performed are likely to remain significantly different. The United States and the Soviet Union, or Japan and Italy, will converge in the sense that their bureaucratic efficiency, occupational structure, level of education, and per capita consumption of raw materials and energy will become more alike—but their political values, their means of reconciling conflicting interest groups, and their authority patterns in family and social organizations, for example, are likely to remain significantly different.[74]

VII. PROSPECTS

In seeking to envision the configuration of Soviet society as it is likely to evolve in a near future that may be thought of in terms of ten or fifteen years, it is important to make a distinction between those features of the current pattern that appear to be relatively stable and those that seem likely to undergo considerable change.

The international environment, which has played such an important role in the formation of the Soviet pattern of modernization, will in its general outlines be more stable than in the period since the end of World War II. The earlier period from 1945 to 1967 has seen a revolution in the balance of power, the accession to power of Communist parties in twelve other states, including China, and the emergence of no fewer than fifty countries from colonial rule. There has also been a rising incidence of modernizing revolutions and other political convulsions of various types in the countries of Asia, Latin America, and Africa. No changes of comparable significance appear to be in preparation for the near future. There are still some forty colonial territories, most of them very small, but the process by which they gain independence will probably follow the relatively stable pattern already set by their predecessors. In many of the newer states there will be revolutions and *coups d'état*, probably no fewer than a dozen a year for the foreseeable future, but it does not seem that their consequence will be to add greatly to the world influence of any of the major powers. The proliferation of nuclear weapons will add to the perils that military technology has already contributed, but the degree of consensus already achieved between the United States and the Soviet Union on this issue appears to be adequate to prevent a major catastrophe.

Within the framework of this anticipated relative stability in world politics, there is good reason to believe that the sense of insecurity that has shaped many Russian attitudes both before and since 1917, is giving place to a greater sense of security and assurance. In a technical sense, the turning point in this regard can be placed at 1956 when, as a result of the development of Soviet military technology, Khrushchev declared that war was no longer "fatalistically inevitable" and that the fear of "capitalist encirclement" need not continue to be a central feature of Soviet strategic planning. Increasingly in the past decade, Soviet officials of the younger generation have approached the outside world with greater self-confidence, and in a number of international crises the U.S.S.R. has played a role of mediator. Notable Soviet successes in international relations and in outer space have served to promote a sense of security, and the maturing of the economy has also placed a premium on international stability and on increased foreign trade as necessary for continued Soviet prosperity.

In the realm of domestic politics the prospects for structural change do not appear to be significant. The main features of the party-state bureaucracy appear to be functioning more effectively and rationally than ever before; and as a new generation of officials rises through the ranks, the top leaders are likely to be increasingly less erratic and more concerned with the smooth operation of the administrative apparatus. Within the framework of this institutional structure, however, significant changes may well take place. The Central Committee will probably play a larger role in party affairs, and may even reach the point of electing the members of the Politburo on the basis of competition among candidates. The domination of the party over the state apparatus, however, including the Supreme Soviet, is likely to continue with little change.

The security restrictions on all forms of expression, significantly relieved in their harshness since the 1950s, will probably continue to be lightened within the present framework of party vigilance and state paternalism. There is no indication that the party-state bureaucracy will significantly alter its monopoly of power, or permit the type of criticism that might lead to the organization of centers of opposition within the country. The ideological role of Marxism-Leninism continues to give evidence of vigor, and is indeed becoming more rational in its successive revisions. The abstractions of the doctrine have assumed greater concreteness as Soviet institutions have come to develop stable forms, and there appears to be no reason why Soviet leaders should not continue to regard Marxism-Leninism as the only ideology that corresponds to reality.

Similarly, the characteristic pattern of modernization that places primary emphasis on heavy industry and technology and relegates consumer goods to a secondary position is likely to continue. In the current Five Year Plan (1966–70), expansion is provided for in all sectors of the economy, but the proportion of investments devoted to consumer goods and services is about the same as in earlier plans. Eventually a shift in emphasis to consumer goods and services similar to that in the advanced societies is contemplated, but such a shift is not yet apparent in plans thus far made available.

When one seeks to depict economic and social trends in the near future in greater detail, the essential question concerns the assumptions one should make regarding these developments. The characteristic of projections in this context is that they assume no change in rates of development. Predictions, on the other hand, generally assume changing rates of development. The choice of one method over the other depends on the credibility of the assumptions that one can make regarding rates of change.

A projection of economic growth to 1975 based on the high growth rates of the 1950s, indicates that Soviet gross national product would be $455 billion in 1975 as compared with $121 billion in 1957, but that its position of second in rank would not change. It is interesting to note in this connection that the rank of the United Kingdom would drop from third to sixth, that of West Germany and China would rise from fourth and fifth to third and fourth, respectively, and that of Japan would rise from ninth to fifth. On a per capita basis, the U.S.S.R. would rank fifteenth in 1975 with $1,627, as compared with twenty-first in 1957 with $600. In this period the U.S.S.R. would thus surpass Venezuela, Finland, and the Netherlands. Australia, New Zealand, and Kuwait, ahead of the U.S.S.R. in 1957, are not included in this projection.[75]

Since these projections were made, it has become apparent that Soviet rates of growth in the 1960s are substantially lower than in the 1950s and the above projection must accordingly be discounted. It would appear that in its over-all economy the Soviet Union will continue in the near future to grow at about the same rate as the more advanced countries. The U.S.S.R. may well close some of the gaps, although in the mid-1960s it fell behind slightly in its race to overtake the United States.

The leap from projections to predictions is a big one, and it cannot be said that any predictions have been made that have the credibility of the projections just cited. It is interesting to note that the official Marxist-Leninist doctrine goes so far as to predict unequivocally that "Calculations based on comparing average annual figures of the development of the economies of the U.S.S.R. and the U.S.A. over a long period show that in 1980 the national income per capita in the Soviet Union will exceed the U.S. future national income per capita by at least 50 per cent."[76] Soviet scholars currently working on problems of comparison have made no such predictions, however, and even Soviet propaganda has adopted a much more modest attitude toward this question.

In the social realm, it is estimated that the U.S.S.R. will have 21.4 per cent of its labor force employed in agriculture in 1975 as compared with 48 per cent in 1959, and will rank twentieth instead of twenty-sixth below the country with the smallest labor force in agriculture. As regards inhabitants per hospital beds, the U.S.S.R. will in 1975 be one of nine countries with the highest ratio of one bed per 70 inhabitants, as compared with a ranking of seventeenth in 1960.[77]

The proportion of the age groups 15–19 and 20–24 enrolled in Soviet schools will be substantially higher in 1970 than in the West European countries, but lower than in the United States and Canada. Enrollment for the age group 5–14, however, will still be considerably lower in the Soviet Union. The enrollment ratio for the entire age group 5–24 in 1970 will be about the same in the Soviet Union as in Western Europe.[78] The Soviet Union is likely to retain its predominance in enrollments in higher and secondary education over Western Europe through the 1970s, although it does not appear that it will equal the United States and Canada in this respect.

The near future is also likely to see a further absorption of the various minority peoples of the Soviet Union into the dominant Russian culture. It is a natural process that is probably encouraged but does not need to be enforced. This process in the Soviet Union resembles that in the United Kingdom in earlier periods rather than that in the United States, and, as in the United Kingdom, is likely to lead to the diminution of ethnic differences.

The areas of most rapid change in Soviet society in the near future are likely to be in the institutional adaptation to a more complex industrial society. The methods of economic organization and social control did not change a great deal from the late 1920s to the late 1950s, but the harsh and arbitrary methods that could be made to work in the earlier period are no longer effective. Khrushchev, despite the association of his name with a number of these changes, belonged essentially to the old school of leaders who worked largely by intuition, assumed that the population was

rather passive, and tended to equate socialism with rapid industrialization. The demands of agriculture, housing, scientific management, and a consumer-oriented light industry can no longer be
neglected despite a continued emphasis on heavy industry, and they
introduce complexities not known to the earlier period.

This experimentation with institutional change can now take
place in an international environment in which Soviet leaders see
their country as a peer among the great powers and no longer isolated in a world of hostile countries. Although the burden of defense expenditures is still very heavy, the relative relaxation of
concern regarding national security provides the environment for
more permissive domestic policies than in any period since the
early 1920s.

At the same time, this process of institutional adaptation will
take place within the framework of a system tightly controlled by
the party-state bureaucracy, will continue to be oriented primarily
toward heavy industry, and will preserve a rather sharp distinction
between a university-educated leadership group and a large body of
industrial and agricultural workers. The rapid movement from
manual to nonmanual labor is likely to diminish, and a greater
stability established between leaders and led.

In the world of nations the Soviet Union will be less of a threat
and also less of a model. Its leaders will be more concerned with
their own problems, and less concerned with ideological abstractions. They will also come to realize that they face major problems
in seeking to promote the further development of Soviet society,
and that they will be doing very well if over a long period they can
maintain the rate of growth of the more advanced countries.

PART TWO

The Formation and Control of Policy

Introduction

The following essays are addressed to five key areas of potential change in policy formation and implementation in Soviet society. Any assessment of the Soviet future must begin with the nature of the Communist Party and its relationships with the larger society, and Jeremy Azrael's opening essay considers this essential matter. He places special emphasis on the factors that may be expected to enhance or diminish the party's mobilizational capacities over the coming years.

A second concern is with the internal functioning of the party, and especially how it copes and will cope with the problems of conflict resolution that inevitably arise in complex political organisms. Although the party has traditionally depicted itself as a monolithic organization, at one with the society, we know that hard-fought policy decisions, representing the clashing interests of different groups and fundamentally affecting developments throughout the system, take place within party circles. Sidney Ploss illuminates the dark and complicated nature of these policy exchanges—which are still weakly institutionalized—and suggests how the further development of interest-group politics is related to the need in an advanced society, even an authoritarian one, to handle perennial conflicts over the allocation of resources and power.

Leon Lipson's analysis of the legal system concerns an unresolved question of the post-Stalin era: how to maintain a viable civil order through increasing resort to legal procedures without at the same time restricting the party's freedom of extralegal maneuvering. Lipson draws a distinction between *legality* and *legalism*, the latter constituting an elaboration of legal forms which are genuine enough but which fall substantially short of placing the political system itself under the rule of law. The Soviet choice between these alternatives is crucial, for the outcome involves no less than the entire style of dealings in the future between the party and government on one side and the populace on the other.

The question of the influence of significant constituencies in the formation and control of policy will assume growing importance as the further development of Soviet society leads to ever more entwined interrelations among its functionally specialized components. The military, which is the subject of Thomas Wolfe's analysis, is a particularly intriguing case. Its existence implies an ever-present potential for disruptive conflict within the society: not only does the military possess an operational monopoly over the means of force, but the very nature of an officer corps sets aside an important segment of the professional population as a special group with highly focused interests. Moreover, the rapid development of technology in warfare not only leads to new problems in civilian (i.e., party)–military relations, but also aggravates traditional tensions within the military establishment. Whether and how the party is succeeding in its management of these multiple tensions provides a clue to the outcome of parallel issues of political control that transcend the specific case of the military.

The final issue treated here is one of the original, and continuing, dilemmas of Soviet policy: how to adjust to the consequences of the substantial presence of national minorities widely differing in cultural, educational, and political development. Vernon Aspaturian's essay on the nationalities serves as an important reminder of why it is so important to look beyond the European "center" of Soviet affairs in dealing with the prospects for Soviet society. Vast, comprehensive, and accelerating changes are under way which will irrevocably alter the fate of peoples, their dealings with one another, and the quality of their future roles in the system.

3.

The Party and Society

JEREMY R. AZRAEL

I. ADAPTATION VERSUS MOBILIZATION

To assess the Communist Party's future role in Soviet society requires, first of all, an appreciation of its origins in the pre-revolutionary period, as well as an evaluation of recent developments.

No feature of Russian history has been more frequently or more deservedly remarked than the wide gulf that divided the Tsarist state from the society over which it ruled. While the point has often been stressed too far, it is fair to say that the degree of reciprocal influence between society and polity rarely rose above the bare minimum essential to the maintenance of the over-all system. Stable channels of communication between the two spheres were few and only intermittently effective. This lack of integration, in turn, was a major source of alienation among the Russian intelligentsia.

The elimination of the prevailing dualism was part of the intelligentsia's "mission," common to Bolsheviks and non-Bolsheviks alike, and served as one of the principal foci of solidarity for the intelligentsia. For the Bolsheviks, however, the objective was nothing less than the absolute obliteration of the barrier between society and polity. Their program looked toward the complete "withering away of the state" and the emergence of a self-coordinating, self-regulating system of associational life in a free and open classless society. The only question was how this objective was to be realized.

To this single question, the Bolsheviks gave two radically different answers. Both entailed revolutionary seizure of power and the subsequent introduction of a transitional "dictatorship of the proletariat," but in almost all other respects they were diametrically opposed.

On the one hand, as Lenin made abundantly clear in his famous pamphlet *State and Revolution*, the Bolsheviks conceived of the "withering away of the state" as a completely spontaneous and essentially unilinear process that would come to fruition in relatively short order and would be accompanied by a rapid and progressive decline in political coercion. Indeed, the "dictatorship of the proletariat" would be unprecedentedly democratic and libertarian from the very start, for it would be directly and immediately representative of and responsible to the vast bulk of the population. Its policies would accord with the felt needs and perceived interests of the citizenry at large. Even the need to coerce the bourgeoisie would quickly disappear, freeing the state of "purely political" functions and introducing a completely "non-political" era in which "the governance of men would be replaced by the administration of things and the management of production." The vision was of a smooth, steady movement from extensive liberty to almost unqualified freedom. The focus was on society's capacity for self-emancipation through democratic political participation and the exercise of individual and group responsibility.[1]

The other Bolshevik vision posited a lengthy and pre-eminently "dialectical" process that could come to fruition only thanks to the systematic containment and redirection of the forces of endogenous social change by a theoretically enlightened, ideologically militant, and politically omnipotent ruling elite organized in a single, monolithic party. The party would, of course, make every effort to acquire a mass base. In fact, it would unceasingly strive to penetrate all sectors of social life. However, its representative functions would be largely symbolic, and it would treat any tendency toward social accommodationism, or "tailism," as a sign of political decay. Far from devoting itself to the articulation and aggregation of society's perceived interests, the party would function throughout the transitional period as a true vanguard, a crusading military formation or "organizational weapon," poised to "combat [social] spontaneity" and to manipulate and mobilize society for the sake of ideological goals which would rarely enjoy more than latent popular support and would often encounter mass hostility and resistance. Moreover, far from relaxing intraparty discipline as its penetration of society increased, the party would have to become progressively more vigilant, since every expansion of its mass base would increase the danger of loss of revolutionary dynamism. Such dynamism would have to be maintained until society had been completely restructured, for any relaxation short of the goal would culminate in the rapid collapse of the entire edifice of "socialist construction." Lenin stated the position in his well-known essay *What Is To Be Done?*, the first and fullest statement of his authoritarian-mobilizational conception. "The more widely the masses are drawn . . . into the struggle and form the basis of the movement and participate in it," the more difficult and essential it becomes for the party to safeguard its character as *"an organ of revolutionaries* capable of maintaining the energy, stability, and continuity of political struggle." It was clearly with this imperative in mind that Lenin chose as the epigraph for *What Is To Be Done?* Lasalle's famous maxim: "A party becomes stronger by purging itself."[2]

Lenin never acknowledged the contradiction between *State and Revolution* and *What Is To Be Done?*; perhaps he did not perceive the incompatibility of their visions. In the real world, however, and especially in the world the Bolsheviks faced on the morrow of the October Revolution, choice was inevitable. While there was a natural tendency for the inconsistencies of theory to become the compromises of practice (and practice undoubtedly would have eventuated in chaos if it had not in fact provided for a substantial measure of compromise), the survival of the Bolshevik regime required a clear-cut policy regarding the party's relationship to the surrounding society. Whatever tactical deviations might prove necessary, at the strategic level it was essential to decide whether the party should be essentially representative and play an essentially adaptive role or, on the contrary, should adopt a predominantly authoritarian role and seek to serve primarily as an agency of social mobilization.

While advocates of both alternatives were found within the party leadership, there was never great doubt about the nature of the ultimate decision. Although *State and Revolution* was written on the very eve of the Revolution, a full fifteen years after *What Is To Be Done?*, it was the vision of the latter that had inspired Lenin to attempt the seizure of power, and this inspiration was not likely to wane quickly. Nor did Lenin fail to have his way within the party. In the event, the improbable did not occur. The new Soviet regime wasted little time before making a decisive commitment to the authoritarian-mobilizational tenets of Bolshevik ideology. These tenets shaped the operational code of the Leninist system.

II. FROM LENINISM TO STALINISM

No doubt the Leninist system provided for a considerable amount of adaptation. As I have already suggested, the Bolshevik regime could not otherwise have survived, and survival was the highest imperative in the Leninist canon. Thus, when it became clear that the mobilizational zeal had to be curtailed in order to prevent economic collapse, Lenin boldly introduced the famous New Economic Policy (NEP), which sanctioned a wide-ranging accommodation of forces of economic "spontaneity." At the same time, however, the NEP was explicitly labeled a tactical retreat, and a rigorous effort was made to limit its scope and impact. Even in agriculture, the regime never went so far as to "give the peasant nag its head," and in industry the regime not merely retained control of the so-called commanding heights, but in fact managed to develop an increasingly effective system of centralized administration and planning. Moreover, and more importantly, the NEP was never allowed to spread beyond the economic realm.

Far from signaling a general withdrawal, the economic "retreat" was accompanied by a rapid and comprehensive advance on the social and political fronts: the introduction and strict enforcement of a ban on "factions and groupings" within the party; the conduct of a massive party purge; the transformation of the full-time functionaries of the party *apparat* into an inner-party elite; the centralization of the *apparat* under an increasingly powerful party Secretariat headed by Joseph Stalin; the proliferation of secret police and party control throughout the machinery of the state; the terroristic suppression of all non-Bolshevik political organizations; and the conversion of most of the major secondary groups and voluntary associations into centrally controlled "transmission belts," subservient to the purposes of the regime.[3] These purposes, in turn, remained pre-eminently revolutionary, and the "transmission belt" system was utilized as an instrument of social "reconstruction" as well as of social control, helping to insure that the Bolshevik regime would be able to stabilize its power without ceasing to be a "movement-regime."[4]

The authoritarian and mobilizational orientation of the Leninist system makes it very tempting to argue that the rise and consolidation of full-fledged Stalinism did not represent a brand new "second revolution," as Stalin once alleged, but rather an extension and rapid acceleration of a "first" revolution, the October Revolution, which was permanent in principle and had never actually ended. Certainly, the Leninist and Stalinist systems were not as radically discontinuous as some analysts contend. Even though Lenin "disinherited" Stalin in his last testament, the record leaves little doubt that Stalinism was a perfectly logical (which is not to say inevitable) outgrowth of institutions, procedures, and principles established during the preceding period. Indeed, there is no compelling reason to challenge Stalin's claim that he, rather than his multifarious rivals and opponents, deserved the title of Lenin's best and most consistent pupil. Still, the fact of major continuities should not obscure the equally important point that the rise and consolidation of full-fledged Stalinism wrought a massive transformation in virtually all sectors of Soviet life.

No brief essay can enumerate, let alone analyze, the many changes that marked the transition from Leninism to Stalinism. It must suffice merely to remark such well-known and critically important changes as the forcible collectivization of agriculture; the imposition of a program of forced-draft industrialization based on the absolute priority of heavy industry; the creation of a hyper-centralized economic and administrative apparatus; the institutionalization of a system of parallel, competing bureaucracies engaged in mutual surveillance and reciprocal cross-espionage; the curtailment of the authority of the party *apparat* relative to that of the state bureaucracy and secret police; the formation of a pseudo-charismatic "cult of personality"; the "reinterpretation" of the chiliastic tenets of Bolshevik ideology along conservative lines; the rejection of social egalitarianism and the active official sponsorship of a highly privileged new class of important state functionaries and party bureaucrats; the suppression of the vestigial autonomy of almost all secondary groups and voluntary associations; the proliferation of terror on a truly mass scale and its transformation into a primary technique of social control and mobilization; and, finally, the radical intensification of the "permanent purge" within the party and the use of physical liquidation as a major purge technique. While recourse to the last measure was delayed for a number of years by vigorous resistance within the Central Committee,

Stalin's will ultimately prevailed, and the Great Purge of 1936–38, which was the product of his victory, cleared the way for the definitive rise of an all-embracing personal autocracy.[5]

Provided that one takes account of the fact that many of the most salient features of Stalinism had been prefigured in Leninist practice or anticipated in Leninist theory, it is perfectly plausible to argue that the transition from Leninism to Stalinism should be viewed as a process of systemic, as opposed to within-system, change. The cogency of such an argument will vary from case to case, but it is easy to imagine analytical reasons for assigning the two systems to different political species or types.[6] Indeed, the more conventional procedure of treating both Leninism and Stalinism as examples of a single totalitarian type is of doubtful utility unless it is accompanied by an explicit recognition of the degree to which Stalinism transcended its Leninist origins and introduced radically new methods into many areas of Soviet life. In other words, it is essential to recognize that Stalinism was an almost perfect incarnation of a totalitarian "ideal type" of which Leninism was at best a fairly remote approximation.[7] Moreover—to return from the methods of analysis to analysis proper—it is probable that the contrast would have grown even greater had it not been for Stalin's sudden death in March 1953. While it was possible during the war and immediate postwar periods to argue that Stalinism was becoming somewhat less totalitarian, from 1947 on the trend was definitely in the other direction. By late 1952 it was evident that Stalin was planning a new blood purge that would have brought the system unprecedentedly close to the totalitarian ideal.

III. STALIN'S HEIRS

There is no better illustration of the uncertainty introduced by Stalin's death than the fact that the successor regime ended its first official announcement with an appeal to the population to abstain from "disorder and panic."[8] Rarely, if ever, has the leadership of a proud and mighty nation been reduced to such a humiliating public confession of its insecurity and isolation. Unlike the population of East Berlin, however, whose behavior relegated it to the new Ulbrichtian category of a population "unworthy of the confidence of its government,"[9] the Soviet population did not rise up in open insurrection. Instead, it made the transition from Stalinism without recourse to violence and spared the Soviet government the choice between suppressing its citizens with tanks or following Bertolt Brecht's sardonic advice to the East German regime to elect itself new citizens. Nonetheless, if Soviet society remained relatively tranquil, it was by no means completely quiescent. On the contrary, the accumulated grievances of the population found expression in steadily mounting pressure for greater personal security, individual privacy, consumer welfare, professional autonomy, local initiative, and cultural tolerance. While these hitherto repressed claims and demands were often interpreted differently and assigned different priorities by various groups, they were very widely shared and in most cases the pressure exerted on their behalf emanated from all levels and segments of society.

The first official response to this upsurge of social pressure was at least adaptive, if not actively receptive. Such moderation was perhaps inevitable during the legitimacy crisis introduced by Stalin's death and the determination of the dominant group within the new collective leadership to curb the power of the secret police, but it derived from more positive sources as well. Almost all of the leading figures in the new regime seem to have recognized that many Stalinist techniques of rule had become politically redundant and economically counterproductive, and some of them evidently favored extensive concessions to the socio-economic imperatives of a mature industrial society. At the same time, none of the leaders wanted adaptation to go too far, for they were determined to prevent the sort of social demobilization that would allow the growth of genuine group autonomy and independence. Such a development would threaten the regime's monopoly of political power, which was of vital concern to all of Stalin's heirs. The question, therefore, was how to maintain the requisite degree of social mobilization while abjuring mass terror and sanctioning important concessions to popular claims and demands. It remained to be seen whether Stalin's heirs could agree on an answer to this question and whether any answer could in fact be translated into effective action.

Shared interests did not prevent Stalin's heirs from succumbing to internecine conflict. Although they must have realized that their behavior would weaken the regime's capacity for social mobilization, the members of the Presidium became involved in an increasingly bitter succession struggle. What is more, this struggle assumed a particularly debilitating form. The chief contenders for power were Khrushchev, whose main source of strength lay in the party *apparat*, and Malenkov, whose power derived primarily from the state bureaucracy. By intensifying the already considerable competition between the two principal instruments of central control, such an alignment of forces was bound to open up an unusually wide sphere for autonomous social action and greatly to heighten the danger that a prolonged succession struggle would lead to a major devolution of power. As it turned out, the succession struggle ended quickly (by mid-1958), and access to the arena of political power remained confined to leaders of major elite groups. Moreover, far from revealing the emergence of a system of countervailing power, the outcome of the succession struggle suggested that, in a contest with the *apparatchiki*, other groups in Soviet society are apt to fail not only as counter-elites but also as veto groups, even where their own most vital interests are at stake. While the period 1953–58 witnessed significant challenges to *apparat* primacy from the side of the secret police, the managerial elite, and the military high command, the end result was a decisive victory for the *apparatchiki* and their leader, Khrushchev, who promptly rewarded his supporters by subjecting the entire state bureaucracy to unprecedentedly comprehensive *apparat* control.[10]

If the rapid resolution of the succession struggle increased the probability that the regime would be able to retain its monopoly of political power, the victory of Khrushchev and the *apparatchiki* substantially enhanced this prospect. Not only were the *apparatchiki* more likely than members of other elite groups to accept the authoritarian-mobilizational tenets of Bolshevik ideology, but their hegemonic role in the society could only be legitimized by insisting on the relevance of these tenets for current policy. Both of these factors (which will subsequently be discussed in more detail) greatly increased the likelihood that the Khrushchev regime would make a vigorous effort to contain adaptation within strictly circumscribed limits, and their impact was further reinforced by Khrushchev's own increasingly evident desire to aggrandize dictatorial power. While this desire was less all-consuming in Khrushchev's case than it had been in Stalin's, it was nevertheless quite intense, and could only be achieved by means of organizational and personnel policies that would destabilize "normal" patterns of behavior so as to prevent the consolidation of insulated pockets of authority and power. It is not surprising that the "Khrushchev era" witnessed a marked reactivation of authoritarian-mobilizational tendencies that had been relatively dormant during the preceding five years. This trend found expression at almost all levels of the system and in many different spheres.

Within the political sphere proper, the authoritarian-mobilizational changes that occurred during the "Khrushchev era" included the recentralization of many of the functions that had earlier been delegated to lower- and middle-level officials; the legislative rehabilitation of the "ritual of liquidation" as a procedure for settling leadership disputes; the propagation of a new, Khrushchevian cult of personality; the introduction of a policy of perpetual administrative reorganization; the prosecution of an intensive campaign of ideological purification stressing the struggle against both East European "revisionism" and Chinese "dogmatism"; and, finally, the institutionalization of a permanent bloodless purge that cost tens of thousands of officials their jobs and careers. To be sure, where party functionaries were concerned, the purge was associated with a variety of electoral reforms that could be construed as democratic. But what was actually involved was not a revival of intraparty democracy but a more or less plausibly disguised attempt to enhance central control. Much the same point holds, too, for the regime's related policy of expanding the party membership and recruiting party members in a more representative fashion. This policy, which culminated in a new doctrine according to which the party was henceforth a "party of the entire people," was analogous to the so-called Lenin Enrollment that Stalin sponsored in 1924–25, and, like its predecessor, was designed above all to facilitate rapid circulation within the elite and to increase the party's utility as a centrally controlled "transmission belt." Although Marxist orthodoxy would seem to require that the transformation of the party into a "party of the entire people" be interpreted as a prelude to the party's "withering away," the regime unabashedly proclaimed that its actual goal was *a further enhancement of the role and importance of the Communist Party* as the leading and guiding force of Soviet society."[11]

The regime sought to obviate the problem of the "withering away" of the party by means of an ex cathedra proclamation that the party was a "public organization" rather than an organ of state power. In fact, it was pronounced, the party was the most public of all public organizations and as such was destined to maintain its leading role, directing and coordinating the work of all lesser public organizations, including not only such well-established institutions as the trade unions and the Komsomol but also such new bodies as the comrades' courts, public meetings, volunteer militia brigades, anti-parasite tribunals, and Komsomol raiding groups.[12] Such para-police and para-judicial organizations were depicted, in turn, as primary organs of Communist self-government, and their proliferation during the post-1958 period was heralded as an index of the rapid democratization of the system. In fact, however, what was at issue was not democratization but rather the institutionalization of a kind of vigilante justice and the mobilization of group pressure as a technique of political domination. This technique had acquired particular importance because of the curtailment of mass terror, and there is no doubt now that the new "public organizations" were created to help fill the void left by the decline of the secret police. At the same time, their main purpose was to extend the hegemony of the party over spheres of life that had proved relatively inaccessible to more formal instruments of control, and clearly entailed a considerable increase of systematic party involvement in the daily living patterns of many Soviet citizens whose personal relations and intimate behavior became objects of growing "public" scrutiny. The professed goal was that "every citizen should not merely obey the law himself . . . and observe the norms of the socialist community, but also demand that other citizens do the same and struggle against all antisocial acts."[13] In short, every citizen was to become a policeman, thereby fulfilling and overfulfilling Lenin's old aspiration that "every Communist shall be a Chekist" and ensuring the repression of all deviant behavior, however private.

At the same time that it used the "public organizations" to launch a major invasion of personal privacy, the regime also mounted attacks against a number of enclaves of social autonomy. Among these "islands of separateness" were the churches, closed in large numbers during the course of a violent anti-religious campaign which also witnessed the imprisonment of many clerics and believers; private property, increasingly restricted by law and substantially diminished by a policy of forcible confiscation and expropriation; and the family, directly attacked when it served as a repository of religious or other overly "heretical" values (for example, many devout "believers" were deprived of their "parental rights" and had their offspring remanded to state custody), and seriously threatened as a socialization agency by the boarding school program and similar educational policies. All cases involved a militant drive to uproot retrograde "bourgeois" instincts and to eradicate undesirable "survivals of the past." Because this campaign took place at a time when the party had programmatically committed itself to the more-or-less imminent realization of full-fledged communism, the accompanying rhetoric often echoed Lenin's *State and Revolution*, but the dominant spirit was that of *What Is To Be Done?*—the spirit that Khrushchev projected so frankly when he warned a plenary meeting of the Central Committee, "Spontaneity, comrades, spontaneity is the deadliest enemy of all."[14]

IV. Continuity and Change

To focus attention on the reactivation of authoritarian-mobilizational tendencies during the Khrushchev era is not to deny that, on balance, the decade after Stalin's death was a decade of adaptation. On the contrary, what stands out in any comparison of 1953 and 1963 are such changes as the elimination of mass terror, the rise in the standard of living, the cessation of "bacchanalian" planning, and the spread of a multifaceted cultural thaw. These changes undoubtedly signify a massive curtailment of the "permanent revolution." Moreover, the active phase of this process was by no means confined to the period prior to 1958. Though the mix was somewhat different, the same combination of official receptivity to the increasingly compelling imperatives of technical rationality, indecisiveness and lack of cohesion within the leadership, and growing public self-confidence and self-assertiveness that had worked to further adaptation under the successor regime continued to operate after 1958. The entire Khrushchev era saw the spread of accommodation to a number of new areas and additional changes in some of the areas where accommodation was already well begun. Nonetheless, the Khrushchev years provided a graphic demonstration of the existence within the system of still powerful impulses toward one-man dictatorship, political militancy, and social mobilization. Indeed, if anything, the evidence suggests that these impulses became progressively more powerful, though they did not begin to approximate Stalinist levels. A marked reactivation of authoritarian-mobilizational tendencies did occur, and unless this is taken into account, interpretations of the post-Stalin decade and prognoses of the future course of Soviet development are apt to be misleading. At a minimum, the history of the Khrushchev era shows that the forces of adaptation in the Soviet system must contend with extremely powerful counterpressures. "Permanent revolution" has deeper roots than many analysts realize. Comprehensive adaptation may be a distant prospect indeed.[15] And the ouster of Khrushchev does not diminish the pertinence of these lessons.

The first thing to be noted about the ouster of Khrushchev is that it was the result of a conspiratorial palace *coup* in which participation was confined to a mere handful of top leaders. Moreover, the conspiracy appears to have been motivated by relatively narrow considerations of political power; it is by no means evident that the conspirators were opposed to all or even most of the mobilizational components in Khrushchev's general policy. To be sure, the Brezhnev-Kosygin regime has called off the most far-reaching of Khrushchev's mobilizational campaigns, the campaign against private property, and greatly moderated the tone of most of the others, but moderation is exactly what one would anticipate from a new and still unconsolidated regime. Current policy does not necessarily prefigure developments to come. It is at least conceivable that the present and putatively moderate leaders will be superseded by a younger and more ruthless version of Khrushchev, who might succeed where Khrushchev failed: liquidating rivals in the leadership, transforming the party Secretariat into a personal appendage, and using the "permanent revolution" from above as a means to autocratic power. No doubt the economic costs in such a process would be greater than ever before, but even now Soviet society is still too atomized and malleable to resist the will of a determined and united dictatorship. Moreover, even a less determined or less united leadership is likely to take steps to prevent comprehensive adaptation and to ward off the society's potential for political self-determination. This will be true so long as there is not a sharp decline in the primacy of the party *apparat* or a major transformation in the *apparat*'s political outlook. Neither condition is now present or is likely to materialize in the immediate future.

While the ouster of Khrushchev has inevitably resulted in more open access to the political arena for other elite groups, it has not seriously weakened the political-power position of the party *apparat*. Groups such as the military high command and the economic ministers have undoubtedly acquired a greater voice in the formation of policy and a wider range of operational autonomy, but the party Politburo remains an inner sanctum of leading *apparatchiki*, and *apparat* control over administration and management remains ubiquitous. Moreover, there is little question that the *apparat* could overcome any efforts to challenge its sovereignty or to transform limited autonomy in the conduct of day-to-day administrative operations into political independence. Even if the outbreak of a new succession struggle were to spark such efforts, the result would almost surely be a vigorous reaffirmation of the lesson taught by the post-Stalin succession struggle. Whatever doubts there once may have been, the *apparat* is now unquestionably the chief custodian of the symbols of legitimacy within the system (a crucial factor in any succession struggle), and the organizational resources at its disposal are at least equal to those it had available in 1953. The really decisive question, therefore, would appear to be how, not who—not the political potency of the *apparat*, but the *apparat*'s potential for *internal* transformation. Here, above all, is where the critical unknowns lie; here, above all, one must penetrate in order to estimate the forces of continuity and change that will shape the development of the Soviet system for the foreseeable future. In the short and medium run, at least, the decisive variable is not the disembodied "logic" of socio-economic maturation but the character of the emergent political leadership. In the words of George Kennan, "what we are discussing boils down to the Party's future recruitment program; if the Party can enlist enough people whose ideas and opinions coincide with its own, then perhaps . . . [totalitarianism] can last for a very long time. [The question is] . . . is this actually possible?"[16]

The composition of the *apparat* has undergone some dramatic changes in recent years, particularly in connection with the recruitment of large numbers of young technical specialists as party secretaries. Without such specialists, *apparat* control over the increasingly sophisticated economy would have become purely nominal, and Khrushchev was not one to be deceived by names. Nevertheless, the leading party secretaries are still predominantly middle-aged men of the Stalinist vintage, and political criteria continue to bulk large in the recruitment of their younger colleagues and future replacements. The regime is well aware of the critical outlook of some segments of Soviet youth and is constantly on guard against deviations toward revisionism or technocratism—the most common forms of criticism among educated youth—among young *apparatchiki*. Such deviations have not been completely eliminated; but the regime's vigilance, which has become more rather than less intense since Khrushchev's ouster, means that they are quickly suppressed. Nor is there reason to believe that they occur with great frequency. Potential deviants are in any event peculiarly likely to exclude themselves from the *apparat* recruitment process, and those who fail to do so can be excluded without compunction. The regime has a sizable pool of more orthodox candidates from which to draw.[17]

A wide range of sustained contacts with the present generation of Soviet youth has convinced me that this group contains a substantial number of individuals who qualify for most practical purposes as "new Soviet men." Raised in many instances in affluent and privileged homes, educated in the best Soviet schools, and assured of promising careers from the outset, these young people are basically satisfied with the existing system and are convinced that further "progress" can and must be attained without departing from the fundamental tenets of Marxism-Leninism or deviating in any essential respect from doctrinally sanctioned goals and procedures. While they are prepared to engage in some "creative" interpretation of conventional doctrine and are well aware of the actualities of power and the imperatives of modern technology, their initiative and their realism are circumscribed by a broader ideological commitment and find expression primarily in the enterprising implementation of the established party line. In short, although there are significant differences in the way the various components are combined, none of these youths' evaluations of the present, or aspirations for the future, transcend the limits inherent in a blend of Marxist idealism, Leninist fanaticism, Stalinist authoritarianism, and Khrushchevian pragmatism. The net effect is a political outlook characterized by intense devotion to the Soviet system and a deeply internalized and more or less militant commitment to the basic principles of social, economic, and political organization that the system embodies. To judge by the available evidence, young men who hold this outlook constitute the bulk of the manpower pool from which the *apparat* has been and is being replenished and who are most likely to rise to leadership positions in the near future.

The acquisition of power will undoubtedly affect the outlook of these "new Soviet men," but it is unlikely to bring a rapid erosion of the authoritarian-mobilizational impulses that their world view implies. These impulses could quickly atrophy only if efforts to translate them into action proved so unsuccessful as manifestly to invalidate the underlying ideological postulates. But for this the society would have to become much less tractable to authoritarian domination and mobilization than it is at present. As it is, society is restive and recalcitrant, but in most areas it still lacks the capacity to resist sustained pressure from above. So long as this is the case, ideological commitment is likely to survive "reality testing" and erosion is likely to be a slow process at best. Indeed, up to a point, the very recalcitrance of society only tends to confirm ideological expectations and to strengthen ideological commitment, for the ideology explicitly incorporates a hostile environment into its definition of reality—the reality that can and should be overcome and reconstructed in conformity with the tenets of Marxist-Leninist theory.

If the growth of ideological agnosticism is apt to be a relatively slow process among all convinced Communists, it is likely to be particularly slow among the *apparatchiki*, for whom the self-perpetuating tendency of ideological conviction is certain to be strongly reinforced by the logic of personal and political self-interest. It is precisely by stressing the continuing need to remold society and to juxtapose consciousness to spontaneity that the *apparatchiki* can best hope to legitimate their political sovereignty and the hegemony that they exercise over all facets of Soviet life. The very fact that "de-Stalinization" and other recent developments have brought the *apparat*'s right to rule increasingly in question makes it more than ever imperative, both psychologically and politically, that the *apparatchiki* attempt to justify their power and privileges. Men who must constantly justify themselves tend often to become more militant protagonists of the justificatory principles that they propound. This propensity, then, provides yet another reason to doubt that the authoritarian-mobilizational impulses within the Soviet system will soon cease to operate. Considered in conjunction with the process of elite socialization and recruitment and the prevailing equilibrium of political power, it provides grounds for believing that a long, uphill struggle will be necessary before the forces of adaptation within the system can be credited with a conclusive victory. Given the underlying logic of socio-economic maturation and the increasingly numerous manifestations of this logic in recent Soviet practice, it may well be that these forces will ultimately prevail. But their progress will be interrupted by major reversals. The final demise of the "permanent revolution" is many years away.

If "creeping adaptation" is the greater likelihood, "galloping adaptation" is nonetheless a real prospect in the event of a prolonged and violent succession struggle or a major economic breakdown. But it should not be confused with the chimerical prospect of rapid democratization of the Soviet system, which some analysts have taken to be imminent. Even if the Soviet system were to succumb to comprehensive adaptation in the near future, it would almost certainly be characterized by heavy elite dominance by men of basically authoritarian outlook, devoid of any real commitment to such values as popular self-government, national self-determination, civil rights, social pluralism, and the stable rule of law. While these and related values have some devoted adherents within the ranks of the Soviet intelligentsia, they are largely alien to the leading members of the "new class," and it is to this class, and more particularly the upper strata of the various strategic elites that comprise it, which would command whatever power gravitated downward in consequence of the definitive withering away of the "permanent revolution." There is no reason to believe that the rest of Soviet society has any substantial commitment to democratic values or that it would incorporate such values into the claims and demands addressed to a nonrevolutionary regime.

Although a significant degree of uncertainty must attach to any generalizations about consensus in Soviet society, the available sources yield no evidence of strong popular opposition to the highly undemocratic principles which presided over the foundation of the Soviet system and have been incorporated into its pivotal institutions. Acceptance of these principles was prevalent even under Stalin, and one of the major reasons that the regime was able to manage the social pressures unleashed by Stalin's death without recourse to violence is that most of society's claims and demands were circumscribed by wide-ranging consensus on official policies and purposes. This consensus did not apply to many Stalinist techniques, and it was far from all-embracing on programmatic or substantive issues. Yet it was quite extensive, often quite intense, and sufficed to restrict most of the pressure to which the regime was exposed to pressure for within-system change. While the change which ensued in consequence of this pressure is usually referred to as liberalization, true liberals or even near-liberals were rarities in Soviet society, and the bulk of the population was not disposed to reject such constituent principles of the established order as collectivism, central planning, comprehensive socialization, and single-party rule.[18] This situation has persisted to the present day.

Some segments of Soviet society undoubtedly are becoming more critical as they learn more of alternative belief systems and patterns of social and political organization; but most groups and strata appear to remain firm in their acceptance of the Soviet way of life, and many have come to accord it increasingly active support as the established system proves its ability to relieve many of their most intense grievances and complaints. To speak on this basis of the emergence of a truly consensual totalitarianism is to go much too far, but the lack of accord within the system is not, with rare and infrequent exceptions, informed by a genuinely liberal or democratic spirit. And without active commitment to liberal or democratic goals by significant segments of the population, there is little prospect that the Soviet system will soon come to embody an open society and a free regime.[19] On the contrary, and quite apart from the high probability of continuing strong elite dominance, the absence of such a commitment virtually assures that the outcome of the withering away of the "permanent revolution" will still be highly authoritarian. If history teaches anything, it is surely that democracy does not come of itself or as an automatic consequence of economic modernization (which carries with it, at least, highly ambiguous and often quite repressive political implications), but arises only as a result of dedicated and active support by politically significant groups.

In sum, if and when adaptation does at last encompass the Soviet system, it is probable that the emerging sociopolitical configuration will not reflect the "law" of self-sustaining change in a liberal or democratic direction but rather what can be called, following Mosca and Michels, the "law of social inertia." In the case of the Soviet Union, this law portends the continued existence of a highly repressive system which will hold freedom at a heavy discount and place a high premium on conformity and compliance.

4.

Interest Groups

SIDNEY I. PLOSS

I. INTRODUCTION

Group action is a significant force in politics, and it has always been based upon distinctions of economic and personal power as well as collisions of varying world views. Over the past half-century, the diversities introduced by economic specialization and growing state intervention into social processes have compounded the traditional divergences and yielded, in democratic political systems, an array of private groups formed by persons who share certain attitudes, or "interests," and who seek to influence governmental action.

In the United States, perhaps fifty major organizations, and ten times as many minor ones, attempt to satisfy particular needs that the consensus-oriented political parties cannot routinely advocate. The organizations do not fit any simple pattern of membership or unity, but are aggregates, shaped in large measure by the internal cleavages of labor, agriculture, business, the professions, and other bodies. Despite the varying degrees of cohesion which the interest groups command and the difficulty of precisely evaluating the impact of their agitation on public policy, a study of their activities is essential to an understanding of the factors that affect political and social life.

In the Soviet case, authoritarian theory obscures the existence of a comparatively narrower circle of interest groups which struggle behind the scenes to wield influence within the single-party structure. The doctrine of the ruling Communist Party of the Soviet Union (CPSU) states that in Soviet society there is no class conflict, but a community of the general interests of all citizens.

Such general interests are said to include the building of a prosperous, and militarily powerful, classless society. This doctrine of shared concern is, above all, the means of rationalizing the dominion of the single political party in the U.S.S.R.

Nevertheless, party literature qualifiedly elaborates that "special interests" (*osobye interesy*) of a class and bureaucratic type do exist in the U.S.S.R., and that they arise from interlaced matters of politics and economics. Such differences of interest include the priorities to be given in the allocation of investments between branches of the economy, fixing the prices of manufactured goods and agricultural products, and the choice of the industrial profile most suitable for various territories. Some representatives of the governing bureaucracy, we are told, favor the maintenance of traditional patterns of capital investment which emphasize forced saving and industrial reproduction, while others stress the value of raising productivity by offering bigger material incentives to the labor force. Urban residents desire lower retail prices on foodstuffs, while peasants quite naturally want more profit. Certain regional administrators strive to ensure local self-sufficiency at the expense of all-union interests as determined at the center. Special interests occasionally clash with general interests, producing conflicts ("nonantagonistic contradictions") which are solved without violent upheavals. Official spokesmen further recognize that Soviet society is beset with complex problems of political and economic organization that generate "struggles of opinion" among leaders of diverse experience and knowledge.[1] In short, inequality of material and human resources admittedly breeds social friction under Soviet rule, and there is intraparty debate over the method of government.

The historical record indicates that official claims concerning the mildness of social conflict are highly misleading. Indeed, severe disparities of privilege have repeatedly weakened the motivation of workers and peasants to labor efficiently, and the topic of their material improvement has been a contentious issue in the closed system of bureaucratic politics. The question of what constitutes a desirable rate of growth in the population's real income has been compounded by others related to funds and functions, and has often spilled over into the area of foreign affairs. The lengthy register of party bosses who have risen and fallen after the settlement of political disputes, and the many *post facto* defamations, also give the lie to propaganda about the amicability of conflict resolution at the apex of the dictatorship. The Kremlin doctrine on social collaboration thus reminds one of Daniel Bell's definition of ideology as "the facade of general interest and universal values which masks specific self-interest." The analyst who wishes to identify the forces at work in the Soviet political process must, accordingly, disregard the Communists' ideological pretense of concord and inquire into those conflicts of self-interest in the body of the nation which have become the stuff of factional politics in the CPSU.

This essay delineates the kinds of special interests that are to be found in the effective organs of Soviet government and may be expected to influence the making of policy in the near future. It will suggest that these interests are ultimately philosophic, with rival ideas about how to govern the society and conduct foreign relations being championed by nonassociational groups which recruit followers in all the centers of administrative power. This is to say that both the authority of a few thousand political activists and the fortunes of millions of people in the U.S.S.R. and abroad are at stake in recurrent intraparty battles over practical political issues. Communication among the interest groups is essential to their functioning, and will be examined from the standpoint of how dialogues are conducted and access gained to the locus of decision-making. Conclusions will be offered about the range of possibilities for development in the Soviet Union, as suggested by a study of contemporary Soviet politics.

II. Habits of Dissension

The Soviet political personality has, over the course of time, exhibited some notable consistencies of behavior. Any typology of interest groups, issues of group conflict, and modes of political discourse must, therefore, be viewed in historical perspective. *Gruppirovki*, or groupings, were the basis of the leadership of all political parties of the revolutionary movement in nineteenth- and twentieth-century Russia. The early history of Bolshevism, according to Leon Trotsky, was a record of internal group struggles, and to his way of thinking, political struggles are in essence struggles of interest. Whatever the truth of that comment, the Bolshevik leaders agreed, once their party took the reins of government, that internecine feuds could no longer be tolerated because they constantly threatened "bifurcation" (*razdvoenie*) or "splintering" (*rasshcheplenie*) of the state administration. Lenin hoped to eradicate canvassing and secret negotiations in the party with his famous resolution "On Party Unity," passed at the Tenth Party Congress in 1921. This edict outlawed factionalism and established severe penalities for violators. However, the cardinal fact of Soviet politics is that Lenin's decree excluding factionalism has always been honored more in the breach than in the observance.

Throughout the 1920s there were nation-wide party groups unified under programmatic slogans, and more diffuse local groups which clustered for reasons of personal and professional ambition. The nation-wide groups made controversies over such issues as economic management, administration of the party's internal affairs, and planning for economic growth. In international policy, some perceived a dilemma over whether to concentrate on problems of internal construction or to make more strenuous efforts on behalf of world revolution. All of the heated debates on these questions would be revived in the decades ahead, long after the "professional revolutionists" had left the scene, but with tough-minded considerations of power and prestige dwarfing those of proletarian idealism. The spectrum of opinion in such disputes over policy guidelines usually conformed to the time-honored division of Left (combative), Center (ambivalent), or Right (adaptive). These orientations would also be discernible in future struggles within the party command.

As early as 1921, the political differentiation of Communist Party members along occupational lines was an important feature of the emerging pattern of governance. N. I. Bukharin, a candidate member of the Politburo, remarked in his analysis of factional conflicts among delegates to the Tenth Party Congress that the Bolshevik organization was hardly single-minded, but "a number of columns with different shadings of opinion." He continued, in amplification:

> There have crystallized military officials, soviet officials, officials in trade unions, and strictly party officials. This specialization has gone quite far. You are all familiar with the basic Marxian proposition that an individual's manner of life determines his mode of thought. This specialization of officials will exert an influence on future reality as well. This specialization has fragmented our party, which was previously unified in its psychology, into a number of groupings which are characterized by various psychological deviations.[2]

Generational and regional cleavages were soon alluded to by G. E. Zinoviev, party leader of Petrograd, who categorized many of the local groups as nonpolitical cliques when he reported to the Eleventh Party Congress in 1922: "What sort of groups are these?

All kinds. We may roughly describe them as the more youthful vs. the more elderly; rural vs. urban; party vs. state; men of the regional economic councils vs. those of the trade unions; and, contrarily, regional food committees vs. regional economic councils."[3] The intimate connections of central officials with those in the provinces, however, would make it appear that Zinoviev's dichotomy between political and nonpolitical groups was a false one. L. B. Krasin, who immediately after the Revolution had industrial responsibilities in the party's Central Committee, soon urged that state economic agencies be freed of operational interference by the party apparatus, which he thought should apply its energies to political indoctrination of the workers. Krasin, therefore, shared the attitude of certain particularist elements in the lower echelons, and voiced their aspirations in an upper-level forum. There is also evidence that Krasin, as the spokesman of the business executives, was active in a political movement critical of any instigation of revolutionary aggression which might have discouraged Western governments from authorizing loans to Soviet Russia for its industrial recovery.[4]

The forums of intraparty debate in the 1920s were variegated. The Party Congresses met almost annually and, in addition to open clashes on the floor, delegates wrangled and bargained at private meetings. Central Committee sessions were held regularly to augment the weekly deliberations of the Politburo, and secret roll-call votes were taken. The party press was under the control of diverse groups in the leadership and offered different slants on the news. Not until 1929 were more stringent rules laid down to circumscribe factionalism. Stalin demanded at the Plenum of the Central Committee and Central Control Commission in April 1929 that appropriate measures be taken forbidding members of the Politburo, when speaking publicly, to deviate in any way from the line of the party and the decisions of the Central Committee. Press organs were to conform fully to the line of the party and the decisions of its leading bodies. This tightening-up in the organizational field was to some extent a corollary of the political decision to wage a campaign of modernization which required popular sacrifice of even the necessities of life and not the slightest hint of disarray in the power structure.

As long as Stalin lacked the ability to terrorize members of the inner governing circle, he could neither dissolve the *gruppirovki* nor stand above their struggles. In 1932 a group of Old Bolsheviks, N. B. Eysmont, V. N. Tolmachev, and A. P. Smirnov, held conversations about the removal of Stalin from the post of General Secretary of the party. (Smirnov, leader of the group, was jointly a Secretary of the Party Central Committee and Commissar of Agriculture for the Russian Republic in 1928–30.) An excerpt from Stalin's unpublished speech on the group at the January 1933 Plenum of the Central Committee and Central Control Commission indicates that these oppositional discussions were over inseparable questions of power and policy that affected the lives of all Soviet citizens. Alluding to the hardships of industrialization and wholesale collectivization of agriculture which were straining popular loyalties, Stalin remarked, "It is only enemies who can say that Stalin should be removed and nothing will come of it." We may infer from this incident that, in spite of all formal rulings, the party leadership was not entirely insensitive to outside pressure and that some expressed the desire of ordinary citizens to restore normality in the country.

Stalin's hurdling of this challenge to his leadership may be explained by his astuteness at balancing competing groups in the hierarchy, a skill which he proved in the 1920s. In May 1932 he unexpectedly and apologetically approved of a project of General M. N. Tukhachevsky to re-equip the army. Only two years earlier, Stalin had angrily rejected the project on the grounds that it would lead to "Red militarism."[5] This change of heart during the economic crisis of 1932 suggests that Stalin made a political alliance with some leaders of the army, the prototype of others which occurred under similar conditions of limited one-man rule in the 1950s and 1960s. Moreover, the agitation of Smirnov's defeated group was not completely ineffectual, since a marked shift of investment priorities to aid the consumer was decreed at the Seventeenth Party Congress in 1934. By that time, there may have been a new movement of bureaucratic opinion for the dismissal of Stalin.[6]

The *gruppirovki* were not eliminated after Stalin established his personal dictatorship in the blood purges of 1937–38, but were compelled to vie with one another for the favor of the master. Just how vicious that phenomenon was may be gauged from the charge that L. P. Beria, at the beginning of the Soviet-German war, deliberately withheld communications equipment from guerrilla units in the Ukraine in order to impress upon Stalin that his centralized security service did more for the war effort than the local party apparatus of N. S. Khrushchev, a fellow member of the Politburo.[7] It would be wrong, however, to think of the group conflicts under Stalinist absolutism in the 1940s and 1950s as merely sordid intrigues without relevance to the affairs of state and society. These conflicts were often fought out over such traditionally vital issues of domestic policy as the relationship between production and consumption, and compulsion and spontaneity. There was also divided counsel over the most advantageous sort of foreign-political undertakings for the regime.

The party press served as a vehicle for intergroup disputes of the Stalin era. Rival lieutenants of the dictator commissioned agents to publicize their distinctive viewpoints, and press organs fell under the control of feuding groups.[8] Moreover, the past had indicated that, as in all polities, the grievances of those on the lower rungs of the bureaucratic ladder would tend to rise up and receive a sympathetic hearing by some leaders. One key sign of mounting discontent in the party appeared in June 1950, when Stalin, as part of a discourse on linguistics, indirectly but unmistakably reproached advocates of sweeping internal change ("comrades who have a weakness for explosions"). The issues were soon definable as industrial accumulation *versus* popular welfare; coercion *versus* persuasion; and centralized *versus* decentralized management of agriculture. A voice which ostensibly belonged to an economist called for the overthrow of the austerity doctrine of the preponderant development of heavy industry.[9] Another expressed belief that the coercive slogan of "dictatorship of the working class" was an outmoded concept.[10] Still a third proposed to relinquish state control of farm machinery and to channel savings into the consumer goods industries.[11]

The appeals for reconciliation of the Kremlin and the people which were made in 1951–53 eventually found their way into the speeches of those who steered the work of the party directorate. After Stalin, G. M. Malenkov, and later Khrushchev, sought to discard the policy of all-out production of capital goods to the detriment of the food and light industries. Khrushchev succeeded in nullifying the harsh slogan of proletarian dictatorship and substituted for it the milder theory of the "state of the entire people." Similarly, Khrushchev decentralized the management of farm equipment and stimulated money relations between town and countryside, a technique inimical to the professed aims of Marxism and Soviet authoritarianism. These later developments clearly illustrate how unorthodox views on policy, which are repudiated in the official press, in fact offer valuable clues to ideas and attitudes germinating within the ruling circle.

The same is true of the controversy over estimates of the world situation after World War II. The most notorious dispute involved Academician E. S. Varga, who in 1946–49 argued that Western economies were stabilizing; that opportunities were arising for the workers of Western Europe to achieve social reforms without revolution; that colonial peoples would gradually be emancipated; and, most important, that wars involving the U.S.S.R. or only the Western powers were no longer inevitable. Varga's assumptions implied that the proper strategy for the Kremlin was to avoid political or military probes of Western positions, and to explore avenues of cooperation with forces as diverse as Western governments and socialist parties, as well as nationalist reformers in the emerging "third world." The opposite theses of Varga's opponents among the ideological functionaries prevailed at the time and tended to legitimize the harsh practices of Cold War and self-isolation of the U.S.S.R.

While the Varga controversy raged, the Party Congress, which formally charts the immediate course of general policy, was not convened. Stalin indeed obstructed the execution of two decisions which the Politburo adopted in 1946–48 to convene the Congress.[12] Since the controversy involved all of the major issues of general policy, and we know that the widespread practice of patronage (*sheftsvo*) extends into the realm of publishing, it may be hazarded that this controversy was the outward reflection of a protracted behind-the-scenes struggle to influence Stalin's final decision. The political memoir of a minister in the coalition government in postwar Hungary, who was in Moscow at the time of negotiations on the Marshall Plan, inclines us to surmise that A. I. Mikoyan and V. M. Molotov were champions of the pro- and anti-Varga positions respectively.[13] An eventual upshot of the Varga controversy was Khrushchev's explicit slogan of 1956 regarding the noninevitability of world war. This doctrinal formula, like all others, served a justificatory purpose, namely, the release of more investment funds from the military-industrial to the civilian sector of the economy. The origins of post-Stalin courtship of Western social-democrats and leaders of the new states of Asia and Africa may also be traced to the Varga dispute.

This short sketch of the argumentation in the postwar period has outlined the divergences over methods of government and foreign policy, which would be the starting point of group conflict after the death of Stalin. On the basis of Stalin's deeds and polemical materials of the day, a polarization of viewpoint on interrelated questions of domestic and foreign affairs evidently had taken place. The classic Leftist alignment insisted at home upon the utmost build-up of industrial-military potential and the centralized command of economic processes necessary to enforce that scale of priorities. Abroad, the Stalinist Left favored constant thrusts against Western outposts and continuing estrangement from liberal democrats. Opposing this combative approach, and patronizing such reformist intellectuals as Yaroshenko and Varga, were leaders of the Center and Right. In varying degrees, these leaders saw merit in creating an effective system of labor incentives, granting some autonomy to local economic enterprises, and reaching limited accommodation with non-Communist foreigners.

A hint that these differences over public policy transcended bureaucratic limits is provided by evidence of the career standing of various officials at the close of the Stalin era. Variation among business executives was denoted at the Nineteenth Party Congress in 1952 by the symbolic tokens of merit which Stalin awarded to some associated with heavy engineering, and his ritualistic degrading of others who had records of long service in the food and light industries. About that time, there were symptoms of disarray in the party apparatus, whose specialized segments for the surveillance of various areas of public life tend to create departmental attitudes and put them under pressure to advance partial interests. (One objective of Stalin's large private Secretariat was probably to overcome departmental interests in party headquarters and to counteract the influence of political groupings which stood behind them.) Some party officials sharply denounced reformist heresies in the press while others kept silent, a response to sensitive matters that has been factionally interpreted as "double-dealing." Of course, the choice of Leftist policies required much indoctrination and thought control by the party apparatus, and if that choice was made, party officials would be less prone to meddle in the work of business executives. Consequently, there took place a synthesis of bureaucratic and philosophic interest among partisans of the Left wing of the CPSU.

III. The Current Phase

The major political question raised by the death of Stalin was inheritance of the leadership of policy and administration. Constitutional provisions for the solution of this question were nonexistent, and power was initially diffused among ten members of the Central Committee Presidium. The role of leader would devolve upon the member who could most effectively combine the *gruppirovki* into majorities within the Central Committee of 150 members. Such majorities were never dependable throughout the post-Stalin period, and Khrushchev's accession rested upon his imperfect skill at playing off diverse groups. A boss who lacked in historically recognized achievement and was unable or unwilling to conduct blood purges as a means of gaining political independence, Khrushchev was the first of what promises to be a long line of post-Stalin leaders, rather than absolute heads of the U.S.S.R. This condition of oligarchic rule makes especially pertinent an understanding of the nature and weight of various interest groups in the Soviet elite.

The functional groups are the party, state economic, military, and police apparatuses. A collective ambition to maximize its authority and reputation characterizes each of these arms of bureaucratic power. At the same time, each is a repository of conflicting ideological, sectional, generational, and personal interests. Such intramural divisions allow the representatives of different apparatuses to work together in certain matters and to contract professional alliances. These points may be briefly illustrated. First, the collective interest of the party apparatus was manifest in all of the denouements of post-Stalin conflict. The senior party secretaries closed ranks against the leaders of other apparatuses in June 1953 (against the police), June 1957 (against the state economic bureaucracy), and October 1957 (against the military). (Khrushchev's party reform of 1962, it will be suggested, was seriously at variance with the group interest of the party apparatus as understood by most of its leaders and heavily contributed to the demise of the Party First Secretary.)

Second, the bloc of party secretaries which rallied at intervals of crisis usually enlisted allies in the state apparatus in order to drive out inconvenient security policemen, business executives, and generals. The state economic bureaucracy and military, for example, joined with the party men against the police in 1953, suggesting that all members of the coalition shared an interest in establishing some kind of rule of law. Moreover, the party bloc often lured volunteers away from its particular target group in the state apparatus. A. N. Kosygin, Deputy Chairman of the U.S.S.R. State Planning Committee, for example, opposed fellow economic administrators in the clash of June 1957. The other side of the coin is the ability of state ministers to gain the adherence of certain party officials on individual questions of mutual concern. In 1960, for example, K. T. Mazurov, Party First Secretary of Byelorussia, publicly upheld the administrative prerogatives of the U.S.S.R. Ministry of Agriculture on the eve of its conversion into a rural extension service. Thus, complicated webs of intrigue are spun throughout the world of Soviet bureaucracy, and the threads invariably lead to contenders for power in the Kremlin itself.

The tactical alliances of the groupings have been over issues which fall under the broad heading of "de-Stalinization," or the manner and rate of modifying the Leftist practices of full-blown Stalinism. The role of the Communist Party apparatus is one of the foremost issues of de-Stalinization. Specifically, it involves the question of whether the regional party secretaries are to continue to perform the political function of exacting obedience to stringent demands of the center, or whether theirs will be a functional role of cooperating with local specialists to implement economic plans which reconcile all-state and local interests. The question of the party role also concerns the feasibility of applying strictly legalistic and technocratic modes of judgment in regulating economic and administrative affairs. Economics is another basic ingredient of Communist politics, and modernizing the command economy is an important issue of de-Stalinization. This focuses upon such traditionally controversial problems as allotting raw materials and appropriations for different branches and sectors of the economy, pricing industrial and farm products, and choosing managerial and planning standards. Cultural de-Stalinization concerns the boundaries of social criticism in literature, and artistic self-expression generally. In foreign policy, disputes have raged over kinds of commitment which would entail minimum risk to national security and still serve to enhance the world-wide glory of the U.S.S.R. The official labels of "conservative" and "pragmatist," which have been affixed to defeated groups in post-Stalin conflicts, would appear basically appropriate. But perhaps more useful in establishing factional alignments and periodic swings in policy is the scale of Left-Center-Right.

The restoration of oligarchy has spelled revival of the policy-making forums which were moribund under Stalinist despotism. The party Politburo and *ad hoc* commissions of the Central Committee Plenum and Congress regularly deliberate on policy proposals. In the case of the Politburo, proposals are made in written declarations submitted by central and local party leaders, government ministers, scientists, and men of letters. Commissions of the

Central Committee Plenum and Party Congress act on draft resolutions tabled by the Politburo and its expanded sessions which are held before the Central Committee plenary meetings. The editorial boards of press organs remain under factional influence, and the topmost leaders continue to inspire partisan articles. This relative broadening of the forum of policy-making has itself been a source of dissension as it comes to involve the prerogatives of Politburo members.

Interests and Issues

The party apparatus is the most important of the bureaucratic interests, holding about one-third of the membership in the Central Committee. This reflects the extraordinary political function of the regional party secretaries, whose vocation it is to ensure local fulfillment of the general plans of transforming society. The regional party leaders must preclude the possibility of state agencies working at cross-purposes, and are called upon to help instill loyalty in the nation-wide cause by organizing the political indoctrination of all citizens. This political function has made of the regional party leaders an exclusive group which overreaches those whose members are immersed in the complexities of administration or the applications of science and technology. Professional detachment is indeed regarded as essential for the party secretaries to be capable of rebuffing "local interests" in their regions. The center's insistence upon such professional detachment has been tacit recognition of the usual divergence of all-state and local interests as these are understood in the bureaucracy and in the population at large.

The substitution of a technical for the political function of the party apparatus was one of Khrushchev's abortive reforms which had significant implications for the workings of the dictatorship. Khrushchev in 1960–62 was hampered by a resurgence of ministerial obstruction of his efforts to renovate industry and agriculture through managerial decentralization and experimentation with new techniques. The complacency of state administrators in meeting their responsibilities to care for the most elementary needs of the people was still another reason for massive party intervention in the everyday business of government. Khrushchev apparently hoped to use the party apparatus as a driving force to smash the barriers of departmentalist red tape which stood in the way of his ambitions.

The splitting of the party apparatus into industrial and agricultural components in 1962 was, therefore, an emergency measure which engaged party officials in the hurly-burly of economic management and public administration. It promptly gave rise to complaints within the apparatus that it was undergoing nothing short of "depoliticization."[14] The anger of local administrators may be gauged from the defensive remarks of a central ideological functionary who addressed a local party meeting during the course of the short-lived reform: "Some comrades may wonder why a Central Committee secretary for ideology is talking at plenums about dining halls, bath houses, and kindergartens. Isn't he taking bread from the mouths of the leaders of soviet and economic organizations, the leaders of trade and communal services, and other officials whose job it is to be concerned about serving the daily requirements of the people?"[15] Moreover, the professional detachment of party workers was jeopardized by the reform, for there was a genuine danger of their absorption by local interests. The prospect could not have escaped Khrushchev, who simultaneously urged measures to increase local participation in the formulation of national economic plans (about which more will be said below). Thus, party functionalism was conceived as part of a broader scheme of reconciling all-state and local interests.

Most of the regional party secretaries vigorously resisted "depoliticization" of the local party apparatus, because they perceived it as a threat to status and livelihood. By no means are all the party secretaries capable of holding their own as technical experts in dealings with specialists. The future boded ill for the veterans among them when it was declared that a major purpose of the party reform was the promotion of more youthful and energetic cadres.[16] After the reversal of the reform in November 1964, heavy emphasis was put on the traditional supervisory, coordinating, and indoctrinating activities of party officials. The new leadership condemned "drift," and Khrushchev's pragmatic bent was implicitly censured in the Stalinist idiom as "commercialism" and "narrow practicism."[17]

This episode of Khrushchev's party reform demonstrates the present-day conflict between factors promoting and inhibiting change in the Soviet system. The idea of party functionalism had its roots in the war and immediate postwar years, reflecting appreciation of the urgent need to cope with practical problems in the economy. It also expressed a materialistic conviction that increasing production is more likely to win popular loyalty for the regime than is exhortation. The conservative viewpoint of the opposition in Moscow was, to be sure, based on pressing considerations. Their fear of loss of control by the center may be inferred from the noted attack on "drift" made just after the overthrow of Khrushchev, as well as from the subsequent revival in modified form of the central economic ministries. Here, the growing interplay of interest groups was a mechanism which braked movement toward the hurried renewal of policy and institutions. A technologically unskilled group of power-lovers in the regional party apparatus, which was being demoralized, found ambitious patrons in central party headquarters; and the latter, in turn, linked up with the protectors of harassed planners and administrators of the state machine (resulting in the coalition of Brezhnev and Kosygin).

The thwarting of Khrushchev's scheme for conversion of the party apparatus into a technically functional agency pointed up the serious ideological cleavages among party officials. It also showed both the determination of senior business executives to uphold the challenged orthodoxy of centralized economic planning and their ability, as about one-fifth of the Central Committee membership, to wield political power in league with more cautious party organizers. Khrushchev's quarrel with the group of central managers and planners over pre-eminence and power was of long standing. Joseph Alsop reported Khrushchev's comments on the law of May 10, 1957, which transferred the operational management of most industries from central to local organs: "As Khrushchev himself pointed out to me, the plan was and is a direct attack on the vested interests of 'tens of thousands' of the most highly placed officials, technicians and administrators in the Soviet Union. . . . As Khrushchev said with sardonic cheerfulness, 'These gentlemen are now to be sent out into the provinces to do more productive work.' "[18] A proposal also made at the time for the election of factory directors at worker meetings was sharply criticized by a propagandist, who was demoted after the rule of Khrushchev grew stronger.[19]

The issue of unified *versus* decentralized economic planning became lively shortly after Khrushchev usurped the premiership. A party and government decree adopted on May 4, 1958, enabled union-republic planning committees and regional economic councils to advise the U.S.S.R. State Planning Committee on the drafting of national economic plans.[20] Khrushchev may also be held responsible for having incorporated into the 1961 Party Program the idea of increasing the role of local organs in planning:

"Centralized planning should chiefly concentrate on working out and ensuring the fulfillment of the key targets of the economic plans with the greatest consideration paid to recommendations made at lower levels; on coordinating and dovetailing plans drawn up locally."

Khrushchev in 1962 took a further step toward the possible goal of drafting national economic plans which, on the West European model, would combine centralized projections with a broad measure of local autonomy. The Premier told the Central Committee in November 1962 that planning and the implementation of plans should be exclusively the task of union-republic planning committees and economic councils. The central planners were to have only a "small apparatus" to work out long-range plans and provide forecasts for economic development. The union republics, proceeding from these forecasts and tasks, were to draw up local plans. "The U.S.S.R. State Planning Committee," Khrushchev declared, "should make a comprehensive study of the plans submitted by the republics and, so to speak, dovetail them, compiling an all-union plan, while seeing to it, in particular, that the economic plans of the union republics and of the country as a whole ensure a balanced development of the economy."[21] A party and government decree in January 1963 directed the U.S.S.R. State Planning Committee to compile draft five year plans by "dovetailing" plans submitted by the republics.[22] Still another joint decree adopted in May 1963 authorized the setting up of local commissions and councils to ensure the drafting of more sensible economic plans.[23]

After the fall of Khrushchev, the new premier, Kosygin, emphatically restored the role of the central planning bureaucracy in originating detailed recommendations for economic development, rather than reconciling local proposals. Kosygin told a conference of managerial and planning associates in March 1965:

> You will recall the invention that the U.S.S.R. State Planning Committee should only "dovetail" plans which come from the republics. Such a primitive notion of planning was created by people who had no idea of how plans must be compiled. Unquestionably, a great deal was accomplished in the localities. But this work was not always in harmony with general state interests, especially when localist tendencies were strongly manifest in the plans. And this display of localist tendencies was provoked to a notorious degree by the idea of so-called dovetailing of the plans at the center.[24]

The clash between Khrushchev and Kosygin over economic planning may be assessed as a potential landmark in the development of the Soviet regime. Khrushchev's position suggested the existence of a current of elite opinion in favor of dismantling the central planning bureaucracy and introducing a socialist market economy of the Yugoslav kind. The possible adoption of that course of action was further suggested by proposals made during the far-reaching economics discussion which opened with the appearance of Professor Liberman's controversial plan to use profit as the main indicator of plant performance, in *Pravda* on September 21, 1962, and temporarily closed with Academician Trapeznikov's article on the self-regulation of industry, which *Pravda* carried on August 17, 1964.

Quite logically, welfare economics went hand in hand with this attempt to introduce the play of the market to an extent unseen in the Soviet Union for more than thirty-five years. The welfare question was and is a burning one, for producers' goods account for as much as three-quarters of total industrial output and less than one-fifth of the heavy-industry sector is devoted to consumers' goods. Such official statistics are indicative of the extent to which special interests in the government may for a time trample upon "social forces" (popular aspirations) under the circuitous process of interest articulation: by the beginning of the 1960s, the chasm between the growth rates of heavy and light industry was even wider than at the end of the Stalin era and a smaller part of heavy industry was being put to work for the manufacture of consumers' goods. In September 1964, Khrushchev held that the "main task" of the economic plan for 1966–70 should be "the further improvement of the living standard of the people."[25] Here, too, however, the thrust of radical reformers was blunted by some party organizers as well as industrialists, and probably generals too. The investment pattern approved after the fall of Khrushchev showed no dramatic shift in favor of light industry, and party publicists who were scornful of "risky experiments" again rebuked Malenkov for having believed that "the development of heavy industry has ceased to be the main link in creating the material-technical base of communism" and that "light industry must be given preponderant development."[26]

Whatever the immediate outcome of the investment controversy, the record instructs us to anticipate renewed effort by a section of the party apparatus to curb the influence and privilege of the upper-level business executives. This may take the form of proposals to abandon unified economic planning by Moscow and to establish a structure of "workers' self-management"—under the firm guidance of local Communist Party officials. A ploy of that kind to win the confidence of the rank and file would probably be accompanied by the increased output of incentive-building consumers' goods.

The bureaucratic quarrels over industry are matched by others over how to handle the chronic peasant question. Specifically involved is the share of national wealth to be allocated to the production of equipment and to the work force in payment for its labor, and the degree to which farm organization is to be personalized. Under the impact of stagnation in the socialized sector since 1958, and a steady rise of the urban population, the post-Khrushchev leadership agreed to revise the scale of investment priorities and the terms of trade between industry and agriculture so as to meet at least halfway the pressing need for more inputs and incentives. No such consensus was forthcoming on the structure of farm management, however, which has remained basically centralized throughout the post-Stalin period. In tackling this nagging question, party reformers have not hesitated to demand the creation of a union of collective farms on the national level. Such a union, in the opinion of an astute observer of the Soviet scene, "could become for the peasants a symbol of their distinct class interests as opposed to those of city people."[27] The proposal for a nation-wide union of collectives to ensure decentralized management and the pooling of scarce farm resources was made by several members of the Party Presidium during the rule of Khrushchev and reintroduced shortly after his deposition. Opposition was initially voiced by the head of the State Ministry of Agriculture, but certainly it also fed upon the deep-rooted suspicion of the peasantry within the more influential party apparatus.[28] Our incomplete knowledge of this dispute between the partisans of stark centralization and a form of local independence in agriculture suggests that a worsening of agrarian difficulty combined with a rise in the status of certain political forces may eventually result in the vitalization of the dormant cooperative element in socialized agriculture. It may be added that the prospect of genuine farm cooperatives has become more realistic in the wake of heated debate over the expediency of substituting a "free market" for the centralized planning of agricultural production.[29]

Deep divisions over the scope to be given to the activities of writers and artists have frequently arisen in political circles, where final decisions are reached about what should and should not be published or exhibited. These divisions have been created by such diverse considerations as pride and ambition, and the effort of reformist chiefs to throw light on social ills as a step toward creating a climate of bureaucratic opinion which is favorable to the adoption of innovative policies. On the most crass level, it is alleged that the central party secretary in charge of cultural affairs in 1956–57 sought personal popularity and hence made concessions to rank nonconformists among the intelligentsia.[30] On a programmatic level, signs of diverse attitudes have often emerged after the release of literary works which deal with the theme of oppression under Soviet conditions. Khrushchev, for example, reportedly overrode colleagues who in 1962 opposed the publication of Alexander Solzhenitsyn's famous novel about Stalin's prison camps. The reservations of dissidents were later expressed by a party official in terms of worry about the effect on youthful readers.[31] Of course, the relatively more permissive attitude of reformist leaders toward cultural controls must not be exaggerated. There is the contented remark in Khrushchev's speech to the Central Committee in June 1963 that well-known intellectuals who signed a letter deploring any and all censorship had reconsidered and recalled it. But whatever the particular outcome of these intraparty battles, they have tended to discredit the unhappiest products of Stalinist policy in the arts, and are having far-reaching effects in stimulating critical thought and longing for social justice among the public. Despite detours enforced by conservatives, the progressive political tendency in the field of cultural affairs has been so enduring as to seem almost irreversible.

The clause in the 1961 Party Program making the achievement of welfare goals dependent on international tranquility suggests how arguments over investment policy are conducted with special reference to global developments. As already noted, industrial proportions during recent years have been overwhelmingly shaped by the needs of the producers' goods and armament industries. The pattern has been basically a centrist course in foreign policy, ruling out negotiated agreements with the West on questions of security arrangements in Europe and disarmament. Furthermore, the Kremlin under Khrushchev embarked on a series of risky politico-military adventures in the Middle East, Africa, and Latin America. At the same time, Khrushchev, prior to his setback in the Cuban missile crisis, now and then improvised moments of atmospheric change in order to cope with economic disruptions on the home front.

The idea of concentrating resources on development of the industrial-military potential and seeking aggrandizement overseas by truculent gestures may be regarded as far more than the private whim of a single leader. It seems to correspond, rather, to the expressed interest of certain party, economic, and military groups. This line of reasoning is supported by an examination of the adaptive moves of Malenkov and Khrushchev in domestic and external affairs in 1954 and 1964, respectively, and the factional recriminations which were surreptitiously hurled at them after they were driven out. Malenkov's policy of accelerating the output of consumer durables was only an inchoate tendency, but one which required the illusion of calm in international affairs. The Malenkov regime in 1954 conducted vigorous diplomatic activity to redefine European security arrangements and prevent the adherence of West Germany to NATO. Malenkov tried to make it appear that risk-taking in foreign policy was unthinkable, alleging the mutually suicidal nature of modern weapons of massive destruction. This proved to be a transient slogan, and, soon after the premiership fell into more aggressive hands, there was criticism of "weak-nerved" leaders who might fall prey to Western dictation.[32]

Similarly, Khrushchev in 1963–64 took the line of pulling up the consumer sector of the economy and adopted a cautious position of détente in relations with Washington. Around the time of the signing of the nuclear Test-Ban Treaty, the Soviet leader told the U.S. Secretary of Agriculture that funds would now be directed away from defense.[33] A year later, when domestic welfare was to be the "main task" of the new economic plan for 1966–70, Khrushchev sought to normalize relations with Bonn and appeared to look toward political disengagement in Southeast Asia. These interlocking projects for détente and abundance were at least temporarily wrecked by the junta which replaced Khrushchev. The junta at first resumed the centrist foreign policy course of 1955 and 1964 and, along with the indirect accusation that Khrushchev was guilty of "narrow practicism" at home, the press criticized "pragmatism" and "faintheartedness in transacting the business of external affairs."[34]

The more orthodox elements, which were victorious in the interrelated disputes over foreign and investment policy leading to changes of government in 1955 and 1964, were to be found mostly in professional party and military quarters, and we may assume that their views were shared by those executives responsible for the heavy and defense industries. Khrushchev had initially rallied his party collaborators on behalf of an investment program that stressed the value of forcing heavy industry for the dual purpose of bolstering defense and agriculture. Brezhnev, also of the party apparatus, later made the same kind of appeal in his bid for leadership. At each juncture, the leaders of the army displayed a reluctance to tamper with the usual order of economic priorities and perhaps were apprehensive about the fate of the Soviet base in East Germany. In any event, after the ouster of Khrushchev, the army leaders urged a new round of heavy industrialization by affirming the primacy of external over internal considerations of policy.[35] Once more, the interplay of interest groups aborted a turning point in public policy.

Communications

Despite the many personal initiatives of Khrushchev which became law, Kremlin policies throughout the post-Stalin era generally grew out of compromises and adjustments among diverse bureaucratic groups and their interests in society.[36] The re-emergence of more broadly based techniques for promoting particularistic causes, and mechanisms for negotiation and agreement, has signified a remarkable departure from the narrow court politics of Stalinism. As pointed out, the new arrangements are still relatively limited and the bureaucratic constituencies are perhaps no larger than those, say, in medieval England. Nonetheless, the persistent recourse to collectivist norms of decision-making, along with the rise of younger and more audacious officials, may offer the promise of greater responsiveness to impulses for change within the population.

An important vehicle for the conduct of polemics on current issues is the exchange of memorandums (*zapiski*) among senior executive officials. Over twenty-five memorandums dealing with agriculture are known to have been sent to the Party Presidium by Khrushchev in his capacity of Party First Secretary. The recommendations in Khrushchev's published memos are often set forth argumentatively rather than in language which brooks no challenge. As for the unpublished memos, a few sent to the Presidium in 1958 and 1962 treated managerial problems, and the evidence of turbulence surrounding them suggests the resort to suppression to guard Khrushchev's reputation as leader. Interestingly, the managerial forms adopted in each instance were consonant with the authoritarian-centralist viewpoint which U.S.S.R. Minister of Agriculture V. V. Matskevich expressed in a private memo on agricultural administration circulated to Central Committee members in 1959. The varied sources of origin of these memorandums and the unpredictable nature of their exchange are also demonstrated by certain events in 1963. The Presidium then rejected a written appeal of Byelorussian leaders for the allocation of 106 million rubles for land expansion in their area. But it acted favorably upon the letter of agricultural scientists who advised lowering a long-range target for chemical fertilizer production which Khrushchev had earlier proposed in one of his memos.

In a thinly veiled manner which sustains the fiction of political unanimity, the press still reflects the differentiation of attitudes within the oligarchy. Some of the more dramatic clashes have occurred during periods of struggle for political succession. Divergence over investment priorities between Malenkov and Khrushchev rose to the surface in December 1954, when the government newspaper, *Izvestiia*, and the party daily, *Pravda*, covered the topic with varying emphasis. A fight over literary controls among the holders of power evidently broke into the open in September 1965, when the chief editor of *Pravda* directly criticized *Izvestiia* for trying to throttle literary exposés of social discord. Moreover, theoretical economists writing in the press took conflicting stands on the politically sensitive theme of growth rates for the producers' and consumers' goods industries. The striking continuity of role performed by these economists in 1953–54 and 1965 again demonstrated the variety of Communist philosophies in the elite.[37]

The press also signals high-level conflict in the phase of limited one-man rule, under which animosities in the Politburo heighten until a new political scandal erupts. A usual instrument of agitation is the press "discussion." In 1962, for example, *Pravda*, *Izvestiia*, and *Ekonomicheskaia Gazeta* opened their columns to industrial technicians, business executives, and economists for an airing of views on planning and management. Letters were sent to party headquarters and all of the proposals were relayed for analysis to the planning agencies and Economics Institute of the U.S.S.R. Academy of Sciences.[38] This overt debate may be regarded as the genesis of the decision taken in mid-1964 to introduce market-type relations between trade organizations and enterprises producing about one-quarter of all clothing and shoes. Khrushchev's failure to push through more extensive measures may be ascribed to the complicated situation which then prevailed in ruling circles.

The precise way in which decisions are reached is obscure, and presumably varies from one occasion to the next. A general picture of Kremlin decision-making may be reconstructed from official sources pointing to "verbal battles" over policy choices, which are often won in accordance with the principle of "Whose voice is louder?"[39] The Politburo is certainly the foremost theater of political operations. It is there that policy initiatives are mounted and intrigues contrived to malign the dependents of antagonists, infiltrate hostile apparatuses, and secure an edge in the intraparty discussions over ways and means to govern. Unlike the practice under Stalin, the Politburo is now said to meet at least once a week. Different points of view are usually expressed and if a consensus is not reached, the problem at hand is decided by a simple majority vote. "Very heated debates" sometimes arise in such discussions.[40] Minutes of the sessions of the Politburo are taken and distributed to regional party leaders,[41] which suggests that Politburo members work on Central Committee members in order to persuade them of the rectitude of distinctive outlooks. Central Committee members are sometimes invited to the deliberations of the Politburo, especially on the eve of Committee plenums. The U.S.S.R. Minister of Defense has intimated that the Politburo formulates military policy after conferences with representatives of the general staff.[42] Khrushchev may have been alluding to such liaisons when he told John McCloy in July 1961 that he was under strong pressure from his "scientists" to resume nuclear testing in the atmosphere.

The Central Committee plenary sessions have sharply increased in regularity, from a total of two or three in the seven-year period 1946–53, to an average of three annually in the thirteen-year span of 1953–66. The conduct of sessions which are unrelated to the delicate business of personnel changes has been modified in the direction of slightly more openness and far greater argumentation. Under Stalin, decisions to call plenums were cloaked in secrecy; during the session in February 1947, the autocrat held a separate gathering of Politburo members and gave orders about the written directive. Nonorganizational plenums held under Khrushchev were usually announced beforehand and were preceded by discussions in the press. While the sessions had the outward appearance of production seminars designed for the enlightenment of hundreds of local practitioners who were in attendance, important hearings took place behind closed doors. Draft decrees composed in party headquarters were examined in special commissions of up to ninety persons. The give and take in "editorial commissions" was not publicized, but it was remarked that drafts were amended, and the meaningful character of some revisions may be established by collating formulas in keynote speeches and plenary decrees. The heirs of Khrushchev have preferred to organize Central Committee sessions without prior announcement, and have restricted attendance to members of the Committee. But they too find it useful to release censored minutes, if somewhat belatedly, and claim to have improved the preplanning of the gatherings.[43]

The quadrennial Party Congress is likewise a different kind of affair from what it was after the consolidation of Stalin's leadership. The abject subordination of the nominally supreme Congress to the will of Stalin was first expressed in 1934, when delegates to the Seventeenth Congress voted for a uniquely terse resolution on the Central Committee accounting report which Stalin had delivered. This resolution merely endorsed the Central Committee's policies and activities, and advised party organizations to execute the tasks set forth in "the report of comrade Stalin." The break with consultative tradition was perpetuated at the Eighteenth Congress in 1939 and the Nineteenth held shortly before the close of the Stalin era. While it is true that the open sessions of the post-Stalin Congresses, like those of 1934–52, have featured no genuine debate, commissions are formed to prepare lengthy resolutions on the report of the Central Committee. As is the case with *sub rosa* proceedings at the Central Committee plenary sessions, the occurrence and nature of bickering in these commissions may be adduced by contrasting the phraseology in their handiwork with that in the main report. Thus, at the Twenty-second Congress in 1961, a less favorable estimate of the military power of the Eastern bloc was offered in the resolution on Khrushchev's accounting report than in the report itself.

The reluctance of the party command to abandon its clandestine procedures for policy-making has stirred discontent in the rank and file, and official recognition of the problem may foreshadow eventual changes in this crucial area of Soviet operations. Understandably, Khrushchev's reform group was the first to attack the conspiratorial mentality of Stalinism. Shortly after the death of

Stalin, Valentin Ovechkin, an essayist who had worked in Khrushchev's Ukrainian apparatus, upbraided local party officials for "the discussion in secret conclave of problems that should be solved together with the people." The same criticism was retroactively directed much higher in 1961, when an editorial in the magazine *Kommunist* charged that the group of Malenkov and Molotov were "accustomed to the secretive, antidemocratic discussion and decision of the most important problems." Although little happened to alter the situation, this item remained on the political agenda. A party journalist in 1965 cautioned that much debate and time were required in order to develop more democratic political forms and institutions, as well as the sort of popular tradition essential for their success.[44] One potential step in the direction of eventually giving meaning to the presently empty constitutional forms might be the approval of a suggestion made in 1966 by the President of the Armenian Republic that political awareness and responsibility be increased through nominating more than one candidate for each seat during elections to the Supreme Soviet.

IV. The Realm of Possibility

Uncertainty has been one of the most striking characteristics of Soviet policy since the death of Stalin. A mainspring of discontinuity has been the absence of a Supreme Leader who adeptly manages the bitter controversies and intrigues of factional politics. Many important decisions have consequently been improvised in conformity with the shifting exigencies of struggles for power, rather than predetermined by one man's concept of the vital interests of society. As a result of this constant improvisation, the Soviet Union is now a kind of halfway house between Stalinist orthodoxy of the Communist Left and Yugoslav reformism of the Communist Right. The unsatisfactory nature of this arrangement has compelled Khrushchev's successors to acclaim time and again the virtue of laying a "scientific" foundation beneath all major decisions of internal and foreign policy. However, the quiet acceptance of pressure-group politics during the past decade or so makes it likely that extemporization and fluidity, rather than scientism and certitude, will characterize political life in the Soviet Union during the years ahead.

Political disputes will continue to rage over a broad gamut of issues affecting domestic evolution. The outcome of these disputes will hinge on the interaction of many random variables, and this cautions us to forego specific predictions in favor of outlining the range of governmental possibilities which loom ahead. This may be done by schematically proposing questions and alternatives which will confront Soviet policy-makers in the near future. In all likelihood, no pure solutions will be forthcoming. But the general impact of the most distinct alternatives may be perceived.

What kind of role should be performed by the Communist Party apparatus? The unadventurous forces in the apparatus may be expected to demand that it undertake the political tasks of regulating the state administration, selecting its officials, and indoctrinating the population. Within this frame of mind will be shadings between those who would grant more operational autonomy to local bodies and others preferring reliance on detailed control by the center. The ascendance of this conventional belief in a politicized party would mean less recourse to legalistic and technocratic modes of judgment, as compared with a situation under which the state officials held sway. The vast attractiveness of this faith in politicism is evident from the impetus which it gave to the careers of three generations of party leaders—namely, Stalin, Zhdanov, and Brezhnev.

Although now discredited, Khrushchev's bold idea of the entrepreneurial party might make a comeback if self-satisfaction were especially marked in the state bureaucracy. This pragmatic radicalism has the effect of degrading ideology to the level of practice and thereby affording greater leeway for experimentation in all walks of life. Under party technicism, sectional feeling might also tend to rise in the industrial and agricultural departments of the apparatus, and perhaps more equitable compromises would be reached between urban and rural interests for the sake of ensuring regime unity. A larger infusion of youthful and technically skilled talent into the apparatus is an organizational precondition for the revival of this school of thought.

A third possibility, which became a probability and almost a reality in June 1957, is that the topmost representatives of the state bureaucracy will exert more influence than their opposite numbers of the party apparatus. In that event, the apparatus would presumably devote its energies to political training and other activities of a civic character. The statists might embark on a course of paternal rule inclining toward centralism, tempered by increased resort to juridical procedures. The fear of a party usurper bent on risky action, or some crisis affecting the industrial-military interest, might encourage a power thrust in this direction.

What is the best way to realize the potential of the economy? A modest departure from the centralized command of industry began in earnest only after the psychological, if not physical, crisis of declining growth rates during the early 1960s had acted as a catalyst. The basic directions which the incipient reform will take are obviously unknown to its sponsors, and a rich variety of possibilities is evident from the ongoing debate. One drastic option is a retreat to the Leftist position of stark centralism, executed with the aid of computer technology and hence afforded the respectable guise of progressivism. This choice would hold an appeal to predisposed and vacillating elements if local machinations turned out to be especially disruptive, or if foreign tensions should require massive endeavors to speed the output of armaments and/or to develop the Siberian hinterland at forced draft.

The other extremist course is to put the command economy on market rails and let centralized planning serve as an auxiliary director. Unthinkable only a short time ago, we can expect to hear much more of the decentralists' implicit slogan of "What is good for the enterprise is good for the state!" Ever greater pressure for the unbinding of the producer in industry and agriculture will be exerted by a curious combination of Left-Right opinion which includes such diverse types as party veterans of the radical stripe, factory and farm managers, Western-oriented economists, and youthful syndicalists. The effectiveness of their agitation will depend on the extent to which calls for enlarging the forum of decision-making are heeded, the edge taken off the sharp social antagonisms, and the arms race slowed down. The contemporary fury of majority polemics against this radically innovative group is only likely to increase the growing number of its followers.

On the other hand, the ambiguity of political centrism may be sustained in the economy for some time to come. Just as Stalinist lethargy heaped up a mass of domestic troubles which eventually compelled the elite to vote for Khrushchevian dynamism, so the adverse reaction to a variety of panaceas may have sunk deep roots. While the immediate legatees of Khrushchev extended local rights and took measures to enhance popular welfare, none indicated verbally that in the struggle for succession he could expect to gain from the Central Committee anything more than a mandate for the conduct of a cautious public policy. This, of course, may have reflected to some extent the limited involvement of Moscow in the military conflict in Southeast Asia. But it may be assumed on the basis of contradictions in the official press that differences were also rife over this aspect of the equation of internal and foreign policy.

What means should be used to gain international advantage? The varied schools of reformist thought desperately need some form of limited accommodation with the United States in order to realize their goals of economic efficiency and abundance. The word "limited" must be emphasized, because neither the annals of Soviet foreign policy transactions nor the polemical literature of the CPSU affords the slightest hint of the existence of any influential strand of opinion which views the U.S.S.R. as a champion of the international *status quo*. Of course, that may yet come. But that thrice happy turn of events now seems to be as much a phantom as does its opposite: a surprise thermonuclear attack on the West. Somewhere between these poles lies the terrain of global struggle on which the two major powers will long be joined.

The future cleavages between reformers and conservatives may be patterned along the lines which had hardened by the 1960s. The partisans of reform are apt to contend that the zone of national influence must be expanded by the force of example, and that the regime must be able to convince malcontented outsiders that the Soviet version of socialism ensures vast strides toward human betterment. This group will feel constrained to persuade the United States to stabilize the arms race and lower barriers to trade with the Soviet Union. It may favor symbolic cooperation in individual undertakings of science and technology, but nationalistically demand a fierce competition for the political and moral solidarity of non-aligned states. The reformist group would probably consider the mutual assistance treaty with Communist China an utter formality and, largely for the sake of discrediting internal rivals, it would not hesitate to denounce a bellicose Peking.

The image of a hostile America has always been conjured up for ulterior reasons by the tough advocates of stringent internal control and an iron wage for the multitude. The insular tendencies of this group will probably spur its members further to oppose any sort of accommodation with the West, and their aggressive opportunism may intermittently gain the upper hand, much to the danger of world order. This conservative group may be expected to look with favor upon continuation of the military alliance with an anti-American regime in mainland China (but fail to honor the provisions if ever confronted by the peril of U.S. nuclear retaliation) and otherwise try to keep the surface unity in the Eastern bloc. Only the introduction of more representative institutions may serve to neutralize those who are prone to this expediently militant disposition.

*   *   *

If our classification of the forces which are now active in the arena of Soviet politics has some merit, the Soviet future promises to be no less exciting than the present. At a time of increasing interplay of domestic and foreign policy, the initiatives and responses of American statesmen will certainly help to shape the configuration of tomorrow in Moscow. Initiatives which may redound to the benefit of more reasonable leaders on the Soviet side will be contingent on our knowledge of the political difficulties which they must confront. Hopefully, this understanding will not be derived from intuitive reasoning, but from the branch of Sovietology that continues the healthy tradition of political historians, exemplified in the following quotation: "The careful study of the opinions of magistrates and influential generals, and of the composition of groups of senators which supported them, has gone far to explain variations of Roman policy and to reveal the rivalries and ambitions of members of the nobility."[45]

5.

Law and Society

LEON LIPSON

In the period of Khrushchev the reigning ideologists, hoping to live down Stalinism without repudiating it, were in the position of the vainly discriminating thinkers depicted in Zen Buddhism as washing off blood with blood. They tried to combine several currents of Soviet thought. The utopian strain pushed them toward what they called a transition from Socialist statehood to voluntary Communist self-government; the revulsion from Stalin's (and their own) past led them to certain improvements in legal procedure; the habit of rule and the claims of daily life, as well as another part of the ideology, demanded the strengthening of the apparatus.

Thanks to the endeavors of an army of Soviet writers, the meaning of the transition from Socialist statehood to voluntary Communist self-government has remained unclear. Of the three stages in the journey, the present and second stage, Socialist statehood, need not be fully described here. (The transition from the first stage, the dictatorship of the proletariat, to Socialist statehood or the state of all-the-people was proclaimed in 1961.) The distant goal, voluntary Communist self-government, is clearest where it is least specific; and the clouds of doubt obscure the way from the censored present to the prudently veiled future. Yet it is essential to have a goal, and that the goal to require authoritative and frequent interpretation by a controlling elite is held politically desirable by that elite.

Under Khrushchev the transition was to be marked partly by the progressive transfer of state functions from the organs of the state to nominally unofficial bodies. Except for legal institutions, the one example always pointed out was that of the administration of physical culture. Bit by bit, according to at least some versions of the theory, the sphere of state action would be taken over by voluntary organizations. The famous old words about superseding the governance of persons by the administration of things would be made flesh.[1]

Practical men, including some of the theorists, hastened to add compelling qualifications to the theory. First, the state was not about to permit itself to weaken even if some functions were about to be transferred to other hands; the state was rightly becoming stronger and must continue to become stronger. Second, the voluntary organizations in many cases would need the help of state organizations, just as in many cases they were to give help to the state organizations. Third, watching over the voluntary organizations and the state alike would be the party, which was not to wither but must flourish. Fourth, some functions would remain in the hands of the state for an indefinite future.

As the Soviet leaders begin to pay more attention to the quality of life in the Soviet Union, the ends to which the instruments of policy are directed will change. At least the number of those ends will grow; addition is likely to be more frequent than subtraction. Whether this diffusion of sub-goals must be accompanied by plurality of organizations and pluralism of power-sharing is a moot point. We may also conjecture that change in specific ends is more likely than is change in grand goals or change in the means used toward the specific ends.

Thus, the chief slogan implicit in the perennial fight against crime changes from "Criminals must be put away" (late 1940s and early 1950s) to "Crime is decreasing but not fast enough" (mid-1950s to early 1960s) to "Crime shall be abolished" (early 1960s) to "Crime must be studied" (mid-1960s). Emphasis is now placed on the need to do away with various new, and some not-so-new, social ailments or symptoms, be they the high rate of births out of wedlock (said to be one in nine), the school dropouts (said to be one in four, in Moscow), the role of drunkenness in crimes of violence, the feeding of bread to cattle, the rising pollution of rivers and lakes, the negative attitudes of writers, or bad manners on the telephone or omnibus.

To cope with these and other problems the Soviet weapon of choice is still the imperative issued from above.[2] More than one form will be used: besides the party directive there will be the penal law, the municipal ordinance, the newspaper campaign, the residential drive. But though the variety of forms is important, the assumption that wisdom resides at the top and center has not been called into question there. Whatever may be occurring in the economy, the Soviet citizen still lives in a command polity.

What is now called voluntarism or the subjectivist approach was spoken of during Khrushchev's chairmanship as "creativity." Creativity was the quality that was brought into play as the means of coping with the changes wrought by "life itself," which had "prompted" the reforms being celebrated. In the field of law reform, at least, little is heard now of creativity; but another quality has taken its place. What is now needed is discipline, and the way to achieve discipline is by showing "disciplinedness" (*distsiplinirovannost'*).[3] The emphasis is on control, regularity, proper subordination, less exuberant creation of organizations or institutions, and more predictable operation of those that exist.

Under present Soviet conditions, room for creative work in the law would be somewhat cramped even if the word had not come down to lay stress on discipline.[4] Soviet legal reformers have been set a three-cornered course by their history; the poles at the corners may be thought of as three conflicting objectives, roughly those of subordination, popularity (in the sense of public participation), and due process. The norms, institutions, and procedures of the law must continue to be subordinate to political decision ("the decisions laid down by the party at a given Congress"). Yet the administration of justice must be made more popular in the broadening of public participation and acceptance. Orderly and rational administration,[5] however, as well as individual equities, require more attention to that meaning of "socialist legality" which comes closer than its other meanings to due process of law. The poles are far apart, and movement toward any one threatens to entail retreat from one or both of the two others. Three illustrations may make the point clear.

Subordination versus *Popularity*. Alarmed by the high frequency of crimes of violence, Soviet authorities have recently lengthened the prison sentences applicable to aggravated rowdyism ("hooliganism")[6] and established a stern procedure for the incarceration and compulsory treatment of troublesome drunkards.[7] It is just such offenders, however, who appear as the commonest beneficiaries of two modern procedural devices designed to bring the local collectives more intimately into the processes of the administration of justice: probational release to the collective, without or after conviction, and the lay civic defender assigned by his collective to convey to the court the community's opinion of one party to the case (usually, the defendant).[8] If more and more applications for probational release are denied in court or discouraged at their source, and if civic defenders are ignored or disparaged, the policy of repression prevails over that of encouraging public participation. The conflict is not simply one between two approaches to a fight against crime, but between two views of the relationship between the legal system and the citizenry.

An illusory resolution of the conflict is attempted by encouraging or pressing the local collectives to designate not civic defenders but civic accusers, so that the public will seem to have aligned itself with the thrust of the new legislation. But to judge by exhortation in public print, the local collectives need continual reminders to keep pressing their cases.

Popularity versus *Due Process*. In the late 1950s and early 1960s a Khrushchevian "creative" initiative overspread the statute books with anti-parasite legislation, under which local collectives were empowered to try antisocial offenders, living on unearned income, and sentence them to exile and forced labor for terms of up to five years. The evils of wayward and haphazard administration provoked a series of explanatory essays, ameliorating directives, and amendments; their general effect has been to lodge more of the initiative in the office of the public prosecutor and more of the deciding power in the regular courts, thus reducing both the benefit from popular participation and the dangers from the hostility of the mob.[9]

Subordination versus *Due Process*. The trial of the Soviet writers Siniavsky and Daniel in early 1966 on charges of sending abroad literature intended to bring discredit on the Soviet form of government was a variant of the show trial, with a closely restricted audience but a wide reading public. Its foreordained conclusion was intended to demonstrate the limits still hedging round the questing spirit of the artist. At the trial itself, though the smuggled unofficial notes[10]—no record having been made public by Soviet authorities—indicate that the accused made a spirited defense of a lost cause, the conduct of the counsel for the prosecution and particularly the attitude of the judge show a casual harsh prejudice that recalls the administrative tribunals attached to seventeenth-century monarchical absolutism more than it answers to the ideal of impartial dispensers of justice. Care, however, must be taken to avoid a too narrow interpretation of the ways of Soviet justice.

When Siniavsky and Daniel are cut off by the court in their attempts to show the literary seriousness of their work, or when dissident Baptists celebrating their rites in public are convicted of crimes in spite of the constitutional language about freedom of religious worship, the trouble is not so much that good laws are being ill used; it is rather that officials are acting, perhaps in good faith, to defend the system that sustains their power and privilege.

Legality and Legalism

To the observer from a society with more differentiated institutions and more formal methods of adjusting the claims to interest and power on the part of competing groups, the forms of Soviet law seem underdeveloped. This is not because Soviet authorities have exalted the spirit above the letter; it is to be remembered that one of the chief draftsmen of the Soviet Constitution of 1936 (which is still in effect) was one of the chief victims of Soviet justice, convicted in good and due form, in 1938.[11] It is rather that law as a whole has occupied a minor place in the Soviet view of the institutions supposed to move and regulate conduct. If law is underdeveloped it is not because the law is primitive, but because the regime as a whole has subordinated the legal system to policy as laid down by the political leadership.

No complex society lacks restraining mechanisms in the sense of inhibiting disapproved conduct and of curbing the excesses of a temporary majority or minority. The Soviet Union has numerous and powerful (but not all-powerful) instruments for inhibiting disapproved conduct; some of these instruments are part of what an outsider would consider the machinery of law. Increasingly serious efforts are made, for instance, to raise the technical efficiency of the discovery, investigation, and solution of crimes. The main focus is on supervision of police and criminal investigators by the public prosecutors.[12]

Similarly, the Soviet Union has some instruments for curbing the excesses of temporarily prevalent minorities, but almost all of these are outside (not, of course, against) the law. So far as we know—and the limits on our knowledge are relevant to the effectiveness and the adequacy of the system—these instruments take the form primarily of secret bargains among groups (who have widely varying scope for maneuver) in a small elite. Law has relatively little to do with the process of bargaining, the terms of the bargains, and the sanctions (especially including threats of deprivation) by which the bargains are enforced. The party serves as the forum, arena, umpire, and scoreboard, besides being one— or several—of the chief claimants.

Nor are legal elements prominent in the myths by which the society lives. To judge from the official press, current literary works, and informal evidence of popular attitudes, the law is not looked to as the guardian of liberties or a check on the mighty. Indeed, the predominant official thought seems to be that in Soviet circumstances the right answer to the classical question *"Quis custodiet ipsos custodes?"* is "No one needs to." The official reason justifying the answer is that the holders of power watch one another closely enough, or rather, to use more conventional Soviet terms, that the party takes care to see that its members act with a consciousness of the high duty their membership imposes.[13]

Within the party, to be sure, there is a system of adjudication intended to correct certain kinds of abuses. The details of its operation are not public; it would be reasonable to suppose that values protected by the system are in the first instance the power and discipline of the party itself rather than the rights of the people, though cases are known where a mild party sanction has been imposed on a party member for high-handed conduct toward the public.

In the formal legal system the office of the public prosecutor maintains general supervision over the legality of governmental actions. At the same time the party has formal authority (which in practice may be exercised by groups within the party) both over the governmental actors and those whose business it is to supervise them. According to a standard Bolshevik tenet, the party, while it is supposed to lead and inspire the administrators, is not supposed to administer; observance of that tenet has always been compromised by the overlap of personnel, the supposed unity of doctrine, and the political claims generated by organizational constituencies.

For almost ten years Soviet legal scholars have attempted to harmonize the supremacy of the party with the need for a stronger legal order. As it has been out of the question to set bounds to the first of these, the legal order has either to be subordinated to, or justified by reference to, party supremacy. In times of political need, and such times are frequent, the legal order is subordinated: a recent example was the retroactive application of the newly increased penalties for economic crimes in 1961–62. Some foreign analysts have taken this to be not so much a defeat for the legal order as an ill-advised legal decision: bad law, rather than weak law, and thus to represent progress.

The second device justifies the interests of a stable legal order by reference to the will of the supreme political leadership. It lays the main stress not on justice, which is claimed as an incidental benefit derived from the Soviet order in general, but on administrative calculability. The notion is that legal stability is important, first, because the party has ordered it and, second, because the party needs it in order to be able to count upon orderly execution of its other policies. (The argument may be intended mainly for the eyes of the party apparatus, for which the *partiinost'* [party-ness] of a proposed policy is a necessary condition of its acceptability.) Legality is praised but comes down to the "unswerving execution of the laws."[14] The slogan is "A law is a law," with "law" rendered by *zakon* (equivalent to *lex, Gesetz, loi*) and not *pravo* (equivalent to *ius, Recht, droit*); the scope of "law" in this use is rather like that in the street signs in some cities in the United States that read "The Law: Clean Your Sidewalk—Curb Your Dog." Still, it is significant that attention is drawn to the law, and not only the latest Party Congress, as the source of even such precepts.

A few straws imply a stronger breeze. In early 1967, it was suggested by Soviet legal writers that law enjoyed a certain independence from the socio-economic base, even though that independence was only relative and partial.[15] Similarly, in a chapter of a collective work published in 1966 on the general theory of Soviet law, another author called for "principles assuring that administration will be under the control of the people and that officials are elective, subject to removal, and strictly responsible." He went on as follows: "Only under these conditions can we have truly a single law for all, a single legality, a single discipline for those who lead as well as for those who are led."[16] If these general ideas were translated into institutions and habits, Soviet "socialist legality" would be greatly changed. Nothing now in sight suggests that this will happen quickly.

The Asymmetry of Repression

In the dynamics of law-making and law-wielding, metaphors can mislead. One example is furnished by the contrast between repression and relaxation. On the face of it, repression requires more effort than relaxation; to clamp down takes strength, to let go is easy. In sad fact the political muscles do not work that way. Repression both in legislation and administration seems to be easier than relaxation to initiate, practice, defend, and sustain. This relationship holds good for many societies, though the quantities standing in that relationship may differ widely. Thus, we do not equate McCarthyism, Nazism, and Stalinism by pointing out that it was easier to enter than to terminate the McCarthy era, easier to Nazify than to de-Nazify, and easier to impose Stalinism than to dig one's country out of it.

The reasons for this asymmetry lie deep in the natures of government and of man. One of them has to do with the acuteness of the emergency that is perceived as justifying current action: energy is lent to repressive measures by the emergency conveniently found to hand, but nothing "positive" seems to call for measures of relaxation. Another has to do with the inertia of governmental apparatus: just as a theory survives long after its brains are knocked out,[17] institutions and organizations often persist after the initial reasons for their creation have disappeared. Governmental institutions in general are seldom set up to *remove* restraints.

The tighter the system, the greater the difference between the relative ease of further tightening and the relative difficulty of loosening. Without a thoroughgoing revision of basic myths and institutions—a revision more thorough than, say, that which accompanied the revolutions of 1917—Soviet legal reform will probably remain partial and precarious.

6.

The Military

THOMAS W. WOLFE

Like many other countries, the Soviet Union finds itself today in the throes of adjustment to the changing technological and political environment of the modern world. Among Soviet institutions, perhaps none has been more immediately affected by this process of adjustment than the armed forces. The process has worked in two directions. The Soviet military establishment has been obliged to adapt its traditional ways to the demands of the nuclear-missile age. At the same time, the role of the military as a sociopolitical force in Soviet society has presented the regime with a series of problems, some familiar from the past and others growing out of the changing conditions of the contemporary world.

The broad problems arising from the role of the military in Soviet society and its influence upon political affairs are by no means unique. Such factors as technological advance, industrialization, and the wider scope and importance of collective security arrangements have tended to give the military institution in the modern world a new power, which, as one student puts it, "protrudes into the political fabric of contemporary society" and creates universal problems of "maintaining traditional forms of political controls" over the military.[1] Recognition of the pervasive spread of the military factor in the international and domestic affairs of states in the present age is reflected, for example, in Harold Laswell's words that "the arena of world politics is moving toward the domination of specialists on violence."[2] The proliferation of military regimes among the emerging new nations is another aspect of the same phenomenon. Despite certain universal trends, it also remains true that the context in which they operate differs from one society to another; and it hardly needs saying that this applies to the Soviet Union, where a "socialist" system organized along totalitarian lines has taken root in a particular historical and cultural milieu handed down from the Russian past.

This chapter is primarily concerned with institutional and policy considerations bearing on the role of the military in Soviet life, especially under the new conditions of the nuclear age. Necessarily, many aspects of Soviet military development lie outside this inquiry, which touches either tangentially or not at all upon such matters as specific military capabilities, force structure, and weapons technology. The matters dealt with here fall broadly into the following categories.

There is the question of political-military relations, involving, among other things, the central problem of how to reconcile political control with professional military efficiency, and the role of the military as a pressure group. The internal military scene is another broad subject, including both tendencies which heighten the cohesion of the military community, and institutional attitudes and groupings which tend to dilute the seemingly monolithic character of the armed forces. Finally, the chapter takes up the military policy debate which was carried on during the Khrushchev era over the problems of adapting Soviet military theory and posture to the changed environment of the nuclear-missile age and which is continuing under the new regime.

I. Political-Military Relations

The problem of exercising political control over the armed forces without impairing their professional efficiency and morale is a familiar one in most states. This has been a central and long-standing problem in the Soviet Union, where the military is both an indispensable instrument of the ruling one-party regime as well as a potential threat to the party's power. The threat has lain less in direct rivalry from the military for political power than in dilution of the party's hegemony over all the institutions in the society by the gradual emergence of the military as a professionally autonomous group. The nuclear-missile age has introduced new sources of strain between political authority and the military and has aggravated some old problems.

From the party's viewpoint, there never has been any doubt that the principle of political supremacy over the armed forces must come first. At the same time the party's responsibility for national security has made it imperative that this principle be honored without prejudice to military capabilities. Its attitude toward the armed forces reflects the sometimes ambivalent effort to satisfy both goals.

On the one hand, the party has sought to integrate the armed forces into the totalitarian state structure in order to prevent them from developing any sense of separate identity. It has laid great stress upon *splochennost'*—solidarity—between the party and the military, welcoming senior officers to places on the Central Committee and other political organs, and enrolling upwards of 90 per cent of the officer corps in the party or the Komsomol.[3] However, with the exception of Marshal Zhukov's brief tenure in 1957, the party has closed its highest sanctum, the Presidium (or Politburo), to military men, and it maintains a pervasive network of party and police controls within the military establishment.

Such practices testify to the party's keen awareness of the armed forces' superior potential for internal coercion, and to its preoccupation with controlling this potential. These and other notions tend to dilute the pursuit of military effectiveness within the armed forces. The party's traditional requirement that the armed forces should be "a school for communism" means that they are burdened with ideological and political indoctrination activities that compete with military-technical training. The party also sanctions such diversions from military preparation as patronage (*shefstvo*), which involves using military personnel to work on local economic and construction projects.[4]

On the other hand, it can hardly be said that the party has intentionally slighted its responsibility for developing Soviet military power. Within the constraints imposed by economics and technology, and subject to the strategic predilections of the men who have ruled the party, more than a fair share of resources has been allocated toward building up an industrial-technical base capable of supporting powerful armed forces. Khrushchev, chancing to exercise his rule at a time when the Soviet Union was entering the missile age, sought to free military doctrine and strategic thinking from the sterility into which it had fallen in Stalin's last days. As the major architect of Soviet military policy and strategy during most of the past decade, Khrushchev carried through military reforms for which many professional officers were undoubtedly grateful—although his policies also antagonized substantial elements of the military and may have contributed to his downfall.

From the viewpoint of the Soviet military command, political-military relations have often left much to be desired. Although not disposed to challenge openly the policy-making prerogatives of the party, the military leadership has sought a larger measure of autonomy in professional matters and has looked upon excessive political intrusion into its affairs as a threat to military effectiveness. Although the military leadership was cowed into passivity under Stalin, especially by the purges of the mid-1930s, since his death it has been drawn occasionally into the political arena. At the same time, the military-technical revolution has placed a higher premium than ever before on professional expertise. Both developments have aggravated the issue of military influence upon the formulation of Soviet policy and strategy. The party has tended to resist expansion of the military's sphere of influence, while the officer corps has sought to win wider legitimation for its professional role in assuring the country's defense.[5]

More precisely, there are three areas in which military influence on Soviet policy may be potentially felt. The first is party-state policy formulation. The second is the development and management of the military establishment itself. The third is internal Soviet politics.

Role of the Military in Party-State Policy

Active participation of the military at the party-state policy level traditionally has been limited, even on decisions affecting defense arrangements. Such basic questions as the share of national resources to be allocated to the armed forces and the uses to which military power may be put have been determined by the political leaders. The role of the military at this level is to furnish professional advice and to assist in the process of integrating military strategy with state policy, rather than to participate directly in national decision-making. Glimpses into the policy process at this level have tended to corroborate the view that the military role is essentially advisory, although the weight given professional advice is a contentious matter. For example, articles by two senior Soviet military men on the occasion of Khrushchev's seventieth birthday in 1964 drew contrasting images of the situation.[6] Marshal R. Ia. Malinovskii, the Minister of Defense, stressed that high-level decisions involving defense policy were reached only after consultation by the Party Presidium with professional military advisors. Marshal A. A. Grechko, Soviet commander of the Warsaw Pact forces, indicated on the other hand that decisions flowed from Khrushchev's personal initiative and expertise in military affairs, implying that military men had relatively little to do with the decision-making process before the fact.

Whatever the indirect influence of the military may be, the continuing absence of military membership at the summit of the Soviet policy-making structure attests to the formal primacy of the political leadership. Military membership on the party Central Committee[7] and in the Supreme Soviet has a symbolic significance, of course, but the members rarely have a direct voice in policy. While there currently seems to be a fairly standard practice of allotting about 10 per cent of representation on various party bodies to military men, one should probably not read too much into this percentage as a measure of political influence.[8]

The body in which the professional military voice can be heard most regularly at the upper echelons of policy-making in peacetime is evidently the Higher Military Council (*Vysshii Voennyi Sovet*), which brings together both leading political and military officials.[9] Its role may be more to furnish recommendations on matters raised within the Politburo than to initiate policy on its own account. It is possible, however, in view of Politburo-level membership mentioned by Soviet sources, that the Council may be a forum for important policy decisions.[10] Khrushchev chaired the Higher Military Council, which suggests that Brezhnev, in assuming the post of First Party Secretary, may also have taken over this job.

Military influence at the top level would undoubtedly increase in wartime; but even then, as past experience suggests, the leadership would rest ultimately in the hands of political men. One of the few Soviet discussions of command arrangements in a future war indicates that the responsibility for over-all policy and direction of the country's efforts would be vested in an agency similar to the State Defense Committee headed by Stalin in World War II, which included no military members.[11] The World War II *Stavka* (Supreme Headquarters of the Supreme High Command), which exercised direct leadership over the armed forces and was also under Stalin's chairmanship, was the highest agency of strategic leadership in which professional military men sat. Presumably, a *Stavka* would be set up again in the event of war. It is not clear, however, how the unity of political-military leadership at the very top that was concentrated in Stalin's person in World War II—and for which Khrushchev had again laid the basis— would be arranged under the current rulers.[12]

Military Influence at the Professional Level and Attempts To Extend It

In the planning and direction of purely military activities in peacetime, the military professionals have enjoyed considerable autonomy. During the past decade, beginning with Zhukov's installation as Minister of Defense in 1955, this post has been occupied by a *bona fide* soldier, and the Ministry of Defense is staffed at virtually all levels by professional military men rather than civilians. This is not to say, of course, that the military leadership has held uncontested sway in the professional realm. Not only have the missions of the Soviet armed forces and the general policies governing their development been laid down by political authority, but secret-police and party controls have pervaded the armed forces themselves.[13] The power of the party to veto promotions of the military cadres has been an especially potent device to dampen any illusions the military leaders might entertain about running their own show.

Nonetheless, the tendency of the military to seek greater institutional and professional freedom from the party has been fairly constant, however varied in form. It can be seen in a long series of efforts to define the working relationship between military professionals and political workers within the armed forces. More significant, in terms of an implicit challenge to the party's policy-making prerogatives, have been the attempts during the past few years to establish the importance of "objective" professional contributions to the formulation of military theory. In essence, the military leadership has utilized a more or less discreet debate over the theoretical foundations of Soviet military doctrine, science, and strategy to wage a subtle campaign for greater influence upon policy decisions affecting national security.

The party has recognized here an incursion into its own policy-making preserve, and periodically has moved to counter it. In 1958, for example, following Zhukov's dismissal for having been, among other things, too vigorous a proponent of the military, measures were taken to reassert the principle of party primacy.[14] Again, after the Cuban missile episode in October 1962, which apparently had aroused criticism in some military circles, another campaign was set in motion to emphasize that the political leadership "alone has the competence and the jurisdiction to solve the problems of developing the armed forces."[15] Following Khrushchev's ouster, the military side of the question was revived in early 1965 when several prominent military figures publicly stressed the importance of professional expertise and "objective" military judgment in the formulation of defense policy.[16] Details of this recurrent contest for jurisdictional rights in the "gray area" where political and military competence overlap in national security matters have been discussed elsewhere by the author and need not be repeated here.[17] However, the essential points at issue merit brief elaboration.

One might note first that the principle of party primacy in military affairs remains formally inviolate. According to the theoretical model, the party sets policy and the military, as managers and technicians, carries it out. In practice, the situation is by no means this simple. Problems arise from the fact that military doctrine and strategy, as well as military power itself, must be articulated with Soviet political strategy.

Putting it another way, the question at issue is what should be the weight of Marxist-Leninist political philosophy on the one hand, and of military-technical considerations on the other, in the development of Soviet military theory and policy. In an age in which the links between political and military power are subject to the stress of technological and other forms of change, it is perhaps not surprising that the extent to which military considerations can be allowed to influence political strategy—and vice versa —should have become a vexed question.

In the Soviet case, an unsettled internal dialogue goes on, with the military seeking ways to make professional thinking and influence felt in the policy process without seeming to infringe upon the party's prerogatives in this domain. One should distinguish here between substantive disagreements over military doctrine and policy (which will be taken up below) and what might best be called attempts to improve military leverage upon the policy process itself. A revealing example of the latter may be found in the work of a prominent Soviet military theorist, Major General S. Kozlov.

Writing in 1964, before Khrushchev's downfall, Kozlov stressed the relationship between doctrine and military science: "To ignore the conclusions of military science and thereby find oneself with a defective doctrine can place the country in a difficult situation."[18] Kozlov seemed to be hedging his acknowledgment that party-approved doctrine enjoys the last word in the policy domain by arguing that if doctrine strays too far from the "objective" findings of military theorists it can be weakened by "sub-jectivism"—that is, by the uninformed or inexpert personal judgment of individual political leaders.

To judge from this and similar expressions of the military view-point in the post-Khrushchev period, one may say that the party leadership can expect to find itself under continuing pressure to heed professional military counsel more closely than was gen-erally the case under Stalin and Khrushchev. So long as no single political figure attains the personal prestige and authority once en-joyed by these leaders, professional military expertise and advice probably will command more attention in any event. Furthermore, the increasing complexity and interpenetration of military affairs with other aspects of the country's life undoubtedly lend weight to the military claim for a larger voice in relevant policy decisions. However, a trend toward greater military influence on policy—whether to promote the national interest as the marshals perceive it or to serve parochial military interests—does not necessarily mean that the military is apt to pit itself against the political leadership in a struggle for political power. On the contrary, barring radical changes in the military's image of its role in Soviet political life, this is an unlikely prospect.

The Military and Internal Soviet Politics

One finds little evidence that the Soviet military elite has ever had serious aspirations to formal political power. Like the military class in Tsarist Russia, though perhaps for different reasons, the Soviet military has maintained an essentially apolitical orientation within the society.[19] Nevertheless, two problematical examples should be cited. In the mid-1930s, Stalin seemingly feared the political potential of the military elite (allied with elements of the party opposition) to such an extent that he was willing to risk serious weakening of the armed forces by widespread purging of the military command. The case of Zhukov in the late 1950s may have posed the threat of a military leader moving toward an in-dependent base of political power capable of decisive intervention in party and political affairs. Although these examples belong in the category of potential threats, they suggest that one should not too hastily rule out circumstances in which the apolitical self-image of the military could undergo major change.

What does seem quite clear from the record is that the Soviet military leadership, almost in spite of itself, has become a political balancing force of some consequence since Stalin's death. Rivalry and maneuvering for position within the post-Stalin "collective leadership" drew the military into the political arena as one faction courted the support of military leaders against another. This first became apparent at the time of Beria's arrest and execution in 1953 for alleged plotting to unseat the other collective leaders, next in early 1955 when Malenkov was deposed by Khrushchev's faction, and again in Khrushchev's 1957 showdown with the "anti-party group" of Molotov, Malenkov, and others.

While the details of the military involvement in these episodes have not been established, intervention by the marshals was clearly important.[20] Marshal Zhukov's prompt elevation to the highest political councils immediately after the anti-party group affair probably resulted from the backing he gave Khrushchev, just as his downfall a few months later must have been at least partly related to Khrushchev's concern that he might make a habit of playing "kingmaker," perhaps on someone else's side in the future. Zhukov's dismissal in the fall of 1957 signaled a decline in the political influence of the military, and until Khrushchev's own sudden ouster seven years later the question of military involvement in the internal Soviet political process lay largely dormant. In the aftermath of Khrushchev's ouster, the question is again alive, although there has been little evidence to suggest that the marshals had a direct hand in his removal.[21]

Whether the Soviet military gained or lost ground in connection with Khrushchev's overthrow is not yet clear. There is no reason to believe, however, that the party's jealous grip on its political prerogatives was substantially loosened in the crisis, or that the new regime finds itself beholden to the military for help in turning Khrushchev out.

With regard to the political potential and ambitions of the Soviet military, several observations may be offered. First, the trend toward increasing professionalization in the military appears unlikely to be reversed. In part, this trend rests on the growing importance of technical expertise in the military applications of nuclear energy, missiles, electronics, space flight, and other technological advances. It is reinforced by the dependence of modernized societies on the services of professional groups generally —managers, economic specialists, scientists, and so on. Despite efforts of the party to check what might be called a nascent "pluralism" among these institutional groups, a long-run tendency in this direction seems likely to continue. Along with other changes in the society, such as some diminution of ideological *élan* and reduction in the use of raw terror as an instrument of rule, these trends seem to be creating conditions which are likely to heighten the Soviet military's self-awareness as a group with a professionally autonomous identity and its own set of interests and values.

How all this may bear on the military's emergence as a political entity and its inclination to participate more actively in the internal political process is the critical question. Several factors could operate to draw the military more deeply into the political arena. One of them is the matter of succession politics. In a system where there is no formal or constitutional arrangement for transfer of power, the potential of the military either as an aspirant to political power in its own right or as a "balancer" of competition among rival factions probably increases. The potential has tended to take the latter form in the Soviet case.

The Soviet military might also become concerned about the implications of collective leadership for other problems of special significance in the nuclear-missile age, such as the question of ultimate command and control of nuclear weapons—or, whose finger belongs on the button. Conceivably, if the political leadership should find itself at odds on this question, the Soviet military might precipitate a showdown over where the real authority resides.

A variety of other circumstances can be visualized in which military professionalism might move from protecting the integrity and efficiency of the armed forces against political intrusions, as in Zhukov's case, to taking a political stand on what is best for the country. Since the Soviet military is a repository of strong national and patriotic sentiment, its conception of how the country's interests can best be served may at times differ from that of the party, even though the military elite may share in general the goals and values of the political leadership. Political-military differences over national security issues like the allocation of resources have in the past prompted the military to lend support to a particular faction, for example, to Khrushchev *versus* Malenkov in the 1953–55 period. These differences, however, have not been translated into a frontal challenge against the political leadership as a whole, although it is perhaps possible that this will happen in the future.

In certain extreme cases, such as the possible collapse of party rule in the massive disorganization of Soviet society in a nuclear war, it might be supposed that the country itself would turn to the

military—whatever the latter's own political ambitions might be—
to restore order and pull the society together again. Under a condition of somewhat less convulsive political instability, such as that
foreseen by Zbigniew Brzezinski if other social institutions besides
the party "succeed in attracting the society's talent and begin to
chafe under the restraints imposed by the ruling but increasingly
mediocre *apparatchiki*,"[22] the military might also play a role in
casting off party restraints and reconstituting the political order.
However, neither mediocrity of party personnel nor a glut of
creative political talent in the military seems close enough at hand
to make this a real prospect in the short term.

Looking at the other side of the coin, one can find various
grounds for questioning whether the emergence of the military
as a more autonomous professional group necessarily points to its
active entry into internal politics. Professionalism connotes a
certain career preoccupation with mastering the demands of the
military trade, which can lead to divorce from the mainstream
of civil life. The upcoming generation of Soviet military leaders, as
we shall see later, exhibits this tendency to some degree. There is,
moreover, the powerful influence in the Soviet case of a tradition
of noninvolvement in the domestic political arena. While institutional and policy differences between the party leaders and the
marshals can be expected to arise, as in the past, it is by no means
a foregone conclusion that they will erupt into rivalry for political
power. Indeed, a more thoroughly professionalized military group
may evolve in a still more apolitical direction, conceiving its duty
to be unswerving submission to whatever political authority holds
sway. For the party, this prospect is not altogether an unmixed
blessing. While a submissive military is certainly a party ideal,
an autonomous military class that resists internal politicization of
military life and that might passively accept a change of political
leadership is not. In a sense, Khrushchev felt the sting of this political "non-interventionism" when the military failed to rally to
his support in October 1964, as it had done during the "anti-party"
challenge to his rule in mid-1957.

These, then, are some of the pros and cons concerning the future
political potential and ambitions of the military. In my opinion,
although the Soviet military is likely to have an intimate interest
in such matters as the problem of succession and the adoption of
policies congenial to a strong military posture, there seems to be
little prospect of a major break with the Soviet tradition of military

subordination to political authority. Unless party rule degenerates greatly, the military elite will probably continue to eschew any quest of formal political power on its own account.

II. The Internal Military Scene

Along with other institutions in Soviet society, the military is in the process of internal transition, reflecting the influence of modernization, the turnover of generations, new social trends, and other phenomena. This process of change entails elements of cohesiveness as well as the interplay of competing interests and values within the military community.

In general, strong binding elements of discipline and duty give the Soviet military community a greater cohesiveness and sense of common purpose than is perhaps to be found in most segments of the society, with the exception of the party *apparat* itself. As already indicated, innate tendencies toward professional autonomy have been strengthened by the military-technical revolution, and have further heightened the military's sense of group identity. At the same time, however, the military establishment, like most large bureaucracies, has its fair share of divergent internal interests and groupings. Seen close up, it is by no means the model of monolithic solidarity customarily pictured in Soviet accounts.[23]

Social Solidarity of the Soviet Military

Although nominally classless, the Soviet Union has patently produced a society with a new class structure of its own. The military elite, occupying a place somewhere among the privileged upper strata of this society, has taken on many of the attributes of a separate military caste. Various factors account for this: the ingrown nature of military life common to most societies; efforts by successive Soviet leaderships to reinforce the loyalty of the military through material rewards, social status, and prestige; recognition of the military's wartime services to the country; the military's own sense of a special calling, and so on.

As it has evolved under the Soviet regime, the military elite has acquired an increasingly homogeneous character. At its outset, the officer corps of the Red Army contained a large proportion of former Imperial Army officers, as high as 75 per cent according to some accounts.[24] Throughout the 1920s, these "military specialists" of non-proletarian origin were still numerous,[25] providing the real professional core of the Red Army, although they were rather closely watched over by military commissars with proper revolutionary credentials. The development of a new officer corps drawn from the "workers and peasants" social category was undertaken in the early 1930s under Marshal Tukhachevsky—himself a former nobleman. The Great Purge of 1937, which claimed about 35,000 military victims, or about half of the officer corps at that time,[26] wiped out most of the remaining former Imperial officers as well as the Old Bolsheviks who had taken up military careers. The purge had the effect, however, of opening the officer corps to younger personnel from noncommissioned ranks, and largely of worker-peasant origin, thus greatly accelerating the social homogeneity of the new officer class. The upper reaches of the military elite today are still populated with men who begain their career advancement as officers in that period.

The mid-1930s was also the period in which the new officer corps began to press for, and was gradually granted, a restoration of traditional military ranks and other hierarchical privileges.[27] In the face of the gathering threat of Hitler's Germany, Stalin found it expedient to elevate the prestige and authority of the Soviet officer corps in a system which, originally suspicious of standing professional armies, had accorded the career officer scant respect. With this development, the egalitarian ideas of officer–enlisted men relationships that had carried over from the Civil War years were laid aside. The growing gap between officers and ordinary soldiers was codified with the introduction of the Universal Military Service Statute of 1939, the essential provisions of which remain unchanged to the present day.[28] The statute ended selective call-up on the basis of social background, but at the same time it laid down strict disciplinary standards for the relationships between officers and men, superiors and subordinates.

Other practices which clearly marked the emergence of the military elite as a privileged group also date from the late 1930s. Special stores were set up for officers and their families, affording access to goods hard to come by in a scarcity economy. A network of "cultural" institutions—clubs, theaters, rest homes—was established for the military. Salary scales, even more than the new regulations, emphasized the growing social distance between officers and enlisted men, with the differential between the pay of a marshal and a private exceeding 100 to 1.

The war years brought an enormous expansion of the armed forces, including the officer corps, which reached a peak of around a million men. Although many wartime officers were later demobilized, many also stayed on in the larger military establishment maintained after World War II by the Soviet Union. The senior echelons of the military command, whose members comprised a comparatively young group in the thirty- and forty-year age bracket during the war, emerged, of course, with new laurels and prestige.

Although Stalin acted promptly after the war to suppress the political potential of the military and to deflate the personal popularity of some outstanding war heroes like Marshal Zhukov,[29] the favored standing of the military as a social group was not essentially affected. Such privileges as special stores, clubs, and access to scarce housing for officers' families were not withdrawn, and the military continued to have its own popular and professional press, which, even though muzzled, provided a means for generating a distinct body of military opinion on many issues of the day. Moreover, the military was now inseparably linked with a victorious wartime tradition, and despite recurrent attempts of party historians to play down the armed forces' share of credit for victory,[30] this tradition helped to swell the self-confidence and solidarity of the military class.

The population certainly continued to hold the military in high esteem, and even though the average citizen's lot compared quite unfavorably in the postwar years of reconstruction with that of an officer, little open resentment was displayed. Anyone who witnessed the Red Square parades on major Soviet holidays, for example, could hardly help being struck not only by the respectful attitude of sidewalk crowds, but also by the sharp contrast between the burnished ranks of officers and cadets in their smart uniforms and the drab lines of workers who followed them past the reviewing stand. The deference customarily paid high-ranking officers in trains, hotels, and other public places also attests to the favored class status of the military in the society.

The postwar modernization and training of the Soviet armed forces has necessarily stressed a higher level of professionalism; it also has been marked by other trends that contribute to the elitism of the officer corps. The process of selection and education of officer personnel is a pertinent example. The Suvorov and Nakhimov cadet schools, established during the war along lines recalling a similar institution of Tsarist times, have been continued. They furnish 12 years of education to boys chosen mostly from families with a military background, after which the youths are enrolled in officers' schools. While graduates of the cadet schools are a small minority of the total officer group, they do provide the basis for a new, semi-hereditary caste of highly indoctrinated military leaders within the officer corps.

The road remains open to officers' training schools from non-commissioned ranks and from the regular secondary school system, although education, political acceptability, nationality background, and other factors operate to discriminate against some and favor the selection of others. Theoretically and legally, minority nationalities have an equal chance with others to rise from private to marshal,[31] but as some accounts suggest,[32] cultural and educational factors have operated to leave the officer corps dominated mainly by Great Russians and Ukrainians. Occasionally, talented individuals from minority groups, especially Armenians and Georgians, rise to the top.

At the upper levels of the military educational system, the General Staff Academy and other higher academies are geared to produce a professionally qualified and well-educated military elite. Selection for these institutions requires, of course, not only a satisfactory military record, but thorough assimilation of the Communist outlook.

As conditions in Soviet society improve for the population at large, some of the material and social advantages which have made an officer's calling attractive are likely to diminish. The attitudes of the new generation of Soviet youth toward military life, which I shall discuss presently, suggest that this is already happening. At the same time, other factors which have given the military elite a strong sense of social solidarity seem likely to be more persistent, such as the tendency toward hereditary careers, intermarriage among military families, and the clannishness of garrison life, which tends to draw career officers and their families together.[33]

The military elite does not remain isolated from other privileged groups in the society. In fact, there seems to be a good deal of "elite interpenetration," which takes several forms. A large proportion of the officer corps, as previously noted, belongs to the party; many of the senior officers, indeed, have held party cards longer than the post-Stalin generation of political leaders. In a sense, therefore, the military elite merges with the party elite, or at least enjoys easy access to it, although the distinction between a military professional and a party *apparatchik* is still a real one. In another dimension, there is a network of official and informal associations between military leaders and scientists, industrial managers, and others concerned in one way or another with national security matters. Although the subject has not been intensively studied, one may speak in the Soviet context of a phenomenon already described in Western countries as the "military-industrial-scientific complex." The internal movement and influence of the Soviet military elite within this complex is considerable, as the known tendency to conduct a great deal of the Soviet scientific and technological effort in close association with military institutions attests.[34] Another dimension of communion of Soviet elites may relate more to generational than to institutional or social-group outlook. It has been suggested, for example, that there is a "cohesive brotherhood" at the upper elite levels, which tends to ally itself "horizontally" along lines of age and shared experience rather than "vertically" by institutional affiliation.[35]

Although the military is a relatively close-knit social group, it has made little direct effort to translate its class privileges into political power. Indeed, "elite interpenetration" in its various forms perhaps serves as an antidote to the strong group solidarity of the military; if one may hazard a guess for the future, it will probably continue to be a major factor in keeping the military from acting as a separate political entity.

Turnover of Leadership Generations in the Military

The leadership of the Soviet armed forces has been dominated for the past two decades by a generation of officers whose formative military experience and first taste of major responsibility were acquired in World War II and the Stalin era. Today, most members of this top Soviet military leadership group in the important command and policy posts are in their sixties, with the average age around sixty-five.[36] This aging leadership stands in the way of a younger generation of officers less conditioned by the experience of the last war and possibly more pragmatic and less doctrinaire than their elders. While the strain between generations at the High Command level has hitherto remained a rather muted theme, one may suppose that it will grow sharper should turnover at the top remain overdue.

The age structure of the dominant military leadership, which suggests considerable stability and a low rate of elite circulation in the top stratum of the Soviet High Command, contrasts with that of the upper political elite. The average age of the party Politburo's regular members is fifty-seven, while that of candidate members is just under fifty-two.[37] In the Central Committee, the next echelon of political leadership below the Politburo, only about one-sixth of the membership is over sixty, and more than half is under fifty-five. This age differential is perhaps less significant in itself than what one might call a "cultural" gap between the military and political elites. A fairly large portion of the latter got its main intellectual conditioning after World War II, and in some cases attained significant authority only in the post-Stalin period. Thus, the outlook of the senior military elite may be somewhat more fixed and less receptive to new ways of doing things than the political elite finds convenient.[38]

The process of replacing the senior military command with younger men may be complicated by the problem of finding suitable younger officers prestigious enough to step into the marshals' boots. The nominal "replacement pool" has been the military district commanders, but these men are also only marginally removed in terms of age, being in their upper fifties and early sixties. However, rejuvenation of the top military command will be difficult to postpone much longer.

The consequences of a takeover by a new military generation are difficult to predict. Although still sharing the "heroic" wartime military tradition, the upcoming generation now in its forties and early fifties has found it necessary to seek career advancement by concentrating its energies on meeting the professional military demands of the modern age.[39] In the process, it not only has developed an outlook less doctrinaire than that of the older generation, but also has tended to be somewhat divorced from the mainstream of postwar Soviet civilian life. These factors could contribute to a more pronounced professionalism that may give the political leadership trouble. On the other hand, the new generation's relative lack of wartime prestige and its evident indifference to the interplay of domestic politics may make it easier for the political leadership to deal with them than the seasoned marshals now in command.

Political Workers and Military Professionals

The history of tension between these two groups, reflecting the perennial problem of reconciling political control with professional military efficiency, is among the better-documented features of the internal life of the Soviet military community.[40] Conflicts between political workers and military professionals have persisted despite the fact that both wear the uniform. Throughout the evolution of the institution of the political commissar within the armed forces, representatives of this party-oriented species have been marked off from the professional breed of military men,[41] and efforts to achieve harmony have been attended by something less than lasting success.

The dichotomy between political workers and the professional military, which arises in the first instance from the differing focus of their day-to-day duties and activities, is accentuated by separate lines of accountability, recruitment, and promotion for the two groups. The Main Political Administration (MPA) in the Ministry of Defense, which supervises the activities of party-political organs in the armed forces, also recruits, trains, and confers military ranks upon the personnel who do its work.[42] The MPA itself is traditionally an extension of the party Central Committee's staff within the armed forces,[43] and its head bypasses the Minister of Defense in reporting directly to higher political authority.[44]

One of the more serious transgressions attributed to Marshal Zhukov during his tenure as Minister of Defense was that he had sought to neutralize the watchdog role of the MPA and to "liquidate" indoctrinational and other activities of political workers in the armed forces.[45] Marshal Malinovskii, Zhukov's successor, evidently tried to avoid the latter's mistakes, but his own career suggests that he, too, sometimes displayed the tendency of career military men to put their professional values ahead of the requirements of political control.

From time to time efforts have been made to pursue a policy of interchanging military and political officers in order to erode military professionalism at its foundation. Such a policy was reinstituted in early 1959, as one of a series of reforms undertaken shortly after Zhukov's dismissal two years earlier.[46] There was some military resistance to these reforms,[47] however, and subsequently military professionalism re-emerged in the form of emphasis on the principle of *edinonachalie* or "single command" under the new conditions of nuclear-missile warfare.

Edinonachalie, long the rallying principle of the professional cadres against the intrusion of the *zampolit* or political deputy into military command affairs, lays stress on military professionalism as against "collective" or collegial sharing of command with political deputies in the armed forces. Partly in reaction to the party's "political supremacy" campaign which unfolded in the wake of the 1962 Cuban episode,[48] many military men in late 1963 and 1964 began to argue the case for *edinonachalie* in new terms, on the grounds, as one writer put it, that "further strengthening of single command is dictated by the increasing role of firm, centralized control of troops in nuclear-missile war."[49]

It is of some interest that both the Soviet Union and Communist China, which rely essentially on political-ideological controls over their armed forces rather than the constitutional-legal controls prevailing in the West, have experienced similar problems of handling military professionalism. The Chinese, who openly acknowledged in 1957 and 1958 that they had much to learn from the Soviet Union about political controls within the armed forces,[50] have found it necessary to continue to warn their professional military cadres to stay in line.[51] In the Soviet case, although the issue of professionalism has been treated in somewhat subdued fashion lately, the past history of friction between political workers and military professionals suggests that this is an endemic problem, unlikely to disappear in the future.

Traditional Commanders and the Challenge of the New Technicians

One of the striking consequences of the modern technological revolution in warfare is the rise of a new *homo technicus* in uniform. The new generation of "military specialists," largely engineers and technicians indispensable to the manning of missile forces and other advanced elements of a modern military establishment, has mushroomed within the ranks of the traditional officer community where the time-honored military virtues and qualities of courage and leadership have counted more than mere technical expertise. In the Soviet case, the trauma produced by this cultural collision between technologists and traditional commanders has cut across the lines of other conflicts between the leadership generations or between the military professionals and party workers.[52]

Soviet discourse points to two areas of tension. One centers on relations between the new officer-technologists and the party apparatus in the armed forces. While in some ways the two groups share a community of interest in overcoming the latent hostility of the traditional professional officer caste, their relationship appears also to involve an unusual amount of friction. Spokesmen for the technologists have complained that they should be less burdened by political activities in order to devote more time to their complex military tasks.[53] Grumbling by the party workers, on the other hand, has singled out the "military technologists," along with some "staff officers," as the main source of "obstructionism" and resistance to party activities in the armed forces.[54] In late 1964, the deputy chief of the MPA noted that some progress was being made in correcting "erroneous" views "among engineers and technologists," but that it remained "extremely important" for various reasons to overcome their tendency to regard their technical work as the only thing that matters.[55]

The second area of tension arises between the new generation of technically oriented, engineer-trained officers and old-line "combined arms commanders"—mainly ground force officers—who represent the archetype of the professional military leader bred in the old school of military tradition. Not only do the latter tend to feel a natural resentment over an upstart group, but they fear that their once dominant position and their career prospects are threatened by the growing influence of the more highly educated military specialists. The threat to the traditional commanders is compounded by the fact that they have generally been the first to feel the effect of the personnel cuts carried out periodically by Khrushchev. Older men in this category of officers, having invested most of their adult lives in military service, are likely to look upon Soviet civilian society as an inhospitable world with little prospect of rewarding new careers.[56] By contrast, the younger specialists, whose skills are in demand in Soviet industry, are able to look without trepidation upon a return to civilian life. Those who stay in service, however, are not altogether satisfied with their lot. Among the new generation of technical officers there is impatience to be recognized as full-fledged members of the military family capable of being placed in positions of command as well as pursuing their specialties.

In consonance with the general trend toward a better-educated officer corps that has accompanied modernization, one might expect that as time goes on, the technical officers will gradually win greater acceptance, blurring the edges of the conflict with the old-line commanders and strengthening the corporate character of the officer corps.[57]

High Command Cliques: Rise and Decline of the "Stalingrad Group"

From the time Khrushchev engineered Malenkov's ouster in early 1955, he began a process of packing the upper echelons of the Soviet High Command with military men who had been associated closely with him at Stalingrad and in the Ukraine during World War II.[58] The process was not completed until about the spring of 1960, but after that it became clear that credentials as a member of the "Stalingrad Group" were the best an ambitious Soviet officer could have. Virtually all the top military posts in the Soviet Union under Khrushchev wound up in the hands of the Stalingrad Group, which included, to name a few of the most prominent, Marshals Malinovskii, Biriuzov, Zakharov, Chuikov, Grechko, Bagramian, Moskalenko, Yeremenko, Rotmistrov, Krylov, Yakubovskii, and Sudets.

Why Khrushchev chose to pack the High Command with men who chanced to be associated with him during his wartime days as a political commissar may be explained in various ways—he knew their qualities, he had often interceded for them against "arbitrary" orders from the wartime Moscow *Stavka* and thus felt he could count on their loyalty and cooperation. This obvious favoritism slighted many other equally capable military leaders who happened to make their mark in World War II on other fronts— Moscow, Leningrad, Berlin. It aroused resentment, jealousy, and bruised egos among the less favored groups of officers, even though military discipline and a fundamental camaraderie may have kept the officer corps from splitting into open warring factions.

Since Khrushchev's ouster, a decline in the status of the Stalingrad Group has become apparent. There has been a tendency to present Stalin's wartime role in a somewhat more balanced light than it was painted while the process of de-Stalinization was at its height.[59] As an offshoot of the refurbishing of Stalin's wartime reputation, there also has been some chipping away at the wartime records of various marshals associated with Khrushchev's Stalingrad clique, among them Chuikov and Yeremenko. At the same time, Marshal Zhukov—who was not a member of the Stalingrad Group and whose career suffered total eclipse in 1957 under Khrushchev—has not only been publicly restored to grace,[60] but allowed to strike back in his memoirs at some of his detractors among the Stalingrad marshals.

Although no major demotions of men who enjoyed Khrushchev's patronage have taken place to date, the anti-Stalingrad tone detectable in recent military memoirs may presage an intention by the new regime to spread the honors and responsibilities of high military office more judiciously than did Khrushchev among what remains of the several rival World War II groups.

Changing Outlook of Soviet Youth Toward Military Life

The Soviet armed forces, with an over-all manpower strength of somewhere around 3 million,[61] are made up of both career and conscripted personnel. The former, representing mainly the officer and noncom corps, account for perhaps one-fourth of the men in uniform; the remaining three-quarters at any given time consists mostly of youthful draftees, conscripted under Soviet law for terms of service averaging three years.[62] Each autumn a new class of young Soviet conscripts is called up for duty and a roughly comparable number returns to civilian life.

The outlook, interests, and, increasingly, the educational background of the Soviet youth entering the armed forces have undergone considerable change. Whereas formerly the annual draft of young people was a predominantly rural, marginally literate, and essentially uncritical cross-section of the country's youth, now a better-tutored generation is showing up for induction each year. As one Soviet source has put it: "The young people coming into the army and navy today possess broader political and cultural views than was formerly the case, and they have an inherent diversity of interests and capacity for questioning."[63] Furthermore, according to other Soviet sources, young soldiers today not only represent a "more literate and educated generation,"[64] but they are prone to "defend their own views vehemently, if not always reasonably."[65]

This new generation probably provides manpower of better quality than its predecessors. From a strictly military viewpoint this is an asset in a modern military establishment, with its demands for a wide range of skills, technical competence, and initiative. From a social and political viewpoint, however, the new generation is creating problems of morale and assimilation into military life on a scale hitherto seldom encountered in the Soviet Union. Thus, one finds a growing literature of official concern over the attitudes which Soviet young people bring with them into the armed forces. These attitudes reflect not only the conflict of generations, but other forces of change at work in Soviet society; they range from relatively harmless tendencies toward nonconformity and self-assertion to more disturbing phenomena, such as disregard for traditional authority and disenchantment with military life in general.[66]

A frequent theme of the official literature is that Soviet young people, now a generation removed from the "heroic struggle" of their fathers in World War II, look upon military service as a waste of time—an unwelcome break in the development of a normal career. Marshal Bagramian has complained that young people often come into the army "without an understanding of their highest state obligation," which leads them "to regard military service as a temporary and unfortunate nuisance."[67] Numerous articles in *Red Star* during the past few years have brought to light the existence of similarly negative attitudes toward military life, such as the advice proffered to a young man who was thinking of taking up a military career: "Don't be stupid, Igor—only failures put on a gray overcoat voluntarily, and you are one of our outstanding lads."[68] Even the prospect of an officer's career evidently fails to overcome the reluctance of some young men to enter the armed forces. The authors of a *Red Star* article describing the "romantic" attractions of such a career noted that one frequently encounters "perfectly good fellows" who, upon being offered a chance to attend officer candidate school, reply no thanks: "I'm better off going to an institute where I can acquire a reliable specialty and still be at home."[69]

Another frequent theme in the military press is that Soviet young people have come to regard the experience of their elders as no longer pertinent in the space age. A dialogue about their senior officers between two young lieutenants, reported by a *Red Star* correspondent, illustrates the point:

—It's no use talking to them.
—There are sputniks, missiles, and electronics all around, but they go on blathering about the importance of internal routine and their frontline experience.
—Who needs frontline experience now?
—All that is long since hopelessly out of date. You can read that in any newspaper.[70]

The conflict of generations is also in evidence between the veteran noncoms and the young soldiers in their charge. Many articles in the Soviet press suggest that a prime source of discontent is the "rude and contemptuous" treatment often suffered by young recruits at the hands of old-timers, whose penchant for unimaginative drill routines (*mushtra*) and rough discipline tends to breed resentment among the better-educated new generation.[71] A still more disturbing tendency appears to have arisen in some cases from the de-Stalinization campaign against the "cult of personality." Stating, for example, that "some politically immature people" have tended to identify "the cult of personality with any higher authority," a Soviet military writer went on to say that "the party's struggle against the cult of personality has somehow been taken as meaning rejection of all authority and as an avenue for weakening leadership."[72]

The Soviet leadership has displayed some uncertainty as to how the attitudes of Soviet youth toward discipline and authority in the armed forces might best be corrected. One tendency has been to reject as "absurd" the idea of making allowances for a qualitative change in the outlook of the new generation, and to insist that Soviet youth be strictly enjoined to adhere only to "a single Marxist-Leninist world view."[73] The prevailing tendency, however, particularly since the introduction of training reforms under Khrushchev in 1960, has been to stress the need to instill "conscious discipline" in young soldiers by "various means of persuasion," rather than resorting to the old methods of discipline by rote.[74] This approach rests in part on the argument that the nuclear age places a premium on initiative and firm morale, and that only a high level of "conscious discipline" will yield these qualities and "stand up under the test of modern war."[75]

The effort to inculcate a proper martial spirit in Soviet youth through the method of "conscious discipline" evidently has met awkward competition from the regime's rather strident anti-war propaganda campaign. With its oversimplified treatment of problems of war and peace, this propaganda threatens to confuse the young Soviet fighting man. The deputy chief of the Main Political Administration of the armed forces has pointed out that in its ideological work great care must be devoted to "the skillful elucidation of the problems of war and peace," since "oversimplification of these problems . . . leads either to underestimating the danger of aggression or to overestimating the strength of imperialism."[76]

Other military commentary, directed both to youth and an older audience, has sought to counter trends which arose during Khrushchev's tenure to question the possibility of victory in nuclear war and the continuing validity of war as an instrument of politics.[77] The countering line of argument, which has been revived since the new regime took power, is exemplified by the words of one Colonel Rybkin, who wrote in 1965: "An *a priori* rejection of the possibility of victory is harmful because it leads to 'disarmament of morale' . . . to fatalism and passivity."[78]

The concern of Soviet military leaders over the effect of anti-war propaganda on their troops is paralleled by their sensitivity to pacifist and anti-military trends in Soviet art and literature. Addressing a group of Soviet writers and artists in February 1964, Marshal Malinovskii criticized "incorrect tendencies" in portraying the last war, charging that various artistic works contained "pacifist themes and abstract negation of war."[79] On an earlier occasion, Malinovskii complained that "negative artistic images" of servicemen "can be transferred to every person who wears a military uniform. This," he said, "does not promote the indoctrination of the Soviet people, and especially young people, in a patriotic spirit, the spirit of respect for military service."[80]

The failure of Khrushchev's successors to make much headway in bringing the skeptical younger generation back into the ideological fold[81] may have the effect of prompting the party leadership to turn to the military for more help in the "patriotic education" of Soviet youth. Slogans advanced in connection with the 1965 anniversary of the Revolution called upon military veterans "to take a more active part in the public and political life of the country, in the education of young people in the revolutionary, militant, and working traditions of the Soviet people."[82] Meanwhile, within the armed forces, senior military leaders continue to stress the need for "strengthening military discipline" and to urge that commanders guard against the spreading "mold that has penetrated healthy officers' circles, where we see cases of drunkenness and amoral behavior."[83] The problem of alcoholism, while by no means exclusively a problem of youth, is a symptom of the general malaise often linked with "ideological immaturity" and "moral uncleanliness" among young people.[84]

These various signs of concern over the ideological laxity of the younger generation in general and its attitudes toward military life in particular suggest that serious long-term problems may be brewing. It would probably be unwise to conclude, however, that these problems are beyond the capacity of the regime to handle, or that Soviet young people in uniform would prove unwilling to give their best for their country in the event of war.

Interservice Competition

The Soviet armed forces consist of five major branches or force components, plus a variety of administrative and technical services and miscellaneous commands.[85] The organizational unity provided by a single powerful Ministry of Defense and a comprehensive General Staff, together with the principle of political supremacy over military affairs, is supposed to preclude the emergence of interservice rivalry and policy controversy within the Soviet armed forces. Between theory and practice, however, there is often some discrepancy.

Historically, the ground forces have been the dominant element on the Soviet military scene, and it is clear that members of other services have occasionally felt their interests jeopardized by the land-warfare orientation of the High Command. In recent years, the rise of the strategic missile forces to a place of pre-eminence has been resented within some of the other services, whose traditional role has been dimmed somewhat by modern technological developments.[86] Not only have the missile forces acquired great prestige at the expense of the older services, but they have become major competitors for scarce resources.

How sharp interservice competition may be in the Soviet Union is a matter difficult to define. Not only are there traditional constraints against the kind of public airing of interservice differences that often occurs in the West,[87] but there are some forms of "exemplary" rivalry which are officially encouraged, such as the practice of setting aside special commemorative holidays dedicated to the various branches of service. Nevertheless, although the form it takes may be less open than in some Western countries, interservice competition is not absent from the Soviet scene.

Generally speaking, the root of interservice rivalries is competition for resources. While this is by no means a new phenomenon, in its contemporary form it reflects new conflicts of interest arising from the radical changes brought about by modern instruments of warfare in both military theory and in the structure of the Soviet armed forces. One notable feature is that the pattern of conflicting interests and viewpoints has not developed strictly along service lines; rather, the military policy debate, to which we now turn, has cut across the interests of particular services, producing several divergent schools of thought.

III. The Military Policy Debate

The military policy debate of the past decade has been carried on by military theorists within the armed forces, but at times has spilled over into policy differences within the Soviet leadership as a whole. The debate began as a reaction against Stalinist military theory and developed under the strong influence of Khrushchev's strategic thinking and military reforms. Rival schools of thought arose, polarizing around what may be called "modernist" and "traditionalist" outlooks, with various shades of "centrist" opinion occupying the ground in between.[88]

The modernists argued for radical adaptation of the fruits of modern technology to military affairs, and suggested that this approach might lighten the strain on resources—that quality, so to speak, could replace quantity. In practical policy terms, the modernist school—with some reservations—aligned itself with the policies espoused by Khrushchev from the late 1950s until his downfall in 1964. These policies resulted in a shift of resource allocation from theater ground forces to strategic offensive and defensive forces, and were accompanied on the conceptual level by a shift from almost exclusive preoccupation with continental land warfare to a growing emphasis on the problems of intercontinental strategic war and strategic deterrence. Successive programs to reduce the manpower levels of an oversized traditional military establishment, by reliance on the vastly increased firepower of modern weapons, were put forward by Khrushchev in early 1956, in 1960, and again at the end of 1963.[89]

The traditionalists, while conceding the impact of technology on military affairs, nonetheless argued against discarding tried and tested concepts too hastily. Although for the most part they accepted the dominant role accorded the strategic nuclear-missile forces under Khrushchev, they held out for the continued importance of large traditional forces and resisted Khrushchev's efforts to economize at their expense.

Although the debate has been the subject of considerable Western commentary, Soviet writers, until recently, shied away from open admission that it existed in fact. Their reticence, however, has gradually diminished, and several Soviet accounts have identified some of the issues.[90] According to one account published in the spring of 1964, the debate has left many issues still unsettled, and "even as before, no unified view yet exists."[91] While regarding this as "unfortunate," the account conceded that controversy over military issues "must be recognized as a normal phenomenon," accompanying the "constant process" of change in military technology.[92]

By the end of the "Khrushchev decade" in October 1964, neither the modernists nor the traditionalists had gained uncontested ascendancy. Although it could be said that a body of theoretical views and practical decisions reflecting the outlook of Khrushchev and the modernist school had come gradually to dominate the picture, there were signs of a mounting counter-trend. Some prominent military figures began to suggest in early 1964 that Khrushchev's "one-weapon" emphasis on ballistic missiles was being carried too far. These critics pointed to the danger that "calculations based on the anticipated results of using a single new type of weapon alone can lead to erroneous conclusions," and expressed concern that exaggerated doctrinal emphasis on missiles threatened to cripple the "creative development" of other forces and of Soviet military theory in general.[93]

For several months after Khrushchev's ouster, the military debate subsided as the new regime went through a period of consolidation. The adoption of a "stand pat" defense budget in December 1964 and the announced aim of the new leaders to tackle such problems as Soviet economic ills and the Sino-Soviet rift suggested that issues relating to defense posture and policy had been temporarily shelved.[94] Around the beginning of 1965, however, roughly coincident with the deepening of the crisis in Southeast Asia, the military policy debate again revived.

One of the first signs was a doctrinal attack in January by two military writers on the Khrushchevian tendency to stress the "possibility of preventing war" through the deterrent effect of nuclear-missile weapons rather than the possibility that war might occur.[95] As implied in the article and later made explicit by one of its authors,[96] overemphasis on war deterrence could lead to neglect of all-around strengthening of the armed forces and to questioning of "the need to spend large resources" on them.

Once the moratorium on the defense policy debate was broken, a series of theoretical arguments for shifting policy priority to the needs of defense appeared in the military press. In general, these arguments sought to make a case for a broad and well-balanced military establishment, and especially for having adequate forces-in-being prior to the outbreak of a war. Assertions that technology had not reduced manpower requirements for modern war were combined with warnings that the only safe policy, even for "a non-aggressive country like the U.S.S.R.," was to devote the requisite effort and resources to preparing itself beforehand for either a short, decisive war of the kind which modernist spokesmen considered more likely or a protracted war along lines which traditionalist opinion tended to envision.[97]

At the same time that military lobbying strove to make the

point of there being no ruble-saving shortcuts to Soviet security, there were signs of divergent views on the question of resource priorities for defense within the political leadership itself. Statements by one group of leaders, including N. V. Podgornyi, A. P. Kirilenko, and D. S. Polianskii, tended to place priority on resource allocation for internal economic development, while a second group, including M. A. Suslov and A. N. Shelepin, stressed the need for further strengthening of Soviet defenses to meet the external threat posed by a deteriorating international situation.[98] The two most influential members of the collective leadership, Brezhnev and Kosygin, took positions roughly midway between the others, speaking out for both strengthened defense and domestic economic improvement.[99] A formulation given by Kosygin in July 1965 seemed to reflect the ambivalent attitudes within the political leadership on the problem of resource priorities. Kosygin pointed out that the upkeep of a modernized Soviet military establishment "demands very large expenditures which we would gladly devote to other branches of the national economy." However, he went on to say: "In the present situation, to economize on defense would be acting against the interests of the Soviet state and the Soviet people."[100]

The announcement in December 1965 of the new budget for 1966 suggested that neither the advocates of major defense increases nor the proponents of domestic economic priority had managed to prevail. A modest increase of five per cent in defense expenditure was provided, 13.4 billion rubles compared with 12.8 billion for 1965.[101] This increase, which reversed the pattern of slight cuts in the defense budgets for the two previous years, was attributed by Kosygin and other spokesmen to "aggravation of the international situation" and stirring up of a "war psychosis" by the United States.[102] It appeared to be mainly a compromise move, intended for the time being to bridge differences of view within the regime.

The precise direction which the debate on military policy may take in the future remains to be seen, for the last word has not been heard. The Soviet regime will continue to be faced with the kinds of issues which have hitherto fueled the debate—ranging from the perennial problem of determining the over-all share of resources for defense to troublesome questions of how such resources may best be used and apportioned among the various elements of the armed forces.

*   *   *

At this point, in assuming that neither in the third world nor in Europe will the situation get so far out of hand as to bring on the ultimate catastrophe of a nuclear war, what may be said about the role that military power is likely to play as an instrument of Soviet policy in the decade ahead? Is there a reasonable prospect that major changes either in Soviet society or in the outlook of the Soviet leadership itself may lead to marked depreciation of military power and instrumentalities for support of Soviet policy objectives?

Any answer is necessarily speculative, and subject to one's own conception of the process of sociopolitical change. To begin with, one can dismiss the chances that in the next decade—or even in the more distant future—Soviet society will arrive at the utopian Communist stage envisioned in Marxist-Leninist scripture, where all institutions of state power, including the military, were expected to "wither away." Military power will probably continue to be regarded by the Soviet leaders as an essential ingredient of Soviet policy, performing much the same functions it serves today.

These functions are several. Most essential, perhaps: to deter an opponent from launching an attack or to wage war if it should occur—a function which is sometimes described as providing a shield for the security of the Soviet Union and its allies against the "designs of imperialism." Next in importance: to ensure good conduct from Soviet partners within the Communist world, where emergent nationalisms may breed disrespect for Soviet interests. To these outward- and inward-looking functions, another of major significance may be added—that of discouraging Western military resistance to Communist political and proxy warfare, or what may be called the "counterdeterrent" role of Soviet military power as a political weapon.[103]

But let us suppose there are some surprises in store, and that during the next decade or so the Soviet Union not only sheds its revolutionary aspirations far more readily than one has assumed, but also accepts with good grace a more or less conventional great power role in world affairs. What then?

Plausibly, one might expect the "counterdeterrent" value of Soviet arms, as back-up for a strategy of Communist political advance that would be essentially inoperative, to decline in the eyes of the Soviet leadership. It seems doubtful, however, that the other functions of Soviet military power would shrink to marginal importance, either in terms of Soviet security from external attack or the assertion of Soviet interests against the national pretentions of other states, including those ruled by Communist regimes. In the latter connection, the "containment" of Chinese encroachment upon Soviet interests could well become a growing problem in the next decade, counseling the continued maintenance of a strong Soviet military posture, even though the chances of an outright military collision between the two Communist powers should remain remote.[104]

So far as internal Soviet development bears on the status of the military, a slackening of revolutionary *élan* and some loosening of the party's hegemony would probably not mean a decline in the institutional position of the military. On the contrary, one might expect that Soviet evolution in this direction would be accompanied by a rise in the influence of the military, along with that of other major institutional groups in the society.

7.

The Non-Russian Nationalities

VERNON V. ASPATURIAN

The most striking characteristic of the Soviet population is its ethnic diversity: the Soviet Union is a country of more than 100 different nationalities, tribes, and linguistic groups, according to the 1959 census. To be sure, there is a propensity for the Soviet authorities to exaggerate the ethnic heterogeneity of the U.S.S.R. for propaganda purposes by even including "nationalities" numbering fewer than 1,000 souls. Nevertheless, the ethnic diversity of the country remains impressive. Twenty-two of the nationalities enumerated in the 1959 census number more than 900,000 each, and account for 95 per cent of the total population. The other 80 or more "nationalities" total fewer than 10 million, and only 20 of these number more than 100,000 people each.

The Soviet multinational population was a legacy of the Tsars, whose expanding empire absorbed but never fully digested this variegated and mutually antagonistic collection of races and nationalities. In Imperial Russia the Russians were not only numerically preponderant but the ruling nationality as well. Russia was a "prison of nations," not a multinational commonwealth in fact or fiction. It is generally acknowledged that one of the principal factors contributing to the Revolution of 1917 was the disaffection of the major non-Russian nationalities, and especially of their educated classes. All the revolutionary parties of Russia counted among their leaders outstanding individuals of many nationalities. The failure of Imperial Russia to grapple intelligently with the nationality question was instrumental in accelerating its demise in the midst of national agony and crisis.

When Lenin assumed power in 1917, the Bolsheviks fell heir to the "prison of nations" and its unresolved problems. Of all the revolutionary parties, the Bolsheviks were perhaps best prepared to deal systematically with the nationality question, since they alone had devoted serious attention to it. Both Lenin and Stalin were specialists on the national question, and Lenin must be accounted one of the chief and original expositors in the twentieth century of the principle of national self-determination, a concept which found its way into President Wilson's famous Fourteen Points some years after the Bolsheviks had incorporated it into their own political program.

Lenin shrewdly recognized the qualitative distinction between the defensive character of the nationalism of oppressed nationalities and the chauvinistic and aggressive nationalism of a ruling nation. He refused to condemn all nationalism as equally retrogressive and perceived in the aspirations of the smaller nationalities of Russia a progressive character and a revolutionary potential. To this day, Communist doctrine continues to draw a basic qualitative distinction between the nationalism of the oppressed, which is praised and supported, and that of ruling nationalities, which is condemned as retrograde. It is a distinction often overlooked by Western observers and statesmen. Although Soviet behavior sometimes resembles oppressive chauvinistic nationalism, and Soviet leaders are notoriously unable or unwilling to acknowledge it, this should not obscure either the objective significance or the moral implications of the perceptive Marxist-Leninist distinction between the nationalism of oppressed and oppressing nations.

Lenin also recognized that under conditions of Tsarist oppression the Bolsheviks could attract the support of the discontented nationalities only by promising them the right to secede and form their own national states, although he was, in principle, against the dismemberment of the Russian Empire once it passed under Bolshevik control. As early as 1903, when national self-determination was incorporated into the Bolshevik program, Lenin acknowledged that it "cannot be interpreted otherwise than in the sense of *political* self-determination, i.e., the right of secession and the formation of an independent state."[1] Since then, the right of secession has remained a cardinal principle of Soviet nationality policy and has continued to find juridical expression as a fundamental tenet of every Soviet constitution.

The Bolshevik espousal of national self-determination was designed to achieve four interrelated purposes: (1) to prove to the non-Russians that the Bolsheviks were not simply another Great Russian party; (2) to diminish the attractiveness of the local nationalist movements and recruit their intellectuals into the Bolshevik organization; (3) to encourage secessionist movements which would weaken the Empire and hasten the revolution; and (4) to prepare the foundations for a future reconciliation between the Great Russians and their former subjects on the basis of equality, once the revolution was accomplished. It is noteworthy that except for point (3), which is recognized abstractly in the Constitution but is ruthlessly suppressed in practice, current Soviet nationality policy continues to pursue essentially the same aims, but in order to stabilize and preserve the *status quo*, not to disrupt it.

Although Lenin was more perceptive than most in recognizing the moral distinction between the nationalism of the oppressed and the oppressing nations, he completely miscalculated its unreasoning, visceral, emotional side. He hoped that Bolshevik policy would be sufficient to persuade the leaders of the national minorities of Bolshevik sincerity and that, once given the right to secede, the nationalities would suddenly recognize the wisdom of not exercising it. After the Bolsheviks assumed power, Lenin and Stalin issued *The Declaration of the Nations of Russia*, which virtually invited the border nationalities to secede by gratuitously recognizing "the right of the peoples of Russia to dispose of their own fate even to the separation and establishment of an independent state."[2] The impotent Soviet regime was cruelly disappointed when the border nations, taking the invitation at its word, responded with declarations of secession and independence. Countries like Georgia, which before the Revolution rarely thought of independence, and peoples like the Byelorussians and Cossacks, who were hardly aware of their separate national identity, suddenly discovered that they were invested with the right to secede. So-called National Councils sprang up all over Russia, even in purely Great Russian areas, and under the guise of "regional national self-determination," asserted this new-found right.[3]

If the policy of national self-determination accelerated the disintegration of the Tsarist system, it was now an even greater threat to the existence of the Soviet state. Secession quickly spread to all parts of the country. Lenin failed to foresee not only the irrational character of nationalism, but also the inherently disruptive and centrifugal nature of the doctrine of national self-determination for a multinational state. Valuable as an instrument of revolution, it was equally a menace to stability and, once set into motion, assumed an undirected and uncontrollable momentum of its own. In order to preserve Bolshevik power, it was necessary to arrest the disintegration of the Soviet state by introducing a countervailing principle, which would halt though not repudiate the disruptive course.

The magic formula was federalism, an idea generally spurned by Marxists as incompatible with their imperative of a centrally organized and planned society, but now seized upon by Lenin as a device which could arrest secession and promote re-amalgamation in the name of national self-determination. To implement the first aim, the R.S.F.S.R. came into being, while the second purpose was served by forming the U.S.S.R. after the Red Army had successfully installed Soviet regimes in some of the disaffected border regions, notably in the Ukraine, Byelorussia, the Caucasus, and Central Asia. The reassembling of the fragmented parts of the Russian Empire into a multinational federal state was substantially accomplished by 1925, after the re-incorporation of the Far Eastern Republic and the full integration of Bukhara and Khorezm into the Soviet state.

I. THE ETHNIC COMPOSITION AND DISTRIBUTION OF SOVIET SOCIETY

Most of the Russian Empire was preserved intact as the U.S.S.R., although Poland, Finland, and the three Baltic states managed to secure their independence, and Bessarabia was annexed by Rumania. The federal solution to the nationality problem, however, was eventually subverted by the political policies and ideological goals of the Soviet regime and could only be considered a limited success before World War II. The nationality problem is in many ways a matter of life and death for the Soviet state because of the strategic location of the border nationalities. The geographical balance and distribution of the nationalities of the Soviet Union give rise, in fact, to a "Russian" problem as well as a "Soviet" problem.

The Great Russians, occupying the continental interior of Eurasia, are fringed on all sides by a virtually uninterrupted belt of non-Russian nationalities which form a buffer on the international borders of the Soviet Union. Along virtually the entire Baltic coast of the U.S.S.R. are the Estonians, Latvians, and Lithuanians, while the Byelorussians, Ukrainians, and Moldavians inhabit the territories bordering Poland, Czechoslovakia, and Rumania. In the Caucasus, the Georgians, Armenians, and Azerbaidzhani Turks inhabit the regions bordering on Turkey and Iran, while in Central

Asia, the Turkmen, Uzbeks, Kazakhs, and Kirgiz occupy the border areas adjacent to Iran, Afghanistan, and the Sinkiang Province of China, and a multitude of Turkic, Mongol, and Tungusic tribes occupy the border regions with Outer Mongolia. Only in the Soviet Far East do Russians inhabit territories adjacent to international frontiers, and this is a region remote from the heartland of the Russian nation.

Because of the strategic location of the border nationalities, their loyalty to Moscow and their relationship to the Russian people has always been a vital factor in Russian and Soviet security considerations. The federal solution whereby each major nationality was organized into a separate republic with its own language, culture, constitution, and other symbols of nationhood, was only a partial success in winning the loyalty and reliability of these nationalities. During World War II, the Germans were welcomed in some of the border regions, and hundreds of thousands of Soviet prisoners of war of many nationalities agreed to enlist in Nazi-organized National Legions to fight against the Soviet Union. The nature and intensity of this defection still remains the subject of considerable speculation and controversy, since it is not exactly clear whether the motivations were basically anti-Soviet, anti-Russian, anti-Stalin, or just simple self-preservation, but undoubtedly all of these elements were involved.[4]

Of the 21 non-Russian nationalities which had 900,000 or more people each in 1959, fourteen are organized into union republics with constituent federal rights and are recognized as quasi-sovereign nation-states. Two of the 22 major nationalities, the Poles and Germans, are considered national minorities of other nations, while a third, the Jewish, is territorially scattered and does not occupy a defined national territory. Four other nations, the Tatar, Chuvash, Bashkir, and Mordvin, being located in the interior of the Union and surrounded by Russians, are organized as Autonomous Republics, since one of the criteria for status as a Union Republic is that it must be located on the border so that the abstract right to secede does not become a technical absurdity.

The Russian Presence

The Russian nation accounted for slightly more than one-half (115 million) the total population in 1959. The ethnically, linguistically, and culturally related Ukrainians and Byelorussians followed with 37 million and 8 million, respectively. Thus, the Soviet

TABLE 1
MAJOR NATIONALITIES OF THE U.S.S.R.
1939–59

Nationality	1939	1959
Russian	99,019,000	114,500,000
Ukrainian	28,070,000	36,981,000
Byelorussian	5,267,431	7,829,000
Uzbek	4,844,021	6,004,000
Tatar	4,300,000	4,969,000
Kazakh	3,098,000	3,581,000
Azerbaidzhani	2,274,805	2,929,000
Armenian	2,151,884	2,787,000
Georgian	2,248,566	2,650,000
Lithuanian	—	2,326,000
Jewish	3,020,141	2,268,000
Moldavian	—	2,214,000
German	1,423,534	1,619,000
Chuvash	1,367,930	1,470,000
Latvian	—	1,400,000
Tadzhik	1,928,964	1,397,000
Polish	626,905	1,380,000
Mordvin	1,451,429	1,285,000
Turkmen	811,769	1,004,000
Bashkir	842,925	983,000
Kirgiz	884,306	974,000
Estonian	—	969,000

Union is still an overwhelmingly Slavic country with nearly 160 million, or 80 per cent, of its people made up of the three closely related Slavic groups. The Russians, or more properly Great Russians, are concentrated in the huge central plain around Moscow, the North Caucasus, and the Volga regions, and are settled across Siberia to the Pacific. According to the 1959 census, more than 85 per cent of the Russians were found in the R.S.F.S.R. Elsewhere they constituted from more than 43 per cent of the Kazakh Republic to 10 per cent of the Moldavian. Only in the Byelorussian, Lithuanian, and Armenian republics did they account for less than 10 per cent of the population (see Table 2).

The presence of substantial numbers of Russians in most of the republics guarantees a minimum political and ethnic ballast in the non-Russian regions to counter separatist sentiment. Their diffusion throughout the Union serves, moreover, to accelerate and intensify the process of Russianization. The large influx of Russians has been due not only to the industrialization and modernization program, but also to the collectivization of agriculture, when mil-

TABLE 2
DISTRIBUTION OF MAJOR NATIONALITIES IN THE NON-RUSSIAN
REPUBLICS—1959 CENSUS

Republic	Total	Per Cent
Ukrainian	41,869,000	100.0
Ukrainians	31,852,000	76.1
Russians	7,400,000	17.1
Jews	840,000	2.0
Byelorussian	8,055,000	100.0
Byelorussians	4,444,000	80.0
Russians	729,000	9.1
Poles	539,000	6.7
Uzbek	8,106,000	100.0
Uzbeks	5,026,000	62.0
Russians	1,101,000	13.6
Tatars	445,000	5.5
Kazakhs	335,000	4.1
Tadzhiks	312,000	3.8
Kazakh	9,310,000	100.0
Kazakhs	2,755,000	29.6
Russians	4,014,000	43.1
Ukrainians	762,000	8.2
Georgian	4,044,000	100.0
Georgians	2,558,000	63.3
Russians	438,000	10.8
Armenians	443,000	11.0
Armenian	1,763,000	100.0
Armenians	1,552,000	88.0
Russians	56,000	3.2
Azerbaidzhani	3,698,000	100.0
Azerbaidzhanis	2,481,000	67.1
Russians	515,000	13.9
Armenians	442,000	12.0
Lithuanian	2,711,000	100.0
Lithuanians	2,151,000	79.3
Russians	231,000	8.5
Poles	230,000	8.5
Moldavian	2,885,000	100.0
Moldavians	1,887,000	65.4
Russians	293,000	10.2
Ukrainians	421,000	14.6
Latvian	2,093,000	100.0
Latvians	1,298,000	62.0
Russians	556,000	26.6
Kirgiz	2,066,000	100.0
Kirgiz	837,000	40.5
Russians	624,000	30.2
Uzbeks	219,000	10.6
Tadzhik	1,980,000	100.0
Tadzhiks	1,051,000	53.1

TABLE 2 (*Continued*)

Republic	Total	Per Cent
Russians	263,000	13.3
Uzbeks	454,000	23.0
Turkmen	1,516,000	100.0
Turkmen	924,000	60.9
Russians	263,000	17.3
Uzbeks	125,000	8.3
Estonian	1,197,000	100.0
Estonians	873,000	72.9
Russians	260,000	21.7

lions of recalcitrant peasants were uprooted in the European parts and deported beyond the Urals. The major cities of Soviet Asia are heavily populated with Russians, while Ukrainians are sprinkled across the rural areas.

Ukrainians and Byelorussians

The Ukrainians constitute a compact unit in the southwestern region of the Soviet Union. Except for a very brief existence as an independent state immediately after the Revolution, the bulk of the Ukraine has been united with Russia for many decades. The Ukrainian population of Eastern Galicia, however, has had little political or cultural contact with Russia, having been ruled by Austria since the partitions of Poland in the eighteenth century, and before that by the Poles. The people of this area are predominantly Uniate Catholics who accept the spiritual authority of the Vatican. After the war, the Soviet government forced a renunciation of their ties to Rome and their return to the Eastern Orthodox Church from which they had been separated by the Poles in the sixteenth century. The Western Ukrainians have been exposed to varying degrees of Polonization. The strongest sentiment for an independent Ukrainian state is found in this region.

The Byelorussians occupy the marshy areas of the Pripet River and their republic also borders on Poland. The idea of Byelorussian nationality hardly existed before the Revolution, since the region was one of the most backward in all Europe, and national consciousness was largely absent. The Byelorussians in the west also have been subjected to varying degrees of Polonization, while those in the east are virtually indistinguishable from the Great Russians. Byelorussian nationhood came virtually as a gift of the Soviet regime and in many ways remains artificial.

The Turks and Tatars

The second largest bloc of ethnically related people are the Turko-Tatar nationalities, which total more than 20 million and are divided among nearly a score of tribal and linguistic groups. Nine of these nationalities number more than 900,000 people each. They are predominantly Moslem in faith and Islamic in culture, although some groups have been exposed to Russian cultural influences for longer periods of time than others. Many of the Russians in the Volga and Ural regions appear to be assimilated Tatars or possess varying degrees of Tatar infusion. Most of the Turko-Tatar languages are mutually intelligible.

Culturally associated with the Central Asian Turks are the Iranian-speaking Tadzhiks, found in the Pamir mountains on the borders of Iran and Afghanistan. Dominated by the Uzbeks for many centuries, large numbers have been Turkicized, but under Soviet rule their basic Iranian traditions and culture have experienced a resurgence, and they share cultural and historical traditions with the Persians, Afghans, and Pakistanis.

The Turko-Tatar nationalities are not a single compact group, but are separated in three distinct geographical regions. The largest concentration of Turks is in Central Asia, and they represent the groups which have experienced the shortest period of Russian rule (dating from the mid-nineteenth century). The major Central Asian Turks are the Uzbeks, the Kazakhs, the Kirgiz, and the Turkmen. The second heaviest concentration is in the Middle-Volga and Urals region, whose most important representatives are the Volga Tatars, the Bashkirs, and the Chuvash. The third concentration is located in the Caucasus, with the Transcaucasian Azerbaidzhanis being the most numerous and significant, while smaller tribes are located in the North Caucasus. Other Turko-Tatar groups are found sprinkled across the vast expanse of Central Russia (European and Asian) and represent the backwash of the retreating Tatar tribes after their period of domination was broken by the Grand Dukes of Moscow and they in turn were subjected to Russian expansion eastward.

The most ethnically diluted of the national republics is the Kazakh, where the native population accounts for less than 30 per cent of the total, whereas the Russians and Ukrainians account for more than half. The reduction of the Kazakhs to minority status in their own republic is due not only to the tremendous influx of Russians into the republic in recent years, but also to the fact that, more than any other nationality, the Kazakhs have suffered great population losses under Tsarist and Soviet rule. The 1926 census reported 3,968,289 Kazakhs, but by 1939, the Kazakhs suffered a net loss of nearly a million people, when their number was reported at 3,098,000. The 1959 census shows that the Kazakhs still number 400,000 fewer than they did in 1926.

The Kirgiz are also a minority in their own republic, where they constitute only 40 per cent of the population, whereas the Russians and Ukrainians account for about 37 per cent. Another significant factor in the ethnic distribution of Central Asia is the presence of a substantial number of Uzbeks in all the Central Asian republics, ranging from slightly more than 8 per cent in the Turkmen to 23 per cent in the Tadzhik. The ruling nationality of Central Asia before the Revolution, the Uzbeks are once again emerging as a stabilizing influence in association with the Russians.

The Caucasus: Georgians and Armenians

The Caucasus represents one of the most complex ethnic areas in the world. Although the total population is relatively small, there is an extraordinary number of nationalities and mountain tribes who have tenaciously clung to their separate identities despite their small numbers. The two most important non-Turkic Caucasian nationalities are the ancient Christian nations of Georgia and Armenia, whose people are culturally and racially, but not linguistically, related. Each numbers approximately 3 million, but whereas the Georgians are for the most part concentrated in the Georgian Republic, nearly half the Armenians reside outside the Armenian Republic, which is, however, the most nationally compact of the republics, with 88 per cent of the inhabitants being indigenous. Both nations have strong ties with Russia, which has traditionally posed as their protector from the Moslem Turks, although each maintains its own distinctive alphabet, national tradition, and its autonomous church. The role of individual Georgians and Armenians in Soviet cultural and political life is far greater in proportion to their numbers than that of any nationality including, ironically, the Russians. This was particularly true during the long period of Stalin's rule. Stalin and his secret police chief, Beria, who were Georgians, naturally relied upon kinsmen in the Caucasus as instruments of their rule. Despite the death of Stalin and the execution of Beria, Georgians and Armenians are still in many important secondary positions in the government, the Communist Party, the armed forces, and cultural and educational institutions, although their proportion is decreasing.

The Baltic Nationalities

The three Baltic nations of Estonia, Latvia, and Lithuania form another small, but important, cluster of nationalities. The Latvians and Lithuanians are linguistically related members of the Balto-Slavic group, while the Estonians belong with the Finns. The three nations are the most Westernized of the Soviet national groups; all use the Latin alphabet, but whereas the Latvians and the Estonians are largely Lutheran, the Lithuanians are Roman Catholic. All three share a common background of long Russian political rule and German social and cultural domination. Under the Tsars, the Baltic Germans, descendants of the Teutonic Knights, constituted a local ruling aristocracy, while the indigenous population was largely peasant in character. The cultural life of the three countries thus represents a curious blend of German, Russian, and indigenous elements.

The three countries enjoyed a brief twenty years of political independence between the wars. There was a genuine resurgence of national culture and tradition, and while the political systems were far from democratic, they were indigenous and far more preferable to the local population than foreign rule.

Since the three states cut Russia off from the Baltic Sea, it was axiomatic that once the Soviet Union had recovered its strength it would again seek to open a window on the Baltic—one of the most persistent aims in foreign policy from Ivan the Terrible to Joseph Stalin. The three states were annexed in 1940, after the German elements of the population were returned to the Reich in conformity with the Nazi-Soviet Pact of 1939.

Russian rule, whether Tsarist or Soviet, is deeply resented. With Soviet occupation, the native elites were arrested and either executed or deported to Siberia as were thousands of others who betrayed overt signs of opposition to Soviet control or ideas. Of all the nationalities of the Soviet Union, sentiment for separation is most pronounced in the Baltic countries because the bonds of mutual benefit, protection, language, culture, gratitude, and religion are largely absent. The Ukrainians and Byelorussians are related to the Russians; the Georgians and Armenians accept the Russians as their protectors; and while the resurgent non-Russian nations of Siberia and Central Asia owe their modernization and elevation from social and economic backwardness to the Soviet regime, the Baltic nations do not owe their high cultural and material standard of life to the Russians or to the Soviet regime. In this association, all of the benefits flow in a single direction, to Moscow.

The Alien Nationalities

Four of the 22 major nationalities (the Germans, Poles, Moldavians, and Jews) are in a separate category in that states of the same nationality are located outside the frontiers of the U.S.S.R.; hence, they constitute true national minorities. Before World War II, the largest concentration of Germans was in the Volga-German Autonomous Republic, and other German communities were scattered in the Ukraine and the North Caucasus. After the German attack, they were all gathered and deported to Central Asia and Siberia, because of both real and imagined pro-German sympathies. According to the 1959 census, half of the 1.6 million Germans are reported as living in the R.S.F.S.R., most likely the Siberian regions; the location of the other half is unreported, but evidence from other sources indicates that they have been relocated in the Kazakh and other Central Asian republics. Since the Soviet census has meticulously enumerated the breakdown of various national groups in the individual republics if they numbered 10,000 or more, the failure to account for the location of 800,000 Germans can only be a deliberate attempt to conceal their present whereabouts.

The Moldavians are linguistically indistinguishable from the people of neighboring Rumania, although under Soviet rule their language is written in the Cyrillic rather than in the Latin alphabet. They inhabit portions of the historical province of Bessarabia, parts of which have been assigned to the Ukrainian Republic, while the remainder has been organized into a separate Moldavian Republic. Actually, the Moldavians are a minority, politically and territorially separated from their national state of Rumania, which is now showing a renewed interest in them.

The Jews

The 1959 census reported a population of nearly 2.3 million Jews, a catastrophic drop in the total number of Jews who lived within the prewar frontiers of the Soviet Union and in the areas annexed from Poland. The decimation of the Jews resulted from Nazi policies, and since the war, their existence as a separate national group in the Soviet Union has been precarious. Their position in Russia has never been an enviable one, and the Tsarist pogroms were largely responsible for the migration of Russian Jews to the United States and the organization of the Zionist movement. After the Revolution, the Soviet government took energetic measures to stamp out anti-Semitism, accorded the Jews recognition as a separate nationality with rights of cultural autonomy, legalized the use of Yiddish as the language of instruction in schools located in centers of Jewish population, and encouraged and supported a Yiddish press and theater. Since the Jews were scattered in various urban centers of the country, a genuine Jewish republic could not be established, while the contrived Jewish Autonomous Region organized in a remote area of the Soviet Far East failed to flourish. Despite the cultivation of a Jewish nationality centered around the Yiddish language, most Soviet Jews were on the road to voluntary assimilation before the war.

Two events brought about a fundamental transformation in the status of Soviet Jews. The first was the Nazi occupation, which succeeded in rekindling the ancient and latent anti-Semitism of the Ukrainians and Russians, which had been submerged by Soviet policies. The second was the establishment of the state of Israel, which apparently had an electrifying impact upon many Soviet Jews, indicating to a suspicious Stalin the possibility of a psychological attachment incompatible with Soviet ideological and foreign-policy objectives. The immediate result was the disestablishment of Jewish cultural autonomy. All Jewish organizations, the Yiddish press, theater, publishing houses, and schools were dissolved. Prominent cultural leaders, as well as some political personalities of Jewish origin, were imprisoned and some were executed, while the Soviet press marshaled a thinly veiled assault against Jews in general, calling them "passportless wanderers" and "homeless cosmopolitans," implying that they were malingerers, speculators, black-marketeers, and social parasites.

Jews were purged from sensitive political positions, and informal quotas for admission to institutions of higher learning were set, although the eminently practical Stalin tolerated their continued participation in literary, professional, and scientific activity. One of his objectives was to terrorize the Soviet Jews into recognizing unambiguously that the Kremlin would not tolerate the faintest shadow of sympathy for Israel. Although the ferocity of the campaign has relented since Stalin's death, his successors have continued the policy of extinguishing Jewish cultural autonomy. This official attitude has once again made anti-Semitism acceptable in Russia; and vandalism and excesses against Jewish religious institutions often go unpunished. Judaism and Jewish believers are vilified periodically in the local press and Jewish religious life rendered virtually impossible.

If Israel were a Soviet republic within the U.S.S.R., Jewish religious and national loyalties might not be incompatible with Soviet interests. But Moscow takes special measures against any religion whose spiritual center is located in a foreign country. Since the Soviet government has itself manipulated to political advantage the Russian and Armenian churches, whose spiritual centers are located on Soviet territory, it expects other powers to do the same. Dual loyalties, whether they be sentimental, psychological, cultural, political, or spiritual, are not tolerated by the regime if it cannot manipulate both loyalties. Cultural and national pluralism are compatible with the Soviet system only as long as they are unambiguously subordinated to Soviet ideological and political objectives.

II. The Quality of the Soviet Multinational State

One of the ironies of the Stalinist legacy is that while the stated purpose of Soviet nationality policy has been to further the development of national and cultural autonomy, in fact it has been used to suppress particularistic political self-expression and identity. But the fact that the Soviet nationalities must subordinate their political and national activity to higher social and political goals is far from unique. All states made up of distinct ethnic, regional, or historical constituents characteristically follow such a course. This important fact should not be obscured simply because the norms imposed upon the Soviet nationalities are Communist norms.

The Soviet Union, no less than Canada, India, Switzerland, Belgium, or any other multinational state, frowns upon all manifestations of national separatism; while this may merely testify to the effectiveness of totalitarian controls, it remains the only binational or multinational state in the world which recognizes even the abstract right of its constituent nations to secede and to establish separate national states. History has amply demonstrated that the voluntary character of federations and multinational states is largely a fiction which no state is ready to put to the test. This has been stated most candidly by the Soviet leaders themselves. In the words of Stalin, which have been quoted *ad nauseam* by critics of Soviet nationality policy as eloquent evidence of Soviet hypocrisy, the Soviet position was articulated as follows: "We are in favor of the separation of India, Arabia, Egypt, Morocco, and the other colonies from the Entente. . . . We are *against* the separation of the border regions from Russia."[5]

Although Western countries have not expressed their double standard of national self-determination as systematically or as frankly as have Soviet leaders, it would not be inaccurate to say that they were precisely in *favor* of what Stalin was against and *against* what he favored at the time these words were written. Soon thereafter, the border regions of Russia (Poland, Finland, Estonia, Latvia, Lithuania, Bessarabia) did manage to separate, with the assistance of the Western powers, while at the same time the colonial dependencies of the European powers were increased. The fact that at present all of the countries named by Stalin, and many more, have become independent states, while Russia's border regions, with the exception of Poland and Finland, have been recovered, is a token of the growth of Soviet power and the diminution of West European influence.

In recent years Western spokesmen have attempted, without signal success, to pin the label of colonialism on the Soviet Union and have been mystified and frustrated by the conspicuous lack of favorable response on the part of the new states of Africa and Asia. Perhaps this is because the decline of Western colonialism and the parallel rise of Soviet imperialism are more the consequences of fundamental shifts in the world balance of power since 1945 than reflections of the ideological and political contrasts between East and West with respect to the ethical imperatives of the age. The dismantling of the British Empire is frequently held up as an example of the Western adherence to the principle of national self-determination in contrast to the forcible preservation of the Soviet empire. But the more painful and violent decolonialization processes which overtook the French, Dutch, and Belgian colonial empires and the continuance of Portuguese colonies are often conveniently overlooked.

There is another universal characteristic of multinational states which is sometimes ascribed to the Soviet Union alone. Specifically, it is alleged that Russia enjoys far more rights and advantages than the other nations making up the U.S.S.R. Actually, such charges have been made in connection with virtually every existing multinational state: the French Canadians allege that the English dominate Canada; the Flemish similarly accuse the Walloons in Belgium; the Slovaks (both before and after Communist rule) complain of Czech domination; the Croats and Slovenes traditionally protest Serb control of the Yugoslav state; and the Hindus are charged with seeking to impose their norms upon the rest of India.

There is a kernel of truth, of course, in all these charges to the extent that in any multinational state the benefits and advantages of the union do not flow evenly or register equally. When the balance of benefits becomes disproportionate to the point where the aggrieved partners perceive the possibilities of greater satisfaction in independence than in partnership, then the consensus upon which the state is based begins to erode.

There is little question that under Stalin the Soviet Union was increasingly reverting to a Russian imperial state, though with some significant reservations, and that residues of the Stalinist era continue to color the Soviet multinational system today. The Soviet multinational experience is especially complex because, although in absolute quantitative terms the Russians enjoy more benefits than any other nationality in the union, it is probably also true that in relative or qualitative terms the Georgians and Armenians derive the greatest benefits and advantages. The Soviet contention that the leading role of the Russians burdens them with responsibilities and duties to the other nationalities is undoubtedly true in a sense. In assessing the value of the union to the non-Russian nationalities one must also consider whether as a nation collectively and as individual citizens their aspirations and interests would be better served by an option other than being part of a Soviet state. No doubt, attitudes would vary widely from one Soviet nationality to another.

III. Molding The Soviet Multinational State: Sovietization, Russianization, and Russification

The Bolsheviks inherited a *Russian* state, not an abstract state devoid of ethnic, cultural, or historical identities. They fell heir to Russia's geography, its multinational population, its culture and traditions, its memories of misery and glory, its friends and enemies, and, above all, its complex of collective behavioral responses summed up as "national character." The nations of the former empire, with their diverse religions, cultures, skills, knowl-

edge, ignorance, prejudices, fears, animosities, superstitions, anxieties, and legacies, now became peoples of the Soviet Union. This
was the human raw material upon which the ideological norms of
Marxism were to be imposed and from which the elite wished to
fashion an embryonic universal Communist state. Most of the
new leaders were Russians, and the non-Russians among them were
drawn, for the most part, from the nationalities which played influential roles in the cultural and political life of the empire:
Ukrainians, Jews, Georgians, Armenians, Germans, and Balts. It
was multinational, but far from international, even though the
new Soviet state intended to play a role on the historical stage
which transcended Russia itself. Thus, the universalism of the
Bolshevik states was putative from the outset because it was ruled
not by the Communist International but by the Russian Communist Party (later All-Union Communist Party). Although the
Soviet state was originally envisioned as the spearhead of the international proletariat, no Soviet leader seriously suggested placing
the former Russian Empire under the rule of the Comintern.

A state gripped by messianic and universalist pretensions but
ruled by Russians was inherently imperialistic, the rhetoric of its
leaders and apologists notwithstanding. In the process of reshaping
the Russian Empire into an embryonic universal state, they in fact
created an authentic multinational commonwealth. This was not,
however, the ultimate purpose of the leaders, simply a means to an
end. Nonetheless, some of the peculiar characteristics of the
Soviet multinational system today are legacies of its original universalist aspirations.

Since the new leaders were predominantly Russian, as was the
population, the universal state was bound to be heavily and disproportionately influenced by the Russian element. The Bolsheviks
had inherited an existing imbalance between the Russian and non-
Russian nationalities, and ultimately succumbed to its objective
dictates.

In the shaping of the multinational state, three distinct though
closely interrelated (but often mistakenly equated) processes were
set into motion: Sovietization, Russianization, and Russification.
Sovietization is here defined as the process of modernization and
industrialization within the Marxist-Leninist norms of social,
economic, and political behavior.[6] Russianization is defined as the
process of internationalizing Russian language and culture within
the Soviet Union. While Sovietization was the ultimate objective
of the regime, Russianization was regarded initially as a means

rather than an end. Sovietization and Russianization, however, became inextricably intertwined and the two processes mutually reinforced and contaminated one another.

Finally, Russification, which is often confused with Russianization, is a more limited process; it was not initially conceived as either an end or a means, but occurred as a sociological by-product or consequence of Sovietization and Russianization. It is defined as the process whereby non-Russians are transformed objectively and psychologically into Russians, and is more an individual process than a collective one. Thus while Sovietization is universal in its effects and Russianization almost so, Russification is more restricted.

There is, of course, an obvious evolutionary relationship between Russianization and Russification. Russianization is a prerequisite to Russification, but it can be a terminal process as well, just as were the Hellenization of the Near East in ancient times and the Hispanicization of Latin America. Near Easterners were not transformed into Greeks, nor were the Indians of the New World into Spaniards or Portuguese. Rather, they became Greek-like or Hispanic-like, and their culture became a stabilized blend of indigenous and nonindigenous elements. Whereas Russification is restricted mainly to the educated elites of the non-Russian nationalities, Russianization affects all social classes and groups in Soviet society. Russification is more than a mere intensification of Russianization, since it involves qualitative psychological transformations and can be legally institutionalized by an explicit change in national identity.

All three processes have proceeded at different paces and with different levels of intensity among the non-Russian nationalities, depending on their prior stage of development and the degree of national resistance and immunity to alien doctrines and cultures. The intensity of Russianization which the non-Russian nationalities have been able to endure without succumbing to Russification also varies from nationality to nationality. The important variations in national resistance and susceptibility will be discussed below.

The Russianization of the Soviet Multinational State

Under Soviet rule, Russian has assumed the status of a "world language" alongside English, French, and Spanish. The superimposition of Russian language and culture on the daily life of the non-Russian nationalities has produced a variegated Russianized civilization whose different hues represent the distinctive indigenous elements in the cultural fusion. The Russian language has become the *lingua franca* of the Soviet Union. Educated citizens of all nationalities are able to communicate fluently, and nearly everybody in the Soviet Union understands some Russian. Within a matter of decades, the Soviet population will be effectively bilingual. There will be a gradual erosion of the non-Russian languages, first among the young people and then among the educated classes. This does not necessarily mean that the nationalities will lose their individual identity, though this will undoubtedly happen to some of the smaller groups, and the space of Russification will surely increase among all nationalities.

The Russianization process is far more significant at this state in the evolution of the Soviet system and should be examined not only as a transit point to Russification but also in its sociological function of expanding and intensifying communication and understanding among diverse peoples and cultures. That is, like Hellenization, Russianization should also be examined as an end-product, and as a possible stabilized permanent fusion of cultures, for it is quite likely that many aspects of Russianization will survive the ideological goals of the Soviet system.

The vehicles and instruments of Russianization are many and achieve their effects subtly as well as bluntly. Some are mandatory and even coercive; others are appealing and agreeable in their operation, while many are erosive and corrosive in their impact upon the non-Russian cultures simply because of their functional character.

Institutional Instruments and Manifestations of Russianization

Institutional instruments of Russianization are Russian norms and practices which have been converted into all-union Soviet norms. Invested with a legal character, they are imposed on all non-Russian nationalities. The most important are the following: (1) the adoption of Russian as an official language in all non-Russian areas through the Soviet Union, alongside the local language; (2) the adoption of Russian as the official language of state, diplomacy, and international contact; (3) the adoption of Russian as the single language of command in the armed forces; (4) the employment of Russian inscriptions on all official awards, decorations, medals, postage stamps, and Soviet currency; (5) the identification of all public institutions and localities in Russian as well as in the local languages; and (6) the inscription of the legend "Proletarians of all countries unite!" on the coats-of-arms of all non-Russian republics in Russian together with the native language.

As a practical matter it is, of course, necessary for the Soviet state to have an official *lingua franca*, and apart from the glowing rhetoric and self-serving nature of the explanations offered by Soviet spokesmen, it would be indeed difficult to disagree with their contention that Russian is the logical choice.[7] While the use of Russian as the *lingua franca* of the Soviet Union is eminently functional, it nevertheless objectively results in the Russianization of the non-Russian languages as well, which is welcomed and encouraged by the regime as an important vehicle of Sovietization and community building:

> The Russian language plays a major role in the process of the mutual enrichment of the languages of the peoples of the U.S.S.R., and as a language of fraternal cooperation of the Soviet peoples it contributes to the development of the U.S.S.R. as a single union state united by the community of interests and goals of all the nations and nationalities of our country, by the single ideology of Marxism-Leninism, of proletarian internationalism.[8]

The regime nevertheless is extremely sensitive to the charge of Great Russian chauvinism and even imperialism. Hence, no longer does it sing the glories of Russian as an intrinsically superior language, as it did under Stalin, but stresses its role as a practical choice dictated by objective historical development. Despite the merit in this contention, Soviet observers are still understandably reluctant to be completely candid about the consequences of choosing Russian as the language of "inter-nationality communication."

To avoid the charge of Great Russian chauvinism, the Soviet regime prudently did not insist that full literacy in the Soviet Union could be most expediently and inexpensively achieved by Russifying the educational system with Russian as the only language of instruction. Instead, it chose the more complicated and expensive, but less painful, way of promoting literacy through the medium of the local language, and using that as a base from which to switch to Russian.

The two processes of Russianization and Russification cannot be separated from each other without doing violence to an objective evaluation of Soviet nationality policy. Critics of Soviet nationality policy often emphasize the Russianization process, equating it with Russification, while apologists for the Soviet regime ignore the Russianization process and stress the multinationalization of the Soviet system. Russianization cannot properly be equated with forcible assimilation, although assimilation is undoubtedly one of the by-products, because non-Russians are not obligated to transform themselves into synthetic Russians and are permitted to preserve their national identity. Soviet policy is not based on the principle "learn Russian or perish," but rather "learn Russian and prosper." Emphasis is on the rewards of assimilation, not on punishment for nonassimilation. The regime clearly recognized that both Russianization and Russification would be facilitated rather than hindered by the concurrent development of non-Russian languages and cultures: the more educated in his native tongue, the more likely the non-Russian is to perceive the inherent limitations and narrow horizons of his own language and to recognize the advantage of learning Russian voluntarily.

The singular redeeming feature of Soviet nationality policy which distinguishes it from Imperial nationality policy in the past is that the Soviet system allows its citizens to choose Russian or their native language, or both simultaneously, as their medium of expression and communication. Most imperial systems have, at best, offered their minority subjects a Hobson's choice: learn and be educated in the ruling language or not at all. The simplistic conclusion that Soviet nationality policy is little more than a sinister extrapolation of Tsarist Russification policies should be avoided. As the following quotation demonstrates, Soviet policy is both more sophisticated and benign:

> The Russian language, although it is the common language of inter-nationality communication between the peoples, occupies politically and legally an equal, and by no means a privileged position among the languages of our country. Any Soviet person in any public context from the rural Soviet or the people's court all the way up to the sessions of the U.S.S.R. Supreme Soviet, has the right to speak his own native tongue. The Soviet people may apply to any state agency, in writing or orally, in their native tongue. . . . As has been noted, Russian came to fulfill the functions of a language of communication between nationalities for objective historical reasons. We know that Lenin resolutely objected to making Russian a compulsory "state language" imposed by force. In the U.S.S.R. there is no state language compulsory for all peoples; each people uses both its own language and the language of inter-nationality communication already singled out historically [i.e., Russian].[9]

It must be remembered that the Soviet population as a whole has achieved virtually 100 per cent literacy, and that this is primarily in the native languages. Even in the most benevolent colonial empires, educational opportunities were available almost exclusively in the ruling language, often with a heavy dose of religious indoctrination, and usually without a serious concurrent effort to promote literacy and learning in indigenous languages. As a consequence, when the European colonial empires fragmented into dozens of independent states, they left a small Europeanized native elite as the new governing class, whose only functional medium of expression was a European language. The population as a whole was left in a general condition of illiteracy.

The Bolsheviks, on the other hand, inherited an empire with only 26 per cent of the population literate (and in Central Asia only 1 per cent). In 1959, the official Soviet census reported a literacy rate of 96 per cent and all school-age children enrolled in schools.

These comparisons are made in order to place Soviet nationality policy in general perspective. Otherwise, what is praised as virtuous when done by the West European powers in their former colonies (for example, educating native elites in the imperial language) is often condemned as a vice when practiced by the Soviet regime on an even larger and more generous scale. Regardless of the political and ideological motives of Soviet nationality policy, it should be subjected to uniform standards of judgment. Furthermore, its achievements should be measured against what existed in 1917.

On the other hand, it is equally necessary to compare actual achievements with the exaggerated official claims, especially because Soviet nationality and linguistic specialists, echoing the rhetoric of the regime, portray Soviet policy as an unblemished model to the new countries of Africa and Asia with parallel problems of mass illiteracy, a polyglot population, and unwritten languages spoken by large numbers of people.[10]

Cultural Vehicles and Manifestations of Russianization

The institutional instruments of Russianization blend in almost naturally with the cultural instruments, some of which are quasi-institutional in character while others are almost purely voluntary. In many ways, the cultural patterns of Russianization, which include the educational system, are far more effective because they are optional rather than compulsory, and the inducements are socially rewarding and advantageous.

The Cyrillization of non-Russian languages. The use of the Cyrillic alphabet for non-Russian languages is essentially an indirect form of Russianization. Properly speaking, the Cyrillic alphabet is not a Russian but a Slavic alphabet, and is employed by Ukrainians, Byelorussians, Serbs, and Bulgars. Before the nineteenth century it was also used for Rumanian. In the Soviet Union, however, it becomes an indirect instrument of Russianization, a fact which is frankly conceded by the regime.[11] (The Cyrillic alphabet, however, is not universally employed in the Soviet Union. The Armenians and Georgians retain their ancient distinctive script, while languages which traditionally have employed the Latin alphabet—the three Baltic languages and those of some nonterritorial minorities—have been exempted from Cyrillization. But all these languages account for only about 10 million people.)

The Cyrillization of the non-Russian alphabets was initiated barely two decades ago. At first, after the Revolution, the Soviet regime adopted the policy of using the Latin alphabet to reduce the unwritten language to writing, and to displace the Arabic script traditionally employed by the Central Asian and other Moslem nationalities. While the displacement of Arabic served the political and ideological purpose of rupturing cultural communication between Soviet Moslems and their co-religionists in the Middle East, the adoption of the Latin alphabet could hardly be described as a gesture of Russianization.

In the mid-1930s Stalin ordered the systematic eradication of the Latin alphabet in favor of modified Cyrillic alphabets. This change-over had its more than obvious chauvinistic overtones, was a definite move in the direction of Russianization, and served a further political purpose in erecting an impediment to communication between Soviet Turkic nationalities and Turkey, where Ataturk had dropped the Arabic script for the Latin. It was nevertheless true that the Cyrillic alphabet was a better alphabetical medium for most of these languages than the Latin or Arabic.

The Russianization of non-Russian languages. Simultaneously with Cyrillization of the printed word, the Soviet regime initiated a policy of Russianizing all non-Russian languages by purging them of cultural importations from abroad and infusing them with

Russian loan words. Most of this infusion consists of political, scientific, and technical words, although its total impact is strongly cultural. This process is euphemistically described by Soviet writers as the "mutual enrichment" of languages, although there is precious little reciprocity involved. The degree of Russianizing has been highly uneven, being determined in large measure by the relative richness of the vocabulary and the literary heritage of the target language. With the smaller and less vital languages, and those based upon the recent selection of a dialect as the literary standard (Central Asian Turkic languages, for example), the Russianization process has been more intensive. Nor is it restricted to the infusion of Russian loan words; some of the smaller and weaker languages have been subjected to syntactical and stylistic changes as well. In some cases, only the basic vocabulary and word stems remain indigenous (one could, of course, say almost the same thing about English except that its borrowings have been more diverse), and the language has the appearance of a synthetic and debased version of Russian.[12]

Soviet writers readily admit that the Russianization of non-Russian languages has been deliberate, systematic, and purposive. The nature and extent of the process can be best described in the words of a recent Soviet account:

> The processes of the mutual enrichment of the languages of the U.S.S.R. are revealed most clearly in the development of their *lexical composition* through common words formed chiefly on the basis of internationalization of the vocabulary and word stock of the Russian language: neologisms of the Soviet period . . . philosophical and sociopolitical terms . . . and scientific-technical terms. . . . Calculations show that in the new written languages approximately 70 per cent to 80 per cent of the new sociopolitical and scientific-technical terms derive from the common word stock [i.e., Russian] of the languages of the U.S.S.R. Numerous instances of the reciprocal influence and mutual enrichment of languages are also observed in the sphere of *syntactical* and *stylistic systems*. Common trends and laws of the development and mutual enrichment of languages are clearly manifested in the formation of a special style of sociopolitical and publicistic literature of the Soviet epoch, which took shape under the influence of the Russian language.[13]

And, according to another essay:

> For peoples living in in a single country, in the same sociopolitical, social and economic conditions of the construction of communism, the formation of common concepts, terms, and figurative expressions

reflective of common processes of scientific and artistic thought and development of social consciousness is essential. Disregard of the processes of mutual enrichment of languages paves the way for exaggeration of "national specifics" and the reciprocal isolation of language in sociopolitical, scientific, and cultural life.[14]

The practice of purging a language of alien importations and influences in order to restore archaic indigenous words or to manufacture new words out of native stems is by now a common nationalistic impulse in many countries. The process of language purgation in the Soviet Union is, however, not primarily a means to purification, but a recontamination of the language with selected "impurities." Russian, Byelorussian, and Ukrainian were stripped of Polish borrowings; the Baltic languages of German words; the Armenian and Georgian of Turkish and Persian; and the Central Asian of Arabic and Persian (except the Tadzhik in the case of Persian). To distinguish further between the Soviet Turkic and the language spoken in Turkey, local slang words were elevated to standard usage. During the Stalin era, resistance to the process was condemned as both anti-Soviet and anti-Russian, and thus doubly heinous. "Bourgeois nationalists," it was charged,

> sought to use foreign languages as their models, persistently trying to minimize the importance of the Russian language. Byelorussian and Ukrainian nationalists injected in their native speech elements of the Polish gentry's speech; the Moldavian nationalists tried to drag into their language aristocratic Rumanian drawing-room words; and the Latvian nationalists, carrying out the orders of the German gentry, attempted to Germanize their tongue. The bourgeois nationalists of our Eastern republics infused their native languages with Persian-Arabic and Turkish elements. In essence this was a policy of betrayal of national interests, a policy of cosmopolitanism.[15]

Since then the pace of the Russianization of the non-Russian languages has relented somewhat. Emphasis is on the practical necessity and logical appropriateness of Russian as a Soviet *lingua franca* and as the common quarry from which other languages mine in order to enrich their vocabularies in the modern age. Furthermore, as the non-Russian languages are increasingly diluted with Russian words and forms, the distance between the languages is narrowed and the final choice of a single language will be spontaneously and naturally made by the social and cultural evolution of society rather than by administrative fiat.

The Russianization of the educational system. The single most important vehicle of Russianization in Soviet society is the educational system, which functions more efficiently and effectively with every passing year. The educational establishment at all levels and in all localities is based upon Russian pedagogical traditions and methods, both pre-Soviet and Soviet. Until 1959, Russian was a compulsory second language in all non-Russian language schools; the elimination of this requirement was not so much a ritualistic abandonment of Russianization as a recognition of its superfluity. Before the educational reform of 1958–59, all Russians living in non-Russian republics had to learn the local language as a second language, although there are strong indications that this rule was not always enforced. Actually, only about 6 per cent of all Russians have studied another Soviet language as a second language. Furthermore, in all republics, Russian-language schools, established primarily to serve local Russian residents, existed alongside the native-language schools and were open to pupils of any nationality.[16] These schools have been a powerful Russianizing and even Russifying instrument, and since the educational reform have become even more so. The Russian-language schools, particularly in Central Asia, often enjoyed better facilities; and, along with this obvious advantage, they also attracted non-Russians preparing themselves for acceptance to higher institutions of learning. Non-Russians living outside the republic of their own nationality nearly always chose to attend schools in which the language of instruction was the ruling or inter-nationality language rather than a school in which the language of instruction was another minority language.

The educational reform acts of 1959. On November 21, 1958, the Central Committee of the CPSU and the U.S.S.R. Council of Ministers adopted new theses on education. On December 24, the Supreme Soviet adopted a new educational reform act based upon them; and most of the union and autonomous republics enacted virtually identical laws within the next few months. Under the new law, the compulsory study of Russian in all non-Russian-language schools was abrogated and, correspondingly, the language of the republic in Russian-language schools situated in the republic was also dropped as a mandatory subject. The ostensible reason for the change was that under the old rule students who wished to study a non-Soviet foreign language were burdened with two foreign languages (except, of course, students enrolled in Russian-language schools in Russian-inhabited areas).

The principle of "free choice" adopted in the reform act is best explained in the words of Thesis 19 itself:

> Instruction in the Soviet school is conducted in the native tongue. This is one of the important achievements of Leninist nationality policy. At the same time, in the schools of the union and autonomous republics the Russian language is studied seriously. This language is a powerful means of international communication, of strengthening friendship among the peoples of the U.S.S.R., and of bringing them into contact with the wealth of Russian and world culture. . . . It is a fact that in the nationality schools children study three languages—their native tongue, Russian, and one of the foreign languages. The question ought to be considered of giving parents the right to send their children to a school where the language of their choice is used. If a child attends a school where instruction is conducted in the language of the union or autonomous republics, he may, if he wishes, take up the Russian language. And vice versa, if a child attends a Russian school, he may, if he so desires, study the language of one of the union or autonomous republics. To be sure, this step could only be taken if there is a sufficient number of children to form classes for instruction in the given language.[17]

It should be noted that the new reform law not only exempts nonindigenous pupils from learning the language of the republic, but it also deprives the republics of the right to make the native language compulsory for pupils of their own nationality in Russian-language schools. (Russians had already been evading for years the requirement that they learn the language of the republic in which they were attending school.) The new reform act thus encroached further upon the cherished sovereignty of the union republics. In their own school systems, all they can now do is maintain the native languages as an optional subject in Russian-language schools, but they cannot legally enforce attendance at native-language schools or at native-language classes in the Russian-language schools. The new reform act not only will accelerate Russianization and Russification, but threatens the very vitality and survival of the non-Russian languages themselves in the face of the opportunities, advantages, and inducements which attendance at a Russian-language school can afford. For some of the smaller and weaker nationalities, national erosion may soon become a real problem.

The possibility was quickly evident to many local officials and educators, and it is a sign of the relative political liberality of

Stalin's successors that they allowed the expression of some dissent in the Supreme Soviet discussions. Some representatives of various republics proposed retention of the existing practice of making both Russian and the native language compulsory in all of the schools of the national republics, while another group suggested that Russian be required for all children and that the indigenous language be a mandatory subject for natives of the republic enrolled in Russian-language schools.[18] Generally speaking, the five Central Asian republics and Moldavia offered the least resistance, whereas the Ukrainian, Georgian, Armenian, Azerbaidzhani, Lithuanian, Latvian, and Estonian republics registered the most vigorous opposition, sometimes covertly supported, if not encouraged, by high republic state and party officials. In Georgia, no less a personage than Mzhavanadze, First Secretary of the Georgian party and a candidate member of the Presidium of the CPSU, publicly supported the view that both Russian and the local language should be compulsory in republican schools.[19] And in the Supreme Soviet discussions, another Georgian, Deputy Abashidze, even questioned obliquely the justification for Russian-language schools in the non-Russian republics. He stressed that Georgian was the "state language of the republic," and impassionately appealed to the assembled Soviet deputies:

> Comrade deputies! We must not set up the Russian and the local indigenous language one against another by allowing people to choose between them. For us both languages are native languages, both of them are indispensable, and both are obligatory.[20]

If the Georgians were the most explicit in their opposition, the Armenians were the most eloquent in defending the necessity for making their language compulsory for all Armenian pupils in their republic, while the Ukrainians urged the continuance of the *status quo*. The Azerbaidzhani deputies were more diplomatic in their opposition but, as events were to reveal, also more implacable, while the three Baltic countries vigorously demanded the retention of the non-Russian languages as obligatory subjects in all republic schools.[21]

In the face of widespread opposition, Thesis 19 was not incorporated into the all-union law, and the impression was left that each republic would apply the thesis as it saw fit, adapting it to local conditions and sentiment. With the exception of those of Azerbaidzhan and Latvia, the laws adopted by the Supreme Soviets of the republics were substantially identical in wording and hewed closely to the substance of Thesis 19, which suggests that strong pressure was exerted from Moscow that they "voluntarily" co-opt Thesis 19 as their own. The laws as adopted by the republics established the right of the parents to select the language of instruction for their children and also to decide whether or not the child should learn Russian or his native language as a second language. Since the all-union law does not include a rule on the language of instruction, we may infer that Article 15 of the R.S.F.S.R. law represents the position of the regime and served as a model for the other laws, although it was not the first to be adopted:

> It is decreed that instruction be conducted in the native language. Parents have the right to choose the school conducting instruction in a given language which their children are to attend. In schools which conduct instruction in the language of the autonomous republic, autonomous national region [oblast], or national district [okrug], study of the Russian language is conducted in accordance with the wishes of the pupils. Similarly, in Russian-language schools, pupils who desire may study the national language of the autonomous republic, autonomous national region, or national district.[22]

A substantially similar law was adopted by the other republics, but with some interesting embellishments. The Uzbek, Tadzhik, Turkmen, and Kirgiz laws pledged to improve the teaching of Russian. The Ukrainian law, strangely enough, called for the strengthening of both languages, but made Russian a compulsory language, with Ukrainian optional. Estonia's pattern was similar to that of the Ukraine, but less emphatic. The adoption of the Armenian, Estonian, and Georgian laws, however, was preceded by discussions which made it evident that the laws would be implemented so as to strengthen the native languages rather than Russian.[23]

The Azerbaidzhani law deliberately omitted any reference to the status of the second language. Premier Akhundov in his report to the Republic's Supreme Soviet declared that "the knowledge of Azerbaidzhani as a means of communication" was "vitally necessary" for all children attending Russian-language schools and strongly intimated that Azerbaidzhani would be studied in these institutions as an obligatory subject.[24] The Latvian law was an even bolder challenge to the central authorities. It omitted all references to the language of instruction, and in his report to the Latvian Supreme Soviet, Deputy Premier Berklav explicitly rejected the principle embodied in Thesis 19 and declared that both

Latvian and Russian would be obligatory: "When the Theses
. . . were being discussed, the residents of Soviet Latvia unanimously indicated that in eight-year schools of our Republic it was
absolutely necessary to continue the traditional instruction in three
languages—Latvian, Russian, and one foreign language."[25]

Moscow did not accept the defiance of the two republics grace-
fully. While the regime had abjured the cruder forms of Stalinist
coercion and could tolerate limited expressions of dissent and permit restricted diversity and deviation in the adoption of laws, it was
not yet ready to permit open defiance on the nationality issue,
which remains a sensitive matter during the transitional period of
the withering away of the nationalities. The party and governmental hierarchies in the two republics were rudely shaken up in
a series of actions between June and December 1959, but within
the framework of party and legal procedures.[26] The ostensible
reasons were a wide variety of ideological and economic shortcomings, but the identity of the local officials criticized and sacked
as well as the fact that the Azerbaidzhani law was simultaneously
cured of its deficiencies strongly suggested that the opposition to
the educational reform was a key factor in the shake-ups. The
Latvian law was also apparently rectified by a decree of August
11, 1959.

The lively opposition to the elimination of the native language
as a compulsory medium of communication in the national republics indicated widespread popular opposition to the erosion of
national distinctions. In republics where high local party and
government officials associated themselves with the opposition, it
was also evident that resistance was particularly acute among the
intelligentsia. Greatest resistance, as could be expected, was
generated among the "historic" nationalities which had powerful
national traditions and which were among the most advanced culturally and developmentally. Least resistance came from the "un-
historic" or weakly developed nationalities and particularly from
those republics with large Russian populations, whose governments and party organizations are infested with ethnic Russians in
key positions at all levels.

It is noteworthy, however, that while the nationalities resisted,
in the end they capitulated. The surrender was not entirely due to
coercion and pressure, although this was obviously a factor. The
elites of the various nationalities are forced to play two social roles,
each responding to different pressures and constituencies, often
pulling in opposite directions. Since the political constituency of

the non-Russian Soviet official is in Moscow, though his natural constituency is his national republic, he is more likely to be responsive to the interests of Moscow than to those of his republic. The rare official who chooses his republic's interest over that of Moscow is almost always removed or demoted. The absolute priority of the interests of the center over those of the periphery is made quite clear by a recent editorial in *Kommunist*:

> The interests of the construction of communism require an irreconcilable struggle against any manifestations and survivals of nationalism and chauvinism. Especially intolerable is localism, which expresses itself in opposing of falsely understood interests of "one's own" republic to the interests of the entire state. . . . The party also stresses the inadmissibility of any manifestations of national exclusiveness in the upbringing and utilization of personnel of various nationalities in the Soviet republics. . . . It is necessary . . . to oppose energetically the slightest tendencies toward national narrowness and exclusiveness, the restoration and artificial imposition, under the guise of "national" traditions, of backward customs and morés that hamper communist construction.[27]

The educational reform acts of 1959 will undoubtedly accelerate both the Russianization and Russification of the non-Russian nationalities. Soviet data already indicated that in 1955–56, 65 per cent of all pupils were enrolled in Russian-language schools. Since the 1959 census reported that the Russians made up only 55 per cent of the total population, and on the assumption that virtually all Russian pupils attend Russian-language schools, this means that approximately 15 per cent of the students enrolled in Russian-language schools in 1955–56 were non-Russians. The percentage of pupils attending Russian-language schools varies widely from one national republic to another—in 1955–56, from a mere 9 per cent in Armenia to 66 per cent in the Kazakh Republic, as shown in Table 3 on page 174.

Generally, the more closely the percentage of pupils enrolled in Russian-language schools corresponds with the percentage of Russians in the total population of the republic, the greater the national resistance to Russianization. This must be qualified, however, by the fact that in some of the advanced republics, the presence of substantial numbers of the indigenous pupils in Russian-language schools may actually reflect a larger number of students preparing themselves for higher education. Another qualification is the percentage of the nonindigenous portion of the population, including Russians, for as a general rule, non-

TABLE 3
PERCENTAGE OF STUDENTS ATTENDING RUSSIAN-LANGUAGE
SCHOOLS 1955–56[28]

	A*	B	C	D
Republic	Per Cent in Russian-Language Schools	Per Cent Russians in Republic	Differ-ential	Per Cent Non-indigenous in Republic
U.S.S.R.	65	55.0	10.0	—
R.S.F.S.R.	94	83.2	10.8	16.8
Ukrainian	26 (5)	17.1 (6)	8.9 (7)	23.9 (11)
Byelorussian	22 (7)	9.1 (12)	12.9 (3)	20.0 (13)
Uzbek	20 (10)	13.6 (8)	6.4 (8)	38.0 (5)
Kazakh	66 (1)	43.1 (1)	22.9 (1)	70.4 (1)
Georgian	20 (11)	10.8 (10)	9.2 (5)	36.9 (7)
Azerbaidzhani	23 (6)	13.9 (7)	9.1 (6)	32.9 (9)
Lithuanian	11 (13)	8.5 (13)	2.5 (13)	20.7 (12)
Moldavian	33 (3)	10.2 (11)	12.8 (4)	34.6 (8)
Latvian	33 (4)	26.6 (3)	6.4 (9)	38.0 (6)
Kirgiz	49 (2)	30.2 (2)	18.8 (2)	59.5 (2)
Tadzhik	16 (12)	13.3 (9)	2.7 (12)	46.9 (3)
Armenian	9 (14)	3.2 (14)	5.8 (10)	12.0 (14)
Turkmen	21 (9)	17.3 (5)	3.7 (11)	39.1 (4)
Estonian	22 (8)	21.7 (4)	0.3 (14)	27.1 (10)

* Figures in parentheses represent rank order.

Russians living in republics other than their own choose to attend Russian-language schools. Where the percentage of the nonindigenous population exceeds the percentage of pupils in Russian-language schools, this not only indicates a strong resistance to Russianization but may also show a strong tendency of the non-Russian nationality to assimilate the non-natives in its republic. It may also, however, indicate the presence of schools offering other languages of instruction. The latter is particularly true of the Central Asian republics, which have substantial minorities of kindred peoples. The Uzbeks, for example, make up 8.3, 10.6, and 23 per cent of the population of the Turkmen, Kirgiz, and Tadzhik republics, respectively, while the Georgian and Azerbaidzhani republics have substantial Armenian minorities. Bearing these reservations in mind, we find Estonia registering the greatest resistance to Russianization and the Kazakh Republic showing the least.

The percentage of pupils enrolled in Russian-language schools exceeds in all instances the percentage of Russians in the total population of the republic. The differential between the two percentages ranges all the way from a 0.3 per cent for Estonia to 22.9 per cent for the Kazakh Republic. This differential (Column C) represents the proportion of non-Russians attending Russian-language schools. It does not necessarily mean that the non-Russians attending these schools were of the indigenous nationality, particularly in those republics where substantial non-Russian minorities are present. The total percentage of nonindigenous nationalities, including Russians, is shown in Column D. The only striking correlations among the four variables listed involve the Kazakh and Kirgiz republics. They clearly are the two republics which have been most intensely denationalized if not Russianized. They rank first and second, respectively, in the percentage in Russian-language schools, the percentage of Russians in the population, the size of the differential, and in the percentage of nonindigenous nationalities in their republics. The Kazakhs and Kirgiz have both been reduced to minorities in their own republics, which are, in effect, subsidiary Russian or, at best, multinational republics.

The Tadzhik and Turkmen republics, which rank third and fourth, respectively, in the degree to which their republics have been nationally diluted, do not even approach the national erosion of the Kazakh and Kirgiz republics. This would seem to indicate that once a republic has a large number of Russians *and* becomes a minority in its own republic, it is in danger of losing its national identity, particularly if it was a weakly developed nationality to begin with. In a sense, both the Kazakh and Kirgiz republics have been retrograded, *de facto*, to the condition of autonomous republics within the Russian Republic. The new Constitution of the U.S.S.R. may have to recognize juridically the qualitative changes which have overtaken the two republics and either alter their boundaries to restore the indigenous nationality to a majority, incorporate them into the R.S.F.S.R. as autonomous republics, organize a Central Asian sub-federation, or continue to violate the original rule that the indigenous population constitute a majority. It should be recalled that the Karelo-Finnish Republic was retrograded to an autonomous republic in 1955 on grounds that it no longer qualified for status as a union republic.[29]

Higher education and Russianization. Higher education in the Soviet Union is increasingly an instrument of Russification rather than Russianization. By the time a non-Russian student enters an institution of higher learning, he has already been thoroughly Russianized by the public school system. The educational reform act will accelerate Russianization and will also enhance the opportunities of the non-Russian nationalities for higher education.

Higher educational institutions are distributed unevenly among the republics in both quantity and quality. The institutions in Moscow and Leningrad alone, which are in fact all-union centers, account for about 20 per cent of all graduations from institutions of higher learning. The two most prestigious universities in the country are located in Moscow and Leningrad, and the language of instruction is in Russian; because of the intense competition, all matriculating students must be thoroughly prepared in the Russian language. Recognizing that Russians would have an advantage over non-Russians, particularly those from the remote regions, in having access to prestigious Soviet universities, the Soviet regime has compensated by adopting informal nationality quotas, including preferential quotas for those nationalities whose educational development was retarded, and has restricted enrollment for those nationalities which have been traditionally "overrepresented"—namely, Russians, Jews, Georgians, and Armenians. The Jews, as a nonterritorial nationality and traditionally the most highly "overrepresented," have suffered the greatest percentage decline in the number of students admitted.

The Soviet policy of preferential national quotas and national balance has been subjected to harsh criticism by some Western observers, who at the same time observe that the proportion of Central Asians and other nationalities in universities is below their proportion of the population. Yet it is obvious that the regime cannot remedy the second deficiency without the institution of nationality quotas, which obviously are inequitable to qualified students whose nationality quotas have been exhausted. In spite of these measures, nationalities which have been overrepresented in the past continue to be overrepresented. The increase in the enrollment of the more retarded nationalities, however, has been no less than spectacular, as Table 4 illustrates.

A comparison of the national composition of students in institutions of higher learning in the years 1927, 1959, and 1965 reveals the quantitative consequences of Soviet nationality policy in education. The policy of proportionate balance between the national composition and the student body has clearly been a monumental success, although it reveals some interesting biases. Generally

TABLE 4
COMPOSITION OF STUDENTS BY MAJOR NATIONALITIES
1927, 1959 AND 1965[30]

Nationality	Per Cent of Population, 1926	Students, 1927			Per Cent of Population, 1959	Students, 1959			Students, 1965		
		Thousands	Per Cent	Index		Thousands	Per Cent	Index	Thousands	Per Cent	Index
Russian	52.9	94.5	56.1	1.06	54.7	835.3	62.3	1.13	2,362.0	61.1	1.11
Ukrainian	21.2	24.6	14.8	.69	17.8	179.6	13.3	.75	558.6	14.4	.81
Byelorussian	3.2	4.6	2.9	.90	3.8	33.8	2.5	.69	114.6	2.9	.76
Uzbek	2.7	.5	.3	.11	2.9	30.5	2.4	.82	95.6	2.4	.83
Kazakh	2.7	.3	.2	.07	1.7	22.0	1.6	.94	69.9	1.8	1.06
Georgian	1.2	4.0	2.4	2.00	1.3	23.7	1.7	1.41	70.1	1.8	1.38
Azerbaidzhani	1.2	1.9	1.1	.91	1.4	17.7	1.3	.92	54.0	1.3	.93
Lithuanian	—	—	—	—	1.1	15.8	1.2	1.09	42.8	1.1	1.00
Moldavian	—	—	—	—	1.1	6.6	.5	.45	22.9	.5	.46
Latvian	—	—	—	—	.7	9.8	.7	1.00	21.4	.5	.71
Kirgiz	.5	.1	.06	.12	.5	6.5	.5	1.00	16.2	.4	.80
Tadzhik	.7	.1	.06	.08	.7	6.8	.5	.71	17.5	.4	.57
Armenian	1.1	3.4	2.0	1.81	1.4	20.4	1.5	1.07	61.8	1.6	1.14
Turkmen	.5	.1	.06	.12	.5	5.7	.4	.80	15.6	.4	.80
Estonian	—	—	—	—	.5	7.5	.6	1.20	18.8	.4	.80
Jewish	1.8	—	13.5ᵃ	7.50	1.1	51.6ᵇ	4.1	3.73	94.6	2.4	2.18
Tatar	2.0	—	.8ᵃ	.40	2.4	22.4ᵇ	1.8	.75	67.7	1.7	.71

ᵃ Data for 1929.
ᵇ Data for 1956.

speaking, "overrepresented" nationalities have suffered a diminution in the percentage of students admitted to higher learning, although all nationalities without exception have experienced a
massive increase in the *absolute* numbers of students admitted.

Those nationalities which were underrepresented in 1927 have
experienced the most spectacular increases in both percentages and
absolute numbers. The greatest increases have been demonstrated
by the five Central Asian nationalities and the Moslem Tatars,
and in the first place, the Uzbeks, who have once again emerged
as the dominant and most vigorous national group in Central Asia
and have apparently been selected by the Soviet regime as the
chosen nationality in this area. By 1965, the principle of proportionate representation had been virtually achieved. The only
seriously "underrepresented" nationalities were the Moldavian,
Tadzhik, and Byelorussian. Only five nationalities—Russian, Jewish, Georgian, and Armenian, and Kazakh—enjoyed overrepresentation, and in the last instance, it was slight. The most conspicuous
deviation from the basic trend toward proportionate national representation has been the Russian share of the student enrollment,
as might be expected. The Russians have gone from 94,500 students, or 56.1 per cent, in 1927 to 2,362,000 students, or 61.1
per cent, in 1965. While in 1927 the Russian contingent among
the students corresponded very closely with the percentage of
Russians in the population (52.9 per cent), in 1965 they enjoyed
a substantial increase over their percentage of the population—a
reflection of the major bias of the system. Surprisingly enough,
however, the increased Russian "overrepresentation" was at the
expense not of the smaller non-Slavic nationalities, but of the
Ukrainians and Byelorussians, which enjoyed the dubious distinction of being the only nationalities which were "underrepresented" in 1927 to suffer a decline in their percentage of the total
student enrollment. The Byelorussians stand out as the single
"underrepresented" nationality in 1927 actually to suffer a decline in its index of representation; the Ukrainians avoided this
distinction only because they experienced a sharp decline in their
percentage of the total population (21.2 per cent in 1926 as
against only 17.8 per cent in 1959).

The chronic "underrepresentation" of the Ukrainians in higher
education, which is paralleled in Soviet political and cultural life
generally, was the result of a deliberate policy during the Stalin
years. Perceiving in this intractable and sizable nationality a possible rival center of power to that of Moscow, Stalin pursued a

ruthless policy of keeping it in check. Stalin's successors, especially Khrushchev, reversed this policy, and the Ukrainians have emerged to assume their natural role as the second most powerful and influential national entity in the Union.

Since the Soviet elite is increasingly recruited from the graduates of institutions of higher learning, changes in the national composition of the students in higher education will ultimately alter the national equilibrium in the social and political structure of the Soviet system. These changes are already being registered. As long as national distinctions continue to exist, it is apparently the Soviet objective to achieve proportionate national representation in all aspects of Soviet life and to create an all-union elite which will quantitatively reflect the multinational composition of the population. This would seem to be confirmed by Khrushchev's "explanation" for the catastrophic decline of Jewish influence in the Soviet system:

> At the beginning of the revolution we had many Jews in our party and government leadership. They were very educated and perhaps more revolutionary than the average Russian. Then we recruited new cadres. . . . If Jews wished to have first places in our republics today, it would naturally be annoying to the natives. They would not recognize the presumptions of the Jews, since they regard themselves as no less intelligent and able than the Jews.[31]

Jews, it should be noted, are considered a nationality in the Soviet Union rather than a religion, but as a nonterritorial nationality scheduled for early assimilation because their geographic and social distribution does not lend itself to easy accommodation to the Soviet multinational system with its territorial concept of nationality. Moreover, they are not treated as a nonterritorial *minority* nationality, like the Germans or Poles, but are considered a nonterritorial *Soviet* nationality, which should be assimilated to the territorial nationality of the republic in which they live or to the Russian nationality. It is this muted objective of the regime which accounts for its contrived responses to charges of discrimination against the Jews. The pathetic attempt to tabulate the number of Jews in the intelligentsia, among scientists, artists, and so forth, to rebut the charges merely confirms that currently the Jews play a social and cultural role far out of proportion to their numbers. The diminishing number of Jewish students in institutions of higher learning, however, portends a diminishing role for Jews in the future. The same is true, to a lesser degree, for the

Georgians and Armenians. As territorial nationalities, however, their fate is likely to be happier than that of the Jews even though in future generations their influence and role in the Soviet system will be cut back to correspond more closely to their proportion of the population.

The continuous increase in the number of Russian students, absolutely and proportionately, suggests an enhanced role and influence for the major nationality. As for the Ukrainians, under Khrushchev they experienced a considerable resurgence, but it is not at all clear whether they are slated for early fusion with the Russians or are to remain as the second most influential nationality in the Soviet Union.

Finally, it must once more be emphasized that the Soviet system of higher education is likely to be rather successful in intensifying the Russianization of the non-Russian elites to the point of Russification. National distinctions among the Soviet elite, then, will increasingly reflect national *origin* rather than national self-identification.

From Russianization to Russification

If primary and secondary schooling is the principal vehicle for the Russianization of the non-Russian nationalities, then institutions of higher learning are the main influence in Russifying the national elites. According to the 1959 census, more than 10 million non-Russian Soviet citizens reported Russian rather than their indigenous language as their mother tongue; most of them were probably members of the non-Russian intelligentsia. Russian is the sole or coordinate language of instruction in all institutions of higher learning. The native language is offered as a language of instruction in all universities of the republics, but highly technical and scientific subjects are taught only in Russian. There is also strong evidence to suggest that foreign languages in many institutions can only be taught through Russian because of the scarcity of foreign language textbooks and dictionaries in some of the more exotic non-Russian languages.[32]

The multinationalization of higher education. A further Russifying factor is the increasing "internationalization" of Soviet institutions of higher learning. While the availability of institutions of higher learning varies greatly from one republic to another, there is a generous complement in all republics. What often strikes outside observers as surprising about them, is that in many instances the majority of the students is not made up of the indigenous nationality of the republic. This leads some observers to jump quickly to the conclusion that this condition represents discrimination against the indigenous nationality in its own republic. Since the data presented above show close quantitative correspondence between the national composition of the student body and the Soviet population, the fact that Kazakhs, Uzbeks, Kirgiz, etc., do not constitute a majority of the students in the institutions of higher learning in their republic may simply reflect their presence in the educational institutions of other republics, particularly the Russian, whose centers of learning are essentially all-union in character. It also reflects the presence of sizable national minorities in the republic as well.

The more denationalized and "inter-nationalized" the republican institutions become, the more necessary it becomes to use Russian, the language of "inter-nationality communication," as the chief language of instruction. And, the more non-Russians enter institutions outside their republic, the more likely they are to become Russified. "Inter-nationalization" in this case means essentially Russification of the student body, and this remains the normative goal of the regime.[33]

The degree to which the republican institutions have been "inter-nationalized" can only be approximated since the regime has not released data on the national distribution of students by republics. However, a comparison of total student enrollments in republics with the total number of students of a given nationality will at least demonstrate the minimum dimensions of the "inter-nationalization" process. This is shown in Table 5.

Since the actual national composition of students in republican institutions of higher learning is not available, Table 5 can show only the minimum degree to which republican educational institutions have been "inter-nationalized." In all cases the nonindigenous share of the enrollment is actually much higher, and all Soviet institutions of higher learning have been "inter-nationalized," including those in the R.S.F.S.R. and the Armenian Republic.

The erosion of national languages. Traditionally the most durable and conspicuous evidence of national identity is language. While the adoption of another nationality does not immediately or necessarily result in a change of national identity, especially if other variables such as race, religion, culture, or geographic

TABLE 5

NATIONAL COMPOSITION OF REPUBLICAN INSTITUTIONS
OF HIGHER LEARNING BY MAJOR NATIONALITIES—1965[34]

By Republic	Total Institutions, 1965	Enrollment, 1965	Per Cent of Total, 1965	By Nationality	Total Enrollment, 1965	Per Cent of Total, 1965	Minimum Per Cent of Non-indigenous Students Enrollment in Republic	Non-indigenous Per Cent of Population[a]
R.S.F.S.R.	432	2,353,900	60.9	Russians	2,362,000	61.1	—	16.8
Ukrainian	132	690,000	17.8	Ukrainians	558,600	14.4	19.1	23.9
Byelorussian	27	104,000	2.6	Byelorussians	114,600	2.9	—	20.0
Uzbek	32	165,800	4.2	Uzbeks	95,600	2.4	42.4	38.0
Kazakh	39	144,700	3.7	Kazakhs	69,900	1.8	51.7	69.3
Georgian	18	76,600	1.9	Georgians	70,100	1.8	8.5	38.7
Azerbaidzhani	11	67,000	1.7	Azerbaidzhanis	54,000	1.3	19.5	32.9
Lithuanian	11	46,400	1.2	Lithuanians	42,800	1.1	7.8	20.7
Moldavian	7	36,300	.9	Moldavians	22,900	.5	37.0	34.6
Latvian	10	33,100	.8	Latvians	21,400	.5	35.4	38.0
Kirgiz	8	32,200	.8	Kirgiz	16,200	.4	49.7	59.5
Tadzhik	7	30,400	.7	Tadzhiks	17,500	.4	42.5	46.9
Armenian	11	38,900	1.0	Armenians	61,800	1.6	—	12.0
Turkmen	5	19,800	.5	Turkmen	15,600	.4	21.3	39.1
Estonian	6	21,400	.5	Estonians	18,800	.4	12.2	26.1
				Jews	94,600	2.4	—	—
				Tatars	67,700	1.7	—	—
Total	756	3,860,000	100.0	Total	3,860,000	100.0		

[a] According to census of 1959.

location remain distinctive, a change in language is a *sine qua non*. This is particularly true in the Soviet Union, where more than 10 million non-Russians reported Russian as their mother tongue in the 1959 census. Also, some 230,000 Russians gave a language other than Russian as their native language, which suggests that some de-Russification also still takes place, probably as a result of intermarriage.

The proportion of a given nationality adopting Russian as its mother tongue is an important index of Russification and, when correlated with cultural, educational, and geographical variables, may help assess relative national immunity or exposure to Russification. The 1959 census reported that 124.6 million people, of whom 10.2 million were non-Russian, gave Russian as their mother tongue.[35] But the number of individuals who gave some language other than that of their nationality as their mother tongue totalled 11.9 million, which indicates that more than 1.7 million people reported some language other than Russian as their new mother tongue.

The reported data do not enable us to calculate the number or percentage of all nationalities who chose Russian rather than some other language as their new tongue. A substantial proportion of those who chose a language other than Russian as their mother tongue probably represents the assimilation of kindred cultural or linguistic minorities: Poles in Byelorussia and the Ukraine; the reciprocal assimilation of Turkic groups in Central Asia; and Armenians in Georgia, but probably not in Azerbaidzhan. The Jews, nearly 80 per cent of whom reported a language other than Yiddish as their mother tongue, may also, particularly in the Ukraine, have adopted a language other than Russian as their mother tongue.

With these reservations in mind we shall assume that the percentage of a given nationality which gave a language other than its own as its new mother tongue provides us with a reliable guide to the relative immunity of various nationalities to national erosion and Russification. The range for the major nationalities is wide, spreading from 79.2 per cent for the Jews to 1.1 for the Turkmen. The immunity index of the Central Asians is particularly high, with no nationality having more than 2 per cent of its population reporting a nonindigenous native language. This suggests that the Central Asian resistance to Russification may be complemented by a refusal of Russians to accept Central Asians as Russians. The statistical data represent, however, more the denationalization of

Central Asian territories than the Russification of their population.

Identical statistical trends may in some cases not represent the same sociological consequences, since relative immunity to Russification depends upon certain qualitative variables, which cannot always be accurately quantified. Jews, Georgians, and Armenians, for example, have demonstrated for many centuries that they can preserve national identity in the face of both blandishments and persecution, and that a change in language need not indicate a loss of national identity.

The relationship between Russianization and Russification thus varies from nationality to nationality. Russianization for the kindred Ukrainians and Byelorussians can very easily pass over to Russification, whereas for the Central Asians it is more likely to be a terminal process rather than a prelude to Russification, which might take many generations. Byelorussians and Ukrainians living outside their own republic are viewed by other nationalities as indistinguishable from Russians.

Of the two, the Byelorussians are the most feebly developed as a nation and can hardly be accounted a "historic" nationality. They are barely distinguishable from the Russians, and their language can just as well be called as a dialect of Russian as a separate language. It is therefore not surprising that the Byelorussians show the highest rate of Russification of any major territorial nationality. The 1959 census reported that 16 per cent of the Byelorussians (1,250,000) gave another language as their mother tongue, and this was undoubtedly Russian in virtually all cases.

The Ukrainians are more numerous and have a more strongly developed sense of national identity, yet they represented the largest share, in absolute numbers (4.6 million), of the non-Russians who reported Russian as their mother tongue and ranked second in percentage (12.4). Thus, out of a total of 10.2 million non-Russians who gave Russian as their mother tongue, more than half were Ukrainians and Byelorussians. (This erosion is far more serious for the Byelorussians than for the Ukrainians, since it is conceivable that the former may rapidly disappear as a distinct nationality, whereas the Ukrainians are in no immediate danger.)

Russianization poses little immediate threat to the national identity of the Georgians and Armenians, or to the Lithuanians, Latvians, Estonians, and Azerbaidzhanis, whose sense of national consciousness, linguistic, cultural, and historical heritage is suffi-

cient to allow a wide latitude of Russianization without Russification. In the case of the Armenians and Georgians, Russianization
might even approach Russification in the statistical sense, but still
be wide of the mark in the psychological or subjective sense. Thus,
while 10.0 per cent of the Armenians gave some language other
than their own as their mother tongue (8.3 per cent Russian),
ranking them third in this index, this is accounted for by the fact
that 44 per cent or 1,235,000 of the Armenians live outside the
Armenian Republic, which probably means that a higher proportion of Armenians than any other non-Russian nationality attend
Russian-language schools. On the other hand, the Armenian Republic is the most indigenous of the republics, with 88 per cent
of the population Armenian, which means Armenians in the
republic are among the most immune to Russification while those
outside are among the most likely to suffer loss of national identity.
Georgians and Armenians, among the non-Slavic nationalities, are
thus probably least resistant to Russianization but among the most
highly resistant to Russification. Russianization for Georgians and
Armenians has resulted in greater opportunities and advantages
for individuals of the two nationalities than for any other of the
non-Slavic groups.

National erosion in Central Asia. Russification has proceeded at
a much slower pace in the Central Asian republics, and Russianization is more likely to denationalize the Central Asian areas and
to erode the national identity of their populations than to Russify
them. Of the four major Turkic nationalities, only the Uzbeks
have a strongly developed sense of national identity. The Kazakhs
and Kirgiz were nomadic conglomerations of tribes until very
recently, while the Turkmen are very small in numbers. The
national consciousness of these three Turkic nationalities is only
feebly developed and, under the impact of accelerated Russianization, is likely to be arrested and perhaps crumble. Their existence
as separate nations was largely synthetic and artificial to begin with,
and it is the conviction of many observers that the four could have
and should have been molded within the framework of a single
Turkic nationality, probably the Uzbek.[36]

While the fragmentation of the Central Asian Turks may have
served a useful political purpose, it is at least arguable that the
Bolsheviks were motivated in part by their stated aim of politically
and psychologically emancipating the other Central Asian national-

ities, including the non-Turkic Tadzhiks, from the ruling grip of the powerful Uzbeks. The creation of four Turkic nations instead of one has admirably achieved this objective, without however, creating four equally viable nations. Since Stalin's death, and particularly under Khrushchev's leadership, the Uzbeks have experienced a national resurgence and are now being encouraged to play a leading role in Central Asia. Two Uzbeks, Mukhitdinov and Rashidov, and one Kazakh, D. A. Kunayev, have achieved all-union prominence as members of the party Politburo and Secretariat; both Uzbeks, particularly Rashidov, played a conspicuous role in Soviet diplomacy among the Asian and African states.[37]

In fact, some critics inside and outside the Soviet Union viewed Khrushchev's creation of a Central Asian Regional Economic Council and a Central Asian Party Bureau as devices for eroding national distinctiveness in the region. While this centralization would undoubtedly strengthen Moscow's grip, it would also strengthen the position of the Uzbeks. If the national identities of the Central Asian Turks are eroded, they are more likely to be converted into Uzbeks than Russians or simply into denationalized, Russianized Turks, without any distinctive national spirit.

The Tadzhiks, who reflect a higher sense of national identity because of their isolation among the Central Asian Turks, are also more tolerant of Russianization, although they view the Russians with a certain degree of ambivalence—as their liberators and protectors against the Turks, especially the Uzbeks, but also as a barrier to communication and contact with their ethnic and cultural kinsmen in Iran and Afghanistan.

The presence of large numbers of Russians in the non-Russian republics is often cited arbitrarily as an index of Russianization or Russification. Actually, the effects of the Russian presence vary from one republic to another, depending upon the other variables we have examined. It undoubtedly facilitates both processes in Byelorussia and the Ukraine, and facilitates Russianization in the Baltic states and the Caucasus (though without seriously eroding their national identities). In the Kazakh and Kirgiz republics the consequences are more severe. Both republics have been effectively denationalized to the point that the Kazakh and Kirgiz account for only 30 and 40 per cent of the population respectively in the republics that now inappropriately bear their names; reality has outdistanced both the Soviet theory of national sovereignty and the juridical norms of the constitution, and Soviet jurists concede the need for constitutional revisions, even though they are not in full agreement as to the direction this revision should take.

Table 6 summarizes some of the variables which reflect the Russianization and Russification of the union republics and the non-Russian nationalities; on the basis of the data summarized there, one can appreciate the complicated and complex processes at work and the contradictory trends in operation for particular nationalities.

As a general rule, national immunity is maximized when the nationality in question is concentrated in its own republic and constitutes the overwhelming proportion of its republic's population. Non-Russians living outside their republic are likely to exhibit less immunity than those living in their own republic. Furthermore, republics having large numbers of Russian residents will show a higher rate of denationalization than those which are nationally homogenous. And finally, the closer the nationality is to the Great Russians linguistically, physically, and culturally, the greater its rate of Russianization and Russification.

These relationships are also borne out by data recently released by the Soviet regime. Table 7, for example, shows that only the Ukrainians and Byelorussians reported less than 98 per cent of their nationals giving their own language as their mother tongue, whereas nationals living outside their republics exhibit a wide range of susceptibility to denationalization. About half of all Ukrainians (48.8), Byelorussians (58.1), Latvians (46.8), and Estonians (43.4) living outside their republics offered Russian as their mother language.

Intermarriage and Russification. In the past, intermarriage has been only a marginal vehicle of Russification, but with the progressive Russianization of the population, the Russification of the non-Russian elites, the penetration of the non-Russian republics by Russian settlers, and the steady urbanization of the country, intermarriage is likely to increase and to become an important factor in Russification. Hard data on intermarriage are scarce and fragmentary; but since the regime has discovered the potentialities of intermarriage, Soviet sociologists are demonstrating greater interest in it as an object of study. Intermarriage is described favorably as both a product and a further impetus to the fusion and amalgamation of nationalities. (In almost all instances it facili-

TABLE 6

INDICES OF RUSSIANIZATION AND RUSSIFICATION OF MAJOR NATIONALITIES[38]

Republic and/or Nationality	Population, 1959	Per Cent Indigenous	Per Cent Russian	Dispersal Indices				Russian as Mother Language (10,300,000 in 1959)			
				Total Nationality	Per Cent in own Republic	Per Cent outside Republic	Number Dispersed	Number	Per Cent of Total	Per Cent of Nationality 1959	1939
Ukrainian	41,869,000	76.1	17.1	36,981,000	86.2	13.8	5,129,000	4,585,644	38.50	12.4 (12.2)	8.8
Byelorussian	8,055,000	80.0	9.1	7,829,000	82.3	17.7	1,385,000	1,244,811	10.45	15.9 (15.3)	12.7
Uzbek	8,106,000	62.0	13.6	6,004,000	85.6	16.4	988,000	96,064	.08	1.6	0.4
Kazakh	9,310,000	29.6	43.1	3,581,000	77.0	23.0	826,000	57,296	.48	1.4 (1.2)	0.9
Georgian	4,044,000	63.3	10.8	2,650,000	96.5	3.5	92,000	37,100	.40	1.4 (1.3)	0.5
Azerbaidzhani	3,698,000	67.1	13.9	2,929,000	84.6	14.4	448,000	70,296	.70	2.4 (1.2)	
Lithuanian	2,711,000	79.3	8.5	2,326,000	92.4	7.6	175,000	51,172	.43	2.2	
Moldavian	2,885,000	65.4	10.2	2,214,000	85.3	14.8	327,000	106,272	.89	4.8	
Latvian	2,093,000	62.0	26.6	1,400,000	92.8	7.2	102,000	68,600	.58	4.9	
Kirgiz	2,066,000	40.5	30.2	969,000	76.4	13.6	132,000	12,597	.11	1.3	
Tadzhik	1,980,000	53.3	13.3	1,397,000	75.3	24.7	346,000	26,543	.23	1.9	
Armenian	1,763,000	88.0	3.2	2,787,000	55.9	44.1	1,235,000	281,487	2.36	10.1 (8.3)	
Turkmen	1,516,000	60.9	17.3	1,004,000	92.0	8.0	80,000	11,044	.09	1.1	
Estonian	1,197,000	72.9	21.7	989,000	88.3	11.7	116,000	48,461	.41	4.9	
Others				—				3,795,344	31.88		
(Jews)	2,680,000							1,796,200	15.10	79.2 (76.4)	54.6
(Tatars)	4,969,000							—	—	7.9 (7.0)	2.6
(Germans)	1,619,000							—	—	25.0	
(Chuvash)	1,470,000							—	—	9.2 (9.0)	3.1
(Poles)	1,380,000							—	—	45.5	
(Mordvins)	1,285,000							—	—	21.9 (21.8)	11.3
(Bashkirs)	983,000							—	—	38.3 (2.6)	0.6

TABLE 7

PER CENT OF NATIONALITY REPORTING THEIR OWN LANGUAGE
AS THEIR MOTHER TONGUE[39]

Nationality	In Own Republic (Ranking)	Outside Own Republic (Ranking)
Ukrainian	93.5 (2)	51.2 (2)
Byelorussian	93.2 (1)	41.9 (1)
Uzbek	98.6 (6)	97.4 (14)
Kazakh	99.2 (9)	95.6 (13)
Georgian	99.5 (12)	73.4 (5)
Azerbaidzhani	98.1 (3)	95.1 (12)
Lithuanian	99.2 (8)	80.3 (8)
Moldavian	98.2 (4)	77.7 (6)
Latvian	98.4 (5)	53.2 (3)
Kirgiz	99.7 (14)	92.3 (10)
Tadzhik	99.3 (11)	94.6 (11)
Armenian	99.2 (7)	78.1 (7)
Turkmen	99.5 (13)	92.0 (9)
Estonian	99.3 (10)	56.6 (4)
....*	....	....
Tatar	98.9	91.1
Bashkir	57.6	75.6
Mordvin	97.3	72.7
Chuvash	97.5	84.7

* The last four nationalities are principally settled in autonomous regions.

tates the spread of Russian as the internationality language of the Soviet Union.)[40]

Mixed marriages have been on the upswing in the Soviet Union since World War II and are likely to increase as a counterpart of the Russianization and Russification processes, increased schooling, and a growing intelligentsia. One immediate result will be the number of non-Russians who will give Russian as their mother tongue in future census reports. As their number increases, pressures will probably develop to permit Soviet citizens to formalize a change in their nationality and have it officially recorded in their passports, in which case the Russification processes will have been legally achieved. If this happens, the number of non-Russians giving Russian as their tongue may remain relatively static and perhaps even decrease, whereas the number of citizens reporting Russian as their nationality will correspondingly increase. In all reported cases, the percentage of non-Russians who gave Russian as their mother tongue in the 1959 census increased substantially over that of 1939.

IV. The Soviet Union as a Multinational Sociopolitical System

The Soviet multinational state, as a sociopolitical system, has been subjected to characterizations ranging from condemnation as a colonial empire to glorification as a model of multinational, multiracial harmony. This disparity is due, at least in part, to the fact that the Soviet system has been in flux since its inception five decades ago, and not always moving in a single direction. Like other aspects of Soviet life, the multinational system has moved through a number of phases, each marked by its own peculiar characteristics. The system and the policy must be examined as dynamically evolving phenomena.

The Soviet Union has undergone three distinct phases in its evolution as a multinational state, and is now well along in the fourth. While each phase has been accompanied by an evolutionary change in the juridical and constitutional structure of the state, the phases are not defined in terms of these formal alternations, but rather by the content of Soviet nationality policy.

The first period, 1917–28, was characterized by the organization of the Soviet state into a formal federal system designed to liberate the non-Russian nationalities psychologically and physically from Russian domination. It was marked primarily by a deliberate policy of restraining and curtailing the natural tendency of the Russians to assume dominance in the new state and simultaneously encouraging the non-Russian nationalities to assume greater responsibility and power. Great Russian chauvinism was considered the main danger to the Soviet order and, while local nationalism was frowned upon, it was nevertheless indirectly encouraged by the regime. During this period, however, the Soviet Union was still largely an illiterate, economically and culturally retarded, agrarian, polyglot state. Vast social, cultural, and political voids separated the various nationalities, who were equal only in the most formal sense. The Russians were the most numerous, the most advanced culturally and economically, and the most habituated to political rule. But, under circumstances in which their natural superiority was artificially suppressed and other nationalities were encouraged to come forward, a curious, limited, authentic multinational sociopolitical system soon materialized.

It soon became evident that an authentic multinational sociopolitical system would be impossible unless there was an approxi-

mate economic and cultural equality among the various nationalities. The second period, 1929–36, was characterized by vigorous
efforts to modernize the underdeveloped nationalities. The Soviet
regime chose more advanced nationalities to act as tutors. As the
most numerous, the Russians inevitably contributed the largest
number of tutors, but the presence of large numbers of non-Russians somewhat mitigated the appearance of a revived Great Russian colonialism. Russians, Jews, Georgians, Armenians, Ukrainians,
and Balts assumed key positions in many of the underdeveloped
republics, usually in secondary administrative positions, where
the real power was vested, rather than in the formal posts occupied
by indigenous leaders. The ruling Communist Party was a genuine
multinational ruling elite, but again highly selective and not always
indigenous to the particular republic. It was thus not a precise
microcosmic reflection of the multinational spectrum of the Soviet
population. Indeed, the well-known failure of Stalinist policy to re-
shape dedicated indigenous Communists out of former "bourgeois
nationalists" led, by 1936, to an apparent revival of the Russian
Empire in Soviet form.

The decapitation of the indigenous leadership of the non-Russian republics signaled the inauguration of the third, or "Russianization," phase, which continued from 1936 until Stalin's death in
1953. The least understood period in the development of Soviet
nationality policy, it is primarily responsible for the characteriza-
tion of the Soviet Union as a Russian colonial empire. An essentially transitory phase in the evolution of the Soviet state was
mistakenly assumed to be a terminal phase, and the sharp departure in political policy from the pre-1936 period effectively obscured the uninterrupted continuity in social and economic policies
which were to have long-range implications for the evolution of
the Soviet multinational state into a multinational commonwealth.

Three sub-phases of the period (prewar, war, and postwar) constituted a distinct escalation in the Russification of the Soviet
political order, but not necessarily the *social* system. As a result
of the pre-1936 experience, Stalin was thoroughly disenchanted
with the prospect of a quick materialization of reliable national
cadres. The Soviet generation would still take some time to mature.
Hence, this consummate specialist on the nationalities question
shrewdly reasoned that Sovietization in the non-Russian areas
would have to be executed principally by Russians and nonindigenous cadres. Stalin decided to shift the *national* base of his sup-

port to the Russian nation, since it was to become the national instrument of Sovietization. Inevitably, this meant Russianization, and even some Russification. (The Cyrillization of the non-Russian languages was carried out during the prewar sub-phase.)

Stalin's secondary *national* base was the Caucasus, since Georgia and Armenia were the only two countries which Stalin felt could be reliably governed by their own indigenous elites. They, like the Russian nation, were particularly favored during this period, and some of the favoritism rubbed off on neighboring Moslem Azerbaidzhan. Georgia and Armenia supplied large contingents of loyal Stalinists to serve in his various apparatuses throughout the country. The secret police, for example, was virtually "Caucasianized" by Stalin's compatriot L. P. Beria, as Georgians, Armenians, and some Azerbaidzhanis assumed key positions in the Soviet secret police empire.[41]

It should be emphasized, however, that the basic Soviet social and economic policy of modernizing the underdeveloped nationalities continued without serious interruption or deviation. The various republics were industrialized and urbanized; more and more indigenous children were enrolled in schools; and a new Soviet-educated native intelligentsia was slowly and painfully squeezed through Russianization and Russification screens. But Stalin was implacable in denying the indigenous nationalities any kind of real *political* autonomy, and the formula "national in form, socialist in content" was ruthlessly executed. Local nationalism of any kind was ruthlessly stamped out, as were anti-Russian sentiments and condemnations of Great Russian chauvinism.

This was one aspect of the Great Purge trials of the 1930s when non-Russian party and administrative leaders in all of the non-Russian republics were purged, incarcerated, or executed on sundry charges of "bourgeois nationalism," secessionist aspirations, and collusion with the enemies of the Soviet Union. The purges reached their climax in 1938 when the two Uzbek leaders, Faizulla Khodzhayev (Chairman of the Uzbek Council of People's Commissars) and Akmal Ikramov (First Secretary of the Uzbek Communist Party), K. C. Rakovsky and G. F. Grinko of the Ukraine, and V. F. Sharangovich of the Byelorussian Republic were tried along with Bukharin and the "Rightists" and executed for alleged treason and separatist activities. The indictment implicated local leaders in virtually all ten of the non-Russian republics which had been established by the new Soviet Constitution only two years earlier. Since Sovietization in Central Asia and other underdeveloped republics was carried out principally by Russians and Russianized non-Russians from other regions, and the Moslem religion was suppressed by nominal Christians, Islamic culture was subjugated to Russian, and local nationalism was stifled by alien bureaucrats assigned by Moscow; Sovietization, so far as the natives and the outside world were concerned, was indistinguishable from colonialism, a fact which Stalin himself periodically noted with distress and chagrin.

The German attack on the Soviet Union served to accelerate and intensify the trends which were set into motion before 1936. It was more essential than ever to secure the absolute loyalty of the Russian population, the most numerous of the nationalities and the backbone of the Soviet armed forces. The war period witnessed a positive glorification of Russia and a powerful resurgence of Great Russian nationalism in all aspects of Soviet life. After the war, the glorification of Russia was not much toned down, but the Marxist-Leninist norms of Soviet life, which had been relatively de-emphasized, were revived with renewed force. Marxism-Leninism-Stalinism was emphatically transformed into Russified Marxism. At the same time, it must again be emphasized that, even under Stalin in the postwar period, the social and economic modernization of the underdeveloped republics was stepped up. During the war, when the western territories of the Soviet Union were devastated, the Caucasian and Central Asian republics experienced accelerated development. While this intensified indigenous political development in the Caucasus, it resulted in accelerated Russian political control in Central Asia because of the large influx of refugees from the west. The industrialization of the Central Asian republics brought in hordes of Russians to the metropolitan centers, just as collectivization earlier had resulted in decimating the nomadic Kazakhs and repopulating their lands with Ukrainian peasants deported from the west. But by the time of Stalin's death, a new generation of Central Asians had matured under Soviet rule, a comparatively young and reliable group of native leaders had been recruited. They were Russianized and bilingual; and while probably not completely immune from infectious local nationalism, they seemed to have a greater stake in the Soviet system than in separatism.

The death of Stalin inaugurated the fourth and current phase: transformation of a Soviet Russian empire-state into an authentic multinational, multilingual, federal commonwealth, preparatory to its conversion into a Russianized unilingual, multinational, *unitary* commonwealth.

Beria was the first of the post-Stalin leaders to perceive that the nationalities had come of age: their dissatisfactions and latent national resentments provided a possible power base from which to move against his rivals. Molotov, Kaganovich, Malenkov, and the "anti-party group," if Khrushchev can be believed, still viewed the non-Russian cadres as unreliable and opposed giving them more political responsibility and power, locally as well as in all-union affairs. Among the charges leveled against Beria after his arrest was that he sought to mobilize the non-Russians against the Russians:

> Beria and his accomplices undertook criminal measures in order to stir up the remains of bourgeois-nationalist elements in the union republics, to sow enmity and discord among the peoples of the U.S.S.R. and, in the first place, to undermine the friendship of the peoples of the U.S.S.R. with the Great Russian people.[42]

On the other hand, it was charged four years later that the anti-party group sought to preserve the national *status quo* and opposed a greater role and participation of the nationalities in the Soviet system:

> They were against the extension of the rights of the union republics in the sphere of economic and cultural development and in the sphere of legislation and against enhancing the role of the local Soviets in the fulfillment of these tasks. Thereby, the anti-party group resisted the party's firm course toward the more rapid development of economy and culture in the national republics, a course ensuring the further promotion of Leninist friendship between all peoples of our country.[43]

And at the Twenty-First Party Congress, the Uzbek leader N. A. Mukhitdinov charged: "The anti-party group . . . showed elements of [Great Russian] chauvinism and did not believe in the ability of the cadres of the national republics to solve tasks of the state."[44]

Khrushchev and his successors appear to have adopted a policy midway between the extremes of complete national autonomy and nonindigenous control: to steer a prudent course between the vices of "local nationalism" and the excesses of Great Russian chauvinism. The key elements in this policy are: (1) to strike a more equitable numerical balance among the nationalities in the distribution of posts in the structure of Soviet power; and (2) to enhance

and expand the authority and responsibilities of the national republics. The national elites will increasingly assume greater direction of their national republics and at the same time become
co-opted and more fully integrated into a multinational all-union
ruling elite. Simultaneously, however, the Russianization of the
multinational commonwealth and the multinationalization of the
union republics have also been accelerated.

V. Reconciling Ideology, Russian Nationalism, and Local Nationalism

The modernization and industrialization of Soviet society has
not only introduced a new system of social stratification and created
a new urban-rural equilibrium, but also altered the social equilibrium among the various nationalities. The Soviet political structure
is only now beginning to reflect these changes in the basic social
and national distribution of power and influence. The changing
nationality equilibrium is reflected first in the shifting relationship between Russians and non-Russians, and among the non-
Russian nationalities. During the current phase in the evolution of
the Soviet multinational state, when national distinctions are still
conspicuous (even while eroding and withering in the face of Russianization and Russification), two basic trends reveal themselves:
(1) the steady and disproportionate increase of Russian participation and influence in all sectors of Soviet life; and (2) a move
toward proportionate participation and influence for the other nationalities (except possibly for the Byelorussians and Ukrainians,
who will be encouraged to Russify themselves). The first trend
establishes Russia as *primus inter pares* in the union during the
transition, while emphasizing the direction in which the Soviet
multinational state is ultimately moving; the second stresses the
principle of national equality, or proportionate balance, as long as
national distinctions continue.

Since the Soviet Union no longer conceives of itself as an
embryonic universal state, its ultimate transformation into a terminal, multinational, unilingual commonwealth deprives it of its
former open-ended imperialistic character. With the transformation of the Soviet state into such a multinational unilingual commonwealth, the importance of separate national republics will
diminish significantly. The implications of such a development are
already being examined by Soviet jurists from a variety of perspectives.

The nationalities now enjoy some latitude in registering their national demands upon the system and upon one another. They can legitimately demand greater representation in local and national organs and institutions of the state and party, greater local control over their own national territories, greater investment and resource allocations for services and enterprises in their national locality, and territorial adjustments and claims against other national republics or foreign states. So long as these demands threaten neither the social imperatives of the system nor the external security and territorial integrity of the Soviet Union, they are considered legitimate expressions of national interest. Their realization, however, will continue to depend upon the leverage which each nationality can command, and the degree to which national demands impinge upon the interests of purely social constituencies, particularly the elites.

In recent years, the Soviet government has tried deliberately to eliminate points of friction where the interests of social constituencies intersect with those of national constituencies. The major evidence of this sensitivity to national interests has been the national quota system, which the Soviet regime has been adopting, formally and informally, in recruiting and staffing state and party institutions from top to bottom; in the enrollment of students in institutions of higher learning; and in the periodic adjustments of territorial claims between various national units. The tendency, then, has been to establish proportional national representation in all political and social institutions. The tempo with which this is accomplished varies among individual nationalities in accordance with their significance, size, and development, as well as the degree to which their interests serve the higher social, foreign policy, and security interests of the state.

The interests of the basic social constituencies—namely, the various functional elite groups—continue, however, to enjoy the highest priority in the decisions and policies of the Soviet Union. Consequently, it is the social elite groups within the various nationalities who are likely to benefit most immediately from the new nationality policy. By according the social elites greater influence and participation on the local and national level, the Soviet regime hopes to raise their "loyalty calculus" by creating a bond of common interest among the elites of various nationalities stronger than the bonds among different social classes of the same nationality. Given its ultimate social and ideological goals, the regime hopes that, as social classes are progressively eliminated and all Soviet citizens are raised to the status now enjoyed only by the social elites, national borders and distinctions will gradually decline in importance, and nationalism will automatically lose its force. It is in this spirit that one must interpret the 1961 Program of the CPSU:

> The boundaries between the union republics of the U.S.S.R. are increasingly losing their significance. . . . Full-scale Communist construction constitutes a new stage in the development of national relations in the U.S.S.R., in which the nationals will draw still closer together until complete union is achieved. . . . Communism will call for still greater interconnection and mutual assistance between the Soviet republics. The closer the intercourse between the nations and the greater the awareness of country-wide tasks, the more successfully can manifestations of parochialism and national egoism be overcome. . . . There is a growing ideological unity among the nations and nationalities and a greater *rapprochement* of their cultures. . . . An international culture common to all Soviet nations is developing.[45]

Switzerland has demonstrated rather effectively that a multinational state based upon a common economic interest can inspire a loyalty which prevails over centrifugal loyalties, but this was accomplished without the extinction of national identity or the imposition of a common language. The United States, on the other hand, has demonstrated that it is possible to forge a new nation by transforming the national identity of millions of citizens of a score of different nationalities, by imposing a common language and culture and thus inspiring a loyalty to the new nation stronger than the old loyalties. The American nationalities, however, were uprooted and transplanted from their national patrimony, and this may have been the decisive factor. It is noteworthy that the Americanization process has been least successful where it affects indigenous and territorially rooted American nationalities such as the Indians, Mexicans, and Puerto Ricans.

The Soviet Union aims to forge a new nation out of more than a score of indigenous nationalities; that is, to effect a transformation similar to that of the United States by imposing a common language and culture upon nationalities rooted, however, in their own national territories, like those of Switzerland. Unlike the latter, which considers itself a permanent multinational state, or the United States, which has never considered itself a multinational state, the Soviet Union considers itself to be a transitional multinational, multilingual state which will ultimately fuse into a unilingual state. Whether the Soviet objective succeeds or not depends upon whether the nationalities can be persuaded that it is more in their interest to give up than to preserve their national identities, and this is by no means a certainty. The evolution of the Soviet multinational state is sure to provide some surprises as the nationalities respond to evolving policies with a curious and ambivalent mixture of acceptance and resistance. If the amalgamation process is pressed too fast, it may intensify rather than attenuate local nationalism among some nationalities. In any event, the nationalities are bound to respond and react unevenly, with the balance between acceptance and resistance varying considerably from one nationality to another.

PART THREE

Resources and Their Management

Introduction

The question of productive resources is not only of obvious long-range significance, but, of all the problems currently facing the Soviet leadership, is also of the most immediate urgency. It is no exaggeration to say that a series of gross failures in the economic realm would place the entire political structure in jeopardy in short order, while an economy of abundance and a rising standard of living would go far toward easing tensions in noneconomic areas as well. In the long run, too, the success or failure of the economy will play a determining role in whether or not the party can retain the bases of authority essential to carrying out its wider domestic aims and maintaining its international position.

One problem that the Soviet Union has not had to face—in contrast with many other latecomers to industrialization—is the pressure of overpopulation combined with a shortage of natural resources. Moreover, the relative underemployment of the rural sector has provided a pool of cheap and abundant manpower that could be diverted to the growth of industry. In recent years, however, the Soviet leadership has been required to act with increasing discrimination in exploiting its demographic resources as the size of the population and its rates of growth begin to stabilize, and as the quality of manpower becomes more relevant than its numerical supply alone. Flexibility in this area is of course limited to some extent by essentially biological factors which policy can affect only indirectly and over long periods of time. But how the regime uses what is available to it, how it educates the population, and how it deploys its manpower resources are weighty and immediate matters of public policy. Warren Eason's detailed analysis of the Soviet population sets forth the potentials and limitations that Soviet society now faces as it moves into the future.

The performance of industry and agriculture is directly affected by official policy, probably more so than any other sector of Soviet life. The degree of central control which has emerged in Soviet economic patterns has been historically a major source of mobilizational strength and no doubt is partly responsible for the sometimes spectacular growth of the Soviet economy since the First Five Year Plan. On the other hand, the relative inflexibility, which has also been a part of those patterns (because of both organizational inertia and a highly restrictive economic ideology), raises serious doubts about the ability of the Soviet Union to sustain the level of past performances. Arcadius Kahan and Herbert Levine, for agriculture and industry, respectively, examine the causes of the current economic impasse, evaluate the probable effects of reforms which are under way, and offer prognoses for the further course of the Soviet economy.

Two areas in which the Soviet system has demonstrated impressive strength are education and science. Indeed, given the nature of modern technology, how effectively an advanced society nurtures and uses such resources will largely determine its domestic vitality and its competitive position among nations. It is no wonder that the West, and America in particular, reacts so sensitively to cues about the state of affairs in Soviet science and education or that this concern should lead alternately to over- and underevaluations of actual Soviet accomplishments. William Medlin's contribution is an assessment of present conditions and future prospects for Soviet education at all levels, while Alexander Vucinich provides a comprehensive survey of the many branches of Soviet science and technology and their probable development over the coming decades.

8.

Population Changes

WARREN W. EASON

The Khrushchev era was relatively brief, demographically speaking. But it is an important era through which to approach the broad subject of the interrelationships between demographic variables and the processes of economic and social change: first, because of secular demographic trends related to the process of development which began to be evident in the 1950s; second, because of the population "data explosion," centered around publication of the results of the 1959 census, which is still continuing; and third, because Soviet demographers themselves have begun to give much more attention to questions of this type than at any other time since the 1920s.

These considerations enable us to reach certain conclusions about Soviet population changes over the past thirty-five years (from the start of rapid industrialization), and also to make something more than wild guesses about the next thirty-five years (to the year 2000).

It will hardly be possible to deal systematically or comprehensively with all questions under this heading. A number of them, however, seem particularly worthy of attention in view of their implications for economic development in the future; these are the questions related to the pattern of growth of the population and the size and structure of the labor force. Prospective trends, it will be shown, embody important elements of continuity with the past, a reflection in part of the very nature of the demographic process; but they also embody elements of change. The rate at which some of these changes will take place, moreover, may turn out to be more rapid and accentuated than is generally appreciated, in which case the implications for economic and social development may be correspondingly more profound.

The prospective trends themselves are set forth below. Questions of particular interest related to the trends are grouped under two broad headings:

1. As far as the *pattern of population growth* itself is concerned, the principal questions are addressed to the nature of the underlying factors affecting such crucial variables as the fertility rate, and the role of government policies designed to influence these variables. It is easier to say how Soviet demographers conceive of these questions than it is to report on their answers, because the demographers have, in fact, only begun to give the matter serious attention. Nevertheless, by combining their tentative views with our own interpretation and projection of the data, some indication of possibilities for the future can be given. The results are interesting for what they suggest about social and cultural forces that have already influenced the pattern of Soviet population growth and, since these forces have probably not yet had their full effect, for what they suggest about future trends.

2. As far as the *implications of population growth for economic and social change* are concerned, it should be recognized, first, that the Khrushchev era signaled the start of a period of transition in Soviet economic development that is still unfolding. It is a period of transition from an earlier stage of development, where human resources are "abundant" (initially even redundant) relative to other factors of production and where labor productivity is low, to a later stage where human resources are relatively "scarce" and labor productivity high. These changing relationships are fundamental to the growth process itself, but their appearance is more evident in the Soviet case.

Among the reasons for this, a factor of short duration is the sharp decline in the rate of growth of the population of working age which took place when the "war babies" became of age during the early 1960s. Factors of longer duration continuing into the future include the following: On the demand side, there is the planned growth of the economy, the development of heretofore neglected and underpopulated regions of the country,[1] and the systematic introduction into production of higher levels of technology and more complex organizational forms. On the supply side, there is the emergence of forces that are leading inexorably to a slowing down in the rate of growth of the total and the nonagricultural labor force, and that are leading also, for the first time on a continuing basis, to an absolute decline in the agricultural labor force. Depending on assumptions about the fertility of the population over the near term, these changes in supply could become especially marked during the late 1980s and 1990s.

The pressures and forces implied by these developments are already making themselves felt in policies which recognize the increasing value of the human contribution to production and which are addressed to the problem of raising the "quality" of human resources and of increasing the effectiveness with which they are joined to the work process.[2] These policies include: (a) a sharply stepped-up rate of increase of the system of vocational and semiprofessional education, together with the continued growth of professional education; (b) the redoubling of efforts to raise the quality of education at all levels; (c) greatly increased attention to the problem of "full employment," and to the more effective (re)distribution of the labor force (and population) by area, branch, and occupation; and (d) the widespread discussion and the implementation of reforms of the economic system and of methods of planning, administration, and management.

These policies in and of themselves have far-reaching implications, not only directly for the potential effectiveness of human resources in economic production, but also indirectly for social change. Perhaps even more significant for social change, however, is the movement toward the urbanization of the population which is implied by the prospective decline in the agricultural labor force (not to mention the long-run objective of eliminating the differences between rural and urban life). For much of the first thirty years of rapid economic development, the Soviet labor force remained predominantly agricultural and the population rural. In the next twenty years, or by the 1980s, the agricultural labor force should decline to some 20 per cent or less of the total, at which time, therefore, three-quarters of the population will be living in urban areas.

It is implicit in the subject that demographic changes play the role of both cause and effect in economic and social development, or, more accurately, that they are an intimate and integral part of the whole developmental process. No attempt is made here to unravel the problem in all of its complexities. But even a partial approach that concentrates on the demographic changes themselves can add several important dimensions to our view of the prospects in store for Soviet society in the decades ahead.

I. Demographic Characteristics of Soviet Population Growth

Non-Soviet analysts studying Soviet population growth inevitably call attention to the broad similarity between Soviet experience (reaching back to the late nineteenth century) and that of other industrializing countries: the declining death rate, in response to public and private efforts and the dissemination of knowledge in the fields of medical care, sanitation, etc.; and the declining birth rate, a reflection of changing attitudes brought about by urbanization, education, and related economic and social forces.[3]

Interpretation of the pattern of Soviet population growth since the 1930s has had to rely heavily on analogy with other developing countries, because Soviet demographers, until quite recently, have provided very little in the way of substantial analysis (or even casual commentary). It is true that they have long been concerned with developing the notion of a Socialist Law of Population.[4] The purview of the law, however, is broadly defined to include, according to one formulation, "full employment and the rational utilization of the total able-bodied population, in labor which is socially useful from a socialist point of view; the uninterrupted increase in the material and cultural level of living, free from exploitation; and the expanded (*rasshirennyi*) natural increase of an all-around developed population."[5] Conventional demographic questions related to population reproduction (mortality and fertility) form only part of the law. From this point of view, a Socialist Law of Population is more or less on the same plane with a Socialist Theory of Society, and population problems have become synonymous with social problems.[6]

In any event, for a number of years before and after World War II, especially prior to the systematic publication of vital statistics (mid-1950s), Soviet demographers had very little to say on demographic problems, narrowly defined, in the Soviet Union. When they approached the subject at all in those years, it was to deal with aspects not directly involving reproduction (e.g., employment), or with facts readily explained (e.g., the decline in the death rate), or with methodology; but they skirted the central question of population fertility, except in the context of history or of other countries.[7]

By the late 1950s, the well-known "renaissance" of Soviet statistics was under way, in which the science of demography played a key role from the very beginning.[8] The publication of vital statistics on a regular basis, and of the results of the 1959 census, was accompanied by a gradually increasing number of articles and monographs on various population problems.[9] Even the question of fertility began to be dealt with: in some cases very briefly,[10] in other cases more systematically, if less than comprehensively,[11] and in still others, by way of an attempt to incorporate the question into discussion of the Socialist Law of Population.[12]

The unfolding of scholarly interest in demographic questions has been especially rapid in the last few years. In view of the publication of such important works as those of Professor Urlanis,[13] on problems of fertility and mortality and their implications for population growth, size, and structure, there is every indication that the science of demography is now in the process of being re-established in the Soviet Union, a science which has deep roots in the pre-Soviet and early Soviet years.[14] There has been created within the Ministry of Higher and Secondary Specialized Education of the U.S.S.R. a Coordinating Council for Population Problems (April 1964), and within Moscow University itself, a Problem Laboratory of Population (*Problemnaia Laboratoriia Narodonaseleniia*) devoted to the study of population problems and to the graduate training of demographers (February, 1965).[15] Within the Academy of Sciences of the U.S.S.R., work on population continues in the Institute of Economics; the new Institute of the World Labor Movement is expected to give attention to population migration and to problems of labor resources; and the creation of an Institute of Statistics and Demography is being discussed.[16]

Finally, there is a growing list of conferences and symposiums attended by Soviet demographers and many other social scientists and specialists at home and abroad. These include: (a) in September 1965, the World Population Conference in Belgrade, at which there were 27 Soviet participants compared to 3 at the similar conference in Rome in 1954;[17] (b) in September 1966, the latest in a series of conferences on population problems which include participants from the Communist countries of Eastern Europe;[18] (c) a number of conferences devoted to the population problems of particular parts of the Soviet Union, including Armenia and other republics (April 1963),[19] Central Asia (September 1965),[20] the Far East (September and November 1965),[21] and the Ukraine (October 1966);[22] and (d) the first all-union symposium on the question of Marxist-Leninist population theory (November 1966).[23]

This catalogue of recent developments—taking into account also the on-going preparations for the 1970 census[24]—suggests that the Soviet Union is on the threshold of a new era in the field of demography, and that Soviet demographers, over the next decade or two, may very well make some important contributions to an understanding of population problems under Soviet conditions.[25] Such a prospect, in and of itself, is of great interest to the future of Soviet society.

By the same token, it must be remembered that these developments are still at an early stage; that the data and other information required for the analysis of many questions are inadequate; and that, as a consequence, the articles and monographs which have already appeared must for the most part be considered tentative and exploratory. Urlanis is quite explicit on these points, when applied to the analysis of fertility trends: "there are very few materials at our disposal which can throw light on the influence of the different factors affecting the birth rate, and those which there are must be used with great reservations. . . . although some studies [on aspects of this question] have been carried out in certain institutes, the scale thereof is too small to permit reaching any general conclusions."[26] To exercise due caution, however, does not mean to ignore this rapidly expanding body of primary source material, which offers some extremely interesting commentary. Despite the shortcomings of these sources, in other words, we are still well ahead of the days of analysis solely by analogy with other countries and on the basis of isolated statistics.

Population Growth and Fertility Trends

Let us return to the questions themselves. From the various sources at our disposal, what can we say about the pattern of Soviet population growth, with particular reference to the future? More specifically, since the death rate has already fallen to very low levels by the standards of developed countries (see Table 1), what can we say about trends in the birth rate (*rozhdaemost'*) and in fertility (*plodovitost'*)?[27]

Soviet demographers are giving more and more attention to this question. They are well aware of the evident decline in the birth rate shown by the official data reproduced in Table 1: from a level near 40 per thousand in the late 1920s and again in the late 1930s,[28] to a level of about 25 during the 1950s, after which it

has continued to decline, reaching 18.2 in 1966.[29] They recognize
that the factors which lead through family planning to reduced
fertility, as in the Soviet case, are complex and interrelated.[30] In
attempting to unravel this complexity, they do not necessarily agree
with one another,[31] and they have an understandable tendency to
hedge when considering prospects for the future. Nevertheless,
some degree of a sense of the problem emerges from the literature
published to date.[32]

Among the interrelated factors influencing fertility, reference is
frequently made to the crucial role played by the "cultural level"
of the population. This concept, by its nature, is not sharply defined, but it appears to be characterized in the Soviet literature
by the following attitudes and values when applied to the fertility
question under conditions of socialist economic development and
change.

1. Both continuity and change in the *attitudes* of the Soviet
people toward having children. Continuity appears in the maintenance of certain traditional values, usually implicit in the discussion (except when comparing fertility differentials by nationality
groups within the country). Change appears in such considerations as a diminished view of children as an economic asset, and
a more mature and "morally responsible" view of children for
their own worth and dignity as human beings in a (socialist)
society.

2. A growing awareness of the *resources*, both economic and
otherwise, that are required to raise children according to the
values implied by (1). This includes such things as housing space,
clothing, education and recreation, but also the intangibles that
contribute to a more vital life together as members of a family
and of society.

3. A growing value placed on the meaningful *alternatives* to
raising children. Most often mentioned is the enhanced possibility
for productive, socially useful work by women.

4. A growing knowledge of what might be called the *facilities*
that may implement decisions on child-bearing. Those which serve
to prevent having children include contraceptive devices, abortions, etc. Those which enhance the raising of children would
include nurseries, monetary grants, and privileges for mothers.

The "cultural level" of the population thus described is felt
to be derived in part from the historical heritage of society, in
part from education, formal and informal, and very much from

	Birth Rates	Death Rates	Per Cent of Increase
1926	44.0	20.3	2.37
1927	43.4	21.0	2.24
1928	42.2	18.2	2.40
1929	39.8	20.3	1.95
1930	39.2	20.4	1.88
1931	38.2	19.1	1.91
1932	31.0	18.5	1.25
1933	[28.6][b]	(18.5)[c]	1.01
1934	[26.4]	[18.4]	(0.80)
1935	28.6	16.3	1.23
1936	32.3	18.7	1.36
1937	38.7	17.9	2.08
1938	38.3	17.8	2.05
1939[a]	36.5	17.3	1.92
1940	31.2	18.0	1.32
1949	—	—	1.86
1950	26.7	9.7	1.70
1951	27.0	9.7	1.73
1952	26.5	9.4	1.71
1953	25.1	9.1	1.60
1954	26.6	8.9	1.77
1955	25.7	8.2	1.75
1956	25.2	7.6	1.76
1957	25.4	7.8	1.76
1958	25.3	7.2	1.81
1959	25.0	7.6	1.74

the process of economic and social change itself and from the nature of the system within which it takes place (i.e., from "productive relationships," in the Marxian sense of the term[33]).

Whether fertility is high or low, rising or falling, however, is not determined by the cultural level alone. It is determined,

TABLE 1
BIRTH AND DEATH RATES PER THOUSAND POPULATION
AND PERCENTAGE RATES OF NATURAL INCREASE, U.S.S.R.:
REPORTED, 1926–66, AND PROJECTED, 1970–2000

	Birth Rates	Death Rates	Per Cent of Increase
1960	24.9	7.1	1.78
1961	23.8	7.2	1.66
1962	22.4	7.5	1.49
1963	21.2	7.2	1.40
1964	19.6	6.9	1.27
1965	18.4	7.3	1.11
1966	18.2	7.3	1.09

BIRTH AND DEATH RATES CONSISTENT WITH
POPULATION PROJECTIONS IN TABLE 4

	High Fertility	Low Fertility	High Fertility	Low Fertility	High Fertility	Low Fertility
1970	19.7	13.7	7.1	7.2	1.26	0.66
1975	20.7	12.6	7.3	7.6	1.34	0.50
1980	21.3	13.6	7.6	8.2	1.38	0.54
1985	21.1	14.0	7.7	8.7	1.34	0.52
1990	20.3	13.8	7.8	9.0	1.25	0.48
1995	20.4	13.7	7.8	9.0	1.26	0.47
2000	20.5	13.5	7.8	9.0	1.27	0.45

Sources:
1926–66: from Soviet sources, as set forth in W. W. Eason, *Soviet Manpower* (forthcoming).
Notes:
  a Data from 1939 on are for present territory of the U.S.S.R.
  b Data in brackets are estimated from partial data in Soviet sources.
  c Data in parentheses are derived arithmetically from the other data for the corresponding year.

according to recent discussion, by the interrelationships between changes in the cultural level and in the availability and feasibility of the "resources," "alternatives," and "facilities" described above. Particular attention is given to the *material* or economic manifestations of the latter—i.e., the ability (and interest) of the system to provide housing space, retail services, employment opportunities for women, etc.; and also to make available the means for contraception.

A shorthand employed by Soviet demographers to explain the secular decline in fertility rates through family planning, since the 1920s and 1930s, is to the effect that the *cultural level* of the population has been changing more rapidly than the *material means* made available to the population by economic development. This implies that if more housing, consumer services, nurseries, etc., had been made available, the fertility rate might not have fallen so rapidly. But it is not necessarily meant to imply that fertility otherwise would have remained at pre-industrialization levels, nor that it will return to these levels when the "material means" are forthcoming. The increased sense of moral responsibility for raising children (1 and 2, above) and the meaningfulness of socially useful work (3), as the cultural level rises, plus the sharply reduced rate of infant mortality (i.e., increased life expectancy of all who are born), may preclude a significant increase in fertility even under prospective conditions of material abundance.[34]

Nor would this necessarily be an undesirable state of affairs. Soviet demographers emphasize that moderate (*srednie*) levels of fertility plus low levels of mortality—an "intensive"[35] or "progressive"[36] pattern—have yielded rates of population growth (*circa* 1.5 per cent) to date which are themselves "moderate" and which are, from a number of points of view, entirely respectable.

This leads to the question of whether Soviet demographers have any thoughts on what *will* happen in the future, and any thoughts also on what *ought* to happen. Implicit to consideration of this question is the acknowledged role of the *family* as the decision-making unit in child-bearing. "In the Soviet Union," writes Urlanis,[37] "the state does not interfere in the private, intimate life of its citizens, leaving to them full freedom in determining the size of their family." Thus, family planning—subject to various "assists" from the government (grants to mothers, free abortions in state clinics, etc.)—has been the medium through which the decline in fertility has taken place to date. And in making population projections, ". . . the task . . . is to determine what the decisions of parents will be with respect to the number of children [they will have]."[38]

From a long-run point of view, when "material means" are relatively abundant and the "cultural level" of the population fully mature, there is the generally expressed *desideratum* that the population will more than reproduce itself, i.e., that it will continue to *grow*. It ought to grow, one concludes from the discussion, at something like the "moderate" rate of the 1950s, i.e., sufficient to support the development of the country, which for many decades, it should be added, will remain relatively underpopulated.

On the other hand, there seems to be no great value attached to "maximizing" the birth rate:[39] "It would be incorrect to imagine that our country will be characterized, during the period of building a Communist society, by a particularly high birth rate. We are not at all trying to maximize the birth rate . . . [rather] it should be at a level which secures the growth of the population." In other words, "Socialism does not propose rapid [*burnyi*] population growth, but that level of the birth rate which secures the expanded reproduction [*rasshirennoe vosproizvodstvo*] of the population."[40]

As to the prospect that family planning *will* in fact lead to adequate (moderate) population growth—expressed by an average of, say, three children per family[41]—Soviet demographers are understandably vague. For example:

> . . . the further improvement of the level of living of our people . . . will create the necessary conditions for the birth rate to reach an appropriate [*nadlezhashchem*] level. Along with the increase in the level of satisfaction of material and cultural requirements of the population, there will also be an increase in the level of satisfaction of the natural human requirements as parents to have children.[42]

This seems to say that whatever number of children mature parents are inclined to have, economic and social development in the Soviet Union will ultimately provide the necessary conditions to enable them to do so. But whether this will in fact result in the growth of the population desired by society depends on what is meant by "natural human requirements." The impression gained from the literature is that most Soviet specialists feel that in the long run, when material conditions are sufficient, these "natural human requirements" will yield birth rates which are "adequate" for population growth, even if this implies an increase from lower levels in the interim.[43]

So much for the long run. What of the foreseeable future, say, over the next decade or two? The answer depends heavily on interpretation of the most recent trends, i.e., since 1950, but especially in the last few years. Crude birth rates (as in Table 1) will in all probability continue lower, if only due to the depressing influence of the age-cohorts of "war babies" now in the younger reproductive ages.

Whether underlying fertility rates will increase, decrease, or remain stable in the near future is, of course, problematical. Several types of available information may be briefly considered in order to shed light on this important question: (1) birth rates by sub-regions of the country; (2) birth rates by age-groups, and related reproduction rates; and (3) rural-urban birth rate differentials. The data and commentary in Soviet sources show that underlying fertility rates have been declining in the last few years, and the interpretation seems to be that this trend may very well continue for at least a while.

Birth rates by sub-regions. The stability of the birth rate for the country as a whole in the decade of the 1950s, as Soviet and non-Soviet analysts have observed,[44] concealed substantial differences and different rates of change by major sub-regions and also by nationalities. Compared to an over-all rate near 25 per thousand during these years (see Table 1), regional differences ranged from near 20 and below in parts of European Russia to above 30 in Central Asia and parts of the Caucasus.[45] And declining birth rates in European Russia were "balanced" by increasing rates in virtually all of the republics of Central Asia and the Caucasus, and in certain other sub-regions of the country.

High birth rates in these sub-regions with lower rates elsewhere, "despite uniform economic construction . . . and equal [participation] of the republics in the growth of the economy and culture,"[46] has attracted considerable attention from demographers. Explanations emphasize the "influence and relative firmness of centuries-old traditions and the customs of the past," which continue to exert their influence "despite the fact that there has been a revolution in education and that economic conditions have appreciably changed."[47]

Considerations of tradition, it is observed, are supported and reinforced in these regions by such things as: (a) a relatively high proportion of the population in agriculture; (b) relatively low levels of employment of women in industry and particularly in white collar (*umstvennyi*) work; (c) a somewhat lower educational level among women than elsewhere; (d) the fact that women become fertile (physically) at an earlier age, and also that they tend to marry younger; and (e) the persistence of "feudal" attitudes regarding the role of women in the family.[48] As a result of these fac-

TABLE 2

Age-Specific Female Birth Rates per Thousand, U.S.S.R.: Selected Years, 1926/27–1964/65

Age Groups	1926/27	1938/39	1954/55	1957/58	1958/59	1960/61	1961/62	1962/63	1963/64	1964/65
15–19	38.2	32.8	15.6	23.9	29.2	35.2	29.6	24.1	22.7	23.7
20–24	259.4	214.4	146.9	160.1	162.2	164.8	162.8	162.1	162.6	157.6
25–29	269.0	230.6	172.9	166.7	164.8	160.7	155.8	151.4	145.6	138.9
30–34	224.5	183.5	127.6	116.4	110.1	110.1	105.2	101.3	97.6	95.5
35–39	171.6	131.7	74.4	66.8	66.6	60.7	56.4	54.2	52.0	50.9
40–44	90.8	68.1	35.4	24.7	24.1	23.5	22.7	22.3	21.4	20.3
45–49	23.0	19.0	7.1	5.7	5.0	4.8	3.8	3.7	3.9	4.2
Total, 15–49	159.1	139.5	86.2	86.9	88.7	90.6	87.2	83.2	78.4	73.5

Sources:

1926/27: B. Ts. Urlanis, *Rozhdaemost' i prodolzhitel'nost' zhizhni v SSSR* (Moscow, 1963), p. 42.

1938/39 and 1957/58–1962/63: TsSU SSSR, *Narodnoe khoziaistvo SSSR v 1963 g.: statisticheskii ezhegodnik* (Moscow, 1964), p. 31.

1954/55: G. A. Slesarev, *Metodologiia sotsialisticheskogo issledovaniia problem narodonaseleniia* (Moscow, 1965), p. 104.

1963/64: TsSU SSSR, *Narodnoe khoziaistvo SSSR v 1964 g.: statisticheskii ezhegodnik* (Moscow, 1965), p. 36.

1964/65: TsSU SSSR, *Narodnoe khoziaistvo SSSR v 1965 g.: statisticheskii ezhegodnik* (Moscow, 1966), p. 44.

tors, until recently at least, contraception is practiced to a much lower degree than in other areas and among other nationalities.[49]

Sooner or later, fertility rates in Central Asia and the Caucasus might be expected to decline, in response to forces similar to those which brought them down elsewhere. In the expectation that the "building of the material-technical basis of Communism" will tend to reduce differences between nationalities and areas both in economic and cultural terms, one author conjectures that there will be a corresponding

> drawing together of indices of the birth rate in different republics and regions of the country. . . . this does not mean, however, that these rates will become identical. But it would seem that for the socialist society as a whole in the future there will be *changes* in the birth rate; and that as far as the Uzbek, Tadzhik, Kirgiz, and Turkmen republics are concerned, this will appear as a *lowering* of the [birth rate].[50] (Italics added.)

Is this process, perhaps, already under way? It is a statistical fact that a general decline in birth rates by regions has recently been taking place. In the intervals for which data are available—1960–63, 1963–64, and 1964–65—birth rates declined in virtually every major sub-region of the country, including Central Asia and the Caucasus.[51] Some, if not most, of the decline in all of the regions, however, is due to the "war babies" effect, which should continue to be felt through the decade of the 1960s.[52]

As far as underlying fertility rates are concerned, Kvasha notes that the European parts of the country are at the point where the respective populations are just reproducing themselves ("simple reproduction") or not even reproducing themselves ("contracted reproduction").[53] With this the situation in European Russia, he observes, the fact that the population for the country as a whole has continued more than to reproduce itself ("expanded reproduction"), "is due essentially to the Central Asian regions."[54] But it is also true, as shown below, that net reproduction rates for the country as a whole, although probably still greater than unity, are declining. This suggests that fertility rates in the Central Asian region may also be declining at the present time.

Age-specific birth rates and reproduction rates. Age-specific birth rates, and related reproduction rates, provide a direct measure of the "fertility" of the population. According to the data which are available for the Soviet Union in these terms, the fertility of the

Soviet population has been in the process of a general decline since the beginning of rapid industrialization.

Age-specific female birth rates, for example, reproduced in Table 2, show that this downward movement has passed through four stages (in terms of the years reported):

a) 1926/27–1938/39, a period of *moderate decline* of some 12 per cent, more or less proportionately, in each and every age-group;

b) 1938/39–1954/55, a period of *sharp decline* to almost one-half the 1926/27 rate over-all, with an even greater decline among the youngest (15–19) and oldest (45–49);

c) 1954/55–1960/61, a period of *relative stability*, showing a slight rise in the over-all rate, with declining rates among the older age groups (25 and over) "balanced" by increasing rates among the younger (15–24); and

d) 1960/61–1964/65, a period of *renewed decline*, by about 20 per cent over-all, with each age-group participating to one degree or another. This recent decline in age-specific birth rates is contributing to the decline in crude birth rates (Table 1), over and above the "war babies" effect.[55]

Soviet data on gross and net reproduction rates of females, reported for a few years, necessarily parallel the over-all trend of the age-specific female birth rates for the period as a whole as well as the decline since the late 1950s. These data, together with estimates for certain other years (in parentheses) made from the age-specific female birth rates in Table 2 according to the method described by Urlanis,[56] are as follows:[57]

	FEMALE REPRODUCTION RATES	
	Gross	Net
1938/39	2.10	1.40
1959		1.30
1960/61	(1.36)	(1.27)
1961		1.26
1961/62	1.30	1.20
1962/63	(1.26)	(1.18)
1963/64	(1.23)	(1.16)
1964/65	(1.19)	(1.13)

The decline in female reproduction rates after 1959 implies that marital fertility was also declining.[58] Brackett and DePauw go further, to suggest that marital fertility was declining during the

1950s as well, at a time when female reproduction rates (as may be inferred from age-specific birth rates of females, in Table 2) were relatively stable.[59]

In any event, the decline in fertility rates in the most recent years—to levels approaching the point where the population is tending barely to reproduce itself (in terms of present fertility and mortality conditions)—raises serious questions about prospects for the future. Some possibilities in this respect may be explored after considering one more set of data bearing on the question.

Rural-urban birth rate differentials. It is clear that urbanization has made a major contribution to declining fertility in the Soviet Union, as Soviet demographers emphasize, because the urban way of life tends to focus and accent some of the changes in the "cultural" and "material" considerations referred to above.[60] Thus, the crude birth rate in urban areas has declined from 34.7 per thousand in 1926 to 16.2 in 1965 (see Table 3).

It is also true, however, that the birth rate in *rural* areas has declined as well, from 45.6 in 1926 to 21.0 in 1965, or in almost exactly the same proportion (over the period as a whole) as the urban rate. What is most interesting—and even surprising—is that the decline in the rural rate was initially much *more* rapid than the decline in the urban rate. This is seen, first, in the precipitous drop from 45.0 in 1928 to 32.2 in 1932, or by 30 per cent in four years, compared to a drop of some 10 per cent in the urban rate, and, second, in the fact that the rural rate never again rose above the 1932 level (for the years reported).[61] The relatively greater decline of the rural rate in the early years culminates in the fact that rural and urban birth rates were almost equal to each other in 1940 and again in 1950. Thereafter, the rural rate was stable, until the 1960s, while the urban rate declined somewhat.

These considerations raise the question of whether the real "demographic revolution" in the Soviet case did not take place in the countryside rather than in the cities. Soviet demographers call attention to fundamental economic and institutional changes under industrialization and collectivization to explain the precipitous decline in the rural birth rates after 1928, and it is in the nature of some of these changes that they would have had more than a transient effect.[62]

The situation in the last few years is that birth rates are declining in both rural and urban areas, and that the difference between

TABLE 3
BIRTH RATES PER THOUSAND POPULATION, U.S.S.R.:
TOTAL, URBAN, AND RURAL AREAS, SELECTED YEARS 1926–65

Dates[a]	Total	Urban	Rural	Rural as Per Cent of Urban
1926	43.7[b]	34.7	45.6	135
1928	42.2	30.2	45.0	149
1932	31.0	27.0	32.2	119
1935	30.1[b]	24.6	32.2	131
1940	31.2	30.5	31.5	103
1950	26.7	26.0	27.1	104
1955	25.7	23.5	27.4	117
1958	25.3	22.5	27.9	124
1959	25.0	22.0	27.8	126
1960	24.9	22.0	27.8	126
1961	23.8	21.2	26.5	125
1962	22.4	20.0	24.9	125
1963	21.2	18.6	24.0	129
1964	19.6	17.3	22.0	127
1965	18.4	16.2	21.0	130

Sources:

1926–35: S. G. Strumilin, *Problemy ekonomiki truda* (Moscow, 1957), pp. 193–94, for the European part of the U.S.S.R.

1940–65: TsSU SSSR, *Narodnoe khoziaistvo SSSR v 1965 g.: statisticheskii ezhegodnik* (Moscow, 1966), p. 43.

Notes:

[a] Dates from 1940 on refer to present boundaries of the U.S.S.R.; other dates refer to pre-1939 boundaries.

[b] These rates differ from those in Table 1 because of different primary sources.

the two has increased once again to the point where rural rates are higher than urban rates by about the same relative amount (30 per cent) as in 1926.[63] One gets the impression that Soviet demographers expect a further decline in rural rates, over and above that accountable to the "war babies" effect—as the level of education, the standard of living, and the employment of women in "socialized production," are improved both quantitatively and qualitatively, in the drive to raise productivity on the farms. "Elimination of the difference between rural and urban life," writes Sonin,[64] "will eliminate differences in birth rates by transforming rural conditions [of life] into urban . . . and this will lead to a lowering of the birth rate in the countryside more quickly than in the city."

TABLE 4
TOTAL POPULATION OF THE U.S.S.R.: CENSUS DATA, 1926, 1939, AND 1959; ESTIMATES ON THE BASIS OF SOVIET DATA, 1926–49; SOVIET ESTIMATES, 1950–67; AND PROJECTIONS, 1970–2000
(*In thousands*)

1926 Census[a]	147,028	1960	212,101
1927[b]	147,100	1961	216,101
1928	149,900	1962	219,730
1929	153,100	1963	223,096
1930	155,600	1964	226,253
1931	158,100	1965	229,100
1932	160,700	1966	231,900
1933	(160,600)	1967	234,400
1934	(160,600)		
1935	160,500		
1936	162,200		
1937	164,100		
1938	167,300		
1939	170,400		
1939 Census	170,557		
1940[d]	194,100		
1941	196,400		
1945	172,300		
1949	175,300		
1950	178,547		
1951	181,603		
1952	184,778		
1953	187,977		
1954	191,004		
1955	194,415		
1956	197,902		
1957	201,414		
1958	204,925		
1959	208,662		
1959 Census	208,862		

	Population Projected on the Basis of Alternative Fertility Assumptions		
	Soviet Projection[c]	*High Fertility*	*Low Fertility*
1970	250,000	245,000	239,000
1975	263,000	262,000	246,000
1980	280,000	280,000	252,000
1985		300,000	260,000
1990		320,000	265,000
1995		340,000	270,000
2000	350,000	365,000	275,000

Sources:

1926–67: set forth in W. W. Eason, *Soviet Manpower* (forthcoming).

1970–80 Soviet projection: M. Ia. Sonin, *Aktual'nye problemy ispol'zovaniia rabochei sily v SSSR* (Moscow, 1965), p. 51.

2000 Soviet projection: B. Ts. Urlanis, *Rost naseleniia v SSSR* (Moscow, 1966), p. 36.

1970–85 projections, to nearest million: J. W. Brackett, *Projections of the Population of the U.S.S.R., by Age and Sex: 1964–1985* (Washington, D.C.: U.S. Government Printing Office, 1964), and supplementary tables, "Estimates and Projections of the Population of the U.S.S.R. and of the Communist Countries of Eastern Europe, by Age and Sex" (1959–89). "High" is "A," "Low" is "D."

These three interrelated indices of the birth rate—by sub-regions, age, and rural-urban areas—were examined in order to try to determine whether underlying fertility rates for the Soviet population might be expected to increase, decrease, or remain stable, in the near future. It is certainly no less hazardous to "predict" fertility trends for the Soviet Union than for any other country. Nevertheless, subject to the qualifications already noted, the data themselves and the interpretations thereof by Soviet demographers point to a continuation of the declining fertility rates of the recent past as somewhat more likely than stable or increasing rates.

The reasoning behind this conclusion favors the continued influence, on balance, of (a) factors that brought birth rates down in urban areas in the first place,[65] (b) rural-urban migration, and (c) basic changes in rural life as it takes on more of the characteristics of urban life. Of particular significance is the distinct possibility that these factors may finally become evident in declining fertility rates in sub-regions of heretofore high fertility, such as Central Asia.

The future implications of this view will be seen if the Soviet population is projected in terms of alternative hypotheses regarding fertility. This is done in Table 4, where an "official" projection by the Central Statistical Administration (TsSU) is reproduced together with a projection, on the basis of alternative fertility assumptions, carried out by J. W. Brackett and other specialists of the U.S. Bureau of the Census. "High fertility" in the latter projection embodies a moderately rising female gross reproduction rate (GRR) from 1.27 in 1962 to 1.40 in 1974 and thereafter stable, while "low fertility" embodies a declining GRR to 0.80 in 1974.[66] The "high" and "low" projections should not be taken as "predictions" or as setting limits to possibilities for the future. They are simply illustrative of plausible alternatives that differ significantly from one another.

If it turns out, over the next decade or so, that there is a continuation of the declining fertility rates of the recent past, as

---

1990–2000 projections: made by extending fertility assumptions in same, summarized in text of present paper, from respective levels as of 1989, to 2000.

Notes:
 [a] Census data are December 17, 1926, January 17, 1939, and January 15, 1959.
 [b] Non-census data are January 1, unless otherwise indicated.
 [c] End of year.
 [d] Data from 1940 are for present territory of the U.S.S.R.

suggested above, then the total Soviet population will tend to grow in the direction of the "low" fertility alternative of Table 4.[67] By the same token, the Soviet projection itself tends toward the "high" fertility alternative. More accurately, the Soviet projection—made in the early 1960s, and based on the assumption of "a small [*nebol'shoe*] increase in age-specific fertility"[68]—is really in the nature of an "intermediate" projection in the terms described above.[69] What we are saying, then, is that a Soviet projection of more recent vintage, reflecting the declining fertility rates of the 1960s, would probably tend toward the "low" fertility alternative of Table 4, at least over the short term.

If this approach appears somewhat cautious, it is out of respect for the nature of the problem of population projection in general, and out of respect also for the limitations of our understanding of the factors affecting fertility that are at work in Soviet society. Is there any more compelling reason in the Soviet case than elsewhere, we must ask, why fertility trends might not depart (even radically) from past trends? Consider the fact that now entering the reproductive ages are individuals who were born beginning in the 1950s, after the war and reconstruction, and who, therefore, are the first to have been raised essentially in the climate of the post-Stalin era. Can we say with any certainty that their attitudes toward child-bearing might not be significantly different, one way or another, from those of their predecessors?[70]

Soviet demographers, it appears, also have some doubt about their ability to predict the future, however much their understanding of the past has improved, as recent discussion of population projections indicates:

> We can more or less successfully explain the reasons for the decrease or increase in the birth rate in the past, but for the time being [*poka*] we cannot, with sufficient basis, foresee its future evolution.
> . . . [As far as concrete, quantitative understanding of the factors affecting fertility is concerned, as a basis for projection] it is not possible even approximately to determine by what percentage the birth rate will decrease or increase by 1970. The drawing up of hypotheses on changes in the birth rate in the future is based for the time being on *simple extrapolation* of past tendencies, modified on the basis of judgments of specialists, intuitively evaluating the connection between the birth rate and different socio-economic factors.[71] (Italics added.)

The ordinary difficulties of population projection have extraordinary consequences in the Soviet case because of the fact that such projections form an important part of national economic planning. And planning, in turn, raises the question of population policy (*politika naseleniia*)—policy developed by the government to influence both the quantitative and qualitative aspects of population growth within the broad purview of the Socialist Law of Population.

Population Policy

The types of population policy developed in the Soviet Union that are more or less directly related to fertility are well known. They include financial assistance and privileges to mothers and mothers-to-be, and the availability of devices and facilities for contraception and the termination of pregnancy.[72] A recent Soviet discussion puts it this way:

> a large role in the process [whereby social and economic factors relate to the birth rate] is played by governmental measures.
> . . . On the one hand, the state takes these measures in order to support a *high* birth rate; on the other hand, the fact that the economy and culture are growing at rapid rates and that the material-cultural level of the population is increasing, means the creation of conditions for a *lowering* of the birth rate.
> Is this a *contradiction*? No, it only appears to be a contradiction. It is not a high level of the birth rate which is endemic to socialist society, but rather that which brings about, with a minimum death rate, the expanded reproduction of the population and which is beneficial to the physiological well-being of women.[73] [Italics added.]

This is not a contradiction, in other words, so long as it adds up to the desired (moderate) rate of population increase. Those measures which had as their objective a larger number of births (prohibition of abortions, allowances to mothers) were instituted at times when there was a genuine concern about declining or lowered fertility and the consequences for population growth (during the mid-1930s and at the end of the war). The effectiveness of the measures in raising fertility is difficult to determine because other factors were also operating, but in each instance population growth returned quickly to "moderate" levels. The allowances to mothers were reduced in 1947, shortly after they had been instituted, and the measures against abortions were reversed in 1955, allegedly because of the incidence of illegal abortions.

The prevalence of "moderate" levels of population growth during much of the period since 1928 seems to explain why no great concern has been expressed about population pressures, one way or another, and why discussions about population policy to affect fertility have been carried out in rather general terms.

It is acknowledged, on the one hand, that birth rates might become too high—or even that "moderate" rates might ultimately be considered excessive—with the result that "it will become necessary . . . to limit population growth"[74] under socialism. Or, as pointed out in a recent reference to the Central Asian republics, "The rapid growth of the population cannot be allowed to become an obstacle [*prepiatstvie*] to the growth of the economy, and the growth of well-being and culture."[75] When considering how to deal with such an eventuality, reference is usually made in the literature to the statement of Engels, that "if it becomes necessary to limit population growth, Communist societies can do so without difficulty."[76]

It is clear, in other words, that the state is not seen as keeping its hands tied in the face of excessively high or low rates of population growth. The policy door is open to a wide range of possibilities, but certain extreme measures are ruled out. The approach has been summarized as follows:[77]

> Under socialism, the so-called "radical measures" of limiting the growth of the population by means of artificially limiting births do not constitute an important aspect of population policy. This is not to say, however, that it is necessary to renounce purposeful socioeconomic policies taken to bring about the correct solution to demographic problems.
> The generally accepted concept in the socialist countries is that policy . . . with respect to the birth rate can take different directions depending on the concrete conditions of the country. [Policy] can have as its objective the encouraging of births under certain conditions and the lowering or stabilizing of them in others.
> With this, it must be understood that there is to be excluded the meddling [*vmeshatel'stvo*] of the state in the free will of the family as far as the number of children in the family are concerned.

It is difficult to say exactly what measures, short of "meddling," the Soviet government might resort to if the population problem were considered to be serious. Presently declining fertility rates could give rise to just such a problem, because, as is shown below, they could lead to an absolute decline in the total labor force beginning in the 1980s. The difficulty of developing a policy to raise fertility rates follows from the very nature of the Soviet interpretation of interrelationships between socio-economic factors and fertility, summarized above. One very obvious step, for example, would be to increase significantly the rate at which "material means" are made available to the population. But this might come to naught, if it were insufficient to meet the rising sense of moral responsibility toward having children, as well as to support the other values embodied in the rising "cultural level" of the population.

A particularly intransigent aspect of the problem lies in the opportunities for employment, which have contributed thus far to high participation rates of women in the labor force. The Soviet government would like to maintain or even increase, not to say "maximize,"[78] the participation of women in socialized labor (*obshchestvennyi trud*). Higher fertility rates, however, imply reduced employment of women. The effect could be modified by an appropriate reduction of the number of hours in the normal work week, and also by increased availability of nurseries and related facilities, but the element of choice between the present labor force (women of child-bearing ages) and the future labor force (children) remains.[79]

All in all, if the problem of reduced fertility becomes serious, steps of the type indicated could involve a major reordering of economic priorities and shifts in resource allocation.[80] The interest of the Soviet government in taking such measures, however, might turn out to be equaled only by the inability of Soviet demographers to "predict" with any certainty the results in terms of fertility.

II. Implications of Population Growth for Economic and Social Change

Distribution by Age and Sex

The primary and direct implications of population growth for economic and social change lie in the rate of population growth, already discussed, and in the distribution of the population by age and sex. Distribution by age and sex is related to the pattern of change in birth and death rates, and, in the Soviet case, to the incidence of several national crises beginning with World War I. Table 5 reproduces these data, consistent with the estimates and projections of the other tables, for prewar census years and by five-year intervals from 1945 to 2000.

Table 5
Distribution of the Population by Age and Sex, U.S.S.R.: Census Data and Estimates, 1926–65; and Projections, 1970–2000

Age Groups	1926[a]	1939	1940	1945	1950	1955	1960	1965
Percentage Distribution of the Population of Both Sexes								
0–15	39.7	38.3	37.7	34.4	32.0	30.3	31.4	32.8
16–54(59)	52.1	53.5	53.7	55.1	57.5	58.4	56.2	53.7
55(60) and over	8.2	8.2	8.6	10.5	10.5	11.3	12.4	13.5
Total	100.0	100.0	100.0	100.0	100.0	100.0	100.0	100.0
Amount (in thousands) by which the Number of Males is Greater Than (+) or Less Than (−) the Number of Females								
0–15	+ 400	+ 200	+ 300	− 400	+ 200	+ 800	+ 1,200	+ 1,700
16–54(59)	− 1,800	− 1,900	− 1,700	− 17,300	− 14,900	− 12,400	− 9,000	− 5,800
55(60) and over	− 3,500	− 5,500	− 6,300	− 8,100	− 10,300	− 10,300	− 12,700	− 15,100
Total	− 4,900	− 7,200	− 7,700	− 25,800	− 23,400	− 21,900	− 20,500	− 19,200
Number of Males per 100 Females								
	94	92	92	74	77	80	82	85

Sources:
Same as for Table 4.
Notes:
[a] Notes on dating and territorial coverage are the same as for Table 4.

Age Groups	1970	1975	1980	1985	1990	1995	2000
			High Fertility				
Percentage Distribution of the Population of Both Sexes							
0–15	31.1	29.4	28.6	29.2	29.7	29.9	29.9
16–54(59)	54.1	55.5	56.2	54.7	53.4	52.3	52.5
55(60) and over	14.8	15.1	15.2	16.1	16.9	17.8	17.6
Total	100.0	100.0	100.0	100.0	100.0	100.0	100.0
Amount (in thousands) by which the Number of Males is Greater Than (+) or Less Than (−) the Number of Females							
0–15	+ 1,900	+ 2,000	+ 2,200	+ 2,400	+ 2,600	+ 2,800	+ 3,000
16–54(59)	− 2,600	− 600	+ 3,300	+ 8,600	+ 9,600	+12,400	+10,100
55(60) and over	−17,000	−17,200	−19,100	−22,100	−19,800	−19,400	−14,300
Total	−17,700	−15,800	−13,600	−11,200	−7,600	−4,200	−1,200
Number of Males per 100 Females							
	87	89	91	93	95	98	99
			Low Fertility				
Percentage Distribution of the Population of Both Sexes							
0–15	29.3	24.9	20.8	20.0	20.4	20.9	21.1
16–54(59)	55.6	59.0	62.3	61.4	59.2	56.7	55.7
55(60) and over	15.1	16.1	16.9	18.6	20.4	22.4	23.2
Total	100.0	100.0	100.0	100.0	100.0	100.0	100.0
Amount (in thousands) by which the Number of Males is Greater Than (+) or Less Than (−) the Number of Females							
0–15	+ 1,700	+ 1,600	+ 1,400	+ 1,400	+ 1,500	+ 1,600	+ 1,600
16–54(59)	− 2,600	− 600	+ 3,300	+ 8,400	+ 9,200	+11,700	+ 9,100
55(60) and over	−17,000	−17,200	−19,100	−22,100	−19,800	−19,400	−14,300
Total	−17,900	−16,200	−14,400	−12,300	−9,100	−6,100	−3,600
Number of Males per 100 Females							
	86	88	89	91	93	96	97

Distribution by age. Declining birth rates in and of themselves tend to reduce the percentage of the population in the younger age groups and to raise accordingly the share in the older age groups. Declining infant mortality by itself tends to operate in the other direction; in other words, to have the same effect as a rise in the birth rate. General improvements in the conditions affecting mortality other than infant mortality tend to have a relatively minor influence on the age distribution of the corresponding population.

Between the censuses of 1926 and 1939—even allowing for the population of the territories annexed in 1940—the population by broad age groups remained essentially unchanged (see Table 5). These age groups include the "able-bodied" ages as defined in Soviet use, namely, males age 16–59 and females age 16–54.

The effect of World War II, if we compare 1940 with the estimate for 1945, was to reduce the proportion of age 0–15 from 37.7 to 34.4 per cent of the total, followed by a further decline to 31.4 per cent by 1960; to increase the proportion in the able-bodied ages, from 53.7 to 55.1 per cent, and thereafter to 58.4 per cent in 1955; and to increase the proportion age 55 (60) and over, from 8.6 to 10.5 per cent, a trend which is still continuing. Thus, in spite of war losses approaching 25 million persons among the adult population, the proportion of adults age 16–54 (59) and 55(60) and over was higher after the war than before. The lower birth rates and higher infant mortality rates of the war "outweighed," so to speak, the effect of high military losses and excess civilian deaths.

These implications for age structure were amplified by the fact that there began moving into the working ages immediately after the war individuals who were born during the late 1920s and the 1930s, when the birth rate was relatively high (for most years), and who were probably less affected than any other age group by the war itself.

In the most recent years, the growth of the population of able-bodied ages has been dominated by the entry of the "war babies," born when the birth rate was low and infant mortality high.[81] One effect of these changes is a decline in the proportion of the population in the able-bodied ages, from 58.4 per cent in 1955 to 56.2 per cent in 1960 and 53.7 per cent in 1965.

The Khrushchev era (1954–64) thus spans years of exceptional change in the age structure of the population—change which is even more pronounced when seen in terms of narrower age groups.

A number of his policies, particularly those related to education, were clearly influenced by demographic considerations, and the latter will have their "echo" effects in the coming decades.

The distribution of the population by broad age groups after 1965, as shown in Table 5, depends significantly on what is assumed with respect to fertility rates. Under the assumption of "high fertility," the age structure shifts only moderately toward the older ages between 1965 and 2000 (Table 5), with almost no change in the death rate (Table 1); while under the assumption of "low fertility," the population becomes relatively "old" and the crude death rate rises. (Age-specific mortality can be expected to decline within fairly narrowly defined limits from the present Soviet level. The projections are based on a single, more or less conventional assumption in this respect.)

Distribution by sex. It is statistically correct and undoubtedly valid in other respects to say that the burden of the Soviet revolution and the building of an industrialized socialist state (if we include its defense in this category) fell much more heavily on males than females. At the time of the 1897 census there were approximately the same number of males as females in the population, or a sex ratio of 99 males per 100 females. By 1926, reflecting World War I and the Civil War, there were almost 5 million fewer males than females, or a sex ratio of 94. By 1939, as a result of the conditions of the early 1930s, there were 7.2 million fewer males than females and the sex ratio had declined to 92, although under normal conditions it would have increased.

The effect of World War II on the sex ratio in the Soviet population staggers the imagination. The 1959 census reports 114.8 million females and 94 million males, indicating an absolute deficit of 20.8 million males. By calculating backward on the basis of published birth rates and certain assumptions with respect to the distribution of mortality by age and sex, it may be estimated that as of 1945 there were almost 26 million fewer males than females, for a sex ratio of 74 males per 100 females (see Table 5).

The war-induced deficit of males, now confined to the population about 40 years of age and over, will continue to decline, and will to all intents and purposes be eliminated before the turn of the century. Even then, however, there will remain a "deficit" of some 14 million males among the population of females age 55 and over and males age 60 and over, and a "surplus" of some 10 million males among the population of females age 16–54 and males age 16–59 (the able-bodied ages)—but this will be a reflection of the ages included in the respective groups by sex. Whether this "deficit" or "surplus" is meaningful in socio-economic terms depends on the interpretation placed on the ages separating the groups, e.g., on the extent to which males can be expected to retire at age 60 and females at age 55, etc. If these age limits are meaningful, then it is important to note that the actual deficit of males in the able-bodied ages will disappear shortly after 1975, while the deficit in the older population will increase until about 1985 (22 million) and remain sizable thereafter.

The Size and Structure of the Labor Force

It has already been pointed out that, in terms of over-all quantitative relationships between human and other resources, Soviet economic development has been passing through a fundamental stage of transition—from a period in which human resources were relatively abundant and cheap, to a period in which the rising economic value of the human factor of production places a rising premium on the development of more sophisticated manpower policies. The reconsideration and reformulation of a number of these policies was recently made more urgent by the sharp slowing down in the rate of growth of the labor force during the early 1960s, against the high rate of growth maintained during the 1950s.

It is to be expected that the rate of growth of the labor force is now returning to about 1.5 per cent per year and that it will remain close to this rate for some 15 or 20 years. Thereafter, the pattern of growth will depend on what happens to birth rates in the meantime, and also on assumptions with respect to the percentage of the population in the labor force (participation ratios).

A projection of the labor force by five-year intervals to the year 2000 is reproduced in Table 6. This projection begins with the labor force participation ratios by age and sex estimated from the 1959 census, and is based on the following assumptions:

1. The percentage of the population age 10–15 in the labor force will decline to zero by 1975, from levels of 7 per cent for males and 5.9 per cent for females in 1959. This assumption reflects the successful implementation of programs for secondary school education on a full-time basis.

2. The percentage of males age 16–59 in the labor force will

TABLE 6
TOTAL LABOR FORCE, U.S.S.R., MALES AND FEMALES:
1926 AND 1959 CENSUSES; 1960–65 ESTIMATES; AND PROJECTION BY FIVE-YEAR INTERVALS, 1970–2000
(*In thousands*)

	1926	1959	1960	1965	1970	1975	1980
Males	45,300	52,400	52,600	56,000	61,900	68,300	75,500
Females	39,100	56,600	56,600	57,000	59,500	62,600	65,500
Total Labor Force	84,000	109,000	109,200	113,000	121,400	130,900	141,000
Females Per Cent of Total	46.3	51.9	51.8	50.4	49.0	47.8	46.5

	1985	1990	1995	2000
High Fertility				
Males	81,300	85,200	89,900	94,800
Females	66,600	67,900	69,500	72,900
Total Labor Force	147,900	153,100	159,400	167,700
Females Per Cent of Total	45.0	44.0	43.6	43.5
Low Fertility				
Males	79,100	79,300	79,200	78,900
Females	64,900	63,500	61,500	61,000
Total Labor Force	144,000	142,800	140,700	139,900
Females Per Cent of Total	45.1	44.5	43.7	43.6

Sources:
Data other than projection: Same as for Table 4.   Projection: Method summarized in text.

decrease from 88 per cent in 1959 to 83 per cent in 2000. This assumption is based on an estimate of the increase in the number that can be expected to be attending specialized training institutions (in higher education and specialized secondary education) on a full-time basis during the course of the next 35 years. It should be noted that the figure of 88 per cent of males age 16–59 in the labor force in 1959 is itself relatively low, primarily because of the number physically disabled from World War II (and unable to work). Allowance is made for the reduction of this number—through the aging of the population—to a minimum by 1985.

3. The percentage of females age 16–54 in the labor force will decline from 87.0 in 1959 to 65.0 in 2000, also because of expected increases in full-time specialized education. If efforts to draw more women into the labor force ("socialized labor") succeed, the percentage would decline at a slower rate, or conceivably even increase. Rising fertility rates, on the other hand, could imply a more rapid rate of decline.

4. The percentage of males age 60 and over (48.5) and females age 55 and over (37.0) in the labor force as of 1959 is assumed to remain unchanged.

The somewhat arbitrary nature of these assumptions, especially with respect to such a long period of projection, is only too evident. The purpose, of course, as with the underlying projection of the population itself (Table 4), is not to "predict" but to enable us to see the implications of certain hypotheses about the future relationships between the labor force and the population. Given the range of conceivable assumptions about participation rates, however, the dominant influence shaping the quantitative dimensions of over-all labor supply in the future is the size and structure of the population itself.

The implications of these several considerations for the future growth of the labor force are as follows: (a) The rate of increase of the total labor force will remain near 1.5 per cent per year until about 1980. Under the assumption of "high" fertility, the labor force will then grow by 1 per cent per year or slightly less between 1980 and 2000, while under the assumption of "low" fertility, after 1985, the labor force will decline absolutely by about 0.2 per cent per year. (These percentages are set forth in Table 8.) (b) The percentage of females in the labor force will decline, from 50.4 in 1965 to about 43.6 in 2000, primarily because of the "normalization" of the sex ratio, but also because of the assumption of a more rapid decline in the percentage of females age 16–54 than males 16–59 in the labor force.

As far as the *structure* of the population and labor force is concerned, we shall confine ourselves to two basic measures: the distribution of the population by rural and urban areas, and the distribution of the labor force by agricultural and nonagricultural occupations. From the data by these measures in Table 7, several observations may be made about the pattern of growth and redistribution to date:

1. The over-all rate of increase of the nonagricultural labor force, as well as of the urban population, after 1928, appears relatively high, although there is variation by sub-periods. Average annual rates of increase of the nonagricultural labor force, from the data in Table 7, are as follows:

1926–39	8.7
1940–50	0.5
1950–60	4.0
1960–65	3.0

The rate of increase of 8.7 per cent per year between 1928 and 1939 is greater, for example, than for any ten-year period in United States experience. On the other hand, the rate of 4.0 per cent per year between 1950 and 1960 and 3.0 per cent between 1960 and 1965 is of an order of magnitude of increases in the United States for several decades during the nineteenth and early twentieth centuries.[82] The increase of only 0.5 per cent per year between 1940 and 1950, of course, reflects the war.

2. The percentage distribution of the labor force between agricultural and nonagricultural occupations has also changed more rapidly than in other countries. Restricting the comparison to countries where the pre-industrialization data indicate a proportion of the population in agricultural occupations of 70 per cent or more (in 1928 in the Soviet Union it was 82 per cent), using ten-year intervals, and beginning with the earliest data available for the other countries, the proportion of the labor force in agricultural occupations declined to below 50 per cent in the course of three decades in the Soviet Union, but took four decades for Sweden, five for the United States, six for Japan, and ten for France.[83]

3. The pace of urbanization is seen in the fact that the urban population by 1965 was at a level (121.7 million) more than four times that of 1928 (27.6 million). On the other hand, the rural

TABLE 7
POPULATION BY URBAN AND RURAL AREAS AND THE LABOR FORCE BY AGRICULTURAL AND NONAGRICULTURAL OCCUPATIONS, U.S.S.R.: ESTIMATES AND AS REPORTED, 1926–66; AND SOVIET PROJECTION, 1970–80
(In thousands)

	Population			Per Cent		Labor Force			Per Cent	
	Total	Urban	Rural	Urban	Rural	Total	Nonagri-culture	Agri-culture	Nonagri-culture	Agri-culture
1926[a]	147,028	26,314	120,714	17.9	82.1	82,300	13,500	68,800	16.4	83.6
1927[b]	—	—	—	—	—	84,200	14,500	69,700	17.2	82.8
1928	149,900	27,600	122,300	18.4	81.6	86,100	15,500	70,600	18.0	82.0
1929	153,100	29,200	123,900	19.1	80.9	87,400	16,400	71,000	18.8	81.2
1930	155,600	30,900	124,700	19.9	80.1	89,500	18,100	71,400	20.2	79.8
1931	158,100	32,000	126,100	20.2	79.8	88,000	21,400	66,600	24.3	75.7
1932	160,700	36,200	124,400	22.6	77.4	88,600	24,100	64,500	27.2	72.8
1933	160,600	39,700	120,900	24.7	75.3	88,800	26,000	62,800	29.3	70.7
1934	160,600	41,000	119,500	25.6	74.4	89,100	25,900	63,200	29.1	70.9
1935	160,500	—	—	—	—	89,300	27,100	62,200	30.3	69.7
1936	162,200	47,000	115,200	29.0	71.0	90,900	28,600	62,300	31.5	68.5
1937	164,100	—	—	—	—	89,600	32,600	57,000	36.4	63.6
1938	167,300	—	—	—	—	89,700	34,700	55,000	38.7	61.3
1939[a]	170,557	56,125	114,432	32.9	67.1	89,800	34,800	55,000	38.8	61.2
1940[d]	196,300	62,000	134,300	31.6	68.4	100,800	40,800	60,000	40.5	59.5
1941	198,700	62,800	135,900	31.6	68.4	—	—	—	—	—
1950	178,700	68,700	110,000	38.4	61.6	94,400	43,100	51,300	44.3	55.7
1951	181,800	72,100	109,700	39.7	60.3	—	—	—	—	—
1952	184,900	75,500	109,400	40.8	59.2	—	—	—	—	—
1953	188,100	78,900	109,200	41.9	58.1	—	—	—	—	—
1954	191,100	82,300	108,800	43.1	56.9	—	—	—	—	—

1955	194,500	85,700	108,800	44.1	55.9	101,300	51,300	50,000	50.6	49.4
1956	197,900	89,100	108,800	45.0	55.0	—	—	—	—	—
1957	201,400	92,600	108,800	46.0	54.0	—	—	—	—	—
1958	205,000	96,200	108,800	46.9	53.1	—	—	—	—	—
1959[a]	208,827	99,978	108,849	47.9	52.1	—	—	—	—	—
1960	212,300	103,800	108,500	48.8	51.2	109,200	64,200	46,800	57.1	42.9
1961	216,200	108,300	107,900	50.1	49.9	—	—	—	—	—
1962	219,800	111,800	108,000	50.9	49.1	—	—	—	—	—
1963	223,200	115,100	108,100	51.6	48.4	—	—	—	—	—
1964	226,400	118,500	107,900	52.3	47.7	—	—	—	—	—
1965	229,300	121,700	107,600	53.1	46.9	113,000	74,500	38,500	65.9	34.1
1966	231,900	124,800	107,100	53.8	46.2	—	—	—	—	—
Soviet Projection[c]										
1970	250,000	144,000	106,000	57.6	42.2					
1975	263,000	165,000	98,000	62.7	37.3					
1980	280,000	190,000	90,000	67.9	32.1					

Sources:

1926–66: from Soviet sources and estimated, as set forth in W. W. Eason, *Soviet Manpower* (forthcoming).

1970–80 Soviet projection: same as in Table 4.

Notes:

[a] Census data (see Table 4 for dates).

[b] January 1, unless otherwise indicated.

[c] End of year.

[d] Data from 1940 are for present territory of U.S.S.R.

population declined by only 8 million, or 7 per cent, during the 1930s, and it has remained essentially unchanged (absolutely) during the entire postwar period to the present. In other words, virtually all of the decline in the rural population was confined to the period of collectivization and World War II. The agricultural labor force displays somewhat the same pattern of change, although declining on the average to a greater degree, implying an increase in the nonagricultural population as a percentage of the rural.

As a result of this pattern of change, the percentage of the population in rural areas (51.2) and the percentage of the labor force in agricultural occupations (42.9) at the beginning of the 1960s was still remarkably high.

The underlying explanation lies in the fact that the proportion of the labor force in agricultural occupations (and of the population in rural areas) at the start of rapid industrialization was so high. The higher the proportion of the labor force in agricultural occupations—for a given rate of growth of the total labor force, and a given change in the agricultural labor force—the greater can be the percentage increase in the nonagricultural labor force. Where the total labor force increases, for example, by 1.5 per cent per year, and the agricultural labor force remains constant, the percentage increase in the nonagricultural labor force is related to the agricultural labor force as a percentage of the total as follows:

Agricultural labor force as percentage of the total	Annual percentage increase in the nonagricultural labor force
85	10.0
50	3.0
15	1.7

Broadly speaking, this illustrates the Soviet case. In the early years of rapid industrialization (1928–39), a relatively rapid rate of increase in the nonagricultural labor force took place (8.7 per cent per year)—with a relatively modest decline in the agricultural labor force (1.8 per cent per year) and a very slow rate of increase in the total labor force (0.5 per cent per year).

During the 1950s, when the proportion of the labor force in agriculture was roughly 50 per cent and when the total labor force was increasing by about 2 per cent per year, a rate of increase of the nonagricultural labor force took place (4 per cent per year) which was less than half of prewar, at the same time that the agricultural labor force declined only moderately, and the rural population was essentially unchanged. During the early 1960s, however, the rate of growth of the total labor force slowed down sharply (the "war babies" effect), and the pace of growth of the nonagricultural labor force was maintained only by virtue of an exceptionally large drop in the agricultural labor force.

The prospects for the future can be seen with reference to the alternative projections of Table 8, and the prospects are rather different from the past. Rates of increase of the nonagricultural labor force as high as 4 per cent per year, or even 3 per cent, are simply untenable for any length of time because what was a relatively large manpower pool in agriculture has become relatively small, dropping from 42.9 per cent of the total in 1960 to 34.1 per cent in 1965.

From a point of departure of 34.1 per cent in 1965, several alternative future trends may be examined and the nature of the constraints on Soviet planners in this respect set forth.

1. Would it be *possible* to maintain a 4 per cent rate of growth of the nonagricultural labor force after 1965? To maintain this rate would require a decrease in the agricultural labor force of 4.8 per cent per year between 1965 and 1970, of 8.6 per cent per year between 1970 and 1975 and 25.3 per cent per year between 1975 and 1980. Shortly after 1980 at this rate, moreover, there would be no one left in agriculture. Clearly a 4 per cent rate cannot be maintained for more than a few years, without making very unreal assumptions about prospective increases in agricultural labor productivity.

2. Even a rate of increase of 3 per cent per year in the nonagricultural labor force would require substantial improvements in agricultural productivity, permitting decreases in the agricultural labor force of 3.4 per cent per year between 1965 and 1970 and 5.3 per cent per year between 1970 and 1975. The corresponding rate from 1975 to 1980 would have to be 10.5 per cent per year, and by that time the agricultural labor force would be reduced to 10 per cent of the total. The 3 per cent rate is also not realistic for more than five years or so.

3. An attempt is made in Table 8 to illustrate a somewhat more feasible path of action for Soviet planners. In the first of the two examples, a "balanced" pattern of change combines a rate of increase of the nonagricultural labor force which declines gradually

TABLE 8

SELECTED ALTERNATIVE PROJECTIONS OF THE LABOR FORCE BY AGRICULTURAL AND NONAGRICULTURAL OCCUPATIONS, U.S.S.R., BY FIVE-YEAR INTERVALS, 1965–2000

	Assuming "Balanced" Rates of Change of the Agricultural and Nonagricultural Labor Force					Assuming Rates of Change Similar to the U.S. After 1905				
	Annual Average Percentage Rate of Change of Labor Force			Agricultural Labor Force Per Cent of Total		Annual Average Percentage Rate of Change of Labor Force			Agricultural Labor Force Per Cent of Total	
	Total	Nonagri-culture	Agri-culture	End of Period	Equivalent Year, U.S.	Total	Nonagri-culture	Agri-culture	End of Period	Equivalent Year, U.S.
1965	—	—	—	34.1	1905	—	—	—	34.1	1905
1965–70	+1.4	+3.0	−3.4	26.7	1921	+1.4	+2.5	−0.6	30.7	1911
1970–75	+1.5	+2.8	−2.2	22.2	1931	+1.5	+2.4	−0.7	27.6	1919
1975–80	+1.5	+2.5	−2.4	18.2	1938	+1.5	+2.3	−0.6	24.8	1923
High Fertility										
1980–85	+1.0	+2.0	−4.3	13.9	1950	+1.0	+2.0	−2.5	20.9	1932
1985–90	+0.7	+1.5	−4.9	11.7	1954	+0.7	+1.8	−4.0	16.3	1942
1990–95	+0.8	+1.3	−3.8	8.3	1958	+0.8	+1.6	−3.7	13.1	1951
1995–2000	+1.0	+1.3	−2.4	7.0	1962	+1.0	+1.5	−2.4	11.0	1956
Low Fertility										
1980–85	+0.4	+1.3	−3.6	14.8	1948	+0.4	+1.8	−3.8	20.0	1933
1985–90	−0.2	+0.5	−5.3	11.4	1956	−0.2	+0.7	−4.6	16.0	1942
1990–95	−0.3	+0.2	−4.6	9.2	1958	−0.3	+0.6	−5.8	12.0	1953
1995–2000	−0.1	+0.4	−5.4	7.0	1960	−0.1	+0.8	−7.9	8.0	1959

Sources: Methods and absolute data are set forth in W. W. Eason, *Soviet Manpower* (forthcoming).

from a 3 per cent rate in the first five years to a rate of 1.3 per cent at the end of the century. The implied decline in the agricultural labor force is of an order of 2 or 3 per cent per year until 1980, and even this is perhaps an optimistic view of the possibilities for raising productivity.

In any event, the picture necessarily tightens after 1980 because of the slowing down in the rate of increase of the total labor force due to the lowering of the birth rates presently under way. (Only substantially higher rates of fertility in the next two decades than are assumed in our projections can change this factor.) To the extent, on the other hand, that "low fertility" pertains, the rate of increase of the nonagricultural labor force will tend to fall well below 1 per cent per year—while the total labor force declines absolutely—and only then can be maintained by rather heroic assumptions concerning progress in agriculture.

4. The second example given in Table 8 patterns Soviet trends after those of the United States from 1905, when the percentage of the labor force in agricultural production was essentially the same as in the Soviet Union at the present time. This alternative implies a slower rate of increase of the nonagricultural labor force to 1980—and very modest declines in the agricultural labor force —and permits thereby somewhat greater flexibility in the two decades prior to the year 2000. This pattern of change, although it involves a rate of change of the nonagricultural labor force which is a good deal lower than in recent years, is consistent with a number of statements in the Soviet literature to the effect that the agricultural labor force will change relatively little in the next decade or so.

5. According to Soviet population projections in Table 7, the rural population will decline to 32.1 per cent of the total by 1980. Compared to the second projection of the labor force in Table 8 (paralleling American experience), this implies a stable to rising agricultural labor force as a percentage of the rural population. Compared to the first projection ("balanced" rates of growth), it implies a declining percentage, as has been the case since the early 1930s and especially in recent years.

All in all, the upshot of these illustrations and comparisons is to place a *much* greater premium on raising productivity per worker —in agricultural as well as nonagricultural branches—than at any time in the past. This particular set of factors, which is tied to the demographic variables, serves to reinforce the conclusion that can be reached on other grounds: the Soviet Union must make major strides in raising productivity if its forward momentum in economic development is not to be threatened. And since some of the principal instruments to this end involve fundamental reforms of the economic (and social) system—in both rural and urban areas—the illustrations from the data in Table 8 put the spotlight on the degree of pressure the planners are under to make these reforms work. It is in this sense that the demographic variables may have a crucial influence on the pattern of economic and social change in the Soviet Union over the next few decades.

9.

Education

WILLIAM K. MEDLIN

The "golden thread" running through the entire Soviet effort at educational reconstruction since 1917, linking all periods together in common design, has been the attempt to make learning of practical value—to fashion the school as a gateway to the world of economic specialization and material production. Marx had stressed that knowledge must prove its worth in practice, and Lenin looked to the schools as a means to disseminate and apply knowledge toward the modernization of a backward society. To function as an agent of material progress in an environment undergoing industrialization was, and continues to be, a paramount task of the new Soviet school.

Because Marxists viewed man's consciousness as a reflection of the material environment, they felt challenged to reconstruct man's psychological and moral nature. To build a "new Soviet man," with a "Communist consciousness," who would work for the common good in restructuring economic and social institutions, became a major goal of Soviet teachers and schools. The state, as the embodiment of the will of the proletariat, was to serve as the catalyst to make possible the new roles and to achieve the goals of society.

The educational efforts launched more than half a century ago are still under way. A review of their relative success, of the performance of Soviet schools, and of the problems facing Soviet education illuminates the current role of the educational enterprise and the emerging trends in the interaction between school and society.

"We can build communism," Lenin declared in 1920, "only on the sum of knowledge, . . . only on the stocks of forces and

241

means left to us by the old society." Appealing for practical schooling, Lenin advised youth: "It is not enough to understand what electricity is; it is necessary to know how to apply it to industry and to agriculture. We must learn this ourselves, and teach it to the whole young generation of toilers."[1] A new army of teachers, he predicted, would lead the people into the modern world and to communism. Later, on the eve of the Five Year Plan, Stalin asserted: "In order to build, we must have knowledge, mastery of science . . . we must learn . . . both from our enemies and from our friends, especially from our enemies . . . , not fearing that [they] may laugh at us, at our ignorance, at our backwardness. Before us stands a fortress . . . called science, with its numerous branches of knowledge. We must capture that fortress at all costs. It is our youth who must capture that fortress, if they want to be builders of the new life, if they want to be real successors of the old guard."

What did the central leaders expect the schools to do? How much would change, and how fast? How would an educational network be created, what would be taught, and to whom? The response to such basic policy matters began to concern the leadership immediately after the Revolution.

A number of fundamental decisions were set forth in policy and legislation during 1917–19. Schools would be administered in a decentralized system, but under a central authority; they would be socially nondiscriminatory and tuition-free, compulsory to age 17, coeducational, and secular. Pupils were to receive material aid, and would be encouraged to relate schooling to work experiences. Teachers were expected to inculcate ideological loyalty and Soviet patriotism, and the schools would serve also as centers to promote adult literacy and cultural programs. They were to emphasize a materialistic and scientific curriculum, aimed at providing manpower resources needed in an industrializing society. Schools and teachers would be primarily architects of change in a modernizing environment.

These principles came to be embodied in the system of "polytechnical education," or the "unified labor school." The quest for its implementation has never been fully realized, but as an aspiration it has influenced Soviet educational philosophy and programs from the beginning, and has recurred in various forms throughout the several periods of Soviet rule. The instruction of pupils through a series of steps linking scientific information with technical skills, followed by training in a vocational specialty, emerged from the early years of Soviet Marxist experimentation as the main format of Soviet polytechnical education. Scientific and technical theory, supported by general education in traditional academic subjects and accompanied by practical exercises and actual productive labor, became the central concern of Soviet educational development. Soviet educational programs, then, developed in a climate of cultural revolution from above. Campaigns for industrialization, secularization, and nationalization ("Sovietization") aimed to supplant traditional institutions. Direct participation by the schools in these huge social programs meant that they were regarded also as political instruments; indeed, the idea that education might lie outside politics was unthinkable in Lenin's view. Soviet policy committed the schools to a radical departure from the old ways, and projected an aggressive educational system into virtually every area of Soviet life. Educational achievement at each rung of the academic ladder took on a transcendent value in society, functioning as a passport to preferred positions. The tangible rewards available in Soviet society have been increasingly linked to educational success.

I. INSTITUTIONAL PERFORMANCE OF SCHOOLS

The frenzied experimentalism of the early period, based on ambitious ideas of polytechnic education and on pedology, ended in the 1930s with a return to more sober practices. Sharply limiting access to secondary education, the government concentrated its resources first on primary schooling and instituted a highly selective policy for further academic opportunities.

By the law of August 14, 1930, primary schooling was made compulsory for the first time in Russian history. Four years of primary education (begun at age 8, later at 7) were required. From 1933 on, annual promotion examinations were held in every grade, and, after 1944, a final examination was required at the end of the 4th, 7th, and 10th grades as a condition of graduation. The legal bases of the 7-year (incomplete secondary) and 10-year (complete secondary) schools were approved in 1934, but since universal primary enrollments were achieved only in 1949 (after the serious wartime interruption), only in the postwar period did a significant expansion in post-primary education occur throughout the Soviet Union. In 1949, a minimum of 7 years of schooling became obligatory, and at least in the urban areas, 10-year education was substantially in effect by 1956. In 1958, however, the government legislated 8 years of schooling as the universal minimum, making the completion of secondary education (11 years, more recently 10) an option only for some.

Soviet educational planning continues to emphasize scientific and technical training. All students going on to secondary school devote some 45 to 50 per cent of their time there to the "hard" subjects—mathematics, science, and technical instruction. Secondary school graduates handle these subjects well enough to proceed to advanced work at university-level institutions which compare favorably with those in Western Europe. The long-standing limitations on access to secondary schools have tended to feed them only the better students, and the high achievement levels are at least partly attributable to this selectivity at admission. The increase in enrollment since about 1954 has somewhat diluted student quality.

Higher Education

Soviet higher schools early became instruments of the five year plans. Over the past thirty years, these institutions have been producing planned quotas of specialists for the professions. Influenced by the prevailing traditional European dualism in educational philosophy, Russian theory assigns the tasks of higher education to two types of institutions: the university, where pure, theoretical sciences and the humanities are primarily taught; and the specialized institute offering courses in the applied disciplines. The proportion of students enrolled in the regular universities has averaged about 8 to 10 per cent of the total number of students at higher levels, the others being in specialized "practical" programs of the institutes.

Qualified engineering and technical observers from the United States and Western Europe have been favorably impressed by the quality of Soviet higher education in many fields, and point to rising competence and important achievements. Programs for specific occupational "profiles," to be sure, are somewhat narrow and utilitarian, while some institutions are poorly equipped. Yet, in the aggregate, they have created well-trained technical cadres, and, in fields of pure science and theory, the international reputation of Soviet scholars attests to their success.

The Soviet student advances to "areas of specialization" in his fourth and fifth years of study (the equivalent of American graduate levels). For example, physics as taught at Moscow in a 5-year program of study is a curriculum academically comparable to a 4-year undergraduate plus about a 2-year graduate program in a first-rate American university. Admittedly, Soviet schools vary in quality from region to region, but educational policy aims through rigid standards to raise the quality of all.

The bifurcation of Soviet higher education, and the intense specialization demanded in advanced programs, are to some extent "bridged" by activities in various research centers and by professional academies. At their apex is the U.S.S.R. Academy of Sciences, supervising a network of affiliates, branches, and basic research institutes across the Soviet Union. (See Chapter 12.)

The more specialized and professional academies are organized to advance scientific and technical work in their respective fields: architecture, education, fine arts, medicine, and the like. In education, the Academy of Pedagogical Sciences in Moscow, under the Russian Republic Ministry of Education, administers nine research academies and scores of experimental schools. The main task of the Academy is to solve theoretical and methodological problems related to governmental policies in education.[2] Pedagogical research institutes having close relations with the Academy are located in other republics. As of 1965, the Pedagogical Academy had nearly 100 members: 36 "full" members, and 61 corresponding ones.[3] An effort in recent years to enlist outstanding teacher-scientists from the more substantive academic fields in the ranks of the Academy reflects a policy decision to strengthen its scientific character and prestige during a period of transition and new educational developments.

Teaching personnel (professors and instructional assistants) in higher education are normally drawn from among advanced degree-holders and research personnel. At the end of 1963, 65 per cent of all those employed in higher education had postgraduate degrees.[4] To hold one of the two university teaching positions, professor and docent (equivalent to the assistant or associate professor), one must normally have the candidate degree. In 1963, there were approximately 11,400 professors and 42,900 docents employed in higher education in the U.S.S.R., and nearly 74,000 teaching assistants. Salaries in these positions, as in research work, are good, ranging from about 250 (new) rubles per month up to 600 rubles per month for professors in leading institutions.

Teacher Education

The levels of teacher preparation for primary and secondary schools, in terms of the amounts of formal education required for certification, compare well with those in Europe and in the United States. Although the quality of education appears to be inferior in the area of social sciences, and no "liberal education" is offered, instruction in the sciences is emphasized and is of good quality.

Kindergarten and primary (grades 1–4) teachers are prepared in two-year pedagogical schools, following on 10 (or 11) years of general education. In 1963–64, there were 260 schools in the U.S.S.R.[5] Their programs concentrate on language, arithmetic, and teaching methods for small children. For grades 5–10/11, teachers must complete a higher education of four years. For a short period (1957–63) educational ministries sought to raise the program to five years, but in view of expansions in post-primary enrollments and the need for increased staffs, it was moved back to four years.

Over the past decade, professional training (educational theory and method) for secondary teachers has declined both absolutely and in relation to substantive subject fields of teaching. The following data on instructional hours for certain education courses illustrate the trend:

Course	1954	1959	1963
Pedagogy (theory)	119 hrs.	100 hrs.	80 hrs.
History of Pedagogy	72 hrs.	72 hrs.	60 hrs.
Methods of Teaching History	116 hrs.	90 hrs.	70 hrs.
Methods of Teaching Literature	133 hrs.	70 hrs.	50 hrs.
Methods of Teaching Russian Language	134 hrs.	100 hrs.	80 hrs.

Source: *Sovetskaia pedagogika*, XXX (January 1966), p. 111.

These sharp declines in the theory and methods of instruction show not only a reduction in professional emphasis, but also a relative contraction of time available for methods of indoctrination in the humanistic subjects. During 1967, a full re-evaluation of pedagogy courses was initiated.

In terms of the proportion of secondary school teachers, however, who have completed a higher education (that is, from 4 to 6 years of education, depending upon the original specialty), there is evidence of steadily rising levels of academic preparation. In the senior grades (9–11) as of 1963, between 85 and 90 per cent of the teachers had completed higher education.[6] For the middle (5–8) grades, however, the percentage was still significantly lower, about 58 per cent. In the foreseeable future, it seems, the overwhelming majority of post-primary teachers will be college trained.

In addition to the 4-year pedagogical institutes, the universities, particularly since 1955, have supplied increasing numbers of secondary school teachers for single-subject work. A significant change in teacher education has been a trend extending training for primary-school teaching to 3- and 4-year post-secondary programs, which should raise the quality of primary instruction accordingly.

Meanwhile, temporary measures are being taken to supplant primary teaching staffs with newly prepared teachers. These measures appear to be related to the manpower shortage, which may well have diverted some teachers and prospective teachers into other employment, as well as to educational factors: the tendency of primary teachers to upgrade their qualifications for service in secondary schools, the increasing numbers enrolled at the primary level, and the expansion of educational facilities in rural areas. Currently, therefore, the ministries of education are arranging 1- to 2-year education courses for graduates of secondary schools in order to qualify them for primary school positions. These courses are being arranged at secondary schools as eleventh and twelfth years of study.

II. Quantitative Levels of Attainment

Enrollment of nearly all eligible children of primary age in Soviet schools has been largely realized during the past generation despite the setbacks of World War II. In 1940, about 90 per cent of the children born during 1930–33 were enrolled in grades 1–4 throughout the U.S.S.R. (including the once-backward Muslim regions); and in 1960, the primary school enrollments were 96 per cent of those born during 1950–54.

Retention rates in post-primary schooling have increased steadily, again with some fluctuations due primarily to the war. The capacities of middle and upper secondary schools to absorb masses of children became significant by 1940, and then again rose rapidly after 1949 when 7-year education became the official minimum. The proportions of youth retained in post-primary grades can be seen in Table 1, which shows a restrictive policy toward upper secondary (college-preparatory) enrollments up to 1955. A sharp drop in eligible age groups (due to lower birth rates during the war) caused a decline in enrollments and also an ensuing labor shortage. Comparing carefully estimated age groups with numbers enrolled in grades 8–9–10 of the secondary school, we find that about 18 per cent of the age group was enrolled in 1959 in the *regular* program. About 1.5 million were also studying in special programs at the upper secondary level for young workers and adults.[7] Because of demographic fluctuations, the number of graduates from secondary school has also varied—for example, from 1.6 million in 1958 to 900,000 in 1963. In 1954, about 12.5 per cent of the age group graduated, and in 1959 this figure was about 21 per cent. In comparison with West European education generally, the Soviet school system has performed quite favorably. Soviet administrators are still concerned, however, about a drop-out rate of 8 per cent by the eighth year.

TABLE 1
TRENDS IN U.S.S.R. PRIMARY–SECONDARY SCHOOL
ENROLLMENTS, 1914–64

Year	Total	Per Cent in Different Grade Levels		
		1–4	5–7/8	8–10/11
1914/15	7,896,000	93.6	4.9	1.5
1922/23	7,322,000	90.3	8.4	1.3
1927/28	11,369,000	87.2	11.7	1.1
1940/41	34,510,000	61.9	31.2	6.9
1946/47	28,506,000	79.2	17.4	3.4
1950/51	33,198,000	59.2	36.3	4.5
1955/56	28,101,000	48.3	33.0	18.7
1959/60	31,000,000	60.0	31.1	8.9
1961/62	35,800,000	52.8	34.6	12.3
1963/64	40,500,000	48.4	42.7	8.4

Sources:
    Narodnoe khoziaistvo SSSR, 1961, pp. 675–78; and *NKh*, 1963, p. 558.
    I. Z. Kaganovich, *Ocherk razvitiia statistiki shkol'nogo obrazovaniia v SSSR*, 1957, p. 86.
    Kul'turnoe stroitel'stvo v SSSR, 1956, pp. 122–23.

Students drawn into secondary technical schools (*tekhnikums*), which are parallel to and in many cases are continuations of general secondary schools, have increased steadily from slightly more than one million enrolled in day courses in 1950, to almost 1.5 million in 1963. Including part-time students, enrollments in 1963 increased to over 2.9 million. In recent years, Soviet schools have been producing between 1.5 million and 2 million young people per year with a secondary certificate. This rate is a significant one, both historically and in comparison with other nations.

These two school systems (general education and special secondary education) account for roughly 50 per cent of the age group eligible for secondary education. The large majority of enrollments have been in the urban areas, with approximately one-third in the rural districts. The remaining youth have pursued a variety of educational and vocational programs, mostly on a part-time basis after completing grade 7 or 8. The following tabulation shows the rising importance of such remedial general education, as well as short-term occupational training:

PART-TIME ENROLLMENTS BY YEAR*

Type of Program	1950	1960	1963
General Education	1,437,800	2,769,000	4,203,500
Vocational Training	439,400	741,000	915,000
Totals:	1,931,200	3,510,000	5,118,500

* Vocational enrollments indicate completions of training courses lasting one year or less.

In addition, the Soviet government also arranges for on-the-job training at a low vocational level. This is not genuine schooling or formal training, but is only intended to raise somewhat the worker's job qualifications. In 1950, about 5.5 million workers (including workers in mechanized agriculture) took advantage of this. Quite obviously, these efforts have attempted to make up for deficiencies in general and vocational education. The implications for worker qualifications and effectiveness can only be guessed at. That these remedial measures are not acceptable, in the long run, is evidenced in the channeling of workers in recent years toward adult schools of general education to qualify them at the middle and upper general secondary school levels. During 1929–63, the Soviet vocational training program prepared only 15 million workers in *specific* occupational skills. The vast majority of workers entered the labor force with little more than primary education.

In an over-all effort to raise worker productivity, educational and manpower policies since the mid-1950s have sought to increase rapidly both the number of youth who continue their secondary education on a part-time basis, and those who enter vocational schools and apprenticeship programs following 7 or 8 years of education. Between 1950 and 1963, students and trainees in these categories have nearly trebled in number, from 2.8 million to 8.3 million, an expansion rate that probably will have a notable effect on manpower productivity.

Similarly, advanced training of managerial, professional, scientific, and other elite personnel in higher institutions has progressively expanded. In recent years higher schools have been enrolling well over 300,000 new students per year in day (regular) programs of study. In the fall of 1963, 340,000 *new* enrollees registered, of whom 52 per cent had fulfilled the 2-year work experience requirement.[8] The summer 1963 graduation figure (from *all* types of university programs) was 300,000. Quantitatively, the educational data place the U.S.S.R. population in highly competitive standing among European and North American countries. In 1958 the Soviet Union ranked third in the percentage of youth aged 15–19 enrolled in schools, and fifth for the age group 20–24 so enrolled, among European nations and North America.[9] In very recent years, however, expansion in secondary schools and higher education of West European countries has been narrowing the Soviet margins.

The steady rate of growth in Soviet higher education can be measured further in terms of both the number of new enrollments per 1,000 population and the number of graduates per 1,000. The following data indicate this rate over the 1940–63 period, and the rough attrition rate over a 5-year period (1958–63) between total number of entrants and graduates.

TABLE 2

NUMBER OF ENTRANTS IN HIGHER SCHOOLS PER 1,000
INHABITANTS AND NUMBERS OF 1ST DEGREE
CANDIDATES PER 1,000 INHABITANTS

Program	Entrants in a Given Year			Graduates in a Given Year		
	1940	1958	1963	1940	1958	1963
Day	.8	1.0	1.5			
Evening/Correspondence	.5	1.1	1.9	.5	1.4	1.5
Total	1.3	2.1	3.4			

Seen through other figures, the growth has meant a steady rise in higher education enrollments.[10] Similar demographic changes in education can only be compared with developments in the United States, although some European countries are now rapidly following suit.

TABLE 3
RISE IN EDUCATIONAL ENROLLMENTS PER 1,000 POPULATION

	Higher Education		Technical Specialized Secondary Schools	
	All Programs	Day Alone	All Programs	Day Alone
1950	6.9	4.5	7.1	5.8
1963	14.4	6.0	13.2	6.5

Students who graduate from 4- or 5-year (or similar) programs with a diploma, and who have passed the final state examinations with outstanding marks or have otherwise demonstrated high ability, may apply by examination for graduate study (called *aspirantura*). This advanced program may be offered by a university, an institute, a research center, etc. After about 3 years of study, the student may present a dissertation before a panel of examiners. If successful, he receives the traditional degree, "candidate of sciences" (*kandidat nauk*, reintroduced in Russia in 1934), which is roughly equivalent to an American Ph.D. It is confirmed by the Higher Attestation Commission of the U.S.S.R. Ministry of Higher and Special Secondary Education. In 1964 there were approximately 122,000 persons holding this degree. The highest Russian degree is the doctor (*doktor*) of sciences, and is awarded sparingly to scholars who have made significant contributions in their field. There were (as of 1964) only about 13,500 doctors of science in the entire Soviet Union.

The rate of graduate (*aspirantura*) training has risen sharply in recent years: between 1960 and 1963 the number of students seeking the candidate's degree doubled, reaching a total of 73,105. Of that number, however, 41 per cent were enrolled while they continued working. The fields of specialization of graduate students for 1959 and 1963 show clearly the overwhelming scientific-technical orientation of Soviet education. (See Table 4, p. 252.)

There is no indication that these proportions or allocations in advanced education are undergoing any significant modifications. The regional distribution of these graduate enrollments shows

TABLE 4
FIELDS OF *Aspirantura* SPECIALIZATION
(*In per cents*)

Field		1959		1963	
Physics-Mathematics	⎫	11.3	⎫	10.3	⎫
Chemistry	⎪	5.9	⎪	5.6	⎪
Biology	⎪	4.8	⎪	6.3	⎪
Geology	Sciences	3.7	⎪	3.4	⎪
Medicine-Pharmacy	&	7.4	= 78.8	6.5	= 78.8
Engineering	Technology	37.4	⎪	37.6	⎪
Geography	⎪	.9	⎪	1.0	⎪
Agriculture-Veterinary	⎭	7.4	⎭	8.1	⎭
History-Philosophy	⎫	4.4	⎫	5.0	⎫
Economics	⎪	7.5	⎪	7.5	⎪
Pedagogy	Humanities	2.5	= 21.2	2.5	= 21.2
Law	&	.9	⎪	1.0	⎪
Philosophy	Social	4.0	⎪	3.5	⎪
Arts	Sciences	1.9	⎭	1.7	⎭

Source:
NKh, 1963, p. 596; DeWitt, 1961, p. 754.

a significant educational increase in what were once culturally backward areas, and particularly in Central Asia. In 1963, for example, 14.2 per cent of all *aspirantura* in the U.S.S.R. were studying in that region, which accounts for 17 per cent of the total Soviet population. This high level of investment in advanced scientific training among a population that did not know modern education a half century ago is a remarkable development, whether in the U.S.S.R. or elsewhere in the world.

The success rates in higher education are consistent with established Soviet practice for that level, where standardized exams for leaving secondary school and university entrance exams are required. For day-program students, the success rate, according to available statistics, is about 95 to 96 per cent—a figure which the U.S.S.R. Minister of Higher and Secondary Specialized Education holds as the constant goal. Based on estimates of children born in a given year, the successful students from the *day* programs represent between 7 to 8 per cent of an *original* age group; including the *evening* program students, the figure is about 10 per cent; and with the dubious addition of those finishing correspondence programs, a figure of 12 per cent is possible. These are respectable figures in comparison with educational results in Western Europe and even in the United States.

Educational performance may also be shown according to the

levels of formal schooling *completed* by the total population, and
by the employed segment. In 1959, the *total* population over 10
years of age had completed an average of 4.5 years of schooling;
while 3.3 per cent of the *employed* population had completed
higher education, and 4.8 per cent had finished special secondary
(semiprofessional) training.[11] By 1964, these two figures increased
respectively to 4 per cent and 5.8 per cent. Nearly 10 per cent of
those employed in 1964, therefore, were members of the professional and technical ranks as defined by educational level. There
is a sizable cultural gap between this group and the masses, and it
remains an important educational task to close this gap. Comparatively, in 1957 the U.S. population aged 14 and over had
completed an average of 10 years of schooling per person.[12]

The distribution of the highly skilled and professional personnel
reflects the decidedly scientific-technical character of the Soviet
intelligentsia as compared to West European and American elites.
The rate of annual graduations from university-level programs
nearly doubled between 1950 and 1963. Since about 75 per cent
of these graduates are trained in the pure or applied sciences (natural, physical, technical), the character of intellectual leadership
in the Soviet Union will remain science-oriented for some years
to come.

The age character of the Soviet intelligentsia, as represented by
professional and semiprofessional personnel in 1959, is significant
for its *youth.* Seventy-five per cent of those educationally qualified
as members of the intelligentsia are between the ages of 20 and
45; 49 per cent are under age 35, and 63 per cent are under 40.[13]
The new knowledge and skills required for modern Soviet society
are largely concentrated—and increasingly so as the rates of training rise sharply—in the young men and women of the country,
a factor with important intellectual and sociological implications
for the future.

III. Educational Trends

To recapitulate the salient features of Soviet educational development, one can indicate the significant functions it has performed in an environment undergoing industrialization, as well as
the major problems and likely developments in the years ahead.

Of major importance has been the role of education in the
transformation of a traditional agrarian society into a modern,
industrial one. Schools have virtually replaced the more traditional

social units in forming the behavior of youth and orienting them to the adult world. There has been substitution of a scientific, technical, and materialistic humanism for a more traditional set of values. They have initiated a process of selection and differentiation of the talents of young people for occupational roles, based in part on a competitive academic system.

The educational process has included the function of modernizing and "Europeanizing" the minority peoples whose traditions, such as the Muslim, were essentially medieval prior to the Soviet period of forced modernization; selected elements of cultural heritage were, however, maintained for purposes of historical identity and social continuity.

Some of the problems facing the educational system appear to be problems of program differentiation and new curriculum development (particularly in view of the limited success of the *polytekhnizatsiia*), and of comprehensive secondary schools *versus* institutional pluralism. There is official concern about rural educational facilities and a desire to upgrade their quality and availability; there is concern with the moral-ideological training of youth and the spread of delinquent behavior. Soviet leadership in the academic world also must consider manpower needs in the current and subsequent five year plans, and allocate job placement accordingly.

Among the more recognizable trends in the educational sphere, one can see an increasing use of orthodox (Western) social theory as well as behaviorism in educational research, departing from stereotyped attitudes phrased in Marxist-Leninist terminology. There are new roles emerging for educational personnel, including both a trend toward some administrative autonomy and the application of new methods to changing teaching tasks. Special interest groups are becoming more articulate in educational affairs, attempting to shape school policies for particular advantages.

Almost all of these problems and trends are similar, even identical, with those common to Western industrial societies. Some elaboration will help to illustrate this resemblance and indicate the main directions in which Soviet schools appear to be moving.

Secondary Education

Expansion of secondary academic and technical schools in urban areas has brought about mass education at this level. The same claim cannot be made for rural facilities, however. In 1963–64, when 47 per cent of the Soviet population still lived in rural areas, the number of youth in *urban* secondary schools was nearly double the number in rural schools. Yet high school education is rapidly becoming more universally accessible, and educational policy-makers are faced with the problem of how best to differentiate the programs in accordance with regional, societal, and occupational needs, as well as the capacities of students. In struggling with and debating the problem since the mid-1950s, educators have identified the main alternatives as: providing three or four different "tracks" in the high school (such as physical science, natural science, technical science); requiring polytechnical education and a vocational-type skill of all pupils; retaining the general academic program for a portion of the youth, while developing special, professionally oriented training in the *tekhnikums*, specialist schools, and vocational schools for others.[14] In 1963 policy discussions intensified, and a "Commission on the Study of Differentiating Instruction" under the Pedagogical Academy was appointed to guide the deliberations. It recommended a 3-track system with retention of the polytechnical training concept.[15]

What has emerged from these policy dilemmas is a mixture of various proposals and new programs. A number of "special subject" secondary schools in mathematics, sciences, and foreign languages, on the model of the traditional general academic school, have been established for students particularly gifted or interested in those subjects.[16] Administrators of vocational and technical secondary schools have also succeeded in getting funds and resources to expand their programs.

In January 1966, and in subsequent legislation, the government unveiled the future form of primary-secondary education, which will be a sequence of 3 years-5 years-2 years. The middle and upper secondary grade levels will offer considerable options in basic subjects (sciences and humanities), as well as in electives such as arts, commercial skills, a second foreign language, vocational shop, etc.[17] Secondary education is now offering a much wider choice for Soviet youth, ranging from academic preparation in special subject areas at one extreme, to vocational-technical education and training for work at the other. These varied programs may be had in some schools under the same roof, or in particular schools that offer unique or special programs for a particular student body.

This pattern of differentiation has come about not so much as the result of deliberate policy, as through trial and error, revisions of original plans, experimentation, and the development of special educational programs strongly supported by certain administrators and professional groups. Legislation has merely tended to confirm the end result. This kind of policy evolution, in the context of Soviet planning methods, appears the most significant aspect of secondary educational development in recent years. It reflects the inability of the planners to predict in any precise form the shape and content of secondary schooling. Changes come about as much through mutual accommodation as they do through deliberate planning.

Soviet educational authorities expect to have 50 million school children enrolled in 1970, a figure which would represent over 95 per cent of the age group 7–16 years (41.3 million eligible for grades 1–8, and 10.2 million eligible for grades 9–10).[18] To provide *general* educational facilities for all those eligible for upper secondary schooling in 1970, the capacity of existing schools and the number of teachers will have to expand about fourfold. The facilities of technical and regular secondary schools would probably have to double. This latter goal appears reasonable. The quality of school expansion, however, remains to be seen. Current policies give only vague indications. Qualifying factors, particularly the level of academic standards, will be discussed in connection with professional manpower selection.

One singular sociopolitical factor emerges from this brief review of institutional developments: the early policy aim of the Soviet government to create a single unified, or common, school system for all children, that would provide instruction in all branches necessary to the modern man, has been modified by *many* alternative solutions and, apparently, by social interests at odds with the unified school concept. Certain professional and intellectual groups managed to develop educational channels leading inevitably to stratified, hierarchical positions in the society.

Education in Rural Areas

The major "drag" on Soviet educational development is the state of rural schools. As recently as 1964, authorities complained of woefully substandard conditions in some rural 8-year schools, where 80 per cent or more of the schools had no special science rooms.[19] One reason for these conditions is the smallness of the schools; many have but 10–15 pupils in grades 1–4, while 8-year schools may have as few as 50 pupils.[20] Authorities plan to regroup rural communities and their schools so that several thousand villages will merge into several hundred resettled communities. The initial changes are to be made by reorganizing the schools, and equipping them with better facilities.[21] A plan for geographic redistribution of technical and semiprofessional schools is also under way, in order to raise the quality of education accessible to the rural population.[22] If the necessary resources and teaching personnel can be relocated to "barren" rural regions, it would improve the schools greatly. A recent change in salary policy, which equalized the primary schedule with the secondary, may also contribute to upgrading the rural primary and 8-year schools.[23]

Moral-Ideological Training

The attempt of Soviet educators to shape behavior in accordance with the regime's expectations still remains at the forefront of Soviet social concerns. In 1963 the youth leader, Pavlov, recounted a whole series of laxities and nonconforming traits among the youth of Komsomol age.[24] Moscow educators say that in Soviet urban centers the delinquency rate is around 8–10 per cent.[25] A number of press reports on youth behavior reveal an opportunistic attitude toward education, suggesting an interest in gaining prestige and success—with all of the "middle-class" benefits—because it is socially the thing to do, and not because such achievement benefits socialist society. Studies of youth programs suggest that the political use made of youth organizations is in good measure responsible for the limited success of the regime in attempting to insure good, "positive" behavior on the part of all young people.[26] A group of university students was recently polled about their habits in seeking political advice on controversial matters, and not one of them indicated that the Komsomol leaders' guidance would be asked!

Young people seem to have become bored with and unresponsive to exhortative techniques of indoctrination. Consequently, in recent years some Soviet educators have turned to a serious study of Western, particularly American, principles and methods of moral and ideological education.[27] Their researchers are also finding that the standardized instructional material used in the social studies are inadequate to the task, and that most children seem to learn their values from the social environment of their families.[28]

Authorities are attempting to expand the services of schools to care for and thereby influence children during after-school hours, such as the "prolonged-day" program.[29] Renewed attempts are being made to revitalize and expand the attractive features of the Pioneer and Komsomol activities through student clubs and activity centers.[30] Boarding schools, which had among their objectives the provision of a wholesome moral climate, appear to have encountered a host of problems that were not anticipated.[31]

Certain signs in the behavior of Soviet youth suggest that greater individualism and avenues for self-expression will be the most pressing demands by young people. As Soviet society becomes more affluent, the ranges of choice open to the young increase, and contacts with other cultures multiply. Such manifestations of social change are harbingers of new cultural values and patterns.[32] Greater nonconformity to authoritarian impositions on youth may be expected in the future.

Ideological pluralism is also evident in the "survival" of traditional religious beliefs. In Orthodox, Protestant-Evangelical, and Islamic rites in particular, throughout the Soviet Union, the careful visitor can gather ample indications of this fact. The press frequently reports that schools and cultural agencies need to be more vigilant in handling manifestations of religious belief and activity.[33]

Another, and perhaps more powerful, source of pluralism that resists integration into Communist conformity is national identity. Especially in those regions where a high degree of native homogeneity persists, in Uzbekistan, for example, it appears that the nationality school operates as a powerful instrument of native solidarity and cultural identification with the national republic, Soviet ideological aims to the contrary notwithstanding.[34] While there is obviously significant ambivalence among some native elites, who choose to "Russify" as a means for political and social mobility, the available evidence suggests that the vast majority of Uzbeks, for example, strongly identify with native cultural values. Barring mass Slavic immigration into such areas as Uzbekistan, Tadzhikistan, Georgia, Armenia, and Azerbaidzhan, one can anticipate continuing effects of national feeling in education during the decade ahead.

An additional area of ideological dilution lies in scientific and independent thinking. Leading Soviet scientists have come out for more flexibility and freedom to work against the stifling and uncreative influences of bureaucratic methods in scientific education and research.[35] Recent trends in this direction have appeared in educational research, discussed below, where a sharp increase in the use of genuine social science methods has occurred. It is probable that in the future the academic elites will enlarge the area of free thinking and scientific autonomy, while the capacity of the regime to make policy independently of the academic, scientific, and technical elites will significantly diminish.

Demographic and Cadres Trends

The potential increase in student enrollments at all levels will seriously tax the capacities of Soviet schools and teaching personnel in the coming years. In primary-secondary schools of general education, enrollments have been increasing at rapid rates: from 29.6 million in 1958, to 40.5 million in 1963, and to a possible 48–50 million by 1970. These increases will naturally provide more applicants for special training in university, professional, and technical schools.

Plans for expanding the training of special cadres (professional and semiprofessional) include the graduation of some 7 million persons during 1966–70—or an average of 1.4 million a year.[36] The economic managers wish (as they have for years) to increase the ratio of technical aides to professional personnel. A common complaint has been that too many specialists with higher education must work at technician levels.[37] To reach the ambitious goal, the number of technical graduates over the next five years will have to more than triple over the present number of higher school graduates; training programs in the five year plan would have to graduate approximately 5.5 million technical personnel, as compared to some 1.5 million professionals. But if the annual increase in day-program registration levels off at around 350,000 for higher education, it is very unlikely that the goals can be reached.[38]

Selection practices for upward educational mobility have undergone several revisions and promise to be controversial in the future. In 1963, an attempt to "democratize" entrance into higher education (VUZ) and to stimulate secondary school achievements by giving a certain weight to the *average* high school marks was opposed and subsequently reversed.[39] Under the 1965 rules, however, rectors have wide discretion, and competitive entrants must take four entrance examinations, including two in their major field. These measures suggest that traditional academic qualifications will probably prevail in Soviet education for some years to come. Social pressures aiming to reduce that exclusiveness, however, could well influence this policy.

While Soviet policy has in recent years pushed for expansion in correspondence education (enrollments rising by 75 per cent and 180 per cent during 1958–63 in higher schools and special secondary schools, respectively), authorities are by no means satisfied with the results. Attempts are again under way to improve the methods and facilities used in correspondence education,[40] but the history of these programs raises real questions about the wisdom of continued investments in expanding them.

With the aim of controlling more closely the employment of graduates, the government has established commissions on job placement to interview and assign young specialists. Commission responsibilities include also graduates of academic secondary schools who do not continue on to specialized education.[41] As an additional control measure, institutions withhold the graduate's original diploma or certificate, which is granted only upon one year's service in the occupation assigned. Unless the professional and semiprofessional employment market improves radically, it appears that the former policy of limited self-selection in job placement will be temporarily inoperative. The new policy could have, according to views expressed by some young people, negative effects on motivation and performance.[42]

IV. New Educational Roles

As Soviet education has moved to levels of maturity and complexity comparable to those of Western industrial nations, new functions and responsibilities have emerged for educational personnel. The party has begun to call on educators to undertake research projects essential to educational progress.

One of the most significant points of change has been the rapidly growing use of social science research rather than the dogmatic application of political ideology to educational administration. A sharp attack by *Pravda* against dogmatism and the slavish use of quotations from the "bibles" of Marxism-Leninism in the name of research appears to represent a growing consensus in the central party circles in support of genuine social science research.[43] One should not overlook the persistence of the doctrinal point of view,[44] yet the demand that researchers attack the "problems of reality," that they abandon the habit of reducing social research to "a mere exegesis of . . . resolutions" and that "the striving for truth stands above all," is an appeal that resounds strongly. Official education journals and the party press have soundly criticized the "lack of a truly scientific method for analyzing and generalizing the facts of teaching practice."[45]

As mass education practices have begun to swell the ranks of secondary schools, many new and serious problems have arisen. Some of the main problems identified are: personality and character development; moral values; lack of student self-appraisal; sociological problems in school-community relations (especially as these affect the drop-out question); study of the physical growth and mental maturation of the child; proper relations between general education and practical, productive work; problems of foreign-language training; usefulness of the historical and comparative (cross-cultural) study of education; the economic value and costs of education; and others.

The drop-outs and grade-repeaters in the 8-year schools have occasioned some systematic sampling and questionnaire techniques bearing on the problem.[46] Origins of the drop-outs, which reach between 10 and 12 per cent of those enrolled in grade 8 during that school year, are being studied in terms of their individual histories and social background. The social environment of children, particularly that of the family, is now coming under special scrutiny.[47] Traditional psychological positions, anchored in Pavlov's conditioning theory, are yielding ground to some new research pursuits.[48] Serious attention and research concerning problems of sexual behavior and proper sex education of youth have been reported by educators in recent years.[49] The school's role as a significant social forum for youth is being recognized and utilized for the moral health of young people.

Analytical, critical thinking which builds scientific and research attitudes is apparently one aim of new methods being encouraged in teacher-pupil relationships. One lead editorial called for lively interaction in social studies classes, so that "habits of independent analysis" could be nurtured.[50] A still more serious approach to the research method in teaching both natural and social sciences, stressing hypothesis-formation and proof, has been urged by the Academy of Pedagogical Sciences.[51] The demands for scientific improvement include revision of the standard biology text (by E. A. Veselov) to include up-to-date findings in genetics. Soviet authorities have also, mainly through the press, renewed a lively interest in educational experimentalists and theorists of the 1920s (Lunacharskii, Shatskii, Blonskii, Pinkevich, Vygotskii, etc.) who stood for scientific inquiry.

These and still other new concerns signify an important modification of the traditional role of the school in Soviet society. If more experimental and dynamic functions emerge and are able to gain the same measure of political confidence and prestige as have the traditional ones, it seems likely that Soviet educators will acquire positions of influence and decision-making that they have not had in the past.

There is also the emergence of distinct interest and pressure groups, articulating and using cultural means to further the aims of the social "consensus." It is a fact, for example, that certain groups have insisted from the outset of the national debates on educational reform in 1956, that special schools for artistically and intellectually gifted children be provided. Another social stratum, apparently less articulate but which made its voice known, opposed such a policy in favor of a more unified and socially egalitarian school pattern.[52] The 1958–59 reform legislation did *not*, as a result, explicitly provide for such special schools. As educational affairs have actually worked out, however, special schools have been established for those youngsters particularly endowed to profit from them. The military hierarchy and the party hierarchy are other clear examples of special interest groups whose children receive special educational privileges.

Finally, there is at least one sign that the teaching profession is exercising a degree of independent, responsible authority that it has never before enjoyed. In 1962 a plan was developed to allow working educators to elect their own supervisory personnel.[53] Nominations of qualified persons are made by educators and related personnel in party, government, trade union, and youth organization agencies. It is not clear yet to what extent this has, in fact, resulted in representative, professional selection of administrative leadership in Soviet education. As in Western industrial societies, the emergence of a professional "class" typified by educators along with other academicians would coincide with a managerial "class" who together might have a significant influence on the composition of the political elite governing the country.

All of these considerations, taken collectively, point to a growing leverage of power and influence exercised by the educated "products" of the schools and by the professional personnel in charge of the educational system itself. As agents of change, schools and teachers will continue to perform key roles in the social and cultural reconstruction of Soviet society.

10.

Agriculture

ARCADIUS KAHAN

The impact of wholesale political changes in the Soviet Union would surely entail drastic consequences for agricultural institutions, but the first responsibility of the economist is to deal with the more certain signs of change that are already abundantly in evidence. Let us assume, as a matter of probability, that the basic political features of the Soviet system will remain intact in the foreseeable future, or that they will change only very gradually.

In agriculture, this means that the Communist Party leadership will continue to be the supreme decision-maker; that its political goals will continue to be given priority over the economic interests of particular institutions or sectors of the economy or of localities and that the criteria in reaching decisions affecting agriculture will be derived, as they are now, from over-all policy objectives for the economy as a whole.

Within this framework, however, we can expect highly significant changes in the agricultural sector itself. For 1970, the Soviet leaders have set as the goal of agricultural development an increase in output of 25 per cent over 1966. The targets for the major agricultural commodities compare as follows with the average yearly gross output of the preceding five-year period:

AVERAGE YEARLY AGRICULTURAL PRODUCTION
(Official figures in millions of tons)

Commodity	Actual Output, 1961–65	Planned Output, 1966–70
Grain	130.3	167
Potatoes	81.6	100
Sugar beets	59.2	80
Cotton	5.0	5.6–6.0
Meat (slaughtered weight)	9.3	11
Milk	64.7	78
Eggs (billion eggs)	28.7	34

Such an increase will depend upon changes in one or more critical factors:

1) Resource allocation in the agricultural and nonagricultural sectors of the economy and its relations to total agricultural output.

2) The efficiency of the planning process in agriculture and its responsiveness to the needs of agriculture.

3) The organization of the farms and the scale of their operations.

4) The output-mix resulting from inter-regional and inter-farm specialization.

5) The input-mix: (a) substitution among inputs; and (b) technological improvements.

6) Absolute and relative prices of particular agricultural commodities and their impact upon the profitability of farm operations in general and of particular commodities.

7) Governmental policies and their relation to the income of the agricultural population.

I. RESOURCE ALLOCATION

One must begin with the question of overriding importance for the performance of every economic unit in the Soviet Union, as elsewhere: the allocation and planning of resources. In the past, the prevailing policy of allocation[1] supported the maximum transfer of resources away from agriculture and into the other sectors of the economy and prevented by political means a price increase of agriculture's main resource: labor. Moreover, Stalin's policy entailed such a severe system of taxation on agriculture that it was deprived of the opportunity even to bid for resources. Capital inputs were limited to quantities that barely enabled the agricultural sector to function, and were restricted to branches of agriculture whose additional output was needed for the expansion of industry or where capital could substitute for the large amounts of labor being transferred out of agriculture. It was a policy of "calculated subsistence," channeling forced savings into the industrial sector for investment in producer goods industries.

Over the years these policies led to a decrease in the volume of savings above the "subsistence level," to stagnation of agricultural output, and to the specter of a repetition of the experience of the 1920s: the gripping (but at that time largely imaginary) fear that the supply of agricultural commodities to the urban areas would fall behind the effective demand for food and fibers. While, in the earlier period, the blame could be laid to the *kulaks* (rich peasants), by the 1950s the fear was better founded and stemmed from the incentive crisis in socialized agriculture. Stalin's successors had to follow one of two paths: to introduce rationing or to institute significant changes in the existing pattern of resource allocation.

During the Khrushchev period the harshest tax features of the Stalin policies were abolished. Prices paid to farms for their output increased appreciably, although not sufficiently and not for all commodities, so that both the general level and the relative prices within agriculture still left much to be desired. Meanwhile, the supply of agricultural machinery, mineral fertilizers, construction materials, and other inputs was rising. Until 1957/58, then, the inflow of resources was rising, relative to the outflow. Optimists could hope, by extrapolating the trend, that agriculture would ultimately receive nearly the market equivalent for its output. However, during the subsequent period the Soviet government began sharply to "economize" on direct investment in agriculture. The first step was to sell the equipment of the Machine Tractor Stations (MTS) to the collective farms at a relatively high price in order to keep agricultural prices from rising above the level of the previous procurement costs (inclusive of the state expenditures on the MTS) and to raise the prices of machinery and spare parts. The second major step in this "economy" campaign was to deduct a substantial portion of the investment in the mineral fertilizer industry from the outlays marked for agriculture. (Although not admitted officially, this seems to have been the logic behind the Khrushchev policies during the later years.) Although it cannot be documented with precision, the inter-industry flow of resources during the latter part of the Khrushchev period was, in the short run, turned against the agricultural sector and probably contributed to the decline in the rate of its output growth. It was left for Khrushchev's successors to redress the balance, so that another period of more rapidly rising agricultural output could get under way.

II. The Efficiency of the Planning Process in Agriculture

Any system of planning involves a set of successive activities which follow the statement of general goals submitted to the planners by the top decision-making authorities. These activities encompass the flow of pertinent information about past and present economic performance, which in turn provides the basis for the choices involved in making alternative decision-proposals, the means to verify the expected consequences (effects) of the defined alternatives, the transmission of the final decisions and the accompanying directives on how to implement the decisions, and the control over the execution of the decisions.

In the past, Soviet planning emphasized the implementation of decisions and the control aspects to the detriment of information-gathering, alternative solutions, and verification. This particular "style" stemmed from the structure of Soviet political institutions and from the lack of a functional division of authority within the government. Indeed, the history of planning since Stalin's death can be described as a slow, evolutionary process of establishing the proper functions and characteristics of a planning system and diminishing the "special" or "extraordinary" features which it had acquired in its Soviet form.

The socialization of agriculture in the Soviet Union initially brought the agricultural sector of the economy within the sphere of influence of the central planning authorities during a period of extraordinary stress. The Soviet economy was then involved in the strenuous effort to expand its industrial base and to build up its basic capital industries (fuel, electricity, ferrous metallurgy, and heavy machine building) and had shifted from broad target-setting of general economic indicators to specific target-setting of output in physical terms. This entailed a system of direct physical allocation of the most important raw materials, labor, and equipment. The new system of planning purported to overcome the difficulties arising from intense inflationary pressures. Its real causes, however, were, on the one hand, the suspension of the operation of the price system in both the factor and product markets and, on the other, the irresistible temptation to use the simple mechanism of physical planning in the case of selected, homogeneous products (for which the technological production coefficients were known) and to consider the remaining products as residual claimants for resources. Thus, agriculture came under the jurisdiction of the planning authorities during a period of extreme primitivism in the concepts, methods, and practice of centralized planning.

It used to be fashionable among Western economists to blame some of the shortcomings of Soviet agriculture upon the rote application of industrial planning methods. But this ascription needs to be qualified if one is to fix more precisely the sources of agriculture's problems. In fact, Soviet industrial planning was by and large successful in those industries high on the list of the planners' preference scale, where the products were relatively homogeneous, where the technical coefficients were known, and the problems to be solved were of an engineering rather than economic nature. However, in industrial branches involving multiple or joint products, choices between end-products, or between end- and intermediate products, the system of industrial planning ran into trouble for lack of a proper price policy and lack of a flexible incentive policy, or because of the rigidity of centralized control.

Basically, agriculture resembles the second type of industry. In areas of monocultures (for example, cotton), where other crops were strictly limited by climatic conditions or by government decree, planning was fairly successful in providing the necessary inputs (water and fertilizer) and in making the price and income incentives operative. But in most agricultural areas, where a given acreage of land and an existing stock of machinery and labor permitted a diversified output or allowed many choices, the system of centralized planning—conducted without proper consultation of local management and often at variance with the local interests and conditions—resulted in poor decisions and inferior results.

The ineffectiveness of Soviet agricultural planning, then, is attributable not only to the rigid use of industrial planning methods but to the inherent weaknesses of a centralized system of planning when it interferes with the minutiae of local production decisions and choices and proceeds without proper information about the complexity of local conditions. The poor performance of the planning process in agriculture is explained by two additional factors: the relatively low priority of agriculture on the preference scale of the decision-makers;[2] and the uncertainties of the weather, which often plays havoc with production targets and procurement plans. The point is that agricultural planning is better served by ranges than by fixed quotas.

A further difficulty stems from the information-gathering activities of the planning authorities (including the Central Statistical Agency), which have been inadequate and often deliberately circumscribed or limited to data that revealed the marketing production capacities of the farms to the exclusion of other aspects of their economic performance. Certain types of information were neither collected nor solicited; the planning authorities were left in the dark about such fundamental matters as productivity and incomes. Indeed, one has the impression that target-setting in agriculture during much of the Soviet period has borne precious little relation to reality. It has even been difficult to ascertain whether the targets for agricultural production were the product of the planning agencies, of the agricultural section of the party hierarchy, or of the party's propaganda section. The range of possible authorship indicates their limited value as a policy or planning guide.

The lack of internal or external criteria to judge and evaluate alternative solutions has had a detrimental effect upon the quality of the decisions arrived at or proposed by the planners. It was only very recently that Soviet planners began to include in their considerations the very important (although elementary) idea of complementarity of inputs to achieve a certain level of output.

> In the plans and estimates of production as well as in the evaluation of particular projects, the calculations were invariably made with reference to a single factor to which the expected production increase was attributed. The planners of a particular irrigation project acted as if water were the only source of the expected increase in yield. The fact that a combination of irrigation, larger allocations of mineral fertilizer, and perhaps insecticides might produce an effect higher than the sum of effects of the three inputs when applied separately somehow did not enter the minds of the planners. To the extent that complementarity did not become a part of the economic calculus, resources were squandered and capacities remained underutilized; on the other hand, coefficients were wrongly estimated by attributing the production increase to one factor, while ignoring the simultaneous application of other inputs which did not appear in the original calculation. It is only very recently that factor complementarity was recognized and is slowly being integrated in the planning system in Soviet agriculture.[3]

Improvements in the information flow and handling of alternative solutions are mandatory for more accurate planning.

The quality of decision-making in Soviet agricultural planning has suffered from two other major shortcomings. One is the tendency to generalize from limited experience. Because the planners could coerce the farms into following commands, errors were inflated to a very large scale. The list of such monumental blunders is very long indeed. It will suffice to mention the planting of rubber-yielding *kok-saghyz*, the planting of cotton on unirrigated lands in European Russia and the Ukraine, the expansion of corn to the north, or the plowing up of summer fallow in the east, as examples of the magnitude of damage inflicted by the planners and decision-makers. The second shortcoming stems from the nature of mass campaigns to which either all farms or a large number were inappropriately subjected. Such campaigns included a shelter-belt planting program, the attempts of universal introduction of the grassland system, the indiscriminate conversion of meadows into plowland, and the like.

One result was to prevent regular crop rotation schemes on Soviet farms.[4] The damage to crop rotation alone involved such high losses in output that even the occasionally successful campaigns could not compensate for them.[5] Nor does the present system of agricultural planning possess built-in safeguards against a repetition of such decisions.

The implementation of the planners' decisions requires a specified chain of command for the transmission of guidelines, and a smoothly functioning system of material supply to the farm units. I have already suggested that guidelines are preferable to commands since they leave much more room for local decisions on important details. However, in order for the planners to give up their rigidity as a command-issuing group, the decision-makers will have to modify their notion of Soviet society's monolithic nature and their simplistic conception of an instantaneous, always predictable response by the local management or labor force. Considerable progress along such lines may well take place. If so, we can expect a clearly differentiated incentive system to replace the current unsophisticated methods of securing compliance with the goals of the decision-makers.

Some aspects of the problems of the supply of materials to agriculture are treated elsewhere in the essay; here suffice it to point out that the main feature of the system—centralized monopoly— makes it unresponsive to the needs and demands of the farm units. Although officially, the Agricultural Supply Organization (*Soiuzsel'khoztekhnika*) is an agency which is supposed to transmit offers from industry to the farms, and orders of the farms for the output of industry, in reality it became a monopolistic distributor for the agricultural machinery industry, a supply organization servicing farms with the available industrial output. Thus far the demand on the part of the farms has had only a marginal effect upon the composition and quality of supply, and farms are forced to accept whatever items are proferred or face the prospect that no supplies at all will be forthcoming. Needless to say, in order to remedy the existing situation the centralized agency would have to be broken up into smaller, autonomous units to permit more direct dealings between farms and industrial marketing institutions. Perhaps a measure of competition ought to be allowed within the industrial branches supplying agriculture, since only within a decentralized setting of marketing can the preferences of the farms be taken into consideration. When producers are allowed to compete for the available market, the usual result is the introduction of alternative products and goods of higher quality. Such an arrangement no doubt would involve short-run headaches for accountants in the state planning agency, but it is bound to save them much effort in the future by eliminating guesswork about the quantities and qualities of inputs on each of the tens of thousands of farm units.

The decision to purchase large quantities of grain from abroad is a major departure from traditional policies and one that may well be repeated in the future. This deviation does not invalidate the long-run goals of self-sufficiency or even surplus in grain production. But it indicates that Soviet policy-makers may in the future be more realistic and less autarky-motivated. It may lead, political conditions permitting, toward a re-examination not only of foreign-trade policy, but more fundamentally to a shift to specialization in areas of production where the U.S.S.R. possesses a comparative advantage. That this realization is a slow, piecemeal process for a generation brought up on ideas of the virtue of autarky is reflected in the long time it took to give up the idea of growing oranges in the Soviet Union at greenhouse costs. But at least there are now precedents for the more rational alternative.

It is inconceivable that Soviet policy-makers will simply dispense with the services of the planning agencies, but it is possible that the work of the planning authorities will increasingly reflect concern with long-range planning.[6] In fact, there is no inherent reason why the Soviet Union, or any other country, ought to deprive itself of long-range planning of agricultural output as a policy instrument to regulate the supply of food and fibers both for domestic use and foreign trade. Indeed, a significant change is already taking place in the time-horizon of Soviet agricultural policy. The timetable for an increase in agricultural output and incomes in general has been shortened. Adequate levels of consumption for the population cannot be put off until *calendas graecas*, until the indefinite maximum development of the industrial potential. This was made clear by Khrushchev, who declared that a high standard of living, and not simply a high index number of steel output, is a precondition for the advent of a new stage in social development. The intention was to narrow the gap between the growth rates of producer and consumer goods. However, under Khrushchev there was an equally unsatisfactory shift to the opposite extreme: emphasis on immediate results at the cost of permanent gains.

The Soviet planners and decision-makers of the post-Khrushchev period have given up gambling on the yearly grain harvest, on corn, on pulses, on sugar beets, on Lysenko's fertilizer-manure mixes, on Jersey bulls and other "trick" measures intended to solve long-run problems overnight. A much more solid, mature, and rational attitude now prevails in the area of agricultural policies. A time span shorter than that under Stalin for the goals of output and incomes is being combined with an apparently longer-time-horizon for the gradual improvement of efficiency in agriculture. The persisting problem, however, is how to minimize the degree of active interference with producers' decisions and to choose the measures that will insure the attainment of desired social goals at the least cost. Certain developments in Soviet agricultural planning already indicate the beginning of a hopeful trend. Recent announcements of long-range procurement plans have specified the floor or bare minimum of marketable supply that the state will claim from the farms at set, current prices, conveying to the farms the magnitude of their minimum obligations, but leaving room for some freedom of decision regarding the rest of the net output. A still better technique would be to announce long-term procurement prices instead of procurement quotas. Nevertheless, the small changes in planning that have been instituted may become cumulative in the long run, while increased measures of rationality will permeate the planning process and perhaps erode some of the most obvious violations of economic efficiency.

III. Farm Organization

One of the fundamental problems with which the Soviet policy-makers will have to contend is the adjustment of organizational structure to the demands of a modernized, intensive agriculture in order to promote a more rational utilization and combination of resources than ever existed before in Russia. Most likely all three presently existing types of farms (state, collective, and auxiliary private plot) will be preserved, but with certain changes.

The proportions or the relative shares of each type may shift somewhat, but it seems certain that the Soviet policy-makers have finally learned the lessons of the past, when disastrous results followed rigid adherence to dogmatic principles and antiquated organizational methods, or when the mechanical, indiscriminate application of half-developed schemes based upon limited experience led to frequent and destructive organizational shake-ups.[7] The policy-makers will need some measure of flexibility in order to be able to deal more effectively with new problems as they arise.

One of the key factors in the institutional problems (which are basically problems of organization and management of the production process) is the question of autonomy at the farm level. With appropriate modifications, the present system can tolerate a very substantial autonomy of farm decisions even under the constraints of procurement quotas or fixed prices. A continuation of the current practice of direct intervention or "paternalism" over the farm, however, will only become an increasingly irritating and retarding factor.

With respect to the state farms, a much greater degree of decentralization is called for. According to the official definition, a state farm is an organizational framework for the use of national (state) property to produce agricultural output in a manner analogous to nationalized industrial establishments. Soviet economists and policy-makers have preferred the state farms over other types because they represent the most "socialized" form. But as part of a vast, bureaucratic machine, the individual state farm has had no control over its own product-mix or the degree of specialization, was largely indifferent to its own cost-structure, and was limited in the provision of incentives to its labor force. (Most of the basic decisions determining output, specialization, size and composition of capital stock, wage bill, and the like, were made by a centralized authority.) Virtually the only motivation to increase production came from the bonus system for the farm manager (director), while other items for financing the farm operation—both fixed assets and operating capital—were provided by the central authorities according to a system of norms, normative coefficients, and the like. Capital investment was provided interest-free, deficits were covered by budgetary subsidies, and most of the farms' profits were appropriated to the state budget.

Operating under the umbrella of the state budget and within a framework of a centralized apparatus, the local farm management suffered from a severely limited scope of action. If we add the fallacious "success indicators," such as output per worker engaged directly in production (instead of profitability), gross output (instead of usable net output), we can understand the state farms' low productivity and high production costs despite the favors extended them by the state.[8] It is only very recently that a change in the *modus operandi* of the state farms has taken place. Instead of relying on the state budget and interest-free investment allotments, the state farms will now have to provide for their investment and production expenditures out of their retained profits or through bank loans. In addition, state farms will be charged for the use of fixed assets, a measure which ought to improve their utilization. It remains to be seen whether the new arrangements will also increase the discretion of farm managers.

The problem of freedom of decision-making at the farm level is also of major concern for the second type of socialized farm, the collective, or *kolkhoz*. A collective farm is an organizational unit that formally has ownership rights over a volume of fixed assets (including land) but has to purchase capital goods and current inputs from a monopolist (the state) and has to sell most of its output to the monopsonist (the state). From the proceeds of its sales the collective farm has to pay taxes and wages and set aside a certain percentage for the replacement of and additions to its capital stock. The paradox of the existing situation is that the collective farms, although legally under cooperative ownership and control, are subject to manifold forms of government intervention and control (which, incidentally, lack any legal basis) over their everyday activities. No wonder that under such circumstances government intervention has been not only burdensome but also arbitrary. Thus, until 1955 openly, and from 1955 to 1964 in a somewhat veiled form, party and government authorities at various levels not only prescribed the product-mix and procurement plans, but often even the dates of planting and harvesting, the size of the livestock herd, the composition of the machinery and equipment, and so forth. Yet the most minute fulfillment of all the initial demands often would fail to satisfy local authorities, and many collective farms were helpless when faced with additional procurement quotas and suddenly changing instructions which wrecked crop-rotations. The harm of uncertainties imposed by such interventions in the past exceeded by far the impact of market uncertainty in unplanned economies.

A guarantee against constant intervention by government agencies in the production and distribution processes of the collectives is an absolute prerequisite for their more efficient functioning. One ought not to overlook the fact, however, that in the past many useful changes in the output mix of the collective and state farms occurred primarily as a response to positive government command or action and to some extent as a reaction to changing conditions of the agricultural producers to their own consumption needs.[9] But the consequences of government demands were negative as well as positive, depending upon the strength of incentives and rewards.[10]

Much has been written in the past about the small auxiliary farm plots and livestock holdings of the farm population. Most non-Soviet observers emphasize the fact that these small farm plots produce at least a third of the gross agricultural output[11] and an even larger share of the net output. Soviet writers, not entirely denying the contribution of the peasants' plots and livestock to the food supply of the country, stress the labor intensity of their operations, the competition for labor with the socialized sector, and their antagonistic aspects with regard to large-scale socialized farming.

I have pointed out elsewhere that

during the Stalin period the private economy provided the peasants with the bulk of their income, thus allowing the collective farms to pay an artificially low remuneration for the labor of their members in the socialized sector. But much more significant is the fact that, apart from grain and some feed, neither the Soviet state nor the prevailing agricultural institutions were under any obligation to supply the rural population with food products. The reliance upon the output of the private sector (as much as it may have been denigrated by the policy-makers in their official pronouncements) allowed the socialized sector not only to market a high percentage of its output, but also to achieve a higher degree of specialization and increased productivity in various branches of agricultural output. Thus, the private household sector in Soviet agriculture, contrary to the view of some Soviet economists and policy-makers, does not play an antagonistic role with regard to the socialized sector, but is complementary in the sense that it contributes significantly to the total output, it enables the socialized sector to specialize, to economize on labor and to keep labor costs relatively low. The interesting feature of the private sector is that, using very little capital, its crop yields and livestock output per animal are substantially higher than in the socialized sector.

. . . Therefore, as long as the socialized sector of agriculture is not sufficiently supplied with capital and skilled labor and is not in a position to attract labor by the relative level of wages, its dependency upon the private household sector will continue. This also might be the reason why any attempt to restrict the private sector, particularly of the collective farmers, in the past had repercussions not only in terms of decreased incomes of the farmers but in reduced incentives to raise productivity in the socialized sector. Any attempt to tamper with the private household sector affected the complementarity of the two sectors and ultimately was bound to harm the socialized sector.[12]

If the above views are correct, and if the liquidation of the private household sector could add only insignificantly to the labor supply of the socialized sector (as it appears from the sex and age composition of labor in the household sector),[13] a policy of nonintervention on the part of the government ought to be a minimum condition for the functioning of the agricultural sector of the economy in the future. It is difficult to set an optimal size for the land and livestock holdings of the peasant household and also to argue for an expansion which would not infringe upon the labor requirement of the socialized sector (which is the limiting factor). But given the historically declining size of rural households and the rural labor force, the lack of capital, and the consumption orientation of the household plots, holding peasant land and livestock at their present size might supplement peasant income until labor incomes on collective farms are raised to "competitive" levels.

Any comparison of the huge socialized farms with the very small household farm plots is bound to raise the nagging problem of optimal size of farm operations in the various regions of the Soviet Union. Unfortunately, very little research has been done on this question, and most of the research was designed to justify the existing, or larger size, of farms rather than to probe into the rationality of the prevailing policies. Under conditions where "investment justified itself," land was not considered a really scarce factor (rent is not charged for land), and management was evaluated in terms of its ability to exercise control and to fulfill procurement plans rather than in terms of profitability of farm operations; in consequence, there was not much room for discussion or experimentation with optimal size. The reasoning was very primitive: more and larger machines are good, therefore the size of farms ought to be increased to suit the new machines, which in turn requires more and larger machines. The present average size of the state and collective farms (7,700 hectares and 3,150 hectares of sown area, respectively) not only exceeds the size of successful family farms elsewhere, but exceeds even the size of corporate farms outside the Communist countries. Whatever gains from increasing scale that Soviet authorities can claim are certainly more than offset by the losses in efficiency resulting from the difficulties of managing excessively large units.

One of the arguments frequently used to justify the size of agricultural and industrial enterprises in the Soviet Union is the necessity to spread scarce managerial resources. The inadequacy of this argument is underscored by the fact that whereas managerial resources evidently are increasing, the average size of the farms simultaneously increases. Therefore, one is inclined to seek explanations elsewhere, for example in the nature of the farm manager's job, which now attracts only low-quality personnel. More rationality in agricultural policies would include greater managerial freedom, the attraction of higher quality talent, and a thorough revision of the attitude toward the size of farm units. An optimal farm size is just as compatible with a socialized as with a private mode of production. Gigantic farms, which have somehow been regarded as evidence of "victory" in the economic race between the East and the West, will presumably lose their pride of place under a more rational administration.

IV. Inter-regional and Inter-farm Specialization

Changes in the output-mix have already occurred as results of shifts in the production of various crops through the designation of special regions as the chief producers of particular crops.[14] Regional policies in agriculture, unfortunately, have seldom been grounded in adequate research or economic analysis, and resulted in serious mistakes of judgment and losses to the national economy.[15]

Moreover, policies of regional autarky were often at loggerheads with proclaimed aims of efficiency and specialization. In addition to patently contradictory policies of agricultural planners, there have been two major reasons for the failure to develop an efficient system of regional specialization: the frequency of policy changes, already mentioned, and the supremacy of the state procurement policies.

The state procurement of agricultural products, elevated to the primary obligation of socialized farming under Stalin, remained

supreme during the Khrushchev period and, in a more sophisticated form, continues to exert a powerful impact.[16]

The state's procurement policies determine the product-mix and
interfere with farm specialization primarily by insisting on the
production (and sale) of a wider range of products by regions and
farms than would actually be profitable to them. For individual
farms, the existing system of state procurement prevents further
specialization within any specific branch of agricultural production
by the insistence upon the completion of the production cycle
within each particular farm.[17] This loss in efficiency can be remedied only by abolishing the principle of procurement from each
farm. A system of voluntary contracts between state purchasing
agencies and specialized farms producing the end products, accompanied by encouragement of inter-farm trade, would lead to
an exchange between, and division of labor within, specific
branches of production and would permit regional specialization
as well as an increased output in general and by the most efficient
producers in particular.

V. The Changing Composition of the Input-Mix

The planned goals of agricultural production for 1966–70 call
both for some increase in total inputs (as well as improvement
of the quality of inputs and their more economical use) and for
changing proportions of the various inputs. Modernization of
agriculture is usually reflected not only by rising levels of output
but also by substantial changes in the input-mix. These changes
are taking place in Soviet agriculture, and one can safely predict
the course of their future movement. Alongside increases of inputs
originating outside the agricultural sector, one would expect shifts
of the proportions of the various inputs originating within agriculture itself.

The future will see a decrease of labor inputs, and an unchanged
or perhaps somewhat decreased input of land (as a result both
of the abandonment of marginal land and of the substitution
of irrigated and reclaimed land). So far as capital is concerned,
a rational policy would set priorities in the following order: agricultural machinery, structures, and productive livestock, in each
case with increased emphasis on quality and lesser reliance upon
sheer numbers. Among the purchased inputs, chemicals (mineral
fertilizer and insecticides) and electric power will most probably

be of major importance. A short review of changes in and substitution among inputs reveals in greater detail the past and future patterns of changes in the input-mix.

Substitution Among Inputs

Labor is by far the largest input in Soviet agricultural production. It accounts for more than one-half of all measurable inputs. Indeed, Soviet agriculture is the most labor-intensive among the developed countries.

In the past, labor was treated as an abundant resource, and official policy reinforced this view. Given the size of the agricultural population and the government's measures to restrict its mobility, agricultural labor was relatively cheap and its alternative uses restricted. Changes in the conditions of agricultural employment, however, are bound to have an increasing impact. In this connection two features of the labor supply in Soviet agriculture should be noted. One involves the age and sex distribution of the labor force and its levels of education and skill. The high proportion of women in the agricultural labor force in the past reflected the cumulative effect of the policies of rapid industrialization and the population losses during World War I and World War II, while the increasing median age was due to the urbanization process which siphoned off the younger, more mobile elements of the agricultural labor force. The relatively low levels of education and skill of the agricultural labor force can be attributed to the heritage of traditional agriculture and to the differential maintained by training and educational policies that favored urban dwellers.

Another feature of the labor input is the existing pattern of its seasonal distribution. Soviet agriculture was unable in the past to eliminate its huge seasonal peak of farm employment, and the insufficient emphasis on livestock production accentuated the peak. In order to cope with the demand for labor during the peak season, labor was limited in its mobility and underemployed during other parts of the year. The destruction of cottage industries during collectivization and the lack of a developed processing industry in rural areas prevented the off-season employment of labor resources in the countryside.

But the demographic changes under way in the Soviet Union, coupled with the process of urbanization and the slowly rising levels of education and skill of the agricultural population, present a challenge to the Soviet policy-makers. Not only will policies of income incentive have to replace the reliance upon the restriction of mobility, but a qualitatively better and more productive labor force will be needed instead of mere numbers, or volume of muscle power.[18] Substitute inputs for labor must be sought.

Substitution for labor in agriculture can take a number of forms. The most widespread is the substitution of capital for labor (introduction of machinery to substitute for farm operations previously performed manually). In the past such substitution applied primarily in crop production (particularly in grains), but there is a clear indication that, in the future, capital-labor substitution will also include livestock production.

In order to pass judgment on the feasibility of further capital-labor substitution it is necessary to review the record of capital input. The capital stock in agriculture comprises such physical assets as buildings and structures, machinery and equipment, as well as the draft animals and basic herd of productive livestock. During the period of 1953–65 the value of the total capital stock increased threefold; the value of fixed assets and machinery increased about 3.2 times and of the basic herd of productive livestock about 1.65 times.[19] The services from the use of this stock provide the contribution of capital to agricultural production. It is not only upon the size of total capital but also upon the composition of capital that the flow of productive services depends. In contrast to U.S. agriculture, the composition of capital in Soviet agriculture is weighted more heavily in favor of buildings and structures than of machinery and equipment. Although such an allotment of capital may be conditioned by a number of factors (climate, for example), it nevertheless indicates that the extent of substitution of capital for labor is smaller in the Soviet Union than in the United States.[20]

The Soviet farm machinery policy was for a long period biased in favor of types of machinery which substituted for draft animals; it exhibited a preference for large-size tractors and machines, and efficiency was judged in terms of the industry's ability to supply uniform, mass-produced runs of equipment. Due to the monopolistic position of the industry, demands of the farms were neglected and the actual performance of the machinery or its contribution to agricultural production was only of secondary importance. Lags in the modernization of technology and scarcities in the supply of machinery were supposed to be remedied by increases in the horsepower of the machinery, by forcing the farms to keep obsolete machines on their books, and by attempts to use the machines for longer periods during the year.[21]

By independent standards the agricultural machinery inputs are still insufficient to meet the requirements of timely field operations and to substitute for labor in areas where such substitution would be profitable.[22] The new Five Year Plan for 1966–70 envisages a supply of 1,700,000 tractors, 550,000 combine grain harvesters, and 1,100,000 trucks. Given the existing rates of depreciation and, the age of existing stocks of agricultural machinery, the net increase would amount to about 400,000 tractors (a 25 per cent increase), 200,000 grain combine harvesters (a 35–40 per cent increase), and 500,000 trucks (about a 50 per cent increase).[23] Such an increase, in view of the expected area in crops and its composition, ought to contribute to more timely schedules of plowing and harvesting; it ought also substitute for much labor in crop production, particularly in grain and feed. But while there is sufficient attention paid to big "mechanization"—in the sense of giant tractors and the like—insufficient attention has been given to simpler labor-saving devices, both in crop and livestock production. A more attentive approach to the real needs of the farms on the part of industry might provide a more effective capital-for-labor substitution, which will become urgent in Soviet agriculture during the next decade.

The supply of mineral fertilizer has been recognized the world over as one of the crucial inputs without which modern agriculture cannot meet the demand for food and fiber in industrialized societies. Thus, in order to "slay the Malthusian devil," to maintain or increase the fertility of the soil, agriculture has to resort to purchases of mineral fertilizers and other products of the chemical industry.

In the Soviet Union, due to a number of factors, the development of this branch of industry was delayed, while other less expensive measures for increasing soil fertility were tried. It was the failure of the substitutes for mineral fertilizer and the tapering-off of yields and output that convinced Soviet decision-makers that an accelerated program of mineral fertilizer production is essential. The current program of mineral fertilizer production not only provides for a relatively rapid growth rate of the volume, but also for a considerable shift in composition, notably the growth of the share of nitrogen at the expense of phosphates.[24] The indicated trends to increase the supply of liquid nitrogen, of granulated, combined fertilizers, and of increasing the concentration of nutrients in the bulk of fertilizers produced are also significant.[25] In the future a more positive response to the increasing supply of mineral fertilizer will probably result in some increase of crop yields, while the use of insecticides and chemical weed-killers will not only directly affect the yields but also decrease the labor inputs in the industrial crops.

Electric power is another of the inputs that agriculture purchases from the industrial sector of the economy. Here, too, Soviet agriculture lags behind other industrialized countries. Agriculture was for a long time deprived of a reasonable share in the spectacular growth of electric power in the Soviet Union. Until 1953 collective farms, regardless of location,[26] were in fact prohibited from using electricity from the state electrical network. Thus, electrification of the farms depended upon construction of local, small, inefficient, power stations with a capacity of 30–50 kilowatts. Given both the virtual rationing of fuel and the high costs of operation, the small power plants worked irregularly and were inadequate to provide electricity for agricultural production processes and for household needs. In 1953 the draconic restrictions were removed and, depending upon the means at the disposal of the farms and upon their location, the electricity consumption increased substantially.[27] The new Five Year Plan envisions an increase of about 200 per cent in electricity consumption in agriculture. If achieved, this would go a long way to provide electric power for production processes which now depend upon other forms of mechanical or muscle power. It may also provide a larger quota for rural households, significantly influencing the way of life in the countryside and providing the agricultural population with amenities that so far have been at the disposal of urban dwellers only. The increased supply of electricity from the state-operated network will lower its unit costs and make it more attractive to the farms to invest in the construction of links with the state network.

Land is still regarded as a major input in Soviet agricultural production. Although its relative importance may decrease over time, in absolute terms the sown area has been rising through most of the period of socialized agriculture, contrary to the experience of other economically developed countries. It is probably fair to assert that each turn in farm policies since the inception of collectivization, regardless of its specific target, was based upon the belief that land is a relatively abundant factor in the Soviet Union and that increased agricultural production ought to be either achieved through or accompanied by an expansion of the land area under cultivation.[28] Thus, the underlying assumption has been that land is an effective substitute for capital, that expansion of agricultural land or even improvement of existing land can be achieved with merely a token of capital investment, and that Soviet agriculture can grow as a basically extensive type of production. Recognition of the facts that quality land is limited under the climatic conditions of the Soviet Union and that only in combination with heavy capital investments could land be made more productive has been slow in occurring to the Soviet decision-makers.[29] Consequently, the program of land improvement announced in 1966 marks a major departure from past attitudes and policies. The principal efforts are in two directions, land irrigation and land melioration.[30] Among the noteworthy features of the program is the planned location of grains on irrigated lands and the restoration to eminence of the old livestock-producing area in the central and northwest regions of the Soviet Union, neglected since the beginning of collectivization. The program appeals to the decision-makers because of its anticipated contribution to reducing dependency upon the weather in grains and feed production. It should also appeal to the Soviet farmers, because it is concentrated largely in the traditional agricultural regions. While the land irrigation program will be carried out primarily by state organizations and in a centralized manner, with only modest involvement on the part of the farms, the bulk of the reclamation program will necessarily involve existing farms not only in the process of land improvement but also in integrating reclaimed lands in their crop rotation, in changing the output-mix, and in decisions about specialization and economic calculation. The over-all impact of the programs will be an expansion of the combination of capital and purchased inputs with land.[31] Land inputs will increase in terms of quality, and not in terms of marginal acres as in the past, which ought to place output increases upon a more solid foundation.

Technological Improvements

Technological improvement in modern agriculture is brought about largely by the supply flow from the nonagricultural sector in response to the demand from agricultural enterprises. The following process is typically involved: (a) articulation of the needs of the farm sector; (b) invention and production efforts by the research institutions and industrial enterprises, followed by testing of methods and products under field conditions; and (c) acceptance of the new technology and its diffusion within the farm sector.

The Soviet case was peculiar in the past because official spokesmen for the agricultural sector implicitly accepted agriculture's role as only a residual claimant for resources, which made the demands and articulation of the farm sector's needs very ineffective.[32] Not only was the voice of the agricultural sector weak, but the flow of ideas from research institutes and industrial enterprises tended to be minimal and often of negative value to the farms.

Until very recently, research in biology and genetics in the Soviet Union was strongly affected by the monopolistic hold of doctrinaire schools. The damage of Lysenkoism and similar schools to the Soviet economy runs into billions. Not only were progressive ideas about hybridization and breeding rejected, but a whole generation of geneticists, soil scientists, and agronomists, was trained to reject alternative approaches and solutions to scientific problems. To undo the damage will take many years and enormous cost. To make matters worse, the entire episode has convinced farmers to regard agricultural research as irrelevant, if not injurious, to their everyday tasks. It will require effort and tact for the research establishment to win the confidence of the farmers.

At the same time the relationships between industrial establishments and the agricultural enterprises which they were serving has been far from satisfactory. Although industry invariably was portrayed by official spokesmen as the benefactor of agriculture, industrial establishments have preferred to supply simple, somewhat obsolete equipment or products and to avoid the risk of new products or technological processes. Thus, the gap between foreign and domestic technology was accentuated by a gap between the laboratory or drawing-board and the production line.

The process of acceptance of new technology on the farms has also been retarded by the monopolistic tendencies of the industrial enterprises and the technical deficiencies of their products, combined with high prices and lack of spare parts, as well as by the lack of technical proficiency among farmers themselves. The net result is that the rate of introduction of technological improvement in agriculture has been slow and less effective than might be expected under the conditions of large-scale farming prevailing in the Soviet Union.

VI. FARM PRICES

The level of absolute prices of farm products in the Soviet Union reflects, albeit imperfectly, the demand for agricultural products and the changes in the costs of production of farm units. We may assume that the prices paid by the state for the bulk of the marketable farm output reflect the general domestic price level and the efficiency with which various inputs (given their costs) are combined in order to make it profitable for producers to continue.

Since collectivization began, farm prices have had an upward trend.[33] By comparison with prices prevailing in other countries, the Soviet Union is at a disadvantage in selling its exportable surplus to compete in the world market.[34] The high prices do not necessarily indicate a rise in profitability or higher returns to particular factors of production.

It is difficult to predict the future levels of prices and costs of agricultural products in the U.S.S.R. On the one hand, the growth of population and the urbanization of the country will increase the demand for most foods and fibers; on the other hand, with a rise in per capita income, the income-elasticities of demand for food ought to decline. (Although the relative share of food in total consumption may be expected to decline, absolute expenditures will undoubtedly increase, in part due to a shift from lower-value products to higher-value products.) It is less as the result of diminishing demand than as a result of increasing supply that one ought to expect prices to decline.

How realistic is it to expect that the increasing supply will be accompanied by declining costs?[35] The past history of Soviet agriculture indicates that the low incomes of the farm labor force were to a large extent responsible for the low labor productivity and high labor costs of farm output. The relationship between farm prices and the cost of production (except labor cost) was of utmost importance for the income position of farm producers. Since labor cost (at least in the collective farm sector) was treated as a residual after the deduction of other production costs and investment expenditure allocation, the level of farm prices became a co-determinant of the farmers' incomes.

Soviet planners will be unable to reduce agricultural costs until farm wages and incomes can be linked to productivity instead of constituting merely a residual from farm prices. The decline in costs ought not be achieved at the expense of the labor income (although labor costs per unit of output could decline while labor incomes are growing), but by cost reduction of some inputs other than labor and by substitution of inputs which would increase output per total value of inputs. There are a number of areas in which major improvements of this type can be achieved; feeding efficiency is an excellent example.

The determination of relative prices in agriculture has affected agricultural production in the past and will have an important influence in the future. It is also an area which was relatively neglected by both Soviet and Western students of Soviet agriculture. During the Stalin period, when reliance was put upon commands and not incentives, and farm management and producers were expected to fall in line behind every government policy, relative prices were considered of no importance, or of very limited importance as a tool of agricultural policy. It was only with the general price rise during the Khrushchev period that prices of agricultural products had to be brought into a better relation one to another. It was difficult, however, to expect a rational policy of relative prices in the absence of clearly defined criteria that would have been available in a free market. The possibility of using world market prices as criteria, or the market prices of other countries, or the prices of the pre-collectivization period did not appeal to the policy-makers.

Prices were therefore set on the assumption of expected future, rather than present, cost relationships. The major price changes in 1953–54 and 1958–59 were heralded as "finally establishing the correct relative prices"; each time, the planners discovered, within a few years, that the price relations were neither "final" nor "correct."[36] It turned out that in many cases the price level not only was below the rising level of costs (as with many livestock products), but the relative prices did not stimulate the output of particular commodities.

The distortions resulting from inappropriate relative prices can be seen in the following two examples. During the pre-collectivization period Russia was one of the leading producers of hard wheat. As a result of a lack of a price differential between hard and soft wheat, hard wheat was replaced by higher yielding soft wheat and hard wheat literally disappeared, making it imperative to import it. It was only a few years ago that a 40 per cent price differential was established to revive the production of hard wheat. The fact that consumers were virtually deprived of lamb can easily be explained by the uniform price for all types of mutton. If, in addition, one takes into consideration the pressure upon the farms to increase the livestock herds, it becomes clear why only a limited supply of lamb was forthcoming.

There were, however, cases when wrong relative prices tended to distort the output-mix beyond the wishes of the planners. An example of such a distortion was provided by the case of pulses. Khrushchev, concerned about the protein content of the feed supply, ordered that the price of pulses, particularly peas, should be increased. The effect of this price increase exceeded the expectations of the planners and surprised them in a rather embarrassing way, since wheat lands were diverted to the growing of peas. Indeed, following the ouster of Khrushchev, one of the measures of the new regime was the reduction of the price of peas. The setting of relative prices, or the opportunity for the various commodities to find their relative price in the market, is a powerful policy tool when applied not only in the short run but also with long-run objectives in mind.

The problem of relative prices of agricultural products and producers' goods for farm activity purchased from the industrial sector is important, since it not only represents the terms of trade between the two sectors but also influences the profitability and income position of the farm enterprises.[37] A review of this problem leads to the conclusion that in the past the Soviet government's pricing policies with regard to machinery, fuel, and construction materials sold to the agricultural enterprises were designed to appropriate to industry or to the state budget most of the increases in the efficiency of production of such goods. Thus, at times of increasing farm prices, the prices of such inputs kept rising. A Soviet economist characterized the movement of relative prices of agricultural products and producers' goods purchased by agriculture as follows:

> Until 1949 the wholesale prices of industrial goods increased and the procurement prices of agricultural products remained very low. From 1949 to 1953 there was some decrease of the wholesale prices at an unchanged level of agricultural prices. And finally from 1953 to 1963 a process of two-sided regulation took place. Procurement prices increased substantially and the wholesale prices of industrial goods exhibited a tendency to decrease, although in particular years prices for spare parts and agricultural machinery increased somewhat.[38]

The esteemed economist leaves out of his summary a few pertinent details. First, he does not mention the level of retail prices.[39]

Second, he fails to mention the size of the price decreases and increases.[40] Instead, he expresses the prices of various producer goods in terms of tons of wheat at the current price in order to prove the benefits of the wheat-machinery exchange to the farms.[41] Thus, it becomes clear that, at least in the past, prices of some major inputs in agricultural production did not contribute to any major extent toward the cost reduction of agricultural output and that the government, or industry, forced the farms to pay a monopoly price.

It will take a number of years and a special effort to make the relative prices operative in the right direction. As with other areas of agricultural policy, it will require a diminution of outright interference with the conduct of activities at the farm level; it will also involve an expansion of facilities to provide various branches of agriculture with a volume of supply commensurate with existing demand—facilities which in many cases only the government can provide.

VII. Farmers' Incomes

One of the goals of socialized agriculture in the Soviet Union, and perhaps one of the motives of collectivization, was to provide for growth of agricultural production independent of changes in the incomes of agricultural producers. Harnessed to the needs of forced industrialization, agricultural output became a major source of the total savings and investment in industry, while farmers' incomes were kept low by institutional arrangements. These arrangements kept income payments to the farmers as a residual after the state received its desired share of output at a price largely determined by the state itself.

As long as the state was able to extract the desired volume of food and fibers, and as long as the agricultural population constituted the numerical majority of the total population, one could not deny the logic (the justice is another matter) of taxing the peasantry heavily and subjecting it to near-subsistence conditions.

However, when the growth of agricultural output and the volume of taxation of the agricultural population became insufficient in terms of the desired goals of industrial development and when the disincentives of low incomes, accompanied by a decrease in the labor supply in agriculture, became apparent, the logic upon which the previous policy was based no longer applied. Policy was due for a change.

Soviet policy-makers have learned from their experience that income incentives can play a crucial role in determining not only the volume of work performed but also its quality. The latter is particularly important in agriculture, for operations cycle annually; one has to live with the consequences of shoddy operations for a whole year before anything can be repeated or corrected. The end of the Stalin era coincided with the beginning of a trend of rising agricultural incomes intended to overcome the disincentives of a system designed to facilitate the acquisition by the state of a constantly growing share of the agricultural output. In addition, the Soviet policy-makers had to recognize the hard fact of weather uncertainties and resulting fluctuations of the volume of output and agricultural incomes. The remedy, which could both protect the level of incomes from fluctuation in output (in the absence of compensation payments or fluctuating prices), and at the same time abolish the principle of payments to farmers as income residuals of the farms, was found in the institution of a guaranteed minimum income (wage) for the collective farmers.

The institution of a guaranteed minimum wage in the collective farms was preceded by a ten-year policy of raising prices of the marketable output of the farms, thus stimulating an increase in the total output, and particularly its marketable share, simultaneously with the increase in incomes. The reasoning was based on the assumption that the value of other inputs would remain stable and therefore the increment in total agricultural income would accrue to the agricultural labor force. This expectation was roughly correct until about 1957–58, but after this date the growth of agricultural inputs obtained from the nonagricultural sector of the economy exceeded the rise in agricultural output, thus causing the labor incomes to stagnate or even to decline in 1959 and 1960. In addition, the growth in the volume of marketable grain affected the level of payments in kind to the collective farm members, thus checking their ability to market grain or to use it for expanding livestock production for sale at higher prices in the collective farm market.

To the extent that various government measures prior to 1965 reduced the size and profitability of the auxiliary private plots of the collective farmers, the real increase in their incomes was less than expected and insufficient to provide an incentive to increase output.

Still another element, stemming from the prevailing outlook of the policy-makers, namely the doctrine that increases in labor productivity ought to precede increases in wages, was not without an effect on policy. The reform carried out during 1965–66 removed most of the shortcomings of the previous Khrushchevian policies. Agricultural prices were increased again, a guaranteed wage was instituted, and restrictions over the private auxiliary plots removed.

The income situation of the state farm workers has also improved recently. As long as the labor-supply was relatively abundant, the wages of the state farm workers were low by comparison with the industrial labor force, but the income differential in turn between the state farm workers and collective farmers was sufficient to assure a labor supply for the state farms. In fact, the state farms very often served as a transition stage for the collective farmers who moved ultimately to industry. As long as the state farm sector was relatively small, even this large labor turnover did not materially affect the level of output.

However, the tightening of the labor market and the increased educational level of the rural population has meant that recruitment and retention of a labor force for the state farms depends upon a substantial increase in the relative wages of state farm workers. Such an increase took place in 1957; during the period 1958–65 the average state farm wage increased by 38.6 per cent, reaching a level of 71 per cent of the industrial wage in 1965 *versus* 61 per cent of the industrial wage in 1958.

It is difficult to estimate the relative incomes of collective farmers, state farm workers, and industrial workers in the Soviet Union, since the incomes from private auxiliary plots vary for the different categories, and the social benefits differ widely. It is much easier to estimate the relative wages received from the socialized sector for the three categories. Thus, for 1965 the state farm wage per man-day was 71 per cent of the industrial wage. Given the fact that in 1965 the collective farm man-day was valued at about 90 per cent of the state farm man-day and that the number of man-days worked in a collective farm is about two-thirds of the state farm man-days per year, the yearly wage income of the collective farmers from the socialized sector amounted to about 60 per cent of such income of the state farm workers and about 44 per cent of the wage income of an industrial worker.

The current plans for 1970 envisage an increase of 20 per cent in the industrial wage by comparison with 1965, and 40 per cent for the man-day on the collective farms. Thus, the wage differential between the collective farmers and state farm workers will be greatly reduced or eliminated, while the wage differential between the industrial sector and state farm sector will be retained.

The main question that arises with regard to the envisioned wage or income policy is whether the actual and promised income rises in the agricultural sector will result in additional and higher-quality effort on the part of the labor force, a more optimal combination with other production factors, and a larger agricultural output. It would be premature to answer the question with certainty, but there is a distinct possibility that the new policy will succeed. In any event, it is clear that a future solution to the Soviet Union's protracted agricultural difficulties will to a large extent depend upon the response to income incentives. Russia may thus join the group of economically developed countries where protection of the income position of the agricultural labor force is substituted for the earlier exploitation of the agricultural sector for the sake of industrialization.

11.

Industry

HERBERT S. LEVINE

In considering the prospects for Soviet industry, let us first trace the main features of Soviet industrial growth from the beginning of the era of planned economy.

The Soviet economy of the mid-1920s was dominated by the raging debate over the form and pace of optimal development. During the period of the New Economic Policy (NEP), the economy had been restored to its prewar capacity; further growth, however, would require a substantial amount of new capital formation. Opinions differed on how this was to be accomplished, on the composition of the capital stock, and on how rapidly the capital stock and the economy should grow.

The solution finally adopted by Stalin, which called for very rapid, forced economic development, represented an extreme outside the range of proposed solutions, yet it was consistent with the Russian historical pattern. Alexander Gerschenkron has shown that the Russian state, when frustrated in its foreign policy because of military weakness resulting from economic backwardness (for example, during the period of Peter the Great), tends to force a rapid economic development in order to attain power parity with its adversaries among the advanced nations.[1] How central this goal was to Stalin's program of forced-draft economic development is reflected in his oft-quoted statement: "We are fifty or a hundred years behind the advanced countries. We must make good this distance in ten years. Either we do it, or they crush us."[2]

Industry performed the principal role in the attainment of this goal: the terms economic development and industrialization were synonymous. It was industry upon which national power would be built, and which would provide the implements for national defense and the means for further economic growth. Moreover, the Bolsheviks' ideological priorities favored the urban components of economic growth, and tended to ignore or downgrade the role of the countryside. In transforming the Soviet economy from a relatively backward, primarily agricultural economy into an advanced, powerful, industrialized economy in as short a time as possible, the emphasis was almost exclusively on the rapid growth of industrial output.

I. The Record of Economic Growth

How well has the Soviet economy performed? From 1928 to 1958, very well indeed.[3] Table 1 gives two indices of industrial growth.[4] The first uses constant Russian prices of 1937 (adjusted to approximate costs of production). The second uses changing weights (prices of the initial year of each period) in order to derive a measure of the growth in the ability of Soviet industry to produce the product mix, or "market basket," of the last year of each period or subperiod.[5]

Soviet rates of industrial growth by either index are quite high. When the rates for 1928–58 are contrasted with those for the United States in a comparable period of development (the last three decades of the nineteenth century), the Soviet performance is clearly superior: 8.6–11.7 per cent per year for the Soviet Union, compared to 6.1 per cent per year for the United States.[6] Other

TABLE 1
AVERAGE ANNUAL RATES OF GROWTH OF INDUSTRIAL OUTPUT
IN THE SOVIET UNION, 1928–58
(*In per cents*)

Type of Index	1928–58*	1928–37	1950–58
1937 Cost-of-Production Price Weights	8.6	10.1	10.2
Capacity to Produce the Output Mix of End Year of Period or Subperiod	11.7	17.9	10.5

* World War II is excluded by considering period to be 26 years long.
Source:
R. Powell in Bergson and Kuznets (eds.), *Economic Trends in the Soviet Union*, pp. 155, 178–79.

non-Communist countries, to be sure, have had for short periods in their history rates of industrial growth similar to those of the Soviet Union. Even so, the Soviet accomplishments have been sustained over a longer period than in other countries, with substantially less help from the outside in the form of foreign investment and labor immigration. (It is true, however, that the Soviets have benefited significantly from borrowing advanced foreign technology.) Finally, the Soviets have been able to achieve these high rates even while sustaining a heavy burden of military production. In brief: although the rates of growth attained by Soviet industry in the period 1928–58 are not unprecedented, they are nonetheless impressive.

How was it accomplished? Since economic output is produced through the application of the factors of production: labor, land, and capital, an analysis of Soviet industrial growth must necessarily consider changes in the quantity, quality, and use of these input factors. But productive resources also have to be organized and administered, and decisions made concerning the allocation of available resources. It is this organization and administration of productive resources, of course, that constitutes the economic system. Let us turn to it first.

An economic system can be viewed essentially as a communication mechanism in which messages are transmitted from those in a position to make demands (a function of the society's social and political system) to the producing units. The producing units, in turn, send various types of messages to the factors of production attached to the producing unit, and to outside factors of production and producing units. Messages flow back and forth and, in response to them, factors of production are combined and goods and services produced and distributed.

There are many possible types of such systems and variations on them. The price-profit, market system is one. The Soviet leaders, however, after deciding on a course of rapid growth and development, chose instead a centralized system of organization and administration in which the dominant preferences, those of the political leaders, were communicated directly to producing units, and these units were severely constrained in their freedom of response in fulfilling the commands of the center. Although Marxist beliefs partly account for this choice, it is important to realize that in the Bolsheviks' situation a turn toward centralized control was neither necessarily inappropriate nor without historical parallels. For when the aim is to change rapidly the entire face of the economy, the appropriateness of a market system is at least questionable. The stable parameters which are needed to make the price-profit type of calculations are themselves variables, and uncertainty is quite rampant. The concentration is on the rapid development of new industries, new products, and new regional complexes. All this creates difficulties in making close, marginal calculations, and makes independent calculations by autonomous production units relatively less useful. Furthermore, when an economy is mobilized in the pursuit of a clearly established goal, the indirectness of the price-profit system and the slowness of its trial-and-error procedure make it unattractive. This has been the case not only in the Soviet Union, but also in the Western nations, including the United States, in times of recent major wars.

The primary contribution made by centralized planning to the economic and industrial growth of the Soviet Union has been in the gross, "macro" aspects of resource allocation rather than in the fine, "micro" aspects.[7] Centralized planning has enabled the dictatorship to change forcibly, in a remarkably brief time, the structure of output and the structure of productive inputs in both quantity and quality. In 1928, producers' goods comprised only 40 per cent of gross industrial output; this proportion was raised to 58 per cent by 1937, and to 72 per cent by 1958. Comparable figures for the U.S. are not readily available, but rough calculations show that in 1919 (and also in 1929 and 1939), the relative share of producers' goods in the American gross industrial output was about 50 per cent, while in 1947 it was on the order of 60 per cent.[8] The rapidly growing concentration in Soviet industry on producers' goods was a crucial element in the high rates of growth achieved not only in industry but also in the entire economy. It is the reflection within the industrial sector of the decisions taken by the Soviet leaders to force a high rate of investment on the economy, that is, to devote a high share of total output to the production of capital goods. However, it was not only the high rate of investment which led to high economic growth, but also the direction of a relatively large share of these capital goods to use in the industrial sector itself (generally about 40 per cent in the U.S.S.R. during the 1928–58 period, compared with less than 20 per cent in the U.S. at the turn of the century).[9]

The Soviet regime also used its powers of centralized control to increase rapidly the size of the industrial labor force. In the period from 1928 to 1937, at a time when the population grew by a little less than 10 per cent, the industrial labor force almost doubled.

The regime was able to accomplish this by forcing a net migration of over 15 million people from the countryside to the cities in those nine years alone, and by pressuring an increasing number of women into industrial employment.[10] Over the entire period 1928–58, the industrial labor force increased about 280 per cent, while the total population increased less than 40 per cent.[11]

The Soviet leaders were concerned as well with the quality of the labor force, with increasing its productivity. Education and technical training were stressed. Advanced production methods in foreign countries were studied and adapted to Soviet industry; and, of course, there was a high rate of increase of capital per industrial worker. As it turned out, the rate of growth of capital per worker in industry was by and large equal to the rate of growth of output per worker (another way of saying that the capital-output ratio in industry remained constant).[12] Since the expectation from concepts of diminishing returns is that output per worker would grow more slowly than capital per worker, the parity of their growth shows that the Soviets were able to achieve a significant increase in the levels of technology, efficiency of resource use, and labor skills.

A revealing way to measure this growth in technology, administrative and planning efficiency, and labor skills is to compare the growth in output with the growth of all inputs combined. If output grows more rapidly than the combined inputs, total productivity is said to have increased. Powell, in his study, found that total productivity in Soviet industry in 1928–58 grew at about the same rate as did total productivity in American industry during comparable periods in our history; Balassa has shown that in the period 1950–58, total productivity in Soviet industry grew on a par with that in the best performing industrialized countries, Japan and Germany. Both authors also argue that the Soviets, given advantages of borrowing foreign technology and exploiting economies of scale, should have had an even greater growth in total productivity than the other countries, but this judgment may be unduly harsh.[13] In considering the low level of skills of much of the labor force, its unfamiliarity with industrial life, and the chaotic conditions of the times, the fact that Soviet growth in total productivity in industry was equal to the best in the capitalist world ought to be taken as a sign of rather high dynamic efficiency of Soviet industry in this period.

These results do not mean, however, that Soviet centralized planning led to the same level of efficiency of resource use in Soviet industry as in the leading industrialized countries. It is clear that this is decidedly not the case. The growth in total factor productivity is a dynamic concept, while the efficiency of resource use in its most usual sense is a static concept. In fact, the *presence* of static inefficiency may be an element in the increase of dynamic efficiency, if the degree of static inefficiency decreases over time. This may have been one of the factors involved in the growth of total productivity in Soviet industry.

II. Slackening Growth Rates in Recent Periods

Although the performance of Soviet industry was generally impressive in the period of centralized planning up to 1958, its subsequent performance has been a cause of increasing concern to the Soviet leadership. Since 1958, general rates of economic growth, including the rate of growth of industry, have been decreasing. According to some recent calculations, the rate of industrial growth fell from 10.6 per cent per year in the period 1950–58 to 8 per cent per year in the period 1958–64, and even down to 7.3 per cent per year in the last three years of that period.[14] The causes of this rather sharp drop in the rate of industrial growth are clearly of fundamental importance in any discussion of the prospects for Soviet industry. We shall, therefore, examine them in some depth.

With respect first to the changes in labor supply and labor productivity, the data show that the rate of growth of employed workers in industry fell from 4.2 per cent per year in the period 1950–58 to 3.8 per cent per year in 1958–64.* The drop in the rate of growth of industrial employment reflects the decrease in the birth rate during the war. To some extent the Soviet leaders protected their high priority industrial sector against the impact of the low birth rate in the war years, as evidenced by the fact that the rate of growth of (civilian) employment in the economy as a whole decreased relatively more than it did in industry.[15] However, this advantage was offset by the program (which began in the 1950–58 period and ended by 1961) of reducing the length of the working day in industry. The reduction in the man-hours worked by each employed laborer led to a decrease in the rate of growth of man-hours of industrial labor services from 3.1 per cent per year to 1.6 per cent per year. The greater decrease in the

* Until otherwise indicated, paired figures pertain respectively to the periods 1950–58 and 1958–64.

rate of growth of man-hours compared to the rate of growth of employment had the reverse effect on measures of productivity. While the rate of growth of output per *worker* fell from 6.1 to 4.0 per cent per year, the rate of growth of output per man-hour fell only from 7.2 to 6.2 per cent per year.

The change in the rate of growth of output is compounded of the change in other rates of growth: of workers employed, man-hours per worker, and output per man-hour. Regarding the role of each of these three factors in the total decline in the rate of growth of industrial output, it can be said that the fall in the rate of growth of industrial workers accounted for a little less than 20 per cent; of man-hours per worker for a little more than 40 per cent; and of output per man-hour for a little more than 40 per cent.[16] It would be tempting to conclude from this that the problems now faced by the Soviets are not so severe, for the rate of growth of employment will pick up again very soon as the postwar baby crop comes of age, and since 1961 there has been no further reduction in the length of the working day. This combination, it might be assumed, should take care of almost 60 per cent of the drop in the rate of growth of industrial output. However, the situation is not so simple. After the reduction in the working day had been completed (the average working day in industry is said to be now slightly under 7 hours and the work week, 40 hours), the rate of growth of output per man-hour plummeted from a very high (see Table 2) 8.7 per cent per year in 1958–61, to a very low 3.8 per cent per year in 1961–64. Thus, the termination of shortening the length of the workday in fact did not help. Indeed, the drop in the growth of man-hour productivity in the three years after 1961 compared with the three years before was so great that it overcame the substantial increase in the growth of man-hours: the rate of growth of industrial output was actually lower after the termination of the program. The high level of growth of man-hour productivity achieved during the period of decrease in the length of the workday[17] was very likely a result of greater efforts on the part of labor per hour worked, and better management at the enterprise level, in response to the pressure of the reduction in the length of the workday. It may also be that these effects served to counter some negative influences on productivity which were beginning to develop at the time. In any event, it is clear that after 1961, the key factor in the fall in the rate of growth of industrial output, so far as labor is concerned, is the fall in the rate of growth of man-hour productivity.

One of the reasons frequently advanced for the fall in the rate of growth of industrial labor productivity (and output) in the years 1958–64 is the drop in the rate of growth of fixed investment in industry. It dropped from 11.5 per cent per year in 1950–58 to 8.9 per cent per year in 1958–64.[18] Certainly, this is of some importance; but because of the relative magnitudes of the numbers involved and because of a reduction in the rate of retirement of old capital,[19] it has not actually led to a drop in the rate of growth of the stock of fixed capital in industry (see Table 2). What is important in the recent period, however, is the serious deterioration in the productivity of this capital stock.[20] As pointed out in the previous section, even though Soviet planners maintained a rapid growth in industrial capital over the period 1928–58, they were able to keep output growing at almost the same rate. But in the period after 1958, while the stock of fixed capital in industry continued to grow at approximately the same rate, the rate of growth of industry fell below this level. The resulting fall in output per unit of capital was at a rate of 3 per cent per year. According to one Western specialist, the amount of additional capital per worker needed in industry to raise output by one unit doubled in the period 1958–64, compared with the amount needed in the period 1950–58.[21]

The effects of both the changes in labor and capital can be illustrated through a comparison of the growth of industrial output and the growth of aggregate inputs, labor (man-hours) and

TABLE 2

AVERAGE ANNUAL RATES OF GROWTH IN SOVIET INDUSTRY, 1950–64
(*In per cents*)

	1950–58	1958–64	1958–61	1961–64
Output	10.6	8.0	8.6	7.3
Employment	4.2	3.8	4.6	3.1
Man-Hours	3.1	1.6	−0.1	3.4
Man-Hour Productivity	7.2	6.2	8.7	3.8
Capital Stock	11.3	11.3	11.5	11.1
Capital Productivity	−0.7	−3.0	−2.6	−3.4
Combined Inputs (Man-Hours and Capital)	5.3	4.2	3.0	5.5
Combined Factor Productivity	5.0	3.6	5.4	1.7

Source:

Based on data in J. Noren in Joint Economic Committee, *New Directions in the Soviet Economy*, Part II-A (Washington, D.C.: GPO, 1966), pp. 282, 316.

capital combined.[22] In the period 1950–58, while output grew at the rate of 10.6 per cent per year, the combined inputs grew at a rate of 5.3 per cent per year, which means that output per unit of combined inputs grew at an annual rate of 5.0 per cent. In the period 1958–61, the rate of growth of combined inputs fell to 3.0 per cent per year, reflecting the sharp decline in the growth of man-hours, and the increased rate of growth of man-hour productivity grew slightly to 5.4 per cent per year, as the increase in the rate of growth of man-hour productivity overshadowed the increased rate of fall in capital productivity. But in the period 1961–64, while the rate of growth of combined labor and capital inputs reached a high of 5.5 per cent per year, combined factor productivity dropped precipitously to a low of 1.7 per cent per year, reflecting the sharp drop in the growth of man-hour productivity and the further augmenting of the rate of decrease of capital productivity. *The picture that emerges, then, with regard to the role of labor and capital in the recent decrease of Soviet industrial growth is not one of a shortfall in quantity of inputs, but of the effectiveness of their use.* In the most recent years of the period under review, the growth of factor productivity fell to an alarmingly low level.

In analyzing the causes of these difficulties in factor productivity, we can separate a group of causes that were specific to certain policies and developments during the period concerned from the more fundamental causes stemming from the historical development of the Soviet economy.

Among the specific causes there is, to begin with, the reorganization of industrial administration along regional lines begun in 1957, and abandoned in the fall of 1965. The regional form of organization had certain advantages in increasing the efficiency of use of local resources and in reducing some of the wastes of departmental duplication. But it also had many weaknesses. Over-all coordination and control proved to be extremely difficult. The industrial supply system for key materials became highly confused. Equally important, the ability of the center to force the introduction of new technology was seriously hampered because the important research and development organizations were subordinate to state committees which were organized centrally by branch of industry, but which did not have sufficient power over the enterprises within their branches since the enterprises were subordinate to regional organizations. In addition to these weaknesses within the system itself, the way in which organizational arrangements and changes were handled could not help having serious consequences for economic performance. The economy was in an almost constant state of administrative change. One organizational reform followed another so rapidly that managers did not know from one day to the next from whom their commands would come—an environment hardly conducive to efficient economic operation.

A second specific factor was the expansion of the Soviet military and space program after 1958. The expansion of the military program has not involved so much an increase in numbers of military personnel (actually they have decreased) as in the development and production of sophisticated military weapons and equipment. Not only has this meant that industry received less capital equipment than it otherwise might, somewhat decreasing the rate of growth of investment in industry, but also that industry had less access to advanced equipment, and reduced opportunities for improvements in the quality of its capital stock. Furthermore, as mentioned, the decreasing rate of investment evidently entailed more retention of old equipment in the capital stock. To make matters worse, the expansion of the military and space programs absorbed a significant number of the best scientists, engineers, and managers from the civilian sector. In an economy where such skills (especially those of engineers and managers) are less prevalent than in advanced Western economies, and where they are more critical to the successful and smooth operation of an industrial enterprise because of the generally lower level of knowledge and experience of the workers, negative effects are likely to follow when such skills are diverted to other needs.

Third, the quality of the labor force was further affected by the coming of age of the "thin" generation born during the war, and by the ways used to handle this problem. In the period 1958–64, civilian nonagricultural employment increased by 14.8 million (2.5 million more than the increase in the previous eight-year period) while the working-age population (15–64 years of age) increased by only 6.2 million. The difference was made up from a one-half million decrease in the armed services, a 2.5 million decrease in agricultural employment, and a 5.6 million decrease in nonworkers.[23] The decreases in the two latter sources undoubtedly lowered the over-all quality of the labor force. Furthermore, the policy adopted in 1958 of reducing enrollments in secondary and higher education in order to bolster the labor force also tended to lower the quality of labor.[24]

A fourth specific cause of difficulties in factor productivity is connected with the fact that the high priority sectors of chemicals, oil and gas, and complex machinery were in a period of transition to substantially new technologies and more sophisticated goods. The problems of transition proved to be quite formidable. There were difficulties with new designs and other construction problems related to new technology, with the result that the backlog of uncompleted construction grew substantially.[25] Complaints were heard especially about the crash program of investment in the chemical industry which not only retarded other projects but did not allow enough time for the producers of machinery for the new chemical plants to develop and master the essential new technology.[26] Further, there were complaints that new plants were having difficulty in bringing production up to capacity. For example, Kosygin noted that a new chemical combine, two years after it opened, was operating at only 17 per cent of capacity.[27] And Baibakov, the chairman of Gosplan, reported at the Twenty-third Party Congress that out of 500 new enterprises studied, more than half of which had been operating for at least two years, only 12 had reached planned capacity while about half were operating below 75 per cent of capacity.[28] The drain of skilled engineers and managers into the military and space programs and the confusion of the supply system under the regional administration of industry, especially in regard to new enterprises, may well have exacerbated these problems.

The effects of these specific factors may be temporary, for they result from organizational decisions which have already been altered, policies which may be changed, and from the transition to new technologies which may pass in time. However, there are more serious and more durable causes of the present productivity difficulties as well. The Soviet economy and Soviet industry today are vastly larger and more complex than they used to be, which, as both Western and Soviet economists have frequently pointed out, makes it difficult to plan and control the economy with the centralized methods used in the past. Furthermore, industry is being called upon to turn out products which are more sophisticated and which demand higher quality and precision in their manufacture. This is not a question merely of the transition to a new technology, but of the consequences of the new technology itself. Goods that require great precision and special design for special uses are not easily produced by the mass production methods which have previously marked Soviet industry. This development, ironically, results precisely from the past successes of the Soviet economy. The rates of growth in output and productivity that were achieved in the production of simpler and less differentiated goods and services will now be far more difficult to attain.

III. Reform of Soviet Economic Planning

In response to the problems now facing the Soviet economy, concern with reform has assumed a central position in the Soviet economic world. In books, newspapers, journals, in conferences and round-table discussions, and at official party and government meetings, the practices of Soviet economic planning are criticized and suggestions for improvement put forth.

Economic planning, in the full sense of the term (and as practiced in the Soviet Union), is composed of two separate but related processes: the process of plan construction and the process of plan implementation. In Soviet planning practice each process entails serious deficiencies, which tend to be of different types. An important complex of deficiencies in Soviet plan construction has to do with the inability to take "best advantage" of a situation and to make "optimal" use of the available resources. The effects of these deficiencies are to be gauged in terms of opportunities foregone, which are difficult to measure, since they are not empirically observable. In addition, however, the centralized construction of plans in the Soviet Union suffers from defects which are more obvious. Not only are plans not optimal, but often they are not even internally consistent. Because of the multitude of interrelations in a large-scale economy, the diversity of producing units, and the primitiveness of the planning techniques employed, Soviet plans do not assure a sufficient balance between planned outputs and the supply of inputs required for their production. Indeed, it is literally impossible to fulfill the plan as constructed! The deficit supply of inputs at some producing units leads to underfulfillment of output targets, with potentially serious secondary effects through the economy, while other producing units receive excessive inputs which they hoard or use wastefully. Finally, Soviet plan construction suffers from the many ills of overcentralization, resulting from the great distance between the planners at the center and the producing units at the periphery. Because the planners are unfamiliar with the idiosyncracies of individual producing units they often issue thoroughly unsuitable assignments; because enterprises receive commands from diverse planning bureaus located far away, the commands (concerning outputs, inputs, deliveries, labor, finances, and the like) are often mutually inconsistent; because communication lines are long and the information needed at the center great, there is a multiplicity of paper work.

The deficiencies in plan implementation are more manifest still. They are largely the consequences of the incentive mechanism, which pays substantial monetary rewards for the successful fulfillment and overfulfillment of assigned targets by economic units at various levels in the economy. Because they have been thoroughly discussed in the literature,[29] the remarks which follow will be brief and pertain to the situation as it existed before September 1965.

One defect in plan implementation results from the fact that rewards are for relative rather than absolute performance, that is, for performance relative to targets. The enterprise manager therefore strives for high performance and low targets and attempts to limit overfulfillment in order not to give the planners a pretext for raising future targets. This entails a reluctance to innovate, for its rewards are short-lived and the risks great. It also leads to the intentional understatement of production potential, information sorely needed by the central planners for the purpose of effective plan construction. A second group of deficiencies results from the dominance of the quantity of output target as a reward criterion. Because of this, Soviet firms tend to be interested only in their own production rather than with the actual needs of those who purchase and use their products. Under the pressures of such a reward system, quality is cut, assortment and delivery agreements violated, the supply system is made unreliable, and little thought given to improving products so as to make them more useful to the purchaser. (Indeed, when innovation is successfully forced on a firm it is usually innovation in productive processes rather than in products.) Finally, great wastes derive from using inappropriate physical measurements as production targets: with tons as the unit of measure, enterprises preferred to produce heavy rather than light machinery.

These defects are of long standing, and have been described in the Soviet literature since the 1930s. Why, then, the current agitation for reform? There are two main reasons: the planning defects are magnified by the growth and development of the

Soviet economy; the weaknesses of Soviet centralized planning are no longer as strongly counterbalanced by its strengths as they used to be.

The growth and development of the economy, as I have suggested, greatly increases the difficulty of planning and control from the center. As the number of firms grows, the number of interrelationships among them may grow as the square of the number of firms. As the number of specialized product types grows, the number of interrelationships among products may grow as the square of the number of products. The increasingly sophisticated new products require highly specific inputs, narrowing the range of tolerable quality variations and general input substitutability in interrelationships among products.[30] Economic growth and development has, then, both an extensive and intensive effect on centralized planning. It increases the required size of the planning force and demands from it much more precision. Academician Glushkov, who predicted that, at present trends, by 1980 the entire Soviet labor force will be required for planning and administrative work, was telling only half the story.[31] Not only the quantity, but the quality of centralized planning would have to improve substantially.

But the strains on centralized planning caused by growth and development are only a part of the present agitation for reform. A second important element, as I have pointed out, is that the deficiencies of centralized planning are less tolerable than they used to be because they are no longer as strongly counterbalanced by equivalent strengths. These strengths, which have included the ability to enforce the preferences of the political leaders on the economy, to accomplish gross movements of resources, and to restructure the composition and use of output, are at the present stage of development of the Soviet economy no longer such important advantages. The original goals of the Soviet leaders when they embarked on the industrialization drive and first employed centralized planning have by and large been achieved. An industrialized economy has been created (as measured by most criteria, with the exception of the large role of agriculture in GNP and in the labor force). The task now is not further massive changes, but growth within the present (or slowly changing) structure. This can be accomplished only through more efficient use of resources. The priorities in terms of particular industrial commodities are no longer as simple and clear as they used to be. In a developed industrial economy, a wide array of goods and services are involved in the process of production and growth, and in their competition for attention they increase the pressure on the (limited) resources available. Khrushchev's attack on the sacrosanct citadel of steel at the November 1962 meeting of the Central Committee of the Communist Party was a symbolic indication of this realization. Without a few obvious, high priority sectors on which to concentrate, and low priority sectors to absorb the shock of errors, centralized planning is in difficulty. In an environment where the need is for micro-efficiency, where myriad choices have to be made, the strengths of centralized planning are blunted and its weaknesses highlighted. Micro-efficiency requires that economic decision-makers make fine calculations comparing numerous sets of alternatives and that they review their decisions frequently as conditions change. For such purposes planners must either have and be able to effectively use enormous masses of information, or the decision-making locus must be moved closer to the periphery. Furthermore, the rise in the standard of living of the Soviet consumer has allowed him to become somewhat more selective. This adds a further need to planning problems, the need both for knowledge of consumer desires and for flexibility in responding to these desires.

These basic changes, and the seriousness of their consequences, have been dramatically brought to the attention of the Soviet leaders by the recent decreases in the rates of growth of output and factor productivity. Of particular importance has been the decrease in the productivity of capital.[32] The growth-producing power of a forced high rate of investment has been the core of Soviet growth policy under centralized planning. Soviet leaders view its erosion with alarm.[33]

It is against this background that the proposals for economic reform have been coming at a substantial and increasing rate. Let us briefly review some of the major ones and ask what they augur for Soviet industry.

Mathematics and Computers

Soviet discussions of mathematical methods and computer techniques in economics began soon after the Twentieth Party Congress in 1956.[34] During the early stages, many looked upon mathematics and computers as a possible way to render centralized planning more effective and to preserve it in the face of an increasingly sophisticated economy. Schemes were developed for huge, computerized systems of data collection, handling, processing, storage, and retrieval. Input-output methods were suggested as means to improve the attainment of internal consistency in centralized plan construction and in the elaboration of the state supply plan. Linear programming techniques were advocated to improve the efficiency of resource use at all levels and to promote plan optimality. Some even dreamed of a large-scale economic cybernetic system which would combine all of these advantages and would control the entire economy, automatically, on a huge computer network.

Soon, however, the centralizers began to give way to the decentralizers in the mathematics discussions. Although plans are still being pushed for a computer network for data collection and processing, less and less is heard about huge cybernetic schemes, and they are no longer taken very seriously. Large-scale linear programming models are being constructed, but again the possibility of using them to construct centralized optimum plans seems remote. Even input-output methods, which at first seemed so relevant to the needs of Soviet planning practice, now appear to be many years away from direct (as distinguished from auxiliary) use in actual plan construction.

The use of computers for data-handling purposes will undoubtedly increase and will require a thorough overhauling of data and information system design. But the computer is not an alchemist; it alone cannot turn all the lead in centralized planning into pure gold. The major impact of mathematical methods will be at the firm and small group or regional level, where programming techniques and computers will be used for the solution of small-scale problems in which the data difficulties are not so great, but where the payoff in improved utilization of resources would be significant. Furthermore, linear programming may play a useful role in generating more meaningful prices, an important step in any movement toward decentralization.

Libermanism

The discussions of use of mathematical methods primarily (though not exclusively) have concerned problems of plan *construction*. Reform in the realm of plan *implementation* is the major objective of the types of proposals generally identified (at least in the West) under the heading of Libermanism. The aim of Liberman's proposals was to improve the operation of the incentive system to enable the industrial firms to accomplish better what the political leaders, through the central planners, had been ordering them to do. Liberman suggested that the number of obligatory targets (commands) given to the firm be reduced to three: volume and assortment of output; delivery schedules; and utilization levels of major input materials (although he was vague on the question of the system of centralized supply). The firm would be given bonuses in relation to its profitability, measured as the difference between value of sales and cost, divided by fixed and working capital; and the reward schedule would be established for an extended period of time. Moreover, the achievement of planned profit would be more highly rewarded than the achievement of above-plan profits. In these and other ways, Liberman proposed to correct many of the weaknesses of the incentive system. For example, the use of value of sales, rather than value of output, to measure profit would lead the firm to be more interested in quality and in the needs of customers. The taking into account of cost of production would encourage the firm to economize on the use of resources. Relating profit to capital would induce the firm to use its capital more efficiently and would discourage it from ordering unneeded capital. Establishing reward schedules for extended periods would undo the harmful practice of penalizing the successful firm by raising its next year's target to the level of this year's performance, and would also promote innovation. And by having the achievement of planned profit more highly rewarded than unplanned profit, Liberman's proposals would encourage the firm to disclose its true productive potential.

Essentially, Liberman was intent on strengthening what is called the planning principle, by stripping away unnecessary and often conflicting orders ("petty tutelage") and creating an incentive mechanism in which the good of the individual firm would coincide with the good of the national economy.

Consumers' Goods

Closely related to Libermanism were developments in the consumer goods industries. Special problems arose in regard to consumer goods in the latter part of the 1950s. The Soviet consumer, no longer plagued by completely empty closets at home, no longer bought all the things put up for sale in stores, and consequently, unsold stocks of certain goods began to pile up. The need to pay heed to consumer tastes soon became obvious. The producing factories, however, were still faced with physical output targets. They preferred to fulfill targets and earn bonuses rather than adjust their production to the changing tastes of consumers. It was not until Liberman's suggestion concerning the use of profitability in industry in general that a possibly effective way of handling this problem was seen. In July 1964, two clothing firms were freed from established output targets. They were to arrange their output through a system of direct ties with the retailer and were to be rewarded in relation to their profitability. These reforms were extended to many clothing, textile, shoe and leather producers beginning in 1965. The reforms in the consumer goods industries, then, have some resemblance to Libermanism in their use of profitability, but their key feature—the direct ties with retailers and the absence of centrally constructed output targets—is not in fact part of Libermanism. Furthermore, when the experiment was extended in early 1965, the bonus was tied to the fulfillment and overfulfillment of sales plan rather than the fulfillment of the profit plan. This was done because of difficulties with the price system, in order not to penalize managers who responded to consumer demand but produced goods on which profit rates were low.[35]

The September Plenum

At a Plenum of the Central Committee of the Communist Party in September 1965, Khrushchev's successors announced a series of economic reforms.[36]

First, it was decided to abolish the regional form of economic administration and to return to the branch line, ministerial type. Although the reform generally resembles the original form, Kosygin claims that it will operate differently because firms will be on a different incentive system and because of the expected growth of financially independent associations (multi-enterprise firms) within ministries which will have direct administrative power over their member-enterprises.

Second, the number of obligatory targets established for the firm was greatly reduced, and an indicator of volume of sales was substituted for the gross output indicator in the enterprise plan. However, output assignments for the most important products will continue to be made, and the centralized system of supply will be retained. Volume of sales will be the primary criterion of success, although profitability and profits will also be an important incentive for the firm.

Third, the manager's freedom to handle labor questions was greatly increased with the abolition of the assignments for number of workers (the manager's ability to fire workers was also increased, although it did not become unlimited), labor productivity, and average wages. Only the assignment of the wage fund from above was retained.

Fourth, a charge on capital, to be taken by the state as a deduction from profit, was established. Furthermore, investment goods are henceforth to be paid for by the firm using long-term credits, rather than receiving them free. The firm will also have a fund to use on its own initiative for the "technical improvement of production" into which it will put a portion of profits and part of the depreciation allowance. Kosygin stated that this fund will reach 4 billion rubles in 1967, which, on the basis of a rough estimate, might approximate almost 10 per cent of gross fixed productive investment outside of agriculture in that year (assuming current rates of growth of productive investment).[37]

Fifth, it was announced that the new ministerial system would be introduced immediately, but that the new operational and incentive system for the firm would be introduced by stages (first in well-working firms and then gradually spread to others).

Although Libermanism was not fully adopted by the Plenum, some of its proposals were, and the tone of many of the speeches, including Kosygin's, strongly reflected the views and phrases of Liberman and the Libermanites. The importance of profitability was emphasized, and the basic policy of freeing firms from "petty tutelage"—the idea that the effectiveness of central control might be improved by restricting it to essential indicators rather than spreading it to all indicators—has caught on. The problem now, of course, is to determine how many and which are the essential indicators.

Prices

The success of any type of decentralization depends upon the meaningfulness of the price system. Discussions of price reform, which have been going on in the Soviet Union for the last decade, often are clouded by Marxist niceties, but three schools may be identified.[38] The first regards the traditional method of constructing prices (basically, labor costs, material costs, depreciation and planned profit, no interest on capital or rent, and an excise tax on consumer goods) as useful, but proposes that prices should also be coordinated with prices of substitutes, should encourage new technology, and should in other ways vary from underlying "value" so as to improve the efficiency of operation of the economy. It believes that prices may and should be revised from time to time, but that the basic method of price formation should not be changed. A second group is concerned with levying the excise tax on producers' goods as well as consumers' goods, and proposes different ways of doing this. A third group, the mathematicians and mathematical economists (most notably Kantorovich and Novozhilov) argues that prices should be derived from linear programming solutions of optimization problems, since these prices if used by firms in the proper way (profit maximization) would also bring about the optimum use of resources (this optimum usually is in relation to party-established policies). This group has brought fresh currents into Soviet price discussions in the form of concepts of marginal cost, opportunity cost, and valuation of all productive resources available in limited supply. Their linear programming methods have become of such great interest, especially to young economists, because of this entirely novel, logically meaningful, and satisfying view of value and price which they bring.[39]

At present, however, there appears little prospect of significant reform in regard to methods of price formation. The words of Kosygin and of the heads of the State Committee on Prices have a traditional ring.[40] To be sure, interest payments on capital have been established, but they are to be deducted from profits, not added to cost. Thus, they will not be reflected in price. Rent charges will be instituted in some extractive industries, and prices in such cases will be set at the level of the high-cost firm. This, the economist argues, is as it should be. But, by and large, the new industrial prices (which came out in July 1967) were based on the traditional methods.

One important source of difficulty in price formation is that prices can be used to *evaluate* performance and also to *guide* performance, but the two are often in conflict. This is what is at stake in the marginal cost *versus* average cost argument. The economist argues that prices should be set at the level of the high-cost firm in an industry so as to reflect the cost of producing an extra unit of output (on the assumption that the least efficient firm in the industry would produce the last unit of output). The administrator argues that if prices were set in this manner all firms could easily earn profit and thus the power to force efficient operation on the firm would be weakened. However, the crucial question in regard to prices, if they are to be used to guide decision-making, is not so much the bases upon which they are formed, but the frequency with which they are changed in relation to economic or "market" conditions. For prices to meaningfully reflect relative scarcities, they must be used and adjusted regularly in response to experience. This is what is involved in the concept of market equilibrium. The Soviets have not in the past been able to revise centrally established prices with any reasonable speed. This may prove a serious roadblock in the future. Effective decentralization will depend upon effective prices, and since Soviet prices are not effective, the Soviets are reluctant to embark upon extensive decentralization. They are faced by a serious dilemma: prices are not used because they are unusable; but they are unusable because they are unused. This circle will have to be broken if Libermanism and other forms of decentralization are to be spread.

* * *

What does this portend for Soviet industrial growth? The Eighth Five Year Plan (1966–70) calls for a rate of growth of industrial output of about 8.4 per cent per year.[41] On the surface, at least, this is not a particularly demanding target. The plan also states that labor productivity is to grow by 6.2 per cent per year, which means that industrial employment is to grow by only 2.1 per cent per year. The latter is a fairly low figure (see Table 2) whereas the former is slightly below the rate of growth in man-hour productivity (as calculated by the Soviets) achieved in the period 1956–60, but above the rate achieved in the period 1961–65.[42] Capital stock in industry is to grow by 9.9 per cent per year. This is somewhat less than in the past (reflecting to some extent the increased attention being paid to agriculture). Yet it is greater than the planned rate of growth of output, thus indicating that Soviet planners expect capital productivity to continue to decrease, although at a lesser rate of decrease than in the recent past. Thus, while the output target does not appear to be excessively high, it may be hard to reach, for, given the low planned rates of growth of factor inputs, combined factor productivity will have to grow at a rate substantially higher than in the most recent past (1961–64). It may turn out that factor inputs into industry, labor and capital, will in fact grow faster than planned. But as the plan stands, its fulfillment depends upon a significant increase in factor productivity. Here, of course, is where the recent reforms come in.

The extent of increase in factor productivity depends on how effective the reforms turn out to be. There is perhaps a good chance that they will be effective enough over the period of the next five years. The return to the ministerial system is bound to have a salutary effect on the administrative problems of the last few years. It will help raise the system of industrial supply from the very low levels to which it had declined and will especially help in assuring the supply of new enterprises, particularly in such important fields as new chemicals and complex machinery. The switch of the dominant target to value of goods sold may improve the quality, relevance, and timeliness of products, thus making them more useful to purchasers and increasing over-all resource productivity. The new emphasis on cost and profit may encourage firms to avoid obvious waste, of which there is apparently an abundant supply. And the removal of some of the controls over the manager's handling of labor will in all likelihood have a positive effect on labor productivity.

A crucial element in the effectiveness of the reforms is their ability to promote the development of new technology in order to stem the decline in capital productivity. The development and inculcation of new technology is viewed as the key element in the return to high levels of growth. Kosygin, at the Twenty-third Party Congress, went so far as to argue that the competition between socialism and capitalism depends "to a tremendous degree" on the ability to develop and employ new technology.[43] A number of elements in the reforms are relevant to this problem. The return to ministerial forms will place the developers of new technology again in a position where they have more power to enforce its adoption. The charge for capital might induce the manager to pay more attention to capital use, especially if profitability takes on a more important role in his own bonuses. And the freedom to use his own enterprise funds to buy capital, and the necessity to borrow at interest for his other investment, will cause the manager to pay more attention to capital use and productivity. The question here, as elsewhere, is, will it be enough?

IV. Implications of the Reforms

Thus far, the reforms have not been very radical. But it is quite clear that the changes are not viewed as complete, to be followed by only minor adjustments. Rather they are seen as the beginning of a series of reforms to be introduced step by step. Kosygin, for example, speaks of decreasing the list of centrally planned goods "when economic ties among enterprises are well organized."[44] Liberman speaks of the "progressive development" of reform, first freeing the manager from limitations on the wage fund, then from centrally planned products, finally going over to a system of state wholesale trade.[45] The directives of the new Five Year Plan speak of preparing "for the gradual transition to the planned distribution of equipment, materials, and semi-finished goods by means of wholesale trade."[46]

The road to reform may not turn out to be as smooth and as simple as these statements would anticipate. There are many who oppose the reforms, who are convinced they will not work, who are happy doing things the old way and fear personal failure doing things the new way, or who may lose their positions in a new decentralized, profit-oriented system. It may be impossible to overcome this opposition gradually, for in a gradual reform the entrenched opposition is in a position to sabotage each small reform. It may turn out to be necessary to introduce the new system quickly, all at once.[47] Or, in the face of opposition and the difficulties and setbacks occasioned by reforms for decentralization, the regime may well find it easier to slip back into familiar and comfortable centralization than to move ahead to a new stage of decentralization.

It would appear, however, that the problems faced by centralized planning at the present stage of development of the Soviet economy are too basic to allow the system of economic planning and control to go unchanged for very long. Much will depend on what happens to the objectives of the political leaders. If the international situation substantially worsens, then the Soviets may again move toward mobilization and centralization.[48] But in the absence of such a development, the objectives of the regime may well become more moderate. I have already cited Gerschenkron's observation of the historical pattern characterizing the Russian state, in which foreign policy aims create intense pressure toward rapid development of the economy. There is another aspect as well: after the achievement of military parity with the advanced adversaries, and after the internal population is exhausted (and, one might add, after the instigator of forced development has departed), the pressure for growth exerted by the regime wanes.[49]

Russia may be repeating that pattern today, for even though its industrial output is by its own count only about 65 per cent of American output,[50] it has to all intents and purposes attained military parity with the United States. If the regime does in fact relax its extreme pressure for maximum growth, this would be of crucial importance to the successful operation of decentralization in Soviet industry. For if the opposite were to be true and the regime were to maintain strong pressure on the economy, then the shortages and strains created by excess demand might make decentralization ineffective. A decentralized system needs full pipe-lines, buffer stocks, and at least a little unused capacity to absorb the fluctuations of the trial-and-error process of decentralized market responses. It also needs a regime which does not feel that maximum growth is the only goal of the economy; it needs a regime which will be able to accept some short-term setbacks, and temporary malfunctioning of the economy (inherent attributes of market processes), in the interest of long-range benefits.

Has the Soviet regime modified its pressure for maximum growth? One sign in this direction is the repeated talk about the need to readjust the balance between investment and consumption, with an increased emphasis on consumption. Kosygin, at the Twenty-third Congress, spoke of the "simultaneous growth of both accumulation and public consumption."[51] It is true that growth is not being denigrated (although an economist writing in *Pravda* recently advanced the infrequently heard argument that under the new conditions it is better to observe the plan faithfully than to overfulfill it[52]), and the rate of growth of producers' goods in industry in the new Five Year Plan is again higher than that of consumers' goods. However, the gap between the growth of producers' and consumers' goods is much narrower, and more of the producers' goods, it is said, are to be used for the future production of consumers' goods. It is also argued that if there is an increase in the productivity of capital, then with the fall in the capital-to-output ratio, it will be possible to decrease the output of producers' goods and increase the output of consumers' goods without sacrificing industrial growth. The Five Year Plan, in addition, calls for per capita income to grow 50 per cent more than in the previous five-year period. This, coupled with the fact that money income has been growing faster than consumer sales in recent years, will put further emphasis on consumption.[53] Finally, the economic environment since the September 1965 Plenum seems to have shifted toward a greater emphasis on personal consumption as a goal of economic life. This shows up consistently in the economic literature on aspects of economic planning and, in particular, in the more mathematical literature in discussions of such matters as "criteria of optimality." It also appeared in a recent, rather unusual, Soviet study, which showed that in comparison with other Soviet-bloc countries, real consumption per capita in Russia was very low—substantially lower than in East Germany and Czechoslovakia, and somewhat lower than in Hungary and Poland. Of the countries studied, only Bulgaria was surpassed, but by only 1 per cent.[54]

The Soviet economy today finds itself in a situation that bears some resemblance to that on the eve of NEP. The economy has just come through a struggle, successfully, but the people are tired of struggle and want some pleasure in life. And the economy has reached an impasse, where the planning and control methods of the past are fetters on continued progress. Moreover, the industrial capital stock, built in a hurry through the 1930s, and rebuilt at the end of the 1940s and early 1950s, now is aging and inflexible. It was designed to produce yesterday's simple products and cannot produce today's complex ones.

Support for decentralization reforms is strong. The prospects for such reform, however, depend on a number of factors. First there is the ideological opposition to the rule of markets and pursuit of profits. The opposition has been countered by the argument that, when operating a socialist economy, these tools can be made to serve man rather than harm him. The cybernetic approach has been applied to the use of markets as a substitute for Adam Smith's "invisible hand." Moreover, the regime, in its own attacks on the "voluntarism" of the past, has supported the economists who are calling for a scientific, rather than just an ideological, approach to economic questions—scientific in that it explores the logical relationships between means and ends and in that it builds upon actual data which describe reality and not upon wishful thinking about the world.

Secondly, for decentralization to grow in any meaningful way, prices must be made to respond to given market conditions. A system of centrally established prices is probably too cumbersome and inflexible, and, therefore, individual units at the periphery will probably have to be given the right to set and alter prices. But there are dangers in this. The introduction of markets is not synonymous with the introduction of perfect markets. Monopolistic elements are bound to appear and the pursuit of profit in monopolistic markets with decentralized price-setting would not bring unmixed blessings. Furthermore, under conditions of full employment, decentralized price-setting might have a strong inflationary bias. Thus, we might say that the prospects for decentralization in price-setting in Soviet industry in the near future entail the power of firms to set and alter prices only within pre-established ranges, with the necessity to go to the center to shift the range.

Finally, there is the question of the dynamism, the inner logic of decentralization, and the problem of the maintenance of party control over the economy. It is often argued that there are no halfway houses. The argument is that, just as in the early reforms in the consumer goods industries, it was not enough to free only garment producers from centrally established output targets, but it was also necessary to extend this freedom to the textile firms which supplied the garment makers, thus indicating that some decentralization will inevitably demand total decentralization and this will mean loss of party control. In my opinion, however, this is an unwarranted expectation. The world is filled with mixed-systems where elements of market coexist with elements of plan. Without entering into the debate concerning the convergence of economic systems,[55] an important consideration in the mixed-systems is whether a market is used to correct (or implement) the plan or whether a plan is used to correct the market. In the Soviet Union, in the foreseeable future, it will certainly be the former.

A sketch of the prospects for the operational system of Soviet industry in the not-too-distant future might, then, have the following features. The plan will remain, but it will be implemented with the aid of market mechanisms. Most of the controls exercised by the regime will be indirect—taxes and subsidies, interest rates, rents, price ceilings, profit rates—and will relate to such major aspects of economic life as the "determination of the basic branch and territorial distribution of production, the relationship between production and accumulation in national income, the distribution of the labor force, the volume of personal consumption, etc."[56] In such a decentralized system populated by profit-seeking firms, the regime could still maintain substantial control over the pace and direction of Soviet industrial development by exercising control over the indirect levers indicated, by the possible extension of government contracts,[57] and occasionally by the issuance of direct commands.

The future of industry in the Soviet Union is largely dependent on how economic reforms are carried out and on developments in other areas of Soviet society relevant to the central issue of the relationship between the individual and the state.

12.

Science

ALEXANDER VUCINICH

In the Soviet Union science is regarded as "the most important component of nonmaterial culture" and as the most significant index of cultural progress. To understand the dynamics of the Soviet scientific establishment in recent years, it is therefore imperative to examine the dominant trends in science not only as a body of systematic knowledge and as an institutional complex, but also as a world view.

I. A System of Knowledge

In contrast to most other modes of inquiry and bodies of knowledge, the prime characteristic of science is that its wisdom is accumulative and its development is marked by progress. The constant search for efficient procedures of investigation and the critical re-examination of the existing body of knowledge produce new, and more precise and reliable, scientific facts, theories, and laws. Once established, each science, through its legitimate custodians, seeks to improve its research methods, patterns of logical explanations of substantive data, and conceptualization. Each develops its own "logic of growth"—or inner momentum—which not only leads to more precision in the acquisition and systematization of knowledge, but also opens new avenues of research and widens the perspectives of inquiry.

In the growth of individual sciences two distinct processes are detectable: the process of fission and the process of integration. Fission leads to the emergence of new disciplines primarily through the splintering of established sciences; integration produces similar results by the pooling of the methodological, conceptual, and substantive resources of two or more established sciences to meet the challenging problems requiring interdisciplinary research.

Soviet scholarship has kept pace with modern scientific developments and undoubtedly has contributed to the birth of new disciplines carved either from the areas of classical sciences or from traditional no-man's-lands in the border areas between established sciences. Even a cursory look at the institutional changes in the Academy of Sciences of the U.S.S.R. and of individual republics bears this out. In the years immediately following World War II, chemistry, for example, was a generic label for a whole array of relatively broad disciplines, such as physical chemistry, astrochemistry, biochemistry, geochemistry, and radiochemistry; today entire research units are organized to deal with narrowly defined chemical disciplines ranging from the electrochemistry of semiconductors to quantum chemistry. One of the basic functions of the scientific councils established after 1959 within the Soviet Academy of Sciences is to keep up with and expedite the emergence of new disciplines. Soviet awareness, active interest, and participation in the development of new disciplines through the process of fission is equally well illustrated by the emergence of new scientific journals, including in recent years *Problems of Transmission of Information, Technical Cybernetics, Autometrics, Radiobiology,* and *Economics and Mathematical Methods.*

Soviet scientists have been equally alert to the emergence of new disciplines through the methodological and theoretical interaction of various sciences. Perhaps the most striking example is their keen interest in cybernetics, a discipline built upon the foundations of several branches of modern mathematics, symbolic logic, linguistics, and neurophysiology. The rapidly growing literature on cybernetics has many aims: to popularize the discipline as a science of information processes; to explore its basic contributions to materialistic monism; to present it as a most effective instrument for "the rationalization of human activity" in a complex industrial society[1] and to show its methodological value for biology and several other sciences. But most of all it is expected to serve as a sure path to such important unexplored areas as the control of complex dynamic systems and the transmission, storing, and processing of information. The full acceptance of cybernetics as a legitimate science has had some very important results in the Soviet Union; it has introduced mathematical models into many scientific disciplines that previously either ignored mathematics or were closed to most of its logical-algorithmic and probabilistic-statistical approaches. In their endorsement of cybernetics, Soviet scholars emphasize that it is not a label for a mechanical aggregate of related disciplines but a new synthesis, a "qualitatively new system of knowledge" providing a unified scientific approach to the study of specific problems of control.[2]

To talk about the progress of science carried on the wings of its own momentum—its own "logic of growth"—is not to minimize the role of the scholar as a motive force in the enrichment of scientific thought. The function of the scholar is to detect, comprehend, and explore the new avenues of research—to transform the latent logic of internal development into an active source of scientific knowledge. All this is to say that the inner momentum or logic of development is only the indicator of the future paths to be traveled by individual sciences and science in general; it is the scientist who determines whether or how successfully each path will be traveled.

Because of the essentially international character of science, it would be exceedingly difficult to determine precisely and comprehensively the contributions of Soviet scientists in the opening of new areas of scientific research and in developing new scientific theories. Their pioneering work in probability theory, theory of models, theory of superfluidity, the analysis of general relativity, quantum radiophysics, and lepton conservation has been widely acclaimed. It is a generally accepted view that the quality and the scope of the pioneering work of Soviet scientists in many branches of physics and related sciences are second only to the breadth and quality of American scholarship. The unprecedented upsurge of exploratory work of Soviet scientists has benefited from two significant developments since the early 1950s: the intensification of contact of Soviet scientists with the scholarly world of the West, and a tangible curtailment of ideological control over the adoption of theoretical innovations—previously particularly strong in biology.

Although acknowledging the wide proportions of current scientific expansion in their country, some leading Soviet scientists admit that there are certain institutional expectations that tend to direct the attention of scholars to the well-blazed paths of inquiry and away from the areas where pioneering work could be done. In the disproportionate emphasis on "practical results" they see one of the most negative influences. In the words of Academician V. A. Kotel'nikov:

I could mention many of our scholars who have originated new theoretical ideas but have failed to pursue them until they have become stylish—and a subject of intensive research—in the West. This practice slows down the tempo of our scientific development. Our scholars usually tell us that they have neither the time nor the means to give immediate and earnest attention to their new ideas. I think the reason lies elsewhere. Often we stay away from the work in unexplored areas for fear that we may not come up with practical results. But when we read in foreign studies about the practical significance of the ideas that we have abandoned, we return to them with such energy that we have no time to search for new ideas.[3]

Kotel'nikov's protestation indicates an awareness among leading Soviet scholars of the danger of overemphasizing technological research to the pioneering work in scientific theory. It is also a concrete manifestation of the growing role of the scientist in the assessment of the social and ideological problems of scholarship. It is perhaps less significant as a record of a chronic problem of Soviet science than as an indication of a change in the intellectual climate in the U.S.S.R., which gives the scientific elite at least a limited opportunity to defend its right to play a leading role in setting up the division of labor in science that is most natural to a normal growth of scientific thought.

The criticism of leading scholars in policy matters affecting scientific work has become a common occurrence and has many origins. It is part of a general, if limited, relaxation of thought control in the country's intellectual life. It is a tangible and logical result of the loosening of the ideological and philosophical hold on science. And it is a concession to the academic elite by the government in recognition of its mounting contributions to the rising stature of Soviet science as a source of national prestige. Many complementary factors have combined to make international recognition of the high quality of Soviet scholarship inevitable. The grand achievements of Soviet space technology have been all too obvious. The Nobel Prizes—since 1908 when Ilia Mechnikov was honored for his work in immunology—have come to Soviet scholars at a most propitious time and in relative profusion. At present five members of the P. N. Lebedev Institute of Physics of the Soviet Academy of Sciences are Nobel Prize winners. The international recognition of the high status of Soviet science is best manifested in the rapidly growing number of Russian scientific works that are translated into West European languages. From 1960 to 1965, more than 200 Soviet scientific books have been translated into English alone. The American Institute of Physics translates regularly ten leading Russian physics journals, cover-to-cover, and a private firm translates and distributes forty-eight Soviet journals outside the field of physics. The number of Russian articles summarized in the *Chemical Abstracts* in 1964 was second only to the number of English articles.[4] Today, Russian is "the second language of science."[5]

All this should not obscure the fact that the growth of Soviet science has been exceedingly uneven and that entire disciplines have been crippled by the rigid limitations of ideology. In recent years much has been said about the urgent need to raise the neglected disciplines to Western standards. Encouraged by ideological relaxations and favorable party pronouncements, the responsible institutes and their professional staffs have been busily engaged in remedial work in several neglected scientific areas.

New Attention to Neglected Disciplines: Genetics and Psychology

The first area is made up of the disciplines—typified by genetics and psychology—which have suffered from undue emphasis on relatively narrow orientations. The case of Lysenko, whose Lamarckian ideas ruled supreme since they were given undivided party backing in 1948, is well known in the West. In early 1965, M. V. Keldysh, President of the Soviet Academy of Sciences, censured publicly "the scholars headed by Lysenko," who ignored "a number of the most important theoretical orientations in modern biology" and imposed their views on other scholars even when they were contrary to the achievements of modern biology and to experimental facts.[6] It has been admitted that entire areas of biology were theoretically impoverished because of the intransigence and dogmatism of Lysenko's ideas.[7] By virtue of party support that gave his ideas an unchallengeable position in biology, Lysenko wiped out the great gains of Soviet genetics made under the influence of N. I. Vavilov, distorted the theory of the evolutionary growth of the organic world, and disrupted the normal growth of several branches of biology.

Keldysh made it clear he did not attack Lysenko's right to his ideas; he concentrated on Lysenko's dogmatism and unfounded scientific claims. The displacement of Lysenko is the greatest victory for science in the Soviet Union in the post-Stalin era. Just as the ascendency of Lysenko in 1948 signified a victory of ideology over science, his dethroning symbolizes a victory of science—and its spirit of criticism and cultivated skepticism—over the inflexible tenets of ideology. As the Soviet community of scholars prepared to commemorate the 100th anniversary of the publication of the first major paper of Mendel—the father of genetics and the main target of Lysenko's pernicious attacks—Soviet biologists began to redouble their efforts to catch up with the world of ideas barred to them through no fault of their own. Their task has been somewhat eased by the fact that neither the harsh institutional limitations nor the intransigent ideological pressures had entirely prevented at least some of the leading scholars from following very closely, but quietly and in relative isolation, the whirlwind of ideas and experiments that make up modern genetics.

The demise of Lysenkoism actually began as early as 1956 when the Central Committee of the Communist Party called on the scholars to declare war on all "idealistic, vulgar-mechanistic and pseudoscientific views in biology and the agricultural sciences."[8] It also gave them time to review the previously suppressed scientific legacy of N. I. Vavilov, whose work—particularly his studies on the origin of industrial crops and the immunity of plants— brought much international prestige to Soviet genetics.

A mixture of ideological pressure and the burden of Pavlovian tradition has kept Soviet scholars from many areas of psychology. Now it is admitted that "the dogmatization of the Pavlovian theory" has hurt both Soviet physiology and psychology. Physiology has been hampered by the extension of Pavlov's theory of the higher nervous system to the entire field of neurophysiology, while psychology has suffered from an exaggerated dependence on reflex physiology. In the opening speech at the All-Union Conference on the Philosophical Questions of Higher Nervous Activity and Psychology, held in Moscow in 1962, Academician P. E. Fedoseev pointed out the narrow physiologism and reflexological extremism of Soviet psychologists and pleaded for research not only in the physiological foundations of psychological phenomena but also in their social foundations.[9]

Social psychology—a science which in the West has provided a meeting ground for genetics, individual psychology, sociology, and cultural anthropology—is virtually nonexistent in the Soviet Union. With so much ideological emphasis placed on the formation of a "new Soviet man," as a product of new cultural values and social dynamics, it is difficult to comprehend why social psychology in the Soviet Union has remained an intellectual wasteland. Until recently, Soviet psychologists concentrated on the study of the *individual* and not on the formation and the dynamics of *personality* and its social and cultural determinants. The problem of the formation of personality has been a domain of belles-lettres where, until recently, characters were divided into heroes and villains, depending on whether they had internalized the officially defined values of the new culture or had been victimized by an inability to rid their minds of the "survivals" of "capitalist psychology."

An important by-product of the general liberalization of thought during the past decade has been the growing awareness of the importance of a scientific study of the maze of problems covered by social psychology. Today there is much demand for the development of a general theory of the formation of personality, the psychology of professions, industrial psychology, and the psychology of deviant behavior. The first studies show that the Soviet scholars are very much aware of the rich problematics of social psychology but that their methodological tools and conceptualization are still rudimentary by Western standards. It is now recognized that many unnecessary errors in the planning of social and cultural change could be avoided if the ideological categorization of human behavior is replaced by careful scientific study.

If the present intellectual climate continues, Soviet social psychology may well become a source of important empirical data on Soviet social dynamics treated in psychological terms. Despite the charms and challenges of the new social psychology, however, it is very likely that physiological psychology (with a reflexological bent)—an area in which the Soviet scholarship is of unmatched quality—will continue to be the primary concern of Soviet psychologists. Meanwhile, the psychoanalytic tradition is still regarded as a bourgeois aberration and as a mixture of psychological biologism and philosophical idealism.

Cybernetics

In other areas of scientific endeavor Soviet scholars have concentrated on the modernization of research methods, particularly on the adoption of modern mathematical-statistical techniques in the disciplines where previously they were not employed or were used sparingly and in the most elementary form. The expanding mathematization of science in the U.S.S.R. has been particularly influenced by the widespread acceptance of cybernetics, which is credited with major contributions to complex changes in the views on science as a method of inquiry and an instrument of social change.

Cybernetics has brought "pure" and "applied" science into direct relationship, and has ensured the application of the most abstract mathematical methods to the most practical problems in electronic communication. Soviet experts argue that cybernetics has categorically disproved the old and bizarre notion that the more abstract a science is the more removed it is from the practical needs of technology. At the same time, they claim, it has legitimized many branches of mathematics, including the theory of games, the mathematical theory of communication, information theory, linear programming, and statistical decision theory, previously underemphasized or ignored because of their apparent remoteness from practical application. There has also been a reevaluation of the importance and functions of symbolic logic. For a long time treated as an "inwardly oriented" discipline with the task of bringing order and clarity into the rising edifice of mathematical knowledge, today it is viewed also as an "outwardly oriented" science contributing to the enrichment of the disciplines clustered around cybernetics. In addition to expanding the scope of mathematical analysis in the physical sciences, cybernetics is credited with stimulating an intensive mathematization of the biological and social sciences.[10]

Today mathematics has become the principal methodological tool in such dissimilar fields as biophysics, linguistics, and economics. Soviet scholars readily admit that before it acquired the rights of citizenship in these disciplines, mathematics underwent an internal transformation of large magnitude: it shifted its emphasis from the search for absolute measurements to relativistic and probabilistic calculations. Now, at long last, Soviet mathematicians recognize the merit of J. L. Doob's dictum that mathematics is only a part of the theory of probability.[11]

Mathematical Economics

The introduction of modern mathematical methods in economics has been long overdue in the Soviet Union. Until the middle of the 1950s, Soviet economists devoted most of their efforts to descriptive studies of regional economies and economic institutions, or to the legalistic and empirical amplification of the general principles of the official political economy. Mathematical

methods were used sparingly and only in a few branches of economics. The economist could not apply the refined mathematical
methods even if he wanted to because the quantitative data came
to him through government handouts and were fragmentary and
most elementary. Even when he had quantitative data at his disposal, the economist of the Stalin era was discouraged from using
the methods that transform "economic qualities" into "mathematical quantities." Stalin looked at any elaborate mathematical
analysis in the social sciences—particularly in economics—as an
ideological conspiracy or a form of academic escapism. As the
chief custodian of political economy, Stalin did not want the
economist to communicate in a language that was totally incomprehensible to him. He leaned on Lenin's dictum that the general
mathematization of science could lead the scholar into the trap
of idealistic philosophy in which "the matter disappears, only
equations remain." Many statisticians of the Stalin era regarded
even the mathematical law of large numbers and the theorems
derived from it as useless in the study of national economy; they
contended that since this law deals with random variables it is
totally incompatible with the exactness and precision of economic
planning.[12]

Today the economist is encouraged to use mathematical models
in the analysis of relevant data, but he is reminded that his science
deals not only with quantifiable data but also with qualitative
categories not conducive to mathematical treatment. A leading
Soviet economist states: "While acknowledging the correctness
and fruitfulness of mathematical methods in various concrete investigations, we should not allow their absolutization, as the
positivists are inclined to do."[13]

Academician N. P. Fedorenko noted in 1964 that the mathematical orientation of Soviet economics is a recent development
and that the application of mathematical methods and models
has produced promising results in several localized areas of industrial and transportation management. The successes thus far
achieved are considered only as preliminary steps toward the development of a system of optimal economic planning and industrial
control on a national scale.[14] A strong argument in favor of the
mathematization of economics has been put forth by the experts
who claim that the quality of Soviet industrial management has
lagged appreciably behind the modern technology of industrial
production.[15]

Mathematical economics is expected to gather momentum when

an integrated national system of computer centers is built and when computers of much higher quality are manufactured. The mathematical methods of economic analysis will take the economists far away from the rigid categories of traditional economic description and will bring them closer to the very pulse of the Soviet economic system. New, refined methods will undoubtedly bring more objective and precise knowledge of direct utilitarian value—but how much of all this will reach the academic market is a different question.

Sociology

The widening of scientific horizons in the Soviet Union has gone beyond the unfreezing of theoretical orientations previously suppressed on ideological grounds in some disciplines and the modernization of research methods in the others. The official recognition of sociology as a legitimate and independent academic field typifies the opening of significant new areas to scientific treatment. The last book of the Stalin era to carry the label "sociology" in its title, and to recognize sociology as a special discipline, was published in 1931. Written by S. A. Ofanasi, *The Basic Questions of Marxist Sociology* viewed sociology as a science of the laws of social development and as inseparable and indistinguishable from historical materialism. Subsequently, Chapter IV of Stalin's *History of the All-Union Communist Party (Bolshevik)* became the breadth and the depth of Soviet sociology and social philosophy.

The word "sociology" reappeared in the titles of a few Soviet pamphlets published during the late 1940s and limited exclusively to attacks on the leading Western sociological theories. It was not until the end of the 1950s that sociology was allowed to rejoin the academic world as a respected discipline with a clearly defined subject matter and unique methodology. Methodologically and theoretically, it is still a very much impoverished discipline, seriously hurt by its uncomfortable proximity to official ideology and philosophy and by a dearth of competent personnel. The ice is broken, however, and even though recent work is too fragmentary and embryonic to give us a clear picture of its main emphasis, sociology may have a promising future in the Soviet Union. It will undoubtedly leave macrosociology—the "theory" of social structure and social change—to the philosophy of historical materialism and will concentrate on microsociological problems of current import. A sample of the studies published in 1964 and 1965 reveals that the attention of Soviet sociologists is focused on such problems as methodology, relationship of sociology to history, economics and demography, the dynamics of social stratification, the family, the social correlates of technology, the social determinants in personality development, and the formation of precise sociological concepts.

To the traditional historical and ethnographic methods, Soviet sociologists have begun to add the more refined techniques of mathematical statistics.[16] However, here as in economics, the scholar is reminded that "the complexity of social phenomena and their specific features cannot be expressed only by means of mathematical formulas."[17] The scholar's passion for quantifiable data will not be allowed to take him away from the nonquantifiable tenets of the Soviet creed.

The reappearance of sociology must be interpreted as official recognition of the acute need for empirical studies based on modern scientific methodology of such diverse social problems as crime, family instability, the fluidity of the labor force, youth discontent, the proliferation of informal groups in large organizations, the technological conservatism of *kolkhozniki,* and the social content of persistent religious ritualism.

II. The Institutional Complex

Recent changes in the organizational network and the institutional base of Soviet scientific work have many explanations. Some changes have been mere adaptations to the growing volume and complexity of scientific research, the emergence of new sciences, and the enormous growth of personnel engaged in science. Others have come as a part of general de-Stalinization that has affected every aspect of Soviet culture. Some have been designed to make scientific institutions more flexible and at the same time more firmly integrated into the Soviet political system. Important changes have also been made in the institutions facilitating the flow of scientific knowledge to industry.

Although in recent years there has been a great deal of experimentation in the search for new institutional supports to scientific work, many organizational problems have not as yet been satisfactorily resolved. Changes, however, have been extensive and have affected every component of the scientific establishment. Our discussion will be focused on important changes in the over-all administration of scientific work, the geographical distribution of research organizations, the internal structure of the Soviet Academy, the relationship of science to industrial production, the reproduction of a scientific elite, and the dissemination of scientific knowledge.[18]

The State Committee

Since 1959, the Soviet government has concentrated on the establishment of a functionally integrated and administratively centralized system of scientific institutions—a gigantic system which in 1963 consisted of 4,476 research agencies employing 580,000 persons classified as scientists. The State Committee for the Coordination of Scientific Work, established in 1961, instituted new mechanisms for a systematic and unambiguous control over the implementation of government decisions relevant to scientific inquiry.[19] It set up broad channels for the coordination of scientific work on a national basis, for avoiding duplication in major research activities, and for ensuring an uninterrupted flow of scientific knowledge from research institutions to production units through such intermediary agencies as design and development bureaus, and experimental and testing laboratories. The Committee was the central agency aiding the government in the preparation of annual and long-term plans for the expansion of scientific institutions and research, and it prepared plans for organizational changes in scientific institutes to bring them more in line with current developments in their particular fields.

The Committee and the complex network of boards subordinate to it and attached to economic councils had two distinct features. They were vested with no administrative authority, which prevented them from maintaining direct formal contact either with scientific institutions or industrial establishments. Serving only in advisory capacity, they became a source of confusion and delays in the administration of intertwined research operations. In the second place, the attention of the Committee and subordinate boards was centered on the coordination of major research projects rather than on the technological implementation of scientific discoveries.

The post-Khrushchevian recentralization of economic administration led to the transformation of the Committee for the Coordination of Scientific Work into the State Committee for Science and Technology. The new Committee operates through special agencies organized in every economic ministry and vested with decision-making prerogatives. Its function is not only to formulate the main lines of scientific and technological development in the country and to direct the major research projects but also to select the most promising scientific discoveries for technical application and to exercise general supervision over the flow of scientific information to industry. It centralizes both the coordination and the administration of national effort in industrial technology. The huge proportions and the dynamics of the Soviet scientific establishment will limit the work of the new Committee to the coordination and sponsorship of major research orientations and undertakings, to the preparation of technological priorities, and to a search for the general lines of interaction between research scientists and industrial technologists.

The new administrative reforms have not produced spectacular changes in the organizational network of Soviet science. They have helped solidify an institutional system that has grown gradually and has had some loose and amorphous ends. They have consolidated government control over the scientific establishment, and at the same time have introduced additional channels through which the critical voice of the scholar—particularly of the academic elite—can be heard in matters affecting the world of science.

Academy of Sciences

By virtue of its pre-eminent position, high prestige, and close relations with the central government, the Academy of Sciences of the U.S.S.R. has figured prominently in the forging of the centralized administrative system of scientific institutions. The reforms that have made the State Committee the administrative center of the entire system of institutions dedicated to various phases of scientific work have contributed to a consolidation of the Academy as the guiding center of institutions engaged in basic research in the natural and social sciences.

The major step in the reorganization—or de-Stalinization—of the Academy was the government decision in 1959 to abolish the Department of Technical Sciences founded in 1931 to alleviate Stalin's pathological distrust of "pure" science and to provide direct scientific assistance to the initial five year plans of economic development. This move has relieved the Academy of many research tasks in applied science and has amounted to the official acceptance of the time-honored view held by most scientists that, at any given time, the power of science as a national asset is expressed primarily in its theoretical wisdom and in the quality of human and material resources assigned to fundamental research. If the scope of the Academy's work had shrunk, it did so at the expense of activities not essential for the advancement of scientific knowledge.

While the range of the Academy's work has been narrowed in one area, it soon began to expand in another. A government ruling of 1961 placed the basic assignments of the Academy under four headings: exploratory work in all sciences; guidance of all scientific institutions engaged in similar work; maintenance of active relations with foreign scientific institutions; and selection and training of the leading cadres in scientific work.[20]

The real scope of the expanded administrative jurisdiction of the Academy has been spelled out in a special government directive issued in 1963.[21] It assigns to the Academy such burdensome administrative functions as the preparation of annual plans of basic research in the entire country. The Academy is the central coordinating agency of basic research, regardless of the auspices under which it is carried out. It is also the chief planning agency for the future expansion of scientific institutions dedicated to fundamental research.

The transformation of republic academies—employing more than 23,000 scientists—into a functionally and structurally integrated network of research complexes, headed by the Academy, has been the major initial result of the new administrative centralization. The growth of these institutions is presently dictated by two equally stressed sets of needs: local economic and cultural needs, and the national need for the expansion of research facilities for individual sciences. The Academy of Sciences, as the commanding institution in this network, decides on the proposals for the establishment of new institutes, laboratories, and publications in republic academies and keeps a close and critical eye on the quality of their output. It plays a decisive role in the selection of new regular and corresponding members of republic academies as well as the directors of their institutes. It also rules that the presidents of republic academies must be selected from among the members of the Academy.

The Republic Academies

All the republic academies have been reorganized on the model of the Soviet Academy. The coordinating and supervisory activities of the Academy are carried out on many levels: primarily by the Presidium, departments (unifying the institutes of neighboring sciences), and institutes. Three special sections—each covering an aggregate of departments—have been established at the Presidium of the Academy to take care of purely administrative matters connected with the coordination of research. While the control by the Presidium is vertical, affecting every institutional component of republic academies, the guiding and supervising activities of departments and institutes are horizontal and limited to their counterparts in republic academies.

The new measures are designed to update republic academies and make them modern institutions feeding new knowledge into the mainstream of scientific thought. The republic academies may have lost in their local autonomies—which have always been limited—but they are most likely to gain in stature as active contributors to the swelling current of scientific thought. In its annual progress report for 1964, the Latvian Academy, for example, reported intensive work in magnetic hydrodynamics, the mathematical synthesis of logical systems, and polymer mechanics.[22]

The rapid growth of these academies in recent years has resulted in the enormous expansion of the most important institutional base of exploratory research in the Soviet Union—a base made up of over five hundred institutes and other research units and 47,000 scientists. The university base of exploratory work, in comparison with the academic base, is still diffuse and unwieldy. The trend is not toward the formation of a university research system but toward a more efficient coordination of basic research under the auspices of the academies and universities. Thus far this has been true primarily for the universities located in cities with academies.

Geographical Decentralization

The process of administrative centralization of scientific work has gone hand in hand with the equally significant—and equally deliberate—process of geographical decentralization, to which the rapid expansion of theoretical and experimental research in republic academies bears witness. While centralized administration allows for an effective coordination of the national effort in science, geographical decentralization is part of a long-range plan to achieve a more rational territorial distribution of all the productive forces, to ensure a more extensive tapping of local talent, and to bring scientific research closer to regional economies. Keldysh informed his colleagues in May 1963 that the practice of building new institutes primarily in Moscow and Leningrad has been the major flaw in the development of the Soviet Academy in recent times and that a decision had been reached that no new institutes be built in Moscow in the near future. He proposed that such first-class organizations as the Institute of the Physics of Metals in Sverdlovsk and the Chemical Institute in Kazan become nuclei for the development of new scientific centers "at the periphery" and that these be guided by the departments of the Academy.[23]

The Siberian Department of the Soviet Academy is the most formidable product of the policy of the territorial decentralization of scientific institutions.[24] In 1963, six years after its founding, it had thirty-two institutes and three branches employing more than 4,000 scientists. It occupies a unique position in the formal organization of the Academy: it is the only department defined as a geographical unit (all other departments are defined as disciplinary units); it is the only department headed by a Vice-President of the Academy (all other departments are headed by academician-secretaries); and it is the only department equated with a republic academy. The growth of the Siberian Department is associated with the large-scale economic development of Soviet North Asia, but much of the work is also dedicated to general scientific problems reaching far beyond immediate regional needs. Here, for example, is one of the most complex Soviet computer centers. Computer mathematics, cybernetics, mathematical economics, automatic programming, and the mathematical theory of communication are some of the areas emphasized by the scholars working in the Institute of Mathematics. There is no doubt that the Siberian Department—counting fourteen academicians among its members—is earmarked to become a full-fledged academy. The new Novosibirsk University is directly linked with the Siberian Department, the two providing a model of cooperation between academic and university centers.[25] Unencumbered by tradition, outdated theoretical commitments, and institutionalized work habits, the Siberian Department is heralded as a prototype of the future centers of coordinated and collective exploration in the most challenging and promising areas where the problems of theory-building are very closely linked with the logical and epistemological riddles of mathematical methodology. It is, for example, the national center for the development and testing of mathematical-statistical methods to be used in sociology.

The Soviet scientific establishment is thus a very complex system of intertwined institutional components. The formal organization of the establishment has all the earmarks of a modern bureaucratic pyramid, yet it possesses unusual flexibility and looseness. The lines of authority originating at the administrative summit are combined with the lines of authority originating at lower academic councils: the idea of "democratic centralism" has been felt in the Academy of Sciences considerably more than in other Soviet institutions. More academic positions have become elective, and the elections for the first time are regular. Since 1959, academic councils have often voiced serious criticism of administration policies and projected changes. Criticism, however, seems to have been a monopoly of academicians.

The Scientific Establishment

The Soviet Academy has two kinds of institutional components: those that are permanent and occupy definite positions in the organizational pyramid, and those that are temporary, cut across the lines of permanent components, and combine with the scientific and industrial agencies outside the system.

The institutes and departments are the representatives of the first category: the institutes concentrate on specific disciplines, the departments are aggregates of institutes engaged in related disciplines. While the institutes are sensitive to the processes of fission that splinter modern sciences into new branches, the departments are sensitive to the processes of integration—to the growing need for interdisciplinary research. While the institutes continue to be the basic research units, the departments have acquired new importance as the prime movers in the coordination of basic research on the national basis.[26]

The second category is represented by scientific councils which have no place in the formal organization of academic authority and are presently labeled "social organizations." After much experimentation, the present tendency is to anchor scientific councils to departments, although in exceptional cases—as, for example, in the case of the Scientific Council on Genetics, and the Scientific

Council on the Philosophy of the Natural Sciences—they may be attached to the central authorities of the Soviet Academy.[27] As an organizational unit, the council consists of representatives of different sciences engaged in specific inquiry requiring interdisciplinary research. It not only crosses the boundaries of individual departments but also goes beyond the limits of the Academy seeking cooperation of scientists working in research institutes of individual ministries or in universities. The scientific councils may search for new theoretical openings in the unexplored areas of scientific interest requiring the concentrated work of several disciplines, or for a new flow of scientific knowledge into industry; or they may undertake to modernize the science curricula of the institutions of higher education.

The scientific councils are the academic answer to the massive effort of the Communist Party to attach special "social organizations" to every institutional component of the Soviet state. In a sense they are neither a formal nor an informal part of the academic administration. They are not formal components because they are vested with no authority; they can only make recommendations to appropriate authorities. They are not informal units because they cannot exist without official approval and are guided by the directives originating in the offices of the formal organization.

The scientific councils are still very much in flux, and it would be premature to try to pinpoint the main lines of their future development. Thus far their main function has been to inject new blood into the collegial side of the Academy's organizational equation, to provide an apprenticeship for promising young scientists in the important matters of the organization and administration of research, to keep the doors of the Academy open to the larger community of scholars, and to help institutes stay close to basic research by relieving them of some of the more practical chores.

The basic advantage of scientific councils, according to an official progress report, "is that they establish personal contact among scientists and thus provide the most flexible method for the coordination of the research activities of scientific institutions in and outside the Academy."[28] The "personal contact" is necessary not only for the cross-fertilization of ideas but also as a dynamic force working against the perennial tendency of institutes toward relative isolation. Academician Kapitsa argues that neither the scientific councils nor any other components of the Academy strengthen the personal element in the Academy's web of social relations. He feels that the human equation of the academic community cannot find full satisfaction in official channels of communication which operate within a coercive framework and lack the most basic elements of spontaneity. In his words:

> I have said many times that what we need is a scholars' clubhouse where we could gather and talk about the essential problems of our work in an atmosphere free of any coercive elements. When I worked in England, I observed that the most interesting discussions about the leading current scientific problems took place in colleges at meal times. There we discussed the questions that crossed the boundaries of many sciences. This helped us to widen our horizons and to comprehend the current significance of individual scientific orientations.[29]

Kapitsa did not elaborate on his plea in behalf of the informal *kruzhok* (circle) as a source of free and spontaneous exchanges of ideas, but his concern with the overbureaucratization of the Academy is unmistakable and is shared by at least some of his colleagues. In a talk on the present state of Soviet physics, Academician L. A. Artsimovich, head of the Academy's powerful Department of General and Applied Physics, digressed from the main topic to express a profound concern with the gradual transformation of the Academy into a "ministry of science."[30] An important product of this transformation has been the renewed emphasis on technological research. "An impression is created," said Artsimovich, "that by abolishing the Department of Technical Sciences we have actually transformed the entire Academy into it." Kapitsa says that the tightening of bureaucratic controls has weakened the authority of institute directors in the use of funds. He argues that financial flexibility is essential for the adaptability of research bodies to new personnel needs and scientific developments and that because of bureaucratic restrictions many leading scholars refuse to fill the positions of institute heads.[31]

The Academy has only one administrative system to cope with two qualitatively different major tasks—the advancement of science and the coordination of basic research on a national basis —each requiring special talent and a unique style of work. The organization of sections as the major subdivisions of the Academy handling the administrative chores of the coordination task would seem to indicate that the Academy will gradually develop an essentially separate bureaucratic machinery to administer research on a national basis. The Academy is not likely to become a "ministry of science," nor is it likely to become a "monastery of science" (a label invented by Keldysh); most probably it will strike a middle course and continue to provide opportunities for employment to a widening range of talent. This middle course, however, would not change the status of the Academy as a typical Soviet institution devoid of genuine attributes of institutional autonomy.

Recruiting and Training

In addition to its vital functions in the advancement of knowledge and coordination of scientific effort, the Soviet Academy has many other tasks. Two of these are particularly important: the selection and training of the future leaders of Soviet science and the maintenance of active and diversified contact with the world of scholarship outside the U.S.S.R.

The academic system shares with the university system the important task of training research scientists and granting the higher academic degrees to persons of established talent. In the Soviet Union, as in other countries, the future of science depends not only on attracting sufficient numbers of students to various scientific fields but also on selecting the most gifted to carry on scientific work at the highest level of theoretical exploration. In recent years the authorities have shown much interest in developing adequate institutional safeguards to facilitate the search for talented young scientists. The reproduction and expansion of the scientific elite is one of the most acute questions discussed in academic councils. The government has introduced several measures to improve the quality of postgraduate studies, particularly with regard to the selection of topics for, and the defense of, dissertations. Participation of examiners from "neutral" institutions at the defense of all theses has become mandatory.[32] The State Certification Committee, which places the final seal of approval—or disapproval—on every dissertation, has been reorganized and ordered to apply more stringent criteria in adjudging the merits of completed theses.

It is now recognized that the formal certification of academic accomplishment is not a sufficient proof of creative ability in science and that it is imperative to explore new methods and safeguards to ensure as correct a recruitment and placement of young talent as possible. In recent years many research institutions have organized special "pools" of carefully selected and highly recommended young science graduates. After two years of probationary employment, the most promising persons are retained by the respective institutions. The higher the status and prestige of an institution, the more stringent are the selection criteria. The duty of the lower institutions is not only to fill their quotas but also to channel the exceptionally talented to higher echelons. If the practice of discovering and placing talented young scientists becomes established, the Soviet Academy would be backed up by a "farm system" assuring the most creative scientists of reaching the "big league" with a minimum waste of time.

The new system, it is hoped, would take the recruitment of scientists deep into the provinces, which at present are largely ignored. It would also help the republic academies and other scientific institutions to stimulate interest in science among various national groups without rich scientific tradition. While, for example, there are 270 and 261 native scientists for each 100,000 Georgians and Armenians, respectively, there are 81 native scientists for the same number of Ukrainians, and 54 for Tadzhiks and Kirgiz.[33] The new system is two-pronged; it widens the territorial and institutional base for the recruitment of scientific talent and provides the safeguards to ensure the most promising young persons of special attention and most rational placement.

Since the new system has been defined only in most elementary outline, the universities, institutes, and academies located outside the traditional centers are encouraged to devise their own techniques for attracting young talent. The Siberian Department of the Soviet Academy, for example, has sponsored a series of "All-Siberian Olympics" in physics and mathematics to select promising young people for special training, and the Novosibirsk University has established special dormitories for the champions. The new recruitment techniques do not replace, but supplement, the established practice of equating "talent" with the acquired academic degrees and of recognizing the importance of the academic standing of institutions granting the degrees.

Some leading Soviet scholars think that the new practice of organized scouting for science talent is predicated on the unrealistic assumption that the abundance of talent is the best guaranty for an even development of *all* sciences and for the achievement of full self-sufficiency of Soviet science. The critics say that the availability of talent is only one of many factors bearing on the exploratory work in science; the inner momentum of individual sciences at different phases of development and institutional traditions supporting various disciplines are equally if not more important. Kapitsa, Semenov, and Artsimovich share the idea that, instead of searching for untried talent to raise the level of underdeveloped sciences, the academic system should give more attention to the institutes blessed "with powerful men and great scientific traditions."[34] The future of Soviet science, they think, is not in a massive search for untested talent to be spread over the entire scientific spectrum but in the full support of scholars of tested and affirmed talent concentrated in traditionally strong areas of scientific work. They believe that the administrative leaders of the Soviet academic system should abandon the dream of Soviet scientific self-sufficiency in the near future and should never forget that modern science transcends the boundaries and contributions of individual countries. The Soviet Union, they say, could best make its contribution—and pay its debt—to this international scientific pool by giving special support to its strong sciences.

International Dimensions

Academician V. I. Veksler argues that the discovery of bright young persons is one thing and attracting them to scientific work another. The reason for this is, according to him, the quite common (unofficial) opinion in the Soviet Union that the sciences—unlike the arts and the belles-lettres—do not require special talent.[35] It is unfortunate, says Keldysh, that in the Soviet Union the newly coined expression "creative intelligentsia" refers to "musicians and poets" but not to scientists.[36] He could have added, however, that in this respect his country is not atypical.

The debate as to whether the true strength of science is in its national or international attributes is actually a mild academic controversy: in practice, the unrealistic search for "national science" goes hand in hand with the very realistic—and constantly expanding—reliance on the international pool of knowledge. Because of the centralized institutional setting of its science, the Soviet Union is in a good position to maintain a coordinated, systematic, and regular inflow of the current scientific contributions of foreign scholarship. In 1965, the All-Union Institute for Scientific and Technological Information published 160 monthly or bimonthly journals of abstracts from scientific works (books or articles) originating in 102 different countries. These abstracts inform the interested reader of the substantive, theoretical, and methodological contributions in each subdivision of the major sciences. The same institute publishes seventy series of *Express Information* providing a speedy dissemination of the latest foreign developments in science and technology in the form of translated technical papers supplied with all the tables, charts, and illustrations.[37] The journals dedicated to the current progress in individual sciences—such as *Progress in the Physical Sciences, Progress in Biology,* and *Progress in Chemistry*—often contain translated articles on basic theoretical issues. In 1961, a typical year, 279 books in various natural sciences were translated into Russian.

The Academy is not only the principal recipient of the avalanche of scientific knowledge from the outside world, but is also the central mechanism for arranging visits by Soviet scientists to foreign lands in pursuit of scientific investigations and personal contact with the world of scholarship. In 1964, according to official sources, 2,287 scientists working in the academic system visited a total of sixty foreign countries to participate in scientific congresses, conferences, or symposia, to lecture, to pursue specific fieldwork, to observe and work in laboratories, or to serve in an advisory capacity; in return the Academy was host to 3,200 scholars from 83 foreign countries.[38]

Soviet scholars are encountered in many countries busily engaged in various highly diversified research projects. In recent years research teams or individual scholars have traveled to Greenland to study complex geological problems, to Cuba in search of oceanographic knowledge, to Mali to gather ethnographic and linguistic information, to the construction sites of the Aswan Dam to conduct archaeological excavations, to several East African countries in search of geographical and economic data, and to hundreds of other places. The traveling scientist brings back huge quantities of new information, some of purely scientific interest, some of intelligence value, but mostly to serve the overlapping cause of science and intelligence.

The most intensive and diversified contacts are, indeed, with the countries of "the socialist camp." Scientific cooperation within the Communist world is carried out mainly through two formal channels: the scientific cooperation plans signed by the Soviet Academy with the academies of individual countries, and the joint research projects under the auspices of the Council of Economic Mutual Assistance. Since 1962, the academies have held annual conferences, at which the lines of active cooperation are explored. The Soviet authorities are less interested in joint research than in the establishment of regular channels for a continuous and un-restricted flow of scientific information from the periphery of the Communist world to the Soviet Academy of Sciences. The periphery, however, can expect to benefit most from the Soviet experience in the organization of group research, the formation of institutional bonds between science and industry, the complex approach to the training of scientific cadres, and the development and utilization of the most modern instruments of laboratory research and the techniques for storing and disseminating scientific knowledge.

III. A WORLD VIEW

The officially articulated Soviet *Weltanschauung* recognizes scientific attitudes as dominant among Soviet values. As a system of knowledge and an attitude, science is considered the true source of "the profound optimism" of the Soviet world view, "based on the unconditional acceptance of the idea of the essential knowability of the world."[39] Academician N. N. Semenov states that social progress is measured in terms of man's command over the forces of nature and their utilization for human welfare and that "the most important role in the solution of these problems is played by natural science."[40] No nonscientific mode of inquiry has an official place in Soviet culture unless it is viewed as compatible with science. Religion and all branches and orientations of philosophy antithetical to science have been officially abandoned. The arts may differ from science by their unique—esthetic—approaches to reality, but they share with science "the cognition and reproduction of reality" and "an undivided world view."[41] Soviet artists and writers are called upon "to reveal the essential, rather than the ephemeral, in life and to have clear ideas about the development of society."[42] A good artist must know the "scientific" laws of social evolution and the sociological axioms of the structure of Soviet society. The poet may not know the laws of physics or the intellectual strengths of the scientific method, but he must not direct his verses against the scientific attitude and mode of inquiry.

Our present task is to survey the philosophical, sociological, and historical explanations of the pre-eminent place of science in Soviet culture and to indicate recent changes in the refinement and amplification of these explanations.

Dialectical Materialism

The philosophical explanation rests on the unqualified identification of dialectical materialism—the core of Soviet ideology—with science and the scientific method. "Marxist philosophy," we are told, "has never aspired to be a substitute for any of the individual sciences; at the same time it has never divorced itself from them—it has always been organically united with them."[43] Sensitive to and dependent upon all the accumulated wisdom of science, dialectical materialism provides the sciences with a codified world view and an integrated philosophy of science. Indeed, dialectical materialism and science are placed in a symbiotic relationship. Dialectical materialism is alleged to rely on accumulated scientific knowledge to ward off the danger of becoming an outdated, sterile, and dogmatic philosophy. In return, it is presented as giving science a comprehensive theory of "the process of acquisition of scientific knowledge," a general method of inquiry, an integrated interpretation of new scientific achievements, and an understanding of the social and cultural role of scientists.[44] According to its spokesmen, it shows the limitless compass and power of scientific knowledge.

In the post-Stalin era much has been said, written, and done on behalf of a more effective and fruitful interaction between philosophy and science. This movement has been dominated by one idea: the elimination of superfluous ideological and philosophical barriers standing in the way of a normal development of scientific thought. In the waning years of the Stalin era—the years of the official crusade in favor of an ideological purification of science—both scientists and philosophers were pressured into a hysterical verbal war against the idealistic philosophies of some of the leading scientists of our age. Einstein, Bohr, and Heisenberg headed the list of philosophical villains.[45] The theory of relativity and quantum mechanics became the solid core of modern Soviet physics; but, at the same time, their founders became the targets of a relentless philosophical attack. The founder and modern proponents of modern genetics fared even worse: their theories were condemned on both scientific and philosophical grounds.

Stalin's concentrated attack on the philosophical ideas of the founders of modern physics did not last long enough to hamper seriously the work of leading Soviet scientists in the rich new areas of theoretical inquiry opened by quantum mechanics and the theory of relativity. Most established scholars, particularly academicians, gave a nominal endorsement to Stalin's philosophical crusade but continued to carry on their work in the branches of physics and chemistry "contaminated" by philosophical idealism. Others, typified by Landau, refused to honor the crusade even with a nominal endorsement. All this does not mean that the campaign for the ideological purification of science did not produce damaging effects. It created an atmosphere of intellectual ambivalence in many vital research areas in physics and chemistry. It discouraged young, meek, and insecure scholars from full and wholehearted commitment to research in the ideologically sensitive and philosophically unsettled research areas. It prevented a wholesome popularization—and a normal diffusion—of the greatest achievements of modern physics. The delightful and thoughtful *Evolution of Physics* by Einstein and Infeld was not allowed to be translated into Russian because it asserted that all ideas are free products of human intellect. Stalin's philosophical campaign gave the leading Soviet scholars much to worry about, for it revealed in clear and disturbing terms one of the basic weaknesses of the institutional setting of Soviet science: the growing articulation and consolidation of control over science by persons and institutional mechanisms with no affinity either with the ethos of science or the inner logic of scientific inquiry.

After Stalin's death the ideological crusade rapidly lost impetus and a grand reversal began to take shape. The philosophers of science were ordered to take another look into the epistemological orientations of the great Western scientists of our age. The essence of this turn was stated succinctly in an editorial of *Problems of Philosophy*:

> In their criticism of idealism in the creative work of eminent scientists in capitalistic countries, many of our philosophers and natural scientists do not take note of progressive materialistic moments in the world views of such leading scholars as Einstein and a number of others. They have been guilty of substituting superficial criticism, occasionally reduced to simple name-calling, for the creative analysis of the real content of new scientific theories. It is necessary to examine objectively the changes in the views of leading scientists in capitalistic countries without making the least concession to idealism and mysticism.[46]

To make their grand reversal as painless as possible, the Soviet philosophers of science claim that in recent years many leading Western scholars have abandoned their strong "idealistic" positions and have gravitated toward materialism. We read, for example, that "Bohr and Einstein, the founders of twentieth century physics, have criticized several neopositivist views on science" and that Bohr "fully recognizes the objective nature of atoms" and opposes the Newtonian concept of causality rather than the idea of causality in general.[47] We also read that Max Born, "who previously shared many ideas of positivism, now occupies a position in philosophy which is in many respects close to dialectical materialism."[48]

The grand reversal goes a step beyond the reinterpretation of the philosophical views of the great modern physicists. The streams of thought unleashed by the theory of relativity and quantum mechanics are now interpreted as *scientific* validations of the basic claims and postulates of dialectical materialism. Bohr's principle of complementarity is interpreted as a most telling example of the dialectical working of physical processes. Heisenberg's principle of indeterminacy is viewed as an unfortunate term for a fortunate discovery in physics: the recognition of the existence of so-called statistical or probabilistic determinacy and its dialectical relationship to the causality of Newtonian mechanics. Despite Einstein's early identification with logical positivism, the theory of relativity, we are now told, is a grand confirmation of at least four ideas built into dialectical materialism: the existence of space and time as forms of matter, the indissoluble unity of matter and motion, the dialectical unity of the absolute and the relative in nature, and the material unity of the world.[49] The contributions of DeBroglie, Dirac, and Pauling have gone through similar reassessments.

In order to reduce the interference of philosophy with the normal flow and acceptance of modern scientific ideas, the scientists are now advised to follow three simple and straightforward rules. The first rule states: do not allow the philosophical bias of a scholar to stand in the way of an objective assessment of his scientific ideas. The fact that Bertrand Russell and Whitehead are "neopositivists" and "idealists" should not detract from their major contributions to the development of symbolic logic.[50]

The second rule states: do not look for philosophical implications in every theory—do not take the struggle between materialism and idealism into every scientific thought.[51] The mechanism of inheritance studied by modern genetics is an important yet philosophically neutral problem.

The third rule states: recognize a clear boundary line between science and philosophy. The scientist and the philosopher of science must know "that just as natural science cannot by itself solve the general theoretical, methodological, and epistemological problems, so philosophy, as a rule, cannot directly give final explanations of concrete scientific questions."[52] All this boils down to a simple dictum that philosophy should not try to resolve the problems that can be resolved within the framework of special theoretical or experimental investigations. The philosopher continues to attack the ideas of "the annihilation of matter," "indeterminacy," "logical constructions," and many other commitments of "neopositivism," but his criticism is veiled in philosophical bombast and carefully isolated from the substance of science.

In the last days of Stalin's reign, scientific thought was attacked, reinterpreted, and on occasion suppressed when it was viewed as incompatible with Soviet ideology. At the present time the practice has been conspicuously reversed: now it is maintained that ideology is flexible enough to accommodate itself to the new advances of scientific thought and that the main function of the philosopher should be to provide a logical and dialectical justification for this accommodation. While under Stalin the philosopher was the ideological watchdog in the house of science, presently he serves—at least on a part-time basis—as a spokesman of science in the fortress of ideology. His basic function is to extol the virtues and powers of scientific thought and to defend the role of science as the core of Soviet culture. He must retreat whenever his philosophizing stands in the way of expanding scientific horizons.

Dialectical materialism is a flexible philosophical system, extremely sensitive to changes in both ideology and science. At times it is primarily a passive tool of ideology; at other times it is concerned mostly with working out sensitive ideological endorsements of the achievements of modern science. It is a philosophy of the past and not of the future; it is not sufficiently resourceful and critical to search for new paths of intellectual development or for new openings in the stream of scientific thought. Hence, it fails to perform the most important task of a philosophy preoccupied with the epistemological problems of science. "It is no accident," states Thomas S. Kuhn, "that the emergence of Newtonian physics in the seventeenth century and of relativity and quantum mechanics in the twentieth should have been both preceded and accompanied by fundamental philosophical analyses of the contemporary research tradition."[53] In relation to science, dialectical materialism is essentially a conservative philosophy—a philosophy too much committed to the proposition of harmonious relations between established ideology and established science to search for and propose new avenues in the development of scientific theory. The primary task of dialectical materialism is to consolidate sacred and secular—ideological and scientific—thought, and to spell out, defend, and extol the superiority of science as a mode of inquiry and a world view. It overlooks the fact that science does not thrive on the dedication of uncritical worshippers but on the work of critical protagonists, whether their labors be in science or in philosophy.

Sociological Factors

The idea of the paramount role of science in Soviet culture has also a sociological explanation, which is usually contained in general statements on the social correlates of modern scientific and technological developments. The present-day technological and scientific revolution is interpreted as an unprecedented synthesis of rapidly growing technical innovations and radically new technological orientations. The Soviet authorities do not claim that this revolution is a unique Soviet phenomenon; indeed, the Program of the Communist Party of the U.S.S.R. states that "mankind has entered the period of scientific and technological revolution connected with the human mastery over nuclear energy, the conquest of the cosmos, the development of chemistry, and many other great achievements of science and technology." They do claim, however, that the Soviet social system is best equipped to meet most effectively the limitless potentialities of the current scientific and technological revolution. This assertion is based on the assumption that Soviet society is dedicated to a harmonious development of all the productive forces and to a progressive elimination of differences between intellectual and physical work, and that it has established a centralized network of scientific institutions meeting the need for coordinated group research dictated by modern science. This, indeed, is not a statement of fact but an ideological pronouncement.[54] It is made in full disregard of the changing pattern of institutionalized research in the West, particularly in the United States. Soviet sociologists of science have not as yet produced a single systematic analysis of the Western experience in the organization of group research, the coordination of scientific activities carried out by individuals, the proliferation of institutions engaged in various phases of scientific inquiry and application of scientific knowledge, the increasing role of government subsidies in fundamental research, the establishment of direct relations between research centers and industry, and the multitudinous efforts to modernize the technological competence of industrial manpower.

Soviet scholars do not conceal their enthusiasm for cybernetics as an important guidepost of the future development of modern social systems. They say that, more than any other modern scientific "orientation," it introduces fundamental changes into the internal structure of management, methods of production, and industrial control, and it brings science and production into an organic union and sets the stage for qualitative changes in both production and science. The current technological revolution is interpreted as a general revolution affecting every science and its interaction with society. The essence of "the cybernetic revolution" is defined by a Soviet academician: "While in the past the machine replaced or lightened man's physical work, at the present time cybernetic instruments can perform complex logical operations, lighten mental work, and raise the productivity of intellectual toil."[55] Cybernetics opens new fields of inquiry and brings science and production into closer and interdependent relationship.

Today, Soviet social theory views science not only as a part of the "superstructure" but also as an integral component of the "base" of the social system—a direct determining factor in the organization of production processes and an "architectural principle" underlying the structure of Soviet society. There is no need here to go into the logic and theoretical merits of this interpretation; what is important, however, is the bold view of science as an intellectual endowment penetrating the entire Soviet social system.

The new interpretation of the social and cultural role of science is, at least in part, justified on the grounds of an enormous widening of the institutional base of science: an expansive continuum of institutes dedicated to theoretical exploration and staffed by a true scientific elite at one end and scientific laboratories operating in individual industrial plants at the other. Between these two extremes are various levels of applied science institutes, development and design bureaus, and engineering and testing laboratories, each requiring a special kind of skill.

In recent years bold efforts have been made to establish all sorts of "social organizations" dedicated to scientific research. The twenty-one scientific and technical societies, organized on a national basis, have 47,000 primary organizations operating in most factories, state farms, scientific institutions, and research and development bureaus.[56] These societies operate on a voluntary basis, their membership consisting of persons with various degrees of scientific training. They vary from research institutes, groups, and laboratories to technological and design bureaus, bureaus of technical information and of economic analysis. Active participation in them is not remunerative on a regular wage basis, but rewards in the form of prizes for outstanding achievement are not excluded. Although they are not formally tied to the network of government institutions engaged in scientific activity, they are part of a grand design for total social mobilization.

That research has been taken as a rallying point for a national network of voluntary organizations is merely another index of the growing prominence given to science as an orientation value of Soviet culture. The practical aim of science societies is to accelerate the general growth of the technical competence of industrial manpower, to marshal human resources to meet the challenge of automation in industry, and, in general, to make science an ever-present ingredient of the daily life of every citizen. To these societies, science is at the same time a dynamic and growing collection of formulas and technical skills and a manner of thinking, behaving, and looking into the future.

The modern relationship between science and production is characterized by the relative speed by which knowledge flows from the desk and the laboratory of a theoretical scientist to the production line. The Industrial Revolution in England actually took place before modern science and industrial technology were wedded. Yet, the two are inseparable: industry is a direct application of up-to-date scientific knowledge, and science is unthinkable without a broad and highly diversified "industrial" base consisting of research equipment of every description and degree of complexity.

The Soviet ideologists envision the future Communist society as a social system based on an absolute unity of science and industry. The future industrial organization is viewed as a complex system dominated by two components: a self-adjusting network of automatic controls and a "conscious" element supplied by "the new man"—a product of perfect rationality.[57] The full realization of this bifurcated dream would depend, theoretically, on two separate but interrelated achievements: the perfection of the branches of mathematics indispensable for the full understanding of such self-adjusting systems as the brain and the industrial firm, and the full triumph of the human understanding of the laws of social development leading to "the unity of human will and behavior." Cybernetics would provide the aegis for the development and refinement of mathematical methodology indispensable for the full victory of self-adjusting systems of automatic controls in the economic life; science societies, along with other voluntary associations, are expected to play a major role in expediting the emergence of the man of the Soviet future. Jointly, the two are expected to render the state an obsolete and unnecessary social category.

It is not our job to discuss the feasibility of the Communist utopia and how much weight the Communist ideologists actually attach to it when they cast their eyes in the direction of the anticipated development of the Soviet social system. Cybernetics and science societies should be judged in terms of their contributions to the Soviet industrial society as it exists today. They may be the ideological guideposts to a more rational future and they may be the symbols of the scientific rationality of Soviet culture, but ultimately their survival will depend on their concrete, measurable contributions to the existing society. Both are designed and employed to bring science closer to society either through a more direct industrial application of scientific discoveries or through the cultivation of the scientific attitude and a wider dissemination of knowledge.

Cybernetics as a synthetic science is not universally accepted in the Soviet Union. Some leading scholars tend to treat it as a sensationalist current in modern scientific thought that derives much glamour from exotic and extravagant promises rather than from the soundness of its theoretical system. Others think it a very exciting but a passing phenomenon. It is possible that an overstressed positive commitment to cybernetics could disturb the normal momentum in the development of Soviet scientific thought in general, just as the overemphasized negative attitude toward modern genetics adversely affected the growth of Soviet biological thought.

All this should not detract from the real intellectual strength and contributions of cybernetics. It has opened the gates for a broader and more fruitful mathematization of science, and has legitimized a symbolic or mathematical logic as a logic of modern science. It has enriched scientific methodology by dealing a mortal blow to Lenin's misguided warning against the mathematization of science as a damaging path leading to a substitution of "equations" for "matter"—and of "idealism" for "materialism."

Cybernetics has helped Soviet scientists to retreat from some of the cruder epistemological and logical elements of Leninist materialism, but it has reinforced their adherence to the ontological foundations of Leninist materialism. The extension of the concept of "self-adjusting complex dynamic systems" to the living world, to the world of social and economic organization, and to the psychological make-up of organisms adds a scientifically sophisticated prop to Soviet atheistic propaganda. Cybernetics has also facilitated the modernization of social science methodology and it has become a prime mover in the proliferation of modern computers and various other types of scientific instruments. In the Soviet Union cybernetics is not only a science, or a scientific method, but also a philosophical vantage point and a social-cultural force of considerable importance.[58]

The scientific and technical societies may not be the prototypes of the scientific institutions of the very distant, and very hypothetical, future. But they are very much a reality today. Their immediate practical aim is to help accelerate the industrial application of recent scientific discoveries, to spur the growth of a scientifically literate industrial manpower, and to bridge the gap between the rapidly advancing industrial technology and the crude and outdated methods of industrial control. Their job is not to enrich science or revolutionize industrial technology, but to help marshal the human resources to meet the challenge of the scientific and technological revolution. They are a "social" safeguard against technological conservatism and against interruptions in the flow of modern scientific information to the factory. Indeed, they belong more to the present than to the future. That they will produce the "conscious"—or human—factor of a future industrial management based on the mathematical-cybernetic model of "self-adjusting complex dynamic systems" is as hypothetical as the scheme of a future Communist utopia.

The scientific and technical societies are not the only voluntary research units. For example, the D. I. Mendeleev All-Union Chemical Society, founded in 1868, has more than 1,500 primary organizations working in scientific and educational institutions, factories, and *sovkhozy*. The Society, which commands a membership of 100,000, is best known for its sponsorship of periodic congresses of Soviet chemists at which selected problems of vital practical importance are discussed. In recent years its primary organizations have founded several thousand voluntary research, development, design, information, and testing bureaus, groups, or brigades.

Whatever the future may hold for the scientific and technical societies and similar organizations, it is clear that they owe their existence to a general recognition of the fact that the industrial establishment is not only a meeting ground of science and technology and an economic institution but also a very complex social organization. This is the rationale behind the growing emphasis on industrial sociology. While cybernetics is expected to contribute to the technical modernization of industrial management, sociology is expected to provide scientific information for the improvement of the human side of the industrial equation. At the general meeting of the Soviet Academy of Sciences held in December 1965, Academician A. D. Aleksandrov stated bluntly that "the questions of economy and management must be rationally resolved on the basis of serious sociological studies." He acknowledged the low level of sociological investigations in the Soviet Union and pleaded for the establishment of a sociological institute in the Academy of Sciences.

Despite the great, and perhaps exaggerated, value attached to sociology at the present time, this subject is not as yet taught in any university and no official list of professions makes a reference to "sociologists." Some universities are currently involved in sociological research and in intensive study of its methodology, including pioneering work in "cybernetic modeling." The teaching of sociology will most probably come after the research institutes have produced sufficient numbers of qualified instructors. It is indeed a paradox that cybernetics and sociology, the two disciplines that not too long ago were treated by Soviet ideologists as the most decadent of all "capitalistic sciences" are today considered the beacons illuminating the path to an ideal Communist society. The burgeoning sociology will concentrate on "the increasing dependence of society on science, the growing proportions of scientific work, and the social nature of science itself."[59]

Although they may occupy the opposite extremes of the scientific spectrum, cybernetics and sociology share two important common features. Potentially, if not actually, they are unique combinations of the most advanced and challenging developments in modern mathematics, and they recognize, in the words of a Soviet writer, that "today science plays an active and irreplaceable role in all the important processes of history: in the development of material production, in government administration, in spiritual life, and in military activities."

Historical Factors

In the Soviet Union, the philosophical explanation of the preeminent place of science in Soviet culture is based on the assumption of the compatibility and essential identity of science and dialectical materialism—the quintessence of Communist ideology. The sociological explanation is based on the idea of the organic dependence of the Soviet social and economic system—as a socialist and a modern industrial system—on up-to-date scientific achievements. The historical explanation that is advanced rests on the claim that science has deep roots in Russian culture.

The study of the history of Russian scientific thought has gradually grown into a huge enterprise without parallel in any other modern society. Symposia, journals, monographs, comprehensive tomes, and articles by the thousands come in a continuous flow from several organizations, but primarily from the Institute for the History of the Natural Sciences and Technology, a component of the Soviet Academy of Sciences. Since 1953, the Institute has published over seventy symposia devoted primarily or exclusively to the history of science in Russia. Complete or selected works of every major Russian scientist of the pre-Soviet period have been republished. Since 1950, approximately fifty monographs or books have been published on Lomonosov alone. A four-volume systematic historical survey of Russian science totalling 2,100 printed pages, and a two-volume history of the Academy of Sciences have been published since 1958. Such popular science journals as *Priroda* ("Nature") and *Nauka i zhizn'* ("Science and Life") regularly publish articles on Russian scientists and scientific institutions of the pre-Soviet era. At least one historical study—in most cases of book length—on every university and learned society has been published since 1950. The life and contributions of the leading scientists have been treated not only on a technical level but also in a popular vein.

Soviet scholars interested in political, social, philosophical, and literary developments in Tsarist Russia pay a great deal of attention to sorting out the heroes and the villains, praising the former and denouncing the latter. The Soviet historian of Russian science is not faced with the same problem, for he regards the history of science in his country as a procession and succession of heroes. Some of these heroes may have made errors of a philosophical nature, but the tendency is either to minimize or to gloss over them. At the same time, an effort is made not to overlook anybody who had written in scientific fields even though his contributions might have been infinitesimal. Equal care is exercised to detect and point out the contributions of scientists to the growth of the Russian tradition in materialistic philosophy.

The postwar emphasis on the history of Russian science received a boost from Stalin's war on cosmopolitanism, which produced a doubtful record of Russian "discoveries" in every major effort of intellectual and esthetic endeavor. In 1948, the Academy sponsored a conference on "the questions of the history of national science" at which one leading scholar after another risked his reputation by producing evidence, in many cases highly tenuous and circumstantial, of the great discoveries originally made by Russian scientists and self-taught inventors and subsequently attributed to Western scholars. The main thesis of Stalin's bizarre anti-cosmopolitan campaign was that the numerous independent inventions show that science is not only a vital part but also a highly original component of Russian culture.

After Stalin's death the war on cosmopolitanism came to an end, but the study of the history of Russian contributions to science had just begun to reach out and gather momentum. As anti-cosmopolitanism faded away, the new historical scholarship rapidly improved in quality and sophistication. The publication of some major collective works, including the *History of the Academy of Sciences of the U.S.S.R.*, was temporarily delayed to allow the scholars to de-Stalinize them. A new breed of talented and excellently trained historians of science showed up in the Academy's Institute of the History of the Natural Sciences and Technology. While not completely free of nationalist romanticism, these experts are taking a new and more objective view of the historical growth of science in their country. Indeed, their numerous publications have given a better and more meaningful perspective for a healthier appreciation of the place of science in Russian intellectual history. Although emphasizing the importance of the scientific tradition, they are careful to avoid the crude Stalinist claims of the national character of Russian science and to reject the sterile search for Russian scientific priorities. However, they have yet to produce a single systematic and detailed study of the paramount role of foreign—particularly German—

scholars in making science an integral part of Russian culture. Nor have they fully overcome the deeply rooted search for materialistic philosophy in the entire Russian scientific legacy, particularly in the works of leading scholars. The history of science is written with the obvious view of reinforcing rationalism—the belief in the inexhaustible power and supremacy of man's intellectual endowment—as a cardinal value of Soviet culture.

*   *   *

Several distinguished members of the Academy of Sciences agree that, despite the deep roots of its scientific tradition, the Soviet Union has not yet produced a genuine community of scientists—a community serving as the chief custodian of the values of science and the scientific legacy. According to Kapitsa: "The building of a healthy advanced scientific community is an enormous task to which we do not pay enough attention. . . . This task," he continues, "is more difficult than the training of selected young talent for scientific work or the construction of huge institutes."[60] He adds that a genuine community of scholarship— and not a bureaucratic organization of science—can best serve as an impartial judge of advancements in science and as a bridge between narrow academic specialization and broad enlightenment. The basic principle of the Soviet scientific establishment is the subordination of scholarship to the bureaucratically organized administration of the state. It is fundamentally antithetical to the principles of contractual autonomy and professional *esprit de corps* without which a true community of scientists cannot exist. So long as the scientist is not the full master of his own house and so long as he is not allowed to enter into free, spontaneous, and critical relations with the representatives of all modes of inquiry, he will be kept away from an important area of intellectual challenge and a vital source of new scientific wisdom.

PART FOUR

Changing Aspects of Social Structure

Introduction

Tracing the sources and consequences of changes in social structure involves some of the most subtle and difficult questions of analysis. The task is made no easier in the Soviet case by the extreme reticence of scholars and officials there to publish, or even to accumulate for internal use, the kinds of data upon which historians and behavioral scientists customarily depend. Nevertheless, the widening public dialogues of recent years on inescapable issues of social organization have provided rich, if necessarily incomplete, information in a number of vital areas—as the chapters in this section reveal.

The question of equality and inequality in Soviet society, the subject of Robert Feldmesser's essay, raises no less than the original and still unrealized promises of the Bolshevik Revolution. Although the intervening years have seen the growth of a stratification system that in certain respects closely resembles those of industrial societies in general, the dream of a classless order still figures importantly both in the rhetoric and in the long-range goals of the regime. Feldmesser's essay illuminates the current version of the dream, and takes account of major impediments to its literal realization.

Few facets of Soviet society have changed as profoundly as the family, yet paradoxically few have remained as inaccessible to direct official action. Despite radical attacks in early years, the family remains unchallenged as the instrument of primary socialization, and the regime has evidently made its peace with an institution which is solidly conventional by contrast with the revolutionary goals originally envisioned. No doubt the need for the reliable nurture of stable personalities lies behind the truce with an institution once denounced as a bourgeois abomination. But the truce is not always an easy one, for individual families social-

357

ize their young in different ways, not all of them satisfactory to the regime. Mark Field and David Anderson outline the tensions that arise in this process and assesses them as a basic source of social change.

Until only a few years ago, any discussion of leisure in Soviet society would have described its general scarcity rather than how it was used, but the gradually rising standard of living and the contraction of the working day have altered the time budgets of Soviet citizens and presented them with increasing allowances of free time. What to do with leisure, especially in urban settings and in a secular age where traditional patterns offer little guidance, is by no means an exclusively Soviet dilemma. But the long-standing predilection in the U.S.S.R. for regulating personal behavior on social and moral, as well as political, grounds makes policy in this area a useful and sensitive index of change (or its absence) with respect to the larger question of individual freedom in a highly regulated society. The *amount* of free time is obviously the first question, but *how* that time is to be used, how the government expects it to be used, and the quantity and quality of facilities to be made available for its exploitation, will deeply affect the content of Soviet daily life. Paul Hollander reports recent discussions of these questions in the Soviet Union, and sees the outcome as a highly significant test case for theories of convergence.

With the exception of Communist China, probably no contemporary society surpasses the Soviet Union in ascribing such importance to the power of ideas to control events, nor have many been more systematic and often ruthless in regulating their intellectuals. Those who are familiar with Russian cultural history will not fail to recognize the deep roots of this orientation in prerevolutionary times. James Billington's searching essay confirms that remarkable continuity and also suggests that a new and perhaps powerful role for men of ideas may emerge from the confluence of the traditional quest for truth with the more recent search for efficiency under modern conditions. His contribution concludes our topical presentations, and we then move to the concluding chapters.

13.

Stratification and Communism

ROBERT A. FELDMESSER

More than in other societies, patterns of social stratification in the U.S.S.R. have been affected by deliberately selected political goals. It would be an exaggeration to say that Soviet stratification has been entirely the outcome of coherently explicated policies; forces beyond the control of the leadership have no doubt played a part. But, even so, their significance has depended to some extent on the degree to which they were taken cognizance of by the leadership, which has been able to give them full play or to resist them. Thus, up to 1961, one can identify five more or less distinct periods, during each of which policies produced a dominant tendency.[1]

The first was the period of War Communism, when the thrust was in the direction of radical leveling. Among the actions that set in motion the leveling process were the abolition of ranks, titles, and uniforms (and even of the three classes of accommodations in railway coaches); the establishment of the party maximum, a ceiling on the income of party members; a high inheritance tax; and the fixing of a maximum ratio between the incomes of manual and nonmanual workers. Differentiation of wages within the working class almost disappeared, and though this was the result of economic processes rather than of deliberate policy, it was welcomed by the party leadership. In some respects, there were efforts to reverse the usual hierarchy of status, in conformity with the concept of a "dictatorship of the proletariat" and with the hostility toward the "alien" or "former" classes which was part of the revolutionary spirit. Workers were favored in the assignment of ration categories—which, under the conditions of War Communism, were more meaningful than money wages—and they were also given preference in admission to the party and to educational institutions, while those who had previously enjoyed high status often lost their property and were subjected to various indignities. On the other hand, the assumption of managerial prerogatives by groups of factory workers was quickly brought to an end when it proved incompatible with the prosecution of the Civil War; and some categories among the "former" classes—especially military, economic, and bureaucratic experts—were protected from loss of status.

While many of these provisions remained in effect during the New Economic Policy (NEP), the net movement during this second period was in the direction of a return to a more highly differentiated status system of a conventional kind. Income differences within the working class, and between it and other groups, were restored. Private control in agriculture permitted the reappearance of the *kulak,* or wealthy peasant, and a similar phenomenon was observed in trade and some branches of manufacturing. Moreover, the critical need to regain stability after the havoc wrought in the preceding years restrained the regime from acting too vigorously against high-status "holdovers" in government and education, even if they continued to be denied prestige in official pronouncements. Perhaps the only significant gain in status for the workers during this time was their indirect representation, through the trade unions, in industrial management.

The beginning of planned rapid industrialization and agricultural collectivization brought a renewal of the revolutionary spirit, which marked the third period. Many of those who had clung to high positions during the vicissitudes of the preceding years were dismissed; some were brought to trial for their opposition to the changes taking place, and a few lost their lives. All were brought under suspicion by a campaign of "spets-baiting" (harassment of technical experts). The *kulak* class was liquidated economically and socially, even physically. Favoritism for workers (and, to a lesser extent, for poor and middle peasants) was reasserted in the form of preferential admission to the party and to educational institutions and preferential hiring for managerial positions. Once again there was a tendency toward wage-leveling, though, as before, it was not altogether of the regime's making.

The third period is generally regarded as having been brought to a close by Stalin's famous speech of June 23, 1931, in which he denounced "equality-mongering" and demanded that the Soviet Union acknowledge the need to have "its own intelligentsia."

From that time, there emerged a system of stratification which bore many of the characteristics associated with industrial societies elsewhere but was intensified, so to speak, by the authoritarianism of the political structure, which deprived workers and peasants of any effective means of resisting the changes in their status. Income differentiation was restored and even increased; the fixed ratio between manual and nonmanual wages was abolished, as was the party maximum. Income taxes were made so low as not to reduce these differences by very much, and the inheritance tax was virtually eliminated. Economic managers were given considerable authority over the enterprises in their charge, though this was limited by their subjection to political commands. The trade unions were emasculated and converted into administrative agencies of the state, with the chief duty of helping to enforce the manager's commands rather than protecting the workers' interests. Not only was discrimination against the intelligentsia in admission to the party ended, but it was they rather than the workers and peasants who were actively recruited; and in other ways, too, they were accorded official honor. Discrimination against their children in admission to educational institutions was also ended and to a degree reversed by the subsequent imposition of tuition fees. Given the greater attraction to education which is generally an attribute of this group (and which had evidently continued despite the previous policies), the children of the intelligentsia enrolled in the schools, particularly at the higher levels, in disproportionate numbers—a factor of increasing significance as the regime made technical competence almost as important a criterion of status as political reliability. These and a host of similar changes (including, for a while, even the reappearance of titles, uniforms, and formal ranks for many occupations) convinced many observers that the Soviet Union was now ruled by a "new class"— to use Djilas' famous phrase.

But with Stalin's death—in part, even while he was still alive— and especially with Khrushchev's advent to power, a fifth period began, marked by renewed efforts at leveling. Among the measures taken toward that end were increased criticism of the high-handedness of managerial and administrative personnel; the use of untrained volunteers to do some of the work of the soviets, the press, the police, and the courts; permission for workers to quit their jobs without the consent of the manager; new powers for the trade unions, including the requirement that they approve the firing of any worker; a rise in the admission of workers and peasants to the party; and adjustments in the wage and tax structure and in payments to the collective farms. These adjustments were in the direction of higher incomes for the lowest-paid groups and lower incomes for those formerly at the top, and included the enactment of a maximum ratio of two to one between wages in the highest and lowest categories of manual-work skills. In the educational system, tuition fees were abolished; the curriculum of elementary and secondary schools was made more "vocational" and less "academic," and most students were expected to work for at least two years before entering a higher educational institution; the method of awarding scholarships was revised to take greater account of the student's material needs; and boarding schools, which were supposed to offer especially favorable educational conditions, were established with preferential admission for children from disadvantaged families. In some respects, these policies were reminiscent of the earlier efforts at "reverse discrimination."

I. Authoritarianism and Differentiation

What this historical sketch suggests is that the Soviet handling of the problems of stratification has been inconsistent. One reason for this instability, and the consequent vacillation in policies, is not hard to locate. On the one hand, the decisions of Soviet political authorities have often run counter to what would probably have been the free choice of the citizenry; at the very least, their decisions have not been the direct result of such choice—which is, of course, characteristic of an authoritarian regime. This has impelled Soviet leaders in the direction of a high degree of differentiation, partly as a "bribe" to assist in the recruitment of personnel to execute unpopular policies under difficult conditions, and partly as a means of putting social and political distance between the executors and those on lower levels who might object to the policies. A degree of status differentiation is apparently a functional requirement of industrial (indeed, of all) societies,[2] which by itself would account for some of the developments in the Soviet Union. However, industrialism as such allows of a range of status differentiation. Industrialism is as compatible with the relatively open stratification patterns of the contemporary United States as with, say, the more rigid division of nineteenth-century England with its "aristocratic bourgeoisie" and a ruthlessly exploited working class. But particularly during the period of late Stalinism, Soviet society resembled the latter situation more than the former, and this "excess" of differentiation can be attributed in part to the imperatives of authoritarianism.

On the other hand, however, an extreme degree of differentiation—indeed, almost any degree of differentiation—also harbors dangers for authoritarianism. If it is to retain its power, an authoritarian ruling group must ensure that those who have been allocated relatively large shares are not thereby enabled to accumulate power and use it autonomously—that is, to challenge the ruling group. Yet a tendency toward accumulation and autonomous use of power is probably an intrinsic consequence of differentiation. In the Soviet case, at any rate, the authority and distance which those in high status enjoyed enabled them to block communications and thus to prevent the regime from keeping close control over their behavior. This is not to say that high-status persons were necessarily "selfish"; some of their actions, as Joseph Berliner has shown in his studies of factory managers, were undertaken for the sake of meeting the regime's demands.[3] Nevertheless, these actions often led to choices—for example, in the allocation of resources—which would not have been made by central authorities had they had the chance to make them. But aside from this, we may assume that in the Soviet Union, as elsewhere, those who have high status are desirous of maintaining it, will not refrain from exploiting and abusing it for their own purposes, and will be the more successful as the perquisites of their status are greater.

Thus, local officials tended to enter into informal groupings for their mutual protection, further frustrating the regime's efforts to control them; they also exerted their influence to shelter their children from the rigors of the selective mechanisms which the regime tried to institute. Hence, the system of stratification both maximized the regime's power and at the same time limited it, and the efforts of the regime to cope with this dilemma resulted in the cyclical alteration of policies which has been described.

Another element must be brought into this interpretation to make it more nearly complete, and that is an ideologically inspired pressure toward egalitarianism. At the very least, Marxism provided a ready justification for reducing differentiation when the regime wished to do so or, as during War Communism, for welcoming it when it seemed to be occurring anyway. But the ideology has surely involved more than that.

An ideology sets up certain expectations that the social structure will take one form rather than another; this is even more the case when the ideology is officially and frequently proclaimed to be the foundation of the social system. When the existing social structure violates these expectations, there is likely to be a felt need to reduce the resultant "dissonance" as far as may be compatible with other goals. For those who are convinced that Marxist ideology no longer plays any significant role in Soviet society (or perhaps never did), it is well to point out that the idea of equality—the notion that there are some degrees and kinds of differentiation which are "morally" improper—is a powerful force in the modern world and has affected even societies in which Marxism has had little importance as an ideology. Nevertheless, in the historical circumstances, the operation of this force in Soviet society can be traced directly to Marxism and we can expect it to be expressed in Marxist terms.

In order to understand the development of Soviet stratification patterns, it is important to recognize exactly what sorts of dissonance Marxism would create. Marx never anticipated that the proletarian revolution would do away with differentiation altogether. Under socialism, the immediate postrevolutionary stage, men would be paid "according to their work"; under communism, the succeeding and final stage of history, they would be paid "according to their needs." But in both cases, he clearly admitted that men would receive *different amounts and kinds of income* or its equivalent.[4] In this sense, a stratified system would remain.

Marx's objections to the evils of "social classes," then, were directed not against differentiation *per se*, but against certain of its forms and consequences. Most broadly, it can be said that he was criticizing the *injustice* typically associated with stratification. His criticisms were chiefly of three specific kinds of injustice. First, he argued, or at least implied, that every individual had some minimum "worth" merely by virtue of the fact that he was a human being, and everyone therefore deserved sufficient income to sustain a decent human existence. Second, he argued that insofar as there was differentiation, it should correspond not to the mere power or prestige of individuals or groups but to a more "rational" and objective criterion. The defects of stratification in capitalism, from this point of view, were that "functionless" property owners enjoyed higher status in both material and nonmaterial terms than the unpropertied; state officials, higher status than those not so employed; "mental" workers, higher status than "manual" workers. Not only were income differentials along these lines unwarranted in the long run but also the differences in the type and location of work done themselves conferred unmerited, "irrational" advantages in the form of related differences in style of life. By contrast, the criterion of status during the transition stage of socialism would be that of contribution to production—payment "according to work." When this motivating force was no longer needed, and when society had attained a sufficiently high level of production to afford it, each individual would receive what he needed, and this type of differentiation would mark the advent of full communism.[5] Even though different individuals would thus be receiving different amounts, each would receive no less than what he required and no more—and in such a situation, after all, without deprivation and without privilege, one can hardly speak of "unjust" stratification.

The third respect in which differentiation would coexist with, or even promote, justice was that what each person received would be dependent strictly on his own labor contribution (or, later, on his need) rather than on arbitrary accidents of fate. The ill, the disabled, and the aged, for example, would not suffer on account of those conditions. But most important, what this meant was that the welfare of a child and the status of the adult would be independent of the family into which he happened to have been born. In capitalist societies, Marx knew, the status of one's parents had enormous influence upon the degree to which one's needs as a child were satisfied and upon the opportunities (for example, in education and employment) to which one had access later in life. Indeed, to a very considerable extent one's whole life chances, ranging from physical longevity to the possibility of refined forms of recreation, were determined by the accident of birth. In the good society which Marx envisioned as the ultimate outcome of the proletarian revolution, this would no longer be true; differentiation would be confined to the individual's own status, and equality of *opportunity* would prevail.[6]

The term *social class* has typically been used—at least in the polemical if not in the scientific literature—to refer to these injustices. We are most likely to say that a society is divided into social classes when there are groups with varied income and with correspondingly varied amounts of power and privilege; when the greatest and least of these especially are not "deserved" by some ethical standard; and when these differences are transmitted more or less intact from one generation to the next through the family.[7] In this sense, Marxist ideology calls for the establishment of a *classless* society, a society with status differentiation but without classes.*

From this perspective, it may be hypothesized that ideological dissonance would be produced in the Soviet social structure when extremely low shares were allocated to some groups, especially if these were manual workers; when differentiation was related to power, prestige, or the character of employment rather than to "merit"; or when birth conferred advantage. Authoritarianism itself would thus be dissonant insofar—and only insofar—as it allowed those in high political office to enjoy higher status than they were perceived as needing or deserving, or to use their high status to obtain benefits irrelevant to their work, or to give their children a more favorable start in life than the children of others had. But it should not be assumed *a priori* that the reduction of dissonance always goes along with a reduction in authoritarianism; certainly social classes do not necessarily disappear under conditions of political freedom. Indeed, Soviet experience suggests that, because of the self-defeating nature of extreme authoritarianism, it may very well be made *more* effective precisely by reducing some of the differentiations that give rise to dissonance—that is, by placing low-status groups in a better position to limit the power of administrators who threaten to become too independent, or even in a position to displace them or their children altogether.[8]

In sum, patterns of stratification in the Soviet Union may be seen as the successive outcomes of the search for ways of developing an industrial society under an authoritarian regime with a minimum of ideological dissonance. The periodic alterations of policy up to 1961 indicate that the search had thus far been unsuccessful.

II. The New Model

The program[9] adopted at the Twenty-second Party Congress in 1961 offered an end to the search by providing the model of a stable solution to the problems of stratification, as one aspect of the "construction of communism" with which the program was chiefly concerned. As a programmatic statement it did not, of course, include all the necessary details. But in the years which

* It is worth repeating here a point made earlier: a demand for an end to class injustice is by no means unique to Marxism, but Marxism is its source for Soviet society.

followed its adoption (and to some extent prior to that), Soviet political leaders, ideologists, philosophers, and social scientists were engaged in elaborating upon it and even testing the precise institutional forms of full communism, and they proceeded far enough to enable us to perceive the major structural features of the system. Admittedly, since Khrushchev's dismissal there has been some doubt that the model is actually going to be brought to life, but I believe that is for reasons extrinsic to the problems which have been discussed above. I shall return to this question below. In any event, there is no doubt that the model was taken with great seriousness at least until October 1964, and an examination of it will show us what Soviet society would have to do in order to create a stable system of classless differentiation under conditions of authoritarianism and industrialism, and it will cast light upon some of the broader prospects of Soviet development.

The Soviet conception of full communism rests upon two premises that have only occasionally been made explicit in the discussions of that subject, though they are vital to an understanding of it. The first premise is that the only ideas that are historically important are those expressing objective facts—"objective" in that they are outside men's minds and cannot be created or changed merely by human thought. The second is that, at any given moment, the Communist Party—or, more precisely, the party leadership—correctly articulates these facts and their implications. Most students of Soviet society would agree that these premises have indeed been evident in Soviet history. I am convinced that they also underlie Marx's theory and that this shared foundation is what permits the Soviet Union to construct communism in the Marxist image.* But it is their consequences rather than their origins which are of present concern. Given these premises, then, what would stratification look like in full communism?

The Division of Labor

One of the characteristics of communism, according to the discussion in the recent Soviet literature, would be the disappearance of significant differences in types of work and in the styles of

---

* We have encountered one echo of this commonality in the preceding analysis: Marx's insistence that status be based upon some "objective" criterion. His belief that this was not the case in capitalism was one reason for his confidence that capitalism could not long survive.

life associated with them—in particular, the elimination of differences between industrial and agricultural work and between mental and manual labor. Part of what is meant, apparently, is the process that has been observed in all industrial societies: the mechanization of agriculture, the automation of industry, a rising level of education in the labor force generally, and the urbanization of life. In addition, however, there are frequent references to "ending the rigid division of labor" itself. This does not imply that everyone would do whatever work he pleases whenever he felt like doing it. "The operation of machinery requires that each person perform his job and meet his social obligations at definite times and in definite ways"; hence, "communist society . . . will be a highly organized and closely coordinated community of men of labor."[10] Nor does it mean that each worker would be capable of handling any job whatsoever. It is recognized that, under the conditions of modern technology, no one individual can "know everything in all spheres of work, or be a master, expert, or virtuoso in all fields. In the distant future, too, we shall have specialization . . ."[11]

But the member of the labor force in communism is described as a *broad-profile worker*. Each worker would learn two or three related skills, so that it would be "possible to move workers systematically from one job to another (within a given trade or branch of production)," and they "will be able to replace each other more easily and quickly."[12] Every worker would be "prepared to change his occupation if the interests of society and his own inclinations require it . . ."[13] Thus, if there is a lag on one production line, extra workers could readily be pulled off of another job to make up for lost time. Or if an occupation is rendered obsolete by technological change, the worker easily shifts to another one he already knows and replaces the obsolescent skill by taking an evening or correspondence course to prepare himself for other such eventualities.

A related attribute of the broad-profile worker is that he would perform, without pay, one or two jobs in addition to his "main" one. The case is offered, for instance, of a music professor who works in a machine-design bureau when his lessons are over and then goes to the factory to help make the machines.[14] Members of the "communist labor brigades," which were supposed to exemplify the new forms of work, kept their own work records, repaired their own machines, performed supervisory functions, served as their own charwomen, and led the way in participating in volunteer "civic activities"[15] (of which more below). Indeed, the many studies of the use of leisure time which have been appearing intimate that Communist man would be expected to devote all his waking hours to "socially useful" activities.

Operationally, then, the "end of the rigid division of labor" seems to mean a more flexible and lower-cost labor force, in which workers will move easily from one job to another during the day and over longer periods of time. We can hardly fail to notice how accommodating this would be to the dynamics of an industrial society. But it is not hard to see how it could be interpreted as an aspect of the classless society as well. If occupation is a major basis of status, as it is in industrial societies, an adult who works at two or more different occupations may not clearly belong to any one class, especially if his main occupation is in manual work and his other is not (or vice-versa). Furthermore, an occupationally derived style of life is often expressed in a characteristic use of leisure time; and if everyone engages in similar "socially useful" (which is to say, "rational") activities during his leisure time, invidious differences in styles of life disappear. Homogenization of styles of life could be expected to lead to homogenization of attitudes as well, with consequences for the rearing of the next generation. This does seem to be the import of such phrases as "equalizing the cultural level of workers and intelligentsia" and "bringing the consciousness of the collective farmer up to that of the worker."[16]

Income Differentials

It is in the context of differences in style of life and in "consciousness" that references to reductions in income inequalities are apt to occur in the discussion of communism. To the extent that these differences are a function of differential access to material goods, they would tend to disappear as incomes are more nearly equalized, and the latter trend has been evident now for about a decade, especially in the form of raising the lowest incomes. This does not imply the sort of leveling that took place during War Communism or at the initiation of the First Five Year Plan; there is no sign of anything as radical as that, and there is abundant evidence that income differentiation is supposed to remain under communism. But it will be recalled that our hypothesis does not require the elimination of differentiation entirely, only of unjust differentiation.

An industrial society probably requires income differentials for the sake of motivating a population of varying abilities to undergo training of varying lengths and complexity that leads to specialized occupations at different skill levels. At least, Stalin's 1931 speech is usually taken (and rightly so) as an acknowledgment that this was the case for Soviet society, and his views on the matter are still being reiterated. Nevertheless, "payment according to work" is bound to be tainted with the suspicion that it is unjust. For one thing, insofar as it is associated with differences in "natural" abilities (for example, the genetic components of "intelligence"), it is the result of an accident of birth. For another, the actual worth of a particular contribution to production is, at best, not self-evident. Thus, it is easy—especially for those whose income is low—to believe that magnitudes of compensation owe less to differences in merit than to differences in power, whether this be power in the market or in the councils of the state or party. Finally, there is the "humanistic" contention that all forms of productive labor or "socially useful activities" are equally valuable; therefore, the only just criterion of compensation is that it fully satisfy the needs of every conscientious producer. Hence, the slogan: "From each according to his abilities, to each according to his needs." But how is this to be reconciled with the motivational function of income differentials?

The importance of cash incentives should not be exaggerated. Even in industrial societies, including those of the West, a great deal of very important work gets done in the absence of a graduated incentive system. The most obvious instance is child-rearing, which parents do because they have learned they "ought" to and without being paid for it in any direct way—certainly not in accordance with the number of children they have or the difficulties presented by particular cases. In this connection, the Party Program and the subsequent discussions have stressed that, in communism, work becomes "a public calling, a moral obligation"[17]—that is, a matter of conscience, like bringing up one's children. Even more than that, work would be "a habit," "as much of a daily necessity . . . as sleep, food, rest, entertainment, etc."[18] It becomes, in short, what one *wants* to do, much as some women want to have children; and when we are doing what we enjoy, we are not so concerned about how much we are being paid for it.

Nevertheless, there probably are limits to what can be accomplished without direct incentives. It may be pointed out, for example, that some adults are not very conscientious about raising their children, and others choose not to have children at all. There has been no intimation that similar phenomena will be permitted in the work sphere. On the contrary, it has been reiterated that, under communism as under socialism, "He who does not work, neither shall he eat"; and, of course, each is supposed to work to the full measure of his ability. Consequently, the problem remains of reconciling work incentives with payment according to needs.

The solution of this problem is that, in the Soviet lexicon, *"need" is not a psychological concept*. However peculiar that may seem to us, it is quite consistent with Soviet premises. What a person needs is not what he wants or what he thinks he needs—those are subjective matters, and so historically unimportant—but rather what is objectively necessary for him to have. As Khrushchev told the Twenty-first Party Congress:

> it must be realized that the needs of people for the means of existence are not unlimited. A person cannot consume, for example, more bread and other products than are necessary for his organism. There are also definite limits to the consumption of clothing and housing. Of course, when we speak of satisfying people's needs, we have in mind not whims or claims to luxuries, but the healthy needs of a culturally developed person.[19]

When to this is added the other basic premise, that the party correctly articulates objective facts, the significance of "payment according to needs" becomes clear. The party would decide what "the healthy needs of a culturally developed person" consist of, and then provide him with enough to satisfy them. When he has received this amount, his needs would be satisfied, by definition, and he could have no legitimate cause for complaint.[20] But as we have seen, differences in needs are not dissonant with ideology; and since the party has accepted the imperative of incentives under industrialism, it would presumably "discover" that the "objective needs" of, say, an engineer are greater than those of a drill-press operator and that those of a highly productive drill-press operator are greater than those of a less productive one.[21] It follows, incidentally, that communism does not require that goods be available in physically unlimited amounts; the "abundance" of communism does not mean that everyone will have as much as he likes, but that everyone's objectively determined needs will be fully satisfied.[22]

Institutions of Socialization

The re-introduction of incentives through the back door, however, once again raises the possibility of the intergenerational transmission of differential advantage. Perhaps the possibility would be reduced if all members of the labor force had "broad-profile" work careers and were engaged in civic activities. But to prevent it altogether, children would have to be raised in such a way that they would be unaffected by their parents' status, which is to say that they must be raised outside the home. Under communism, the family, in the old phrase, should "wither away."

Moreover, what we have seen about the division of labor and income differentials implies that, under communism, each person must learn not only that work is play but also—so that suspicions of injustice may be avoided—that the needs the party has defined as correct for him are indeed the needs he feels. This convergence of duty and desire is, as E. I. Afanasenko, the R.S.F.S.R. Minister of Education, has put it, "undoubtedly the result of stubborn and persistent psychological preparation . . ."[23] Close supervision over the child-rearing process seems called for. But this is difficult when children are brought up in conventional family units, for there is such a large number of families and they carry out their functions more or less privately. Hence, from this starting-point, too, the conclusion emerges that there would be at least a drastic decline in the part played by the conventional family in child-rearing.

Surprisingly, this conclusion is explicitly rejected by most (though not all) of the participants in the discussion of communism. Instead, they assert that "the family will grow stronger under communism."[24] Such statements may be attributable partly to the continued sentimental attachment for the family, and partly to anxiety that Communist child-rearing might be introduced "prematurely," repeating the disaster of the 1920s. We shall see shortly that a kind of "shell" of the present-day family was probably expected to remain under communism, and perhaps this is what is being referred to. In any case, the concrete descriptions of communism and the measures which were said to be bringing it closer made it quite clear that the functions of the family were to be narrowly circumscribed.

One way in which this would be accomplished is through the extension of the *social funds*. Many goods and services which consumers now have to pay for would be furnished through public institutions without direct charge or at low cost. The Soviet discussions cite free education and medical care, old-age and disability pensions, and maternity leaves as already existing signs of the transition to communism. Of course, many of these services are available in other societies as well, and in the same way, under the name of the "welfare state." But the social funds would apparently go well beyond that. For example, the Party Program anticipated that, by 1980, midday meals would be provided "free" to workers and farmers at their place of work; prices for other meals would "decline steadily," to the point where public dining "will gradually take precedence over the home preparation of meals."[25] The aim seems to be, in Peter Wiles' term, "to socialize consumption."[26] That is, decisions about what to eat, for instance, would be taken out of the hands of individuals and entrusted to public authorities. Literally as well as figuratively, the family kitchen would be replaced by the public dining room. A major arena of child-training would thus be lost to the family, while the hand of the political authorities who manage the dining rooms would be greatly strengthened. It may also be noted that socialized consumption would make it much easier to supervise the satisfaction of needs, avoiding both deficiencies and excesses.

Similarly, there have been suggestions for "appliance pools," to permit the "collective utilization" of refrigerators, washing machines, vacuum cleaners, and other household equipment, and there is no reason why these pools could not also furnish the personnel to use the equipment.[27]

> Gradually, as the rapidly expanding network of household service enterprises is converted into one of the largest and most widely developed branches of production, family housekeeping will be reduced to a minimum . . .
> The separate household will be replaced by a large public industry.[28]

It has commonly been pointed out that these measures would make it possible to provide household services much more cheaply than under present arrangements and to allow women to take more "interesting" and "productive" employment, the latter having the further by-product of "improving the cultural and technical level of women and . . . eliminating the residual inequalities between men and women."[29] With both parents working—and Soviet society has already gone much further in the employment of women than other industrial societies have—there would be no one left in the home to socialize the children. Even grandparents might be absent, for there have been many laudatory stories of pensioners taking "voluntary" jobs, such as staffing the public dining rooms.[30]

What would replace the family in child-rearing is, of course, the school, a far more accessible, more "public"—and hence more controllable—institution. "The sooner we provide nurseries, kindergartens, and boarding schools for all children, the sooner and the more successfully will the task of the Communist upbringing of the growing generation be accomplished," declared the Twenty-first Congress.[31] Despite the subsequent modification toward voluntarism in the party program—"The development of the network of preschool institutions and boarding schools . . . will fully meet the requirements of all working people who *wish* to give their children of preschool and school age a public upbringing"[32]—it is clear that children would be expected to begin attending school earlier and to spend more of their time in it during their years of attendance.

Thus, if we may speak of the "socialization of consumption" under communism, so also we may speak of the "socialization of socialization." "An important peculiarity of the boarding school," the director of a research institute at the R.S.F.S.R. Academy of Pedagogical Sciences has written, "is that it is simultaneously an institution and a kind of family. The children study, work, play, and rest here. It is truly a school of organized communist life."[33] The thoroughness of this organization is startling. Preparation for work is emphasized, of course, but polytechnical education is a pale shadow of what that means. "We set it as our goal," writes a school principal, "that work should become a passion, an enthusiasm on the part of each child, that it should give him a profound moral and esthetic satisfaction, and that the child should seek to engage in the work he loves in his free time, forgetting about time."[34] The consistency of such training with the adult work roles described above is obvious. And if work is to be more than just a single job in adult life, the child must be prepared for that, too. Scores of "extra-curricular" activities are organized and the pupils are kept continually busy, to the point where a school inspector feels he has to remind school heads that they "must . . . take all measures to organize a daytime nap for the children, as is required by the decision of the Central Committee of the CPSU and the Council of Ministers of the U.S.S.R."[35]

On the basis of Soviet premises, there is no more reason to allow

every adult to raise children as he wishes than there is to allow
him to consume anything he wants to. There is an objectively correct outcome of child-rearing and an objectively correct way of
achieving it; the party knows what they are; and it is the party's
obligation to history to see to it that every child is raised accordingly. Logically, this might imply that the party should also provide the physical facilities, but it would be more practical to
"permit" parents to continue to provide sleeping space for their
children—and in fact the number of places in boarding schools
has not risen as rapidly as the number in "prolonged-day" schools,
where children spend only their waking hours.[36] It is in this very
limited sense that the household would continue to survive. But
the basic principle, as Afanasenko has put it, is: "Family upbringing is not a private affair."[37] Perhaps there are still some members
of Soviet society who do not appreciate this, but that is because
full communism has not yet arrived. "Some people still live according to the antiquated precept, 'My home is my castle,'" said
Il'yichev in 1963. "It is not because of this that such survivals of
the past as religious prejudices, drunkenness, hooliganism, money-
grubbing, and incorrect attitudes toward women and children feel
especially at home in everyday life?"[38]

Political Controls

Yet early socialization might not be invariably successful, even
in public institutions; and in any event, socialization in a modern
society extends well beyond childhood and adolescence. The planners of communism took cognizance of these facts and outlined
suitable mechanisms of control in adult life which would be, at
the same time, the institutions for preparing the present generation of adults for life in Communist society. Most often cited in
this connection are the so-called public organizations: the volunteer militia, the anti-parasite tribunals, and the comrades' courts.
The personnel of these organizations consist chiefly of unpaid,
nonspecialized, "lay" citizens, usually members of the same "collective" (a work group, a Komsomol unit, the residents of an
apartment building), who serve on them after "working" hours—a
major form of the participation in civic activities.

The acts under the control of these organizations are rather
vaguely defined. They include not only routine offenses such as
property damage, drunkenness, currency speculation, and black-
market dealings, but also such "non-crimes" as "poor quality
work," coming late to work or otherwise failing to display a "con-

scientious attitude" toward one's job, violating the rules of apartment life, failing to bring up one's children "properly," and "other antisocial acts not entailing criminal liability."[39] The punishments they could impose are on the whole rather minor (the most severe ones, such as resettlement, required the approval of the local soviet or people's court); it has been reported that about 80 per cent of the anti-parasite cases resulted in only a warning or reprimand to the offender.[40]

Perhaps most important in the present context, the public organizations were apparently intended to be agencies of prevention at least as much as of punishment.

> Comrades' courts [reads the statute which authorized them in the R.S.F.S.R.] are . . . charged with actively contributing to the inculcation in citizens of a spirit of a communist attitude toward labor and socialist property and the observance of the rules of socialist society. . . . The chief duty of the comrades' courts is to prevent violations of law . . . to educate people by persuasion and public influence, and to create an intolerant attitude toward any antisocial acts.[41]

Similarly, of the volunteer militia it was said: "The most important aspect of their activity is prevention of violations of public order. Therefore, explanatory work and character-building are central to the attention of all the personnel. They regularly conduct lectures and group discussions at the places they patrol . . ."[42] But "creating attitudes" and "building character" are precisely what the socialization process is supposed to accomplish. What we have here, then, is the counterpart, at the adult level, of the replacement of the family by the school.

How far the work group is expected to go toward becoming a "family" is indicated in the reports about those "scouts of the future," the Communist labor brigades. We find these brigades collectively celebrating their members' birthdays, visiting sick members, going on outings together, attending classes, museums, and libraries together, helping one another to become "regular newspaper readers" or to give up smoking, drinking, and "foul language."[43] One brigade "voted unanimously" to spend the entire amount of a recently received bonus on furnishing a newly married member's apartment.[44] In another,

> the features of new wedding customs are already to be seen. The members of the work brigade . . . participate in making the wedding dress, preparing the food, buying the rings. The fellow-workers choose a best man and matron of honor in the old tradition. . . .

When a child is born the mother's entire communist work brigade are named honorary parents. . . . On the day when the child's birth is officially recorded . . . a solemn ceremony is held at the factory involving . . . a pledge by the collective to assist in raising the child . . .[45]

It was this brigade, too, that set up "special committees on home problems," whose members "are always up to date on the personal problems of the working women and give them the necessary assistance at the appropriate time."[46] It is perhaps surprising that no warnings have appeared in the press that the brigades are not to interfere in their members' choice of spouses.

None of the planners of communism has suggested that the existence of the public organizations entails any real dilution of authoritarianism. As Khrushchev put it:

The transfer of many important government functions to public organizations and the gradual evolution of persuasion and education into the basic method of regulating the life of Soviet society do not and cannot imply a relaxation of control over strict observance of the norms of Soviet law, labor discipline, and everyday living.[47]

These "norms" of law, labor, and life would continue to emanate from the highest authorities. Since the "highest authorities" have generally been identified, in Soviet history, with the party, and since party membership has generally been regarded as a privileged status in the stratification system,* it is important to learn what role the party would play in Communist society.

The striking generalization that seems to emerge from a consideration of this question is that Communist society would overcome the distinction between party and non-party, exactly like the distinctions between mental and manual labor, and urban and rural employment. That is, the party would lose its character as a separate, specialized organ. There are "many people," Khrushchev said, "who do not hold party cards but whose entire beings are imbued with lofty *partiinost'*," while, on the other hand, "there are some people who do have party cards, but all that remains to them of *partiinost'* is the party card and nothing more. . . . If a person who considers himself a party member clings to an incorrect position after the party has expressed and defined its

---

* The privilege involved in party membership should not be exaggerated; in some ways, it is a burden with little reward. Nevertheless, there is no doubt that membership has been a condition of advancement in many career lines and especially of appointment to high office in the political and economic bureaucracies.

attitude on a given question, if he insists on his own way, to all intents and purposes he ceases to be a member of the party."[48]

In other words, formal membership in the party is meaningless; what counts is whether one accepts party policy. Further, he said, "In our times non-party people, too, are actively building communism arm in arm with Communists, and the overwhelming majority of them reason like Communists."[49] Even more flatly, he declared: "Strictly speaking, there is no *bespartiinost'* in [our] society"[50]—no one who lacks party spirit. It seems reasonable to interpret these statements as a mixture of belief and aspiration —something like "all men are created equal"—but the purpose seems quite clear.

One interesting portent of the trend was that party bodies, like other organizations, were having part of their work done by unpaid civic activists who were not themselves members of the party.[51] On a grander scale there was the proud boast that 73 million people had participated in the discussion of the draft of the 1961 Party Program,[52] though total party membership at the time was less than 10 million. This mass discussion produced no substantial alteration in the program, but that is precisely what reveals the essential nature of the change to take place. It is emphatically not the case that the policies announced by the party leader would no longer enjoy a special authority. Rather, the obligation of conforming to the demands of the party leader, of behaving like a party member, would fall equally on all citizens, party and non-party alike.[53] When the party leader has spoken, all would be expected to obey. If the party did not altogether wither away, it would become simply another administrative arm of the leader. This is evident in Khrushchev's vivid exclamation: "Comrades! We have 10,000,000 Party members, 20,000,000 Young Communists, 66,000,000 trade union members. If we were to put all these forces into action, to utilize them for purposes of control, even a mosquito's flight would not escape notice."[54]

III. The Model in Action

The model of communism that has been described appears to meet most of the conditions set for it. The operation of the social funds, together with continued economic growth and the already evident willingness to raise the incomes of the lowest-status groups, would eliminate a major source of ideological dissonance as all members of society were brought up to a minimally decent standard of living. The differentiated incentives necessary to an industrial society would remain, but they would not create ideological dissonance because they would be defined as payment according to needs and because, in the absence of familial socialization, they would not lead to the intergenerational transmission of advantage. Authoritarian control would continue to be exercised, if anything even more stringently than it is now; moreover, in a system which hardly distinguishes between the economy and the polity, it would not be difficult to extend the definition of "needs" so as to allow higher payments to those holding important political offices.

Nor is it far-fetched to believe that the model could work passably well. Perhaps this point can best be demonstrated by some hypothetical examples of how the individual might actually function within it. The formula for individual decisions would presumably be adapted from the slogan which has long been used to describe Soviet nationality policy: "national in form, socialist in content." With socialism superseded by communism, and with the disappearance of national distinctions (for the same reasons that class distinctions would be overcome, and in similar ways), this formula would no longer be applicable. Though it has not been stated in so many words, it is not unreasonable to anticipate that it would be replaced by the slogan, "individual in form, Communist in content." That is, each person would be required to behave like a Communist but to exhibit his devotion to communism in his own way.

Now consider average Communist Ivan at breakfast in the public dining room. Khrushchev predicted that, by 1980, when the "material basis" of communism was to have been created, the production of eggs would be 365 per capita annually,[55] or one egg per person per day. We might assume that a certain number of eggs—say, one per person per week—would be set aside to be consumed in cakes, puddings, etc. Consequently, Ivan's norm of correct consumption—that is, his objective need—would be set at six whole eggs a week, and his collective, seated with him at their table in the public dining room, would see to it that he ate that number, for his own good. He himself, however, would decide how his consumption of eggs would be distributed over the week and whether he would have them boiled, scrambled, or sunnyside up. *Ergo,* "individual in form, Communist in content." One can envision the issuance of "consumption books," kept in the possession of the collective, in which would be noted down all such free choices as well as the individual's diligence in following the dietary pattern which is correct for him.[56]

Two objections may be raised to the feasibility of this model. First, no such model could work perfectly; no degree of planning or control could avoid occasional deviance. What is to be done, then, with the person who refuses to eat his six eggs, or who tries to eat more, or whose behavior in some other way is not "Communist in content"? It is a measure of the realism of the post-Stalinist leadership that such possibilities were frankly admitted and that the inadequacy of handling them through coercion was fully recognized.

But the solution to this problem is latent in the premises that were mentioned earlier. The policies announced by the leader are regarded not as choices among arguable alternatives but as historical necessities incontrovertibly derived from objective facts. And what is to be said of the person who repeatedly denies the truth of objective facts—who insists, for example, that he is too ill to work when a physical examination reveals that there is nothing wrong with him, or who has a craving for eggs beyond what is healthy for him? Khrushchev asked the question and answered it:

> Can there be, under communism, breaches of public order and deviations from the will of the collective? There can be. But evidently they will be individual cases. It cannot be supposed that cases of psychological disorders will be precluded and that the rules of community life will be safe from being violated by persons who are mentally deranged . . . but there will obviously be some means of curing the outbursts of lunatics. Even today there is the straitjacket, which they put on lunatics and thereby restrain their wildness and stop them from doing harm to themselves and to those around them.[57]*

Thus, the deviant in Communist society—at least, the serious and persistent one, who refuses to heed the warnings and reprimands of his collective—would be sent to a mental hospital to be cured of his unfortunate illness. Several allusions did appear in the press to writers who were being treated in this way after having stubbornly rejected party guidance, and to "mentally defective" persons who were victims of religious propaganda.[58]

This brings out the second ground for doubt about the feasibility of the model: It appears to call for a degree of "thought con-

---

* "The will of the collective" has always been, in Soviet society, a euphemism for the command of the leader. Calling it the will of the collective confers upon it the appearance of democracy, deflects hostility away from the leader, and gives him a convenient means of changing policy and controlling its implementation, by saying, when necessary, that the "collective" has made a wrong decision.

trol" that is simply unrealizable. Deviance from authoritarian commands would not be regarded by the population as "mental derangement" unless virtually everyone accepted the commands as correct and proper and unless disagreement were so rare ("individual cases") that it would indeed be looked upon as "queer." Moving closer to issues of stratification, such near-unanimous acceptance would also seem to be necessary to prevent differentiated payments from being perceived as injustice—that is, each person would have to believe that his own payments and everyone else's actually did correspond to their respective needs. How likely is it that this "homogenization of attitudes" could be brought about?

One answer is that it need not be. The viability of a social system, at least in the short run, requires not that people *think* the right way but that they *behave* the right way—and there is a good deal of evidence, including some from Soviet experience, that a given mode of behavior is compatible with quite a wide range of attitudes.[59] It would not be necessary for all Soviet citizens, or even most, to feel the way the Party Program says they should feel, or to believe "deep down" that the leader is infallible. All that is necessary is that they should act *as if* they felt that way and *as if* they believed it.

Consider, as another hypothetical illustration, the situation of parents who are deciding whether to send a new-born infant to a public preschool institution. We have seen that the Party Program said that only those parents "who *wish* to give their children of preschool . . . age a public upbringing" need do so. Yet it is clearly intended that, when full communism is reached, all parents *would* do so, voluntarily; and this would be, moreover, necessary to prevent the injustices of social class. Now, to begin with, our parents, knowing that they are *supposed* to want to send the infant off to a nursery, might well reason that refusal to do so would raise suspicions about their motives. Under such circumstances, they would be apt to feel that sending him is *dobrovol'no-obyazatel'no* ("voluntarily obligatory"), as Soviet citizens have said about voting in an election or subscribing to the state loan. But more than that: with the child taken care of outside the home, it would be easier for the wife to work, and the parents would save the expense of child care.* Finally, if their chief concern was for

---

* Note that, directly or indirectly, they will have to pay for the support of the public institutions in any case, whether they send their own child or not.

their child's welfare rather than their own, they could hardly fail to appreciate the advantages, material and otherwise, that would accrue to a Soviet child raised in a public institution rather than privately. I do not find it difficult to believe that they would decide to send the infant away. They might even feel a sense of gratitude to the regime, for having met their needs.

If subsequently, at a meeting of their collective, they were held up as shining examples of people with a Communist conscience who are leading the way to the future, they would not be likely to deny it. Indeed, the theory of cognitive dissonance would lead us to suspect that they might even come to believe it themselves,[60] and it is easy to imagine them loudly insisting that others should do as they have done. The fact that they have done it makes it easier for other parents to do the same, and, as more and more parents go along, it becomes harder and harder for the rest not to. (Applications for places in nurseries have long exceeded the number of places available, and the same has been true of the boarding and prolonged-day schools since they were established.[61]) Eventually, keeping an infant at home would seem as "odd" as sending him away seems now. During this entire process, it is difficult to say what the "real motives" of the parents are— and in fact, it is quite irrelevant.

As a last illustration, consider the case of participation in the public organizations. This, too, should occur voluntarily, out of the urging of conscience. In some cases, given the nature of the socialization experience, no doubt it would. But there are also other motives which would lead citizens to serve on, say, a comrades' court and to render the decisions wanted by the leader. For some, it would be a way of demonstrating their own loyalty and reaping the rewards that follow; others might see in the comrades' courts an opportunity for the development of genuine autonomy, an opportunity they would not want to jeopardize by making "incorrect" decisions. Perhaps most important, many of the cases coming to the attention of the court would involve behavior that the individuals serving on it would have liked to engage in themselves: getting drunk, or selling goods on the black market—or eating a couple of extra eggs, or raising their children themselves, or refusing to serve on the comrades' court! The chance to punish others for doing what one would have liked to do oneself provides both satisfaction to the individual and stability to the social system.[62]

Each member of the comrades' court, however, would be aware of these less "creditable" motives only in himself, if that. So far as each of them knows—and, still more, so far as the fellow hailed before them knows—everyone else has sincerely accepted the leader's policies and is abiding by them. This apparent unanimity among one's peers is surely a more reliable means of social control than threats of coercion from above. The Party Program was on sound ground when it said, "Comradely censure of antisocial acts will gradually become the principal means of eradicating manifestations of bourgeois views, customs, and habits."[63]

But apparent unanimity in a group is also a powerful device for changing the attitudes of dissenters.[64] Indeed, continuous interaction over a long period of time with the same collective—at work, on vacation, in the public dining room, and in the public organizations—is likely to produce a considerable similarity of attitudes, and dissent is not apt to appear.[65] (Even in free societies, family members and friends tend to have the same political preferences.[66]) Thus, the institutions of communism could well bring about that very homogeneity of attitudes which it would require in the long run. When that happens, objectively defined needs would be felt as subjectively correct. Furthermore, there would be no necessity for shielding managerial and administrative personnel any longer from the protests of those under their authority; such protests would be infrequent, and, as with the comrades' courts, the criticisms could be counted upon to be of the acceptable kind. Consequently, there would be no further need for great economic and social distances in the hierarchy of stratification (and additional resources would thereby be freed for raising the level of the lowest groups). The solution to the dilemma of authoritarianism would have been found, its self-limiting nature overcome, and the construction of communism—an authoritarian industrial society displaying no dissonance with Marxist ideology—would be complete.

*   *   *

Consistent and convincing as this picture may be, it must be admitted that relatively little has been said about the construction of communism since Khrushchev's dismissal.[67] There is no evidence that his policies on this score had anything to do with his dismissal, and we should not foreclose the possibility that they will be revived once the new regime gets its bearings. Nevertheless, for the time being, at least, there does seem to be some hesitation about implementing them, and it is appropriate to inquire why this might be so, although there have been no explicit indications to guide us.

Some of the conceivable reasons are ephemeral. For example, neither the general nor the technical educational level of workers and peasants is yet, on the whole, sufficient to permit them to acquire easily a wide range of occupational skills, much less to eliminate the differences between them and the intelligentsia; but this deficiency (due in part to the disruptions of the war) is being overcome.[68] There has also been a problem in providing personnel and facilities in sufficient quantities to allow for the public socialization of all children from birth. Boarding schools, in particular, proved to be very expensive, but they could be dropped in favor of the prolonged-day school, as has already been happening; this would also obviate the necessity of liquidating the family entirely.* Nurseries and kindergartens are something else again; there have never been enough places in them for more than a small proportion of children, and the current leaders might well be reluctant to devote substantial amounts of resources to building them right now. Continued economic expansion, however, might eventually make them possible. Similarly, the production of consumer goods is not now high enough for even the most ingenious propaganda campaign to persuade the people that their needs are being met; this, again, is surely only a matter of time, but the present leaders might believe that since the time is so far off, it is unwise to raise hopes at this point. In addition, a serious qualification must be introduced here. So long as standards of living elsewhere continue to be higher than in the Soviet Union, and so long as the population is aware of the gap, it might continue to be quite difficult for Soviet citizens to believe that they do not need more than they are getting. The implication is that, until the gap can be closed, the construction of communism would require the reconstruction of the iron curtain—and this, too, Soviet leaders might be reluctant to attempt.

Possibly longer-run problems would be presented by planned consumption, which under communism would have an importance equal to that of planned production. If nothing else, it would require an enormous bureaucracy to carry out so massive a pro-

* Western social scientists have expressed doubts that societies could function with personalities molded in public institutions rather than in families. However, this question has not been raised in the Soviet literature; and since the doubts are based upon one variety or another of depth psychology, a discipline which has long been excluded from Soviet social science, I would not expect it to be among the objections to public socialization. Furthermore, it is far from clear that the doubts are valid ones for Soviet society and especially for Communist society as it has been described here.

gram. There are some countervailing considerations: computers could perform many of the operations;* and for the rest, a large bureaucracy might be just what is needed to provide "socially useful" activities in an increasingly automated economy. Still, it can hardly be expected that Soviet leaders would wax enthusiastic about the prospect of creating an even larger bureaucracy than the one that they have found in the past to be so intractable and so diluting of their authority.

Other "middle range" difficulties arise out of the functioning of the public organizations. The civic activist, it has turned out, does not always have the skills or the technical knowledge requisite for efficient and effective performance. Apparently it is still true that the state cannot be run by cooks and housewives. Increased education and a degree of specialization in civic activities (along with the disappearance of the category of "housewives") might eventually take care of that; but, again, the time is probably not yet at hand. Meanwhile the civic activists have shown some tendency to turn their participation to their own ends, and though this often takes the form of overzealousness, as we might expect from what has been said above, the regime is nevertheless distressed by it.[69]

But what seems to be the most serious obstacle to communism, and the one most likely to be permanent, is the enormous burden it places upon the leadership—or, more exactly, upon the leader. The job of being the infallible dictator of a large modern society is a terrifying one, and communism would demand that the person in that position make still more decisions, with still greater consequences. It is not unreasonable to expect that the present Soviet leaders are weary of this burden and less confident of their ability to carry it than their predecessors were. If they wish to lighten it—and the signs are that they do—the price they will have to pay is the return of pluralism, and Soviet society will then become, for better or worse, just one more industrial society.

---

* The reader might give thought to how far it is already possible to check up on planned consumption—and much else—with a combination of computers, credit cards, and social-security numbers. See *The New York Times*, May 21, 1967, Section 3, pp. 1, 14.

14.

The Family and Social Problems

MARK G. FIELD
and DAVID E. ANDERSON

I. FAMILY AND SOCIALIZATION: SOME
GENERAL CONSIDERATIONS

A society may be said to be in a ceaseless state of metabolism as new members are born, grow old and die, and are replaced by others. Yet physical replacement alone is insufficient to insure the survival of the social structure or the persistence of cultural patterns. The metamorphosis of the infant into a socially adequate adult is a long, costly, and problematic process that cannot ever be taken for granted, and the fabric of a society is affected by the quality as well as the quantity of its replacements. Socialization shapes the adult personality, the individual's sense of identity, his ability to communicate and to conceptualize. And, particularly in a changing, industrializing society, socialization increasingly is a process that extends through much of adult life.

Two aspects of socialization may be distinguished: "upbringing" is the transmission to infants and children of basic personality traits, values, habits, and oral language skills. The process of "education" or "apprenticeship," on the other hand, refers to the transmission of subject-knowledge: basic tools such as writing and reading, as well as more specialized skills. The balance typically shifts from a preponderance of "upbringing" in the early years to one of "education" and training in the later years.[1] The prolonged helplessness and the plasticity of the child at birth and for many years afterwards makes both types of socialization necessary and possible.

In most agricultural or nonindustrial societies, the family and the kinship group of which it is a part perform a wide range of functions beyond providing for the early care and socialization of children: in these societies the kinship group actually *is* society for the individual. It is an economic unit, an educational agency, often a military and political organization, and sometimes a "church" all at once. Socialization, in such societies, typically is relatively smooth, reflecting the simple tasks adults must perform, and the child can fairly early be integrated into meaningful tasks. Moreover, the child is surrounded by a range of visible role models with which he can identify and from which he can learn. Finally, by comparison with the process in modern societies, the length of the dependency period is relatively short.

One of the major structural consequences of industrialization has been to transfer a range of activities from the family to more specialized extrafamilial settings. This "loss of functions" means that the individual must operate in situations and locations not controlled by the family, and away from the home. The school, the university, the mill, the factory, the plant, the office are formal groupings of unrelated individuals brought together to perform specific tasks. In them the child and the adolescent (and later on, the adult) are subjected to a variety of values, influences, demands, communications, and competitive situations that may be at variance with the home situation and with one another. Socialization becomes more complex and involves more conflict and may lead to a variety of social and psychological problems and dilemmas. It is a potential source of societal change that rivals in importance the more dramatic and visible developments at the political level.

II. Soviet Family Policy in the Past: Con and Pro

There is no need here to repeat in detail the early history and vicissitudes of Soviet family policy, but a few reminders are in order.

According to the Marxist (and Engelsian) interpretation,[2] the private-property basis of the family under capitalism entails unjust inequality between the sexes (men "own" women as instruments for the production of "legitimate" offspring to whom their private property can be passed) and leads to a double standard—monogamy for women and philandering for men (thereby encouraging prostitution)—and to an unfair stigmatization of women who bear children out of wedlock and of these children themselves.

Early Soviet policy was intended to attack these evils and to transfer the care, education, and maintenance of children from home to society. This would mean the end of the family's socialization functions, and would remove the child from the conservative atmosphere of the patriarchal family to a setting that could be entirely controlled by the regime. True love and a genuinely monogamous family would finally be achieved; a family would consist only of a man and a woman in love, and marriage would automatically be dissolved when love or mutual attraction ceased.

Early Soviet legislation was the most radical of its kind.[3] Marriage consisted of a simple registration at the civil registry (ZAGS), divorces were effected by the simple unilateral declaration of one of the spouses, registered and unregistered marriages engendered equal obligations, differences between legitimate and "natural" children were eliminated, and abortions on nonmedical indications were legalized. Most of these measures, however, were predicated on the idea expressed by Engels that care of children would be assumed by the society. The first stage of this care was to be the maternity house and maternity provisions. The second was to be the crèche in which, according to the Webbs, "from two months old, the infant may be cared for whilst the mother is at work."

> This was one of the ideas on which Lenin most strongly insisted. He described the crèche, in setting free the mother from the burden of a constant care of the young children, and thus enabling her to earn an independent livelihood, as being the "germ cell of the communist society."[4]

Early policy failed, however, to yield extensive results. To begin with, the state could not, because of more pressing tasks and limited personnel and material resources, fulfill the conditions Engels had specified for extrafamilial facilities. Furthermore, the impact of the regime's family policies was largely restricted to the urban areas which, before the five year plans, accounted for less than one-fifth of the population. Yet even the limited results of these policies were sufficiently visible and dramatic to convince the regime that their continuation and extension would directly conflict with the program of forced-draft rapid industrialization. The introduction of the First Five Year Plan strained the economy to the utmost and further reduced resources (including personnel) available to establish extrafamilial institutions. More seriously, anti-family policies were leading to a situation where many children in the first Soviet urban generation simply lacked the kind of socializing experience to fit them intellectually or emotionally to the new society the regime was attempting to build, with its emphasis upon self-discipline and control, perseverance, steadiness, punctuality, and accuracy. While family influence was being undermined, extrafamilial agencies (the school, in particular) had failed to provide a workable substitute, leaving the child prey to the noxious and deviant influences of "the street." As an article in *Izvestiia* pointed out in 1935:

> We must frankly admit that the school has not concerned itself with the education of children satisfactorily . . . out of this there developed hooliganistic escapades which one can observe now and in some cases even criminal acts . . . in every school, in every class one can look for and find disorganizers, "difficult" children . . . at the same time the family, to a greater degree than before, must concern itself with the education of children. . . . The child spends only several hours in school, the rest of the time he is subjected to the influence of the family and the street . . . [5]

Restoration of family responsibility for children (and parallel measures to bolster discipline in the classroom by restoring the authority of teachers) was a main purpose of the changes in family legislation of the mid-1930s. Official recognition was accorded to the importance of early family experience for the child, and signified that the family would henceforth be considered a partner (a junior one, to be sure) in the task of bringing up the new generation. Now it was made costly and inconvenient for parents (particularly fathers) to take a "light-minded attitude" toward their responsibilities, as they were made responsible for the disorderly conduct and the hooliganism of their children.[6] Furthermore, the law of 1936 made abortions illegal except upon strictly limited medical indications, while the freedom of marriage and divorce was seriously constricted. Both parties now had to appear at a ZAGS bureau, graduated fees were introduced for divorce, and the fact of divorce was to be entered into one's passport.[7]

The measures introduced in 1944, toward the end of the war, were even more conservative. From that time on, only marriages duly registered at the ZAGS bureau were to generate rights and obligations for the marriage partners. Divorces were returned to the courts and were made the subject of a complicated adversary procedure without the statutory grounds for divorce even being spelled out. A couple desiring a divorce had first to apply to a lower People's Court, whose function was to attempt reconciliation; if this failed (and it usually did), the case could then be appealed to a higher court, and so on all the way to the highest court. The divorce was granted (if at all) at the court's discretion. Finally, costs and fees for the publication of the divorce proceedings were such as to be prohibitive for most of the population. Children born out of wedlock had to take the mother's name, while the patronymic was left blank on the certificate, restoring the stigmatization Engels had deplored. The mother was denied the right to sue for alimony, support, or recognition of paternity, but was given the option either of receiving some state aid for raising her child, or placing him in a state institution.[8] At the same time, since 1936 and more so after 1944, state aid became available to large families, and parents were granted relief from some taxation, reduction of fees in nurseries, and other assistance. Since Stalin died, only two major changes of a liberalizing nature had taken place (though others have been discussed): abortions were again made legal (on nonmedical indications) toward the end of 1955,[9] presumably to reduce the harm caused by illegally performed operations; and a decree published in December 1965 simplified the divorce procedures as established by the law of 1944. Under the new decree, the cost of divorce is sharply reduced through the elimination of the requirement to advertise the proceedings in the press as well as the fee for the application. More important, the decree gives the lower court authority to grant divorces and to settle questions of custody, alimony, maintenance, and property.[10] It appears, however, that illegitimacy as a status remains, and so does the lack of paternal responsibility for illegitimate children, although now the mother may mitigate the stigma by choosing a patronymic for the child.

III. Family and Soviet Society: Four Types

While in the early years the state-run crèche had been hailed as the germ cell of the future Communist society, from the middle 1930s the family was rehabilitated, reinstated, and officially entrusted with the first-stage responsibility of setting future Soviet citizens on "the road to life." The chronic underdevelopment of extrafamilial socialization agencies required the regime to fall back in large measure on old and tried methods of child rearing. The reinstatement of a strong and authoritarian family pattern in the Soviet Union, however, carries with it (as in every society) the risk that some families will fail to socialize their children in a manner deemed desirable by society and the regime. Indeed, in the 1920s, many families were powerful sources of ideological counterindoctrination and political conservatism. This danger, as Kent Geiger points out, has long since passed, for the family has been substantially "captured" by the regime politically as well as economically. But the subtle and more complex question of "moral education," of character formation, personality traits, and the transmission of values and attitudes, is no less vexing than before. The renewed reliance upon the family poses problems of articulation between family and society that seem to characterize the modern industrial order generally, and assume special forms in the Soviet context. Although quantitative information about them is not readily available, Soviet sources suggest four principal types of families. The amount of official attention given to the "problem" families, particularly in the light of limited newsprint and a controlled press, indicates that they are not isolated phenomena, but representative of the social tensions generated in Soviet society and indicative of an inability on the part of the regime to devise easily applied solutions. We present them, of course, merely as analytical models; no claim is made that such families exist in the "pure type" or that the models are exhaustive. Our purpose is to answer the following critical question: from the society's and regime's viewpoint, how well does the Soviet family perform its assigned tasks of personality formation and character building? What is the quality of its "output?" Makarenko, the Soviet pedagogue, made the point succinctly in 1937 when he said to parents:

> Always remember that a future citizen is in your charge. If you fail, the grief will not be yours alone. The whole country will suffer. If your factory turned out damaged goods you would be ashamed. Isn't it much more shameful for you to give your country a spoiled or bad human being?[11]

The first type, which we name the *ideal* family, represents the Soviet family as regime spokesmen would like it to be and serves as a model for emulation. The other three types—the *bountiful-neglectful*, the *over-protective* and the *under-supportive*—represent major deviations from the ideal norm in that each produces its own kind of "damaged" or "defective goods"; that is, personalities that do not have the desirable traits and qualities. Each deviant type, furthermore, seems to be approximately associated with a given socio-economic level, while the ideal type is presumably to be found at all levels. There is, undoubtedly, a fifth category, the "garden-variety" type of family—neither deviant nor particularly exemplary—which manages to muddle through and to function more or less adequately. (This family is given scant attention in Soviet sources since it is neither target for attack nor model for emulation.) But we believe that more can be learned about the major strains of Soviet society and about possible directions of change from those family types that are clearly identified as problematic.

The Ideal Family

This family conforms to the official contemporary blueprint by turning out "good" Soviet citizens and future Communists. It is defined in the *Large Soviet Encyclopedia* as

> the cell of the Communist upbringing of people. Relationships between members of the family are established on the basis of mutual love, the equality between husband and wife, on the unity of interests of the person and society, on working cooperation and the realization of mutual assistance in life. . . . Care for the family and its strengthening was always one of the most important tasks of the Soviet government.[12]

As depicted in approving descriptions, it is a closely (but not too closely) knit group of people with warm feelings toward one another, living in a spirit of cheerful cooperation and helpfulness, firmly guiding the children in the spirit of "Communist morality." Its code emphasizes Soviet patriotism, proletarian international-ism, Communist attitudes toward work and communal property, socialist humanism, optimism, self-discipline, collectivism, cama-raderie, honesty, and the ability to criticize oneself and others.[13] Such families are said to prepare the child for collective life by stripping him of any vestige of self-centeredness, laziness, and lack of discipline, and by fostering a positive devotion to his society and his neighbors, a desire and motivation to do his best in all situations, to devote his talents to society, to share, to help, and to obey superior authority. It is also understood that the family, as a Soviet collective, must sacrifice its own self-centered interests to those of larger collectivities and to Soviet society as a whole. The products of this type of early socialization should thus be *unspoiled* and *well-guided*.

The Bountiful-Neglectful Family

Because it is characterized by superior material resources, this family presumably appears mainly among the upper strata of Soviet society. It belongs to the power elite or to the higher ranks of the intelligentsia—to the new Soviet "aristocracy" or, better, "meritocracy." The parents typically did not inherit their position, power, or status; they had to work and struggle, often against considerable odds. But some of them seem unable to resist the temptation to provide their children with the "good life" they themselves never enjoyed. The children are brought up with pocket money, cars, vacations, and unearned leisure, in luxurious surroundings apart from the rest of Soviet society, leading lives often sheltered from the scrutiny of the common herd. Education to them is a matter of a social grace, a *sine qua non* for the good life, rather than the means to acquire a profession or occupation that will be useful later on. At the same time, their successful parents are too busy to provide the necessary "moral" guidance and leave their children the impression that, for them, "anything goes." When these children run afoul of law and authority, parents exercise every kind of pressure permitted by their rank to provide protective immunity. From the official point of view, the products of such an "upbringing" often turn out to be parasites, loafers, idlers who will not pull their own oars in the bark of Soviet society, people who sneer at physical work (or any work at all) and for whom life consists primarily of a round of pleasure, a search for thrills, and escape from boredom—including sexual excesses, drug addiction, and even murder. An article in *Izvestiia* entitled, appropriately, "Hiding Behind Papa"[14] illustrates the concern. It relates the escapades of one Valery Novokreshchenov, born in 1945, the son of the Deputy Chairman of the Magnitogorsk City Executive Committee. When Valery was arrested for drunkenness, hooliganism, and insulting militia personnel, his father used all his influence and power to have him released:

> this was not the first time that young Novokreshchenov had been arrested. . . . But each time his father's position had saved the son from punishment. This time the hooligan was brought to trial. On the day of the trial all the telephones and switchboards in the city of Magnitogorsk were working for Novokreshchenov; telephones rang in the court and in the militia office; he [the father] advised

how best to circumvent the laws, which was done: The court's verdict was to issue a warning.

The parents of this *jeunesse dorée* are usually decent enough citizens but have failed to educate their children in the "main thing: high civic mindedness, and intolerance toward egoism, haughtiness, and disrespect for people." From the official viewpoint, these young people (even though their number is small) are doubly disturbing. They symbolize the repudiation, indeed mockery, of the basic values of Soviet society, including the sacredness of work and collectivism; they emphasize that the right parents and the proper connections are often what count. Worse, they constitute a group suggestive of a leisure class, an anathema to Soviet ideology. These parents, as though by default, are training their children for a style of life that is "officially" nonexistent. The human products of such socialization will be *spoiled* and *unguided*.

The Over-protective Family

This family somewhat resembles the "bountiful-neglectful" type, but displays certain distinctive features. It appears to be found predominantly among the middle classes, that is, the middle intelligentsia—professionals and others engaged in white-collar occupations. Members of this class, by virtue of their position, tradition, culture, and occupations, tend to be oriented toward intellectual life, the cultivation of the arts, and a devotion to affairs of the mind that sets them off not only from lower socioeconomic levels but, to some degree, from the *arrivistes* of the "bountiful-neglectful" families. Members of this class, who enjoy a modest standard of living compared with that of the upper socio-economic groups, are unable to indulge their children to such extent, although they undoubtedly would like to do so. They tend to make up for it, however, often by doting on their offspring, and by extreme emotional investment in their children. It is almost as though the dreariness and monotony of their everyday lives impels such parents to look exclusively to the family circle for contentment and satisfaction, and to use the child as an extension of the self in playing out important psychological (and perhaps neurotic) needs. Their behavior is reminiscent of the "maternal over-protection" described by David Levy,[15] that is, an emotional envelopment of the child by the mother that prevents him from fully differentiating his personality from hers.

Moreover, given the "cultural" preoccupations of this class, parents are often tempted not only to consider their child as unique, but also to hope that he may be some kind of *wunderkind*, whether the *wunder* be in music, dance, science, literature, art, or any other "elevated" activity. The product of this attitude often turns out to be a child with an inflated sense of his own worth who believes, with his parents, that his great talent sets him above common children, and who runs a genuine risk of becoming an unhappy misfit in a social system whose code has no place for isolates.

The case of Serezha will serve as an illustration. When his mother brought him to the senior class of a kindergarten she announced, in his presence: "My Serezha is a most unusual child. He models wonderfully well in clay. A sculptor friend says he is talented." The mother left, imploring the teacher not to ask him to do physical work. "We value his hands so!" In truth, the boy (all of six years old) did model exceedingly well, but always the same subject: a horse lying down. In addition, he kept aloof from the other children. Asked why he repeated the same theme he answered automatically: "Mama and Vladimir Ivanovich [the sculptor friend] say this is my best subject and I should stick to it." The teacher later called in the mother, who, expecting to hear Serezha praised, to her surprise and anger was told about her "mistakes in raising her child." The teacher took it upon herself to re-educate *both* the child and the mother by integrating the child with his schoolmates and revealing to the mother the errors of her ways.[16] (It is a reflection of the regime's retention of its primary rights over children that judgments by school personnel are supposed to be accepted by parents.) Soviet sources complain of another consequence of the existence of such inwardly-oriented families: the inability of its members to extend a sense of loyalty to extrafamilial institutions or persons. The case is cited of the wife who has found happiness exclusively in her family world, in the care of her husband and children, and who has given up her job and her membership in the Komsomol. *Pravda* disapprovingly describes this as a kind of bourgeois connubial bliss:

> a small but friendly family where all love each other and each one takes care of the others. However, these cares do not transcend the framework of the small familial world. Vera sees to it that her daughter and husband are dressed and fed. Ivan sees to it that his family should not experience material wants. Having worked seven

hours, Vania comes home, has supper, reads a little ("We do not fall behind life—we subscribe to newspapers")—and goes to sleep. Vera's day begins with shopping. . . . She prepares food, washes, launders, looks after Lenochka, meets her husband in the evening, feeds him—and then also goes to sleep.[17]

There is also the danger that the overly intense emotional bond with parents will bind the child to the family even when he reaches adulthood. A. Protopopova, in an article in *Pravda* entitled "Cultivation of Feelings," investigated the reasons people give for seeking a divorce, and became convinced that in almost every case the reason stemmed from an "incorrect, and even abnormal upbringing of one or both of the former spouses." She cites the case of Lydia, an only child who, from childhood, was denied nothing. "Whatever she did wrong, her parents, blinded by love, accused the neighbors, her friends, her teachers, her acquaintances—anyone but her." The result of such "rearing" was a "vain egoist" who categorically refused to follow her husband to go to the "stupid backwoods" post in the countryside to which he had been assigned as a physician. Lydia herself declared:

> I was born in Moscow, I grew up here, my home and parents are here. He says: "If you love me, you'll go." And I say: "If you love me, you will stay." Does he want to be a hero? Well, I am not a heroine. I want simple happiness. . . . And the child? My parents dote on him. We'll bring him up without a father![18]

From the society's viewpoint, the firm refusal of such families to forego private emotional ties in favor of outside affiliations effectively insulates them from demands for involvement in the economic and social life of the country. The human products of such a family will tend to be *spoiled* and *misguided*.

The Under-supportive Family

This type is met primarily but not exclusively among lower socio-economic, usually manual workers' groups. It is fundamentally unstable and incapable of providing the child with a secure and consistent home surrounding. Typically, both parents work because of financial pressure. They are beset by the all-too-familiar problems of such families in most industrial societies: high rates of desertion, separation, promiscuity, drinking, brutality, and incompatibility, and the ever-present overcrowding that seems to be the lot of the urban poor everywhere. In these families, not only is the influence and the example provided to the child likely to be negative or inadequate (and often emotionally traumatic), but supervision, particularly when both parents work, is haphazard or even nonexistent. The preschool child may be shunted from place to place or left to himself, taking "to the street" and to gangs and the myriad noxious stimuli he finds there. This condition is further aggravated by the perennial lack of adequate housing which affects most families in the Soviet Union. Even if a family has a "private apartment" (that is, one which it does not have to share with other families) seldom does the child have a room of his own where he might invite a friend, build an airplane model, or quietly read, while his parents are often eager to have him out of the way[19] so they can entertain their friends. Once out of the house, he is likely to find a severe shortage of organized recreational facilities.[20] The problem in this case is not so much that of the "wrong" type of socialization as the absence of supervision, control, and guidance by *any* responsible adult and it leads to a condition the Russians call *beznadzora* (lack of care)— children who, from an economic and legal viewpoint are "cared for," in the sense they have a family and a home, yet lack correct moral influence and upbringing.[21] No doubt such conditions are partly responsible for the deviant and delinquent behavior that the Soviets find so disturbing and difficult to cope with.

Drunkenness on the part of the father and community tolerance of that pattern is also held to be an important contributory factor to family disorganization and the lack of a "healthy atmosphere at home." For example, *Komsomolskaia Pravda* reported in 1965, in an article entitled "Papa Hears but Drinks," the sad case of two children from whom their father "stole their childhood." He often came home drunk, abused his wife, and once beat up his daughter so brutally that she was taken to a hospital with fractures and a brain concussion.[22] The inability of such a family to provide its children with companionship and a good example[23] leads to a poorly socialized individual who may be *unspoiled* but is also *unguided*.

These four Soviet family types, then, are turning out quite different kinds of adults. Now we must take a longitudinal view of the socialization process in order to trace the major steps in their development.

IV. The Career of the Future Soviet Adult:
"Orbiting" the Infant, Child, and Adolescent

By the time the individual reaches legal maturity, his future career as an adult is to a large extent predetermined by the prior sequence of events. The number of fundamental options left to him will be limited by his upbringing, personality traits, parental and social class background, education, and the choices he himself will have made by that time or which will have been made for him.

This course of development may conveniently be divided into stages of about seven years each, characterized by a gradually changing "mix" between the responsibilities and the functions of different agencies of socialization vis-à-vis the growing child. The first stage is dominated by the family and particularly the mother; in the second, the socialization process is shared between the family and the school, with the school and party-affiliated children's organizations assuming greater and greater responsibility for the child; the third sees the continuing emancipation of the adolescent from family supervision, and the greater influence of the school, the job, and the youth organizations. (The major exception to this sequence involves orphans and illegitimate children who are placed in state-run institutions almost from birth and for whom there is no gradual shift from a family to an extrafamilial surrounding. We shall discuss this important group subsequently.)

Stage 1 (Birth to 6 Years)

The typical Soviet citizen in an urban area nowadays enters the world via the maternity hospital or ward operated by the health department of his city or district. Even before his birth, his mother had, in most instances, reported to a Women's Consultation Clinic, which watched over her pregnancy and over the well-being of the child in the womb. The mother, if working, was entitled to 112 calendar days with pay and had probably stopped working about a month and a half before her expected delivery date.* She was entitled, without losing her job, to take an additional three months off, but without pay. In addition, she would not lose her seniority status for a year after the birth of the child in case she chose to remain at home during that period of time. The

---

* If she had twins or a multiple delivery or if there were complications, her postdelivery period could be extended from 56 to 70 days.

mother, then, must come to a decision fairly early after the birth of her child on whether she will stay at home and care for him, or make alternative arrangements. If she goes back to work, she is legally allowed one-half hour in every three and one-half to nurse her child, whether the child stays at home with someone else or is placed in a nursery operated by her place of work.

While the mother may place her child in a nursery as early as three months, the more usual pattern is to wait at least until the child is a year old, or to entrust him to another person at home; more likely than not a grandmother (*babushka*). The *babushka* arrangement is not always feasible because of such factors as lack of living space or incompatibility between her and either a daughter- or son-in-law. Furthermore, the extremely crowded conditions under which most Soviet families must live do not present the best prospects for raising children. As a Soviet sociologist remarked: "The elimination of shared apartments and the building of one-family apartments will certainly have positive influence upon the upbringing of children. It is also most important to separate children . . . because for an entire family to dwell in a single room does great harm in terms of the upbringing of children."[24] This, however, is still mostly for the future, since the massive building program instituted by Khrushchev must first deal with the accumulated backlog of a generation of neglect as well as the natural increase of the population. These crowded conditions not only create problems in the development of the child's personality but propel him, once he reaches school age, or even earlier, into activities *outside* the house, either of the type approved by the regime (Octobrists, Pioneers) or unsupervised and deviant activities. As to the *babushka*, the regime is less than enthusiastic over having future generations raised by women who are suspected of conveying to their young and impressionable charges "wrong" ideas (religious convictions, superstitions, and other remnants of "capitalistic consciousness"), and clearly prefers, where facilities allow, that the child be brought up (at least during his mother's working hours) in a state-operated nursery.[25]

Between the ages of one and six, then, some Soviet urban children have the opportunity of being placed in extrafamilial preschool institutions either of the daytime type, such as the nursery, or, for children between four and six, the boarding school kindergarten, where they stay from Monday morning until Saturday afternoon. (Orphans and children of "single mothers," of course, may be placed in institutions almost from birth.) It is thus possible, and probably from the viewpoint of the regime, desirable, that from an early age children be removed for increasing periods of time from their families and placed in state-run institutions where the child will get his first taste of "collectivistic" life and be brought up in the "correct" moral and ideological climate. These institutions, moreover, are supposed to "teach" the parents how to behave and how to raise their children at home. This is especially true of the "over-protective" family (the "bountiful-neglectful" family would not be inclined to entrust children to ordinary state institutions). Yet, from the viewpoint of the society and the regime, the families whose children most need this exposure—the "under-supportive" type—are precisely those that are least likely to place their children, since there is no legal requirement to do so.

Stage 2 (7–13 Years)

When the child reaches the age of seven, there are no more options about extrafamilial schooling: he must go to school, though he may go either to a regular school, or to an extended-day school, or to a boarding school. These schools, in addition to their standard "educational" functions, continue the "moral" education presumably begun in the family (positive attitudes toward work and the collective, for example) and also control and supervise the time and activities of children during (and sometimes after) school hours.

Children are admitted to the Octobrists when they are about seven and stay until they are nine; from nine to fourteen they belong to the Pioneers. These organizations, although officially under Komsomol control, are for all practical purposes run by and for the school authorities. They serve, as Nicholas DeWitt has pointed out, two major purposes: to provide additional training in a specific area of the pupil's interest as a supplement to his education and, perhaps more importantly, to organize the children into a group which can readily be supervised, controlled, managed, and manipulated by school personnel,[26] usually with the assistance of a "co-opted" class member, with meetings convened in the same room in which classes are held. These organizations serve, in theory at least, as a means for the control of their members' activities outside the home, by offering such enticements as club activities, the use of recreational facilities, outings, and summer camps. Given the crowded living conditions under which most Soviet families must live, they provide children a chance for escape, for personal pleasure as well as an opportunity to exercise some choice in extra-curricular and generally approved activities. The very same needs, however, cause some children to seek non-approved activities and, as they strive to emancipate themselves from their early childhood dependency, find scope in deviant or delinquent types of behavior.

An important element, particularly in the latter part of this stage, is that of male identity. For most boys in contemporary industrial society, there is no easily available, constantly present, male role model with which to identify. Brought up mostly by a mother or a grandmother, their subjection to feminine dominance usually extends to the preschool institutions and to the elementary grades where most teachers are women. While this poses few problems for the girls, it does create one for the boys who know that, as adults, they will have to perform in "masculine" roles; it appears that a great deal of the aggressive, rebellious, and deviant behavior of young boys in urban settings may well be an exaggerated attempt to assert an uncertain masculinity. As an article in *Izvestiia* put it: "how many practical jobs connected with attracting children to technology, agronomy, and applied art have never been done, how many athletic competitions never been held . . . because there are too few healthy, vigorous . . . male pedagogues. . . . Youths with more energy than they know how to apply . . . need a firm masculine hand . . ."[27] With the father (and often the mother) away at work, and given the absence of relatives who might supervise and control the child, as well as the familial malintegration frequently produced by this kind of urban living, there are few effective social mechanisms to counteract the growing alienation and isolation of the child. Neither the school, the youth organization, or the "official" agencies (juvenile courts, for example) can do very much at that stage to alter the behavior of the child except through physical restraint. We may assume that it is primarily for children of this type, most of whom must come from "under-supportive" families, that the boarding schools as well as the extended school programs were instituted in the late 1950s. In the boarding schools, control over the total life situation of the child is possible; in the extended-day school, children are kept under school control until their parents have returned home and are presumably capable of resuming their supervision. Indeed, this idea of the desirability of "total" control is central to the boarding school concept:

The basic idea of the boarding schools which distinguishes them from ordinary schools, is that in them the educational training influence of the teachers embraces the entire life of the child from the moment of early childhood when children cease to need direct maternal care until maturity.[28]

Unsupervised or poorly supervised children in this vulnerable and impressionable age group may easily move into modes of juvenile delinquency and gang behavior that often prove harmful to the individual or his society.

Stage 3 (14–20 Years)

This stage is a most decisive one in the career of the Soviet child and adolescent, involving as it does the end of childhood and the initiation into adulthood. Earlier experiences will now culminate in a career decision, while for the less fortunate, difficulties that began to develop earlier will surface in acute form, as the youth grapples with problems of personal identity, his integration in the society, the demands and pressures to "grow up," his needs to rebel, to conform, and to give up childhood dependencies. Also at this third stage, the role of the family as guide, supervisor, and controller dwindles to be almost entirely replaced by extrafamilial agencies. This is a difficult phase in any society, but is even more difficult in those still in the process of changing from agricultural to industrial, where both individual and society are subject to rapid environmental shifts.

This is also the time when many must choose either to continue formal education with its implications for prolonged dependency and delayed gratification for the sake of a better future, or to go straight to work. Let us examine the circumstances faced in either choice.

We already have referred to some of the problems raised by the children of the "bountiful-neglectful" families. For many, education is more an element of social status than a means to acquire necessary training and skills. At the same time these youths occupy educational facilities that could better be used by more capable but disadvantaged adolescents.

The children of the middle classes and "over-protective" families may find themselves under somewhat different pressures, when their parents insist that they continue their education even if, on objective grounds, they are not qualified to do so. Unrealistic goals are set for them; even bribery is attempted. *Izvestiia* once

reported that demand for admission to institutes of higher learning was such that only those who can afford to "pay" (that is,
under the table) can go on, especially among those who are only
average students.[29] In another instance, a girl who had complained
that she had failed to be admitted to a Kiev institute because she
lacked "connections," was advised to work harder and not to
blame others.[30]

It may well be that it is precisely youths from this kind of
middle-class background who form the backbone of student unrest
and protest, who articulate the discrepancies between the official
values and the realities of daily life, and who sometimes find themselves in comrades' courts branded as "parasites"—youths who
have been educated at state expense and yet who are not engaged
in "socially useful labor." Coupled with this is the phenomenon,
so visible for example in medicine, of young professionals who "do
not repay their debts to the people who educated them" and
refuse to report to the positions to which they have been posted,
particularly when these are away from their families and from the
cultural and other amenities of the city. Accounts in the Soviet
press insist that these spoiled youths have not been sufficiently imbued with a sense of dedication to their society, and that the fault
lies in most instances with their families and in ineffective Komsomol organizations whose boring activities fail to shape young
minds in the right direction. As *Molodoi Kommunist* wrote, echoing many a familiar complaint, ". . . dullness and stereotype are
still the hallmark of many meetings. . . . When you see the
boring symmetry . . . the hampering officialism . . . you clearly
sense how inhibition and estrangement are born."[31] To make
matters worse, the regime's steadfast refusal to countenance group
activities over which it has no control makes it difficult for adolescents to turn to groups that have no official sanction, but might
fill their needs to get together informally. *Sovetskaia Rossiia* reports on an informal discussion group that sprang up, the efforts of
the Komsomol in infiltrating and spying on it, and its eventual
disbandment.[32]

Paradoxically, it is the very intensity of state control and party
distrust of outside activities that often aggravates the alienation
of those youths who, according to the regime, are most in need of
proper influence; for the tedium and the boring predictability of
Komsomol activities repel many who wish to find goals worthy of
personal commitment.

It is, however, among those who quit school altogether that

the youth problem is quantitatively most disturbing. The rapidly changing occupational structure of an expanding industrial society produces casualties in the form of the relative unemployability and uselessness of many adolescents, particularly among the poorly trained and the drop-outs. Soviet society, despite its planned economy, is beginning to experience precisely such problems, and the unemployed or underemployed adolescent poses a serious ideological embarrassment as well as a social and economic dilemma. It points to the inability of a society that so often has boasted of its unique capacity to solve the vexing questions that plague the Western world to cope with the existence of the very same problems at home. The most obvious consequence of the drop-out situation is idleness, and this in a society where work is considered man's most important activity. *Kazakhstanskaia Pravda* complained, "It is no secret that our schools have a high drop-out rate. *Many young people do not know what to do with themselves.* In Alma-Ata, we have some upper-grade students who have taken the wrong road."[33]

Enforced inactivity increases the propensity of children and adolescents to delinquency, often under the influence of older children and adults. We are told that "teenagers take to the streets, where they have their 'authorities,' usually slightly older and stronger youngsters who already are familiar with cigarettes, in some cases even liquor and with thieves' jargon. Next step is to get into trouble."[34]

Predrag Vukević, writing in *Politika* (Belgrade), has written almost admiringly of the sonorous string of epithets used in the Soviet Union to designate and stigmatize the idler, the parasite, the *tuneadets*:

> He belongs to the group of speculators, drunkards, hooligans, good-for-nothing fellows, lazybones, egoists, "mother's pets," vagabonds, idlers, sluggards, parasites, loiterers, dawdlers, defrauders, vagrants, thieves, rascals, wastrels, adventurers, ne'er-do-wells, cheaters, slackers, profiteers, middle-men, commissioners, agents, those who abandon work, cunning fellows, despots, plunderers, egoistic businessmen, fortune-tellers, intruders, rogues, knaves, villains, people with smallholders' passions, transport swindlers.

He added that "it is almost impossible to quote or find an equivalent in our language for such a determined category of people or all its types."[35] While Soviet ideologues continue to assert that the roots of juvenile delinquency and crime, of alcoholism and unemployment, of poverty and inequalities of income have been eradicated in Soviet society, the fact of the matter is that growing industrialization seems to intensify these problems without respect to national boundaries.

Efforts to ameliorate the drop-out problem by attaching youngsters to industrial training programs have not been notably successful, for industrial plants are simply not geared to the training of any appreciable number of youths and their efforts on this score tend to be perfunctory. Nor has the system of alternating shift schools been effective. According to *Komsomolskaia Pravda*, "night school is powerless without the support of industry."[36]

In some instances the problem of the drop-outs is masked by encouraging poor students to leave a school under the pretense of their being assigned to a vocational school. *Pravda* reports that an elementary school principal in Moldavia gave his drop-outs papers for further training and then dismissed them, as neat a way as any to get rid of "problem students."

The feeling of hopelessness and superfluity experienced by the drop-outs, the drabness of everyday existence, the lack of recreational facilities, and the inability to derive either from their families or from youth organizations the kind of support and meaningful help they need, constitute a major and relatively new social problem of contemporary Soviet society.

An example of a novel and experimental response to it is the attempt to integrate young workers into an industrial setting through the formation of a council (soviet) in which fathers who are workers at a plant will help their sons learn and adjust to factory life, a sort of apprenticeship in modern garb. As described in *Komsomolskaia Pravda*, "[fathers] ordained the new worker into the working class."[37] This kind of "ordaining" is, however, more the exception than the rule. It is usually simpler and more direct, and the holy liquid used is more likely to be vodka than a gentler fluid. Indeed, one of the traditional responses in Russian culture to "problems" is alcohol, a medium evidently adopted by many young people under the pressures of older workers for whom the downing of a drink is regarded as the badge of manliness. Young workers are challenged to drink "bottoms up" if they want to be accepted. The few Soviet reports we have on juvenile delinquency emphasize that a major cause of juvenile crime, hooliganism, and other types of deviant behavior is the influence of alcohol.[38] There are even reports of the use of narcotics by Soviet youths.[39]

The corrective measures adopted in this area have not proved particularly effective, despite their variety: the enforcement of regulations against the sale of alcohol to minors, limiting the serving of vodka to 100 grams per person, encouragement to drink other types of alcohol such as wine and beer, the preaching of "healthy" recreation, scolding by the Komsomols, and the exiling of parasites or hooligans, or their commitment to corrective labor camps. Indeed, it may well be that at this point in the career of the Soviet youth, the use of coercion, propaganda, comrades' courts, and other means and entreaties, legal and extralegal, only increases rebelliousness and discontent. A study of juvenile delinquency in one of the districts of Moscow reports that 8.9 per cent of the juvenile crimes were committed by youths of fourteen, 51.4 by those fifteen to sixteen years old, and 39.7 by those seventeen to nineteen. Its authors indicate that such statistics confirm the familiar proposition that the most unstable, critical period for children occurs after the age of fifteen:

> Precisely at this time youths, particularly boys, frequently pass from the influence of their parents, teachers, and the public organizations. At this age they acquire a need for some independence, they tend to nihilistically interpret the demands of adults. As a result of this, youths easily fall under bad influences, not being able critically to distinguish the bad from the good. Consequently at the age of 15 begins a period during which the behavior of youths must be especially controlled, particularly since at the age of 15 or 16 the youths, as a rule, are completing the eight-year course and must make decisions concerning their future.[40]

As the Soviet youth rounds the last phases of this third stage, then, the cumulative effects of earlier socialization have left their permanent mark, for better or worse. When adolescents reach adulthood, the legal responsibility of the family ceases as they form families of their own; they in turn will shape the personality and character of their own children. Those who have emerged from the process with serious problems begin to affect the next generation.

V. Soviet Family Policy Today: Dialectical Synthesis and Some Problems

There appear to be no prospects at present for a significant reorientation of Soviet family policy. What may be expected is a synthesis (of a highly pragmatic sort) between the anti- and pro-family policies of the past—a combination of approaches that would continue to entrust the family with major responsibilities in ◄ the early socialization of children, while promoting its consistency with the needs of Soviet society and with the extrafamilial agencies which gradually take over the upbringing of the new generation. This will imply a wide range of institutions and arrangements to complement, supplement, and, in some cases, to supplant parents (as in the case of the "non-supportive" family).

Some of the measures introduced by Khrushchev, and now being quietly abandoned or modified, would have meant a renewal of the assault on the family if carried to their logical conclusion. Attacks on policies of fallen leaders are routine in Soviet-type systems, but even before Khrushchev's deposition, doubts had been raised about their validity and viability.

In this section we briefly examine four basic issues, on which there is now debate. The first two center on the consequences of familial neglect—encouraged in part by the regime's announced commitment to the eventual transfer of socialization to extra-familial institutions; the latter two center on the characterological consequences of institutional upbringing.

The Unwarranted Abdication by Families of Their Responsibilities

While some families, notably the "over-protective" type, hold on to their children and encapsulate them in a tight family circle, some of the "under-supportive" families would gladly be rid of their responsibilities if there were any alternative. Yet this was clearly not the intent of the boarding schools' program, for they were to replace only those families manifestly unable to perform basic socialization functions. *Izvestiia* takes to task the "indifference and thoughtlessness of parents who are stupidly happy at having found a place for their children," reminding them that "no society has the means for education without their direct participation."[41] The article goes on to say that the boarding school was meant to help, not to replace family and parents. *Komsomolskaia Pravda* further notes that "there are families in which parents are of the opinion: the raising of their own children is the sacred duty of society and government."[42]

The import of these remarks is quite clear: raising and educating the new generation is a collaborative venture between family and society; the society is willing to guide, assist and, *if necessary*, rescue the family, but does not give the family *carte blanche* to neglect its duties.

High Economic Costs of Extrafamilial Socialization

Another cogent reason for the reluctance of the regime to put its full weight behind an extensive boarding schools program is cost. Many parents, evidently, are reluctant to pay their fair share of the costs of maintaining their children in the schools even when they can afford to do so. According to *Izvestiia*, it was never expected that the boarding schools would bring up their charges in isolation from their families. While, in the first few years, the youngsters sent there had no supervision at home, "now many of them have very fine [material] conditions at home, their families have moved to new apartments." And the state has the right to demand greater financial contributions from parents: "payment for the upkeep of these children should be regularized."[43] These considerations are probably behind the program of the extended day school (introduced in 1960) which provides supervision of children as long as their parents are not at home. The elimination of the "hotel" functions of the boarding schools will lead to important savings: extended day schools can be operated at one-sixth the per-student cost of the regular boarding school.[44]

The Problems of "Institutionalized" Children: "Maternal Deprivation"

From an economic and "rational" viewpoint it may, in fact, make good sense for children to be brought up in crèches, nurseries, or kindergartens where one woman can take care of several youngsters in order to release mothers for other tasks. But there may be severe social costs in damaged personalities. The Western literature on consequences of institutional (as against familial) upbringing points to a high probability of "maternal deprivation," a situation where an infant or young child is not in fairly constant contact with one human being (usually a mother or mother-surrogate) or is deprived of such interaction because of separation or the mother's death. It is best formulated by Bowlby:

> What is believed essential for mental health is that the infant and young child experience a warm, intimate, and continuous relationship with his mother (or permanent mother-substitute) in which both find satisfaction and enjoyment . . . it is this complex, rich

and rewarding relationship with the mother in the early years, varied in countless ways by relations with the father and with siblings, that child psychiatrists and many others now believe to underlie the development of character and mental health.[45]

According to this theory, which has been re-evaluated, refined, and reassessed but not invalidated,[46] children fare better in (economically) poor homes than in good institutions or, to put it in another way, the "vitamins of love" are just as vital as good nutrition and adequate physical care.* When such attention is lacking, for one reason or another, the child suffers maternal deprivation. The younger the child, the deeper and more lasting the damage. Maternal deprivation before the age of five is likely to affect the child's basic personality, his ability to relate to others, his subsequent emotional maturity and intellectual development. Furthermore, while a nutritional deficiency is easily observable and usually remediable, a deficiency in the "love vitamins" often shows up only after the damage is irreversible. As far as character is concerned, the maternally deprived child tends to be maladjusted, lacking a well-organized, integrated concept of the self, with a poorly developed system of internal controls.

> There is an inability to love or feel guilty. There is no conscience. The inability of these children to enter into any relationship makes treatment or even education impossible. They have no idea of time, so that they cannot recall past experience and cannot benefit from past experience or be motivated to future goals. This lack of time concept is a striking feature in the defective organization of the personality structure.[48]

There may be some evidence that the Soviets are dimly aware of the character problems that follow an institutional upbringing, particularly for very young children, and that plans for mass or universal extrafamilial upbringing of children *à la* Engels may well have been shelved, at least for the near future. A few years ago, *Literaturnaia Gazeta* sounded a cautious note of alarm relating the observation made by first-grade teachers in Leningrad that, compared to children who had been brought up at home, children (presumably orphans) who had been brought up in Childrens' Homes (*Detskie Doma*) appeared to be intellectually and socially

---

* It is interesting to recall that a great deal of the literature of nineteenth century England was also devoted to the cruelties of orphanages and poorhouses. More recently an article describing a center for dependent children near Washington described it as "a great factory of retardation and mental illness."[47]

handicapped in many ways when they reached the elementary grades.[49] An investigation of these institutions showed that two staff members usually took care of fifteen to eighteen children: one was a nurse, the other an aide. Their "procedures" were uninterrupted: change of diapers, feeding, washing, carrying them to the open air, again washing and changing of clothing, feeding, giving injections—a busy assembly line. Conversations with children were minimal and cursory, and could not be otherwise because of time pressures. With older children, there was a little more communication, but the ration for each child was insufficient, perhaps ten minutes a day in the guise of a "lesson." This was contrasted with the almost constant attention a mother gives an infant, and the importance of such contact for early language formation and cognitive processes. The social maturity and development of the institutionalized children are further retarded by the self-contained, "sterile" atmosphere in which the children are raised. They are in contact almost exclusively with children of their own age, not with adults and especially not with adult men; because the women who surround them wear white caps and white medical coats, the children are dismayed when they see street clothing for the first time; they rarely leave the institution (because of the staff's concern lest they catch infectious diseases). In one institution the staff had simply forgotten to hang mirrors, and the children had no idea what they looked like: they could recognize their playmates on a photograph but not themselves. In another institution, a speech therapist incredulously described the scene she found there:

> It was full of children. They pottered in the sand under 'mushrooms.' Each was absorbed in his own interest. A deathlike silence, broken only occasionally by inarticulate muttering. The nannies sat on benches and knitted, from time to time they glanced at the children and shouted at them. In bewilderment the new speech therapist asked the head doctor, "What is this, are they deaf and dumb?"—"No, normal." "Why are they so silent?"—"That's why we asked you here."[50]

One can imagine what might happen if most children were brought up under such conditions: it would almost certainly alter the quality and outlook of new generations, and the fabric of society itself. Soviet statements to the effect that such extrafamilial institutions should be restricted to children who have no family or a grossly inadequate family, and that they must have more and better trained personnel, show some awareness of the danger. Closely related to this question, but of more relevance to the boarding schools, is the "disciplinary" aspect of socialization we mentioned earlier, and its potentially crippling effect.

"Incorrect" Socialization Due to Disciplinary and Collective Emphasis

There seems to be a "symmetry" in family upbringing between love and discipline that an institutional staff, necessarily discipline-minded, simply cannot or does not reproduce. *Izvestiia*, in a 1961 article on boarding schools, recalled the words of a Russian pedagogue, Ushinsky:

> Imagine a child who spends his whole day irreproachably, without once stepping out of the formal, prescribed limits of decorum; who wakes up at the assigned minute, marches to and from the appointed places and, finally, goes off to bed when the bell sounds—in a word, a child who marches at command all his life! . . . When there is too much tutelage, the children we rear are weak-willed milksops, because in their childhood they have never had occasions to rely on their own will.[51]

Discipline may range from the oversolicitous, overprotective curtailment of activity as in the orphanages, to the strictness of military school discipline current in boarding schools characterized by dominance-submission relations between teacher and pupils and among pupils themselves. This authoritarian pattern may stem from the fact that the first pupils of the boarding schools were delinquents who were disciplinary problems at their former schools and at home, but the heritage lingers and includes child-beating by supervisors or by older children used as "trusties." As one description put it: "the children's life is based on the unconditional recognition of the physical strength of older inmates."[52]

The same disciplinary approach is often found in the extended-day-school system. Indeed, in Riga, School No. 3 exists only for the "punishable pupils," a term for boisterous youngsters who particularly annoy the teachers. Knowing of this "system," parents send their children to the group only when they become unmanageable, and when they act like hooligans and receive bad grades.[53]

Recently there has been increased concern for the emotional and intellectual consequences of the disciplinary emphasis in Soviet schools, whether of the boarding, prolonged-day, or ordinary type. One teacher quoted by *Izvestiia* expressed worry about the verbal development of children, many of whom tend to be quiet and silent. "As a result their vocabulary is poor, they cannot express their thoughts. Now that I understand this, I restrain myself when I want to shout 'Quiet, children.'" The article also comments on the "collective emphasis" of the Soviet school, with its insistence on the "we," "our group," "our class" and not "I, myself" or "you yourself." "It is therefore not surprising that the children strive to 'rest from society.'"[54]

All this suggests that there are limits to social engineering and manipulation beyond which the costs in human damage take a heavy toll, and that the Engelsian dream of freeing the family from its socialization functions may be chimerical, even if the solution to its economic aspects is within sight. For the foreseeable future, the Soviets are likely to limit themselves to cautious experimentation, a pragmatic blend of conservatism and radicalism, tempered by common sense and the recollection of the unanticipated consequences of radical family legislation in the past.

VI. Utopia Revisited: Unconditional and Contingent

No society, particularly one of the Soviet type, can rest easily without some image of its future, some delineation of its own utopia. It is to this vision that we now turn.

In an article on the future Communist society, Academican S. Strumilin outlined his idea of the major contours of full communism. The shape of that future society is already visible in the U.S.S.R., he asserted, even alongside the shameful vestiges of a blighted past doomed to extinction.[55] The family, he writes, is the most elementary "collective," the cell or the molecule of contemporary society. It simultaneously answers the need for self-preservation and for the continuation of the race. At its base there are powerful and deep instincts of man, but from it arise social instincts of cooperation and mutual assistance, crowned by young love and capable of any sacrifice and actions. Under capitalism, love and marriage are debased; the "bourgeois" family is increasingly disinclined to fulfill its duty to have children. Under socialism, the family is liberated from the shackles of private property. Husband and wife are free agents who select each other and are equal partners, each capable of earning his or her own livelihood; marriage by design or crass calculation in Soviet society is becoming extinct. In the U.S.S.R. certain trends already presage the Communist future: the constant rise in the welfare of the population and the sharp decrease in mortality accompanying increased production and preventive health work; rising life expectancy for all age groups; increased leisure and improved communal facilities; a proliferation of nursery arrangements that free young mothers for work and cultural exposure and "family joys." Love, writes Strumilin, as the most important element uniting a couple, is becoming constantly more free of constraints and will become completely liberated under full communism. But, echoing Lenin's well-known strictures against the "glass of water" theory, Strumilin carefully adds that love must not be confused with the sexual license of bourgeois morality. Under communism the interests of the family and those of society will be identical. Strumilin concedes that there are still many facilities lacking in the march toward that utopia, especially institutions for the communal upbringing of children and for the collective feeding of the population, but foresees their ultimate plenitude.

Strumilin's utopia, in one sense, is nothing less than Paradise recovered: the primordial innocence of the Garden of Eden with the material benefits of industry. In his section on the family and children, he specifies more precisely the relationship between family, society, and children. Children, he writes, must be born healthy and physically strong, and brought up to become worthy members of the society in which they are destined to live and "build their fate." While the first task (healthy child bearing) can be entrusted in its entirety to the family, the second task can be accomplished more effectively and successfully by society itself. The role of the family, then, should be limited to uniting two people in love and letting them produce healthy babies. But child rearing should be and will be separated from the family because the family is not qualified or equipped uniformly to conduct correct "moral" upbringing or to impart the full range of skills and capacities necessary in the new society.

A strong marital union, Strumilin writes, is, so to speak, egoism *à deux*. The birth of desired children only broadens this familial egoism beyond the framework of the marital pair and leads to a contradiction of interests in which excessive love by the parents destroys the child's capacity to participate fully in Soviet life. The incubus of egoism is that dread disease of children too blindly loved. The end product of such misguided love is the spoiled, self-loving, and self-indulgent person, who believes (usually wrongly) he is God's gift to creation, and who cannot take his place within the ranks of a collectivistic and cooperative society.

And, argues Strumilin, if love toward children be good (and he agrees that children need the "vitamins of love"), then it is selfish for a loving mother, and particularly one who is good with children, to limit herself to her own. She should not hoard but should share her maternal capacities with other children, particularly those who have no parents capable of giving such affection. She should become a "societal" mother.

Strumilin also argues that the kinds of trained teachers and educators who will be available in children's institutions will provide a better, more rounded educational experience for their charges than the small family. He envisages neighborhood communes in which nurseries and kindergartens will be located, but which will have their own separate facilities. Councils of women and mothers will supervise these institutions, while mothers will have limited access to their own children. Strumilin estimates that within the next fifteen to twenty years societal upbringing and education will begin at the cradle and end at maturity: "Every Soviet citizen, at the time he leaves the maternity home, will be directed to a nursery, from there to a boarding-type kindergarten or to a childrens' home; from there he will transfer to a boarding school and from the boarding school he will either go to work in a chosen specialty or will be assigned to study in higher-education establishments." Strumilin is confident that institutions will be devised to provide children the same kind of emotional support as a mother or mother-surrogate, presumably by employing "loving" women and mothers.

As a matter of fact, many of Strumilin's demographic expectations, such as reduced mortality and increased life expectancy, have little to do with "socialist" society but are observable the world over as a result of industrialization and modernization. And his concept of communes, while ideologically "correct," begs the question of the infrastructure of Communist society, and of the connections among these communes in an economy that would be national, societal, or even world-wide rather than local. His views are suggestive of the concept advanced by some analysts of communism as a kind of "retribalization" of society, a "great collectivized commune,"[56] and seem hardly realistic in the light of Soviet experience until now.

A more sober view is advanced by Kharchev,[57] one of the few Soviet sociologists systematically working on questions of the family. He does not foresee the future of the family in quite the radical ways outlined by Strumilin. He points out that under socialism the family has ceased to be an economic group and that its task is mainly the rearing of children. Kharchev further argues that the absence of conflict in a socialist society between family and societal upbringing has never signified their total identity. Family upbringing, as one of the forms of influence of society on the individual, possesses important features of its own, especially its emotional content and "tone," "inasmuch as its main prerequisites are parental love and a corresponding responsive feeling of children for their parents." Kharchev is mostly concerned with the moral or character-building process within the family, and particularly the development of positive attitudes toward work. The development of these attitudes is, however, complicated by the fact that, in the modern, industrialized society, young people are typically kept out of the actual work force until they aie rather advanced: in their late teens, early twenties, and even late twenties. While Kharchev accepts this delay of work participation for adolescents as the necessary price for progress achieved by industrialization, he also sees in it the danger that the family will fail to impart values and attitudes toward work indispensable to the adult.[58]

We have come, then, full circle to the issue raised at the outset, concerning the role of the family in imparting to the rising generation the "right" kinds of values, attitudes, and personalities. The question is not one of some hypothetically perfect articulation between individual and society. Indeed, variations among families —and the individuals they rear—may be absolutely essential to the fund of originality and creativity upon which societal development depends. Formal educational institutions, on the other hand, are more likely to enforce conformity and stifle individuality. It may well be that while Soviet leadership regards the family's functions as residual; it nevertheless recognizes that those it still performs are replaced only at intolerable cost.

VII. A Look into the Future

We have already suggested that there are unlikely to be radical changes in Soviet policy toward the family; rather we foresee a balance, a continuing division of labor, between the family and extrafamilial agencies of socialization. The evolution of the family under Soviet conditions in some respects duplicates the structural changes and differentiation that have marked the advent of industrialism elsewhere. More and more, in Western and in Soviet societies, the family gives up a series of functions it once performed simply because it is not equipped technically, intellectually, or financially to meet the new conditions imposed by the endless complexities of modern life. A father could teach his son how to plow or repair a pair of shoes; a mother can still teach her daughter how to cook and how to diaper a child. No family is equipped to train a youth in brain surgery or the use of intricate computer machinery. Yet, as the Soviets have had reason to discover, substitutes for early socialization by the family continue to be elusive; the soaring visions of the "engineers of the soul" have persistently defied realization. Granted that the fragile family of industrial society sometimes tragically fails its duties toward child and society, experience shows that wholesale replacement of the family entails unpredictable, and mostly undesirable, consequences for the entire society.

Many of the problems of youths and adolescents are not unique to Soviet society, but are increasingly familiar products of the dislocations and discontinuities of urbanization and industrialization. It is noteworthy, too, that the official Soviet reactions to these problems have tended to be singularly ineffective, or, at best, no more effective than those offered in the West. They alternate between the "understanding and condoning" attitude and a "get tough" policy advocating the use of force and punishment to rescue those who have chosen the wrong path.

Perhaps the major source of future change will be the rate and nature of female participation in the labor force. If, with the development of automation and the easing of unrelieved drudgery that has long been the lot of Russian women, they become more and more superfluous in the labor force (especially in low-skill occupations) their energies will have to be channeled elsewhere. The advent of relative affluence in Soviet society may, of course, return them entirely to their domestic functions and the care and feeding of husbands and children. But given the ideological predilections of a Communist regime and the special sensitivities to the "woman question" permanently instilled by the Revolution, it is entirely possible that they will be enlisted in a genuinely new effort to staff a comprehensive network of public services that, at the moment, remains the dream of a Strumilin. The combination of a politically motivated envelopment of young and old in such a network, with the formidable resources of Russian womanhood unchained, might well renew the capacity of an authoritarian regime to create the total society. The details of such a program cannot yet be foreseen, but the enduring influence of utopian images should not be dismissed in anticipating Soviet reactions to problems that are endemic the world over in industrialized societies.

Meanwhile, the basic family unit as we know it will continue to serve under Soviet conditions as an emotional home away from the rigors and the impersonality of a harsh and demanding social system and to provide the earliest socialization for the child. The critical point, particularly in a Soviet-type system, is the shifting balance of loyalties and affiliations from the family to society; and society is likely to remain a jealous mistress.

15.

Leisure: The Unity of Pleasure and Purpose

PAUL HOLLANDER

I. Leisure and Social Change

The process of molding the new man and his Communist consciousness takes place not only while he is working but also in his nonworking time.

Under socialism every worker can make use of his free time as he
sees fit. This does not, however, mean that society takes a passive
attitude toward the ways in which he utilizes his time.
—G. S. Petrosian
Vnerabochee Vremia
Trudiashchikhsia v SSSR (1965)

The subject of leisure in Soviet society belongs to those areas of
inquiry which can be safely characterized, with the mixture of sor-
row and glee appropriate to occasions of scholarly stocktaking, as
underinvestigated. Western, and particularly American, traditions
of Soviet scholarship are tied to and originate in the concern with
the militant, malevolent, and menacing aspects of Soviet society
under Stalin—an image that has hardly invited associations with
the problems of leisure.[1]
Under Stalin, Soviet citizens had little leisure, and its utilization did not, as it does today, present problems worthy of the attention of Soviet ideologues and policy-makers. But it must be
stressed that the new official interest in leisure does not necessarily
signify the mellowing of the system and is not in itself compelling
evidence of the liberalization of Soviet society. Indeed, governmental concern with the free time of individuals is not only consistent with the totalitarian model of social organization, but is
totalitarian virtually by definition. The effort to regulate leisure,

and not merely to provide facilities for its use plus a modicum of guidance, is part of the desire to oversee the entire life of the citizen, including those aspects which in other societies are considered irrelevant by the polity. To the extent that the government considers that it has a right to exercise supervision over leisure, it ceases to be leisure in the full meaning of the term.

This is not to say, however, that recent official interest in leisure is unrelated to post-Stalin changes. As Soviet spokesmen themselves point out, "nonworking time" acquires new importance for the regime, that is, for society and the collective, in proportion with its quantitative increase. The reduct the workday has resulted in the citizens' spending less time than they previously did in such well-defined institutional settings as the work place. Moreover, the general decline in compulsion has led to a measure of independence or separation from other institutional environments, such as those provided by various political and public organizations. We may be witnessing the beginning of a shift in the expenditure of time from the public realm, which includes work, to the private one. If this be the case, we can better appreciate the reasons for the new-found curiosity of the policymakers about how people spend their time when not at work.

The recognition of the political relevance of leisure time must also be viewed as a response to diminished coercion. To the extent that overt coercion has ceased in the post-Stalin period to be the dominant method of exacting conformity and influencing behavior, persuasion has become increasingly important and leisure time provides good opportunities for its implementation. An expression frequently encountered in Soviet writings on leisure, "the rational use of free time," means precisely that that time is to be made functional. A major theme for analyzing Soviet leisure is the interaction between the official intention to make it functional and the popular pressures to make it private and apolitical.

Much of Soviet life may be characterized as an interplay between official policies, values, and desires, and the deviant, recalcitrant, or evasive popular responses to them. Such responses do not imply political or ideological opposition; rather they entail an almost instinctive, inarticulate tendency to improvise techniques of circumvention. This constant interplay is peculiarly relevant to the realm of leisure, where popular attitudes can find the best and politically least suspect expression. At the same time, a political leadership willing to balance its own desires against those of the population will find the area of leisure one where compromise is tolerable and concession pays high dividends in cementing the loyalty of the citizen. It is impossible, then, to pass simple judgments about the role of leisure in Soviet society and the ways official policies influence it.

Leisure is one of the aspects of Soviet society which cannot be understood solely on the basis of a totalitarian model. We have stressed the typically totalitarian nature of the intense governmental concern with leisure, and suggested that many facets of Soviet leisure can best be treated with reference to persisting totalitarian characteristics. But other issues involved in Soviet leisure, specifically those which fall into the category of social problems, call for analysis in terms of the interaction between totalitarianism and characteristics not peculiar to the Soviet Union, but found as well as in other modern and modernizing societies. The most relevant aspects of modernity are secularization and urbanization.

The official concern with leisure already reflects some fundamental changes in Soviet society since Stalin:

1) The reduction of working time, which has resulted from a higher level of industrialization.

2) The rejection of coercion as the predominant and omnipresent method of social control. This is related to the desire of the leadership to secure more than surface conformity, which coercion could easily achieve, and to the long overdue recognition that Communist society, or anything even remotely resembling it, cannot be built until the official social ideals are more thoroughly internalized by the populace.

3) The need to find new and more effective ways of raising the productivity of labor by providing better recreational facilities, and also to use leisure time in order to raise occupational and educational qualifications.

4) The inauguration of a policy designed to increase social solidarity and popular commitment to the regime by means of greater, although still carefully controlled, public participation in communal affairs during leisure time.

5) An increasing awareness of the connection between the leisure activities of young people and the misbehavior of some. (This realization is one of the original reasons for official interest, especially since free time plays a much greater part in the lives of young people and because it has a more profound influence upon the formation of character than is the case for adults.) So-

viet authors particularly stress the relationship between idleness and the development of antisocial attitudes among the young:

> Life without creative work and active participation in the life of society leads to the inability to make rational use of free time, to the inability to fill it with art, sports, and human relationships which deeply enrich the personality. It is then that the notorious bottle of vodka appears. The lack of skill in making use of leisure was re-marked upon . . . by 376 of the respondents [in a youth poll of *Komsomolskaia Pravda*]. They attributed to this lack of skill the source of such negative traits as drunkenness, hooliganism, coarse [*nekul'turnyi*] behavior, and apathy.[2]

6) The official insistence on the proximity of the future Com-munist social order also has implications for the new interest in leisure. "Rationally" expended leisure is said to meet the need for ever higher levels of productivity and efficiency associated with full communism and to contribute to the complete development of the new Soviet man. Thus, the prerequisites of Communist society include both changed values, or complete development of the new Soviet man, and an economy of abundance to provide for his material and cultural needs. Furthermore, the strong utopian elements in Soviet ideology and their use in appealing to an expectant audience, virtually dictate that some account be given of what, besides material abundance and freedom from fatiguing toil, will comprise the "good society" of the future.

7) In a more ironical vein, it may be that the recent interest in leisure represents yet another attempt to catch up with the affluent and leisure-ridden societies of the West, and the United States in particular. To claim that leisure and its uses now may constitute a special problem is to imply that there is plenty of it, and that Soviet society has entered the realm of relatively subtle, refined difficulties that go far beyond the satisfaction of elementary needs. The suspicion is supported by the fact that major Soviet discussions and studies of leisure invariably begin with a survey of Western leisure studies, demonstrating a strong awareness of the existence of the Western leisure problem.

Leisure in any society is one of the best avenues toward an understanding of the social order as a whole. The nature of leisure-time activities reflects personal values and aspirations, which are more genuinely reflective of choice than, for instance, the ways in which people earn their living. Such choices tell us a great deal about the most fundamental aspects of human nature and behavior, as well as about the society itself. They tell us what is available to choose from, and about the purposes served by leisure-time activities (recreation, escape, self-improvement, reflection, status-seeking, companionship, or solitude). And, in Soviet society, the fact that political leaders are directly concerned with it affords considerable insight into their values and aspirations for the system as a whole. The examination of leisure in Soviet society thus exposes issues and problems that transcend the realm of leisure itself, and affords a better understanding of the complex relationship between the official and unofficial worlds of the Soviet citizen.

II. Ideology and Leisure

In communist society, where nobody has one exclusive sphere of activity but each can become accomplished in any branch he wishes, society regulates the general production and thus makes it possible for me to do one thing today and another tomorrow, to hunt in the morning, fish in the afternoon, rear cattle in the evening, criticize after dinner, just as I have a mind, without ever becoming hunter, fisherman, shepherd, or critic.

—Marx and Engels
German Ideology

*   *   *

An unreasonable person might picture for himself the daily life of the citizen under communism as follows: getting up in the morning he begins to ponder, where should I go to work today—in the factory as the chief engineer, or should I collect and lead the fishing brigade? Or perhaps fly to Moscow to conduct an urgent session of the presidium of the Academy of Science? . . . Thus it will not be. But how is it going to be? How should the intelligent reader envisage the liberalization from occupational specialization? . . . the question is exciting. . . .

Kommunist (August 1960)

The theoretical views of Marx and Engels on the disappearance of the specialization of labor under communism raise difficult, if exciting, issues for Soviet adherents a century later. Does the Marxian analysis apply to the period of transition from socialism to communism? What are the implications of the nature of work and specialization for the use of nonworking time? If, as Soviet ideologues suggest, work and leisure are interdependent, the character of work, and not only its amount, has far-reaching implications for the character of leisure.

The Marxian vision of the future implies that work and leisure will merge, or that work will be elevated to the plane of leisure by the removal of the stigma of specialization. It also predicts that under communism it will be a simple matter to change from manual to mental activities, from hunting, fishing, and cattle raising to being a critic. An altogether different prospect for the end of specialization, however, emerges if one paraphrases the words of Marx on the basis of contemporary experience and speaks of the individual's freedom under communism "to be an electronics engineer in the morning, an agronomist in the afternoon, a department store manager in the evenings, and a critic after dinner, without ever having to become an engineer, agronomist, manager, or critic." The prospects for the disappearance of vocational specialization under modern circumstances are rather dim, since each of these occupations requires the acquisition of skills and knowledge far more extensive and specialized than those needed for fishing, hunting, or animal husbandry. Understandably then, *Kommunist* entertains the Marxian conception of the unspecialized renaissance man of the Communist society with considerable reservations. Sporadic, premature efforts to do away with specialization are sometimes explicitly rejected:

> There is the opinion, in our view erroneous, that any elimination of auxiliary personnel is progressive and constitutes nothing less than a "tangible feature of communism." Yet experience has shown that this is by no means always justifiable. A typist is dismissed and necessary papers are typed with one finger by a person with an engineer's diploma who earns twice the typist's salary. Why not make an effort to analyze this, to examine it more seriously from the standpoint of state interests? One must not forget that the birth of the new is a complex process.[3]

The issue of whether specialization will or will not persist in the future is relevant for understanding the current ideological presuppositions and conceptions regarding leisure, the more so since problems of leisure—and their ideological elaboration—are increasingly important as more people have more leisure. The degree to which Soviet citizens remain or cease to be specialized in their work has considerable bearing on their avocational as well as vocational activities. For example, it is likely that the less fatiguing work becomes, the greater the inclination to engage in physical leisure activities (sports, hunting, fishing), while the less specialized—and hence the more satisfying—work becomes, the less the need to make the most of leisure and the less pronounced the contrast between the two.

But, even if specialization were to disappear in the future, technologically advanced society (as Communist society must be)—what of leisure? Can Marx's view be taken as a point of departure in understanding leisure under communism? Evidently he did not envisage leisure under communism as mere recreation, but as a fusion of *work-like* activities with leisure. Marx's uncharitable view of work in the countryside and the mentality it breeds suggests that, in including fishing, hunting, and cattle raising in his inventory of activities under communism, he foresaw a transformation of their quality and connotation once they would cease to be necessities performed under the pressure of making a living. In this he affirmed a principal criterion of leisure-time activities, namely, that they are freely chosen and serve no utilitarian purpose and are pursued for their inherent pleasure rather than for practical results. If our interpretation is correct—and other pronouncements of Marx on the possibilities of complete self-realization under communism support it—he offers limited ideological support for those who are today striving to functionalize the leisure of the Soviet citizen.

To return to the complexities of the present, the emphasis during the current "transition to full communism" is clearly not where Marx would have placed it. The stress today is on the interdependence between leisure (or recreation) and work, rather than on the enrichment of the personality (or self-realization) even though the latter theme is also in evidence. Soviet writers today are increasingly explicit about the contribution well-spent leisure makes to efficiency at work and to raising professional-occupational qualifications. Not even leisure filled with entertainment is free from such associations. A recent opinion poll on the preferences of theater-goers included the question: "Has any production you have seen helped you to decide a vital, personal problem for yourself?" Among the appropriate and exemplary answers we could read:

> After seeing "Irkutsk Story" I firmly resolved to get my husband to return to school for further study even though we had a year-old child and lived in our own apartment. . . . When I saw "Judge Between Us, People" I decided to go to night school. . . . The pro-

duction of "Colleagues" . . . helped me to understand what it means to choose an occupation suited to one's desires and abilities.[4]

Television, regarded by Western intellectuals as the new opiate of the masses and by the masses as a means of pure entertainment, is not considered a waste of time but as a centrally controlled medium of education and propaganda. As an authoritative article pointed out:

> With the help of domestic television it is possible to learn a foreign language, prepare for an examination to a higher educational institution, receive professional education, significantly widen a person's range of interests. . . . Television does not simply bring the masses to art. It is called to train in them high artistic taste, to impart a complex new knowledge and impressions. As the most mass instrument of artistic upbringing, television serves and will serve as a mighty weapon of the propaganda of the beautiful.[5]

The article also sharply criticizes programs without a revolutionary theme, those which are merely entertaining and divert people from the main problems of the present. The prevailing functionalized conception of leisure stresses not so much the needs of the individual as those of society. Well-spent leisure is held to be important because of the contribution it makes to production and the smooth functioning of society in general. It should enrich the individual so that he may enrich society. Enriching the self—in the eyes of Soviet ideologues—is inconceivable without enriching society (a socialist one, at any rate), since in the last analysis there can be no conflict between personal and social interests and benefits. Correspondingly, no matter how satisfied the individual may feel about how he spends his leisure, if the latter is deemed unworthy by qualified spokesmen of the collective, then "objectively" the leisure is not well spent. The attack on dominoes provides a seemingly trivial but highly revealing illustration. For some reason it seems to be very popular among Soviet citizens, as a serious-minded respondent to a survey of servicemen noted:

> Dominoes are a real evil in our unit. . . . As soon as we have any free time our sailors begin to slap down the black tiles. . . . But the most paradoxical thing of all is that even our officers do not lag behind the sailors and spend their free time just as purposelessly, to the knock of the dominoes.[6]

No wonder that even Academician Strumilin, a most dedicated student of the Communist future in its most alluring aspects, brings up the matter of dominoes, though in a more tolerant manner (perhaps because he was discussing the future in a publication produced for readers abroad) :

> No one will object to a quiet game of cards or dominoes [in Communist society]. Nor will anyone interfere with a person who wastes his leisure, or kills time, as they say. Such a person, however, might meet with the censure of his comrades.[7]

If time-wasting citizens of the future need fear only the censure of comrades, in the present more authoritative and stern voices are raised. "Our society cannot reconcile itself to the fact that there are still people who fritter away their free time."[8]

The perception of a relationship between leisure and work is not, of course, peculiar to Soviet thinkers. But Communist spokesmen insist on so transforming the notion of leisure as to make it often unrecognizable to the Western eye. Participation in public life, in communal, political or quasi-political activities, volunteering for extra work, bringing up children, studying—these are some of the activities which, by current Soviet definitions, constitute leisure. It is not difficult to discern the connection between this highly functionalized view of leisure and a totalistic outlook on life that rejects compartmentalization and the separation between the private and public realms, between the purely pleasurable and the useful, between relaxation and work. In this conception every aspect of social life is seen as organically linked to others. Interdependence lurks everywhere.[9]

The emphasis on the special interdependence of work and leisure stems from the paramount importance attributed to work and from the claim that, in socialist society, it has acquired a uniquely satisfactory character owing to the absence of exploitation and alienation. It follows that leisure is also bound to be different than in societies where work is acknowledged by most to be only a necessary evil. For most people, the importance of leisure rises in proportion with the unattractiveness of work. The more tiresome, uninteresting and unsatisfying work is, the more stress there is on making good use of the precious and limited time away from work, on striving to find meaning in other spheres. Even Soviet authorities on leisure persist in attributing primacy to the role of work in man's life, not to leisure-time pursuits.

> Free time is necessary for the harmonious development of the individual. This, needless to say, is in no way to demean the importance of labor for the all-round development of the individual. *Labor,*

having created the individual, *always remains primary and definitive in his development*; the meaning and beauty of life lie in labor.[10]

It is the preoccupation with work, the current interest in leisure notwithstanding, that imposes in the final analysis not only practical, but theoretical-ideological, limitations on Soviet explorations of the leisure problem.

In official Soviet thought, as we shall see, the term leisure itself is infrequently and reluctantly used,[11] almost as if a frivolous connotation would attach to it. Soviet authors refer instead to "free time," of which leisure is considered only a small part. The following definitions illustrate the point:

Nonworking time (*vnerabochee vremia*) . . . [that which] is not directly absorbed by participation in socially productive activities. Nonworking time includes the routine activities of daily life and free time. The rational organization . . . of nonworking time is one of the most important objective indicators of harmonious personality development and hence a necessary element of social planning.

Free time (*svobodnoe vremia*) is the part of nonworking time which includes study . . . voluntary public activities, leisure, hobbies, creative activities, etc.

Leisure is one of the parts of free time connected with the restoration of psychic and physical energies of man.[12]

This utilitarian-instrumental approach to leisure and free time (which we shall use here interchangeably) is highlighted by a warning:

Free time does not amount to idleness . . . . This is the time devoted to study, the raising of [occupational] qualifications, self-education and self-development (attending lectures, cultural groups, museums, the reading of fiction, journals, newspapers, etc.) to sports, and hobbies (hunting, fishing, photography, etc.) to active rest and rational leisure (visiting places of entertainment, walks and excursions, traveling, open air festivals, creative disputes, and bringing up children, etc.) and also to participation in the life of society.[13]

Soviet social scientists believe that leisure is well spent only when it is "rationally" used, according to criteria that do not necessarily include the degree of personal satisfaction experienced.

If, in the time spent on studying, the worker does not learn anything useful and does not raise his qualifications, he spent his time in an irrational way. Time spent on domestic [parlor] games is rational if it is devoted to such interesting and elevating games as chess, riddles . . . crosswords, charades, and so forth. Time spent on entertaining or visiting is rational if it is devoted not to various gossip, scandal-mongering, and guzzling liquor, but to interesting conversation about the accomplishments of science and technology, about international and domestic political events, about the needs of production, to the exchange of experience about the upbringing of children, to the exchange of opinion about books read, films and plays seen, etc.[14]

The reduction in irrational expenditures of nonworking time also leaves the working people more time for relaxation and leisure . . . . Nowadays certain free time pursuits that in 1923–24 still accounted for a big share (religious services, games of chance, etc.) have virtually disappeared. At the same time a large role is now played by expenditures of free time that were insignificant or totally absent in the earlier period: participation in amateur groups, peoples' theaters, peoples' volunteer detachments for preserving public order, universities of culture, etc.[15]

Rationality in the use of free time is said to have four major components: (1) the recreational (it helps to restore energy for production and in general for useful social purposes); (2) that which contributes to the "all-round development" of the personality (that is, to the creation of the new Soviet man described in the 1961 Party Program as one "who will combine harmoniously spiritual wealth, moral purity, and perfect physique");* (3) activities which raise educational and professional qualifications: formal and informal study, reading; and (4) participation in communal-public affairs of direct or indirect political and economic relevance (e.g., volunteering for such communal projects as planting trees, improving housing, building cultural facilities or attending meetings, participating in the work of party or mass organizations and so forth).

A second official prescription for the use of leisure is that it should be organized: planned, collectivized, and integrated with other "socially useful activities." It is thought that the informal social controls inherent in the collective are more effective than those embodied in formal institutions, and that conformity can

---

* The current Soviet vision of the well-rounded man may have its intellectual ancestry not only in Marx's concern with the fully developed human being free of the fetters of private-property relations and specialization, but also in the Soviet preoccupation with *kul'turnost'*, or "cultured behavior," which makes sense only in the context of a population in large part still peasant. *Kul'turnost'* entails good manners, observance of elementary rules of hygiene and sanitation, politeness, respect for (if not actual possession of) knowledge, and cultural attainment.

therefore more readily be exacted through the collective. Collectivized leisure is seen as discouraging excessive individualism, reflection leading to doubt, and the development of tastes for privacy that might interfere with loyalties toward the collective. Well-spent leisure should also be politically relevant to some degree:

> The role and significance of nonworking time [which as noted before includes free time and leisure] and its utilization consists, above all, in that by means of its utilization the mental and physical development of workers can be guided by society in a socialist direction, in the spirit of the great principles of Communist morality, collectivism, love of work, patriotism, the love of humanity, and internationalism, respect for human dignity, manliness, etc. . . . Consequently the use of nonworking time becomes for society an exceptionally important channel for actively influencing the broad mass of workers.[16]

These official prescriptions then, must be understood as arising both from the totalitarian drive for control as well as from a desire to educate the population in a broad sense of the word, and to prevent the wasteful dissipation of energy and time—often seen as a trait of the Russian national character by non-Russian observers. The Soviet policies toward leisure, like the Soviet system as a whole (and many of its totalitarian characteristics), can be viewed as responses to backwardness and not merely as logical extensions of the desire to control.

III. How Soviet Leisure Is Spent

No matter how devoted a person is to volunteer community work, how enthusiastic about and occupied with studies he is, there must be a part of his leisure time devoted strictly to entertainment.

"How do you spend your leisure?"
Komsomolskaia Pravda

*   *   *

The Communist party and the Soviet government have provided all the conditions for optimal utilization of the free time of the workers.

G. S. PETROSIAN
Svobodnoe Vremia Trudiashchikhsia
v SSSR

The leisure of the Soviet citizen is molded by many conflicting pressures. On the one hand, the ideological and practical stress which the regime makes upon work implies that leisure is relatively unimportant, since labor makes man and only through labor can man make the most useful contribution to society and the collective. At the same time, leisure activities are in fact hindered by the persistence of poor living conditions, scarcity of consumer goods and household labor-saving devices, and the time-consuming nature of routine tasks such as shopping.[17] The low standard of living and the priorities of the economy are further reflected in the inadequacy of physical facilities for entertainment and recreation. As Soviet writers put it, demand continues to outstrip facilities for leisure-time activities, particularly in the countryside, smaller urban areas, and the new industrial settlements.

There is, on the other hand, an ever greater popular demand for leisure and for more varied activities with which to fill it. The very drabness and harshness of Soviet life cry out for relief. "Life itself" urges the Soviet citizen to find activities which help him to forget its many unpleasant realities: shortages, regimentation, overcrowding, and the measure of personal insecurity which persists even in relatively "mature" and noncoercive totalitarian societies. Even if Soviet citizens consider their work to be as exciting and fulfilling as the official publications tell us,[18] the quality of life outside the place of work is still something less than satisfactory. Housing is so crowded that even members of a nation observed to have a lesser sense of privacy than Westerners have inevitably get in one another's way. And if the home, in terms of privacy, comfort, and recreational facilities, leaves a great deal to be desired, public places of entertainment become all the more important and alluring. Soviet government policy, although incompletely implemented, aggravates the imbalance by its lavishness toward the public and tight-fistedness toward the private realm.[19]

At least half of the Soviet population now lives in a modern, urban, industrial society, a condition which in itself, regardless of the character of the polity, promotes and predisposes people to certain kinds of leisure-time activities. At the same time, the rural living conditions of nearly half the population inhibit many forms of recreation. The persistence of rural customs in such large segments of the population combines with other factors that challenge the privacy of leisure (i.e., government policy, housing, etc.). In peasant societies and among peasants, privacy is either totally unknown or is an incomprehensible value. The widely remarked Soviet preference for group activities probably derives as much from the surviving traditions of village life as from the official liking for collectivized leisure. The limited resource allocation for private telephones, automobiles, and household articles is also relevant here: all of these goods, services, and facilities, particularly the spacious, uncrowded home and the automobile, are essential ingredients of private leisure. It is particularly interesting to contrast the number of private telephones with that of television sets. There are approximately, and *at the most*, 3 million private phones in the Soviet Union, as opposed to 15 million television sets. The latter of course represent centralized, standardized, one-way communications from the regime to the population, so to speak, whereas private phones are the means of varied personal communications of little public or collective relevance. We should also note here that the recent planned increase of automobile production (from an annual 200,000 to a projected 800,000 by 1970) does not fundamentally alter the role of the car in Soviet leisure. What is apparently envisaged is not making the car accessible to the average citizen, or the "broad masses," but to provide an adequate supply for the elite groups. Certainly the leisure pattern of this minority will be altered by this increase of car production, provided that there will also be a corresponding growth in the number of service stations, repair shops, roadside restaurants, and rest areas, and, above all, good roads. Should such auxiliary facilities lag behind the production of cars, the latter is more likely to become a new source of time-consuming frustrations, than of enjoyment.

In examining the actual expenditure of free time by Soviet citizens, we have to ask how much leisure they have, what facilities are available, which activities seem to be most favored, how people would like to spend their leisure, and what kind of atmosphere (escapist, purely recreational, utilitarian) surrounds various leisure-time activities. Available information supplies only fragmentary answers to all these questions, and must be pieced together from incomplete Soviet statistics, time-budget studies, and the impressions of Western visitors.

Soviet students of leisure time frequently state, as does Petrosian, that the "steady growth of the absolute magnitude of nonwork time is a natural tendency of socialism," while the opposite tendency is characteristic of capitalist societies. According to Petrosian, the working time of Soviet industrial laborers decreased by slightly over an hour in an average day in the period of 1956–62.[20] His study of shifts in the structure of nonworking time between 1923–24 and 1958–61, based upon a tabulation of his own statistics alongside those of Academician Strumilin for the earlier period, shows, however, that while both nonworking time and free time have increased since the 1920s, quantitative increase of the nonworking time in particular did not in fact lead to very significant increases of free time, or what we should call leisure.[21] Petrosian himself observes that the expenditure of free time constitutes only 16.8 per cent of nonworking time, while domestic work and personal care consume 22.3 per cent of that free time. In addition, activities related to work, such as transportation to one's place of employment, or changing from one shift to another, account for an excessive amount of nonworking time; together with domestic work and personal care, work-related activities add up to twice the amount of free time.[22]

Predictably, differences in sex, income, occupation, and place of residence also affect the use of nonworking time. Soviet literature emphasizes in particular the uneven regional availability of facilities. As Petrosian writes:

> The basic reasons for irrationality in the actual use of free time by the workers are still the inadequate provisions of a series of cities with necessary conditions of life—housing, communal, sanitary-medical, commercial, cultural, transport and other kinds of services, and those of children's and pre-school establishments, enterprises for communal nourishment, places of entertainment, and so on—and also insufficiencies in the work of cultural-everyday organizations.[23]

Less is said about variations due to differential income and occupation; even when statistical data are provided, they reveal little about high-income and elite groups. Petrosian's tabulations, for example, include as a final category people earning over one hundred rubles per member of family per month, a classification which obviously fails to reflect income in the upper brackets and the attendant differences in availability and quality of both nonworking and free time. Time-budget studies are usually made in factories and therefore do not include data on highly placed scientists, artists, and government officials. A recent investigation does, however, concern itself with the nonworking time of engineering and technical personnel, urging that it be used to raise professional qualifications, develop an ideological-political and cultural outlook, and encourage participation in the Communist upbringing of the workers.[24]

Although Soviet leisure probably reflects income differentials to a lesser degree than does leisure in pluralistic industrial societies, there are indications that the social stratification of Soviet society finds some expression in recreation. Members of the elite groups tend to be concentrated in the three major cities, Moscow, Leningrad, and Kiev, which possess superior cultural facilities. Furthermore, to the extent that functional importance is reflected in greater remuneration, higher income gives some groups access to certain opportunities not available to the masses: country houses (*dachas*), automobiles, better resorts, trips abroad, expensive restaurants, larger apartments which allow entertainment at home more frequently and on a grander scale,[25] and the cultivation, in general, of more costly tastes. Foreign visitors have often noted these privileges of the Soviet elite, and some have gone as far as to speak of the rise of a new leisure class.[26] It is also true, however, that for elite individuals time for recreation is a problem, since they are more involved with their occupations and greater demands are made upon them. This is, in particular, the case for urban intelligentsia.[27] Such a situation is, of course, not peculiar to Soviet society, and is in fact also observed in American and European societies among people who derive much satisfaction from their work.

The widest gulf between different patterns of recreation is between the rural and urban populations as a whole. Collective farm peasants appear to be the single most disadvantaged group in terms of leisure—if not in the absolute amount of time available, at least in opportunities for its use. The problems of recreation in the countryside are, once more, not peculiarly Soviet, but universal characteristics of economic underdevelopment or backwardness. The present rural, and to some extent even the urban, leisure situation is the product of an uneven modernization which has undermined traditional forms of peasant recreation, yet not far enough to provide substitutes found in the major cities.

This incomplete modernization probably accounts for the sense of cultural confusion and disorientation, and nostalgia for the old rural ways, which may be observed in journalistic and sociological Soviet writings on leisure. Petrosian and the authors of the *kolkhoz* study strongly recommend the maintenance and enrichment of "well-organized," nonreligious, traditional holidays in the countryside, departing for this purpose from their otherwise strict criteria of rationality. In the cities, the vacuum left by the desertion of age-old recreational and ceremonial customs has occasioned such debates as one in *Literaturnaia Gazeta on* "folkways and artificial 'traditions' ":

> Introduce them? How? Issue a decree? Require each person to sign a pledge, signatures to be collected by the apartment house superintendents? Establish control by the volunteer patrol detachments? . . . Only those customs, ceremonies, and rituals that meet the life of the people and are entirely separate from artificial contriving, become genuine popular traditions.[28]

In a much more extreme commentary, a highly controversial article in *Literaturnaia Gazeta* describes the folk past with longing and advocates a return to it as a response to modernization:

> Annual agricultural fairs used to be held in Russia. A host of articles of folk handicrafts were brought, wonderful folk songs resounded, folk games were played, folk dances flowed in bright colors. Perhaps we should revive the tradition of these fairs. The birch tree festival was held for the first time this year . . . a boring introductory talk, a crowd around the buffet, discordant singing of "Moscow Nights." We should give thought to ceremonial rites for this occasion. Why should the young men and women not dress up in national costume? Why should the girls not adorn themselves with wreaths? Mass dances, mass folk games. . . . No one knows them? Has everyone forgotten them? We can remember and learn them. . . . The people are the creators and guardians of folk art, and not simply radio listeners and television spectators."[29]

Another striking discrepancy in the use of free time exists between men and women in all sections of the population. Women, while devoting fully as much time to work as the men do, continue to carry their traditionally unequal share of responsibility for the domestic labor which must be done in nonworking time. The Soviet woman must spend an amount of time on daily household tasks which her Western contemporaries might perhaps comprehend only with reference to memories of the workload of their grandmothers:

> Women in Novosibirsk wash, mend, darn, and iron in the evenings and on Sundays . . . many women also spend their free time in papering walls, whitewashing and painting. . . . How much time does a woman in Novosibirsk work each day after she has put in a normal working day on the job? Two hours are spent standing in lines, two more hours in preparing supper, breakfast, and dinner (in order to be on time for work in the morning, breakfast and dinner are cooked the evening before), an hour in cleaning the apartment and another hour in washing, ironing, and other work. Almost a

whole "overtime" work day! Is this normal? . . . It is necessary to
spend an hour and a half to two hours in the stores after work
everyday just to purchase groceries for the next day. . . . In order
to dine at any dining room in Novosibirsk, it is necessary to stand in
line for two hours.[30]

While the situation in Novosibirsk is possibly somewhat less
"normal" than that in the large and long-established cities, women
everywhere in the Soviet Union seem to carry the considerable
burden of arduous household tasks in addition to full-time employment outside the home. Nearly all time-budget studies urge
Soviet men to help their wives in this respect, and many also
note that the attitudes of men toward domestic work have only
moderately improved since the 1920s. The problem appears to be
more significantly alleviated by the presence in many homes of
persons known in the time-budget studies as "assisting" relatives,
usually grandmothers who can take over from working mothers
such chores as cooking, shopping, and baby-sitting. But it is not
surprising that Petrosian recommends, in order to increase free
time, the reduction of time spent upon the upbringing of children
through the establishment of more boarding schools, children's
clubs, and Pioneer Palaces.

Petrosian's data, drawn from investigations conducted among
industrial workers in six cities (Erevan, Novokuznetsk, Kostroma,
Sverdlovsk, Krasnoyarsk, and Norilsk) illustrate the ways in which
popular preferences continue to outweigh official ones.[31] It is particularly interesting to compare the 3.5 hours per month spent on
"social work" (a term referring to community work, participation
in public organizations, and voluntary quasi-political activities)
with the 33.5 hours spent on "entertainment." A limited preference for the diversions offered by the mass media is also reflected
in the relatively small amount of time devoted to radio and television (6 hours per month) as against frequenting places of entertainment (9.5 hours), and visiting or receiving friends (8 hours).
Another notable fact is that only 2 hours per month are occupied
by sports. Since it is the policy of the authorities to provide sports
facilities and to encourage their use, the low level of participation
cannot be entirely attributed to a lack of facilities. It may be that
the Soviet citizens surveyed still find that their work and domestic
chores leave little surplus energy for other physical activities. A
further explanation may be found in the peasant origins of many
of the respondents, and to the perfectly understandable rural
disdain for unnecessary physical exertion. (The hostility to sports

is, in any case, deplored by Soviet experts on leisure time. The author of one collective farm study castigates such attitudes as a manifestation of *nekul'turnost'*.) In the category of "self-education," a significant discrepancy appears between predisposition to reading (14 hours per month) and attendance at lectures, seminars, and study circles (2 hours). A recent article in *Kommunist* notes the vast contrast between substantial civic participation at the worker's place of employment and little at his place of residence.[32] Such evidence reflects a preference for more private, informal, noninstitutional, and apolitical use of free time.

The tension between official and popular desires is also evident in the work of Soviet social scientists in this area. The attitude of the authorities is expressed by Petrosian:

> Particularly unsatisfactorily organized in some enterprises is mass cultural work—collective attendance at theaters, moving pictures, museums, evenings of rest, touring trips, country excursions and picnics, meetings with well-known people, and so on; public organizations are little interested in the life and daily existence of the workers, and insufficiently influence actively the use of nonworking time. Therefore, as a rule, workers at these enterprises use their nonworking and especially their free time less rationally. The raising of the general level of the work of party, Komsomol, and labor union organizations is an essential reserve of the further rationalization of the use of nonworking time of the workers.[33]

But while this analysis refers only to the low level of rationality in the use of free time among industrial workers, the level is lower still on the collective farms. A recent investigator reports with regret, "the *kolkhozniki* prefer in their free time to sit at home in warm apartments, in a circle of friends or acquaintances over a cup of tea, or, for that matter, over a glass of vodka." It must be added that sitting at home is not regarded as irrational *per se*, but only in light of the further finding that "because of the insufficient penetration among rural workers of such games as the solution of chess and checker problems, crosswords and rebuses, table tennis and billiards, particular success is enjoyed by lotto, dominoes, and cards, which give nothing to the mind or heart."[34]

Both the remarks of Soviet commentators and the impressions of Western travelers are agreed upon the extraordinary importance of reading, by far one of the most favored uses of leisure. Already in the early 1930s, Klaus Mehnert in *Youth in Soviet Russia* described the unforgettable picture offered by a walk down the express train during a long journey through Siberia:

The Germans, American, and Frenchmen traveling first and second class were whiling away the time with a story-magazine, an Edgar Wallace thriller, or a yellow-backed novel; but the Russians in their "wooden class" were reading technical manuals and textbooks of political economy, records of party congresses, agitation pamphlets, works on agricultural science. The entire country seemed to be a vast school.[35]

More recent visitors have had similar impressions: Soviet citizens reading while walking, crossing the street, or standing in an elevator; the waitress, taxi driver, and cloak room attendant perusing serious literature while waiting for customers. One account suggests that, although the origins of the Russians' compulsive love of reading are to be found deep in the prerevolutionary past,

> the avidity with which they read has some practical motivations. Some said that they would probably read less if they had a greater variety of entertainment or some other escape from the cares of their daily lives. For others the reading of certain books and magazines was a means of advancing their careers. And still for others reading was a symbol of having achieved a higher station in life.[36]

Several additional reasons may be proposed to explain the extraordinary popularity of reading. One is undoubtedly the policy of encouragement by the regime. Reading is officially promoted as a highly respectable activity, a most desirable means of acquiring knowledge and proper ideological attitudes, and an indispensable instrument of the "all-round development of the personality." The relative novelty of literacy may be another explanation. We may also suspect that reading is favored because it provides an irreproachably legitimate escape from the unpleasant realities of life, and because it can be highly apolitical. The particular popularity of nonpolitical books (technical, classical, and foreign literature) suggests such an explanation. A *kolkhoz* survey, for example, reports that Russian classics are especially loved among the older generation of collective farmers.[37] And the current vogue of detective, science fiction, and adventure stories, attested to by the press, underscores the escapist quality of some Soviet reading.[38]

Facilities and opportunities, and their limitations, determine to a great degree not only what Soviet citizens actually do with their leisure, but also their aspirations. It would be idle and pointless for most of them to crave such diversions of Western affluence as motor boating, a summer home in a scenic part of the country, or Sunday family automobile rides.[39] The facilities available to the masses of the people predispose them toward some form of public, although not necessarily collectivized, entertainment, or toward such leisure-time activities as can be accomplished in the home. The established city dweller can enjoy nature by walking in municipal parks, which are extremely important for the recreation of the average Soviet urban citizen. Whether they are lavishly equipped "parks of culture and rest" (where there is planned entertainment) as in Moscow and other large cities, or merely places to walk and sit in the fresh air, parks represent an inexpensive, or entirely free, publicly provided opportunity for the use of leisure in an at least partially private way. The popularity of parks also results from the overcrowding of apartments and of indoor recreational establishments.

Reading, going to parks, and excursions are not the only forms of recreation in which official policies and private wishes converge. Evening schools, "peoples' universities," and correspondence courses are also welcome opportunities for the citizen to take advantage of facilities provided by the state. In this case, the harmony between personal and social interests is very close, since the raising of educational levels or occupational qualifications is an obvious gain for both parties. The inclusion of such activities in leisure time may, however, strike the Western observer as odd, since they are quite unrelated to his conceptions of recreation, in which the "fun" or "play" element is prominent. Soviet writers leave little doubt as to the utilitarian and functional assumptions underlying official encouragement of part-time educational institutions:

> It goes without saying that, studying in a correspondence or evening educational institution, the individual subjects himself to an established regime and its demands, fulfills definite obligations. To bourgeois sociologists, who understand free time as inactivity and idleness, it seems that this is suppression of the personality by society, dissolution of the individual in the mass. But in the Soviet Union and other socialist countries, contrary to the world of capitalism, the necessity of subjection of personal aspirations to the interests of society does not prevail over the individual as damnable, but appears as a conscious necessity, as the unity of personal and social interests. The individual consciously, by his own will and desire, gives part of his free time to study, to self-education, to that which facilitates the raising of his cultural-technical level, which polishes his professional qualities. The socialist government creates all the conditions for this, and in all ways encourages the aspiration to knowledge and culture. This indeed is one of the phenomena of freedom of personality and society.[40]

The functionalization of leisure, from the standpoint of official wishes, is occasionally encountered in the most unexpected areas. The recent movement to legitimize and institutionalize hitchhiking, apart from its obvious wisdom in a country in which the system of transportation is overloaded and private transportation extremely limited, had to be justified in the following manner:

> Suppose a hitch-hiker belongs to an aesthetic study circle. . . . Hitch-hiking would give him the opportunity to stop off in collective farms along the way and give lectures to the villagers. If he plays an instrument he may give a concert. If he has a special talent he might give a hand in farm work.[41]

IV. Leisure as a Social Problem

Workers sometimes do not know how to use their free time. It is therefore necessary for the leaders of the relevant social organization [to concern themselves with] the most rational utilization of the workers' free time.

> G. S. Petrosian
> *Vnerabochee Vremia Trudiashchikhsia v SSSR*

*   *   *

The reduction of the working day has found many people unprepared. . . .

> *Kazakhstanskaia Pravda,* translated in
> *Current Digest of the Soviet Press*

It is difficult to assess how serious a social problem leisure has become in the Soviet Union. If Soviet publications were to serve as the only source of information, one would have to conclude that it is a serious problem indeed. The last few years have seen a surprising proliferation of complaints, warnings, exhortations, and exposés of a multitude of problems and deficiencies connected with the utilization of free time. Yet some caution is in order when evaluating these manifestations of concern. The misuse of free time belongs to those defects of social organization to which Soviet policy-makers and ideologues are extremely sensitive. We have already seen how they regard free time as a politically and economically significant resource. At the same time, problems of leisure are comparatively pleasant ones, particularly since their ultimate basis is an abundance rather than scarcity.

Leisure problems are most characteristic—at least on a large or mass scale—of modern societies. (The privileged or leisured classes of the past always had leisure problems which were not seen as particularly troublesome partly because the number of people so afflicted was relatively small, partly because they devised elaborate, if not truly satisfactory, ways to chase boredom away; the latter activities became institutionalized and assumed the character of a life-style that was "naturally" associated with the life of the privileged.) They have two essential sources. One is at least a measure of abundance and ease which allows the reduction of time spent on providing for the necessities of life. The other is the breakdown of traditional values, cultural forms, guides to everyday living. Modern societies, among other things, differ most fundamentally from traditional ones in that societal value prescriptions and customs cease to be self-evident, that more choices have to be made by the individual than in the past. Occupying oneself during his free time is one of these areas of choice. To this extent the problems of leisure are common to pluralistic as well as totalitarian industrial societies, and the problematic aspects of Soviet leisure are indeed quite similar to those found in other industrial or industrializing societies. While there may still be sectors or strata of Soviet society where the problem is the lack of sufficient amount of leisure, the concern voiced by Soviet publications invariably centers on the issue: How should it be spent? Why is it not spent in the right way? What are the right ways to spend it?

To the extent that in every modern society the young, and particularly adolescents, have more leisure than the adults, it is to be expected that the leisure problem of Soviet society (as reflected in Soviet publications) is primarily a leisure problem of the young. However, other considerations are also relevant for understanding the official concern with the leisure of the young. As noted earlier, in the era of the construction of communism the proper ideological upbringing of the future generations of that society is of exceptional importance. As Soviet authors frequently point out, the molding of the new Communist man takes place in his free time as well as at work (especially when his free time assumes more significant proportions). We have already noted that the shift from policies of coercion to policies of persuasion elevated leisure to a new place of prominence in the realm of attitude formation and influence. The rebellious, deviant, and anomic tendencies observable among many Soviet youth lend further significance to the official interest in the use and guidance of their leisure. For all these reasons, we find most of the social problems of leisure among the young, who are unaccustomed to Stalinist coercion, impatient with regimentation, and eager to translate into reality the promises and prospects of a full and rich life which their parents viewed with perhaps a greater measure of disbelief.[42]

Characteristically, the problem is conceived of primarily as one of facilities, resources, and proper guidance—as a practical rather than philosophical matter. The problem of facilities is particularly serious in rural areas and is said to contribute to the departure of the young from the villages: "Young people do not leave the village in search of the 'almighty ruble'. . . . They leave for greater culture in their work, leisure occupation, and life in general."[43] Problems of satisfactory rural leisure are also well illustrated in the debate published by *Literaturnaia Gazeta*. Once more, the question was: What's wrong with the cultural life and leisure of the villages and how can it be remedied? At least one participant suggested that material-technical means alone will not make the spiritual life of the villagers more meaningful:

> Yes, the radio and TV are powerful instruments of culture. But instruments; and an instrument is good only in skilled and experienced hands. . . . When spiritual organization is richly developed, TV and radio are priceless aides. Otherwise, they are substitutes. They help chiefly to speed time, to pass time unnoticeably.[44]

The problem in the countryside may also be related to the novelty of the idea of time for pleasurable pursuits (unrelated to felt needs for recreation):

> The reasonable use of leave is a guarantee of the health of the rural worker. . . . The majority of those who receive leave do not always use it correctly. Most often, the free time of the *kolhoznik*, in the summer period, is spent on domestic work: building . . . repair of homes, preparation of fuel for the winter, pickling and preservation of vegetables, fruits . . . of jam and so on. Many *kolhozniks* have no understanding of what it means to spend one's leave somewhere away, and some of them in their entire life have never left the borders of their villages.[45]

Even when facilities are available, they may not be used to capacity. Existing recreational programs are often poorly organized, those in charge of them untrained, and sometimes such attractions are commercialized (i.e., people are charged admission).[46]

The close interdependence of leisure with the mass media and other organized forms of entertainment raises the question of how satisfactory the latter are. Time and again the recurring theme in Soviet discussion of the various media of entertainment is that of dullness. It appears that the organizers and producers of Soviet films, plays, TV, radio, and club programs are beginning to be haunted by the revolt against dullness by Soviet audiences, and by the young in particular. In the Aesopian language of the officials: "Young people expect from writers, artists, and composers, from the theater and the screen, works which will vividly show our heroic times and will create an image of a contemporary world worthy of emulation."[47]

From the point of view of the authorities, the dilemma has become how to provide the population with "interesting" and stimulating leisure-time activities and facilities while at the same time preserving their didactic, educational functions. How "to give the masses what they want" but avoid the degeneration of Soviet mass media and entertainment into a Western-style "mass culture" with only a thin topping of unconvincing ideological frosting? Or how to stem the tide of popular alienation from the mass media too heavily permeated with edifying contents? Clearly, the present is a period of experimentation, of efforts to find an ideologically acceptable balance between the leisure-time facilities that the builder of communism ought to have and those he wants to have.

The problems and difficulties of Soviet young people often bear an astonishing similarity to the leisure problems of youth in other lands. A study of 1,000 secondary students in Smolensk revealed a number of familiar deficiencies.[48] "The teenagers' weekdays and Sundays were taken up mainly by passive activities: reading, watching television, listening to the radio, etc. Activities requiring active intellectual output . . . were in 10th to 20th place." Only 3 per cent of those polled expressed a desire to engage in public activities. For this in part, the parents were to blame: "In some families, the children are pushed, consciously or unconsciously toward this kind of apoliticism through ironical or skeptical comments about public work." The article notes that "most alarming is the admission by almost half of the youngsters that they do not know what to do in their free time." It concludes with a strong hint at the relationship between the bad use of free time and juvenile delinquency. The connection between boredom, escapism and undesirable uses of free time among the young were also brought out in a recent exchange between the editors of *Izvestiia*, and an anonymous 17-year old who complained about the "main enemy, boredom."[49]

The most visible expression of the leisure problem in Soviet society—besides juvenile delinquency and minor acts of hooliganism—is drunkenness. Drunkenness is certainly no novel phenomenon in Russian society, and people who wanted to get drunk somehow found time for it well before the expansion of leisure time. But its spread to the younger age groups may be new, and reflects both their confusion as to what to make of the new leisure and their greater purchasing power. What is undoubtedly new is the enormous concern of the authorities with the phenomenon and their tendency to relate it to increased leisure.[50]

Thus, among the social problems associated with leisure in contemporary industrial societies, several apply to the Soviet Union, though some only in an incipient form. They may be summarized as follows: In relation to the growing popular expectations, there is a shortage of facilities which is most keenly felt by the young and in the provinces. Among many strata of the population, increased free time has been met with a degree of puzzlement and ignorance as to what should be done with it. Among urban youth, escapist tendencies have been noted (more will be said of this later), but the desire to evade the politicization of free time is not limited to the young and finds expression in the strongly voiced desire for "interesting," diverting entertainment. In the countryside, the erosion of traditional forms of recreation inherent in industrialization creates additional problems as long as their replacement by modern, urban amenities is lacking.

There is every reason to suppose that such problems will magnify in proportion with the rise in the standard of living and with any decline in the effectiveness of regimentation and external pressures.

V. Leisure as a Political Problem

It was decided to counter the Charleston with something offering real beauty and grace. Twelve young men from various enterprises of the city and from various cultural institutions were sent to Alma-Ata with the mission of learning attractive modern dances and teaching them to everyone else. In the past, the Young Communist League had sent out its finest to liquidate illiteracy. Now they were being sent out to teach dancing, to liquidate esthetic illiteracy. In this small detail there is a remarkable logical pattern of development.

> *Komsomolskaia Pravda*, translated in *Current Digest of the Soviet Press*

*   *   *

In science fiction novels, Martians perish upon meeting earthlings because their bodies are not accustomed to combating the microbes to which mankind has already developed immunity. Does not the same hold true in ideology? The man of the future cannot be raised in a bell-jar; it is necessary to foster in him an immunity to all kinds of pernicious microbes. . . .

> *Izvestiia*, translated in *Current Digest of the Soviet Press*

The trend toward Westernization of Soviet leisure raises significant issues. Leisure and its cultural implications represent an area where convergence is least chimerical. Moreover, the diffusion of models of leisure and styles of life from one culture to another is of intrinsic sociological interest. The attention Soviet ideologues give to the problem indicates that it is considered an important one in Soviet society. The Westernization of leisure poses a dilemma for the guardians of Soviet values.

One aspect of the problem is purely quantitative. In this sense "Western" leisure means more leisure and more leisure-oriented consumption. A second aspect is technological: certain forms of leisure, particularly those which make use of the mass media, presuppose a degree of modernization. Finally, we are faced with the questions: To whom do Western models of leisure appeal in Soviet society? Who rejects them, and on what grounds?

As far as the Soviet public and the young in particular are concerned, interest in Western forms of leisure is part of the ambivalent, yet voracious interest in the material and cultural products of the Western pattern in general and Western styles and dimensions of consumption in particular. Western leisure is not only associated with greater material abundance and comforts, but is seen by many as more exciting, more dynamic, and more typically contemporary or "modern." The Soviet reverence for classical literature, music, and high culture notwithstanding, there are many indications that the Soviet public is far from invulnerable to the appeals of Western mass or popular culture, including its vulgar, sensational, and escapist elements.

Such propensities in the population are unwelcome to Soviet ideologues and policy-makers. Borrowing from the West in the realm of leisure is undesirable because it implies the imitation of *values* as well as techniques. Many of the values and attitudes associated with leisure in the West suggest a devaluation of, or indifference to, labor. There is, furthermore, a somewhat subversive and unpatriotic connotation in borrowing forms of entertainment and recreation from abroad, for it implies a *nontechnological* backwardness which Soviet leaders are loath to admit. (It is a different matter with respect to technology, where backwardness as well as the need to import techniques are more readily acknowledged.) Indigenous Soviet forms of recreation are a matter of pride and tantamount to a minor patriotic duty. The unfavorable official attitude toward Western forms and values of leisure is also reflected in the Soviet view that models of behavior and life styles disseminated by Western mass media lie behind antisocial attitudes among the young and are a cause of hooliganism and juvenile delinquency.

Soviet criticism of Western forms of leisure, and even of Western studies of leisure, offers additional proof of ideological relevance and sensitivity and illustrates the familiar phenomenon of projecting upon the West or "capitalist societies," tendencies in fact characteristic of the Soviet Union:

> From its very inception, bourgeois ideology strove to influence the working masses both at work and in their free time.
> . . . the bourgeois conception of free time has an extremely pragmatic, applied and utilitarian character.
> Most of the research on free time in capitalist countries is financed by the bourgeois governments which also control its use.
> By studying the use workers make of their free time bourgeois sociologists are trying to find out about the most effective measures to serve the needs of the industrial enterprise.
> In those bourgeois countries where the means of dissemination of culture is in the hands of the government, they are used by the ruling classes primarily to indoctrinate the population for the support of the capitalist social order.[51]

Western leisure and mass media have become in Soviet eyes a new, secular opiate of the more subtly exploited and disoriented masses; it is fundamentally escapist, wasteful, and lacking in serious purpose. It often entails entertainment that appeals to the most vulgar aspects of a human nature distorted by class society, particularly by means of its stress on excitement generated by dehumanized sex and physical violence. Even a moderately perceptive observer of Western society must agree with many of these criticisms.

But the undesirable use of leisure, including waste and escapism, is not a singular affliction of Western societies. It is, rather, a product of more general trends and processes, such as the improvement of material conditions of life and secularization. As we have already seen, Soviet leisure is beginning, on a small scale, to show the results of these processes. Escapism in the Western sense is, to be sure, not yet a major issue. Escapist tendencies in Soviet leisure are of a more primitive kind: they originate in the desire to escape and forget about the harshness and drabness of life, rather than from the pressure of questions and quests which arise after material wants and environmental harshness have been conquered. The "spiritual maladies—ennui, restlessness, spleen, and general world-weariness—which afflict and always afflicted the leisured classes"[52] are still a long way from afflicting the Soviet masses. But we can already see that they are not invulnerable to them. Huxley's ironic comments on the optimists of his day, such as G. B. Shaw and H. G. Wells, who believed that the "leisured masses of the future . . . will do all the things which our leisured classes of the present so conspicuously fail to do,"[53] invite application to similarly unrealistic Soviet predictions.

It would, however, be unfair either to criticize present-day Soviet thinkers for their unrestrained optimism, once rampant among illustrious Western thinkers as well, or to credit them with unique efforts to uplift and ennoble leisure. Their concerns and attitudes hark back to times when the modernizing rulers of Russia had no time-budget studies or mass media at their disposal, yet took a lively interest in the leisure-time activities of some of their subjects. It is another matter, and perhaps another aspect of historical continuity, that in doing so they modified the concept of leisure itself. Thus, in the early eighteenth century, Peter the Great energetically attempted to introduce European *kul'turnost'* into the free time of the Petersburg and Moscow aristocracy:

> All the dancing partners were obliged to perform the steps in exactly the same way as did the sovereign, and incidentally, he turned out to be a great and ingenious master of this subject. [A contemporary foreign observer writes:] . . . "The Tsar with his characteristic persistence undertook to teach the dancers, and told them to learn the dances quickly. No matter how he struggled, however, things did

not get on well: the pupils barely kept on their feet, but the Tsar hopped and twirled before them tirelessly."[54]

Despite its typically Soviet features, the citizen's leisure represents a way of relating to the world outside. It is an area in which convergence of the American and Soviet systems could take place with the least difficulty, and in which it has indeed already made some progress. We may venture the generalization that a society whose citizenry enjoys a great deal of leisure can be manipulated only with difficulty for aggressive political moves, domestic or international. People immersed in leisure may become "soft" in a not altogether undesirable sense of the word. They may resist, to some degree, mobilization for distant and external goals that threaten to reverse gains made in the realm of leisure and consumption. And there is, of course, a clear association among high levels of consumption, comfort, and abundant leisure. We are not suggesting here that such generalizations are as yet applicable to the Soviet Union. But at least a minor move has been made toward a limited "revolution" of rising expectations in the field of leisure.

The further Westernization of Soviet leisure by the penetration of Western models is most likely. Nor should it be surprising that the more affluent and consumption-oriented societies are the models, for it is there that people have most leisure and the most varied means for its use. The extent to which this Western penetration continues depends upon the regime's future definitions of what constitute harmlessly apolitical forms of recreation. More important than any specific activity, fashion, or fad that might be borrowed from the West would be the transplantation of the idea that leisure is above all a private and personal affair; or, that the choices with regard to its use should be left to the judgment of the citizen. Should Soviet citizens come to think of leisure as an ultimate value, and thus to reject its functional and collectivized connotations, the entire official value system would be brought into question.

This is what Soviet spokesmen have in mind when they complain of the "pernicious microbes" transmitted by the Western mass media and forms of entertainment.[55] Even if many of the Western mass media are free of the deliberate ideological content attributed to them, they do have long-range, "subversive" potential. Although the Soviet leadership wishes to immunize the population against these "microbes," there is a growing recognition that immunization cannot take place without exposure; "the man of the future cannot be raised in a bell-jar." And exposure cannot proceed without a more permissive attitude toward the penetration of Western models and styles of leisure.

If the Soviet citizen is to have more leisure and more freedom of opportunity for its use, he will probably have to pay a price in the form of discoveries or rediscoveries of the absurdities of human existence. He will have to face new questions and new insecurities. The new problem of Soviet leisure will arise in proportion with the improvements in the standard of living and the decline of regimentation. They will be more complicated but in a sense more desirable problems than those generated by Soviet life and leisure today. Difficult as they may be for the Soviet citizen, the emergence of such issues will signify his emancipation from the burden of material needs and the harshness of the social environment. The new problems of leisure will point to the further humanization of Soviet society.

16.

The Intellectuals

JAMES H. BILLINGTON

The classic problem of how ideas influence human events involves both soaring questions of philosophic belief and exacting subjects for sociological analysis. Since one cannot assume any common framework of belief in pluralistic America or amass any very adequate body of data from authoritarian Russia, no discussion of this problem is likely to provide satisfactory, let alone definitive, answers.

A cultural historian called on by social scientists to discuss how intellectual forces may affect the over-all development of Soviet society should perhaps record at the outset both a general note of skepticism about man's ability to "factor," even in retrospect, ideas into measurable vectors of force with predictable consequences, and a sense that cultural tradition has continued to influence Soviet development in important if often elusive ways.[1] His contribution to a comprehensive appraisal of over-all Russian prospects might well begin with three elements of historical background: (1) critical self-examination of the American approach to the study of Soviet cultural ferment; (2) general consideration of the past relationship between cultural ferment and broader social change in Russian history; and (3) special examination of the problems created during the last century by the emergence in Russia of the world's first self-proclaimed, alienated "intelligentsia" in an unevenly modernizing society.

I. PERSPECTIVES AND ANTECEDENTS

The profusion of "cultural Kremlinology" in the West during the last decade has focused considerable attention on the *fact* of ferment in the U.S.S.R., without providing any clear sense of its *meaning* for Soviet development as a whole. Extra-intellectual forces have entered into the American appreciation of this phenomenon, and among many oscillations in perspective may be detected a tendency to undervalue recently what may have been overvalued earlier.

Self-scrutiny of our own peculiar relationship to the phenomenon of Soviet cultural ferment reveals first of all our continuing ignorance. We still cannot distinguish with confidence that which is unknowable from that which we may simply not yet have found out from available but unexamined material. American interest in the subject, moreover, has not kept pace with the rapidly expanding volume of creative and critical writing that is being published; and distressingly little precise study has been made of the concrete workings and structural changes taking place within the various institutions that provide ideological guidance and practical supervision to all cultural activities in the U.S.S.R.[2] With cultural even more than with political Kremlinology, one is entitled to complain, not that it is an improper discipline, but that it remains even more imprecise than it need be.

A second characteristic of our relationship to Soviet culture is our general tendency to project many of our own special problems and preoccupations into our appraisal of foreign phenomena. Our original overvaluation of Soviet cultural ferment was itself born in part of a desire to compensate for undervaluing the significance of intellectual ferment in Eastern Europe prior to the tumultuous events of 1956. The initial infatuation with Russia's restless youth subtly helped, moreover, to relieve our own ideological boredom in the late 1950s, and corresponded with the resuscitation of youthful idealism in the Kennedy era—just as our present mood of skepticism corresponds in many ways to the pragmatic temper of the Johnson era (and perhaps also to the steady growth in prestige of the social sciences at the expense of the humanities in our increasingly technocratic society). Our new skepticism about Soviet cultural ferment seems, however, to have greater self-sustaining possibilities than the previous enthusiasm not only because enthusiasm is always evanescent, but also because we inevitably tend to judge the relative significance of their American counterparts. It has been difficult for us as a nation to believe that poets and professors—as distinct from producers and politicians—really matter in the dynamics of American (and, by extension, any nation's) development.

A third characteristic of the American study of contemporary Russian culture which tends to distract from questions of broader significance results from the dynamics of American academic life. The creation of a new caste of specialists in Soviet literature has spawned a semiprecious literature of internal shop talk that often concentrates on derivative gossip or the assignment of literary merit badges and good conduct medals to half-understood writers, rather than on reading ever more deeply into the literature itself— let alone on relating literary phenomena to broader questions of social development.

One wonders if America must acquire its own alienated intelligentsia and poets of revolution in order to be able fully to appreciate the importance of these phenomena in other lands; and if American academia will bring humanistic imagination as well as social scientific technique to bear on the study of the many unfamiliar cultures now on our intellectual agenda. In the Russian case, however, the continuing fascination with the cultural scene among intelligent observers from many different disciplines pays testimony to an instinctive feeling that cultural ferment in the U.S.S.R. may be a phenomenon of unique, if only dimly perceivable, importance for the future—perhaps not only of the U.S.S.R., but of an ever more interrelated humanity as well.

Any estimate of significance for the future, particularly in the Russian case, requires the perspective of the past. The history of Russian culture illustrates the political nature of culture in the Christian East and a tendency for periods of cultural ferment to coincide with political and social unrest. Taking over from Byzantium a tradition of turning political disputes into ideological polemics (in which it was always assumed there could be but one true answer), the Russians long persisted in the belief that the role of culture was to preserve and beautify the inherited forms of "correct praising" (the literal meaning of *pravoslavie*, Orthodox) while awaiting the coming end of history. Disputes over ritualistic and genealogical details and iconographic priorities became the major form for expressing complex political and economic controversies during the Kievan and appanage period of Russian history. The position of a local prince in a chronicle or of a local saint on an icon screen became matters of critical *political* importance—as they tended to become again with the return to a secularized form of Muscovite ritual in the Stalin era.

The consolidation of autocratic power and centralized control under Ivan III and Ivan IV, as later under Stalin, involved an almost schizoid process of extensive *technological borrowing* from the West and simultaneously intensified *ideological isolation* from it (including persecution of "cosmopolitan" Jews and repopulation of the westward-oriented Baltic provinces). The agony of the "Time of Troubles" which followed this early period of expansion produced a crisis within a powerful but primitive Moscow psychologically unable to accept the logic of a Western-style modernization implied in the educational and reform programs of Boris Godunov, the False Dimitry, and Vasily Shuisky alike.

Russia not only failed to produce a single secular book of any significance or originality during the first century of rule by the Romanov dynasty (which emerged after 1613 at the end of the Time of Troubles), but found its society convulsed and its church split open during the seventeenth century—in part over the very issue of whether to have such books. Like printing, higher education came late and traumatically to Russia. The young American colonies had four universities before ancient Russia acquired its first, at Moscow in 1755; and not until the beginning of the nineteenth century did it acquire a second and begin systematic advanced teaching in the Russian language. At that time, Russia suddenly found itself a great world power hailed as the deliverer from Napoleon and licensed to extend dominion over culturally more advanced regions (Poland, Finland and parts of the Balkans and the Caucasus)—yet profoundly uncertain of its own basic beliefs and identity. The reign of Alexander I was a period of intellectual and spiritual disorientation which saw the florid development of Russian Freemasonry, sectarianism, and pietism further split and dilute Russian Orthodoxy, while political agitation (of which the Decembrist movement was only one expression) testified to a new kind of alienation among the "Pugachevs from the academies." The long and authoritarian reign of Nicholas I was widely viewed (particularly by the defenders of aristocratic neoclassical culture like Pushkin) as a return to relative rationality after the unfathomable mysticism and subjective capriciousness of Alexander.

Far more than his Prussian relatives, Nicholas felt the need to fortify his militaristic rule with the cohesive force of a new ideology. Nicholas paid tribute not only to the demand for one true ideology characteristic of *Byzance après Byzance*, but also to the seductive appeal of new ideas, when he added *narodnost'* (meaning both nationality and "spirit of the people") to "autocracy and Orthodoxy" in the famed ideological trinity of late

Romanov rule. He permitted his newly formed Ministry of Popular Education (no longer "popular education and spiritual affairs" as it had been called under Alexander) to enter the ideological lists with a "thick journal" of its own, the *Journal of the Ministry of Popular Education*, which can properly be regarded (at least in its proclivity, under Uvarov, for magisterial pronouncements on social and spiritual questions) as a remote ancestor of *Bol'shevik* in the high Stalin era.

Those who felt oppressed and alienated under Nicholas tended to view ideology as the weakest and most vulnerable chink in the official armor. Thus there began during Nicholas' thirty-year reign a visionary tradition of protest that expressed itself in some of the most powerful ideological literature of a Europe that was everywhere in ferment during the romantic era. The most (perhaps the only) original political contribution of Russia to this general ferment of ideas in the nineteenth century was anarchism, which (whether in the militant, original form of Bakunin, the quasi-religious form of Tolstoy, or the pseudo-scientific form of Kropotkin) was a kind of foredoomed extremist reaction to the extremist authoritarianism of the Romanovs.

A new—in many ways still contemporary—era was ushered in by the Crimean War and the decade of uncertain reform and irreversible modernization that followed. More socially heterogeneous and uprooted young leaders arose within the growing student population which sought generational identity as "new men of the sixties." They became the first large group in the history of Russia to be enamored with the efficacy of the scientific method; the first in the history of the world to characterize itself as an "intelligentsia."

Intelligentsia is a Russian term that came into general use just a century ago.[3] The passion with which Russians subsequently debated the question *Chto takoe intelligentsiia?* indicates the extraordinary power and appeal of the label in the ideologically charged atmosphere of an empire undergoing sweeping change. The main original usages of the 1860s already reveal some of the distinguishing traits which later came to be associated with the term. The word was used to express a sense of alienation from both the repressive rule of the official bureaucracy and the irrational alternation between passivity and violence associated with the rural Russian masses. It meant both a group of people and a supra-personal force of scientific intelligence. The movement of this mighty force from the abstract mind of man into the dedicated lives of men would literally transform the world, beginning with Russia, and was called (in another phrase co-opted by Soviet ideologists) the "moving force of history."

Victorian England's rise to greatness as described by Buckle's enormously popular *History of Civilization in England* was viewed in the age of the whist-playing, fox-hunting Alexander II as an imperfect model of the coming transformation of Russia to be made by men conscious of material forces, but dedicated above all to the power of intellect to transform crude *muzhiks* into *kul'turnye liudi*—a term taken by Soviet ideologists from the cultural evangelism of the first mass movement of the Russian intelligentsia: the "movement [literally 'procession'—*khozhdenie*] to the people" of the early 1870s.

The term *intelligentsia* had in its initial Russian context little reference to politics (either reformist or revolutionary) or to religion (either Orthodox or sectarian)—though advocates of all these positions in the late imperial period attempted to take over this appealing term and redefine its meaning (as have later historians, who are generally able to find whatever they are looking for in the compulsive conversationalism of this creative period of culture).

The problem of the Bolshevik leaders as they drew up their program in the first years of the twentieth century was not essentially different from that of other forces competing for effective leadership in the confusing conditions of the late imperial period. How could politicians either co-opt or discredit the attractive power of this uniquely gifted and dedicated group? By this time, a kind of saintly mythology had been built around the tradition of the intelligentsia by the epigones of the original "men of the sixties." Like the older hagiography, the new fed on martyrdom—particularly the long Siberian exile of Chernyshevsky, widely called "St. Nicholas," and of the populists whose defense stand in the trials of the 1870s and 1880s was popularly referred to as "Golgotha."

Rather than analyze the ideas of these fallen figures, many uprooted and eager young students in the late imperial period idealized their integrity and identified with their attitude of defiance. They often continued to seek total, utopian answers rather than partial, practical ones, and to seek unity not so much in precise programs as in common opposition to creeping philistinism—the hated *meshchanstvo*—which they felt closing in on them from every side. There was, to be sure, a unified common belief that man must actively serve what Mikhailovsky called "two-sided truth," by seeking both scientific knowledge and social justice. The basic opposition was not between any clearly definable social groups, but between two approaches to life: *intelligentsiia* and *meshchanstvo*.[4]

II. Intellectuals Under the Soviets

Whether or not the coherent existence of an intelligentsia was more of a myth than a social reality by the time of the Revolution, it was as real a force for Lenin, the convinced materialist focused on the problem of power, as it was for its authentic heirs: idealists focused on the search for truth. From the beginning, Lenin viewed the intelligentsia as a perverter of the Russian drive toward revolution and a major threat to the ruthlessly pragmatic revolutionism of his "party of a new type" and its mystique of *partiinost'*. Yet, at the same time, his political instinct recognized the importance of the small educated elite. Subconscious concern over his own anomalous condition as a middle-class intellectual who was the self-appointed leader of the proletariat, coupled with a determination to avenge his martyred older brother, may have contributed to his compulsive desire to supplant the older intelligentsia as the legitimate heir to the sacred task of transforming Russia.[5]

In any event, Lenin's party seems to have sought to graft onto itself the ideological cohesion and selfless dedication (as well as some of the tested slogans) of the older intelligentsia. Hence Lenin's strong sense of identification with Chernyshevsky and a host of other (mostly earlier) Russian revolutionaries whose ideas he usually either did not digest or skillfully distorted; and his hatred for those like Mikhailovsky, who lived on into Lenin's lifetime to contest the apostolic succession.

However, the alliance Lenin forged in the heat of battle with many visionary middle-class intellectuals was at best a precarious one. As earlier in Russian history, the sociopolitical revolution that emerged from the fighting and confusion of the 1914–21 period came in the midst of a profound cultural and intellectual revolution—the productive and Promethean age sometimes known as the "Russian renaissance."

Lenin died before providing any clear guidelines for dealing with the surviving elements of the old intelligentsia, let alone with the autumnal flurry of cultural experiment and modernism that continued into the relatively permissive early 1920s. He claimed to be realizing the "two-sided truth" by providing the new state with both a scientific world view and a dedication to social justice. At the same time, however, he imparted to the leaders of the U.S.S.R. both a personal, puritan aversion to inventive art and a belief in the basic need to enlist all forms of human activity in the disciplined service of party policy. Evident also in Lenin's brief years of peacetime rule was an aversion to the bohemian *Kultur-bolschewismus* fashionable in the West, and a willingness to fall back on traditional Tsarist devices for censorship and control. (The name, as well as some of the functions, of the Tsarist administrative organ for literary censorship, *Glavlit*, was quietly revived as early as 1922.)

Under Stalin, there was a gradual erosion of the practical limitations on interference with cultural matters that had prevailed under Lenin (whether because of principle or preoccupation with other things). Sharing neither the Russian intellectual background nor the broader European vistas of Lenin, Stalin reverted to the older, ecclesiastical model with which he was familiar for dealing with secular culture by combining massive technological Westernization with propitiatory purges of alleged Westernizers in the realm of ideology.

Stalin quite literally killed off the old intelligentsia, forcing those who were supposed to be bearers of its purity to humiliate themselves en route to their places of execution and denying to survivors even the refuge of remaining silent. He systematically liquidated those within his party who could be thought to feel any sense of continuity with the older aspirations and traditions.

At the same time, even Stalin recognized the appeal of the idea of some kind of dedicated intelligentsia as well as the practical need of a modernizing state for higher educational accomplishment. Thus, he sought in the 1930s to raise from humbler class origins a young and altogether "new Soviet intelligentsia," which would bring the dedication of the old to the purely technological tasks of Communist construction in the U.S.S.R.

In terms of numbers of people educated and the general ability to provide technological support for industrialization, this "new Soviet intelligentsia" was a remarkable success.[6] However, in the late years of the Stalin era and under his successors, it has become increasingly apparent that there are some profound, unsolved problems bequeathed to the Soviet leadership—partly by the interrupted renewal under more relaxed circumstances of some of the traditions of the old "truth-seeking intelligentsia" and partly by the increasing demands and rising expectations of a new post-war generation within the "Soviet intelligentsia" created by Stalin: a restive, modernizing group that might well be called the "efficiency-seeking intelligentsia."

Soviet leaders during the past decade have faced the complex task of dealing with a cultural and intellectual ferment that has authentic roots both in older Russian tradition and in the new need for more efficient material construction. The problem of dealing with intellectuals dedicated to higher callings than self-aggrandizement was not solved by Stalin's efforts to create a new breed of technological zombies capable of performing complex mechanical tasks and printing enormous editions of the works of physically and/or spiritually dead writers, but disciplined to block out any higher aspiration than the fulfillment of the five year plan. Since the death and denigration of Stalin, the Communist leadership has had to cope with this still unsolved problem under conditions when it can no longer credibly pretend to be heir and custodian of this semi-sacred tradition of dedication and aspiration.

Khrushchev, an anti-intellectual epigone of the Stalin era, alternated between preoccupied permissiveness, periodic efforts to pose as the benefactor of an easily dramatized force for change, and occasional explosive reversions to Stalinist denunciation. The intelligentsia slowly emerged from his confusing but practically-minded rule as a distinct social grouping which was increasingly placed alongside the workers and peasants as part of the sacred social trinity from which progressive humanity and the Communist Party drew its strength. His and his successors' attempts to draw them back into party activity by promises of a return to "Leninist norms of party life" have been undercut by continuing internal intrigues and public denigration of past leaders. Thus, a corrosive cynicism has developed among educated Soviet citizens at precisely the time when the Communist Party has defined increasingly ambitious tasks and a many-sided exhortative role for Soviet intellectuals in the current "period of the full-scale construction of a Communist society."

III. Current Problems

Moving to the concrete situation of the last few years, one must attempt to distinguish those elements in the ferment which are of objective significance for the development of Soviet society from those which are primarily of subjective interest to a humane observer (such as the dramatic affairs of Pasternak and of Tertz/ Siniavsky). The critical question is: which of the problems raised in this continuing intellectual and artistic ferment have serious bearing on the future development of Soviet society as a whole?

Three seem particularly crucial: (1) the largely submerged but potentially explosive questioning within the Communist Party about the organization's future role in Soviet society; (2) the more widely discussed, but still sensitive problem of how to enlist greater ideological *élan* and popular support for the programs of the Soviet state; and (3) the reinterpretation of the Russian past as a means of redefining present goals and future possibilities.

The problem of defining how the Communist Party can effectively exercise its "leading role" in the new and ill-defined "all-people's state" remains an unsolved legacy of the Khrushchev era. As party membership ballooned with the addition of 4.78 million full and candidate members between October 1961 and January 1, 1965, and the educational level rose markedly, it seemed increasingly probable that the general ferment in society had in some measure infected the party as well. While the infection was probably less advanced at higher levels and among professional cadres, Khrushchev's successors showed a curious compulsion to talk about ideology even amidst their seeming preoccupation with technological and administrative competence. The highest party organs may well have written more about ideological matters in the last few years, yet at the same time offered less clear guidance for practical activity, than at any time since the rise of Stalin.

There was some talk during and after the Twenty-second Party Congress of "ideological commissions" which would be injected into party committees to bring a rebirth of ideological *élan* from below;[7] and later, more authoritative talk of consolidating all the arts into a single union.[8] But these seem to have been only more of the phantom "harebrained schemes" of the Khrushchev era. The last few years of this period brought a veritable frenzy of conferences beginning with the all-union conference on questions of ideological work in late December 1961 and climaxing in the famous June 1963 Plenum of the Central Committee of the party dealing with the same problem.

The remarkable thing about party prose on the subject during this period is not only its verbosity and monotony (in the context of which Khrushchev's earthy "subjectivism" provided a certain amount of relief and even amusement), but the absence of clear

analysis and prescription from the party and the increasing extent
to which the complaints of the heretics came to dominate the attention of even the most orthodox party discussions. It is from
an official *doklad* at a party conference by the Komsomol head and
rising party leader, S. P. Pavlov, that we first learn that many
speak of a new "fourth generation," apparently even within the
party, distinct from those which successively made the Revolution,
launched the five year plans, and defeated Hitler.[9] At the same
forum the definitive exposition of the required "Leninist style
in the direction of the press" was largely a negative exposition of
what Leninism became under Stalin and never should have
been.[10]

There have been in the last few years occasional echoes of a
tougher conception of party interference: notably in the speeches
of Suslov, in articles of late 1965 celebrating the sixtieth anniversary of Lenin's seminal article on "Party Spirit in Literature,"
and in the groveling tone with which the liberal journal *Yunost'*
responded in April 1966 to criticism launched at the Twenty-
third Party Congress.[11]

But the dominant (or at least the most noticeably accelerating)
trend is that of increasingly sophisticated and frank discussion in
party organs of the ideological problems raised by the "de-heroi-
zation" (*degeroizatsiia*) of the best contemporary Soviet literature,
or by the tortured extrapolation of a positive message from such
unlikely phenomena as burgeoning Soviet science fiction. Though
solemnly said not to be a part of a Communist's "logical and
scientific training (*trening*)," Soviet science fiction is hailed as
free from the love of destruction in its bourgeois equivalent, and
able to inspire "optimism, confidence in one's capabilities as a
man shaping his own future."[12]

In the absence of strong reassertion by one recognized leader
of the ultimate right to interfere and pronounce judgments on all
questions (a role which Khrushchev faithfully carried over from
Stalin even while denouncing him as a person), it seems hard to
see how the party leadership will be able to sustain the "artificial
dialectic" by which threats and inducements were skillfully alternated to hold cultural ferment within acceptable limits.[13] It may
be a sign of things to come that—almost for the first time on the
question of *ideological* discipline—the major initiatives for a
harder line on writers and artists throughout 1965 came not from
Pravda but from the government paper, *Izvestiia*.

The party may indeed be feeling its way toward some new role as a mediating and harmonizing force, not so much between clearly defined interest groups as between conflicting impulses and attitudes within society as a whole.

The situation of the post-Stalinist Soviet leadership bears some similarity to that of the Russian leadership after the death of Alexander I. Then, as now, there was a deepening disillusionment with the postwar hopes for political and spiritual renovation worthy of Russia's exalted great power status and ideological pretensions; then, as now, the passing of a reformer-turned-reactionary did not lead to fundamental liberalization by successors, but did require them to provide a new ideological formula for rule. Thus, Uvarov's formula of Autocracy, Orthodoxy and Nationality (*Narodnost'*) of 1833 reduced the hitherto dominant, but increasingly irrelevant, religious ideology to but one of three principles of rule. Recent Soviet writings have coined a new trilogy of their own: *Intelligentnost'* (intellectuality), *Partiinost'* (party-spiritedness), and *Narodnost'* (a term preserved from Uvarov's formula, though more in the sense of "spirit of the people" than of "nationality").[14] This trilogy reduces the hitherto supreme concept of *partiinost'* to being merely one of three principles. To be sure, neither Khrushchev nor Brezhnev is a Nicholas I, and the day of primary reliance on "third sections" may have ended; but there is no reason to believe that the waning of older, religious beliefs will necessarily make the new administered and automated society of the U.S.S.R. in years ahead any more humane than the bureaucratized and militarized despotism of Nicholas I.

While there will no doubt continue to be much talk of consumer benefits and the common good, we may be heading not for the liberalization that many now expect and that as most Western intellectuals had expected in the wake of Catherine and Alexander, but rather into another period in which, as then, *le bien-être général en Russie* could be bitterly translated: "It is well to be a general in Russia."

If the muffled debate in the U.S.S.R. over the nature of the party's "leading role" in the years ahead can be largely confined to party circles and perhaps ultimately resolved by new rationalizations for authoritarian rule, the problem of ideological reinvigoration involves of necessity broad segments of the population and extra-administrative prescriptions.

The degeneration of Leninist ideology into catechistic grotesquery under Stalin and capricious rationalization under Khrushchev has left the party with a hard core of discredited wooden ideologists, and an image of Marxism-Leninism as an intellectual labor-saving device rather than an effective instrument for eliciting fresh enthusiasm. However, the fundamental fact that the exercise of Communist Party power is still based on an ideology (rather than on inherited tradition or measurable popular consent) provides a continuing imperative for neo-Leninist revivalism reaching flood proportions on the occasion of the fiftieth anniversary of the Bolshevik Revolution. Since ideological vitality lies largely with non-party intellectuals who are widely recognized to be mirroring the moods of less articulate members of society, perceptive and ambitious elements within or near the ruling circles are continually tempted either to court their favor or to imitate their methods of communication with the people at large.

Thus, one finds (particularly in the organs of the Komsomol, but also increasingly in *Kommunist* and other party journals) periodic surveys on what people actually think about various issues. There are also increasing appeals for cadres to be more imaginative and sympathetic in responding to popular moods, and more aware of the complexities of the artistic and spiritual media from which heresies are to be expelled.

But if party courtiers of the new intelligentsia pride themselves on their increasing denigration of Stalinist monumentalism and exhortative realism as obligatory styles, they are hardly prepared to welcome the intellectuals' wholesale flight (particularly that of the Soviet stage) to a diametrically opposed emphasis on satirical and ironical art.

Brecht has been since 1964 the most frequently performed playwright in Moscow; and Soviet literature has in the past few years moved dramatically forward from "Aesopian" satire (using veiled language, remote fairy-tale settings, and an attenuating tone of whimsical fantasy and happy endings) to increasingly bold portrayals of contemporary realities. In the 1964–65 season one could see dehumanized women on a collective farm getting down on all fours to imitate cows (in Nagibin's widely shown, and apparently much-censored movie, *The Chairman*); a satire on the parasitic Soviet new class (in Aksenov's play *Always on Sale*); a satire on the omnicompetence of the scientific method (which is likened to the sound of a neighing horse "I go-go" in the review of that name at Obraztsov's puppet theatre); and extraordinary spoofs on Soviet statistical claims and even the pretentious procedures at Soviet party meetings (in Raikin's review *Magicians Live All Around Us*).[15] Intelligent Russians seemed, moreover, generally able and willing to quote at length a first-rate satirical parody of postwar Soviet political history based on Pushkin's *Skazka o Tsar-Saltane*. Listening to it and to the partly satirical, partly elegaic folk-singing which has also grown up recently in the U.S.S.R., one is reminded of the hardy survival of oral epics throughout Russian history. Reliance on and reverence for precise oral transmission was a necessary expedient of popular culture in a society where the government traditionally had a monopoly on the acts of writing and printing.

The last major period of systematic crackdown, which began with Khrushchev's tempestuous visit to the exhibition of experimental art in December 1962 and continued through the special Plenum of the Party Central Committee in the early summer of 1963, had the effect of easing some of the more vulnerable and manipulable writers into new exercises to aid the government in its search for ideological rejuvenation.[16] But Yevtushenko, for instance, seems to have found more ideological inspiration in his visits to Cuba than in those to the Bratsk hydroelectric station; and the selection from his mammoth, leaden epic "Bratskaia GES" (which provided the text for Shostakovich's bombastic *The Execution of Stenka Razin*) received approving but modest applause from a student audience at the performance with Shostakovich and Yevtushenko present that I heard in Moscow in January 1965.

A major element in Khrushchev's campaign to find new sources of moral authority and spiritual appeal for party programs was a kind of neo-populist appeal to the wisdom of "the people" and of *narodnost'* ("the spirit of the people"). His own itinerant political style, heavy reliance on folk proverbs, continued vilification of the "paper-sickness" (*bumagamorenie*) of the urban bureaucracy, and his constant exhortations to overcome "separation from life"—all establish him as an authentic neo-populist. His formal redefinition of the U.S.S.R. as an "all-people's state" (*obshchenarodnoe gosudarstvo*) carried within it the implication that efforts would be made to broaden the range.of popular participation in the business of government. By increasing the number of party members and proposing some regularized rotation procedures, he indicated a serious intention of giving substance to this idea.

Neo-populism, like populism before it, offers an emotional appeal more attractive to those, like Khrushchev, with an essentially rural mentality, than to the more urbane and urban mentality of the new efficiency-seeking intelligentsia. Yet so great was the continuing need for some new source of higher sanction that the post-Khrushchev leadership did not entirely reject the neo-populist approach in the course of rejecting Khrushchev's "subjectivism." The term "all-people's state" was neither reaffirmed nor repudiated, but was simply not mentioned at all in the proceedings of the Twenty-third Party Congress in 1966. Despite the reinstitution of Stalinist terms like General Secretary and Politburo, there seemed to be an acceleration of the trend begun under Khrushchev to invoke the statements of ordinary workers as the only contemporary figures worthy of being quoted alongside the divinized Lenin.[17]

Much stronger than vestigial neo-populist appeals in the immediate post-Khrushchev era was the intensified tone of deference to professional competence by party ideologists. One finds hagiographers of Lenin going to some length to prove the master's great concern for the working conditions of the scientific intelligentsia even during times of revolutionary upheaval;[18] party ideologists lingering on the term "intellectuality" (*intelligentnost'*)[19] as a new amalgam of technical knowledge and sympathetic imagination which party activists must cultivate in order to forge closer links with non-party intellectuals; and Pavlov berating critics of his insistence on Komsomol participation in purely scientific and cultural activities for "raising the scarecrow of *kul'turnichestvo* (cultural work divorced from politics)."[20]

From the early fall of 1965 through the late spring of 1966 there seemed to be a general return to repression. The quiet departure of Rumiantsev from the editorship of *Pravda*, the denunciations and trial of Siniavsky and Daniel, and the difficulties which both *Yunost'* and *Novyi Mir* seemed to be having with the authorities—all indicated the continuing power of hard-line forces. However, the campaign was halting, and accompanied by plaintive appeals for more inspirational art and expressions of distress at the shrivelling numbers of genuine party-line writers and the significantly dwindling readership of many official journals. Some indication of the creeping pragmatism and internationalism with which party ideologists must contend was revealed in an article in *Izvestiia* in June 1966, which discussed how "Two or three years ago certain workers in the theater and the arts were arguing quite seriously about a 'single style of the epoch' . . . the same in New York as in Moscow, in Bonn as in Prague, in Rome as in Sofia."[21]

If the pragmatism of the new efficiency-seeking intelligentsia was clearly the main obstacle to Leninist revivalism by party leaders, there was also considerable resistance from elements of the more traditional truth-seeking intelligentsia. The vigorous defense of "large" *versus* "small" truth by the editors of *Novyi Mir* in connection with their fortieth anniversary in September 1965, and the defense pleaded by Siniavsky and Daniel at their trial early in 1966,[22] as well as the growing intensity of the antireligious campaign that had already begun in the Khrushchev era —all bespoke continuing ideological opposition of a more traditional sort that seemed to touch some resonance in the younger generation as well.

In the area of education, where any systematic effort to promote ideological reinvigoration would have to begin, no clear pattern has emerged. Khrushchev's effort to help budding young intellectuals overcome their "separation from life" by an obligatory two-year work period between secondary and advanced schooling was a characteristic mélange of neo-populist anti-intellectualism and shortsighted grubbing for additions to the work force. Such a sweeping program clearly required too many exemptions to be fully implemented in a society bent on further and more sophisticated economic development. More durable and potentially important in the Khrushchevian program was the introduction of the *internaty*, or boarding schools, which seemed in some ways a revival of the Tsarist elite training schools set up by Catherine the Great and Alexander I to add around-the-clock supervision to the usual curriculum. These have grown impressively in number and could potentially provide the vehicle for a massive effort to produce the "new class of men" that Ivan Betskoy, the eighteenth-century reformer, foresaw coming from the quasi-monastic houses of secular education (*vospitatel'nye doma*) that he set up primarily for orphans and bastards who were thought to provide the ideal *tabula rasa* for enlightenment. However, in the absence of any fresh surge of ideological commitment in the U.S.S.R., the *internaty* seem more likely to end up being desirable academic centers for those seeking assured entry into the best universities and disposal places for privileged children of the new ruling class: in short a massive imitation of the Eton that so impressed Khrushchev on his visit to England.

Recent educational changes seem to be weighted in the direction of increasing diversification, with the appearance of new institutes, regional centers and more curricular flexibility within established institutions. The hard outer shell of a monolithic ideology seems to bear increasingly less relationship to the contentious and at times incipiently pluralistic intellectual life that goes on within. The continuing influx of foreign tourists and exchange visitors has whetted the appetite of this artificially isolated people for more information about the outside world, which entrepreneurial publishers and academic politicians in turn quietly seek to encourage. Thus, despite the perpetuation (and even periodic reintensification) of many restrictions and obstacles, a kind of cultural Libermanism has arisen which tends to give the consumer of ideas and art forms increasing influence upon, if not yet firm leverage over, the development of cultural life in the U.S.S.R.

Last but not least among the major questions of intellectual ferment relating to the broader development of society is the many-sided debate about the Russian past.

In the relatively monolithic culture of Russia, the interpretation of history has always been a major area of dispute and a virtual substitute for political debate in its authoritarian state structure. One need only look at the uncritical, historical theology of the Russian church or the almost umbilical attachment of rebellious intellectuals to some reassuring philosophy of history—whether Schellingian, Hegelian, Comtean or Marxist (the principal ideological infatuations of successive generations of nineteenth-century Russian radical intellectuals).

Disputes over who was responsible for victory in battle were always specially important in Russia, because the successes or failures of the Russian cause were presumed to be part of an unfolding divine plan, and the charisma of authority came largely from identification with those deeds which revealed visible signs of providential favor. The decisive factor in the break-up of the superficially impressive Muscovite state of Ivan the Terrible and the disintegrative interregnum of the Time of Troubles was not Ivan's cruelty or stupidity, but his breaking of the sacred line of succession that he himself had done so much to embellish. It was not his atrocities, but his destruction of the rationale for them— the myth of infallibility—that was politically decisive in bringing into being the long tradition of opposition to the ruling powers in the name of some "true Tsar."

Likewise, it was not the fact of Khrushchev's revelations about Stalin's crimes (which was in any event partial and has never been published in the U.S.S.R.) or any shock effect produced by lurid revelations on a long-suffering people, but the breaking of a new myth of infallibility that was politically decisive. In the midst of the spiritual confusion and disorientation caused by this "death of gods" in the U.S.S.R., the re-examination of past history became the closest approximation in the public media to a debate over desirable future alternatives for Russian development. As in the nineteenth century, when debates about Peter the Great were really directed at programs for the future rather than facts of the past, the initial discussion of the internal controversies within the early Social Democratic movement were politically loaded. Incipient revisionism was exercised by extremely harsh denunciations of Burdzhalov's modest efforts to reconsider the role of the Mensheviks in the Revolution of 1900 and efforts were made to transfer the myth of infallibility to the party whose "Leninist norms" had allegedly been violated in the Stalin era.

But the steady and substantial increase in the academic popularity of history and in the number of historical journals and historical novels has stimulated a broadening popular discussion of the richness and variety of Russian (and to some extent Western) historical experience. Moreover, there is an apparently continuing discussion, particularly among the young, of the question that Khrushchev's selective castigation of Stalin's "cult of personality" left unanswered: where, why, and how could things have gone so wrong? Some are apparently inclined to blame the second, Stalinist, revolution (and particularly agricultural collectivization); others apparently sympathize with the critique of Leninism by Rosa Luxemburg and/or the Worker's Opposition in the early days of Soviet rule. There is much interest in the range of social and intellectual alternatives that still seemed possible in the late imperial and early Soviet periods; and there are, of course, as Yevtushenko's poem reminded us, still many "heirs of Stalin" who may be looking for some kind of true Tsar-deliverer to lead men back from current confusion to familiar hierarchies and rituals. Except for the receding latter group, all seem agreed that the degeneration had been profound under Stalin and view this fact merely as the starting point for more searching analysis and tentative prescription.

One cannot, of course, predict what the outcome will be of this debate, the most important part of which is not conducted in public, and its final resolution will in any case depend on extra-intellectual developments. But one must insist on the critical importance of this discussion for a nation that still has a sense of common tradition, but has not yet found in the post-Stalin era any clear sense of common identity or purpose. Controversies over

Russian history will thus probably remain more important than those about art or literature. The regime could continue to function as an effective autocracy even while tolerating far more jarring styles than the realism it has already begun to question, and even bolder satirical criticism of specific policies and shortcomings. One could indeed simply give up on writers and artists as effective cheerleaders for the Soviet assembly line, and hope that they would (as many might) devote more energy to entertainment than agitation. The Soviet regime is not based on a theory of art, but it still purports to be based on a philosophy of history. Moreover, history is something in which all Russians have an intimate sense of involvement, whereas those who feel deeply involved in the arts have always been (even in Russia) only a sophisticated minority. Thus, historical debate continues to deal with present power as much as past facts and has—of all purely intellectual matters—perhaps the most importance for the Russian people.

All living Russians beyond their late twenties have experienced history in a traumatic personal way (as many were killed in Russia as the other major allies had in uniform during World War II). Russians have, moreover, suffered so much at the hands of their own leaders before and since the war that there is a growing desire to make some sense—come what may in terms of disillusionment or disgust—about their own past before pledging any new allegiance to remote goals in the future.

IV. THE FUTURE

In attempting to offer conclusions, which amount to stated or implied predictions, one begins with the essential note of caution. Any predictive process depends on a far greater body of data and a far more precise and comprehensive framework of interpretation than we yet possess in the still virginal field of the history and sociology of ideas. One must recognize as well the dangers of underestimating either the power or the resourcefulness of the ruling elite of the U.S.S.R. in dealing with the problems posed by disaffected intellectuals. This is, after all, a problem with which Russian rulers have long experience, and perhaps little basic reason to fear unless re-enforced by other forms of internal or international unrest. It is possible, moreover, that even if the problem is never solved, it may simply be bypassed as a better administered authoritarian oligarchy eases the U.S.S.R. by controlled stages into a new post-ideological era of increasing material abundance.

Nevertheless, the historian has an obligation to point out that great dreams and pretensions rarely die without final struggles and attempted revivals; and that richly ensconced priestly classes rarely accept passively the dismemberment of their realms of authority. Indeed, it seems likely that the power elite of the U.S.S.R. will periodically lash out severely, as well as accommodate and harass the intellectual elite; and that many party leaders will feel attracted by the idea of a more thoroughgoing revivalist crusade against creeping pragmatism and ideological decay. Many will feel the need to rival the Chinese in providing some new sense of ideological uplift[23] which would (1) prevent the *embourgeoisement* of the postwar generation at home, and (2) provide fresh appeal to ideologically intense elite groups abroad.

From the other side, the prospects for continued intellectual ferment seem securely rooted—not only in human nature, but in the economic imperatives that the Soviet leaders have set for themselves and in the unresolved "identity crisis" they share with the entire Soviet people. The roots of the ferment, moreover, go far deeper than simply into the nineteenth-century intelligentsia; they go back into the older religious traditions of Russia. Marxism in part and Russian tradition in greater part may still have within them the dormant, but potentially infectious virus of older and deeper faiths. It may be that those who have known systematic dehumanization and perversion of the means of communication will be better able to discover a new humanism and fresh forms of speech which will enrich all people in the process of fulfilling the long-frustrated hopes of the Russian people.

The struggle between *intelligentsia* and *meshchanstvo* may indeed be part of a broader drama in which we are all involved. If the revived tradition of the old truth-seeking intelligentsia can be joined with and tempered by those of the new efficiency-seeking intellectuals, intellectual ferment in the U.S.S.R. may be able to direct some of the old sense of selfless dedication into less self-defeatingly utopian programs than the intellectuals produced in the late imperial period. *Dolgoterpenie*—long-suffering in the hope of spiritual purification and illumination—was an historical characteristic of Russian spiritual culture; and the fumblings as well as the lashings-out of party ideologists in the U.S.S.R. seem likely to encourage the already noticeable sense of identity between the old truth-seeking and the new efficiency-seeking intellectuals.

The advantage that the restless intellectuals have in the Soviet Union may well be the very fact that the *intelligentsia* is not, any more than it was in the late imperial period, an easily definable social group, but a kind of authentic "higher principle," a unique source of recognized integrity in a society that has done so much to debase the traditional political and moral language of the Judaeo-Christian tradition and the aesthetic standards of the classical heritage. The fact that Russians have a sense of common destiny and common involvement in the inner spiritual life of their country may again produce *dvoiniki* and *raskol'niki* within the new ruling elite that will soon emerge. The sense of unity within Russian culture between scientists and humanists is greater than within Anglo-American or indeed most European cultures.

A new generation of leaders may feel increasingly split between the official actions which they perform for the state mechanism and the heretical ideas and ideals to which they secretly feel an inner attraction, if not commitment. The sheer boredom of official Soviet life with its prematurely crumbling, prefabricated cities lends a continuing fascination to the life of the spirit and the imagination. As scientific education spreads, the ferment of ideas may well become more and not less intense.

In any event, well-fed suburban America has little right to be patronizing about the creative potentialities of a culture that has produced in the last century or so the novels of Tolstoy and Dostoevsky, the art of Stravinsky and Kandinsky, the poetry of Blok and Pasternak, and a host of traumatic but often inventive social experiments and political upheavals for which there are few parallels in our experience. Few Western observers would have thought any of this remotely possible in the early nineteenth century, when the accepted image of Russia was that of a powerful but frozen and uncreative giant.

What can be dimly foreseen cannot be confidently predicted, not only because we see through a glass darkly and lack critical data on ferment in the U.S.S.R. today, but also because the Russians of the new "fourth generation" seem surer of what they oppose than of what they favor. They still look abroad for ideas and examples; and much will depend on avoiding a marked remilitarization of the international situation and on the development of a sympathetic Western relationship with the forces of evolution in the U.S.S.R. There will probably be no return to private ownership of the basic means of industrial production, and little inclination to imitate the forms of traditional liberal democracy. But remarkable changes may well be in store, and could come with the unpredicted suddenness that is so characteristic of Russian history and is invariably later seen to have been predictable.

PART FIVE

Prospects

17.

The Soviet Union in the
International Environment

JOHN C. CAMPBELL

One question about Soviet foreign policy is perennially asked and never satisfactorily answered: Is it a strategy of world revolution inspired by Marxist faith, or is it the pursuit of national interests by a secular national state? In support of the first proposition, one can cite innumerable official declarations, from Lenin's early calls to the proletarians and oppressed peoples of the world to the latest pronouncements of contemporary party leaders, and the ties with Communist parties all over the world. In support of the second, there is evidence in any number of specific acts, from the Treaty of Brest-Litovsk in 1918 to the pact with Hitler in 1939 to the mediation between India and Pakistan at Tashkent in 1965. If Winston Churchill could describe Soviet foreign policy as a riddle wrapped in a mystery inside an enigma, he could also find one consistent line running through it, Russian national interest.[1]

It is impossible to give a clear answer either by coming down on one side or the other or by finding some fixed ratio between the two. There is no doubt that the leadership of the Soviet Union, from Lenin onward, has been made up of convinced Marxists who took seriously the mission of this world's first socialist state to lead the cause of socialism to its inevitable triumph over capitalism. Nor is there any doubt that their day-to-day policies have been concerned with protecting and advancing the security and immediate interests of the Soviet state. The state, of course, can be pictured as the center and guiding force of the revolution, though it would probably be more in accordance with

473

the historical record to say that the ideology and apparatus of the world revolution have been harnessed to the interests of the Soviet state. As heir to the land mass and peoples of imperial Russia, the Soviet Union followed similar policies with respect to frontiers, control of peripheral seas, and the like, mixing Marxist reasons with geopolitical ones in support of its conduct. But the concerns of Soviet foreign policy have ranged far beyond the traditional interests of Russia.

What concerns us here is the way in which the Soviet Union acts in its relations with the rest of the world. It may be possible to get closer to the realities by seeing what the leaders of the Soviet government and of the party have in fact done, uncertain though we may be as to the particular motives and reasoning behind their acts.

World War II introduced a new era in Soviet foreign policy. Despite the great strains and losses of the war, the Soviet Union came out of it as one of the two great powers in the world, owing to the eclipse of Germany and Japan and the grave weakening of Britain and France. Stalin attempted to take advantage of that situation to expand the area of Soviet control and strengthen the Soviet Union by acquiring new positions beyond its borders. In Europe he established dominance over the East European states and those parts of Germany overrun by the Soviet armies, and tried to reach further westward through diplomacy and subversion. In the Mediterranean and Middle East he used the same methods in attempting to extend Soviet power. In the Far East he regained, with Western consent, the old positions held by Tsarist Russia before its defeat by Japan in 1905, while Soviet troops, and Soviet political control, flowed into North Korea.

The Soviet Union simply annexed certain adjacent territories to which it laid claim on historical or strategic grounds. In areas beyond the new borders in Europe it set up satellite regimes in the shadow of its overwhelming military presence, either with the consent of the Western powers or over their ineffective protests. These governments were run by the local Communist parties, called themselves "people's democracies," and set out on the road to socialism on the Soviet model. This managed social revolution in areas on the Soviet periphery, Soviet pronouncements told the world, represented the first great expansion of socialism at the expense of capitalism since the October Revolution, a giant step toward its triumph in the whole world. It could as easily have been called a giant step in Soviet imperialism, for these great gains for socialism were all won in territories which were close to the Soviet Union itself and within reach of its military and police power.

Three significant points bear on any judgment of Stalin's policy. First, as we have indicated, he tried by diplomacy, subversion and pressure to push the zone of Soviet control further outward where ever there seemed to be weak spots. Second, when he ran up against strong Western resistance, he took the setback and avoided a showdown. When he saw that the West would not give the Soviet Union a voice in control of the Ruhr, a trusteeship over Tripolitania, or a base in the Dodecanese, he retreated from those demands. When he saw that the Communist parties in Western Europe could not take power by themselves, that the Greek Communists could not win their civil war, or that Turkey and Iran, backed by the West, could not be brought to yield tamely to demands compromising their independence and integrity, he refrained from backing his ambitions by force. He gambled at Berlin in 1948, but accepted his failure when the airlift broke the blockade. He gambled again in Korea in 1950, but carefully refrained from military action after the United States intervened with its own forces.

The third point was the relative indifference of the Soviet leadership to the cause of revolution in the colonial and underdeveloped areas. Stalin's policy was centered on Europe, and his attempted thrust into the Near East was an effort to outflank Europe. Despite his past writing on the subject, Stalin had no strategy based on either nationalist or Communist revolution in Asia, Africa and Latin America. He made no attempt to win over or support bourgeois nationalists like Nehru and Sukarno. Nor did he give any effective support to Communist movements in revolt against the new national governments. His concern was with the power position of the Soviet Union. If a nationalist movement or a socialist revolution did not contribute to Soviet power, and was not under Soviet control, it could be more troublesome than useful. The break with Yugoslavia in 1948 made clear that Stalin was in favor of Communist regimes only if they were under his control. No doubt he had his hesitations and fears about China, where the Communists won out in spite of the Soviet Union rather than with its help.[2]

Limited as the aims of Soviet foreign policy under Stalin may seem in retrospect, the steady pressures with which they were pursued and the strong responsive reaction of the West, led by the United States, combined to create a climate of total hostility and tension between two seemingly irreconcilable blocs. Both sides increased their military strength in Europe; Germany's division hardened, making impossible any progress toward a treaty settlement on Germany or, at the time, on Austria; the Soviet Union became a nuclear power, but no advance could be made on the control of weapons; the United Nations was little more than a sounding board for cold-war issues; the Cold War itself took on the form of a clash of ideological absolutes which gave every crisis, indeed every disagreement, the color of a preparatory phase of a war of survival.

Both powers, but especially the Soviet Union as the weaker of the two contestants, were exposed to real dangers as a result of the very intensity of the struggle. Much more than was realized in the West at the time, Soviet moves were often in the nature of reactions to moves by the Western powers which seemed to threaten Soviet security.[3] But Soviet threats and intransigence brought only greater Western unity, and the absorption of West Germany's economic and military potential in a Western alliance growing ever tighter and more formidable was a disturbing prospect. The Nineteenth Congress of the Soviet Communist Party, held in 1952, indicated a turn toward a more flexible policy which would give the Soviet Union more chance to maneuver and make its influence felt within the non-Communist world without carrying a big stick. Stalin himself had refurbished the idea of inevitable conflict among capitalist states, and with it came opportunities for greater use of divisive diplomacy, popular-front techniques, and such propaganda devices as the "peace campaign."[4] Especially important was the reappearance of the theme of national liberation in the colonial areas and the beginnings of the shift from Zhdanov's concept of a "two-camp" world to one of three camps: socialist, imperialist, and the peoples of the colonies and less developed states.[5]

I. Foreign Policy After Stalin

The transition from Stalin to his successors gave more immediate evidence of continuity than of drastic change. Even so, the record of two years following Stalin's death contained some startling new initiatives. From the beginning, the new "collective" leaders were focusing their attention on their positions at home, including their relations with one another. Together, they felt the need to relieve some of the dangerous pressures which had been building up in Soviet society, and also to ease the tension of an international situation in which the Soviet Union, its European satellites, and a China only beginning to be organized by its new Communist masters faced a largely hostile world at many points of real danger. They proceeded to take some of the heat out of relations with immediate neighbors, withdrawing the claims made on Turkey in Stalin's day and assuring Iran of their desire for normal and friendly relations. The Soviet government returned to the four-power conference table in 1954 to consider the future of Germany, albeit without making any concessions to reach agreement. It helped to end the war in Indochina. The year 1955, when Khrushchev emerged as the most powerful of the Soviet leaders, saw the withdrawal from the Soviet military base in Finland, the acceptance of an independent and neutral Austria, and the dramatic reconciliation with Yugoslavia. It was the year of the Warsaw Pact, a defensive reaction to West Germany's admission to NATO, but also of the summit conference in Geneva where the tacit understanding was reached to rule out nuclear war as an instrument of national policy. In 1956, at the Twentieth Party Congress, Khrushchev revised Leninist doctrine on the inevitability of war with the capitalist powers.

All this, to the accompaniment of much talk of peaceful coexistence, was evidence of new techniques and greater imagination in the conduct of Soviet foreign policy. Basically, it was an adaptation of policy to changing world conditions rather than an overhaul of strategy. Among them were challenges to Soviet domination within the Communist world itself, the increasing strength and solidarity of the Western position in Europe, and the rise of nationalism and neutralism in Asia and Africa. Meanwhile, with the growth of nuclear weapons, the Soviets began to perceive the full implications of going to the brink; but they were also aware of the possible gains to be made by an active policy short of that point. This is the background against which Soviet policy in the Khrushchev period can be considered in its three main aspects: the struggle for leadership in the Communist world, the direct confrontation with the West, and the Cold War in the new and underdeveloped nations.

In almost no time at all after Stalin's death it became apparent that his empire could not be maintained when the emperor was no longer there to run it. The main instruments of Soviet power in Eastern Europe were still present, but the combined uncertainties of leadership in Moscow and in the satellite states themselves, not to speak of the pressing need to escape from the strait-jacket of Stalinist policies, made it impossible to use those instruments as Stalin had. The relative free play which Moscow allowed to competing forces in the satellites, and especially the alternation of relaxation and repression, led inexorably to the open challenges to Soviet authority in Poland and Hungary in 1956. Henceforward, the Soviet leadership felt compelled to find a new basis for socialist solidarity in which compromise and consent found a place alongside the continuing preponderance of Soviet power. Not wishing to provoke further resistance and revolt, the Soviet Union was ready to provide economic aid to its allies instead of merely exploiting their economies for its own benefit, to seek an agreed basis for the stationing of Soviet forces on their territory, and to give them greater freedom in the conduct of their own affairs.

"Unity in essentials, diversity in details" became the accepted formula,[6] but it was still the Kremlin that reserved to itself the decisions on the essentials, and therein lay the problem. Ever since Tito's challenge in 1948, Moscow's position as the fount of Marxist truth and the ordained leader of the world Communist movement was vulnerable. Call it revisionism, reformism, national communism, or whatever; as the years passed, it became an established fact that no doctrinal *ukaz* from Moscow could win the automatic and unquestioned acceptance of Communist parties in Eastern Europe and elsewhere. Especially after Khrushchev himself tore down the authority of Stalin and Stalinism at the Twentieth Party Congress in 1956, he could hardly succeed in his attempt to maintain ideological leadership while denouncing dogmatism on one side and revisionism on the other, meanwhile steering his own uncertain course in both domestic and foreign policy. His manner of dealing with Yugoslavia was characteristic. Whether he denounced Tito as a revisionist or made up to him as a brother socialist, he called attention to Yugoslavia's heretical ideas and spurred their impact on Eastern Europe.

Among the Communist parties of Western Europe, the largest, that of Italy, led the way in the assertion that the world Communist movement had to be "polycentric" to survive in its various individual national environments. What Palmiro Togliatti implied in his statements after Khrushchev's denunciation of Stalin in 1956 came to full expression in his "testament," the memorandum made public after his death in 1964. It meant that the Communist parties themselves were engaged in the process of emancipation from the status of mere instruments of Soviet foreign policy which had been their lot since the early 1920s. The "nationalization" of Yugoslav or Polish or Italian Communists was rooted in the conditions of these countries, but its appearance at this juncture and the forms it took owed a great deal to another challenge to Moscow, that posed by Communist China.

We know now that the Soviet-Chinese dispute existed all through the Khrushchev period, although it was not clearly visible to the outside world until 1960. From then on it has been a standing refutation of the axiom of the solidarity of Communist states and of any recognized Soviet leadership of more than a part of the world Communist movement. China, from the moment of takeover by the Chinese Communist Party, presented Moscow with an insoluble problem. The Soviet Union had either to make vast contributions to building the industrial and military power of China, as a brotherly Communist state, or else incur China's resentment and enmity. It did give important support, especially in supplying entire plants and essential technical services. But the Soviet leaders did not choose to divert to China resources which they needed for their own defense effort, their domestic economy, and the support of their foreign policy in other parts of the world. Nor was it evident that they wanted to see China develop into a powerful state. Certainly Stalin had reservations about the Chinese Communists, and Khrushchev's regime, after efforts to conciliate them by giving up the special Soviet positions in Manchuria in 1954 and agreeing to help them in developing nuclear weapons in 1957, soon gave up the idea that China would become a cooperative member of the new "socialist commonwealth" he was trying to build on the ruins of Stalin's empire in Eastern Europe. Indeed, as China challenged Russia on doctrinal matters and tried to build strength on the basis of its own wild theories of the "Great Leap Forward," while looking to Moscow for active support of Chinese policies of dangerous confrontation with American power in the Far East, Khrushchev reacted by cutting off Soviet help on the Chinese nuclear program and withdrawing Soviet technical advisers from Chinese industries.[7]

The charges and countercharges of dogmatism and revisionism intensified the conflict and had a devastating effect on the Soviet Union's pretensions to ideological leadership of the world's Communist parties and on its international position in general. They enabled Peking to assert itself as a rival center of authority and to contest Soviet influence both among Communists and among the nations of the third world. Underneath the doctrinal disputes, moreover, was the fact of China's assertion of its potential as a great power, with interests and policies which could and probably would be antagonistic to those of the Soviet Union. It forced the Soviet leaders to view the world as a triangular structure in which they faced two major enemies, rather than as simply divided between the contending forces of socialism and capitalism. It was bound to affect their relations with the West, but more immediately it showed itself in sharp Soviet-Chinese rivalry in the third world.

The early 1950s witnessed scattered signs of a new Soviet strategy; one of cooperation with nationalist movements and governments in the colonial areas and the new nations of Asia and the Middle East against imperialism and colonialism, that is, against the Western powers long dominant in those areas. But the real change came with Khrushchev in 1955; the flamboyant journey with Bulganin to India and Burma, the follow-up of the Bandung Conference (where Chou-En-lai was preaching peaceful coexistence to the neutrals), the arms deal with Egypt and other moves to court the nationalists and neutrals of the third world came at the same time as the peaceful overtures toward the West leading up to the summit conference at Geneva. But they had the very different purpose of opening up a new front in the Cold War where the Western powers were already on the defensive and opportunities for Soviet gains were beckoning.

This was not really a new but an old strategy, dating back to the early years of the Bolshevik regime. But the circumstances of the 1950s were not those of a generation before. The Soviet Union had become one of the two greatest world powers; and the European empires in Asia and Africa were melting away. Many leaders of revolutionary nationalist movements had now become rulers of sovereign states. They still had ambitions, fears, and grievances which poisoned their relations with the West. Once they saw the opportunity, they could play the Soviet card against the West, without the need of either a formal alliance or an acceptance of communism. For Moscow, the possibility of cutting down Western influence and substituting its own was very tempting.

The tactics were well worked out. Certain key countries were chosen—India, Egypt, Indonesia, and later Iraq, Ghana, Guinea and Algeria—which were important for reasons of size, location, or influence beyond their borders, or had special circumstances easily exploited. The means comprised arms shipments, loans, trading arrangements, diplomatic support against neighboring states or against the West, and a great deal of talk about independence and progress. Not that the policy was confined to these few states. As more and more new states won independence, the Soviets wooed all but those who rebuffed them by showing a clear preference for the West. They preached respect for sovereignty, anticolonialism, and cooperation for peace. Khrushchev, at the Twentieth Party Congress in 1956, spoke of a vast "zone of peace" in which the socialist countries would stand united with the colonial and newly liberated peoples of Asia and Africa against the imperialist West.[8]

Khrushchev seemed remarkably free of ideological concerns in pursuing his chosen line. The question of the advantages and dangers of supporting bourgeois nationalists in the colonial areas had been debated in Soviet and Comintern councils from the time of Lenin's first manifesto to the "toilers of the East" after the October Revolution. Basically, the question was one of means and ends, of how Soviet policies at a given time fitted into the long-term aim of the advance of socialism. Lenin's "Theses" adopted by the Comintern in 1920 had approved working temporarily with bourgeois nationalists against imperialism, at the risk of strengthening anti-Communist forces but with the ultimate intention of pushing them aside so that true Communists could take power.[9] Variations on this theme have since filled the thoughts and the writings of Soviet scholars and ideologists and of Communists from the countries of the third world.

In the late Khrushchev period the phrase of the day was the "national democratic state," which found its way into the statement of the 81 Communist parties gathered in Moscow in 1960 and the program of the Twenty-second Party Congress in 1961. Communists were to join with all progressive elements, including anti-imperialist bourgeois parties, various kinds of socialists, trade unions, peace groups, and others, in order to dispose of the reactionaries and their foreign masters. The concept was subject to fluctuating definition as the theorists struggled to keep up with practice amid the changing conditions in different countries.[10] Whether and when the Communists were to discard their allies and seize leadership and control of the national democratic state, perhaps along the lines of the Communist seizure of power in Eastern European countries, was never clearly stated. There were times when Khrushchev pushed the cause of the native Communists, as when he told Gamal Abdel Nasser that they were good progressive people and should not be persecuted. Yet for long periods Moscow seemed indifferent to the fate of local Communists, even when their parties were outlawed and they were thrown into jail. In Iraq in 1959, when the local party had a chance to reach for power, the orders from Moscow forbade even trying. By their actions the Soviet leaders left no doubt that they were far more interested in the non-Communist ruling groups than in the idea of Communist revolution. On the side of Marxist theory, it was sufficient that the radical states like Syria, the U.A.R., Guinea or Mali were anti-imperialist and had "taken the non-capitalist road." That their "Arab socialism" or "African socialism" bore no resemblance to the theories of Marx and Lenin or to the practice of "scientific socialism" in the Soviet Union itself did not appear to be important.[11]

The great hope of Nikita Khrushchev was to contain the Chinese challenge while making a decisive change in the relative positions of the Soviet Union and the United States. Success in the third world could contribute to it, but the critical element in the equation was military power, and the critical place was Europe. Soviet nuclear weapons had already provided a counterbalance to those of the United States, and the tonic effect of the appearance of the first sputnik and of Soviet intercontinental missiles in 1957 was evident in Khrushchev's strategy of the following years. He seemed intent, as he continued to preach peaceful coexistence, on exploiting the situation for the military and political advantage of the Soviet Union. But the Soviet Union did not in fact have a strategic advantage, and the space feats and boasting only spurred the United States to increase its superiority. The reaction to the threat to Berlin which Khrushchev put forward in 1958 proved that the Western powers could not be forced into retreat by the mere fact of growing Soviet nuclear capabilities. For Khrushchev to have carried through his threat to sign a peace treaty with East Germany and leave Western access to Berlin to East German hands would have meant a showdown by force. He pulled back.

The Soviet threat hung over Berlin and the Western powers for four years. In 1961 the situation reached a new high level of tension as Khrushchev tested the new American president. But in the end the lesson learned was the same as in 1948 or 1958: neither side could push the other into acceptance of a basic change in the territorial *status quo*. Both knew that Berlin was not an isolated problem, to be settled by tidying up the map. The future of Berlin meant the future of Germany, and Germany was the key to the balance of power in Europe.

It was apparent from Khrushchev's statements in 1959 that the only united Germany which the Soviet Union could accept was a Communist Germany, and there is room for doubt whether this was regarded as a possible or even desirable outcome. The strongest motivation for the pressure on Berlin was the immediate need to consolidate East Germany, not the distant goal of winning West Germany. Once the drastic step was taken to insulate Ulbricht's state and to imprison its people by building the Berlin wall, the pressure began to ease. It was ironic that although both sides were trying to consolidate rather than to expand, they came to the brink of war. Moscow was mainly concerned with its hold on its European "commonwealth" of which East Germany was an essential member, but a member with a wound in Berlin that was draining its life blood. To the Western powers, the *status quo* in Berlin, anomalous as it might seem fifteen years after it was set up as a temporary arrangement, was an essential part of the larger *status quo* between East and West in Europe, which they could abandon only at their peril.

Why Khrushchev and the Soviet leadership, after the cautious avoidance of a direct military challenge at Berlin, made the reckless gamble of placing nuclear missiles in Cuba, we cannot be sure. In any case, he evidently did not foresee that the United States would see it as a brazen attempt to shift the existing balance of power and would seriously debate only two possible responses: military action against the missile bases themselves or a demand for their removal coupled with a blockade to stop any more from coming in. Fortunately for the world, Khrushchev was left with an avenue of retreat, which he took.

The Cuban crisis temporarily cleared the air and led to some rethinking of Soviet policy. As the quarrel with China moved to a new climax, the Soviet leaders decided that a measure of détente with the United States was called for. Thus it became possible to conclude the limited test-ban agreement of August 5, 1963, and a series of lesser agreements which were reached within the next year (the "hot-line," the mutual cutback of production of fissionable material, and the ban on military uses of outer space). The Soviet government accepted those agreements because its leaders found solid reasons of national interest for doing so, not because they had decided on a general policy of cooperation or were ready to negotiate seriously on major political problems.

Nevertheless, the last two years of Khrushchev's reign were remarkable for the possibilities of change they seemed to hold. He was obsessed with the conflict with China and determined to mobilize against it the Communist states and parties through the world, even as he saw the Chinese making great gains among them. He deepened Soviet commitments in the third world, especially to the Arab states, but without realizing any commensurate gains. In attempts to take advantage of the weakening of NATO and of increasing signs of nationalistic policies in France and in Germany, he encouraged General de Gaulle but also planned a new approach to Bonn. More than before, his performances were less predictable and his policies more personal. And this was a principal reason why his colleagues finally turned against him.

II. Foreign Policy After Khrushchev

How far was Khrushchev's foreign policy responsible for his downfall? Official statements and press editorials appearing after the event referred to harebrained schemes and failure to conduct policy through the regular channels. Whether the moves which brought on the Cuban missile crisis of October 1962 were in the "hairbrained" category has not been specified. From what happened or did not happen after Khrushchev's removal we know that in at least two aspects his international course met with disapproval: his proposed visit to West Germany and the meeting of Communist parties he had scheduled in December 1964 to deal with the challenge of China. The new Brezhnev-Kosygin regime consigned the German visit to oblivion. It tried very hard to be conciliatory toward Peking, calling for an end to public polemics and abandoning the international meeting, which the Chinese would not have attended (and which would have shown, incidentally, how far from unanimous the other Communist parties were in their attitudes toward the Soviet-Chinese conflict).[12] On the side of military policy, the new regime also sought to appease the military establishment by reversing the Khrushchev policy of heavy cuts in the conventional forces.

On the whole, these were minor changes. Khrushchev had not proposed a change in Soviet policy on Germany but only a visit to Bonn.[13] The shift on China related to tactics, not to substance; and since the Chinese kept right on with their own polemics, displaying their scorn for "Khrushchevism without Khrushchev," the tactics did not work. All in all, the point to note about the post-Khrushchev foreign policy of the Soviet Union is its similarity to what went before. But Brezhnev and Kosygin had to face also the problem of the Vietnam war, with all its complicating effects on the Soviet Union's policies toward its two main adversaries, the United States and Communist China.

Above all, the Vietnam question sharpened the horns of the dilemma which already confronted the Soviet leaders. During a period in which they were trying to stabilize the situation in Europe and to extend their influence in the third world, all without undue risk of conflict, they found themselves faced both with American acts of war against North Vietnam, and with constant verbal attacks from the Chinese Communists charging abandonment of the revolution and collusion with the imperialists. They could not go very far in the direction of a *modus vivendi* with the United States without giving substance to the Chinese charges; and they could not try to equal or outdo the Chinese in revolutionary militancy without running too great risks and without ignoring their own convictions on how best to pursue the Soviet Union's interests. The Soviet government felt compelled to send substantial aid to North Vietnam, and it could not bring itself to take the lead in bringing about a negotiated peace. But it was careful to limit its commitments, to continue to talk of peaceful coexistence with Western nations, and to keep open the channels of negotiations with the United States on disarmament and other matters.

Despite the diversions of the Chinese, the real tests of Soviet foreign policy had to do with the relationship to the principal adversary, the United States. Although nuclear war was pronounced on both sides to be unthinkable, the military balance between the two powers remained central to the relationship. Both, presumably, would strive for a scientific breakthrough which would nullify the other's deterrent and confer a decisive strategic superiority. The new men still faced a difficult choice: whether to strive harder for equality or superiority, or to settle for a position which was admittedly second best but still gave adequate deterrence for security.[14]

It would be as foolish for Americans to predict whether or not the Soviet Union will gain superiority as it is wise to do what can be done to prevent such an occurrence. The greater probability is a continuance of mutual deterrence by which the likelihood of a major war is greatly reduced. But even under a nuclear umbrella, the strength and disposition of armed forces set a framework within which the political competition is carried on. The relative military positions in such an area as the Eastern Mediterranean, for example, could have a major influence on the shape and outcome of crises in that area, as they did in 1958 and again in 1967. Thus, the Soviet Union could be expected to carry on its campaign to get U.S. forces out of Europe, the Mediterranean, Southeast Asia, and elsewhere, and seek to bring its own military power to bear on these same areas. Aware, however, of the limitations on the use of force, the Soviet leaders have chosen as their main methods of competition the time-honored means of influencing governments: diplomacy, propaganda, appeals to the hopes, fears and interests of other nations, economic and military aid. These methods bear the mark of controlled competition, not of unlimited conflict.

Since the pressure on West Berlin was relaxed by Khrushchev in 1962, Moscow has presented neither a military nor a revolutionary threat to Western Europe. Officially, the policy is peaceful coexistence with countries of different political and social systems, but with no compromise on ideology, for communism must carry on the struggle against bourgeois values, capitalism and imperialism until the inevitable victory. In fact, while the ideological struggle may occupy the party propagandists, it has little to do with foreign policy and diplomacy. Foreign policy is largely directed to weakening NATO and preventing the appearance of a strong, united Western Europe, including a reunited Germany. Diplomacy is devoted to turning Europeans against the United States and against one another. The war in Vietnam has provided opportunities to exploit European disagreements with America, and the policies of de Gaulle's France have admirably served the Soviet purpose of promoting division in the West. By conciliatory moves toward some Western European states while denouncing and trying to isolate others, notably the Federal Republic of Germany, the Soviets attempt to deny the latter a leading role in the West and to maintain indefinitely the partition of Germany. The propaganda campaign against German "militarism" and against any access by the Federal Republic to nuclear weapons serves a variety of purposes, from protecting the security of the Soviet Union to gaining prestige and recognition for the East German regime.

When Soviet spokesmen preach the need for the solution of European problems by Europeans (their Europe includes the Russians but certainly not the Americans and perhaps not the British), they appeal to pride, to nationalism, to the ambitions of leaders, and to the anti-Americanism already apparent or latent among Western European peoples. Not that they have really believed that a European settlement could be reached in America's absence. Not that they wanted Western Europe to unite, even on a platform of independence of America. What they wanted was to undermine the two pillars of successful Western policy in the past two decades: Western European solidarity and the leadership and support of the United States.[15] Nationalism, represented in France by President de Gaulle and in Germany by men of the stripe of Franz Josef Strauss, was as useful to Moscow in Western Europe as it was dangerous in Eastern Europe. Courting de Gaulle served two purposes. It gave strength and prestige to the one statesman in Western Europe who had become a symbol of independence, indeed defiance, of America. And it struck at the new Franco-German friendship, reviving fears in Germany of a new Franco-Russian alliance directed against Germany's reunification. As in Lenin's day, Germany continued to be the key to Europe in Soviet eyes. A reunited Germany, allied with America or even by itself, would represent a clear and present danger to the Soviet Union.

The Kremlin, however, does not face Western Europe from a position of strength. Regardless of the weakening of NATO ties, the nuclear balance still rules out any Soviet military adventure in Europe. The Soviet Union no longer deals with Western European states as the head of a solid Communist bloc. The economic strength which accompanied the rise of the European Economic Community has not been matched in the East. The East European states, some of them increasingly independent of Moscow, are turning to the West to meet their pressing needs for modern equipment and technology. They are establishing trade and other ties even with the Federal Republic of Germany, including projects involving intimate economic collaboration, whether Moscow likes it or not. The difference from the time of Stalin is striking. Then, Eastern European governments and Western European Communist parties were instruments of Soviet policy. Both have been slipping out of control. The big Communist parties of Italy and France keep their ties with Moscow. But the Italian party, for example, has not only abandoned any revolutionary role, it has also abandoned Soviet guidance except when it conforms to the Italian leaders' views of what is necessary and desirable in the light of conditions in Italy and in Western Europe. The Soviet government has promoted the idea of a Europe for the Europeans as a device to eliminate America's presence and influence. Yet if some new kind of Europe, including states of Western and of Eastern Europe should arise, there is no guarantee at all that it would meet Soviet desires and specifications. The likelihood is that the Kremlin will find it safer to work against any consolidation of Europe, whether confined to the West or stretching further eastward.

In the third world, the regime of Brezhnev and Kosygin carried on in the pattern set by Khrushchev. But somehow the great opportunities which had seemed to open up in the 1950s had dimmed, and the problems were ever more complicated. The simple formula of common action by the socialist states and the revolutionary new nations to sweep the remnants of colonialism and Western influence from Asia, Africa, and Latin America proved not so easy to apply. Ten years before, Moscow had not anticipated having to fight off the opposition of Peking, both in the "international workers' movement" and on the level of governmental relationships. Now, putting political interests ahead of ideology, they did not hesitate to support India against China, but in doing so they were merely following a line parallel to that of the United States. Further afield, conflict with the Chinese in dozens of countries and polemics with them in such organizations as the Afro-Asian Peoples' Solidarity Council tended to bewilder and disgust the Asian and African representatives and break down the whole concept of Communist-nationalist cooperation. The "second Bandung conference," scheduled for Algiers in June 1965, was the subject of wrangling between Soviets and Chinese and ultimately was not held at all. The immediate occasion for the postponement, the overthrow of Ahmed Ben Bella, was an illustration of the shaky foundations on which Moscow was trying to build a policy. Ben Bella was the type of new, radical, anti-Western leader who looked both to Moscow and to Peking, taking arms and economic aid from both and seeking to share revolutionary leadership on the world stage, and whose career ended abruptly in disaster stemming from political opponents at home. Nkrumah, Ben Bella, Sukarno—the roster of fallen "great leaders"—was testimony to the fragility of their power.

The Soviet leaders had learned some hard lessons in their dealings with the third world. In one country after another they saw how fleeting success could be. None ever became a tool of Soviet policy, subject to dictation and control. The Soviets could not count on a political "payoff" from their aid programs any more than the Americans could. In the Middle East they saw Syria and the U.A.R. goad Israel into a war in which Soviet prestige went down with the defeat of the Soviet-supplied Arab armies. The natural advantages which Moscow had over the West in playing on the theme of the struggle against imperialism and neocolonialism were limited by other factors: the strong economic interests which many third-world countries shared with the West; the heavy cost of supporting the national economies of client states in addition to providing them with arms; and the preponderant military power of the United States in regions such as Southeast Asia, the Middle East and Latin America, which made it impossible for the Soviet Union to use its own military power to make and consolidate political gains.

The Soviet "success" in Cuba and developments in the rest of Latin America point up the problem.[16] Fidel Castro has his own ideas on spreading the revolution in Latin America which are closer to the Chinese than to the Soviet line. Where Moscow and the Communist parties which it controls have courted existing governments and non-Communist forces in hopes of forming popular fronts, stressing nationalism and anti-imperialism, Castro's agents have actively promoted and supported guerrilla movements in Guatemala, Venezuela, Peru, Bolivia and elsewhere. All the while, the Soviet Union has to subsidize the Cuban economy to the tune of three to four hundred million dollars a year. It may be asked whether the Soviets really desire a successful Communist revolution in a Latin American country, as they would then have to support the new regime without really controlling it. Could the Soviet Union take on the cost of the economic development of Brazil? There remains the question of the reaction of the United States, where the doctrine of "no more Cubas" would be likely to prevail over the doctrine of nonintervention.

The Soviet leaders, even more frankly than Khrushchev, have accepted the fact that their brand of "scientific" socialism has no appeal for the peoples of the third world. Making anti-imperialism the supreme test, they have chosen to support governments and parties almost without regard to form and character, calling them "progressive" or "socialist in outlook" or "on the non-capitalist road," and even urging Marxists to work with religious and other groups "under conditions where anti-Communist attitudes are in evidence."[17] As a result, the most revolutionary elements tend to look to the Chinese, who keep up a drumfire of propaganda against the "modern revisionists" of Moscow and their betrayal of the cause of revolution. Nor does Peking leave Moscow in sole possession of the cause of "national liberation." It cites Soviet conduct in the Cuban crisis of 1962 and the Arab-Israel war of 1967 as a combination of cowardice and collusion with the imperialist enemy.

Stung by China's criticism, the men in the Kremlin may be driven toward excessive risks in the competition with the West and toward abandoning the peaceful coexistence policy. On the other hand, they have defended that policy publicly before Communist critics as serving the struggle against imperialism; and they have made plain to the West that peaceful coexistence does not apply when it comes to struggles for national liberation.[18] They also seem to believe that the measures of détente with the West have in fact served Soviet interests. Undoubtedly there are differing tendencies within the Soviet leadership, with some favoring greater militancy and others stressing the need for caution. But none, it seems, really supports the Chinese line of all-out conflict with the West, and none is ready to accept a true peaceful coexistence with the West. Both their basic Marxist outlook and their view of the interests of the Soviet Union as a great power drive the Soviet leaders to a course of continuing competition and tension with the United States. They are also forced, so long as the implacable challenge of China exists, into a struggle to beat back Chinese influence within the international Communist movement all over the world and to contain the expansion of Chinese power in Asia. That middle position is hardly a firm foundation for a decisive and successful policy. It tends to breed inconsistency and to promote compromise between aims and realities. But it is likely to continue for some time to come.

III. The Scope for Change

The Soviet approach to the Western world remains dominated by the idea of struggle. Many times over the past half century, the question has been raised whether the dynamic expansionism, rooted in the concept of permanent hostility between the heartland of socialism and the capitalist powers, might not fade as the Soviet Union adjusted itself to the world community and began to act as a state like other states. The debate in the West has been carried on largely between those whose wish was father to their interpretation and those already convinced that there could be no change.[19] So it was when Lenin introduced NEP, when Stalin brought the Soviet Union into the League of Nations, when the Soviet Union and the West fought together against Hitler, and when Khrushchev proclaimed himself the champion of peaceful coexistence. So it has been as Khrushchev's less spectacular successors try to concentrate on pressing internal problems and temper their belligerent talk with considerable restraint in action.

Objectively, there is no immutable reason why Brezhnev and Kosygin or their successors should not come to see the true interest of their country in discarding the myth of the plans of the imperialists to enslave the world and of their own mission to lead it to communism, and in joining with non-Communist states to build a more secure world environment for all. Yet there is no prospect that any Soviet regime for years to come would or could make such a change. Fifty years of history lie behind the official myth. The document put out by the Communist Party to mark the fiftieth anniversary of the Bolshevik Revolution spoke in the old familiar terms of capitalism's inevitable doom (still approaching, as it was in 1917) and the struggle between socialism and imperialism as "the pivot of world politics," but added the current theme of peaceful coexistence.[20]

An anniversary document, of course, is a propaganda statement intended to set the line for the speech writers and sustain the enthusiasm of the party faithful. But it illustrates how firmly fixed the old line is in the regime's concept of itself, how its position at home and the Soviet Union's role in the world are wrapped up in the same set of myths. There is no evidence that the Soviet leaders do not believe their basic ideological explanation of world developments. The more pertinent question is the gap between pronouncement and practice, and whether it may grow to the point that the ideological motive in foreign policy becomes more or less irrelevant. The difficulty here is that there is no necessary correspondence between the erosion of ideology and progress toward reconciliation or *modus vivendi* with the West. By all indications, whatever may be thought or said about capitalism and socialism, Soviet policy will continue to be a combination of confidence and fear: confidence in the growing strength of the Soviet Union and fear that the "ruling circles" in the Western world, especially in the United States, do in fact plan its destruction.

One decisive factor, often neglected by those who concentrate on the ideological or geopolitical motivation of Soviet foreign policy, is the international environment with all its limitations on the action of any one state and its obstacles to the steady and consistent pursuit of any global strategy. So far as the ultimate goal of world communism is concerned, the Soviet regime may consider itself the instrument of history, but it is not required to hold to any fixed schedule in reaching history's ordained goal. Nor is it propelled by any death wish to use its full military power to advance the cause of communism—and wreck much of the world, including the Soviet Union, in the process. So it plays the game of world politics, seeking security, military advantage, territorial gain, political influence, client states, and even votes in the United Nations. The area of choice, in the complex world of today, is often narrow. Soviet success, or lack of it, depends in large degree on the decisions and acts of other states beyond the reach of Soviet control: not only its principal adversary, the United States, but all other nations which seek to protect their own interests and follow their own roads to salvation. The Soviet regime, George Kennan has pointed out, is "enmeshed in a veritable welter of contradictions and problems, internal and external; torn by conflicting compulsions it is unable to resolve or to contain except by the most delicate sort of political compromise; . . . vacillating, weaving this way and that; responsive to the shifts in the world scene."[21]

Now that states which Moscow recognizes as socialist, both in Europe and in Asia, are part of that outside realm which sets limits to Soviet power, the whole conception of history as a struggle between socialism and imperialism is called into question. The published works continue to argue that the harmony among socialist states has introduced a new and higher type of international relations,[22] but when most of the states now in the "socialist camp" are following policies divergent in greater or less degree from those of the motherland of socialism, can the Soviet leaders be thinking seriously of extending the Communist revolution to all of Germany, to Great Britain, or to the United States? Judging from their experience with China, Yugoslavia and Rumania, one may ask whether they look forward to dealing with a Communist Germany or a Communist United States.

The best judgment we can make for the future is that the Soviet Union's conduct of its international affairs will continue to be dominated by the theme of struggle on two fronts: against the main imperialist enemy, the United States, and against the revolutionary rival, China. World alignments have shifted in the past, however, and will shift again. Is it not possible that the pressures and dangers inherent in this uncomfortable middle position will push Moscow toward cooperation with either China or America in order to meet the threat from the other? The more natural course might seem to be a reconciliation with China, once the frenzied era of Mao Tse-tung's leadership is past. The Kremlin has put its hopes in such an outcome of China's internal struggle for power. Yet China is likely to maintain its revolutionary fervor and fanatic nationalism for a long time to come, both at home and abroad; its immense problems and difficulties will only contribute to that trend. It is hard to see the Chinese accepting the leadership of the Soviet Union or even a working relationship with it. Indeed, the fact that both are Communist states makes cooperation more rather than less difficult, because all their secular conflicts and frictions inevitably are clothed in ideological absolutes, and neither can yield on the correctness of its own line and the heresy of the other's.

China as a nuclear power seems almost bound to be a rival, rather than a partner, of the Soviet Union in Asia. Soviet policy in recent years can best be described as containment, to use a term made familiar in other circumstances. The most striking example was in India and Pakistan, where from the outbreak of the Chinese-Indian quarrel in 1959, Moscow took the side of India and continued thereafter to supply India with arms. Then, after the India-Pakistan war of 1965, Premier Kosygin brought off his successful mediation at Tashkent, thus maintaining a position in both countries and limiting Pakistan's rapprochement with China. It was an unprecedented policy for the Soviet Union, this contribution to the settlement of a conflict between two non-Communist states in order to thwart the ambitions of a fellow member of the Communist camp. Perhaps a more significant example was Vietnam, where the fact that both Moscow and Peking were aiding Ho Chi Minh did not disguise the former's purpose of reducing Chinese influence in Hanoi and strengthening its own. A similar struggle for influence was taking place in North Korea.

The fact that both the Soviet Union and the United States were engaged in containing China, however, did not result in Soviet-American cooperation. Vietnam kept them apart instead of bringing them together. Even the Soviet mediation at Tashkent, though not out of line with American interests, was undertaken by the Soviets on their own and for their own reasons, one of which was to achieve a stronger position in both countries at the expense of the United States. And the Tashkent pattern has not yet been copied elsewhere. Soviet policy toward the Arab-

Israel conflict, with China not so directly involved, provided quite a contrast.

There has been a détente in Soviet-American relations since 1962 in the sense that the ultimate danger of nuclear war has found expression in the willingness of both sides to keep international crises below that danger point. The few instances of agreement or parallel action in the field of arms control, from the test ban of 1963 to the proposed treaty on nonproliferation of nuclear weapons, are related to that mutual caution and instinct for self-preservation. Although the spirit of mutual restraint seemed less evident after 1964, thanks to Vietnam, the Dominican affair, and the clash of interests in the Middle East, other agreements which would limit the scale and intensity of the arms race, and thus the economic strain on both sides, remained within the realm of possibility.

Did the change in Soviet policy go deeper? Was the "Soviet threat," on which Western policy and the whole NATO structure had been based, disappearing? There was no doubt that Soviet pressure on Berlin had relaxed and that the temperature in Europe had been lowered. But relaxation of tension, in the history of Soviet foreign policy, has been a tactic, a pursuit of unchanged ends by softer methods which would give way to a hard line when new conditions arose. Was the soft line of the 1960s something different, something more than the tactical shifts of the past? Could the détente, as many Europeans believed, become an entente, a real basis for the settlement of differences and an effective system of security?

Such a fundamental change in Soviet outlook and policy toward the West might come about with the rise of Chinese power to the point of real danger to the Soviet Union's security and its status as a world power. It might come about if the instabilities of a world wracked by local wars, economic chaos, and East-West rivalry created such intolerable burdens of armament and risks of total war that the need for peaceful cooperation would outweigh hope for Soviet gains sought by old methods. One cannot predict that either of these contingencies will materialize in the next decade, for China's nuclear power may be counterbalanced by fatal weaknesses in its economy and body politic, and the prospect of chaos and trouble in the world is still likely to appear in Soviet eyes more as an opportunity than as a danger.

There is a third contingency which stems from Soviet society itself. Can internal changes, such as those discussed elsewhere in this volume, bring about a change in the way the Soviet leadership thinks about foreign affairs? Can they bring about a situation in which regime and people feel less threatened from outside, less compelled to wage a struggle with the West, and more willing to engage in the normal relationships of one state with another in an ever contracting world?

Without attempting an answer to those questions, we may recall briefly some of the changes and trends: the increasing complexity of industrial society and the need for reform; attention to the consumption side of the economy and consequent pressure on available resources; the insistent stirrings of writers and artists for greater freedom of expression; the growing numbers of well-educated and technically trained people not likely to be forever deferential to party bureaucrats; the erosion of ideology; increasing contact with the outside world, and the need for trade and economic cooperation with the West. These trends cannot be directly translated into foreign policy. But it seems evident that they have already found some reflection in it. Several examples may be cited.

First, the inability or unwillingness of Moscow to follow the line taken by Communist China is more than a reaction to Mao's defiance and insults and his threats to Soviet prestige and territory. It is the natural refusal of a relatively advanced society not to jeopardize its progress, its standard of living, and its entire system, to follow dogmas offering a return to Stalinism or worse at home and great risks of war abroad. Second, the competition for resources is real, setting limits on what a society entering the automobile age and the space age at the same time can spend for an uncontrolled arms race, subsidies to "national liberation" movements all over the world, and military and economic aid to allies and clients both Communist and non-Communist. How many Castros and Nassers can the Soviet government afford and still pay heed to the needs of the Soviet people? Third is the old story of the fat Communist and the thin Communist. Without putting stock in the theory that the former will be less bellicose than the latter, one may note the fact that the economic progress the Soviet Union has made tends toward a "have" rather than a "have-not" mentality affecting both the people and the regime; an infusion of new technology through cooperation with the West can become more important than the cause of national liberation in a remote African republic. Fourth, there is the feeling for peace itself, incessantly proclaimed by the regime for its own tactical propaganda purposes, but deeply held by the Soviet people, from peasants to nuclear scientists. It is the party that rules, not the people, but the party leaders may not have an entirely free hand on the supreme issue of peace and war; they may not be wholly aware that the logical consequence of years of peaceful coexistence as a tactic may be a vested interest, over the long run, in having those words mean what they say.

Fifty years of Bolshevik rule have shown that drastic shifts in Soviet foreign policy can take place almost without warning; that the line can turn rapidly from anticapitalist militancy to nonaggression pacts, from proletarian solidarity to popular fronts, from cooperation with democracies to cooperation with fascism, and back again. Such tactical changes have had the consistency only of serving the interests of the Soviet state and the cause of socialism as the men in power at the time interpreted it. The main questions now concern whether more fundamental changes may be taking place; whether ideology may come to be little more than empty ritual rather than a motive force of foreign policy; whether the Soviet leadership may be edging toward a view of its interests in Europe as requiring cooperation with the advanced nations and an end to the partition of the continent; whether relations with the United States can be seen as a problem of adjusting the interests and concerns of two great powers, difficult enough in any case, rather than as a conflict of irreconcilable historic forces that must end in the triumph of one system over another. It seems safe to say that such changes will not appear within the next decade. They are not likely to appear until further transformation of Soviet society itself has taken place. It is enough to note that changes within the Soviet Union cannot be wholly without influence on Soviet relations with the outside world, and that even the precisely visible trends seem to rule out a reversion to a revolutionary militancy which would take the world back to the worst days of the Cold War.

18.

The Future of Soviet Society

ALLEN KASSOF

The reader who has followed each of the preceding chapters is well aware of the extraordinarily complex cross-currents at work in Soviet society today. There is no single or simple answer to the question of social change in the Soviet Union. Nevertheless, certain major themes recur in the essays which, taken together, allow us to trace the outlines of the Soviet social system as it is likely to evolve over the next decade or two.

One of the most important generalizations concerns the relative durability of the formal social, political, and economic institutions in the Soviet Union. When one considers that they emerged under conditions of severe stress and overcommitment, and during a period of the ferocious and often bloody politics of a now discredited leader, their viability in the face of changing domestic and world conditions is the more impressive. This is not to suggest that these institutions will not continue to change, and perhaps substantially, but to assign a low probability to their breakdown under the pressure of internal and external conflicts. Of course, no one can predict with certainty that there will not be sudden and radical shifts in a severe emergency, or guarantee against such a cataclysmic event as war. Nevertheless, the institutional stability that seems likely to prevail will undoubtedly exert a powerful influence on how, and how fast, the society as a whole changes.

The will and capacity of the Communist Party to maintain its mobilizational style and its relative success in imposing this pattern on the larger society must be counted as key factors in future developments. As Jeremy Azrael points out, although the party's record on this score since Stalin's death has been less than perfect, by and large its allegiance to the mobilizational principle is undiminished and the requisite power and personnel to carry out its policies are almost certain to remain at its disposal.

It is not only the past record of the party that points to its continuing domination over Soviet affairs, but the likelihood that it will adapt reasonably well to future contingencies. I suggested in the Introduction that one of the vulnerabilities of the Soviet system in the face of change stems from the rigidity of the Communist Party in coping with cross-pressures generated by the increasingly complex and vocal "constituencies" that arise in a society dependent upon the services of indispensable functional groups—managers, scientists, military professionals, and the like. The nature of these pressures and the difficulties that they are already causing are genuine enough. However, Sidney Ploss's analysis of the role of interest group politics within the party should caution us against premature conclusions. Even under the rigors of Stalin's dictatorship, he shows, there were informal mechanisms (severely limited and often suppressed, to be sure) within the party to balance and adjudicate among the demands of various sectors of the society for priority in the allocation of resources, power, and prestige. Since then, the arena for the interplay of interest groups, though still modest, has expanded significantly. If the party in fact is able to institutionalize the techniques to handle political conflicts with minimal destructiveness, it may very well escape the threat of being displaced by a multi-party system in the long run. It is especially noteworthy that the best defined interest group and the one potentially most threatening to the party, the military, continues to accede to the established system of controls. As Thomas Wolfe points out, the very nature of a military establishment under conditions of modern technology and weaponry aggravates traditional strains between soldiers and politicians, but the Soviet leadership has so far been successful in keeping them below critical levels. The willingness of the military not only to accept but to support the *status quo* is one more sign, and a very important one, of the relative stability of current institutional arrangements.

Some of the most persuasive evidence of stability is presented in the essays on the economy by Arcadius Kahan and Herbert Levine. The secular decline of industrial growth rates and the perennial perils of Soviet agriculture are amply confirmed in their reports. Even more significant, however, both analysts conclude independently that Soviet industry and agriculture may function adequately, and possibly at advanced growth rates, if reforms which are already underway begin to be effective. These reforms, moreover, are taking place more or less within the current system of decision-making and control. While they may be expected to result in significant modifications of current procedures, they still will fall far short of the kind of gross decentralization or privatization that is sometimes predicted as the only solution to economic difficulties in the U.S.S.R. The assumption that economic necessity must result in wholesale political change—presumably of a liberalizing or democratizing nature—may or may not be valid. The point is that the assumption is unlikely even to be tested in the Soviet Union if, as Levine and Kahan suggest, the essential reforms are being effected without a substantial abandonment of traditional Soviet approaches.

Another basis for the viability of formal institutions is to be seen in the successful creation of a scientific community second only to that of the United States and supplied with quality manpower by the potent educational system which William Medlin describes. The evaluation presented by Alexander Vucinich, moreover, challenges the assumption that authoritarian systems are necessarily incompatible with scientific progress. Either the hypothesis is incorrect, or the Soviets have managed to escape its consequences by shielding the scientific enterprise at least from the most destructive consequences. No doubt the highly centralized nature of Soviet scientific organization will continue to pose a serious hazard of political interference and disruption, but against this danger must be weighed the demonstrated advantages of a coordinated use of talent and knowledge. Furthermore, recriminations over past episodes suggest that the new leadership has learned some of the virtues of restraint in dealing with an absolutely essential source of national power.

Such a situation of formal institutional stability by no means signifies an absence of change—far from it, as we shall see—but is likely to shape and limit its consequences. Specifically, there appears little reason to anticipate a general political democratization of Soviet society in the sense that this is generally understood in the West, even though the already substantial abatement of the arbitrary governmental practices that were part of Stalinism will surely continue. Further steps in this direction, however, as in the past, are likely to occur as efforts to establish a sound basis for public order and efficiency rather than as concessions to irresistible popular demands, which at best are diffuse and unorganized, or out of a growing allegiance to some abstract ideal of individual rights. Leon Lipson's analysis of Soviet legal developments provides a compelling illustration. There is growing resort to the forms and procedures of law in the interest of orderly conflict resolution at the lower and intermediate levels of the society, but no sign of concession to a rule of law that would bring party or government under the restraint of absolute principle or genuine constitutionalism.

All this means that we must answer one of the main questions posed at the outset by concluding that the Stalinist episode will indeed have permanent consequences for Soviet society and that its influence will be eroded only partially in the process of liberalization. The over-all social changes that may be expected in Soviet life over the coming decades, then, are likely to take place within a still overwhelmingly authoritarian political system, a heavily centralized economy, and in an atmosphere characterized by the continuing (and to some extent successful) efforts of the Communist Party to mobilize and to control the material and human resources of the entire society. This institutional style will be encouraged by the force of tradition; by the absence of clearly articulated alternatives; by the appeal of an attenuated but still encompassing ideology; and by the fact that the Soviet Union, despite its considerable material achievements, will continue to lag behind the West and to struggle and mobilize in order to improve its position.

Within these broad limits, however, there will be vast if gradual social changes. Some of them are highly probable or even inexorable: for example, the demographic shifts which Warren Eason predicts, not only in the quantitative but also in the qualitative sense, including such master trends as increasing urbanization and the prospect of higher educational levels for more of the population. At the other extreme are subtle developments in the intellectual and cultural worlds, the outcome of which is as speculative as it is important. Let us see where these changes may lead.

To begin with, Soviet society will become more homogeneous. The stark contrasts in economic and cultural levels among various segments of the society of course will pose severe problems for many years to come. As the processes of modernization continue, however, the extreme differences between peasant and bureaucrat, between the educated and the uneducated, between European and non-European areas (see Vernon Aspaturian's analysis), will diminish in scope and importance. Soviet society will continue to be affected by the historical currents which have already swept over European societies and the United States. Urbanism will create far-reaching uniformities in life style, educational aspiration and attainment, material tastes, attitudes towards work and family, the uses of talent, the nature of recreation and pastimes. The growth of a common mass culture will be furthered by a spreading network of sophisticated communications technologies.

At the same time, paradoxically, the very complexity of an increasingly modern and productive society will more and more preclude a return to the relatively primitive totalitarianism of Stalin's day and will also militate against the advent of a more sophisticated latter-day variety. Collecting, ordering—and using—all of the information essential to total control over a society (not to mention how to enforce the policy decisions involved) pose insuperable obstacles even in the era of computer technology. It would be going too far to say that the resulting gaps will simply lead to a pluralistic society, but we probably can count on some increases in individual and group autonomy—a kind of freedom by default. Such a prospect, let it be noted, will be profoundly disturbing to a Communist regime still strongly attached to a utopian ideology of complete social coordination and planning and will lead to repressive episodes during periods of conservative ascendancy. But such efforts are likely to retard, rather than stop, the erosion. The alternative of enforcing conformity through terror, apart from the political risks entailed, is no longer a realistic answer in a system more than ever dependent upon the rational use of human resources.

There is a certain irony in this situation, for it is precisely the complexity and interdependence of modern life that is often said to threaten the autonomy of the individual and to augur the atomization and depersonalization of society in Europe and America, where the intensive and detailed coordination that is imperative under conditions of an explosively developing technology is leading to the bureaucratization of many areas of life traditionally regarded as lying beyond the scope of public concern. But in a system such as the Soviet, which is already thoroughly politicized, the mounting difficulties of coordination from above may in fact serve somewhat to insulate the individual and his private life from the demands of the center. One extremely important aspect of this shift is foreshadowed in Robert Feldmesser's analysis of social stratification. The continuing efforts of the regime to prevent the "freezing" of status groups are only partially successful;

the relative persistence of status advantages from one generation to the next promises to sustain family and group subcultures, which, Feldmesser predicts, will contribute to a certain kind of pluralism.

The key struggle over the coming decades, then, will be waged between the regime's traditional and still powerful drive towards comprehensive mastery over the society, and the centrifugal tendencies that seem to be inherent in its increasingly complicated domestic environment. I have already stated my conclusion that the Communist Party will almost certainly continue in its commanding role. But in the process of implementing that role—indeed, precisely in order to make it possible—the party will increasingly face the necessity of compromises, the cumulative results of which will greatly alter the atmosphere of daily life.

The party's initial tactical retreats will occur—have occurred—in areas where the relevance of political controls or the means to effect them are most ambiguous. We have already seen the consequences of this in the arts, where political saliency is difficult to define with any useful precision. No Communist regime will ever simply give up its proprietary claims over these fields (especially in literature and drama, where content can be highly literal and direct) but Soviet ideologists have already shown signs of weariness in jousting with twelve-tone scales and cubist painters, and may grudgingly give up the practice, if not the principle, of always and everywhere carrying on a holy war against an elusive and intangible enemy. As this happens, the uniquely influential but muted role of the Russian intelligentsia (which James Billington assesses in his chapter) is likely to be more forcefully felt. It would be premature to anticipate a victory for freedom of expression, yet the yearnings of artists and intellectuals for professional and creative autonomy and their stirrings of conscience as they struggle to face and account for the Stalinist past will contribute directly and indirectly to a general atmosphere of moderation.

A parallel retreat or compromise will probably also take place in the arena of party control over certain aspects of informal social life, not because of some new generosity on the side of the leadership but because of the growing realization that the long-standing effort to create a new Soviet man, the heroic socialist personality, is both unrealistic and too costly. The attempt to inculcate a uniform and deeply rooted set of civic virtues and a Communist world-view will, of course, continue unabated. There will also be experiments from time to time aimed at extending and re-enforcing public priorities in the formation of national character—as, for example, in the boarding schools. Moreover, the principle of political primacy in the socialization of the young (in the educational system and in the official youth program) will be maintained. But, as Field and Anderson show, no substitute has been found, nor is one likely to be devised, to replace the family as the universal and fundamental context of formative training, and as a source—from the point of view of the regime—of variant and often deviant forms of private attitudes and public behavior. While there is no reason to expect a formal concession from the regime, actual practice already reflects a more flexible understanding of the limitations upon molding human nature and a somewhat greater willingness to live with the attendant ambiguities.

Another centrifugal tendency which is already being felt has to do with the impact of a gradually rising material standard of living. If the experiences of the more advanced industrial nations are a guide, the absorption of emotional energy in the pursuit of personal and family consumption is likely to be antithetical to the high level of public commitment and self-sacrifice which the system has traditionally sought to generate and upon which the maintenance of a mobilizational atmosphere greatly depends. One need only think of the role of automobile culture in the United States (and more recently in Western Europe) in revolutionizing social behavior in order to grasp some implications of a more gradual and limited growth of a consumer economy under Soviet conditions. It is no wonder that the party is so anxious, as Paul Hollander finds, to contain the consequences of individualized consumption within the bounds of public regulation as to its use and context—hence, the dominating concern to keep the expenditure of free time and the uses of leisure insofar as possible within the public realm. The outcome of this tug of war between private tendencies and the officially defined public interest cannot be precisely predicted, but the inherent difficulty of curtailing individual aspiration (without, again, a return to the terror) suggests that the relative weight of private pursuits will grow in the coming years.

Superficially, the projection of such tendencies toward the erosion of important totalitarian features of Soviet life seems to point to cumulative changes so great in the long run as to bring into question the very nature of the society. It is precisely on this point, I believe, that extreme caution is necessary lest the projection be carried out in a merely mechanical fashion, for there are self-limiting factors involved which point to a rather different conclusion: namely, that the generally authoritarian atmosphere and institutional functioning of Soviet life are likely to remain more or less intact even in the face of these extensive changes.

I have already referred to the evidence presented in various chapters to the effect that the formal institutions are in little danger of breakdown despite the expectation that they will gradually change. These institutions, it should be stressed, are organized along highly authoritarian lines; granted that rational procedures and improved utilization of resources will be accorded greater emphasis than in the past, the authoritarian features will probably endure. Then too, we should not think of the party as simply helpless in the face of change even though its choice in some areas will be significantly curtailed. On the contrary, to the extent that various reforms and compromises lead to a more satisfactory life both in material and social terms, the prestige of the party and its capacity to carry on its programs are likely to be enhanced. Most important, many of the fundamental pressures toward change stem from the accumulated grievances of decades of political repression, material deprivation, and individual insecurity. As these grievances are satisfied, the pressures for further change will be substantially diminished. It is primarily in this sense that the rate and extent of change is likely to be at least partly self-limiting. The awareness of living in a closed society and, with it, the sense of moral outrage that militates for a more decent life are likely to be greatly diminished by concessions and reforms that fall far, far short of the Western standards of political freedom and material well-being.

Such an outlook strongly suggests that the future of Soviet society will be determined as much by factors specific to the Soviet experience as by forces universally present in industrial societies. The argument now becomes frankly more speculative in going somewhat beyond the "hard" evidence of the chapters, but my own interpretation is that the admittedly powerful influence of that complex of factors known as industrialism now has left its basic mark on Soviet society, that most of the important similarities generated by industrialism among modern systems are already in substantial degree present in the Soviet Union. These include such essential elements as the nature of contemporary technology; the system of mass education; the key role of modern cities; the highly developed transportation and communications facilities; the dominant position of scientific undertakings; a certain commitment to rational procedure in the organization of production and

the utilization of human resources; a bureaucratic mode of coordination of various social functions; the high (relative to underdeveloped economies) standard of living; the diminished influence
of primary social units such as the family and local community;
and a range of familiar material indices. Indeed, if a hypothetical
observer from another planet were to view all contemporary societies he would surely be more impressed by the similarities
among all industrial societies than by the differences. The question, however, is whether the impact of industrialism will be
responsible for *further* similarities between Soviet society and its
Western, and especially American, counterparts.

In certain respects, especially those having to do with purely
physical appearances—for example, the layout and form of the
modern city and the materials and techniques employed in its
construction—the answer is certainly, yes. In still other respects,
such as the tempo of daily life, fashion, high geographical mobility, access to the pleasures of consumption, and the like, the
answer is also yes. Then too, so large a part of the Soviet population is still rural, and in this degree nonmodern, that its assimilation to the contemporary stream will in itself create increasing
similarities in the obvious quantitative sense.

Beyond this, however, the striking lesson of the Soviet past—
and I dare say of the future—is that, although there are inherent
limits to the kinds of societies that are compatible with the industrial mode, these limits are very broad indeed; the Soviet experience has shown conclusively that the "classical" development of
industrial society under the aegis of capitalism was historically
specific as to time and place, and that other configurations—call
them socialism, or communism, or state capitalism—are equally
compatible.

This being the case, the expectation that tensions generated by
the incongruency between the Soviet system and the imperatives
of industrialism will sooner or later force the Soviet Union to become more "Western" in some fundamental respect rests, I believe, on an unwarranted assumption. The Soviet Union is already
well within the bounds of those imperatives, and the current
process of reform and adjustment is likely to prevent any real
collision that would bring the system down. That the Chinese
Communists have recently replaced the Soviets as the world home
of revolutionary fervor; that the U.S.S.R. is truly more cautious
(though no less energetic) than in the past about involvements
beyond its borders; that the ideology is indeed taken less literally

than once it was; and that the stringency of daily life for the Soviet citizen has somewhat abated—these and similar developments tempt one to go the rest of the way and to conclude that the Soviet episode is about to fade into history to be replaced by something vaguely closer to home. Such a conclusion is further prompted by a certain provincialism which sees the Western pattern of industrialism as a mean towards which all modern societies eventually evolve. Add to this the hope that a Soviet Union more closely resembling its Western counterparts will be easier to live with (perhaps, perhaps not), and it is no surprise that the wish for convergence is easily translated into an expectation. But the petulant Chinese accusation that the Soviet Union has sold out to capitalism is a monstrous and in some ways exceedingly funny historical joke; there is no reason for us to take the charge seriously.

Rather, the evidence presented in this volume suggests the emergence in the Soviet Union of what might be best described as a more or less benevolent authoritarianism of great vitality and long-range durability. For the Soviet people, then, the burning questions concern the content and the limitations of that benevolence, and the political, social, and economic factors that will hasten or retard its growth. On this score, although we can already dimly perceive the probable outlines of the future, it is too early to speak with confidence of any kind of timetable. Nor can we altogether rule out the baneful influence of retrograde tendencies, or the eruption of unforeseen civil conflicts that might once more crush individuals under the weight of monumental social forces and impersonal historical processes. Nevertheless, the prospects for a more decent existence for such a significant portion of the earth's population—and such a talented one—are probably better now than at any time since the tumultous years immediately following the Bolshevik Revolution. That these prospects will assume forms only partly familiar to the Western experience in no way diminishes their significance.

Notes

CHAPTER 2. SOVIET SOCIETY: A COMPARATIVE VIEW

1. The range of problems involved in such comparisons is discussed in Richard L. Merritt and Stein Rokkan (eds.), *Comparing Nations: The Use of Quantitative Data in Cross-National Research* (New Haven: Yale University Press, 1966).

2. Akademiia Nauk SSSR, Nauchnyi Sovet po Kompleksnoi Probleme, "Ekonomicheskoe sorevnovanie dvukh sistem i slaborazvitie strany," *Sorevnovanie dvukh sistem. Problemy ekonomicheskoi nauki* (Moscow, 1963), and *Sorevnovanie dvukh sistem. Ekonomicheskie sopostavleniia* (Moscow, 1965). See also the bibliography on Soviet research on international economic comparisons in Congress of the United States, Joint Economic Committee, *New Directions in the Soviet Economy* (Washington, D.C.: GPO, 1966), pp. 987–88.

3. See the estimates of percentage of national income devoted to defense in 1914, 1921, 1929, and 1937 in Quincy Wright, *A Study of War*, 2 vols. (Chicago: University of Chicago Press, 1942), I, pp. 670–71; and of expenditures on defense as percentage of gross national product in 1955–60 in Bruce M. Russett *et al.*, *World Handbook of Political and Social Indicators* (New Haven: Yale University Press, 1964), pp. 79–80.

4. There is a discussion of this question in Theodore H. Von Laue, "Problems of Modernization," in Ivo J. Lederer (ed.), *Russian Foreign Policy: Essays in Historical Perspective* (New Haven: Yale University Press, 1962), pp. 69–108.

5. U.S. Department of State, *World Strength of the Communist Party Organizations* (Washington, D.C.: GPO, 1966), p. i.

6. These characteristics are discussed in Arthur S. Banks and Robert B. Textor, *A Cross-Polity Survey* (Cambridge, Mass.: Harvard University Press, 1963), pp. 82–84, 88–89, 101, and 106, with detailed analyses in paragraphs 92–100, 112–14, 152–55, and 167–69 of the appended computer printout.

7. Banks and Textor, cited, pp. 85–87, 89–95, 103–4, 110, 113–15, with detailed analyses in paragraphs 101–8, 115–32, 159–61, 174–77, and 184–87 of the computer printout.

8. Russett, cited, pp. 82–87.

9. See Merle Fainsod, "Bureaucracy and Modernization," in Joseph La-Palombara (ed.), *Bureaucracy and Political Development* (Princeton: Princeton University Press, 1963), pp. 233–67, who suggests this typology; also Frederick C. Barghoorn, "Soviet Russia: Orthodoxy and Adaptiveness," in Lucian W. Pye and Sidney Verba (eds.), *Political Culture and Political Development* (Princeton: Princeton University Press, 1965), pp. 450–511; and Robert C. Tucker, "Towards a Comparative Politics of Movement-Regimes," *American Political Science Review*, LV (June 1961), pp. 281–89.

10. John A. Armstrong, "Sources of Administrative Behavior: Some Soviet and Western European Comparisons," *American Political Science Review*, LIX (September 1965), pp. 643–55.

11. *Fundamentals of Marxism-Leninism*, 2nd ed. (Moscow, 1963), p. 645.

12. Simon Kuznets, "A Comparative Appraisal," in Abram Bergson and Simon Kuznets (eds.), *Economic Trends in the Soviet Union* (Cambridge, Mass.: Harvard University Press, 1963), pp. 335–36.

13. Same, p. 337.

14. Russett, cited, p. 160.

15. Kuznets, cited, p. 337.

16. Russett, cited, pp. 160–61.

17. Stanley H. Cohn, "Soviet Growth Retardation: Trends in Resource Availability and Efficiency," *New Directions in the Soviet Economy*, cited, p. 105.

18. Michael Boretsky, "Comparative Progress in Technology, Productivity, and Economic Efficiency: U.S.S.R. versus U.S.A.," *New Directions in the Soviet Economy*, cited, pp. 148–55.

19. Russett, cited, pp. 166–69.

20. On this question see Oskar Morgenstern, *On the Accuracy of Economic Statistics*, 2nd ed. (Princeton: Princeton University Press, 1963); Rolf Wagenführ, *Der internationale wirtschafts- und sozialstatistische Vergleich* (Freiburg-im-Breisgau, 1959), pp. 74–79; Abraham S. Becker, "Comparisons of United States and USSR National Output: Some Rules of the Game," *World Politics*, XIII (October 1960), pp. 99–111; and especially Wilfred Beckerman, *International Comparisons of Real Incomes* (Paris, 1966).

21. Cohn, cited, p. 108.

22. Same, pp. 107–9; see also the discussion in Stanley H. Cohn, "The Soviet Economy: Performance and Growth," *Studies in the Soviet Union*, VI, No. 4 (1967), pp. 24–54.

23. V. M. Kudrov, "Natsional'nyi dokhod SSSR i SShA," *Sorevnovanie dvukh sistem. Ekonomicheskie sopostavleniia*, pp. 101–18, esp. pp. 109–11.

24. Kuznets, cited, pp. 358–64.

25. Janet G. Chapman, *Real Wages in Soviet Russia Since 1928* (Cambridge, Mass.: Harvard University Press, 1963), p. 166.

26. Same, p. 176.

27. Congress of the United States, Joint Economic Committee. *Current Economic Indicators for the U.S.S.R.* (Washington, D.C.: GPO, 1965), p. 122.

28. Same, p. 120

29. Same, p. 119.

30. Same, pp. 55–61.

31. Simon Kuznets, "Quantitative Aspects of the Economic Growth of Nations: VIII. Distribution of Income by Size," *Economic Development and Cultural Change*, XI, No. 2, Part II (January 1963), pp. 20–23.
32. See especially Franklyn D. Holzman, *Soviet Taxation: The Fiscal and Monetary Problems of a Planned Economy* (Cambridge, Mass.: Harvard University Press, 1955), pp. 275–307; and also Abram Bergson, *The Economics of Soviet Planning* (New Haven: Yale University Press, 1964), pp. 118–26; and Peter J. Pettibone, "The Soviet Turnover Tax," *Public Finance*, XIX (1964), pp. 361–82.
33. Kuznets, cited, pp. 344–47.
34. Russett, cited, pp. 54–55.
35. S. M. Miller, "Comparative Social Mobility," *Current Sociology*, IX, No. 1 (1960), pp. 56–59.
36. U.N., *Demographic Yearbook*, 1964 (New York, 1965), pp. 292–335; and G. B. Osipov (ed.), *Sotsiologiia v SSSR*, 2 vols. (Moscow, 1965), I, p. 344. Similar proportions are reflected in comparisons of distribution of employment by economic sector, *New Directions in the Soviet Economy*, cited, p. 111.
37. *Higher Education in Other Countries* (London, 1964), Appendix Five of *Higher Education* (London, 1963), The Report of the Committee on Higher Education (the Robbins Report), p. 16.
38. Russett, cited, pp. 214–16.
39. *Higher Education in Other Countries*, cited, pp. 15–16.
40. Same, p. 9.
41. Same, p. 11.
42. Same, p. 17.
43. Same, p. 18.
44. Same, p. 19.
45. Frederick Harbison and Charles A. Myers, *Education, Manpower, and Economic Growth: Strategies of Human Resource Development* (New York: McGraw-Hill, 1964), pp. 23–34.
46. C. Freeman and A. Young, *The Research and Development Effort in Western Europe, North America and the Soviet Union: An Experimental International Comparison of Research Expenditures and Manpower in 1962* (Paris: OECD, 1965), esp. pp. 11–13, 69–70.
47. Russett, cited, pp. 218–20.
48. *New Directions in the Soviet Economy*, cited, p. 123.
49. Russett, cited, pp. 222–24.
50. Same, pp. 108–10.
51. Same, pp. 120–22.
52. Same, pp. 126–31.
53. *Book Publishing in the U.S.S.R.*, Report of the Delegation of U.S. Book Publishers Visiting the U.S.S.R., August 20–September 17, 1962 (New York, 1963), pp. 27–35.
54. Russett, cited, pp. 197–98.
55. Same, pp. 200–201.
56. Same, pp. 204–6.
57. Same, pp. 208–10.
58. John B. Parrish, "Soviet Womanpower as a Professional Resource," *Quarterly Review of Economics and Business*, IV (Autumn 1964), pp. 55–61.

59. Norton T. Dodge, *Women in the Soviet Economy: Their Role in Economic, Scientific, and Technical Development* (Baltimore: Johns Hopkins Press, 1966), pp. 5–31.
60. Russett, cited, pp. 32–33.
61. U.N., *Demographic Yearbook, 1964* (New York, 1965), pp. 643–46.
62. A pioneering comparative study in this field is International Labour Office, *Report of the Ad Hoc Committee on Forced Labour* (Geneva, 1953), which devoted considerable attention to the U.S.S.R., pp. 82–98, 426–528.
63. Russett, cited, pp. 293–303.
64. Tsentral'noe Statisticheskoe Upravlenie, *Narodnoe khoziaistvo SSSR v 1964 g. Statisticheskii ezhegodnik* (Moscow, 1965), p. 89.
65. Donald H. Niewiaroski, "The Level of Living of Nations: Meaning and Measurement" (Manuscript).
66. Brian J. L. Berry, "Basic Patterns of Economic Development," in Norton Ginsburg (ed.), *Atlas of Economic Development* (Chicago: University of Chicago Press, 1961), pp. 110–19.
67. M. K. Bennett, "International Disparities in Consumption Levels," *American Economic Review*, XLI (September 1951), pp. 632–49.
68. Simon Kuznets, "Quantitative Aspects of the Economic Growth of Nations: I. Levels and Variability of Rates of Growth," *Economic Development and Cultural Change*, V (October 1956), pp. 9–19.
69. Cohn, "Soviet Economic Development in the First Half Century," cited, Table A-1.
70. See references in footnotes 22 and 23 above.
71. *The Growth of the National Economies of Japan and the Soviet Union* (Tokyo: Ministry of Foreign Affairs, 1963).
72. This question is discussed in Irving B. Kravis, "International Differences in the Distribution of Income," *Review of Economics and Statistics*, XLII (November 1960), pp. 408–16.
73. The adaptation of historically evolved institutions to modern functions is discussed in C. E. Black, *The Dynamics of Modernization: A Study in Comparative History* (New York: Harper and Row, 1966).
74. See especially Zbigniew Brzezinski and Samuel P. Huntington, *Political Power: USA/USSR* (New York: Viking Press, 1964), pp. 419–36.
75. Russett, cited, pp. 352–55.
76. *Fundamentals of Marxism-Leninism*, 2nd ed. (1963), p. 694; it is interesting to note that this prediction does not appear in the 1st edition (1961).
77. Russett, cited, pp. 356–61.
78. Seymour E. Harris (ed.), *Economic Aspects of Higher Education* (Paris: OECD, 1964), p. 82.

Chapter 3. The Party and Society

1. V. I. Lenin, *Selected Works* (New York: International Publishers, 1943), VII, pp. 5–111.
2. Lenin, cited, II, pp. 27–192, especially pp. 121 and 138.
3. See Leonard Schapiro, *The Communist Party of the Soviet Union* (New York: Random House, 1960), pp. 178–266, for a detailed discussion of the Leninist system.

4. See Robert C. Tucker, *The Soviet Political Mind: Studies in Stalinism and Post-Stalin Change* (New York: Frederick A. Praeger, 1963), pp. 3–20, for the concept of the "movement-regime."
5. See Schapiro, cited, pp. 267–546, and Merle Fainsod, *How Russia Is Ruled*, rev. ed. (Cambridge, Mass.: Harvard University Press, 1963), for comprehensive analyses of these changes.
6. See Tucker, cited, pp. 3–20, for some interesting reflections along these lines.
7. See Carl J. Friedrich and Zbigniew K. Brzezinski, *Totalitarian Dictatorship and Autocracy*, 2nd ed. (New York: Frederick A. Praeger, 1966), for the "classical" statement of the theory and practice of totalitarianism.
8. Leo Gruliow (ed.), *Current Soviet Policies II* (New York: Frederick A. Praeger, 1953), p. 247.
9. The reference is to the July 1953 uprising in East Berlin.
10. See Wolfgang Leonhard, *The Kremlin Since Stalin* (New York: Frederick A. Praeger, 1962), for an unusually good account of the post-Stalin succession struggle.
11. Leo Gruliow and Charlotte Saikowski (eds.), *Current Soviet Policies IV* (New York: Columbia University Press, 1962), p. 31. See J. Stalin, *Works* (Moscow: Foreign Languages Publishing House, 1953), VI, p. 189, for the view that the party will "wither away" simultaneously with the dictatorship of the proletariat; B. Ponomarev, F. Konstantinov, Y. Andropov, *Kommunist*, No. 8 (1960), for a rare modern affirmation of this view, although the stress is on the impossibility of a "withering away" of a party prior to the arrival of full-fledged communism.
12. See Jeremy R. Azrael, "An End to Coercion?" *Problems of Communism* (November–December 1962), XI, pp. 9–17, for more detailed treatment of the material covered in this paragraph.
13. *Current Digest of the Soviet Press*, XI, No. 10, p. 1.
14. Quoted in Erich Goldhagen, "The Glorious Future," in Abraham Brumberg (ed.), *Russia Under Khrushchev* (New York: Frederick A. Praeger, 1962), p. 626.
15. See Richard Lowenthal, "The Revolution Withers Away," *Problems of Communism*, XIV (January–February 1965), pp. 10–17.
16. In Raymond Aron (ed.), *World Technology and Human Destiny* (Ann Arbor: The University of Michigan Press, 1962), p. 86.
17. See Jeremy R. Azrael, *Managerial Power and Soviet Politics* (Cambridge, Mass.: Harvard University Press, 1966), Chapter V, for a detailed discussion of the evidence on which this and the next paragraph are based.
18. See Alex Inkeles and Raymond A. Bauer, *The Soviet Citizen* (Cambridge, Mass.: Harvard University Press, 1959).
19. See Allen Kassof, "The Administered Society," *World Politics*, XVI (July 1964), pp. 558–75, for a detailed critique of the concept "liberalization" as applied to the development of the Soviet system since Stalin's death.

Chapter 4. Interest Groups

1. Cf. G. G. Gabrelian, *Protivorechiia sotsialisticheskogo obshchestva i puti ikh preodoleniia* (Yerevan: 1962), pp. 34ff.; G. Smirnov, *Kommunist*, No. 1 (1963), pp. 36–48; G. Glezerman, same, No. 7 (1963), p. 32; P.

Rogachev and M. Sverdin, same, No. 9 (1963), p. 14; N. Bikkenin, S. Oduev, A. Pozner, and G. Smirnov, same, No. 5 (1965), pp. 57–74; and P. Kopnin, *Pravda*, February 10, 1966.

2. *Desiatyi s'ezd RKP (b), mart 1921 goda, stenograficheskii otchet.* (Moscow, 1963), p. 230.
3. *Odinnadtsatyi s'ezd RKP (b), mart-aprel' 1922 goda, stenograficheskii otchet* (Moscow, 1961), p. 402.
4. See Boris I. Nicolaevsky, "Vneshniaia politika Moskvy" (Moscow's Foreign Policy), *Novyi zhurnal* (New York), No. 3 (1942), pp. 178–79.
5. S. S. Biriuzov, in M. N. Tukhachevsky, *Izbrannye proizvedeniia* (Moscow, 1964), I, pp. 12–13.
6. The claim of anti-Stalinist sentiment among delegates to the Seventeenth Party Congress is made by L. Shaumian in *Pravda*, February 7, 1964, and A. M. Samsonov *et al.*, in *Kratkaia istoriia SSSR v dvukh chastiakh* (Moscow, 1964), II, 270.
7. *Voprosy istorii KPSS perioda velikoi otechestvennoi voiny* (Kiev, 1961), p. 300.
8. According to the speech of Khrushchev at a conference of agricultural workers held on November 2, 1961, G. M. Malenkov in the postwar period "recommended" to T. D. Lysenko that he write an article which would have the effect of discrediting Khrushchev's viewpoint on the technology of grain farming. "This episode," Khrushchev concluded, "demonstrates how some leaders use authoritative people for their selfish ends." (N. S. Khrushchev, *Stroitel'stvo kommunizma v SSSR i razvitie sel'skogo khoziaistva* [Moscow, 1963], VI, p. 58). On factionalism in the magazine *Bol'shevik*, see my "Political Conflict and the Soviet Press," a paper delivered at the 1964 Annual Meeting of the American Political Science Association.
9. "Concerning the Errors of Comrade L. D. Yaroshenko," in J. Stalin, *Economic Problems of Socialism in the U.S.S.R.* (Moscow, 1952), pp. 65–92.
10. See I. Pomelov's criticism of Sh. A. Kobakhidze, a philosophy instructor who circulated a letter to various organizations demanding an end to the "dictatorship of the working class," in *Kommunist*, No. 2 (1953), p. 62.
11. "Reply to Comrades A. V. Sanina and V. G. Venzher," in Stalin, cited, pp. 93–104.
12. *Pravda*, April 28, 1964.
13. Miklós Nyárády, *My Ringside Seat in Moscow* (New York: Crowell, 1952), pp. 74–78.
14. V. Stepanov, *Izvestiia*, December 19, 1962.
15. M. A. Morozov, *Sovetskaia Kirgiziia*, July 31, 1964.
16. M. Polekhin, *Partiinaia zhizn'*, No. 1 (1964), p. 26.
17. Cf. the editorial article in *Pravda*, October 17, 1964, and V. Stepanov, same, May 17, 1965.
18. *The New York Herald Tribune*, July 8, 1957.
19. M. Sakov, an editor of *Kommunist*, warned against the elections in the magazine's issue No. 8 (1957), pp. 10ff., and was excluded from the new editorial board approved by a Central Committee decree of January 9, 1959, which is in *Spravochnik partiinogo rabotnika* (Moscow, 1959), pp. 534–37.

20. N. F. Kolbenkov, *Voprosy istorii KPSS* (*sbornik statei*) (Moscow, 1959), pp. 56–57.
21. *Pravda*, November 20, 1962.
22. The decree is in *Spravochnik partiinogo rabotnika* (Moscow, 1964), pp. 75–80.
23. Same, pp. 109ff.
24. *Ekonomicheskaia gazeta*, April 21, 1965.
25. *Pravda*, October 2, 1964.
26. N. M. Kiriaev *et al.*, *Leninskaia partiia—protiv revizionizma i dogmatizma* (Moscow, 1965), p. 127.
27. Wladyslaw W. Kulski, *The Soviet Regime: Communism in Practice* (Syracuse: Syracuse University Press, 1959), p. 410.
28. Cf. *Pravda*, December 23–26, 1959; N. Karotamm, *Sovetskaia Rossiia*, July 16, 1965; and L. I. Brezhnev, *Pravda*, March 30, 1966.
29. Cf. G. Lisichkin, *Plan i rynok* (Moscow, 1966) *and Sel'skaia zhizn'*, September 22 and December 21, 1966.
30. See the editorial article in *Kommunist*, No. 10 (1957).
31. N. G. Egorychev, *Kommunist*, No. 3 (1965), p. 18.
32. *Kommunist*, No. 4 (1955), p. 16.
33. Khrushchev, cited, VIII, p. 51.
34. *Kommunist*, No. 12 (1965), p. 7; and S. M. Mayorov, *Leninskie printsipy sovetskoi vneshnei politiki* (Moscow, 1966), p. 6.
35. Cols. V. Rybnikov and A. Babakov, *Krasnaia zvezda*, December 7, 1965. Cf. the vigorous support of the policy of preferential development of heavy industry by Yu. Sadokhin of the U.S.S.R. State Planning Committee in same, May 11, 1966.
36. Unless noted otherwise, the sources for this section are in my *Conflict and Decision-Making in Soviet Russia: A Case Study of Agricultural Policy, 1953–1963* (Princeton, N.J.: Princeton University Press, 1965).
37. Cf. A. Koriagin, *Pravda*, December 29, 1953, and *Ekonomicheskaia gazeta*, February 17, 1965 (pro-light industry); Ya. Kronrod, *Kommunist*, No. 16 (1953), and *Ekonomicheskaia gazeta*, May 12, 1965 (pro-light industry); and A. Bechin, *Voprosy ekonomiki*, No. 7 (1954), and *Ekonomicheskaia gazeta*, March 24, 1965 (pro-heavy industry).
38. Khrushchev, *Pravda*, November 20, 1962.
39. Cf. Khrushchev, *Pravda*, April 26, 1963 ("Chei golos gromche"), and *Ekonomicheskaia gazeta*, June 16, 1965 ("Slovesnykh bataliiakh").
40. Cf. Khrushchev's interview with Turner Catledge, managing editor of *The New York Times*, in *Pravda*, May 14, 1957, and the repetition of this remark by A. F. Vodolazsky in *Pravda vostoka*, June 16, 1961, and by G. I. Shitarev, *Voprosy istorii KPSS*, No. 7 (1964), p. 37.
41. E. I. Bugaev and B. M. Leybzon, *Besedy ob ustave KPSS* (Moscow, 1962).
42. R. Ya. Malinovsky, *Pravda* and *Krasnaia zvezda*, April 17, 1964.
43. Cf. *Partiinaia zhizn'*, No. 19 (1965), p. 5, and F. Loshchenkov, *Kommunist*, No. 15 (1965), p. 49.
44. G. Shakhnazarov, *Politicheskoe samoobrazovanie*, No. 12 (1965), p. 19.
45. Sir Frank Adcock, *Roman Political Ideas and Practice* (Ann Arbor, Mich.: University of Michigan Press, 1964), p. 41, based on H. H. Scullard, *Roman Politics 220–150 B.C.* (Oxford: Clarendon Press, 1951).

CHAPTER 5. LAW AND SOCIETY

1. See Engels, *Socialism: Utopian and Scientific* (selection from his *Anti-Dühring*) (New York: International Publishers, 1966).
2. A West European scholar, commenting on ways to explain the presence in Russian law (at least as early as 1845) of a law making it criminal to fail to come to the rescue of one in danger, conjectures: ". . . the ideals of 19th century liberalism and freedom of the individual hardly influenced Russian law, which therefore, instead of restricting itself to punishing a comparatively small number of clearly defined proscribed acts, aimed chiefly at enforcing and reflecting the officially approved morality. The present Soviet point of view is hardly different." F. J. M. Feldbrugge, "Good and Bad Samaritans: A Comparative Survey of Criminal Law Provisions Concerning Failure to Rescue," *Am. J. Comparative Law*, XIV, No. 4 (1966), pp. 630, 631.
3. See, for example, the tenfold reiteration of "discipline" in the editorial articles in *Sotsialisticheskaia zakonnost'*, No. 3 and No. 4 (1967), or in *Sovetskaia iustitsiia*, No. 3 (1967).
4. On "state and labor discipline" see the resolution of the Central Committee of the CPSU, reported in *Pravda*, December 22, 1966: "at the present stage of Communist construction . . . discipline and good organization become increasingly necessary requirements for strengthening the might of our state, for successful fulfillment of the decisions of the Twenty-third CPSU Congress and of the five year plan . . . for multiplying the public wealth and for growth in the Soviet people's living standard and cultural level." (Translation from *Current Digest of the Soviet Press*, XVIII, No. 51, p. 8.)
5. In Weberian terms the effort of some of the legal theorists may be seen as aimed at substituting a rational-legal myth in part for the routinized-charismatic myth at the base of the claim to the legitimacy of the party. Cf. Mark G. Field, "Soviet Society and Communist Party Controls: A Case of 'Constricted' Development," in Donald W. Treadgold (ed.), *Soviet and Chinese Communism: Similarities and Differences* (Seattle, Wash.: University of Washington Press, 1966), p. 192.
6. *Ugolovnyi Kodeks RSFSR* as of Sept. 16, 1966 (Moscow, 1966), p. 72 (text of Art. 206, Hooliganism) and pp. 210–16 (Decree of the Presidium of the Supreme Soviet of the U.S.S.R., July 26, 1966, and Resolution of the Plenum of the Supreme Court of the U.S.S.R., August 26, 1966). See also I. Tiazhkova, "Voprosy otvetstvennosti za khuliganstvo," *Sotsialisticheskaia zakonnost'*, No. 3 (1967), pp. 29–32.
7. See *Vedomosti Verkhovnogo Soveta RSFSR*, No. 15 (April 13, 1967), Item 333; *Current Digest of the Soviet Press*, XIX, No. 15, p. 11.
8. Lipson, "Law: The Function of Extra-Judicial Mechanisms," in D. W. Treadgold (ed.), cited, pp. 160–62.
9. Lipson, "Hosts and Pests: The Fight against Parasites," *Problems of Communism*, XIV, No. 2 (March–April 1965), pp. 72–82.
10. *At the Trial of A. Sinyavsky and Yu. Daniel* (in Russian) (New York: Inter-Language Literary Associates, 1966).
11. Bukharin, Nikolai, *The Great Purge Trial*, edited by R. C. Tucker and S. F. Cohen (New York: Grosset & Dunlap, 1965), p. xxxv.

12. For a detailed survey, whose comparative candor is encouraging despite the faults acknowledged, see "The Fight against Crime and the Strengthening of the Procuracy's Supervision over Inquiry and Investigation," *Sotsialisticheskaia zakonnost'*, No. 5 (1967), pp. 3–11.

13. M. S. Strogovich, *Socialist Legality, Legal Order and the Application of Soviet Law* (in Russian) (Moscow, 1966), p. 4.

14. S. N. Bratus' and I. S. Samoshchenko (eds.), *General Theory of Soviet Law* (in Russian) (Moscow, 1966), p. 352.

15. This has been noticed by more than one reader of the current Soviet legal literature, including Mr. Andreas Bilinsky.

16. Bratus' and Samoshchenko (eds.), cited, p. 390. The passage appears in a chapter written by Dr. Samoshchenko.

17. T. H. Huxley, quoted in Massachusetts Bonding & Ins. Co. v. United States, 352 U.S. 128, 138 (1956); see Bickel and Wellington, "The Lincoln Mills Case," *Harvard Law Review*, LXXI (1957), pp. 1, 15.

CHAPTER 6. THE MILITARY

1. Morris Janowitz, *The Professional Soldier* (New York: The Free Press, 1960), p. viii.

2. Harold D. Lasswell, "The Garrison-State Hypothesis Today," in Samuel P. Huntington (ed.), *Changing Patterns of Military Politics* (New York: The Free Press, 1962), p. 51.

3. M. Kh. Kalashnik, *Politorgany i partiinaia organizatsiia Sovetskoi Armii i Voenno-Morskogo Flota* (Moscow, 1963), p. 15. See also Iu. P. Petrov, *Partiinoe stroitel'stvo v Sovetskoi Armii i Flote, 1918–1961* (Moscow, 1964), pp. 350–52, 442–43, 476.

4. See Roman Kolkowicz, *The Use of Soviet Military Labor in the Civilian Economy*, The RAND Corporation, RM-3360-PR (November 1962), pp. 1–15.

5. For a fuller discussion of Soviet political-military relations, see the present author's *Soviet Strategy at the Crossroads* (Cambridge, Mass.: Harvard University Press, 1964), especially pp. 91–109; and Raymond L. Garthoff, *Soviet Military Policy: A Historical Analysis* (New York: Frederick A. Praeger, 1966), pp. 29–62. See also Alexander Dallin et al., *The Soviet Union, Arms Control, and Disarmament: A Study of Attitudes* (New York: Columbia University Press, 1964), pp. 82–91. An exhaustive historical examination of the subject can be found in a new study by Roman Kolkowicz, *The Soviet Military and the Communist Party: Institutions in Conflict*, The RAND Corporation, R-446-PR (March 1966).

6. Marshal R. Ia. Malinovskii, "In the Leadership of the Party—Our Strength and Invincibility," *Red Star*, April 17, 1964; Marshal A. A. Grechko, "Mighty Guardian of Peace," *Izvestiia*, April 17, 1964.

7. Thirty-one of the 330 members and candidates elected to the Central Committee in 1961 by the Twenty-second Congress of the CPSU were military men. See Kalashnik, cited, pp. 34–35. Previously, the largest military representation was 26, elected to the Central Committee by the Nineteenth Congress of the CPSU in 1952. At that time, however, the size of the Central Committee was smaller, so that the military percentage of the total membership was 11 per cent, compared with slightly under 10 per cent for the present Central Committee.

8. For a detailed analysis of the current military representation in various party organizations, see Harriet Fast Scott, "The Soviet Military and the Communist Party," pp. 2–11. This presently unpublished paper, whose author has given permission for this citation, offers the thesis that a rather close "politico-military marriage" is to be found consistently at various levels below that of the party (Politburo). It also finds that a military representation of about 10 per cent seems to obtain.

9. Military Councils, combining political and military authorities, have existed at various levels of command in essentially their present form since Stalin set them up in 1938 in the wake of the military purges. Petrov, cited, pp. 305–306. Their functions have fluctuated, but they have generally been employed by party leaders to water down the authority of military commanders. The Higher Military Council at the top Moscow level has been seldom discussed in Soviet materials. One of the charges made against Marshal Zhukov was that he interfered with the work of the Higher Military Council and "tried to subordinate it to the Ministry of Defense rather than to the decisions of the Central Committee . . . despite the fact that it included members of the party Presidium as well as military and political leaders of the army and navy." Petrov, cited, pp. 460, 462. Military Councils at the military district level include the party secretary of the pertinent republic, as well as ranking military authorities.

Following Zhukov's removal in 1957, measures were taken to "significantly increase the role and authority of Military Councils." These measures are discussed at length in Petrov, cited, pp. 465–70, who states (p. 465) that "the Soviet Armed Forces, this gigantic complex organism, would be unthinkable without the work of the Military Councils." A somewhat less enthusiastic description of Military Councils at the military district level was given by General of the Army, P. Kurochkin, in a recent article. Kurochkin described them as "a collegial form for examining important questions," but he also argued that this "collective form of leadership" was "no substitute for the principle of one-man command (*edinonachalie*)" within the armed forces. "Modern Warfare and One-Man Command," *Red Star*, June 5, 1964. See also Kalashnik, cited, p. 16; Joseph Baritz, "The Soviet Armed Forces," *Studies on the Soviet Union*, II, No. 3 (Munich: Institute for the Study of the U.S.S.R., 1963), pp. 24–26.

10. The Higher Military Council is mentioned as an important decision-making body in the celebrated *Penkovskiy Papers*. The high-level composition of the Council described in the Penkovskiy account jibes with that indicated in official Soviet sources. See *The Penkovskiy Papers* (New York: Doubleday & Co., 1965), pp. 209, 233, 239, 310, 331.

The controversy concerning the authenticity of *The Penkovskiy Papers* raises some delicate questions about citing them as a source of information. Although the present writer has no intention of trying to adjudicate this issue, it is his impression that many portions of Colonel Penkovskiy's account ring true. This seems to apply to his comments on the Higher Military Council (which he termed the Supreme Military Council), even though doubt may attach to some other aspects of the *Papers*. For commentary pro and con on the *Papers*, see among others: "Soviet Expert Doubts Validity of Controversial Papers," two-article series by Victor

Zorza, *The Washington Post*, November 15, 16, 1965; Bernard Gwertz-man, "Russians Angrily Attack Penkovskiy Spy Book," *The Washington Star*, November 15, 1965; "Gibney Defends Penkovskiy Papers," letter by Frank Gibney, *The New York Times*, November 17, 1965. "Penkovskiy Papers Defended," letter by Peter Deriabin, *The New York Times*, November 19, 1965; K. Aleshin, "Scandalous Downfall of the Washington Falsifiers," *Izvestiia*, November 25, 1965; "Legacy of a Spy," book review by George Feifer, *The New York Times*, November 28, 1965; "Penkovskiy Reaction," letter by Prof. Samuel L. Sharp, *The Washington Post*, December 3, 1965; "Our Man in Moscow," book review by John Le Carré, and "Penkovskiy's Role: A British Review," *The Washington Post*, December 26, 1965.

11. See Marshal V. D. Sokolovskii, *et al.*, *Soviet Military Strategy*, 1st edition, with Analytical Introduction and Annotations by H. S. Dinerstein, L. Gouré, and T. W. Wolfe (Englewood Cliffs, N.J.: Prentice-Hall, 1963), pp. 67, 494–95.

12. Stalin combined in his person during World War II the posts of party leader, head of government, chairman of the State Defense Committee, Minister (Commissar) of Defense, chairman of the *Stavka*, and Supreme High Commander of the armed forces. Khrushchev at the time of his removal was head of both party and government, as well as Supreme High Commander. With Brezhnev now holding the post of party chief and Kosygin that of premier, which of them might take up the mantle of Supreme High Commander is a moot question.

13. In addition to agencies of party and secret police control within the armed forces, arrangements also exist for independent outside surveillance of military activities and for verification of military fulfillment of party instructions. The Department for Administrative Organs, an agency of the civilian party apparatus which was headed by Major General N. R. Mironov until his death in an airplane crash in Yugoslavia in October 1964, is charged with this function. See L. Slepov, *Vysshie i mestnye organy partii* (Moscow, 1959), p. 107.

14. See Garthoff, cited, pp. 53–57; Kolkowicz, *The Soviet Military and the Communist Party*, cited, pp. 217–36.

15. Colonel General N. A. Lomov, *Sovetskaia voennaia doktrina* (Moscow, 1963), p. 5.

16. One of those who took the lead in hinting that the new regime should avoid Khrushchev's "subjective" errors and give more heed to professional military advice was Marshal M. V. Zakharov, who has been reappointed as Chief of the General Staff in November 1965, following the death of Marshal S. S. Biriuzov. See article by Zakharov, "Imperative Demand of the Times: On Improving Further the Scientific Level of Military Leadership," *Red Star*, February 4, 1965.

17. See Wolfe, *Soviet Strategy at the Crossroads*, cited, pp. 91–104; Sokolov-skii *et al.*, cited, pp. 33–41; and also the present author's "Military Policy: A Soviet Dilemma," *Current History* (October 1965), p. 203.

18. Kozlov's views appeared in two publications in early 1964. One was an article by him entitled "Military Doctrine and Military Science" in *Kommunist vooruzhennykh sil*, No. 5 (March 1964), pp. 9–16. The other was the second edition of a major treatise on military science by four Soviet military men—the same General Kozlov, plus Major General

M. V. Smirnov and Colonels I. S. Baz and P. A. Sidorov, *O Sovetskoi voennoi nauke*, 2nd edition (Moscow, 1964), esp. pp. 382–88. For a fuller discussion of these materials, see the present author's *Soviet Military Theory: An Additional Source of Insight into Its Development*, The RAND Corporation, P-3258 (November 1965), pp. 30–43.

19. See Garthoff, cited, pp. 29, 41.

20. For useful examinations of this question, see Raymond L. Garthoff, *Soviet Strategy in the Nuclear Age* (New York: Frederick A. Praeger, 1958), pp. 18–30, and *Soviet Military Policy*, cited, pp. 47–52; Myron Rush, *The Rise of Khrushchev* (Washington, D.C.: Public Affairs Press, 1958), pp. 80–81; Zbigniew Brzezinski and Samuel P. Huntington, *Political Power: USA/USSR* (New York: Viking Press, 1964), pp. 252, 339–52; Roger Pethybridge, *A Key to Soviet Politics: The Crisis of the "Anti-Party" Group* (New York: Frederick A. Praeger, 1962), pp. 89–90, 103–6, 128–32; Robert Conquest, *Power and Policy in the USSR* (New York: St. Martin's Press, 1961), pp. 330 ff.; and also by Conquest, *The Soviet Succession Problem*, no imprimatur, p. 101.

21. See by the present author, *Impact of Khrushchev's Downfall on Soviet Military Policy and Détente*, The RAND Corporation, P-3010 (November 1964), pp. 28–29; *Note on the Naming of a Successor to Marshal Biriuzov*, The RAND Corporation, P-3025 (December 1964), pp. 13–16. (These papers are hereafter referred to respectively as *Impact of Khrushchev's Downfall* and *Naming of a Successor to Biriuzov*.) See also Nikolai Galay, "The Role of the Soviet Army in Khrushchev's Overthrow," Reference Paper No. 16 (Munich: Institute for the Study of the U.S.S.R., 1964/65).

22. Zbigniew Brzezinski, "The Soviet Political System: Transformation or Degeneration," *Problems of Communism* (February 1966), p. 5.

23. See, for example, B. Borisov and V. Riabov, *Sovetskaia armiia* (Moscow, 1962), p. 111.

24. Colonel N. Piatnitsky, *Krasnaia armiia SSSR* (Paris, 1932), II, p. 116, cited by Garthoff, *Soviet Military Policy*, cited, p. 242.

25. Figures compiled by Garthoff, *Soviet Military Policy*, cited, p. 35, indicate that as late as 1926 men of non-worker/peasant origin constituted over 60 per cent of "higher officers" in the Red Army.

26. Leonard Schapiro, "The Great Purge," in B. H. Liddell Hart (ed.), *The Soviet Army* (London: Weidenfeld and Nicolson, 1956), p. 69. For additional discussion of the military purges, see Erickson, *The Soviet High Command* (New York: St. Martin's Press, 1962), pp. 449–509.

27. Schapiro, same, pp. 66–67.

28. J. M. Mackintosh, "The Soviet Soldiers' Conditions of Service," in Liddell Hart, cited, p. 404.

29. Stalin's Supreme Soviet speech of February 9, 1946, marked the beginning of a new policy line which within two years reduced the stature of the wartime military leadership. See Garthoff, *Soviet Military Policy*, cited, pp. 42–44.

30. For a careful analysis of manipulation of the history of the war see Matthew P. Gallagher, *The Soviet History of World War II, Myths, Memories, and Realities* (New York: Frederick A. Praeger, 1963). See also Kolkowicz, *The Soviet Military and the Communist Party*, cited, pp. 279–353.

31. Borisov and Riabov, cited, pp. 114–15.
32. See *Service Conditions and Morale in the Soviet Armed Forces: A Pilot Study*, Volume I, The RAND Corporation, R-213 (August 25, 1961), pp. 13, 262–63.
33. An interesting picture of the way family and social ties operate to give the military elite a close-knit character is conveyed in *The Penkovskiy Papers*, cited, esp. pp. 48, 302, 322.
34. See Garthoff, *Soviet Military Policy*, cited, p. 39.
35. See Vera Sandomirsky Dunham, "Social Values of Soviet and American Elites," *The Journal of Conflict Resolution*, VIII, No. 4 (December 1964), p. 407.
36. The range of ages among the top group of 30 important Soviet military leaders in 1966 is from 52 (General I. I. Yakubovskii) to 73 (Marshal A. I. Yeremenko), but only three of the group besides Yakubovskii are in their fifties. Yakubovskii, former commander of the Soviet forces in Germany, is probably the most distinguished of the top leadership group who can still be regarded as being in the prime of his career with the prospect of further upward advance within the hierarchy yet before him.
37. Among candidate members, only V. P. Mzhavanadze is over 60, the others ranging from the late forties to the early fifties.
38. In this connection, some data on elite attitudes reported in *The Journal of Conflict Resolution*, VIII, No. 4 (December 1964), are of interest. One finding based on a content analysis of Soviet elite media indicated that the military elite was more disposed than the party-government elite to feel that "nothing is achieved without taking risks" and that "the society that gets ahead will be the society that takes large and frequent risks, even on vital matters." This attitude would seem to be at some variance with the notion that the senior military elite may be more fixed and conservative in outlook than the political elite. See in the journal cited, Robert C. Angell, "Social Values of Soviet and American Elites: Content Analysis of Elite Media," p. 367.
39. Nikolai Galay, "Generational Turnover in the Soviet Armed Forces," paper presented at International Symposium on the Soviet Takeover Generation (Munich: Institute for the Study of the U.S.S.R., September 6–8, 1965), pp. 11–13.
40. See, for example, D. Fedotoff-White, *The Growth of the Red Army* (Princeton, N.J.: Princeton University Press, 1944), pp. 76–100, 348–407; Merle Fainsod, *How Russia Is Ruled* (Cambridge, Mass.: Harvard University Press, 1954), pp. 411–18, 500, and *Smolensk Under Soviet Rule* (Cambridge, Mass.: Harvard University Press, 1958), pp. 325–42; John Erickson, cited, pp. 113–78, 187–91, *passim*; Louis Nemzer, "The Officer Corps as a Political Interest Group," paper read at the 39th Annual Meeting of the American Political Science Association, New York, September 4, 1963, pp. 1–38; Raymond L. Garthoff, *Soviet Strategy in the Nuclear Age*, cited, pp. 18–40; Roman Kolkowicz, *Conflicts in Soviet Party-Military Relations*, The RAND Corporation, RM-3760-PR (August 1963).
41. The flavor of the deep antipathy between military commanders and non-professional party "intruders" during the past war has been graphically conveyed in such literary works as V. Nekrasov's *In the Trenches of Stalingrad*. For an excellent discussion of Nekrasov's work, including

translation of pertinent passages, see Gallagher, *The Soviet History of World War II*, cited, pp. 171–74.

42. Kalashnik, cited, p. 13.

43. A statement on this point in *Kommunist vooruzhennykh sil*, No. 6 (March 1958), p. 8, reads as follows: "Party work in the armed forces is under the leadership of the Central Committee, CPSU, through the Main Political Administration . . . which operates with the rights of the Central Committee, CPSU." See also Petrov, cited, p. 456.

44. The head of the MPA has generally been a party *apparatchik* who dons a uniform and is given high military rank during his tenure in the job. An exception to this rule was Marshal F. I. Golikov, who succeeded A. S. Zheltov in early 1958, and in turn was replaced by A. A. Epishev, a former secret police official, in 1962. Golikov was a bona fide professional soldier who may have lost his MPA post for not having been a sufficiently vigorous guardian of the party's interests.

45. Editorials in *Pravda*, November 3, 1957; *Red Star*, November 5, 1957. See also Petrov, cited, pp. 460–65.

46. *Red Star*, May 16, 28, 1959; Petrov, cited, pp. 461–69, 507.

47. See Kolkowicz, *The Soviet Military and the Communist Party*, cited, pp. 231, 418.

48. See Wolfe, *Soviet Strategy at the Crossroads*, cited, pp. 92–96 ff.

49. Colonel A. Babakov, "On the New Stage in the Development of the Armed Forces of the U.S.S.R.," *Red Star*, May 8, 1964. See also Captain Third Rank V. Puzik, "The Commander's Thinking and Cybernetics," *Red Star*, May 27, 1964; General P. Kurochkin, "Modern Warfare and Single Command," same, June 5, 1964; Marshal M. V. Zakharov, "Single Command and Single Commanders," same, October 12, 1962.

50. Marshal Liu Po-cheng, "The Soviet Army is the Example for the People's Army of the World," *Jen-min Jih-pao*, October 31, 1957, in *Survey of the China Mainland Press* (SCMP), 1647, pp. 26–30; speech by Marshal P'eng Teh-huai, February 22, 1958, same, pp. 26–29. One may note that the Chinese not only talked of adopting reforms to combat military professionalism similar to those instituted in the Soviet Union following Zhukov's dismissal, but that they pressed the parallel further in 1959 by dismissing P'eng Teh-huai himself as Defense Minister for having resisted political interference in the armed forces.

51. See Seymour Topping, "Peking Rebukes Officers Who Resist Party Curb," *The New York Times*, February 8, 1966.

52. For a highly useful discussion of this question see Roman Kolkowicz, *The Impact of Technology on the Soviet Military: A Challenge to Traditional Military Professionalism*, The RAND Corporation, RM-4198-PR (August 1964). (Hereafter cited as *The Impact of Technology*.)

53. See, for example, Colonel General V. Tolubko (deputy commander of the strategic missile forces), "Know Strategic Weapons Perfectly," *Red Star*, January 8, 1963; Lieutenant Colonel P. Baranov, "At the Roadside," same, March 20, 1963; Colonel General A. L. Getman, "The Sympathetic Commander," same, March 29, 1963.

54. Colonel D. Lebchanko, "The Commander and the New Technology," *Red Star*, November 10, 1960; General I. Pliev, "The New Technology and Problems of Strengthening Discipline," *Communist of the Armed Forces*, No. 19 (October 1962), pp. 21–28; Colonel V. Sergeev, "The

Party Spirit of Military Science," same, No. 1, (January 1963), p. 24.
55. Colonel General M. Kalashnik, "Raising the Efficiency of Ideological Work," *Communist of the Armed Forces*, No. 24 (December 1964), p. 4.
56. See Wolfe, *Soviet Strategy at the Crossroads*, cited, pp. 240–42.
57. See Kolkowicz, *The Impact of Technology*, cited, pp. 31–32.
58. As a political commissar with the rank of lieutenant general, Khrushchev had been the chief party representative on the Military Councils of several southern fronts during the war, but the main one in terms of renown was the Stalingrad front. During his early postwar years in charge of party activities in the Ukraine, Khrushchev continued his wartime links with a number of officers of the Stalingrad Group. For an analysis of the Stalingrad clique, see Kolkowicz, *Conflicts in Soviet Party-Military Relations*, cited, pp. 37–48.
59. Khrushchev gave the signal for denigration of Stalin's wartime role in his secret speech at the Twentieth Party Congress in February 1956. The text of this speech may be found in Bertram D. Wolfe, *Khrushchev and Stalin's Ghost* (New York: Frederick A. Praeger, 1957). The relevant passages attacking Stalin's wartime leadership are in pages 164–88. Following Zhukov's dismissal in 1957, it became the fashion to link him with Stalin as being responsible for Soviet unpreparedness on the eve of the war and for faulty conduct of various operations, such as the drive on Berlin in 1945. For a representative sampling of these charges, see *Pravda*, November 3, 1957; *Istoriia Kommunisticheskoi Partii Sovetskogo Soiuza*, 2nd ed., B. N. Ponomarev (ed.) (Moscow, November 1962), p. 541; review of book by General P. I. Batov, *Red Star*, November 1, 1962; editorial, *Communist of the Armed Forces*, No. 8 (April 1963), p. 3; *Military-Historical Journal*, No. 9 (September 1963), p. 24; article by Marshal M. V. Zakharov, *Red Star*, February 16, 1964.
60. Zhukov began to come back into public notice in February 1965, when his name appeared as one of the signers of an obituary in *Red Star*, February 10, 1965. A short time later, a Soviet writer, S. Smirnov, appearing on Moscow television on February 12, made the surprise suggestion that "it would be uplifting" if Zhukov were to lead the 20th anniversary victory parade on May 8. Although he did not lead the parade, Zhukov's rehabilitation was seemingly confirmed on May 8, 1965, when he joined top party and military leaders to hear Brezhnev's victory day speech. Brezhnev's reference to Zhukov on this occasion as one of the "splendid" wartime commanders was greeted with "thundering applause." See *Pravda*, May 9, 1965; dispatch by Henry Tanner, *The New York Times*, May 10, 1965.
61. See remarks by Secretary of Defense Robert S. McNamara, "Major National Security Problems Confronting the United States," in *The Department of State Bulletin*, December 16, 1963, p. 918; *The Military Balance 1965–1966*, The Institute for Strategic Studies, London (November 1965), p. 2.
62. Mackintosh, "The Soviet Soldier's Conditions of Service," in Liddell Hart, cited, p. 408.
63. Lieutenant Colonel M. D'iachenko, "Psychological Conditions for Strengthening Troop Discipline," *Communist of the Armed Forces*, No. 12 (June 1964), p. 46.

64. Colonel S. Il'in, "The Authority of Leaders," *Communist of the Armed Forces*, No. 6 (March 1964), p. 45.

65. Lieutenant Colonel V. Demin, "The Process of Adjustment of Young Soldiers," same, p. 51.

66. For an informed discussion of these trends, see Yury V. Marin, "Morale in the Soviet Armed Forces," in *Analysis of Current Developments in the Soviet Union*, No. 43 (Munich: Institute for the Study of the U.S.S.R., 1963/64); see also Kolkowicz, *The Impact of Technology*, cited, p. 28; *Molodezh Sovetskogo Soiuza*, Report of the XIV Conference of the Institute for the Study of the U.S.S.R., Munich, 1962, pp. 38–53; "Debate on Youth Widens in Soviet Union," *The New York Times*, September 20, 1965. For recent major attacks by the first secretary of the Komsomol on the mood of "indifference" and "rejection of authority" among Soviet youth, see S. P. Pavlov, "The Ideological Persuasion of Youth," *Pravda*, August 29, 1965; *The New York Times*, December 30, 1965.

67. *Molodaia gvardiia*, No. 2 (1964), p. 8. Poor morale among some recruits seems traceable to their having already held responsible jobs in civilian life. Thus, *Red Star* describes the case of a young soldier who was disciplined for insulting his commanding officer, and who defended his conduct by arguing: "Before I came into the army I had a job with 50 people working for me." *Red Star*, August 21, 1962.

68. "Igor Nazarov—Missile Officer," *Red Star*, August 26, 1962.

69. Senior Lieutenant I. Vashevich, "First Step to a Romantic Career," *Red Star*, May 7, 1964. Similar sentiments were reflected in a published letter to Marshal S. Budennyi in early 1962 from several students at a Soviet military academy. Referring to the tendency of some people in Soviet society to disparage the military profession, the students wrote: "They say that even though the officer profession is necessary at present, it is uninteresting and unromantic and that any civilian profession is better than the military." Cited by Kolkowicz in *The Impact of Technology*, cited, p. 29.

70. "Dangerous Delusion," *Red Star*, March 4, 1961.

71. See, for example, the review of the book by Matreshin, *A Soldier's Thoughts*, in *Red Star*, August 14, 1962; V. Nikolskii, "Soldier Nikitin, Sergeant Vlasenko and I," *Iunost'*, No. 7 (1962).

72. Colonel Il'in in *Communist of the Armed Forces*, No. 6 (March 1964).

73. *Red Star*, March 4, 1961. See also Petrov, cited, p. 496.

74. Demin in *Communist of the Armed Forces*, No. 6 (March 1964), p. 51; D'iachenko, same, No. 12 (June 1964), p. 46. See also *Molodezh Sovetskogo Soiuza*, pp. 46–51.

75. D'iachenko, cited, pp. 46–47.

76. Lieutenant General M. Kalashnik, "The Sense of Ideological Work—In Practice," *Communist of the Armed Forces*, No. 24 (December 1963), p. 13.

77. For a discussion of the Soviet debate over war as an instrument of politics, see Wolfe, *Soviet Strategy at the Crossroads*, cited, pp. 70–78.

78. Lt. Colonel E. Rybkin, "On the Essence of World Missile-Nuclear War," *Communist of the Armed Forces*, No. 17 (September 1965), pp. 55–56.

79. *Red Star*, February 9, 1964.

80. *Moskovskaia pravda*, July 2, 1963. For other military criticism of artistic works which failed to provide "heroic" inspiration and were permeated with the spirit of "Remarquism," see Captain A. Chermonys and Lieutenant Colonel V. Fedorov, "Wherein Lies the Beauty of an Heroic Deed," *Red Star*, January 29, 1964; Marshal I. Bagramian, "Mighty Means of Patriotic Education," *Sovetskii patriot*, January 29, 1964; Marshal N. Krylov, "An Honorable Profession Needed by the Nation," *Red Star*, June 9, 1963; Major General M. Kuznetsov, in *Komsomolskaia pravda*, December 25, 1965.

81. For a useful discussion of the new Soviet regime's preoccupation with the ideological estrangement of Soviet youth, see Andrei V. Babich, "Resurgence of the 'Fathers and Sons' Polemic and Party Dissatisfaction with Youth," *Analysis of Current Developments in the Soviet Union*, No. 392 (Munich: Institute for the Study of the U.S.S.R., January 18, 1966).

82. *Pravda*, October 23, 1965. See also Marshal Krylov in *Sovetskaia Rossiia*, October 8, 1965.

83. Marshal R. Ia. Malinovskii, "Perfecting the Political, Practical and Moral Qualities of the Military Cadres," *Red Star*, September 24, 1965.

84. V. Tolstikov, "A Good Specialist and a Staunch Warrior," *Pravda*, September 1, 1965.

85. The five major branches of the armed forces are the ground, naval, air, air defense, and strategic missile forces. The missile forces, created under Khrushchev in the late 1950s, are the newest branch. The air defense forces, also newer than the senior ground, naval, and air forces, are to include antimissile defenses as these are developed, according to Soviet sources. For more detailed discussion of the formal organization of the armed forces, see Garthoff, *Soviet Strategy in the Nuclear Age*, cited, pp. 41–46; *Soviet Russia: Strategic Survey*, Department of the Army Pamphlet 20–64 (Washington, D.C.: December 1963), pp. 173–88.

86. For a discussion of the rise of the strategic missile forces under Khrushchev and the reaction of other less-favored branches of the armed forces, see Wolfe, *Soviet Strategy at the Crossroads*, cited, esp. pp. 153–71. See also present author's article, *Current History* (October 1965), p. 206.

87. See Garthoff, *Soviet Military Policy*, cited, p. 50.

88. For more detailed discussion of the internal alignments in this debate, see Sokolovskii *et al.*, cited, pp. 12–41; Wolfe, *Soviet Strategy at the Crossroads*, cited, pp. 26–37, *passim*.

89. The announced manpower reductions in 1956 and 1960 would have brought the Soviet armed forces down from about 6 million men to 2.4 million, according to figures given by Khrushchev (*Pravda*, January 15, 1960). The 1960 program was suspended before completion, however, leaving the armed forces at around 3 million men or slightly more. No figure was ever announced for the cut proposed by Khrushchev in December 1963 (*Izvestiia*, December 15, 1963). The only strength figure mentioned since Khrushchev's ouster was an ambiguous reference in February 1965 by Marshal Sokolovskii, which suggested that reduction to the 2.4 million level may have been carried out. See discussion by the present author in *Current History*, October 1965, pp. 205–6.

90. Among these accounts, two are especially noteworthy: Colonel I.

Korotkov, "The Development of Soviet Military Theory in the Post-War Years," *Military-Historical Journal*, No. 4 (April 1964), pp. 39–50; and the previously cited work by Major General Kozlov *et al.*, *O sovetskoi voennoi nauke*, pp. 50, 204–16.

91. Korotkov, cited, p. 46.
92. Same, p. 50.
93. Marshal P. Rotmistrov, "Military Science and the Academies," *Red Star*, April 26, 1964; Major General V. Bolotnikov, "Man, Altitude and Speed," same, April 25, 1964. See also by the present author, *Some Recent Signs of Reaction Against Prevailing Soviet Doctrinal Emphasis on Missiles*, The RAND Corporation, P-2929 (June 1964), and *Soviet Strategy at the Crossroads*, cited, pp. 168–72.
94. See discussion by the present author, *Current History* (October 1965), pp. 201–3.
95. Major General K. Bochkarev and Colonel I. Sidel'nikov, "New Epoch, New Conclusions—On Development by the Party of V. I. Lenin's Ideas on War, Peace and Safeguarding the Conquests of Socialism and Communism," *Red Star*, January 21, 1965.
96. Colonel Sidel'nikov, "V. I. Lenin on the Class Approach to Defining the Character of War," *Red Star*, September 22, 1965.
97. Among pertinent articles, see the following: Colonel General S. M. Shtemenko, "The Queen of the Battlefield Relinquishes Her Crown," *Nedelia*, No. 6 (January 31–February 6, 1965); "The Armored Shield of the Motherland," *Pravda*, April 15, 1965; Colonel V. Larionov, "New Weapons and the Duration of War," *Red Star*, March 18, 1965; G. Miftiev, "War and Manpower Resources," same, June 4, 1965.
98. See speeches by Podgornyi, *Pravda*, May 22, 1965; Kirilenko, same, July 25, 1965; Polianskii, same, November 7, 1965; Suslov, same, June 5, 1965; Shelepin, same, July 25, 1965.
99. See Brezhnev reports at the March and September Plenums of the Central Committee, *Pravda*, March 27 and September 30, 1965, and July 3 speech to military academy graduates, *Moscow News*, July 10, 1965. See Kosygin report on drafting of new five year plan, *Planovoe khoziaistvo*, No. 4 (April 1965), pp. 8–10; speech at Volgograd, *Pravda*, July 12, 1965; report at September Plenum, same, September 28, 1965.
100. *Pravda*, July 12, 1965.
101. V. F. Garbuzov, "On the USSR State Budget for 1966 and on the Fulfillment of the USSR State Budget for 1964," *Pravda*, December 8, 1965. Whether the announced or "overt" defense budget figure reflects actual military outlays in the Soviet case is, of course, a matter of considerable doubt, as Western press commentary on the 1966 budget pointed out. See *The New York Times*, December 8, 1965; *The Washington Post*, December 8, 1965. For a more detailed analysis of this question, see Abraham S. Becker, *Soviet Military Outlays Since 1955*, The RAND Corporation, RM-3886-PR (June 1964).
102. Garbuzov in *Pravda*, December 8, 1965; Kosygin interview of December 6 with James Reston, *The New York Times*, December 8, 1965.
103. See Garthoff, *Soviet Military Policy*, cited, pp. 110–11.
104. For a discussion of Sino-Soviet military relations, see the present author's *The Soviet Union and the Sino-Soviet Dispute*, pp. 40–49.

CHAPTER 7. THE NON-RUSSIAN NATIONALITIES

1. V. I. Lenin, *Collected Works* (New York: *International Publishers*, 1945), XVI, p. 507.
2. For the full text, see *Dokumenty vneshnei politiki SSSR*, X (Moscow, 1957), pp. 14–15.
3. Cf. Richard Pipes, *The Formation of the Soviet Union* (Cambridge: Harvard University Press, 1957), esp. pp. 50–113.
4. Cf. Alexander Dallin, *German Rule in Russia, 1941–1945* (New York: St. Martin's Press, 1957); George Fischer, *Soviet Opposition to Stalin: A Case Study in World War II* (Cambridge, Mass.: Harvard University Press, 1952); and Robert Conquest, *The Soviet Deportation of Nationalities* (New York: St. Martin's Press, 1960).
5. J. V. Stalin, *Marxism and the National and Colonial Question* (New York: International Publishers, 1936), p. 298.
6. The most impressive study of the Sovietization, Russification, and Russianization of the non-Russian nationalities during the Stalin era (although it does not draw a distinction between Russianization and Russification) is Frederick C. Barghoorn, *Soviet Russian Nationalism* (New York: Oxford University Press, 1956). One could even make a useful distinction between "Marxification" and modernization in the Sovietization process, since the modernization of the underdeveloped nationalities of the Soviet Union is an objective phenomenon which could survive its separation from the ideological norms which inspired and shaped the course of modernization.
7. See, for example, Yu. Desheriyev, M. Kammari, and M. Melikyan, "The Development and Mutual Enrichment of the Languages of the Peoples of the U.S.S.R.," *Kommunist*, No. 13 (September 1965), pp. 55–66.
8. Same.
9. Same.
10. Same.
11. "The adoption of the Russian script by most of the languages has not only contributed to their development, but has been of notable assistance to the various nationalities of the Soviet Union in their successful mastery of the Russian language and in the assimilation of Russian culture." N. A. Baskokov, "The Development of the Languages and Cultures of the Peoples of the U.S.S.R.," as cited in S. Wurm, *Turkic Peoples of the U.S.S.R.* (London, 1954), p. 48. See also U. Weinreich, "The Russification of Soviet Minority Languages," *Problems of Communism*, No. 6 (1953), pp. 46–57 and J. Ornstein, "Soviet Language Theory and Practice," *Slavic and East European Journal*, XVII (1959), pp. 1–24.
12. According to an Estonian linguist, "examining any one of the languages of the Soviet Union, e.g., Mordvinian, one is shocked by the discovery that it swarms with Russian words, and that often only the suffixes are Mordvinian; the word order, use of cases, etc., are a poor imitation of Russian." Alo Raun, "National in Form, Socialistic in Content," *Ukrainian Quarterly*, No. 2 (1950), pp. 115–16.
13. Yu. Desheriyev, *et al.*, cited.
14. Same.

15. T. P. Lomtev, "J. V. Stalin on the Development of National Languages During the Epoch of Socialism," *Voprosy filisofii*, No. 2, (1949). It was further charged that "bourgeois nationalists artificially bred local words and forms to obstruct the penetration of Russian words and forms." The Great Russian language, Lomtev maintained, "has become the source of enrichment and flowering for the different national languages. . . . The Russian language is . . . the instrument of the most advanced culture in the world. From its inexhaustible treasures, the national languages of the U.S.S.R. draw a life-giving elixir." Compare this with the mellower current view of Desheriyev and his co-authors: "The allegation of certain linguists that the borrowing of forms from other languages demonstrates an underestimation of the native tongues and their possibilities is unfounded. . . . Lenin justly criticized the use of foreign words *where it is unnecessary*. But Vladimir Ilyich never opposed the purposeful borrowing of words and terms. . . . In combating artificial term-coining, we must create terms both on the basis of the native tongue and through borrowings from Russian and other languages (where this is expedient)." For a good description of Soviet linguistic policy during the Stalinist era, see Elliot R. Goodman. *The Soviet Design for a World State* (New York: Columbia University Press, 1960), pp. 264–84.
16. See Nicholas DeWitt, *Education and Professional Employment in the U.S.S.R.* (Washington, D.C.: National Science Foundation, 1961), pp. 112–17, for statistical data and analysis of language instruction in Russian and non-Russian-language schools.
17. "On the Strengthening of the Relationship of the School with Life and on Further Development of the System of Public Education in the Country," *Pravda*, November 14, 1958. The text of the Supreme Soviet law can be found in *Pravda*, December 25, 1958.
18. *Zasedaniia Verkhovnogo Soveta SSSR, 5 soiuza, II sessiia (22–25 dekrabria, 1958 godu) stenograficheskii otchet.* For an excellent description and discussion of the debate in the Supreme Soviet, see Yaroslav Bilinsky, "The Soviet Education Act of 1958–59 and Soviet Nationality Policy," *Soviet Studies* (October 1962), pp. 138–57.
19. *Pravda*, December 2, 1958.
20. *Zasedaniia*, pp. 346–47.
21. Cf. Bilinsky, cited, pp. 140–45.
22. Cf. DeWitt, cited, pp, 556–74, for a textual comparison of the republican laws with the all-union law.
23. Cf. Bilinsky, cited, pp. 145–46.
24. *Bakinskii rabochii*, March 27, 1959.
25. *Sovetskaia Latviia*, March 17, 1959.
26. Cf. The discussion in Bilinsky, cited, pp. 146–47.
27. "Friendship of the Peoples Who Are Building Communism," *Kommunist*, No. 16 (November 1965), pp. 3–13.
28. Data in column A is from *Kulturnoe stroitel'tsvo SSSR: statisticheskii sbornik* (Moscow, 1956), pp. 186–87. See also DeWitt, cited, p. 112.
29. Pravda, July 17, 1956.
30. Basic data is from *Narodnoe khoziaistvo SSSR v 1960 godu* (Moscow, 1961), p. 780.
31. Pierre Lochak, in *Der Monat*, June 1957.
32. This would be inevitable where the smaller and more exotic languages are

concerned. Cf. *Pravda vostoka,* September 4, 1957; *Sovetskaia Estonia,* January 31, 1957; *Sovetskaia Kirgiziia,* November 4, 1957, for illustrative complaints about the lack of scientific and technical textbooks and journals in indigenous languages.

33. Cf. Yaroslav Bilinsky, "Education of the Non-Russian Peoples in the Soviet Union," *Comparative Education Review,* June 1964, pp. 78–89.
34. Adapted from DeWitt, cited, p. 355.
35. *Pravda,* February 4, 1960.
36. Cf. Geoffrey Wheeler, *The Modern History of Soviet Central Asia* (New York: Frederick A. Praeger, 1965); Michael Rywkin, *Russia in Central Asia* (New York: Collier Books, 1963); C. W. Hostler, *Turkism and the Soviets* (New York: Frederick A. Praeger, 1957); Olaf Caroe, *Soviet Empire* (London, 1954); and W. Kolarz, *Russia and Her Colonies* (New York: Frederick A. Praeger, 1952). The view that the Turkic peoples of Central Asia constitute a single nation is about as tenable as the view that all Arab speakers constitute a single nation.
37. Mukhitdinov, who was closely associated with Khrushchev, has since departed from the party summit, while Kunayev was elected a candidate member of the Politburo at the Twenty-third Party Congress in 1966. *Pravda,* April 9, 1966.
38. Data are from the Soviet census of 1959 and from A. A. Isupov, *Natsionalnyi sostav naseleniia SSSR* (Moscow, 1961). Figures in parentheses in the next to the last column represent the precise percentage giving Russian, while the other figures represent the percentage giving "another language," which turns out to be mainly Russian, with a few conspicuous exceptions (Bashkirs). The data in parentheses and in the last column are from Isupov, cited, p. 34, and are incomplete.
39. Isupov, cited, pp. 33–34.
40. Cf. S. M. Abramson, "The Influence of the Process of Increased Contact Between Nations on Family Life in Central Asia and Kazakhstan," *Sovetskaia etnografiia,* No. 3 (1962) and the article on intermarriage in Tashkent by K. Kh. Khanazarov in *Obshchestvennye nauki v Uzbekistane,* No. 10 (1964). In one Tashkent suburb, according to Khanazarov, in 1963, 10.5 per cent of the mixed marriages between non-Russians gave Russian as their language, while 79 per cent of all mixed marriages involving a Russian partner registered as Russian-speaking, for a total of 86.9 per cent of all mixed marriages reporting Russian as their common language.
41. Cf. Robert Slusser and Simon Wolin, *The Soviet Secret Police* (New York: Frederick A. Praeger, 1957), pp. 3–61.
42. *Pravda,* December 23, 1953.
43. *Pravda,* July 3, 1957.
44. *Pravda,* February 1, 1959.
45. *Izvestiia,* November 2, 1961.

CHAPTER 8. POPULATION CHANGES

1. N. S. Khrushchev, in *Pravda,* January 8, 1955, had this factor in mind when he observed that "even another 200 million" people would be insufficient to support the development of the resources of the country.

2. See M. Ia. Sonin, *Aktual'nye problemy ispol'zovaniia rabochei sily v SSSR* (Moscow, 1965), p. 3, for a general statement of this view of the problem.

3. F. Lorimer, *The Population of the Soviet Union: History and Prospects* (Geneva, 1946), Chapter XI, was one of the first to recognize the similarity, as documented in F. W. Notestein, *et al.*, *The Future Population of Europe and the Soviet Union: Population Projections, 1940–1970* (Geneva; League of Nations, 1944). After comparing Soviet prewar experience with other countries, Lorimer based his projection of the postwar population on "the assumption that the future development of population trends in the Soviet Union will conform to previous European experience." P. 175.

4. For example, R. Ia. Besher, *Problemy naseleniia v narodnokhoziaistvennom planirovanii* (Moscow, 1937), pp. 14 ff.

5. D. I. Valentei, *Problemy narodonaseleniia* (Moscow, 1961), p. 115.

6. This wider view of population problems is considered basic to the Soviet approach, as in G. Namestnikova, "Organizovan koordinatsionnyi sovet po problemam narodonaseleniia," *Ekonomicheskie nauki*, No. 3 (1964), pp. 120–22.

7. For example, A. Ia. Boiarskii and P. P. Shusherin, *Demograficheskaia statistika* (Moscow, 1951 and 1955).

8. At a landmark conference of Soviet statisticians, held in June, 1957, the question of demographic statistics was one of the three major questions discussed. See *Vsesoiuznoe soveshchanie statistikov 4–8 iiunia 1957 g.* (Moscow, 1958).

9. A seven-volume series on statistics published by the Academy of Sciences of the U.S.S.R., *Uchenye zapiski po statistike* (Moscow, 1955 to 1963), included a special, supplementary volume entirely devoted to demographic statistics, entitled *Problemy demograficheskoi statistiki* (Moscow, 1959).

10. B. Ia. Smulevich, *Kritika burzhuaznykh teorii i politiki narodonaseleniia* (Moscow, 1959), pp. 142–49.

11. M. Ia. Sonin, "Ob aktual'nykh voprosakh vosproizvodstva trudovykh resursov SSSR," in Akademiia Nauk SSSR, *Voprosy sotsialisticheskogo vosproizvodstva* (Moscow, 1958), pp. 258–64.

12. See in particular A. A. Dol'skaia, *Sotsialisticheskii zakon narodonaseleniia* (Moscow, 1959), pp. 36–49. T. N. Medvedeva, "Nekotorye metodologicheskie problemy narodonaseleniia," *Vestnik Leningradskogo Universiteta*, No. 11, seriia ekonomiki, filosofii i prava, Issue 2 (1965), pp. 140–44, surveys the literature on the "law" and then gives a good deal of attention to the narrower "demographic process" itself. E. A. Arab-Ogli, on the other hand, cited in D. P. Krikun, "Diskussiia po teoreticheskim problemam izucheniia narodonaseleniia," *Vestnik Moskovskogo Universiteta*, seriia VIII, filosofiia, No. 2 (1966), p. 86, sees the demographic process as less subject to forces that might give it "direction" than, say, economics. "The law of population," he writes, "is essentially spontaneous (*stikhiino*)."

13. B. Ts. Urlanis, *Rozhdaemost' i prodolzhitel'nost' zhizni v SSSR* (Moscow, 1963); and *Dinamika i struktura naseleniia SSSR i SShA* (Moscow, 1964).

14. Precisely this link with the past has been marked by the recent publication of the collected works of several distinguished Soviet demographers:

for example, S. A. Novosel'skii, *Voprosy demograficheskoi i sanitarnoi statistiki* (Moscow, 1958), and M. V. Ptukha, *Ocherki po statistike naseleniia* (Moscow, 1960). Several major studies of pre-Soviet population trends have also been published: A. G. Rashin, *Naselenie Rossii za 100 let (1811–1913): statisticheskii ocherki* (Moscow, 1956), and V. M. Kabuzan, *Narodonaselenie Rossii v XVIII-XIX v. (po materialam revizii)* (Moscow, 1963).

15. E. S. Samoilova and A. A. Rybakov, "Ratsional'noe razmeshchenie naseleniia—vazhneishaia narodnokhoziaistvennaia zadacha," *Vestnik Moskovskogo Universiteta, ekonomika*, no. 1 (1967), pp. 87–90, report on a conference sponsored by these two organizations devoted to the subject of population location and distribution. The work of the original academic organization in this field—a "Problem Group Concerned with Population in the Period of Transition to Communism" (November 1962)—is described in D. Valentei, "Problemnaia gruppa 'Narodonaselenie v period perekhoda k kommunizmu'," *Ekonomicheskie nauki*, No. 6 (1962), pp. 123–25. The work of this first organization and the establishment of the Coordinating Council is described in Namestnikova, cited, pp. 120–22.

16. Despite these developments, there are still institutional shortcomings. G. Kiseleva, "Obsuzhdenie problem narodonaseleniia Ukrainy," *Ekonomicheskie nauki*, No. 1 (1967), p. 99, observes that "at the present time there is still no institute devoted to the study of all the complex problems of population [the institute under discussion for the Academy would fill this bill: WWE], no demographic journal, and no institution of higher education [VUZ] training demographers." E. Samoilova, "Teoriia i politika narodonaseleniia," *Ekonomicheskie nauki*, No. 3 (1967), p. 117, reports that the recent symposium on Marxist-Leninist population theory (see footnote 24, below) posed questions on all of these points for the Ministry of Higher and Secondary Specialized Education of the U.S.S.R. and the Presidium of the Academy of Sciences of the U.S.S.R.

17. D. Valentei, "Vtoraia vsemirnaia konferentsiia po voprosam narodonaseleniia," *Ekonomicheskie nauki*, No. 1 (1966), pp. 129–34.

18. B. Iagodkin, "Demografiia—aktivnyi faktor sotsialisticheskogo preobrazovaniia obshchestva," *Voprosy ekonomiki*, No. 12 (1966), pp. 147–50.

19. A. Dzhagatspanian and A. Volkov, "Nauchnyi seminar po voprosam perspektivnogo ischisleniia naseleniia, raspredeleniia i ispol'zovaniia trudovykh resursov v soiuznykh respublikakh," *Vestnik statistiki*, No. 10 (1963), pp. 81–87.

20. R. D., "Vsesoiuznaia nauchnaia konferentsiia po problemam narodonaseleniia Srednei Azii," *Vestnik statistiki*, No. 1 (1966), pp. 78–80.

21. L. Sbytova, "Vsesoiuznoe nauchnoe soveshchanie po problemam formirovaniia naseleniia i ispol'zovaniia trudovykh resursov v raionakh krainego severa," *Voprosy ekonomiki*, No. 2 (November 1966), pp. 150–53; A. Gladyshev and B. Shapalin, "Problemy formirovaniia naseleniia i ispol'zovaniia trudovykh resursov v raionakh severa SSSR," *Planovoe khoziaistvo*, No. 1 (1966), pp. 91–93.

22. V. Piskunov, "Konferentsiia demografov Ukrainy," *Ekonomika Sovetskoi Ukrainy*, No. 1 (1967), pp. 90–96.

23. S. Alchev, "Na povestke simpoziuma—aktual'nye voprosy teorii narodonaseleniia," *Voprosy ekonomiki*, No. 1 (1967), pp. 159–60.

24. Originally scheduled to take place in January, 1969, ten years after the 1959 census, the date of the forthcoming census has been changed to January, 1970, according to an announcement in *Izvestiia*, April 9, 1967. The reason for the postponement has not been given; but it is very likely to be found in the spate of criticisms of the program and methods of the census which appeared preceding and following the postponement, particularly in *Vestnik statistiki*, journal of the Central Statistical Administration. Focus of the criticisms is an article by P. Pod'iachikh, director of the census, "O predstoiashchei Vsesoiuznoi perepisi naseleniia," *Vestnik statistiki*, No. 8 (1966), pp. 38–48.

25. Beyond demographic questions narrowly defined, there is also a tremendous increase in attention to related questions concerning the development and utilization of the labor force. For example: V. G. Kostakov and P. P. Litviakov, *Balans truda: soderzhanie i metodika razrabotki* (Moscow, 1965); and V. N. Iagodkin (ed.), *Osnovnye zakonomernosti vosproizvodstva rabochei sily razvernutogo stroitel'stva kommunizma* (Moscow, 1965).

26. Urlanis, *Rozhdaemost'*, cited, pp. 62 and 64 P. Borisenkov, G. Kiseleva and E. Shiriaeva, "Rastet interes k problemam narodonaseleniia," *Ekonomicheskie nauki*, No. 3 (1966), pp. 130–33, stress the serious shortcomings of primary demographic information, particularly from sample surveys.

27. These expressions are not always used with precision. By "fertility" is usually meant one or another measure which relates the number of births to the number of women in the population, typically with reference to the period of their lives when they are physically capable of bearing children. The "birth rate" usually stands for the number of births in relation to the total population, although there is also the notion of "age-specific" birth rates (see Table 2).

28. Rates higher than 40 in the earlier 1920s are regarded as a temporary "compensatory" rise following World War I and the Civil War; rates below 30 in the early 1930s are also regarded as temporary, due to collectivization of agriculture and the deteriorating food supply; and the decline in 1940 is seen as related to the increasing international tensions, which, among other things, caused marriages to be postponed. See Urlanis, cited, pp. 26 and 28.

29. It is also recognized that the decline in the birth rate was already in progress during pre-Soviet times. See V. Kustova, "Estestvennoe dvizhenie naseleniia v SSSR i zarubezhnykh stranakh," *Vestnik statistiki*, No. 11 (1965), p. 31.

30. The central role of deliberate family planning, in both urban and rural areas, is stressed in a number of sources, including, for example, by A. G. Volkov, director of the demographic section of the research institute of the Central Statistical Administration, in Samoilova and Rybakov, cited, p. 90.

31. Krikun, cited, pp. 85–87, stresses the different views of demographers, in reporting on the work of an ongoing seminar devoted to methodological problems in the social sciences, including demography.

32. What follows is a paraphrased and highly abbreviated summary of views expressed in a number of the sources cited in this paper.

33. Medvedeva, cited, p. 141, however, sees the demographic process as de-

pendent not only on "productive relationships," but on a broader set of factors which are (a) general-sociological, (b) specifically related to a given social system, and (c) concrete-historical.

34. The particular role of the improvement in living standards and its effect on the birth rate has come in for much attention. As indicated by V. V. Pokshishevskii, "Novyi poisk v rassmotrenii demograficheskikh problem sotsiologii," *Voprosy filosofii*, No. 11 (1966), pp. 158–63, in a review of the literature, the well-known Marxian view of an inverse relationship has been modified to include the possibility of a direct relationship. A. D. Kuznetsov, *Trudovye resursy SSSR i ikh ispol'zovanie* (Moscow, 1960), p. 39, puts it this way: "The birth rate [moves] in direct relation to the level of satisfaction of material and cultural requirements of the population of different social groups, and in inverse relation to the requirements and demands" (i.e., to what we might call "rising expectations"). The upshot of this discussion is generally to explain why the birth rate has gone down in the past and why it may go up in the future.

35. Urlanis, cited, p. 3.

36. Medvedeva, cited, p. 141, stresses this "progressive" relationship as an outstanding characteristic of the Socialist Law of Population to date.

37. Urlanis, cited, p. 70.

38. Same, p. 73.

39. Same, p. 74.

40. Valentei, cited, p. 150. The notion of "expanded reproduction" as applied to the population implies a net reproduction rate (NRR) greater than 1.0. This is as distinct from "simple reproduction" (*prostoe vosproizvodstvo*), or NRR equal to 1.0, and "contracted reproduction" (*suzhennoe vosproizvodstvo*), or NRR less than 1.0. The NRR is a hypothetical measure of the number of female children that will be born and survive to their reproductive years, for each female passing through the reproductive years, under age-specific fertility and mortality rates of a given moment in time. An NRR of 1.0, therefore, means that under the given fertility and mortality rates, the population is tending just to reproduce itself. The gross reproduction rate (GRR) is the number of female children that will be born to each female passing through the reproductive years, under given age-specific fertility rates, i.e., not taking into account mortality.

41. Urlanis, cited, p. 70.

42. Same, p. 64.

43. For example, Sonin, cited, p. 42, writes: "when material well-being will be high enough that the birth of a child will not detract from the possibility of a family to satisfy all material requirements, in particular will not worsen the housing [situation], then the dependency of the birth rate on the level of material well-being will assume the character . . . of stimulating the birth rate."

44. For example, N. Esipov, "Chto vliiaet na uroven' rozhdaemosti," *Ekonomicheskie nauki*, No. 5 (1964), pp. 114–19; Urlanis, cited, pp. 34–39; and J. W. Brackett and J. W. DePauw, "Population Policy and Demographic Trends in the Soviet Union," U.S. Congress, Joint Economic Committee, *New Directions in the Soviet Economy*, Part III (Washington, D.C.: GPO, 1966), pp. 650–53.

45. The data are reported in TsSU SSSR, *Narodnoe khoziaistvo SSSR v 1965 godu: statisticheskii ezhegodnik* (Moscow, 1966), pp. 46–47.
46. Esipov, cited, pp. 115–16.
47. A. Kvasha, "Tvorcheskie obsuzhdeniia demograficheskikh problem," *Voprosy ekonomiki*, No. 7 (1966), p. 158, reporting on a meeting of the demographic section of the Scientists Club (*Dom Uchenykh*) of the Academy of Sciences of the U.S.S.R. in Moscow. The Scientists Club is for members of the Academy and the senior research staff of the institutes of the Academy. The demographic section has been a small but vital force in recent developments in Soviet demography.
48. Esipov, cited, pp. 117–19; and Dzhagatspanian and Volkov, cited, pp. 82 and 85.
49. Esipov, cited, p. 118.
50. Same, p. 119.
51. TsSU SSSR, *Narodnoe khoziaistvo SSSR v 1964 godu: statisticheskii ezhegodnik* (Moscow, 1965), pp. 38–39; and *Narodnoe khoziaistvo . . . 1965*, pp. 46–47. An increase is reported only for the Tadzhik republic for each of the intervals of years; and a small increase is reported for the Estonian republic between 1963 and 1964.
52. Kiseleva, cited, p. 98.
53. Kvasha, cited, p. 158. See note 40, above, for definition of terms.
54. Same.
55. Noted in A. Isupov, "Vtoraia vsemirnaia konferentsiia po voprosam narodonaseleniia," *Vestnik statistiki*, No. 6 (1965), p. 39. It is possible that some of the recent decline in birth rates of specific age brackets (e.g., 20–24) could also be due to the "war babies" effect; but the general decline in rates for each and every one of the younger age groups together cannot be so explained.
56. Urlanis, cited, pp. 43–44. Survival ratios required for these estimates are from *Narodnoe khoziaistvo . . . 1965*, p. 45; *Narodnoe khoziaistvo . . . 1964*, p. 37; TsSU SSSR, *Narodnoe khoziaistvo SSSR v 1963 godu: statisticheskii ezhegodnik* (Moscow, 1965), p. 32; and TsSU SSSR, *Narodnoe khoziaistvo SSSR v 1962 godu: statisticheskii ezhegodnik* (Moscow, 1963), p. 31.
57. The GRR and NRR for 1938/39 and 1961/62 are from Kustova, cited, pp. 33–34. The NRR for 1959, 1961 and 1961/62 are from Kvasha, cited, p. 158. Among other things, the substantial decline in infant mortality over the years is evident in the narrowed difference between the GRR and NRR. (See note 40, above, for definition of terms.)
58. The assumption is that the percentage of females who are married, in the reproductive ages, has largely recovered from the low postwar levels (which reflected the loss of males during the war), and is now more or less stable. Brackett and DePauw, cited, p. 653.
59. They reason, in effect, that since the percentage of Soviet women who were married was rising, from the low postwar levels, stable reproduction rates with respect to total females in the reproductive ages (the measure above) implies declining fertility rates with respect to married females. Same, pp. 648–53.
60. For example, Urlanis, cited, pp. 65–67.
61. It is possible, but not at all certain, that the rural rate rose (briefly) above 32.2 between 1935 and 1940; but it is unlikely, in light of circum-

stances, that it did so between 1932 and 1935. It is possible, also, that some of the data may be affected by the under-registration of births, although no Soviet source consulted suggested this possibility. In any event, the rates are mutually consistent for prewar years: given the appropriate population data (from Table 7), the birth rates for the total population may be derived from the respective urban and rural rates.

62. N. I. Shishkin (ed.), *Trudovye resursy (problemy raspredeleniia i ispol'zovaniia)* (Moscow, 1961), p. 15, writes that "collectivization broke up patriarchical land utilization, thereby removing the influence [of the latter] on the birth rate in rural areas." Kuznetsov, cited, p. 35, cites the "breaking up of economic relations in the countryside," and the fact that children were no longer a prime economic asset, as a result of collectivization and the growth of obligatory education. Urlanis, cited, p. 26, refers to the reorganization of agriculture on a collectivized basis, and implies also that the food shortages of the early 1930s had a depressing influence on rural birth rates. Finally, however, it must be recognized that age cohorts born during World War I and the Civil War, when birth rates were low, entered the reproductive ages beginning about 1930, and that this fact alone had a depressing effect on the birth rate, other things equal, for at least a decade or so.

63. J. W. Brackett, *Projections of the Population of the U.S.S.R., by Age and Sex: 1964–1985*, International Population Reports, Series P-91, No. 13 (Washington, D.C.: GPO, 1964), p. 5, writes: "The age structure of the urban population . . . is more favorable to a higher birth rate than is the age structure of the rural population. Thus, the birth rates understate the difference between urban and rural fertility. Estimates of the maternal and paternal gross reproduction rates for 1959, which take account of the differences in age structure, show fertility as being about 55 per cent higher than urban fertility." This compares with 26 per cent according to the crude birth rates for 1959 (Table 3).

64. Sonin, cited, p. 32.

65. Same, p. 40, for example, calls attention to the economic factors, such as housing, "which until now have influenced [the birth rate] and will continue to exact an influence *for a certain period of time* in the direction of lowering the birth rate" (italics mine). Compare this with his "long-run" view expressed in note 43, above.

66. Two "intermediate" projections are also provided ("B" and "C"), but it is sufficient for the purposes of the present paper to deal only with the extreme alternatives ("A" and "D"). Furthermore, the data reproduced in Table 4 (and Table 1) are from what is now an earlier projection. Brackett and Depauw, cited, pp. 657–61, provide a later projection of the U.S. Census Bureau, carried forward from estimated data as of 1965. Examination of the two projections shows differences which are relatively small for the purposes of the present paper, not warranting recalculation of tables using the data, especially those below.

67. This is so, in terms of the projections in Table 4, partly because the fertility of the Soviet population has actually been declining since the date of the projections, at which time the GRR was estimated, on the basis of the latest published data, as 1.27 (1962), compared to 1.19 in 1964/65 (see above in text).

68. Sonin, cited, p. 51.

69. Thus, it turns out to be quite close to the "intermediate" alternative ("B") of an earlier projection of the Soviet population made by the U.S. Census Bureau, based on the assumption that the GRR of 1.30 estimated for 1961 would continue. This projection is set forth in J. W. Brackett, "Demographic Trends and Population Policy in the Soviet Union," U.S. Congress, Joint Economic Committee, *Dimensions of Soviet Economic Power* (Washington, D.C.: GPO, 1962), pp. 557 and 560.

70. Even in the arena of world population growth, according to one prominent U.S. demographer, "population trends before 1960 are largely irrelevant in predicting what will happen in the future." Because of efforts toward fertility control which, in his view, have finally begun to pay off, the "rate of world population growth may be expected to decline with each passing year," to the point where "it will be zero or near zero at about the year 2000. . . . The world population crisis [the population explosion] is a phenomenon of the 20th century, and will be largely if not entirely a matter of history when humanity moves into the 21st century." D. J. Bogue, "The End of the Population Explosion," *The Public Interest*, No. 7 (Spring 1967), pp. 11–12 and 19.

71. E. Belousova and V. Steshenko, "O nekotorykh problemakh demograficheskogo prognozirovaniia," *Ekonomika Sovetskoi Ukrainy*, No. 1 (1967), pp. 83–85.

72. See Brackett, *Dimensions* . . . , cited, pp. 542–54, for a review of the history and development of Soviet population policy.

73. Esipov, cited, p. 115.

74. Urlanis, cited, p. 74.

75. Iagodkin, cited, pp. 149–50.

76. For example, Dol'skaia, cited, p. 47.

77. Iagodkin, cited, pp. 149–50.

78. See Sonin, cited, p. 99.

79. The issue is drawn here in terms of employment in "socialized labor," which is more or less equivalent, in the Soviet context, to the notion of "employment" in other countries, except that it excludes the "self-employed." In a broader sense, however, there is also the notion of "socially useful labor" (*obshchestvenno poleznyi trud*), which includes child-rearing and even housework, and in terms of which the Soviet concept of "full employment" (*polnaia zaniatost'*) is defined. The child-rearing activities implied by higher fertility rates, although perhaps reducing the participation of women in "socialized labor," would nevertheless be considered entirely "socially useful labor." See same, pp. 95–101.

80. Norton T. Dodge, *Women in the Soviet Economy* (Baltimore: The Johns Hopkins Press, 1966), pp. 19–25 and 30–31, explores some of these alternatives.

81. Detailed estimates by single age-groups are given in Brackett, *Dimensions* . . . , cited, pp. 519–27, and in Brackett and DePauw, cited, pp. 610–20.

82. Further discussion of these data may be found in W. W. Eason, "Labor Force," in Abram Bergson and Simon S. Kuznets, *Economic Trends in the Soviet Union* (Cambridge, Mass.: Harvard University Press, 1963), pp. 71–81.

83. S. Kuznets, "Quantitative Aspects of the Economic Growth of Nations: II. Industrial Distribution of National Product and Labor Force," *Eco-*

nomic *Development and Cultural Change*, Supplement to Volume V, No. 4 (July 1957), pp. 82ff.

CHAPTER 9. EDUCATION

1. V. Lenin, *Selected Works*, II-2 (Moscow, Publishing House, 1952), pp. 467–68, 471–73.
2. W. Medlin, "Soviet Pedagogical Academy and the New School Plans," *Comparative Education Review* (October 1958), pp. 12–14; J. Zepper, "Educational Research in the USSR," same (February 1964), pp. 267–72.
3. *Pravda*, March 6, 1965.
4. *Naradnoe khoziaistvo SSSR v 1963 godu*, p. 589.
5. *Spravochnik dlia postupaiushchikh v srednie spetsial'nye uchebnye savedeniia SSSR* (Moscow, 1963), pp. 9–298, 340.
6. *Narodnoe khoziaistvo 1963*, p. 560.
7. *Narodnoe khoziaistvo 1961*, p. 679.
8. *Pravda*, January 24, 1964.
9. Organization for Economic Cooperation and Development, *Policy Conference on Economic Growth and Investment in Education*, II, "Targets for Education in Europe in 1970." (Paris: OECD, 1962), pp. 67ff. R. Poignant, *L'enseignement dans les pays du marché commun* (Paris: Institut Pédagogique Nationale, 1965), pp. 149–206; Unesco, *Statistical Yearbook for 1964*, pp. 342ff.
10. *Kul'turnoe stroitel'stvo v SSSR*, 1956; *Narodnoe khoziaistvo 1963*; *itogi vsesoiuznoi perepisi naseleniia v 1959 godu SSSR*, 1962 (hereafter cited as 1959 census).
11. *Narodnoe khoziaistvo 1964*, p. 34; *Narodnoe khoziaistvo 1963*, pp. 595–96.
12. S. J. Muskhin (ed.), *Economics of Higher Education* (Washington: GPO, 1962), p. 97.
13. 1959 Census, p. 112.
14. *Soviet Education* (International Arts and Sciences Press, N.Y.) No. 7, pp. 25–32, and No. 9, pp. 12–24; G. Shapovalenko (ed.), *Polytechnical Education in the USSR* (Paris, 1963), pp. 55–64; N. DeWitt, *Education and Professional Employment in the USSR* (Washington: GPO, 1961), pp. 19–20; W. Medlin, C. Lindquist, and M. Schmitt, *Soviet Education Programs* (Washington: GPO, 1960), pp. 32–40; G. Bereday, W. Brickman, and G. Read (eds.), *The Changing Soviet School* (Boston: Houghton Mifflin, 1960), pp. 91–98.
15. *Sovetskaia pedagogika*, No. 7 (1963), pp. 144ff.
16. B. R. Vogeli, *Soviet Secondary Schools for the Mathematically Talented* (Bowling Green: Bowling Green State University, 1965) (mimeographed), esp. pp. 8ff.; discussions with Soviet educators in 1959, 1962, 1964, including mathematics professors on exchange in the United States.
17. *The New York Times*, January 12, 1966, p. 45.
18. Data given by educational trade union officials, 1962; *Vestnik statistiki*, No. 8 (1963), pp. 91–93.
19. *Uchitel'skaia gazeta*, August 11, 1964.
20. *Pravda*, May 4, 1966.
21. Same.

22. *Izvestiia*, April 15, 1966.
23. *Uchitel'skaia gazeta;* August 6, 1964; I. Grivkov, *Prospects of education in the USSR* (Moscow, 1961) (mimeographed), pp. 20–22.
24. *Current Digest of the Soviet Press*, XV, No. 29, 17.
25. Discussion with leading Soviet educators in Moscow, April 1964. *USSR* (August 1963), pp. 8–9.
26. Ralph T. Fisher, Jr., *Pattern for Soviet Youth* (New York: Columbia University Press, 1959); Allen Kassof, *The Soviet Youth Program: Regimentation and Rebellion* (Cambridge, Mass.: Harvard University Press, 1965); *Komsomolskaia pravda*, April 20, 1965.
27. Discussions with researchers in the Academy of Pedagogical Sciences in 1959, 1962, and 1964. Cf. an analysis of indoctrination in G. Bereday and B. Stretch, "Political education in the USA and USSR," *Comparative Education Review* (June 1963), pp. 9–16.
28. See discussions in *Sovetskaia pedagogika*, No. 4 (1962), pp. 10–21; No. 4 (1966), pp. 102ff. and pp. 3–84; No. 1 (1966), pp. 24–32, and 54–65.
29. *Pravda*, March 18, 1966.
30. *Vestnik vysshei shkoly*, No. 1 (1966), pp. 60–62; *Komsomolskaia pravda*, December 29, 1963; *Sovetskaia pedagogika* No. 4 (1963), pp. 152–54; Discussions with educational and youth leaders, 1962 and 1964.
31. *Izvestiia*, September 11, 1963; *Partiinaia zhizn'*, No. 15 (1963), pp. 55–61; verbal reports from visitors in the U.S.S.R.
32. See the survey by the Academy of Pedagogical Sciences, *Razvitie samodeiatel'nosti uchashchikhsia v pionerskoi organizatsii* (Moscow, 1959); personal observations and discussions with leaders and children in Pioneer activities, 1959, 1962, and 1964.
33. *Sovetskaia pedagogika*, No. 8 (1965), pp. 54–58; *Izvestiia*, February 4, 1966; and many other instances.
34. W. K. Medlin, F. Carpenter, and W. M. Cave, *Education and Social Change: The Role of the School in a Technically Developing Society in Central Asia*. Ann Arbor, Mich.: The University of Michigan, 1965 (Cooperative Research Reports 1414 and 2620), esp. pp. 167, 221ff., 261ff., 353ff.
35. *Pravda*, December 14, 1963.
36. *Pravda*, April 10, 1966.
37. *Vestnik vysshei shkoly*, No. 6 (1963), pp. 3–6.
38. *Narodnoe khoziaistvo*, 1963, p. 573; *Pravda*, March 20, 1965.
39. *Izvestiia*, March 13, 1963; *Pravda*, February 24, 1964; *Pravda*, March 20, 1965.
40. *Vestnik vysshei shkoly*, No. 1 (1966).
41. *Pravda*, March 18, 1966.
42. *Soviet Life*, No. 19.
43. Kovalev, *Pravda*, May 6, 1966, p. 3.
44. *Pravda*, October 8, 1965.
45. *Soviet Education*, VI, No. 8 (1964), 4; *Sovetskaia pedagogika*, No. 1 (1966), p. 5; *Pravda*, February 13, 1965.
46. *Uchitel'skaia gazeta*, December 22, 1962; J. Pennar, "Five years after Khrushchev's school reform" *Comparative Education Review* (June 1964), pp. 73–77; *Sovetskaia pedagogika*, No. 10 (1965), pp. 84–90.
47. *Sovetskaia pedagogika*, No. 9 (1965).

48. *Sovetskaia pedagogika*, No. 1 (1966), pp. 1ff.; and articles by B. Anan'ev, in same and also in *Soviet Education*, VII, No. 8 (1965), 3–15.
49. *Soviet Education*, VI, No. 11 (1964), pp. 8ff.; H. Redl (ed.), *Soviet Educators on Soviet Education* (New York: The Free Press, 1964), esp. the translation of the article by T. Atarov, pp. 53–77.
50. *Soviet Education*, V, No. 8 (June 1963), p. 15.
51. *Soviet Education*, VI, No. 11 (September 1964), pp. 15–26; same, VII, No. 9 (July 1965), pp. 3–9.
52. The essential details of this group's social pressure, through letters, meetings, and other communications to party and education authorities, were discussed with the writer by Soviet educational officials in 1959 and 1962.
53. *Uchitel'skaia gazeta*, No. 24 (1962).

CHAPTER 10. AGRICULTURE

1. Resource allocation during most of the Stalin period worked by direct physical allocation of a number of products or raw materials considered vital for the fulfillment of the planned objectives in industry. Most of the products not centrally allocated, which were treated as a residual in the national plan, were, however, assigned some supply priorities. Agriculture was considered a residual claimant, relative to other claimants of the industrial production sector, except for the allocation of agricultural machinery, fuel, and inorganic fertilizer.
2. This explains the failure to insure a more accurate and detailed flow of information about the agricultural sector of the economy, apparent in the lack of such elementary tools of information as a land cadaster and soil-maps.
3. Arcadius Kahan, "Changes in Agricultural Productivity in the Soviet Union," Economic Council of Canada: Conference on International Trade and Canadian Agriculture (Ottawa, 1966).
4. According to the data of the Central Statistical Authority (TsSU) for August 1, 1961 three-quarters of the state farms and two-thirds of the collective farms in the R.S.F.S.R. did not have any crop rotation. The situation was similar in other republics. During the years 1962–64 many of the farms which previously had a crop rotation were forced to abandon it under the impact of changing instructions, frequent reorganizations of the farms, and changing fads of the policy-makers. See *Ekonomika sel'skogo khoziaistva*, I, No. 11 (1965), pp. 92–93. "Crop rotations were introduced in about half of the state and collective farms of Kazakhstan, in 18 per cent of the farms of Moldavia, in 8 per cent of Turkmenia, 6 per cent of Estonia." *Ekonomika sel'skogo khoziaistva* No. 3 (1966), p. 59. This information pertains to the year 1965, but does not indicate the duration of the crop rotation.
5. If the full potential damage of such campaigns did not materialize, it was due to the fact that in the Soviet Union, as in most other countries, a dichotomy exists between a state bureaucracy's intentions and achievements. One should never underestimate the traditional resistance to change on the part of farmers nor overestimate the efficiency of a bureaucracy.
6. The emphasis on long-range planning versus short-run planning is due to the fact that much of what was labeled as short-run planning was either

the planners' response to galvanizing decisions of policy-makers or constituted changes in plan targets undertaken on their own initiative. Both had an obviously unsettling effect upon the agricultural producers.

7. The Khrushchev period witnessed a real organizational upheaval of agricultural enterprises, which included mergers of farms, the conversion of collective farms into state farms, etc.,—all measures which were likely to increase the uncertainty on the part of farm management and ordinary farm producers. The following data indicate some dimensions of the organizational changes.

Year	Number of collective farms by January 1 (in 1,000)	Collective farms converted into state farms	Number of state farms by Jan. 1
1957	83.0	5,730	5,098
1958	76.5	1,256	5,905
1959	67.7	2,074	6,002
1960	53.4	5,068	6,496
1961	44.0	2,906	7,375
1962	40.5	402	8,281
1963	39.7	271	8,570
1964	38.8		9,176

See V. G. Venzher, *Voprosy ispolzovania zakona stoimosti v kolkhoznom proizvodstvie*, 2nd ed. (Moscow, 1965), p. 131; TsSU SSSR: *Narodnoe khoziaistvo SSSR*, for the pertinent years.

8. The production costs per unit of output on the state farms were higher than the ones on the collective farms. The following official figures for selected agricultural commodities illustrate the fact:

PER UNIT COSTS OF PRODUCTION ON THE STATE FARMS AND
COLLECTIVE FARMS, 1959–62
(*In rubles per ton*)

	1959		1960		1961		1962	
	Collective Farms	State Farms	Collective Farms	State Farms	Collective Farms	State Farms	Collective Farms	State Farms
Grain (without corn)	36.2	40.4	36.1	42.0	35.6	45.1	37.4	46.4
Potatoes	13.5	23.7	11.8	18.5	13.7	21.1	16.1	23.2
Sugar Beets	29.5	52.8	26.9	49.1	28.1	51.1	37.7	69.3
Milk	103.9	126.3	117.1	131.5	122.4	142.7	129.4	159.7
Beef	748.7	688.2	808.6	729.7	748.1	773.9	833.7	844.0

N. M. Studenkova: *Metodika ischisleniia sebestoimosti produktsii v kolkhozakh i sovkhozakh* (Moscow, 1965), pp. 101–6.

9. Among the classical examples of the first kind is the spectacular growth of cotton output; of the second, the expansion of potato production; and the rise in sunflower seed output could probably be attributed to the combined demand of government and households.

10. The reactions of farms and farmers differed with respect to various crops; while it was positive toward the production of sugar beets, it was negative toward hemp and flax and mixed toward socialized livestock output, depending upon the period.

11. Whether the share of agricultural output produced on the private household plots of the collective farmers, workers, and employees in the total output of Soviet agriculture will remain unchanged is a different question. The official data for the share of the private household sector in gross agricultural output during the last decade are as follows:

SHARE OF THE PRIVATE HOUSEHOLD SECTOR

Year	In Crop Output	In Livestock Output	In Total Output
1953	30.5	56.0	45.4
1958	25.8	52.1	37.0
1962	22.9	44.9	33.1
1963	23.8	45.6	34.2

It is worth mentioning that the use of a different (more realistic) set of price weights would increase the share of the household sector by another 4–5 per cent. In the future the size of the private sector's output will depend upon the extent to which the socialized sector will substitute for the labor-intensive output which has thus far been left to the private sector, as well as upon the availability of a marketable surplus of commodities which have been marketed by the state primarily in urban areas.

12. Kahan, cited, pp. 367–69.

13. According to the population census of 1959, out of 9.9 million employed on the private household plots there were 4.1 million women of 55 years and above, and 0.7 million were of 60 years and older. TsSU SSSR, Itogi vsesoiuznoi perepisi naseleniia SSSR 1959 goda (Moscow, 1962), p. 99.

14. Such shifts were discernible in the cases of winter wheat and sunflower seed in the Ukraine, spring wheat in the Kazakh Republic, sugar beets in Western Ukraine, etc.

15. The non-observance of a rational regional distribution of crops led to some considerable losses in output. A part of the price paid for pushing corn too far to the north was the loss of corn output on an area of 1.439 million hectares in 1961 and of 5.879 million hectares in 1962. N. M. Studenkova, cited, p. 126.

A calculation by Soviet economists revealed that the substitution of corn and sugar beets for grasses and fallow in 1962 increased the operating expenses of the state farms alone by 180 million rubles in comparison with 1961. Despite the increased costs to the farms, the increment in the value and volume of production expected from the change in output-mix did not materialize. N. M. Studenkova, cited, p. 90.

16. The defense of the system of governmental procurements invokes the scarcity of domestic agricultural supply as a justification for maintaining

the system. To this writer, the prevalence of the procurement system appears to contribute to the perpetuation of the scarcity of supply.

17. Thus individual farms are prevented from specializing in such an intermediate process as stock-raising. They must also deliver fattened stock, or vice versa; the livestock fattening farm is obliged to raise its own stock.

18. While the volume of labor inputs (in man-days) or the number of persons engaged in agricultural activity did not change during the last decade, a qualitative improvement took place through the rising number of agricultural laborers using machinery rather than serving as field hands performing manual tasks. One would expect the percentage of laborers servicing agricultural machines to increase sharply, provided that along with training facilities they will be paid high wages as an incentive to remain on the farms.

19. Douglass B. Diamond, "Trends in Output, Inputs and Factor Productivity in Soviet Agriculture," in U.S. Congress, Joint Economic Committee, *New Directions in the Soviet Economy* (Washington, D.C.: GPO, 1966), p. 348.

20. This is no indictment of Soviet policies. It is perfectly rational not to substitute capital for labor when labor is relatively cheap.

21. This is not to mention some Soviet agricultural economists who turned the vice into a virtue by boasting about the land/tractor ratio being the highest in the world and confusing it with actual utilization of the machinery.

22. Some notion of the changes in the supply and stock of agricultural machinery during the last seven years is provided by the data in the table on facing page.

23. Needless to say, a policy of accelerated retirement of machinery which would leave a smaller net increase would provide for a better utilization of the machinery—which would be working in the fields instead of lying in disrepair or awaiting cannibalization.

24.

MINERAL FERTILIZER DELIVERIES TO AGRICULTURE
(*In thousand tons of nutrients*)

Year	Total	N	P_2O_5	K_2O
1950	1,261.0	307.0	532.0	422.0
1953	1,586.4	394.2	673.4	518.8
1958	2,458.4	686.3	1,029.1	743.0
1959	2,576.3	709.5	1,079.7	787.1
1960	2,628.4	768.5	1,093.6	766.3
1961	2,710.0	858.7	1,148.3	703.0
1962	3,083.8	1,069.7	1,188.3	825.8
1963	3,582.3	1,360.0	1,321.3	901.0
1964	5,029.0	1,759.0	1,849.0	1,421.0
1965	6,303.0	2,282.0	2,121.0	1,891.0
1970 (Plan)	12,509.7	5,002.0	4,262.9	3,244.8

Kilograms per hectare of arable land

1964	22.8	8.0	8.4	6.4
1965	28.5	10.3	9.6	8.6

Stock and Supply of Agricultural Machinery in the Soviet Union,
1958–64
(*In thousands*)

	1958	1959	1960	1961	1962	1963	1964	1965
Tractors supplied	157.5	144.3	157.0	185.3	206.0	293.3	222.5	239.5
Net increase	77.0	52.9	68.0	89.7	116.9	113.1	97.0	74.2
Total tractors	1,001.4	1,054.3	1,122.3	1,212.0	1,328.9	1,442.0	1,539.0	1,613.2
Grain combines supplied	64.9	53.1	57.0	70.0	79.2	79.6	78.6	79.4
Net increase	19.0	−7.7	3.2	.9	21.5	−2.4	−4.6	7.1
Total grain combines	501.7	494.0	497.2	498.1	519.6	517.2	512.6	519.7
Trucks supplied	102.1	76.3	66.1	69.7	82.6	68.8	63.0	70.2
Net increase	40.0	29.0	49.0	18.0	79.0	47.0	32.0	28.0
Total trucks	700	729	778	796	875	922	954	982

25. One can probably explain a number of present shortcomings in the supply and application of mineral fertilizer by various factors. Among them I would list the industrial production plans made up in terms of bulk rather than nutrient content, preventing high nutrient concentration; lack of technology and transportation facilities which prevents the manufacture and delivery of liquid nitrogen; lack of storage facilities at the railway sidings and within the farms, which leads to reported losses of at least one-fourth of the total mineral fertilizer supply; lack of detailed soil maps, which prevents the use of combined fertilizers; and the scarcity of machinery to spread and apply the fertilizers. How easily the shortcomings could be overcome, is, of course, anyone's guess.

26. It was a classic example of Stalinist enforcement of priorities.

27.

ELECTRICITY CONSUMPTION IN SOVIET AGRICULTURE
(*In million kwh.*)

	1953	1956	1958	1960	1962	1964
Total consumption	2,176	3,654	5,104	6,417	9,961	12,731
Agricultural production use	n.a.	1,335	3,369	4,166	6,081	8,001
Household and other uses	n.a.	1,319	1,735	2,251	3,880	4,730
Produced by rural stations	1,841	n.a.	4,261	5,735	6,935	6,246

28. Even the corn program was based upon the tacit assumption that the substitution of corn for other grains ought to be accompanied by the expansion of small grains in other areas. So, for example, the Kazakh Republic had to compensate for the wheat lands of the Ukraine, Northern Caucasus, and the blacksoil zone of the R.S.F.S.R., which were converted to corn production.

29. It is true that the shortage of capital made the Soviet leaders reluctant to channel major capital resources into agriculture. But this cannot be accepted as an adequate excuse. They should have foreseen the disastrous consequences of the near total neglect and misguided investment which postponed the essential intensification of agriculture.

30. During the current five-year-plan period about 1.04 million hectares of newly irrigated land in Central Asia, 1.35 million in European Russia, in the Ukraine and Moldavia, and .15 million in the Caucasus, or a total of over 2.5 million hectares, are to be added to the existing irrigated area, and 51 million hectares of arid pastures are to receive water holes for their herds. The drainage program concentrated in areas of excessive rainfall should encompass 6 million hectares (2.25 million in the R.S.F.S.R., 1.6 in Byelorussia, 1.43 in the Baltic Republics and .7 in the Ukraine) of newly drained land; 9 million hectares of cleared and improved land and 28 million hectares need to be limed to counteract the increased acidity of the soils.

31. The use of fertilizers on irrigated land is higher than on nonirrigated lands and so is the application of machinery in the production of crops on irrigated or drained lands.

32. This is apart from the fact that some of the official spokesmen were lacking both in knowledge and training and might have been innocently unaware of specific needs for technological improvement.

33. The level of farm prices for grains and livestock products was kept artificially low during 1928–52, increasing only by about 90 per cent. The only prices allowed to increase more were those for industrial raw materials like cotton, flax fiber, and sugar beets. The following table of farm prices presented in terms of the base year 1952 provides, therefore, a general impression of the tendency during the last decade. Since 1962, all prices have risen again by about 30 per cent.

PRICE LEVEL OF AGRICULTURAL PRODUCTS DELIVERED TO THE STATE BY
COLLECTIVE FARMS AND THE AGRICULTURAL POPULATION
(1952 = 1.0)

	1955	1958	1962
All grains	5.53	6.95	8.43
Sunflower seed	9.87	7.74	8.48
Potatoes	3.68	7.89	10.43
Cotton	.96	1.06	1.20
Total crops	1.69	2.03	2.16
All meat	5.85	11.75	15.23
Milk	3.03	4.04	4.34
Eggs	1.52	2.97	3.39
Wool	1.58	3.52	3.46
Total livestock products	3.19	5.46	6.03
Total crops and livestock	2.09	2.96	3.32

M. Ia. Lemeshev, (ed.), *Ekonomicheskoe obosnovanie struktury sel'skokhoziaistvennogo proizvodstva* (Moscow, 1965), p. 255.

34. This should not be construed as an indication that the Soviet Union ought not or will not export agricultural commodities. In order to conduct its economic activities in other areas the Soviet Union may need foreign currency which might be actually valued much higher than the official exchange rates, particularly in the absence of a convertible currency. It is also possible (at least in the abstract) that the comparative disadvantage of selling agricultural products might be smaller than in exporting other goods. Such an assumption is not very realistic, except perhaps for some few commodities.

35. Costs of production during the last decade tended to fluctuate from year to year; the trend, however, was an upward one, as illustrated by the table (page 546) on production costs on state farms.

36. A glance at changes in relative prices of agricultural products in the Soviet Union reveals not only long-run tendencies of rising relative costs of production of livestock products and potatoes, and encouragement for the production of industrial crops; it also reveals inexplicable distortions of price relationships between meat and milk, or within the meat group between pork and beef. Such erratic movements of the relative prices, as reflected in the table on page 547, provided the farms with poor guidelines for changes in their output-mix or for increases in agricultural production.

37. This phenomenon is often discussed in the United States under the name of "parity" prices.

Costs of Production of Agricultural Commodities on State Farms
(In rubles per ton)

	1955	1956	1959	1960	1961	1962	1964	1965
Grain (except corn)	45.8	32.5	40.4	42.0	45.1	46.1	50.0	66.0
Corn for grain	n.a.	n.a.	57.7	35.2	37.7	37.6	n.a.	n.a.
Potatoes	54.4	47.9	52.8	49.1	51.1	69.3	63.0	61.0
Vegetables	48.7	54.3	61.0	56.6	62.6	68.2	64.0	72.0
Cotton	179.2	158.2	209.3	252.2	244.8	284.8	282.0	291.0
Sugar beets	14.3	16.0	23.7	18.5	21.1	23.2	23.0	27.0
Milk	117.5	127.6	126.3	131.5	142.7	159.7	181.0	163.0
Beef	659.9	700.8	688.2	729.7	773.9	844.0	1,167.0	1,052.0
Pork	977.0	985.8	1,025.0	n.a.	n.a.	1,243.8	1,261.0	1,067.0
Wool	1,575.8	1,846.1	1,910.6	2,063.2	2,219.2	2,733.3	3,096.0	2,907.0

RELATIVE AGRICULTURAL PRICES, BASED UPON AVERAGE
PROCUREMENT PRICES
($Wheat = 1.0$)*

	1913	1929	1940	1952	1955	1958**	1963***
Wheat	1.0	1.0	1.0	1.0	1.0	1.0	1.0
Rye	.98	.72	.54	.61	.71	n.a.	n.a.
Corn	.73	.51	.496	.58	.73	n.a.	1.01
Sunflower	1.2	.96	1.21	1.94	2.5	(2.62)	2.39
Sugar beet	.16	.13	.52	2.02	.42	(.35)	.380
Potatoes	.333	.489	.344	.505	.479	(1.25)	.939
Beef and veal	3.43	2.93	4.82	5.05	5.00	(8.59)	10.57
Pork	4.44	5.01	7.06	6.57	11.96	(13.84)	12.96
Mutton	3.43	3.18	4.56	2.53	5.08	(10.31)	n.a.
Milk	1.01	.856	1.46	2.93	2.13	(1.95)	1.61
Eggs	3.43	4.40	18.07	20.10	6.33	(7.21)	9.26
Wool	11.49	12.46	77.45	97.37	28.08	(51.25)	50.09

* 1913, 1929, 1940, 1952, 1955 data from I. I. Lukinov; *Tsenoobrazovanie i rentabel'nost' proizvodstva sel'skokhoziaistvennykh produktov.* (Moscow, 1964), pp. 404–5.
** Relative prices from the price weights used in the Central Statistical Agency's index of gross agricultural output. Wheat assumed 64 rubles per ton at an average price for grain of 58 rubles, based upon S.G. Stoliarov, *O tsenakh i tsenoobrazovanii v SSSR* (Moscow, 1963), p. 83.
*** Collective farm purchase prices. M. Ia. Lemieshev (ed.), *Obosnovanie struktury sel'skokhoziaistvennogo proizvodstva* (Moscow, 1965), p. 254.

38. I. I. Lukinov, *Tsenoobrazovanie i rentabel'nost' proizvodstva sel'skokhoziaistvennykh produktov* (Moscow, 1964), p. 401.
39. The collective farms until 1962 paid the retail rather than wholesale prices for such goods. The relationship between the wholesale and retail prices for 1961 can be surmised from the following example:

Roofing slate	1 : 1.5
Window glass	1 : 1.65
Nails	1 : 2.35
Cement	1 : 3.15

See D. D. Kondrashev, *Tsena i stoimost' v sotsialisticheskom khoziaistve* (Moscow, 1963), p. 291.
40. The price decrease for machinery and spare parts of 1961 of 40 per cent followed two previous price increases; in 1958 when tractor and machinery prices were increased by 10 per cent and in 1959 when spare parts for trucks rose by 50 per cent and for tractors and agricultural machinery by 90 per cent. The costs of assembling the DT-54 tractor from spare parts in 1960 was 5,070 rubles, or twice the price of a new tractor. See Kondrashev, cited, p. 29.
41. Some of the data were put into a tabular form.

RELATIONSHIP BETWEEN COLLECTIVE FARM WHEAT PRICES AND
WHOLESALE PRICES OF INDUSTRIAL PRODUCTS
(*In tons of wheat per unit*)

	1940	1948	1952	1955	1962
Truck ZIS-5	99	124	156	53	20
Tractor KD-35			218	65	26
Drill SD-24	11	41		7.6	4.7
Gasoline (1 ton)	8.9	8.9		2.0	1.1
Portland Cement (1 ton)	0.88	1.88		0.44	0.19

Lukinov, cited, p. 400.

Although the above table might create the illusion of tremendous savings for the farm producers, we should keep in mind that the price of wheat increased about 7.8-fold between 1940 and 1962 and about 7.5-fold since 1952.

CHAPTER 11. INDUSTRY

1. See A. Gerschenkron, *Economic Backwardness in Historical Perspective* (Cambridge, Mass.: Harvard University Press, 1962), pp. 17–18.
2. J. Stalin, *Selected Writings* (New York: International Publishers, 1942), p. 200.
3. As a card-carrying economist, I find it difficult, on moral grounds, to deal with the problem of the measurement of growth in a completely simple way. Therefore, let me use this footnote to discuss briefly the difficulties and limitations inherent in the economist's measures of growth.

The basic cause of the difficulties lies in the fact that not all industrial sectors grow at the same rate; thus, if we want a measure of aggregate industrial growth, we have to find a meaningful way of putting all the disparate sectoral rates of growth together. The problem is further complicated by the fact that prices (which we use as indicators of the relative importance of the products of the different sectors) change from year to year and do so at dissimilar rates. Since we want to measure the change in output (and not the change in prices), we have to choose one set of weights (prices) and use them to aggregate the outputs at the beginning and at the end of the period we are considering. Unfortunately, if there is a radical change in the structure of output, that is, if there is a wide variation in the rates of growth of different sectors, we will get widely different measured rates of growth of aggregate output, depending on whether we use "early year" prices or "last year" prices. And due to the tendency toward a negative correlation between the rates of output changes and the rates of price changes (those products which exhibit the greatest rates of growth of output have the greatest rates of decrease of relative prices), the measure of growth which employs "early year" prices as weights to aggregate output will normally be higher than the measure which uses "late year" weights, because it gives relatively greater weight to the fast-growing components of the index.

The Soviet economy, and within it, Soviet industry, went through a massive structural change in the prewar plan period, and in this period there is, therefore, a wide disparity between rates of growth using early and late year prices. In the postwar period, the index number problem is, fortunately, almost entirely absent because of the more even growth within industry which took place.

4. Growth is here defined in the sense of the increase in the productive capacity of the industrial sector, rather than in the sense of the increase in human welfare deriving from the use of industrial output.

5. It is necessary to choose a particular product mix because the growth of productive capacity will differ according to the different product mixes an economy could produce. For a discussion of this problem see: G. W. Nutter, "On Measuring Economic Growth," *Journal of Political Economy* (February 1957), pp. 51–63; R. Moorsteen, "On Measuring Productive Potential and Relative Efficiency," *Quarterly Journal of Economics* (August 1961), pp. 451–59.

6. U.S. figure is from U.S. Bureau of Census, *Historical Statistics of the United States, Colonial Times to 1957* (Washington, D.C.: GPO, 1960), p. 139.

7. See H. S. Levine, "Growth and Planning in the Soviet Union," in W. A. Leeman (ed.), *The Soviet Economy in Theory and Practice* (Columbia, Mo.: University of Missouri Press, 1964), pp. 51–95.

8. The U.S.S.R. figures are from *Narodnoe khoziaistvo v 1963 g.*, p. 112. Those for the U.S. are calculated from W. W. Leontief, *The Structure of American Economy 1919–1939: Empirical Application of Equilibrium Analysis,* 2d ed., enlarged (New York: Macmillan, 1951), Tables 5, 6, 24; and from D. Evans and M. Hoffenberg in *Review of Economics and Statistics* (May 1952), Table 4.

9. N. Kaplan in Abram Bergson (ed.), *Soviet Economic Growth: Conditions and Perspectives* (Evanston, Ill.: Row, Peterson, 1953), pp. 52–54.

10. R. Powell in Abram Bergson and Simon S. Kuznets (eds.), *Economic Trends in the Soviet Union* (Cambridge, Mass.: Harvard University Press, 1963), p. 188. The growth of Soviet urbanization was twice as fast in this period as was that in the United States at a comparable stage of our development (W. Eason in same, p. 75).

11. R. Powell and W. Eason in same, pp. 72–73, 188.

12. See R. Powell in same, pp. 155, 165.

13. Same, pp. 170–76; B. Balassa, "The Dynamic Efficiency of the Soviet Economy," *American Economic Review* (May 1964), pp. 491–502.

14. See data in the article by J. Noren in U.S. Congress, Joint Economic Committee, *New Directions in the Soviet Economy,* Part II-A (Washington, D.C.: GPO, 1966), p. 282. I use Noren's figure of 10.6 per cent for 1950–58 (rather than Powell's figures as above) for purposes of comparability with the post-1958 period (which Powell did not cover). It is sufficient to give a single growth figure in one set of price weights because of the relative absence of the index-number, as discussed in note 3, above.

Note: *Unless otherwise indicated* all subsequent figures in this section of the paper are based on the data in Noren's article and are presented in Table 2 in the text.

15. See M. Feshback in *New Directions in the Soviet Economy,* cited, Part III, p. 746.

16. Comparing the rates per year in 1958–64 with 1950–58 (calculated from data in *New Directions in the Soviet Economy,* p. 282):

1) Decrease in the rate of growth of employment: 0.4 percentage point.
2) Decrease (increase) in the rate of growth (fall) of man-hours per worker: 1.0 percentage point.
3) Decrease in the rate of growth of output per-man hour: 1.0 percentage point.

These comprise 2.4 of the total drop of 2.5 percentage points in the rate of growth of output. Ignoring the 0.1 percentage point (which results from the interactions among these three rates), I divided $0.4/2.4 = 16.7$ per cent; $1.0/2.4 = 41.7$ per cent; $1.0/2.4 = 41.7$ per cent. For a discussion of the problems involved in such procedures, see H. S. Levine, "A Small Problem in the Analysis of Growth," *Review of Economics and Statistics* (May 1960), pp. 225–29.

17. Man-hour productivity grows by 8.7 per year in both periods (1955–58 and 1958–61) of the decrease in the workday program. In neither period, however, was this increase in man-hour productivity able to overcome the decrease in the rate of growth of man-hours of labor service in industry.

18. *Narodnoe khoziaistvo v 1964 g.* (Moscow, 1965), p. 513.

19. Noren, cited, p. 299.

20. One of the factors which probably contributed to this deterioration was the aforementioned decrease in the rate of retirement of old capital, which would tend to diminish the general level of quality of the capital stock.

21. S. Cohn in *New Directions in the Soviet Economy*, cited, p. 120.

22. For a discussion of the methods used see Noren, cited, pp. 278–79, 302–15. See also the two articles by E. Domar, "On the Measurement of Technological Change," *The Economic Journal* (December 1961), pp. 709–29; and "On Total Productivity and All That," *The Journal of Political Economy* (December 1962), pp. 597–608.

23. See Cohn, cited, p. 112.

24. Same, pp. 123–24.

25. Uncompleted construction in 1958–64 grew faster than did industrial investment in oil and gas and machinery, but not in chemicals. However, in industry as a whole, the ratio of the growth of uncompleted construction to the growth of investment was higher than that for chemicals and machinery; only oil and gas was higher than the industry average. The relevant ratios are: Total industry 1.14, chemicals .98, oil and gas 1.22, machinery 1.10. (*Narodnoe khoziaistvo v 1964*, pp. 516, 523). Therefore, the growth of uncompleted construction in these three industries, when compared with their growth in investment, is not generally out of line with the industry average. But given their high level of priority, it might have been thought they would do much better.

26. See the article by Ia. Kvasha in V. Venzher, *et al.*, *Proizvodstvo, nakoplenie, potreblenie* (Moscow, 1965), pp. 124–25, 163–64.

27. *Pravda*, September 28, 1965. Translation in *Current Digest of the Soviet Press*, XVII, No. 38 (October 13, 1965), p. 5.

28. *Pravda*, April 7, 1966, p. 5. Translation in *Current Digest of the Soviet Press*, XVIII, No. 20 (June 8, 1966), p. 12.

29. See, *e.g.*, J. Berliner, *Factory and Manager in the U.S.S.R.* (Cambridge, Mass.: Harvard University Press, 1957); A. Nove, "The Problems of Success Indicators in Soviet Industry," *Economica* (February 1958).

30. See J. Hardt, D. Gallik, V. Treml in *New Directions in the Soviet*

Economy, cited, pp. 41–42, and the sources cited there. These authors also report that the number of different types of metalworking equipment produced in the Soviet Union increased from 320 in 1940, to 900 in 1957 and to 1,500 in the 1965 plan.

31. See V. Glushkov in *Literaturnaia gazeta*, September 25, 1962, p. 1.
32. According to Soviet data, industrial output grew as fast as, or faster than, the stock of fixed capital in all periods of centralized planning except 1928–32, 1937–40, and the post-1958 period. *Promyshlennost' SSSR* (Moscow, 1964), pp. 31, 68; *Narodnoe khoziaistvo v 1964*, pp. 68, 124.
    The two prewar periods could be explained away by the newness of the industrialization program under centralized planning and by the preparation for war (and the purges). But the post-1958 developments cannot easily be explained away and thus are a cause for grave concern.
33. See, for example, the comments by Kosygin at the September 1965 Plenum, *Current Digest of the Soviet Press*, XVII, No. 38, p. 5.
34. For a full discussion of this question see J. Hardt, *et al.*, *Mathematics and Computers in Soviet Economic Planning* (New Haven: Yale University Press, 1967).
35. Central Intelligence Agency, *An Evaluation of Experimental Economic Reforms in the Consumer Industries of the USSR* (December 1965), p. 14.
36. *Current Digest of the Soviet Press*, XVII, No. 38, pp. 3–17.
37. Same, XVII, No. 38, p. 9; *Narodnoe khoziaistvo v 1964*, p. 513.
38. Based primarily on M. Bornstein, "The Soviet Price Reform Discussion," *Quarterly Journal of Economics* (February 1964), pp. 15–48.
39. See R. Campbell, "Marx, Kantorovich, and Novozhilov: Stoimost' versus Reality," *Slavic Review* (October 1961), pp. 402–18.
40. See Kosygin in *Current Digest of the Soviet Press*, XVII, No. 38, pp. 3–17; V. Sitnin in same, XVIII, No. 41, pp. 3–6; A. Kuznetsov, *Izvestiia*, November 5, 1966, p. 3.
41. All data on the plan are from the Directives on the Five Year Plan and Kosygin's speech at the Twenty-third Party Congress as reported in *Pravda*, February 20, 1966 and *Pravda*, April 6, 1966. Translation in *Current Digest of the Soviet Press*, XVIII, Nos. 7, 8 and 14. See also Noren in *New Directions in the Soviet Economy*, cited, pp. 301–02.
42. The two rates as reported by Kosygin are 6.5 per cent and 4.6 per cent (*Current Digest of the Soviet Press*, XVIII, No. 14, p. 5).
43. Same, XVIII, No. 14, p. 5.
44. Same XVII, No. 38, p. 7.
45. *Pravda*, November 21, 1965.
46. *Current Digest of the Soviet Press*, XVIII, No. 7, p. 5. Also see the statements of V. Lagutkin, Deputy Chairman of the State Committee for Material-Technical Supply, in *Ekonomicheskaia gazeta*, No. 26 (1966), pp. 4–5.
47. See R. Greenslade in *New Directions in the Soviet Economy*, cited, p. 17.
48. If the military situation in regard to China worsens, then the likelihood that Russia would receive support from the West (covert or even overt) might make a return to centralization unnecessary.
49. A. Gerschenkron, cited, pp. 17–18. See also, H. S. Levine, "Pressure and Planning in the Soviet Economy," in Henry Rosovsky (ed.), *Industraliza-*

tion in Two Systems: Essays in Honor of Alexander Gerschenkron (New York: John Wiley, 1966), pp. 265–85.

50. *Narodnoe khoziaistvo v 1964,* p. 87.
51. *Current Digest of the Soviet Press,* XVIII, No. 14, p. 5.
52. V. Nikitin, *Pravda,* Sept. 20, 1966, p. 2.
53. See M. Goldman in *Journal of Political Economy* (August 1965), pp. 366–80.
54. See the review in *Voprosy ekonomiki,* No. 1 (1966), p. 134. The figures were as follows: U.S.S.R. = 100; East Germany = 150; Czechoslovakia = 138; Hungary = 110; Poland = 106; Bulgaria = 99.
55. See J. Tinbergen *et al.,* "The Meeting of the Twain," *Columbia Journal of World Business* (Summer 1966), pp. 139–49.
56. B. Rakitskii, "Against the Bourgeois Interpretations of Economic Reform in the USSR," *Voprosy ekonomiki,* No. 10 (1965), p. 125.
57. See the system described by V. Nemchinov in *Current Digest of the Soviet Press,* XVI, No. 18, pp. 3–8.

Chapter 12. Science

1. I. B. Novik, "Kibernetika i razvitie sovremennogo nauchnogo poznaniia," *Priroda,* No. 10 (1963), p. 11.
2. For a general discussion of Soviet interest in cybernetics, see Loren R. Graham, "Cybernetics in the Soviet Union," *The State of Soviet Science,* by the Editors of *Survey* (Cambridge, Mass.: The M.I.T. Press, 1965), pp. 3–18.
3. "Nekotorye voprosy razvitiia sovremennoi fiziki (Obsuzhdenie raboty otdeleniia obshchei i prikladnoi fiziki)," *Vestnik Akademii Nauk SSSR* (henceforth cited as VAN), No. 2 (1965), p. 32.
4. Philip H. Abelson, "Translation of Scientific Literature," *Science,* CXLIX (1965), p. 929.
5. Same.
6. "Vstupitel'naia rech' Prezidenta Akademii Nauk SSSR Akademika M. V. Keldysha," VAN, No. 3 (1965), p. 8.
7. "Godichnoe sobranie Akademii Nauk SSSR," VAN, No. 3 (1965), p. 111.
8. *Voprosy ideologicheskoi raboty: sbornik vazhneishikh reshenii KPSS (1954–1961 gody)* (Moscow, 1961), p. 188.
9. P. N. Fedoseev *et al.* (eds.), *Filosofskie voprosy fiziologii vysshei nervnoi deiatel'nosti i psikhologii* (Moscow, 1963), p. 21.
10. I. A. Akchurin, "Razvitie kibernetiki i dialektika," *Voprosy filosofii,* No. 7 (1965), p. 22.
11. L. A. Linsternik and A. A. Konopliankin, "Matematika i nauchno-tekhnicheskii progress," in G. S. Zhdanov *et al.* (eds.), *Estestvoznanie i stroitel'stvo kommunizma* (Moscow, 1965), p. 92.
12. E. Kol'man, "Matematika v novykh oblastiakh znaniia," *Priroda,* No. 1 (1964), p. 17.
13. P. N. Fedoseev, "Filosofiia i estestvoznanie," *Priroda,* No. 9 (1963), p. 7.
14. "Godichnoe sobranie," cited, pp. 95–96.
15. V. M. Glushkov, "O nekotorykh problemakh kibernetiki," in K. K. Khrenov (ed.), *Problemy istorii nauki i tekhniki* (Kiev, 1963), pp. 11–12.

16. N. V. Novikov *et al.*, *Sotsial'nie issledovaniia* (Moscow, 1965), pp. 55–117.
17. V. S. Nemchinov, "Sotsiologiia i statistika," in *Sotsiologiia v SSSR*, I (Moscow, 1965), p. 334.
18. For valuable information on the organizational changes in the network of Soviet scientific institutions, see Alexander G. Korol, *Soviet Research and Development* (Cambridge, Mass.: The M.I.T. Press, 1965), pp. 18ff. See also Nicholas DeWitt, "Reorganization of Science and Research in the U.S.S.R.," *Science*, CXXXIII, 1981–1991 (1961).
19. *Spravochnik partiinogo rabotnika*, IV (Moscow, 1963), pp. 397–403.
20. Same, p. 401.
21. *KPSS o kul'ture, prosveshchenii i nauke* (Moscow, 1963), pp. 532–37.
22. "Nauchnaia deiatel'nost' i struktura Akademii Nauk Latviiskoi SSR," *VAN*, No. 7 (1965), p. 3.
23. M. V. Keldysh, "O merakh po uluchsheniiu deiatel'nosti Akademii Nauk SSSR i Akademii Nauk soiuznykh respublik," *VAN*, No. 6 (1963), p. 12.
24. G. S. Migirenko (ed.), *Novosibirskii nauchnyi tsentr* (Novosibirsk, 1962), pp. 7–27; M. A. Lavren'tev, "Razvitie nauki na Vostoke strany," *VAN*, No. 6 (1964), pp. 3–11; H. Koprowski *et al.*, "A New Science City in Siberia," *Science*, CXLIX (1965), pp. 947–49.
25. I. N. Vekua, "Vysshaia shkola v nauchnom tsentre Sibiri," *VAN*, No. 6 (1964), pp. 12–20.
26. M. V. Keldysh, "Vse sily nauki—stroitel'stve kommunizma," *VAN*, No. 7 (1963), pp. 8–9; M. V. Keldysh, "K tesnomu edineniiu nauchnykh sil strany," *VAN*, No. 3 (1964), p. 6; N. M. Sisakian, "Vazhneishie dostizheniia v oblasti estestvennykh i obshchestvennykh nauk v 1963 g.," *VAN*, No. 3 (1964), pp. 15–16.
27. M. V. Keldysh, cited, p. 20.
28. N. M. Sisakian, "Vazhneishie dostizheniia v oblasti estvestvennykh i obshchestvennykh nauk v 1964 godu," *VAN*, No. 3 (1965), pp. 11–12.
29. "Nekotorye voprosy razvitiia sovremennoi fiziki," cited, p. 18.
30. Same, p. 14.
31. Same, p. 19.
32. *Voprosy ideologicheskoi raboty*, cited, pp. 223–38. See also *Spravochnik partiinogo rabotnika*, IV, pp. 408–12 and 418–23.
33. Korol, cited, pp. 125–26.
34. "Nekotorye voprosy razvitiia sovremennoi fiziki," cited, p. 19.
35. Same, p. 36.
36. Same, p. 44.
37. "Izdaniia VINITI v 1959 g.," *VAN*, No. 1 (1965), p. 135.
38. Sisakian, cited, p. 88.
39. Zhdanov *et al.*, cited, p. 71.
40. N. N. Semenov, "Nauka i obshchestvo v veku atoma," *Voprosy filosofii*, No. 7 (1960), p. 24.
41. "New Organization of U.S.S.R. Academy of Sciences," *The Current Digest of the Soviet Press*, XV, No. 27, p. 19.
42. N. Mikhailov, "Nekotorye voprosy razvitiia kul'tury," *Kommunist*, No. 1 (1960), p. 53.
43. "Doklad Akademika L. F. Il'icheva," *VAN*, No. 11 (1963), p. 19.
44. L. F. Il'ichev, "Metodologicheskie problemy estestvoznaniia i obshechest-vennykh nauk," *Priroda*, No. 12 (1963), p. 16.

45. For a sample, see A. A. Maksimov *et al.*, *Filosofskie voprosy sovremennoi fiziki* (Moscow, 1952), pp. 216ff. and 369ff.
46. "Peredovaia," *Voprosy filosofii*, No. 3 (1962), p. 5.
47. V. A. Fok, "Nil's Bor v moei zhizni," *Nauka i chelovechestvo*, 1963 (Moscow, 1963), p. 519. See also V. A. Fok, "Diskussiia s Nil'som Borom," *Voprosy filosofii*, No. 8 (1964), pp. 49–53.
48. V. I. Siforov *et al.*, "Idei Lenina i sovremennoe estestvoznanie," *VAN*, No. 4 (1965), p. 5.
49. A. D. Aleksandrov, "Filosofskoe soderzhanie i znachenie teorii otnositel'-nosti," in P. N. Fedoseev *et al.*, *Filosofskie problemy*, pp. 127–28. See also "Doklad Akademika L. F. Il'icheva," p. 20.
50. G. A. Kursanov, "Nauchnoe poznanie mira i neopozitivizm," *VAN*, No. 9 (1963), p. 51.
51. A. Bovin, "Nauka i mirovozzrenie," *Kommunist*, No. 5 (1960), p. 101.
52. V. I. Siforov *et al.*, cited, p. 9.
53. Thomas S. Kuhn, *The Structure of Scientific Revolutions* (Chicago: University of Chicago Press, 1962), p. 88.
54. L. S. Rozhneva, "Prevrashchenie nauki v neposredstvennuiu proizvoditel'-nuiu silu," *Vestnik Leningradskogo Universiteta*, No. 17 (1964), pp. 28–29.
55. P. N. Fedoseev, cited, p. 6.
56. M. Lebedeva and A. Smirnova (eds.), *Kul'tura, nauka, iskusstvo SSSR* (Moscow, 1965), p. 112.
57. A. A. Godunov, "Ob osobennostiakh upravleniia sotsialisticheskim proiz-vodstvom," *Filosofskie nauki*, No. 4 (1965), pp. 88–89.
58. For a systematic summary of cybernetic problems treated by Soviet scholars, see A. I. Berg, "Kibernetiku na sluzhbu kommunizmu (Vvedenie)," in A. I. Berg (ed.), *Kibernetiku na sluzhbu kommunizmu: sbornik statei* (Moscow-Leningrad, 1961), pp. 7–33. See also A. I. Berg, "Kibernetika i stroitel'stvo kommunizma," in A. I. Berg *et al.* (eds.), *Kibernetika, myshlenie, zhizn'* (Moscow, 1964), pp. 5–19; and B. V. Birinkov and V. S. Tiukhin, "O filosofskoi problematike kibernetiki," in A. I. Berg *et al.* cited, pp. 16–108.
59. P. A. Rachkov, "Vozrastenie roli nauki pri sotsializme i razvitie ee sotsial'-noi organizatsii," *Filosofskie nauki*, No. 6 (1965), p. 5.
60. P. L. Kapitsa, "Lomonosov i mirovaia nauka," *Uspekhi fizicheskikh nauk*, LCCCVII, No. 1 (September, 1965), p. 168.

CHAPTER 13. STRATIFICATION AND COMMUNISM

1. The following description is drawn largely from Alex Inkeles, "Social Stratification and Mobility in the Soviet Union: 1940–1950," *American Sociological Review*, XV (August 1950), pp. 465–79; and two articles by the present author: "The Persistence of Status Advantages in Soviet Russia," *American Journal of Sociology*, LIX (July 1953), pp. 19–27; and "Equality and Inequality Under Khrushchev," *Problems of Communism*, IX (March–April 1960), pp. 31–39.
2. Wilbert E. Moore, "But Some Are More Equal than Others"; Melvin Tumin, "On Inequality"; and Moore's "Rejoinder," all in *American Sociological Review*, XXVIII (February 1963), pp. 13–28.

3. Joseph S. Berliner, *Factory and Manager in the USSR* (Cambridge, Mass.: Harvard University Press, 1957), pp. 232ff., 329.

4. Karl Marx, *Critique of the Gotha Programme* (New York: International Publishers, 1933), pp. 9–10.

5. Same, p. 10.

6. Same, pp. 7, 10; Karl Marx and Friedrich Engels, *The Communist Manifesto*, ed. Samuel H. Beer (New York: Appleton-Century-Crofts, 1955), pp. 31–32; T. B. Bottomore and Maximilien Rubel (eds.), *Karl Marx: Selected Writings in Sociology and Social Philosophy* (London, 1956), pp. 248–250; A. P. Sheptulin *et al.*, *K. Marks, F. Engel's, V. I. Lenin o nauchnom kommunizme* (Moscow, 1965), p. 414.

7. Bernard Barber, *Social Stratification: A Comparative Analysis of Structure and Process* (New York: Harcourt, Brace, 1957), pp. 73–75. See also Barrington Moore Jr., *Soviet Politics—The Dilemma of Power: The Role of Ideas in Social Change* (Cambridge, Mass.: Harvard University Press, 1950), pp. 236–37.

8. Feldmesser, "Equality and Inequality Under Khrushchev," cited, pp. 37–39.

9. An English translation of the program is conveniently available in Charlotte Saikowski and Leo Gruliow (eds.), *Current Soviet Policies IV* (New York: Columbia University Press, 1962), pp. 2–33. Citations to the program will be made from this translation.

10. N. S. Khrushchev, "O kontrol'nykh tsifrakh razvitiia narodnogo khoziaistva SSSR na 1959–1965 gody,' *Vneocherednoi XXI S"ezd Kommunisticheskoi Partii Sovetskogo Soiuza . . . stenograficheskii otchet* (Moscow, 1959), I, p. 100.

11. F. F. Korolev, "Rounded Development of the Human Personality—The Paramount Task of Communist Construction," *Soviet Education*, IV (January 1962), p. 8. See also A. P. Osipov, "Tekhnicheskii progress i izmenenie professional'noi struktury rabochego klassa," *Sotsiologiia v SSSR* (Moscow, 1966), II, p. 25.

12. E. L. Manevich, "O likvidatsii razlichii mezhdu umstvennym i fizicheskim trudom v period razvernutogo stroitel'stva kommunizma," *Voprosy filosofii*, No. 9 (1961), pp. 23, 26. See also Osipov, cited, pp. 22–23; and in the same volume, M. T. Iovchuk, "Sotsial'noe znachenie pod'ema kul'turno-tekhnicheskogo urovnia rabochikh," pp. 31, 34; and L. N. Kogan, "Problema likvidatsii professional'noi ogranichennosti rabochego," pp. 68–69.

13. Korolev, cited, p. 8.

14. Same, p. 10. See also Vadim Semyonov, *Aim: A Classless Society* (Moscow, n. d.), p. 41; Iovchuk, cited, pp. 39, 45, 49–50; M. N. Rutkevich, "Elimination of Class Differences and the Place of Non-Manual Workers in the Social Structure of Soviet Society," *Soviet Sociology*, III (Fall 1964), pp. 6–7; and V. S. Semenov, "Ob izmenenii intelligentsii i sluzhashchikh v protsesse stroitel'stva kommunizma," *Sotsiologiia v SSSR*, I, 428.

15. B. A. Grushin and V. V. Chikin, "Problems of the Movement for Communist Labor in the USSR," *Soviet Sociology*, I (Spring 1963), p. 33; A. K. Uledov, *Obshchestvennoe mnenie sovetskogo obshchestva* (Moscow, 1963), p. 342; Semenov, cited, pp. 424–25. For other comments on the numbers and functions of unpaid activists, see Howard R. Swearer, "Popular Participation: Myths and Realities," *Problems of Communism*,

IX (September–October 1960), pp. 42–51; H. T. Willetts, "The Public Image of the CPSU," *Soviet Survey*, No. 35 (January–March 1961), p. 72; *Current Digest of the Soviet Press*, XVI (December 30, 1964), pp. 14–16; and A. K. Kurylev, *Preodolenie sushchestvennykh razlichii mezhdu umstvennym i fizicheskim trudom—problema stroitel'stva kommunizma* (Moscow, 1963), pp. 69–70.

16. Saikowski and Gruliow, cited, pp. 14, 20; M. N. Rutkevich, cited, p. 8; M. T. Iovchuk and others, *Pod'em kul'turno-tekhnicheskogo urovnia sovetskogo rabochego klassa* (Moscow, 1961), pp. 16–17; Ts. A. Stepanian, "Osnovnye zakonomernosti i etapy formirovaniia kommunisticheskogo obshchestva," in P. N. Fedoseev *et al.*, *Ot sotsializma k kommunizmu* (Moscow, 1962), p. 18.

17. Saikowski and Gruliow, cited, p. 65.

18. Same, p. 27; E. I. Afanasenko, "Five Years of the Boarding Schools," *Soviet Education*, IV (March 1962), p. 4.

19. Khrushchev, cited, p. 95.

20. This may also be inferred from the following statement by Khrushchev: "It must of course be realized that, under the conditions of socialism, a significant and ever increasing portion of material and cultural goods is already being distributed among the members of society independently of the quantity and quality of their labor, that is, without charge. Society spends large amounts on citizens' free education, on free medical care, on the provision of pensions, on grants to large families, on free services to clubs, libraries, etc." Same, p. 97.

21. See the speech by L. F. Ilyichev in *Current Digest of the Soviet Press*, XV (July 3, 1963), p. 10; and L. M. Gatovskii, "Ob ekonomicheskikh osnovakh perekhoda k kommunizmu," in Fedoseev *et al.*, cited, p. 59.

22. Saikowski and Gruliow, cited, p. 66.

23. Afanasenko, cited, p. 4.

24. Saikowski and Gruliow, cited, p. 105.

25. Same, pp. 23, 98.

26. Peter Wiles, "Will Capitalism and Communism Spontaneously Converge?," *Encounter*, XX (June 1963), p. 89. The phrase has also been used, apparently with the same meaning, by a Soviet economist, who referred to the "protsess obobshchestvleniia v sfere potrebleniia i byta." Gatovskii, cited, p. 64.

27. A. S. Petrov, "Dvizhenie za kommunisticheskii trud i sovershenstvovanie obshchestvennykh otnoshenii," *Sovetskaia etnografiia*, No. 1 (1962), p. 81.

28. E. G. Balagushkin, "Stroitel'stvo kommunizma i razvitie brachno-semeinykh otnoshenii," *Voprosy filosofii*, No. 3 (1962), p. 32.

29. Manevich, cited, p. 22.

30. See, for example, Petrov, cited, p. 81; Murray Yanowitch, "Soviet Patterns of Time Use and Concepts of Leisure," *Soviet Studies*, XV (July 1963), p. 18.

31. *Vneocherednoi XXI S'ezd*, cited, II, p. 532.

32. Saikowski and Gruliow, cited, p. 28; emphasis added.

33. Korolev, cited, p. 15.

34. V. A. Sukhomlinskii, "Labor and Morality," *Soviet Education*, IV (December 1961), p. 37.

35. P. Simakov, "The First Experience of Schools with a Prolonged Day," *Soviet Education*, IV (September 1962), p. 29.

36. Compare the figures and statements in Tsentral'noe Statisticheskoe Upravlenie, *Narodnoe khoziaistvo SSSR v 1963 godu* (Moscow, 1965), p. 556; *Narodnoe khoziaistvo SSSR v 1964 godu*, p. 668; *Narodnoe khoziaistvo SSSR v 1965 godu*, p. 678. See also Norton T. Dodge, *Women in the Soviet Economy* (Baltimore: The Johns Hopkins Press, 1966), p. 90.

37. E. I. Afanasenko, "Concerning the Progress in Implementing the Law on Strengthening the Ties of the School with Life and Further Developing the System of Public Education in the RSFSR," *Soviet Education*, V (November 1962), p. 12. See also V. I. Selivanov, "Pervichnye sel'skie kollektivy i ikh vliianie na formirovanie lichnosti," *Sotsiologiia v SSSR*, I, pp. 460–63.

38. *Current Digest of the Soviet Press*, XV (July 10, 1963), p. 11.

39. Same, XIII (May 24, 1961), pp. 8–9; and XIII (September 13, 1961), 8.

40. Harold J. Berman, *Justice in the U.S.S.R.* (New York: Vintage, 1963), p. 85.

41. *Current Digest of the Soviet Press*, XIII (September 13, 1961), p. 8.

42. Petrov, cited, p. 26. Alec Nove has suggested that the existence of the volunteer militia may account for the fact that the Soviet Union apparently has, "proportionately to its population, slightly fewer police than Great Britain." Nove, *Economic Rationality and Soviet Politics: Or, Was Stalin Really Necessary?* (New York: Frederick A. Praeger, 1964), p. 279.

43. Grushin and Chikin, cited, pp. 19–20; Willetts, cited, pp. 74–75; Petrov, cited, pp. 79–80; G. S. Kostiuk, "Psychological Problems in the Combination of School Learning and Productive Work," *Soviet Education*, III (August 1961), p. 44.

44. Petrov, cited, p. 80.

45. Same, p. 80.

46. Same, p. 81.

47. Saikowski and Gruliow, cited, p. 66.

48. *Pravda*, June 29, 1963, p. 1.

49. Saikowski and Gruliow, cited, p. 114.

50. *Pravda*, March 10, 1963, p. 2.

51. V. Petrykin, "The Volunteer Principle in Ideological Work," *Current Digest of the Soviet Press*, XV (June 5, 1963), p. 15; Willetts, cited, p. 74.

52. Saikowski and Gruliow, cited, p. 110. For a similar phenomenon on another issue—the short-lived division of the party into industrial and agricultural sections—see Uledov, cited, pp. 115–16.

53. "The second congress of the Comintern in its resolution on the role of the communist party in the proletarian revolution noted the fact that after communism had ceased to be the object of struggle, the communist party will dissolve fully in the working class and the entire working class will become communist. This is a logical development. The party is striving for such a growth of the communist consciousness of members of society as will raise all to the level of the vanguard." P. Romashkin, in *Partiinaia zhizn'*, No. 9 (1961), quoted in Leonard Schapiro, "The Party and the State," *Survey*, No. 38 (October 1961), pp. 114–15.

54. *Pravda*, November 20, 1962, p. 7.

55. *Pravda*, March 6, 1962, p. 2.

56. Annual per capita consumption of meat, milk and milk products, and sugar by 1980 were also predicted at the same time (*Pravda,* March 6, 1962, p. 2). A year earlier (*Pravda,* February 5, 1961, p. 1), Khrushchev spoke of 184 kilograms of fresh milk per person per year, or about 0.5 liters a day, as being a "good norm"; the figure had been established by the Food Institute of the Academy of Medical Sciences. In his speech on the 1961 program, Khrushchev said: "Within the next decade *all Soviet people will be able to acquire a sufficiency of consumer goods, and in the following decade* [i.e., by 1980] *the demand for them will be met in full.* According to plan estimates, per capita consumption will increase over the 20 years as follows: clothing and footwear, approximately 250 per cent; articles of cultural and everyday use, 450 per cent. The output of furniture is to rise six- to eightfold. . . . the country's housing must be approximately tripled in 20 years' time." Saikowski and Gruliow, cited, p. 98 (emphasis in the source). See also the remarkable article by F. Iu. Aleshina, "K voprosu o metodologii raschetov nauchno—obosnovannykh norm lichnogo potrebleniia," *Voprosy truda,* IV (Moscow, 1959), pp. 154–72.

57. *Pravda,* March 10, 1963, p. 3.

58. The best-known case, of course, is that of Valeriy Tarsis, who subsequently wrote a book about his observations in the mental institution to which he had been sent: *Ward 7: An Autobiographical Novel* (New York: Dutton, 1965). The translator's note to the book cites (p. 7) other instances; and see also *The New York Times,* February 9, 1966, p. 16. For references to the mental derangement of religionists, see *Current Digest of the Soviet Press,* XIV (July 18, 1962), pp. 12–14. As George Gibian has pointed out, this device is not new in Russian history: "The New and the Old: From an Observer's Notebook," *Problems of Communism,* XVI (March–April 1967), pp. 62–63. See also Timothy McLure, "The Politics of Soviet Culture, 1964–1967," *Problems of Communism,* XVI (March–April 1967), pp. 36, 38. Finally, it is worth noting this press report concerning the departure from the Soviet Union of Stalin's daughter, Svetlana Alliluyeva: "A young working girl in Moscow said the word on the grapevine was that Svetlana was 'strange' in the sense of being mentally unbalanced." *The New York Times,* June 4, 1967, p. 18.

59. Alex Inkeles and Raymond A. Bauer, *The Soviet Citizen* (Cambridge, Mass.: Harvard University Press, 1959), pp. 282–83; Herschel Alt and Edith Alt, *The New Soviet Man* (New York: Twayne, 1964), p. 135.

60. Leon Festinger, "The Theory of Cognitive Dissonance," in Wilbur Schramm (ed.), *The Science of Human Communication* (New York: Basic Books, 1963), pp. 21–22; George C. Homans, *Social Behavior* (New York: Harcourt, Brace & World, 1961), pp. 104, 117.

61. Dodge, cited, pp. 81–82, 88–90; Afanasenko, "Concerning the Progress. . . ," cited, p. 12.

62. The hypothesis is originally Durkheim's, but an especially relevant and interesting discussion is that by Jackson Toby, *Contemporary Society* (New York: John Wiley, 1964), pp. 306–8.

63. Saikowski and Gruliow, cited, p. 28.

64. The classic experiment is that of S. E. Asch, "Effects of Group Pressure Upon the Modification and Distortion of Judgments," in Eleanor E. Maccoby *et al., Readings in Social Psychology* (New York: Henry Holt,

1958), pp. 174–83. See also Richard S. Crutchfield, "Conformity and Character," in Edwin P. Hollander and Raymond G. Hunt (eds.), *Current Perspectives in Social Psychology* (New York: Oxford University Press, 1963), pp. 398–401; and Bernard Berelson and Gary A. Steiner, *Human Behavior* (New York: Harcourt, Brace & World, 1964), pp. 567, 575.

65. Edward L. Walker and Roger W. Heyns, *An Anatomy for Conformity* (Englewood Cliffs, N.J.: Prentice-Hall, 1962), pp. 97–98; Berelson and Steiner, cited, pp. 327–39, 566, 568; Uledov, cited, pp. 342–45, 353–55.

66. Bernard R. Berelson et al., *Voting: A Study of Opinion Formation in a Presidential Campaign* (Chicago: University of Chicago Press, 1954), pp. 88–98; Angus Campbell et al., *The American Voter* (New York: John Wiley, 1960), pp. 147, 492–93; Berelson and Steiner, cited, pp. 562–66.

67. The basic ideas do not appear to have been abandoned, but less has been said about the imminent advent of communism and more about the difficulties and dangers to be avoided or overcome on the way to it.

68. F. I. Il'iashenko, "An Experimental Study of the Level of Culture and Technical Knowledge of Rural Working People," *Soviet Sociology*, III (Summer 1964), pp. 43–44; A. V. Vinokur and R. V. Ryvkina, "Socio-Economic Problems of the socialist rationalization of production," *Soviet Sociology*, III (Winter 1964–65), pp. 5, 7; V. N. Shubkin, "Vybor professii v usloviiakh kommunisticheskogo stroitel'stva," *Voprosy filosofii*, No. 8 (1964), p. 28; Iovchuk, "Sotsial'noe znachenie. . . ," cited, pp. 37, 41; Kurylev, cited, p. 96.

69. *Current Digest of the Soviet Press*, XII (December 7, 1960), pp. 24–25; XVI (June 26, 1963), pp. 28–29; XVI (June 10, 1964), pp. 20–21; and XVI (June 24, 1964), p. 24. Berman, cited, p. 288; Swearer, cited, pp. 49–50; Uledov, cited, pp. 352–53; and A. Shpeier, "Vo imeni kollektiva," *Izvestiia*, September 1, 1965, p. 5.

Chapter 14. The Family and Social Problems

1. See *Soviet Educators on Soviet Education*, edited and translated by Helen B. Redl (New York: The Free Press, 1964).

2. Friedrich Engels, *The Origin of the Family, Private Property, and the State* (New York: International Publishers, 1942).

3. Alex Inkeles, "Family and the Church in the Post War U.S.S.R.," *Annals of the American Academy of Political and Social Sciences*, CCLXIII (May 1959), pp. 33–44.

4. Sidney and Beatrice Webb, *Soviet Communism: A New Civilization?* (New York: Charles Scribner's Sons, 1938), II, p. 825.

5. Reported in *Izvestiia*, April 24, 1936, p. 4.

6. Vladimir Gsovski, "Marriage and Divorce in Soviet Law," *Georgetown Law Journal*, XXXV, No. 1 (January 1947), pp. 209–23.

7. Inkeles, cited, p. 37.

8. Same, p. 34.

9. Mark G. Field, "The Relegalization of Abortions in Soviet Russia," *New England Journal of Medicine*, CCLV (August 1956), pp. 421–27.

10. *The New York Times*, December 20, 1965.

11. Cited in David and Vera Mace, *The Soviet Family* (Garden City: Doubleday and Company, 1963), p. 266.
12. *Large Soviet Encyclopedia (Sem'ia)*, XXXVIII (Moscow, 1955), p. 491.
13. *Soviet Educators on Soviet Education*, cited, p. xxxiv.
14. "Hiding Behind Papa," *Izvestiia*, May 22, 1964, p. 3.
15. David M. Levy, *Maternal Overprotection* (New York: W. W. Norton, 1966).
16. M. M. Skudina, "The Gifted Child," *Doshkolnoe vospitanie*, 1961, No. 4, *Soviet Review* (January 1962), pp. 3–10.
17. *Pravda*, January 6, 1962.
18. "Cultivation of Feelings," *Pravda*, January 31, 1965, translated in *Current Digest of the Soviet Press*, XVII, No. 5 (February 1965), p. 23.
19. Sergei Obraztsov, "Off the Street and to the Stadium," *Literaturnaia gazeta*, December 23, 1965, p. 2, *Current Digest of the Soviet Press*, XVIII, No. 12 (April 13, 1966), Part II, pp. 19–20.
20. L. Kuznetsova, "Where are the Young to Meet?" *Komsomolskaia pravda*, January 7, 1966, p. 2; *Current Digest of the Soviet Press*, XVIII, No. 12, Part II, p. 20.
21. *Soviet Educators on Soviet Education*, cited, p. xxx.
22. "Father Hears but Drinks," *Komsomolskaia pravda*, July 31, 1965, p. 2.
23. For example, "From Monday to Saturday," *Izvestiia*, November 24, 1965, in which a kindergarten teacher urges parents to set a good example for the children; or "The Air of the Family," *Izvestiia*, January 6, 1965, in which the parents are reminded of the effect of the family atmosphere on the child.
24. M. D. Shargorodski, "The Causes and Prevention of Crime," *Soviet Sociology*, III, No. 1 (Summer 1964), p. 37.
25. For example, see article "On Marriage and the Family" in *Krokodil*, February 20, 1964, which points to the old-fashioned nature of *babushkas*.
26. Nicholas DeWitt, *Education and Professional Employment in the U.S.S.R.* (Washington: GPO, 1961), NSF, pp. 126–8.
27. "Important Side of Education," *Izvestiia*, August 18, 1961, in Letters to the Editor, p. 4; see also V. Kvashnin, "Stadiums are not the Solution," *Literaturnaia gazeta*, January 27, 1966, p. 2, *Current Digest of the Soviet Press*, XVIII, No. 12, Part II, p. 20.
28. "Shkoly-internaty," *Pravda*, June 28, 1956, p. 1.
29. "How I was Offered a Bribe," *Izvestiia*, September 28, 1963, p. 2.
30. "Letters with Commentary: Circles in the Water," *Izvestiia*, September 4, 1965, p. 3.
31. "Thirteen Full Days," *Molodoi kommunist*, February 1965.
32. "How They Put Out the Spark," *Sovetskaia Rossiia*, February 25, 1965, p. 2.
33. "What Lies in the Heart," *Kazakhstanskaia pravda*, March 31, 1963, italics supplied.
34. *Pravda*, July 26, 1965, *Current Digest of the Soviet Press*, XVII, No. 30, p. 29.
35. Predrag Vukovic, "Campaign Against People Who Spoil the Reputation of Soviet Citizens," *Politika*, November 21, 1960.
36. "Independence with a Minus," *Komsomolskaia pravda*, May 21, 1965, p. 2.

37. "And the Street Will be an Ally," *Komsomolskaia pravda*, April 26, 1965.
38. Mark G. Field, "Alcoholism, Crime and Delinquency in Soviet Society," *Social Problems* III (1955), pp. 100–9.
39. "Russians to Jail Youth's Enticers," *The New York Times*, July 7, 1965.
40. "An Experiment in the Composite Research of the Causes and Conditions Leading to Juvenile Delinquency," *Sovetskoe gosudarstvo i pravo*, No. 9 (1963), pp. 110–116.
41. "Prepared for Everything," *Izvestiia*, September 11, 1963, p. 3.
42. "And the Street Will be an Ally," cited.
43. "Prepared for Everything," cited.
44. Ivan Bakalo, "Soviet Boarding Schools and Extended Day School," *Studies on the Soviet Union*, IV, No. 1 (1964).
45. John Bowlby, *Maternal Care and Mental Health* (Geneva, 1952), p. 11.
46. *Deprivation of Maternal Care: A Reassessment of its Effects* (Geneva, 1962), Public Health Papers, p. 14.
47. J. W. Anderson, "A Special Hell for Children in Washington," *Harper's* November 1965, pp. 51–56.
48. Bowlby, cited.
49. A. Kotovschikova, "Unusual Children," *Literaturnaia gazeta*, October 29, 1960, p. 6.
50. A. Kotovschikova, "Many People Think About Them," *Literaturnaia gazeta*, July 25, 1961.
51. "Schools with a Great Future," *Izvestiia*, March 7, 1961, p. 3.
52. "You Are Not Worried? You Should Be," *Komsomolskaia pravda*, May 12, 1961.
53. Same.
54. "Pedagogical Reflections: Long and Valuable Day," *Izvestiia*, April 7, 1965, p. 3.
55. "Rabochii byt i kommunizm," *Novyi mir*, No. 7 (1960), pp. 203–20.
56. Albert L. Weeks, Jr., "The Boarding School," *Survey*, LVI (July 1965), pp. 83–94.
57. A. G. Kharchev, "The Nature of the Soviet Family," *Soviet Review*, V, No. 2, pp. 3–19.
58. Same, pp. 16–17.

CHAPTER 15. LEISURE: THE UNITY OF PLEASURE AND PURPOSE

1. The rise of sociological interest in leisure within the Soviet Union in the past decade has not been paralleled by any substantial awakening of such interest on the part of American students of Soviet life. There are further factors accounting for this situation which also apply to the gap in sociological information about many other aspects of Soviet society. Among them are the difficulty of gaining access to data, the impossibility of conducting empirical studies, and the linguistic barrier. American and English articles on Soviet leisure to date are:

David Allchurch, "Diversions and Distractions," *Soviet Survey*, No. 26 (October–December 1958), pp. 49–55.

Jeremy R. Azrael, "Notes on Soviet Urban Attitudes Toward Leisure," *Social Problems*, IX, No. 1 (1961), pp. 69–78.

F. G. Durham, "The Use of Free Time by Young People in Soviet

Society," January 1966, M.I.T. Center for International Studies Monograph.

Murray Yanowitch, "Soviet Patterns of Time Use and Concepts of Leisure," *Soviet Studies*, XV (July 1963).

Paul Hollander, "The Uses of Leisure," *Survey* (July 1966).

Paul Hollander, "Leisure as an American and Soviet Value," *Social Problems*, XIV, No. 2 (Fall 1966).

While Western scholarship in this area is still very limited, a somewhat impressionistic but occasionally revealing picture of Soviet leisure in Western eyes may be obtained from a large number of travel accounts of which use has been made in the present paper.

2. B. Grushin and V. Chikin, *Ispoved' pokoleniia* [compiled from a questionnaire in *Komsomolskaia pravda*] (Moscow, 1962), p. 194.

3. *Izvestiia*, August 31, 1965, translated in "A Criticism of Glib Talk of 'Communism in Our Life,'" *Current Digest of the Soviet Press*, September 22, 1965, p. 16.

4. *Teatr*, October 1964, No. 10; translated in "Theatergoers Polled on Preferences and Wishes," *Current Digest of the Soviet Press*, December 23, 1964, p. 10.

5. *Kommunist* (September 1965), pp. 73–74.

6. *Krasnaya zvezda*, July 7 and October 11, 1964; translated in "Krasnaia Zvezda Polls Soldiers on Army Life," *Current Digest of the Soviet Press*, December 9, 1964, p. 11.

7. S. G. Strumilin, "Your Questions on Communism," *USSR* (December 1964), p. 13.

8. L. Bibik and M. Markovich, *Politicheskoe samoobrazovanie*, No 7 (1962), translated as "Changes Occurring in the Structure of Free Time," *Soviet Sociology* (Fall 1962).

9. The attribution of interdependence as a feature of totalitarian regimes is also observed in Alex Inkeles, "The Totalitarian Mystique," in Carl J. Friedrich (ed.), *Totalitarianism* (New York: Grosset's Universal Library, 1964), pp. 93–94.

10. G. S. Petrosian, *Voprosy ekonomiki* (June 1963), translated in "An Analysis of How Workers Spend Off-Work Time," *Current Digest of the Soviet Press*, September 11, 1963, p. 1. The extraordinary importance of labor in life was demonstrated recently in a *Pravda* news item (November 30, 1965) which reported that an allegedly 153 year-old Armenian woman works on the state farm where she lives with her great-great-grandson, since, as she remarked to *Pravda's* correspondent, she does not "like to rest." Children, too, are not exempt from the demands of work. *Nedelia* invited Moscow school children to evaluate various toys in a round-table discussion with the following results: "It was found that a toy should be: (1) such that one could repair it oneself, and 'the scale should be realistic'; (2) such that when one plays with it, one can imitate real work processes: 'If it is a conveyer, it should carry loads'; (3) fast-moving ('The hydroplane from the Children's World Store creeps along like a turtle; this is wrong and boring.') with variable speeds and steering gear." *Nedelia*, September 8–14, 1963; translated in *Current Digest of the Soviet Press*, February 5, 1964, p. 14.

11. "There is an exact equivalent in Russian for our word 'leisure,' but it is nowadays seldom used except for humorous or archaic effect. With its

suggestions of idleness and frivolity, or at best of doing what you please instead of what you must, it does well enough to describe the lives of old-time gentry and modern parasites, or the off-work hours of bourgeois individualists. For the honest Soviet toiler, 'rest' has superseded 'leisure.' . . . The Russian exhorts his friends to 'rest,' whether in fact they are bound for the easy chair, the theater, or the ski-run." David Allchurch, "Diversions and Distractions," cited, p. 49.

12. *Sotsiologiia v SSSR* (Moscow, 1965), II, glossary pp. 485, 495.
13. G. S. Petrosian, *Vnerabochee vremia trudiashchikhsia v SSSR* (Moscow, 1965), p. 16. Further categories are suggested by Goncharenko in an article in *Nauchnye doklady vysshei shkoly*, No. 1 (1963): "Learning, raising of qualifications includes: lectures, seminars, political enlightenment, universities of culture, self-education; passive rest: walks, visiting parks, gardens, reception of guests and visiting friends, etc.; cultural rest: use of television, radio, attendance at theater, cinema, clubs, etc."
14. Petrosian, *Vnerabochee* . . . , cited, p. 126.
15. Petrosian, *Voprosy ekonomiki*, cited.
16. Petrosian, *Vnerabochee* . . . , cited, pp. 47–48.
17. This is what Markoosha Fischer calls the "complicated business of living" in her *Reunion in Moscow: A Russian Revisits Her Country* (New York: Harper and Row, 1962).
18. In which case "the reduction of working hours becomes simply illogical and probably sadistic in a situation where labor is becoming man's prime want and need." Azrael, cited, p. 77.
19. See Aline Mosby, *The View from No. 13 People's Street* (New York: Random House, 1962), p. 170; Sally Belfrage, *A Room in Moscow* (London, 1958), p. 79; Irving R. Levine, *Main Street, USSR* (New York: Doubleday, 1959), p. 253.
20. Petrosian, *Vnerabochee* . . . , cited, p. 64.
21. Same, p. 78.
22. Same, p. 127.
23. Same, p. 129.
24. V. G. Baikova, A. C. Duchal, and A. A. Zemtsov, *Svobodnoe vremia i vsestoronee razvitie lichnosti* (Moscow, 1965), p. 147. From that study, p. 174: "As the analysis shows, engineer-technical workers who study in a system or correspondence and evening general education, and also in various forms of production-technical and political study, devote much more attention to the training of children, physical culture and sport than those who study nowhere. The social-political activeness of the former is also significantly higher. True, they have somewhat less time remaining for rest and amusement, but for all that, on the whole, the content of their free time is incomparably richer."
25. David Granik, in *The Red Executive: A Study of the Organization Man in Russian Industry* (New York: Doubleday, 1960), remarks that the housing situation inhibits home entertainment even among managerial executives, and that the home is a "place to stay away from." P. 103.
26. See Edward Crankshaw, *Russian Without Stalin: The Emerging Pattern* (New York: Viking Press, 1956), p. 89; and Fischer, cited, p. 73.
27. See Raymond A. Bauer, Alex Inkeles, and Clyde Kluckholn, *How the Soviet System Works* (Cambridge, Mass.: Harvard University Press, 1956), p. 129.

28. *Literaturnaia gazeta*, December 10, 1964; translated in "Folkways and Artificial 'Traditions': Two Feuilletons," *Current Digest of the Soviet Press*, January 13, 1965, p. 17.

29. *Literaturnaia gazeta*, December 3, 1964; translated in "How Can Folk Art and Rural Culture be Fostered?," *Current Digest of the Soviet Press*, May 12, 1965, p. 20.

30. *Trud*, April 27, 1965; translated as "Give Attention and Concern to the Sphere of Service," *Current Digest of the Soviet Press*, June 2, 1965, p. 30.

31. The data which follows is from Petrosian's statistical table in *Vnerabochee vremia trudiashchikhsia v SSSR*, cited, p. 163.

32. A. Krasilov, "Zavod: zhizn', trud, dosug liudei," *Kommunist* (August 1965), p. 55.

33. Petrosian, *Vnerabochee* . . . , cited, p. 180.

34. Baikova *et al.*, cited, p. 267.

35. Klaus Mehnert, *Youth in Soviet Russia* (London: Allen and Unwin, 1933; New York: Harcourt Brace, 1933), p. 25.

36. Fischer, cited, p. 148.

37. Baikova *et al.*, cited, p. 257. Similar reading preferences were found among industrial workers in a survey by L. N. Kogan in "Esteticheskie potrebnosti sovestskogo rabochego," *O chertakh lichnosti novogo rabochego* (Moscow, 1963), p. 190. Favorite writers were said to be Sholokhov, Pushkin, Leo Tolstoy, Lermontov, and Gorky, in that order.

38. In an attempt to turn the popularity of the detective story to constructive ends, *Komsomolskaia pravda* recommended the use of such stories as ideological weapons, saying that "adventure literature should become a powerful means of propagandizing the Soviet way of life." March 31, 1964; translated in "The Detective Story as an Ideological Weapon," *Current Digest of the Soviet Press*, July 22, 1964, p. 13.

39. See Donald Barry, "Russians and Their Cars," *Survey* (October 1965), p. 98; "Boating Highly Organized But the Fun Concept is Alien to Soviet System," *The New York Times*, January 17, 1965; *Ekonomicheskaia gazeta*, October 12, 1963, translated in "The Trials and Tribulations of the Soviet Motorist," *Current Digest of the Soviet Press*, December 4, 1963, p. 13.

40. Baikova *et al.*, cited, p. 166.

41. *The New York Times*, April 12, 1964.

42. See Merle Fainsod, "Soviet Youth and the Problem of the Generations," *Proceedings of the American Philosophical Society*, CVIII, No. 5 (October 1964).

43. *Komsomolskaia pravda*, June 16, 1965; translated in "Bring the Work of the YCL Abreast of the Times," *Current Digest of the Soviet Press*, July 14, 1965, p. 3. On the problems of poor cultural facilities in the countryside and the response of young people to them, cf. *Izvestiia*, December 4, 1964; translated in "450 Interviews at the Village Crossroads: Discussion Continues," *Current Digest of the Soviet Press*, December 30, 1964, p. 28.

44. *Literaturnaia gazeta*, December 31, 1964; translated in "How Can Folk Art and Rural Culture be Fostered?" May 12, 1965, cited.

45. Baikova *et al.*, cited, p. 262.

46. Cf. *Komsomolskaia pravda*, December 29, 1963, translated in "The Palace is not Merely for Show," *Current Digest of the Soviet Press*,

February 5, 1964; *Literaturnaia gazeta*, September 1, 1964, translated in "Over a Cup of Coffee," *Current Digest of the Soviet Press*, November 4, 1964; *Pravda*, "Svobodnoe vremia podrostkam," November 24, 1965; *Pravda*, May 26, 1965, translated as "Club is not a Commercial Enterprise," *Current Digest of the Soviet Press*, June 16, 1965; *Pravda*, "Sel'ski ochagi kultury," November 29, 1964. "Last year there were about 89,000 club leaders in the USSR. More than 35,000 of these did not have high school education."

47. *Pravda*, August 29, 1965, translated in "The Ideological Commitment of Youth," *Current Digest of the Soviet Press*, September 22, 1965; *Izvestiia*, August 11, 1965, translated as "Give Young People the Romance of an Exploit," *Current Digest of the Soviet Press*, September 1, 1965; *Izvestiia*, October 11, 1963, translated as "Commotion in the Temple," *Current Digest of the Soviet Press*, December 11, 1963; *Pravda*, August 19, 1965, translated in "Soviet Television," *Current Digest of the Soviet Press*, September 8, 1965; *Izvestiia*, December 13, 1964, translated in "The Reader's Intelligent Comrade," *Current Digest of the Soviet Press*, January 6, 1965. This last is of particular interest, since it notes that people are still in the habit of dismissing the negative evaluation of critics: "One rarely hears, 'The critics praised it so I must read it.' It is more often said: 'The critics tore it apart, so where can I get a copy?' " The public preference for making free time as different from working time as possible was also voiced by a participant in the debate in *Izvestiia*, February 6, 1964.

48. *Komsomolskaia pravda*, June 16, 1965; translated as "Senior Pupils After Class," *Current Digest of the Soviet Press*, August 25, 1965.

49. *Izvestiia*, November 3, 1965; translated as "Jumping Rope with a Cigarette," *Current Digest of the Soviet Press*, November 24, 1965.

50. For example, *Kazakhstanskaia pravda*, October 31, 1964; translated as "Kazakhstan Alcoholics Face Compulsory Treatment," *Current Digest of the Soviet Press*, December 16, 1964. Also *Sovestskaia Rossiia*, November 20, 1965; and *Kazakhstanskaia pravda*, October 31, 1965.

51. V. N. Pimenov, "Sotsiologia dosuga' i obsuzhdenie problemi svobodnogo vremeni," *Marksistkaia i burzhuaznaia sotsiologiia segodnia* (Moscow, 1964), pp. 439, 440, 446.

52. Aldous Huxley, *Along the Road* (London, 1925), pp. 238–39.

53. Same, p. 235.

54. S. Kniaz'kov, *Ocherki iz istorii Petra Velikago i ego vremeni* (St. Petersburg, 1914), 2nd ed., p. 622.

55. For example, the detective story is seen as "a weapon that has been used long and successfully by our ideological enemies." *Komsomolskaia pravda* June 10, 1964; translated as "The 'Secret' of the Detective Story," *Current Digest of the Soviet Press*, July 22, 1964, p. 16.

CHAPTER 16. THE INTELLECTUALS

1. A classic case for the distinctively Russian roots of Bolshevism is made in Nicholas Berdyaev's *The Origin of Russian Communism* (Ann Arbor: University of Michigan Press, 1960). The roots in traditional Russian culture for both the Stalinist period of Russian culture and the ferment since Stalin's death are stressed in my *The Icon and the Axe: An Interpre-*

tive History of Russian Culture (New York: Knopf, 1966), pp. 536–97.

2. Literature is the only one of the art media in the U.S.S.R. on which there is a real body of "literature" (as distinct from an occasional memoir or monograph) that deals sensitively and concretely with the problems of manipulation and control. An introduction to the literature and the contemporary forms of the problem may be gained from reading Harold Swayze, *Political Control of Literature in the USSR, 1946–1959* (Cambridge: Harvard University Press, 1962); J. F. Matlock, Jr. "The 'Governing Organs' of the Union of Soviet Writers," *American Slavic and East European Review,* XV (1956), pp. 382–99; Priscilla Johnson, *Khrushchev and the Arts: the Politics of Soviet Culture 1962–1964,* edited by Leopold Labedz (Cambridge: M.I.T. Press, 1965); Alexander Steininger, *Literatur und Politik in der Sowjetunion nach Stalins Tod* (Wiesbaden, 1965). In addition to materials cited in *The Icon,* p. 779, note 26, and ff., there are a number of new articles that discuss the problem in the U.S.S.R. in symposia that suggest comparisons with other developing nations: M. Fainsod, "The Role of Intellectuals in the Soviet Union," in *The Texas Quarterly* (Winter 1965), pp. 88–103 (a special issue on "The Role of the Intellectual in Politics"), and J. Azrael, "The Soviet Union," in James S. Coleman (ed.), *Education and Political Development* (Princeton, N.J.: Princeton University Press, 1965) pp. 233–77.

3. See materials referenced in *The Icon,* cited, p. 715–16, note 101; p. 749, note 35.

4. This is the subtitle and theme of one of the best early histories of the tradition, R. Ivanov-Razumnik, *Istoriia russkoi obshchestvennoi mysli* 5th edition, (Petrograd, 1918), a work particularly offensive to Soviet historians because of its suggestion that the radical intelligentsia transcended the traditional framework of class interest.

5. For Lenin's feeling of rivalry with the older intelligentsia, see Adam B. Ulam, *The Bolsheviks: The Intellectual and Political History of the Triumph of Communism in Russia* (New York: Macmillan, 1965). There is an interesting parallel in the even more marked and personal rivalry that Antonio Gramsci, founding father of the Italian Communist Party, felt for Benedetto Croce.

6. M. P. Kim, editor of the official party history of the U.S.S.R. that downgraded Stalin in the Khrushchev era, never lost his characteristically Stalinist zest for discussing culture in terms of statistics (see his *Sorok let sovetskoi kul'tury,* Moscow, 1958), and more recently has implicitly suggested that the Stalin era played a key role in "the cultural revolution" which increased the number of "workers of mental labor" (*rabotnikov umstvennogo truda*) from less than 2.5 million in 1926 to more than 25 million in 1965. See his "Sovetskii opyt kul'turnoi revoliutsii," *Kommunist,* No. 8 (May 1966), p. 53.

Having coined the term "cultural revolution" and devoted much attention to analyzing their own (see, for instance, the report of the sessions held on the subject in the Institute of History of the Academy of Sciences by I. I. Popov, "Obsuzhdenie problem kul'turnoi revoliutsii v SSSR," *Istoriia SSSR* (1965), No. 5, pp. 196–98), Soviet ideologists were clearly distressed at the Chinese Communist adoption of the term (which was always reported in quotation marks), and endeavored to define cultural revolution in such a way as to deny the Chinese claim to be conducting one. See A. Arnol'dov, "Kul'turnaia revoliutsiia—zakonomernost' razvitiia sotsializma," *Pravda*, September 26, 1966, pp. 2–3. For an official, Marxist-Leninist *riposte* to the Chinese "petty-bourgeois adventurists" for putting "a cult in place of culture," see G. Shakhnazarov, "Kul'turnaia revoliutsiia v Kitae i melkoburzhuaznyi avantiurizm," *Kommunist*, No. 3 (1967), pp. 104–13, esp. p. 107. For a deft, pictorial contrast between the growing Soviet interest in restoration of antiquity and the tendency toward destruction and defacement in China, see the pictures in the new and ideologically interesting "illustrated social and political weekly" *RT*, No. 28 (1966), pp. 8–9.

7. D. Zemliansky, and S. Mezentsev, "Ideologicheskie kommissii partiinykh komitetov," *Kommunist*, No. 5 (March 1962), pp. 78–84.

8. See the article by Theodore Shabad discussing this proposal by the subsequently demoted L. Ilichev in *The New York Times*, April 11, 1963.

9. *XXII s'ezd KPSS i voprosy ideologicheskoi raboty* (Moscow, 1962), pp. 141–49.

10. Same, pp. 322–33.

11. See G. Kunitsyn, "Literaturnaia chast' partiinogo dela," *Kommunist*, No. 16 (November 1965), pp. 91–102; and the editorial in *Yunost'* (April 1966), pp. 2–5. The sparse account of the all-Union conference-seminar of party workers called by the Central Committee and devoted to questions of ideological work in light of the decisions of the Twenty-third Congress of the Party from October 18–25, 1966, gives no indication of any new approaches or fresh ideas. See *Izvestiia*, October 26, 1966, p. 1; and *Current Digest of the Soviet Press*, XVIII, No. 43, p. 23.

12. V. Ivanov, "Geroicheskoe v povsednevnom," *Kommunist*, No. 17 (November 1965), p. 75; M. Emtsev, E. Parnov, "Nauka i fantastika," *Kommunist*, No. 15 (October 1965), p. 73.

13. See O. Utis (Isaiah Berlin), "Generalissimo Stalin and the Art of Government," *Foreign Affairs* (January 1952).

14. See A. Rumiantsev, "The Party Spirit of the Creative Labor of the Soviet Intelligentsia," *Pravda*, September 9, 1965, as translated in *Current Digest of the Soviet Press*, XVIII, No. 36, pp. 3–6; also the editorial "Our People's Intelligentsia," *Pravda*, September 19, 1965, as translated in *Current Digest of the Soviet Press*, XVII, No. 38, pp. 31–32. This formula, of course, lacked the full-blown official status of Uvarov's. However, as editor of *Pravda* at the time, Rumiantsev was criticizing a much tougher earlier article in *Izvestiia*, and thus represented (like Uvarov in comparison with some of his immediate predecessors) a return to relative rationality within a framework of orthodoxy.

15. I discuss this season and give my views on the nature of the ferment in an article in *University: A Princeton Quarterly*, and provide further analysis together with references in section VI, part 3 of *The Icon*, cited.

16. The sanction of the *narod* was, of course, invoked by Lenin himself in the early days of the Soviet state when he abolished the ministries of the old repressive state and rebaptized his own administrative divisions *narodnye komissariaty*. Stalin also resorted to it after World War II, when he took over from Kuusinen the phrase "people's democracy" (*narodnaia demokratiia*—first used by Lenin's former personal secretary V. Bonch-Bruevich) and made it the approved variant of proletarian dictatorship

for newly conquered Eastern European countries which generally also had native populist traditions.

17. See, for instance, the lead editorial in *Kommunist*, No. 2 (1966), "Ideinaia ubezhdennost' stroitelei kommunizma," which quotes only ordinary people and Lenin with no words taken from any other political figure.

18. See E. V. Genkina, "O Leninskikh metodakh vovlecheniia intelligentsii v sotsialisticheskoe stroitel'stvo," *Voprosy istorii* (April 1965), pp. 21–42; and S. Iedivkin, "Oktiabr'skaia revoliutsiia i intelligentsiia," *Kommunist* No. 13 (September 1966), pp. 39–49.

19. See, in addition to Rumiantsev's original usage, that of A. Mikhalevich, "Iadro intelligentnosti," *Molodoi kommunist* (1966), No. 6, pp. 46–48.

20. S. Pavlov, "The Ideological Commitment of Youth," *Pravda*, August 29, 1965, as cited in *Current Digest of the Soviet Press*, XVII, No. 35, p. 14.

Even the most leaden of Soviet officials on the most ritual of state occasions now use the term *intelligentsiia*. See, for instance, the reference by Marshal Malinovskii (in his speech in Red Square on the 49th anniversary of the Bolshevik Revolution) to the appearance of "a new generation of our Soviet military intelligentsia," *Izvestiia*, November 7, 1966, p. 1.

21. G. Mdivani, in *Izvestiia*, June 16, 1966, as cited in *Current Digest of the Soviet Press*, XVIII, No. 24, p. 19. For a typical recent rejection of the convergence theory in literature see V. Shcherbina, "Leninskie printsipy razvitiia khudozhestvennoi kul'tury," *Kommunist*, No. 8 (May 1966), esp. pp. 44ff.

Attempts to sustain a sense of national identity have led to extraordinary *agitprop* embellishment of the ideological significance of Soviet space accomplishments and increased discussion of the concept of "Soviet patriotism." See, for instance, A. Nebenzia, "Politicheskoe vospitanie mass," *Kommunist*, No. 10 (July 1966), esp. p. 19. It is also interesting to note that conservative party journals like *Molodaia gvardiia* have opened their pages (in an apparent bid to find some non-Westernizing alternative to the avant-garde modernism of *Yunost'* and other such journals) to the writings of a figure like the ostensibly religious painter of traditional Russian themes and subjects, Il'ia Glazunov. See his "Doroga k tebe," in *Molodaia gvardiia*, Nos. 10 and 12 (1965), Nos. 3 and 6 (1966); also the even more unorthodox praise of Muscovite antiquities by Vladimir Soloukhin in the same journal, Nos. 9 and 10 (1966), as well as the heavy-handed denunciation of these articles by three workers "Net, ne prav pisatel' Soloukhin!" in *Moskovskaia pravda*, December 16, 1966.

The party hierarchy itself expresses periodic interest in the study of Russian antiquity. See, for instance, the speech of Pavlov to the eighth plenum of the Komsomol Central Committee in December, 1965, as translated in *Current Digest of the Soviet Press*, XVIII, No. 1, p. 10 (in the context of an attack on the decadent Westernism of *Yunost'*).

22. The *Novyi mir* editorial, No. 9 (1965), pp. 283–88 is translated in *Current Digest of the Soviet Press*, XVII, No. 47, pp. 9–11; for an alleged transcript of the trial proceedings (apparently received from the Paris-based Polish magazine *Kultura*), see *The New York Times Magazine*, April 17, 1966.

23. See, for instance, the text of the catechistic, neo-Stalinist "Oath of Youth" that was read to a mammoth audience of young people in Red Square on

September 11, 1966, with the young people chanting "We swear!" at the end of each long list of pledges. Picture and text in *Vechernaia Moskva*, September 12, 1966, p. 1.

CHAPTER 17. THE SOVIET UNION IN THE INTERNATIONAL ENVIRONMENT

1. Winston S. Churchill, *The Gathering Storm* (Boston: Houghton Mifflin, 1948), p. 449.
2. Vladimir Dedijer, *Tito* (New York: Simon & Schuster, 1953), p. 322.
3. Marshall D. Shulman, *Stalin's Foreign Policy Reappraised* (Cambridge, Mass.: Harvard University Press, 1963).
4. J. Stalin, *Economic Problems of Socialism in the U.S.S.R.* (New York: International Publishers, 1952), pp. 26–30; Report of the Central Committee to the Congress (delivered by G. M. Malenkov), *Pravda*, October 6, 1952.
5. Philip E. Mosely, "Communist Policy and the Third World," *Review of Politics* (April 1966), pp. 212ff.
6. Alexander Dallin, "The Use of International Movements," in Ivo J. Lederer (ed.), *Russian Foreign Policy: Essays in Historical Perspective* (New Haven: Yale University Press, 1962), p. 338.
7. For a careful appraisal of the economic aspects of the Soviet-Chinese relationship, see Alexander Eckstein, *Communist China's Economic Growth and Foreign Trade: Implications for U.S. Policy* (New York: McGraw-Hill, for the Council on Foreign Relations, 1966), pp. 135–82.
8. *New Times*, No. 8 (February 16, 1956), Documentary Supplement, p. 13.
9. Jane Degras (ed.), *The Communist International, 1919–1943: Documents*, I (New York: Oxford University Press, 1956), pp. 138–44.
10. John H. Kautsky, "Soviet Policy in the Underdeveloped Countries: Changing Behavior and Persistent Symbols," in Adam Bromke and Philip E. Uren (eds.), *The Communist States and the West* (New York: Frederick A. Praeger, 1967) pp. 198–217; Elizabeth Kridl Valkenier, "Changing Soviet Perspectives on the Liberation Revolution," *Orbis* (Winter 1966), pp. 953–69.
11. Mosely, cited, pp. 217–28. As times, conditions and tactics have changed, Soviet analysts have continued to provide a variety of interpretations of the character of national liberation movements, especially their relation to the forward march of socialism; there has even been public discussion of points of disagreement. See, for example, V. L. Tiagunenko, *Problemy sovremennykh natsional'no-osvoboditel'nykh revolutsii* (Moscow, 1966); G. Mirskii and T. Pokataeva, "Klassy i klassovaia bor'ba v razvivaiushchikhsia stranakh," *Mirovaia ekonomika i mezhdunarodnye otnosheniia* (March 1966), pp. 57–69; N. A. Simoniia, "O kharaktere natsional'no-osvoboditel'nykh revolutsii," *Narody Azii i Afriki* (June 1966), pp. 3–21.
12. The meeting, finally held in March 1965, was attended by only 19 parties (not including the Yugoslav or the Rumanian) and did not even tackle the question of excommunicating China. The communiqué has been well described as "a triumph for the heirs of Togliatti over the heirs of Khrushchev," and the outcome demonstrated a serious diminution of Soviet authority even over the parties which were basically on Moscow's side in

the dispute with China (see Kevin Devlin, "Which Side Are You On?," *Problems. of Communism*, January–February 1967, pp. 53–54).

13. Edward Crankshaw, however, believes that he was preparing, as part of his grand design, to sell Ulbricht down the river and reach an accommodation with West Germany; see his *Khrushchev: A Career* (New York: Viking Press, 1966), pp. 285–86.

14. See Thomas W. Wolfe's discussion of this point on pp. 138–40, above.

15. Pierre Le Gall, "L'U.R.S.S. et l'unification européenne, *Revue Française de Science Politique* (February 1967), pp. 28–46.

16. Herbert S. Dinerstein, "Soviet Policy in Latin America," *American Political Science Review* (March 1967), pp. 80–90.

17. R. Ul'yanovskii, "Nekotorye voprosy nekapitalisticheskogo razvitiia osvobodivshikhsia stran," *Kommunisti*, No. 1 (January 1966), pp. 109–19 (especially pp. 118–19).

18. Note Brezhnev's statement at the Twenty-third Party Congress (*Pravda*, March 30, 1966), virtually a repetition of Khrushchev's interpretation of peaceful coexistence in his review of the 81–party statement of 1960 (same, January 25, 1961).

19. See the discussions of this point in Bertram D. Wolfe, "Communist Ideology and Soviet Foreign Policy," *Foreign Affairs* (October 1962), pp. 152–70; Cyril E. Black, "The Pattern of Russian Objectives," in Ivo J. Lederer cited, pp. 3–38; R. V. Daniels, "Doctrine and Foreign Policy," *Survey* (October 1965), pp. 3–13; Henry B. Mayo, "Power and Ideology in East-West Relations," in Bromke and Uren, cited, pp. 3–16.

20. *Pravda* and *Izvestiia*, June 25, 1967, condensed text in *Current Digest of the Soviet Press*, XIX, No. 25, July 12, 1967, pp. 3–10; XIX, No. 26, July 19, 1967, pp. 3–6. The points are roughly the same as those of the program adopted by the Twenty-third Party Congress in 1966. See also V Israelyan and others, "Soviet Foreign Policy and the Contemporary World," *International Affairs* (Moscow, March 1966), pp. 3–20.

21. George F. Kennan, "The United States and the Communist Giants," Walter E. Edge Memorial Lecture, February 25, 1965.

22. See, for example, M. E. Airapetian and V. V. Sukhodeyev, *Novyi tip mezhdunarodnykh otnoshenii* (Moscow, 1964).

Index

Index

CONTRIBUTORS

DAVID E. ANDERSON—Instructor, Department of General Education, Boston University.

VERNON V. ASPATURIAN—Research Professor of Political Science and Director, Slavic and Soviet Language and Area Center, Pennsylvania State University. Author of *The Union Republics in Soviet Diplomacy* (1960) and *The Soviet Union in the World Communist System* (1966). Contributor to *The Soviet Union*, edited by Roy C. Macridis and R. E. Ward (1963).

JEREMY R. AZRAEL—Associate Professor of Political Science, University of Chicago. Author of *Managerial Power and Soviet Politics* (1966).

JAMES H. BILLINGTON—Professor of History, Princeton University. Author of *Mikhailovsky and Russian Populism* (1958), *The Icon and the Axe: An Interpretive History of Russian Culture* (1966). Contributor to *Communism and Revolution*, edited by Cyril E. Black and Thomas P. Thornton (1964).

CYRIL E. BLACK—Duke Professor of History, Princeton University. Author of *The Dynamics of Modernization: A Study in Comparative History* (1966), co-editor of *Communism and Revolution* with Thomas P. Thornton (1964), co-author of *Twentieth Century Europe*, with E. C. Helmreich (1959), editor of *The Transformation of Russian Society: Aspects of Social Change Since 1861* (1960).

JOHN C. CAMPBELL—Senior Research Fellow, Council on Foreign Relations. Author of *The United States in World Affairs* (3 vols. 1947–49), *Defense of the Middle East* (1958), *American Policy Toward Communist Eastern Europe* (1965), and *Tito's Separate Road* (1967).

WARREN W. EASON—Associate Professor of Economics and Chairman, Board of Russian Studies, Syracuse University. Contributor to *The Transformation of Russian Society: Aspects of Social Change Since 1861*, edited by Cyril E. Black (1960). *Economic Trends in the Soviet Union*, edited by Abram Bergson and Simon S. Kuznets (1963), and *Population: The Vital Revolution*, edited by Ronald Freedman (1964).

ROBERT A. FELDMESSER—Associate Professor, Department of Sociology, Dartmouth College. Contributor to *The Transformation of Russian Society: Aspects of Social Change Since 1861*, edited by Cyril E. Black (1960).

MARK G. FIELD—Professor of Sociology and Anthropology, Boston University; Associate, Russian Research Center, Harvard University. Author of *Doctor and Patient in Soviet Russia* (1957), *Soviet Socialized Medicine: An Introduction* (1967), and co-author of

581

Social Approaches to Mental Patient Care (with Morris S. Schwartz and Charlotte Green Schwartz, *et al.*) (1964).

PAUL HOLLANDER—Assistant Professor of Sociology, Department of Social Relations, Harvard University; Research Fellow, Russian Research Center, Harvard University. Author of *The U.S. and the Soviet Union: A Sociological Comparison* (forthcoming) and *American and Soviet Sociology: A Reader in Comparative Social Analysis and Perception* (forthcoming).

ARCADIUS KAHAN—Professor of Economics, Departments of Economics and History, University of Chicago.

ALLEN KASSOF—Associate Professor of Sociology, Assistant Dean of the College, Princeton University. Author of *The Soviet Youth Program: Regimentation and Rebellion* (1965), and contributor to *The Transformation of Russian Society: Aspects of Social Change Since 1861*, edited by Cyril E. Black (1960).

HERBERT S. LEVINE—Associate Professor, Department of Economics, University of Pennsylvania. Author of *A Study in Economic Planning: The Allocation of Materials in Soviet Industry* (forthcoming), and contributor to *The Soviet Economy: Theory and Practice* edited by W. Leeman (1964), and *Industrialization in Two Systems: Essays in Honor of Alexander Gershenkron*, edited by Henry Rosovsky (1966).

LEON LIPSON—Professor of Law and Associate Provost, Yale University. Co-author of *Report on the Law of Outer Space*, with Nicholas de B. Katzenbach (1961).

WILLIAM K. MEDLIN—Professor of History of Education and Comparative Education, School of Education and Center for Russian and East European Studies, University of Michigan. Author of *The History of Educational Ideas in the West* (1964); Project Director and co-author of *Soviet Education Program*, with C. Lindquist and M. Schmitt (1960), and *Education and Social Change: A Study of the Role of the School in a Technically Developing Society in Central Asia*, with F. Carpenter and W. Cave (1965).

SIDNEY I. PLOSS—Associate Research Professor of International Affairs and Member, Institute for Sino-Soviet Studies, George Washington University. Author of *Conflict and Decision-Making in Soviet Russia: A Case Study of Agricultural Policy, 1953–1963* (1965).

ALEXANDER VUCINICH—Professor of Sociology, University of Illinois. Author of *Soviet Economic Institutions: The Social Structure of Production Units* (1952), *The Soviet Academy of Sciences* (1956), and *Science in Russian Culture: A History to 1860* (1963).

THOMAS W. WOLFE—Senior Staff Member, the RAND Corporation. Author of *Soviet Strategy at the Crossroads* (1964), co-editor and translator of V. D. Sokolovskii, *Soviet Military Strategy* (1963).

COUNCIL ON FOREIGN RELATIONS

Officers and Directors
   John J. McCloy, *Chairman of the Board*
   Henry M. Wriston, *Honorary President*
   Grayson Kirk, *President*
   Frank Altschul, *Vice-President & Secretary*
   David Rockefeller, *Vice-President*
   Gabriel Hauge, *Treasurer*
   George S. Franklin, Jr., *Executive Director*

Hamilton Fish Armstrong	Walter H. Mallory
William P. Bundy	Bill D. Moyers
William A. M. Burden	Alfred C. Neal
Arthur H. Dean	James A. Perkins
Douglas Dillon	Lucian W. Pye
Allen W. Dulles	Philip D. Reed
William C. Foster	Robert V. Roosa
Caryl P. Haskins	Charles M. Spofford
Joseph E. Johnson	Carroll L. Wilson
Henry R. Labouisse	

PUBLICATIONS

Foreign Affairs (quarterly), edited by Hamilton Fish Armstrong.
The United States in World Affairs (annual). Volumes for 1931,
   1932 and 1933, by Walter Lippmann and William O. Scroggs;
   for 1934–1935, 1936, 1937, 1938, 1939, and 1940, by Whitney
   H. Shepardson and William O. Scroggs; for 1945–1947, 1947–
   1948 and 1948–1949, by John C. Campbell; for 1949, 1950,
   1951, 1952, 1953 and 1954, by Richard P. Stebbins; for 1955, by
   Hollis W. Barber; for 1956, 1957, 1958, 1959, 1960, 1961, 1962
   and 1963, by Richard P. Stebbins; for 1964, by Jules Davids; for
   1965 and 1966, by Richard P. Stebbins.
Documents on American Foreign Relations (annual). Volume for
   1952 edited by Clarence W. Baier and Richard P. Stebbins; for
   1953 and 1954 edited by Peter V. Curl; for 1955, 1956, 1957,
   1958 and 1959 edited by Paul E. Zinner; for 1960, 1961, 1962
   and 1963 edited by Richard P. Stebbins; for 1964, by Jules Davids;
   for 1965 and 1966, by Richard P. Stebbins.
Political Handbook and Atlas of the World (annual), edited by
   Walter H. Mallory.
How Nations Behave: Law and Foreign Policy, by Louis Henkin
   (1968).

584 *Council Publications*

THE INSECURITY OF NATIONS, by Charles W. Yost (1968).

PROSPECTS FOR SOVIET SOCIETY, edited by Allen Kassof (1968).

THE AMERICAN APPROACH TO THE ARAB WORLD, by John S. Badeau (1968).

U.S. POLICY AND THE SECURITY OF ASIA, by Fred Greene (1968).

NEGOTIATING WITH THE CHINESE COMMUNISTS: The U.S. Experience, by Kenneth T. Young (1967).

FROM ATLANTIC TO PACIFIC: A New Interocean Canal, by Immanuel J. Klette (1967).

TITO'S SEPARATE ROAD: America and Yugoslavia in World Politics, by John C. Campbell (1967).

U.S. TRADE POLICY: New Legislation for the Next Round, by John W. Evans (1967).

TRADE LIBERALIZATION AMONG INDUSTRIAL COUNTRIES: Objectives and Alternatives, by Bela Balassa (1967).

THE CHINESE PEOPLE'S LIBERATION ARMY, by Brig. General Samuel B. Griffith II U.S.M.C. (ret.) (1967).

THE ARTILLERY OF THE PRESS: Its Influence on American Foreign Policy, by James Reston (1967).

ATLANTIC ECONOMIC COOPERATION: The Case of the O.E.C.D., by Henry G. Aubrey (1967).

TRADE, AID AND DEVELOPMENT: The Rich and Poor Nations, by John Pincus (1967).

BETWEEN TWO WORLDS: Policy, Press and Public Opinion on Asian–American Relations, by John Hohenberg (1967).

THE CONFLICTED RELATIONSHIP: The West and the Transformation of Asia, Africa and Latin America, by Theodore Geiger (1966).

THE ATLANTIC IDEA AND ITS EUROPEAN RIVALS, by H. van B. Cleveland (1966).

EUROPEAN UNIFICATION IN THE SIXTIES: From the Veto to the Crisis, by Miriam Camps (1966).

THE UNITED STATES AND CHINA IN WORLD AFFAIRS, by Robert Blum, edited by A. Doak Barnett (1966).

THE FUTURE OF THE OVERSEAS CHINESE IN SOUTHEAST ASIA, by Lea A. Williams (1966).

THE CONSCIENCE OF THE RICH NATIONS: The Development Assistance Committee and the Common Aid Effort, by Seymour J. Rubin (1966).

ATLANTIC AGRICULTURAL UNITY: Is it Possible?, by John O. Coppock (1966).

TEST BAN AND DISARMAMENT: The Path of Negotiation, by Arthur H. Dean (1966).

COMMUNIST CHINA'S ECONOMIC GROWTH AND FOREIGN TRADE, by Alexander Eckstein (1966).

POLICIES TOWARD CHINA: Views from Six Continents, edited by A. M. Halpern (1966).

THE AMERICAN PEOPLE AND CHINA, by A. T. Steele (1966).

INTERNATIONAL POLITICAL COMMUNICATION, by W. Phillips Davison (1965).

MONETARY REFORM FOR THE WORLD ECONOMY, by Robert V. Roosa (1965).

AFRICAN BATTLELINE: American Policy Choice in Southern Africa, by Waldemar A. Nielsen (1965).

NATO IN TRANSITION: The Future of the Atlantic Alliance, by Timothy W. Stanley (1965).

REMNANTS OF EMPIRE: The United Nations and the End of Colonialism, by David W. Wainhouse (1965).

ALTERNATIVE TO PARTITION: For a Broader Conception of America's Role in Europe, by Zbigniew Brzezinski (1965).

THE TROUBLED PARTNERSHIP: A Re-Appraisal of the Atlantic Alliance, by Henry A. Kissinger (1965).

THE EUROPEAN COMMUNITY AND AMERICAN TRADE: A Study in Atlantic Economics and Policy, by Randall Hinshaw (1964).

THE FOURTH DIMENSION OF FOREIGN POLICY: Educational and Cultural Affairs, by Phillip H. Coombs (1964).

AMERICAN AGENCIES INTERESTED IN INTERNATIONAL AFFAIRS (Fifth Edition), compiled by Donald Wasson (1964).

JAPAN AND THE UNITED STATES IN WORLD TRADE, by Warren S. Hunsberger (1964).

FOREIGN AFFAIRS BIBLIOGRAPHY, 1952–1962, by Henry L. Roberts (1964).

THE DOLLAR IN WORLD AFFAIRS: An essay in International Financial Policy, by Henry G. Aubrey (1964).

ON DEALING WITH THE COMMUNIST WORLD, by George F. Kennan (1964).

FOREIGN AID AND FOREIGN POLICY, by Edward S. Mason (1964).

THE SCIENTIFIC REVOLUTION AND WORLD POLITICS, by Caryl P. Haskins (1964).

AFRICA: A Foreign Affairs Reader, edited by Phillip W. Quigg (1964).

THE PHILIPPINES AND THE UNITED STATES: Problems of Partnership, by George E. Taylor (1964).

SOUTHEAST ASIA IN UNITED STATES POLICY, by Russell H. Fifield (1963).

UNESCO: ASSESSMENT AND PROMISE, by George N. Shuster (1963).

THE PEACEFUL ATOM IN FOREIGN POLICY, by Arnold Kramish (1963).

THE ARABS AND THE WORLD: Nasser's Arab Nationalist Policy, by Charles D. Cremeans (1963).

TOWARD AN ATLANTIC COMMUNITY, by Christian A. Herter (1963).

THE SOVIET UNION, 1922–1962: A Foreign Affairs Reader, edited by Philip E. Mosely (1963).

THE POLITICS OF FOREIGN AID: American Experience in Southeast Asia, by John D. Montgomery (1962).

SPEARHEADS OF DEMOCRACY: Labor in the Developing Countries, by George C. Lodge (1962).

LATIN AMERICA: Diplomacy and Reality, by Adolf A. Berle (1962).

THE ORGANIZATION OF AMERICAN STATES AND THE HEMISPHERE CRISIS, by John C. Dreier (1962).

THE UNITED NATIONS: Structure for Peace, by Ernest A. Gross (1962).

THE LONG POLAR WATCH: Canada and the Defense of North America, by Melvin Conant (1962).

ARMS AND POLITICS IN LATIN AMERICA (Revised Edition), by Edwin Lieuwen (1961).

THE FUTURE OF UNDERDEVELOPED COUNTRIES: Political Implications of Economic Development (Revised Edition), by Eugene Staley (1961).

SPAIN AND DEFENSE OF THE WEST: Ally and Liability, by Arthur P. Whitaker (1961).

SOCIAL CHANGE IN LATIN AMERICA TODAY: Its Implications for United States Policy, by Richard N. Adams, John P. Gillin, Allan R. Holmberg, Oscar Lewis, Richard W. Patch, and Charles W. Wagley (1961).

FOREIGN POLICY: THE NEXT PHASE: The 1960s (Revised Edition), by Thomas K. Finletter (1960).

DEFENSE OF THE MIDDLE EAST: Problems of American Policy(Revised Edition), by John C. Campbell (1960).

COMMUNIST CHINA AND ASIA: Challenge to American Policy, by A. Doak Barnett (1960).

FRANCE, TROUBLED ALLY: De Gaulle's Heritage and Prospects, by Edgar S. Furniss, Jr. (1960).

THE SCHUMAN PLAN: A Study in Economic Cooperation 1950–1959, by William Diebold, Jr. (1959).

SOVIET ECONOMIC AID: The New Aid and Trade Policy in Underdeveloped Countries, by Joseph S. Berliner (1958).

NATO AND THE FUTURE OF EUROPE, by Ben T. Moore (1958).

INDIA AND AMERICA: A Study of Their Relations, by Phillips Talbot and S. L. Poplai (1958).

NUCLEAR WEAPONS AND FOREIGN POLICY, by Henry A. Kissinger (1957).

MOSCOW-PEKING AXIS: Strength and Strains, by Howard L. Boorman, Alexander Eckstein, Philip E. Mosely, and Benjamin Schwartz (1957).

RUSSIA AND AMERICA: Dangers and Prospects, by Henry L. Roberts (1956).